W9-BBF-738

Praise for 225 Best Jobs for Baby Boomers

"An invaluable resource for the swelling numbers of baby boomers staying in and re-entering the workforce.... I...have yet to see a more comprehensive resource."

Tammi Midkiff, Project Coordinator
Senior Employment Center—Athens

"If you are a baby boomer thinking of changing careers...changing to a part-time job...or want to make your present job better, you should read this book."

Steve Bridge, CEO
National Association of Working Seniors

"I liked [the book] for its organization and content and the different ways of looking at careers. The 'best jobs' lists were interesting and targeted to the needs of job seekers, such as age-sensitive abilities (poor hearing, strength, visibility, interests) and the best jobs for personality types, and it helped to view careers from multiple angles."

Linda Hopkins, Librarian
Harriotte B. Smith Library
Camp Lejeune, NC

"Full of good information and easy to use. I would definitely recommend it as a useful guide to help baby boomers transition into 'retirement' and make a late career change."

Kathleen Casey-Kirschling, Master's in Health Education
First Baby Boomer

"Job seekers will use this volume to help them self-direct their career decision-making. A valuable addition to the library of any career counselor working with clients 45 and older."

Deborah E. Lipton, Senior Human Resources Generalist/Program Manager
Operation A.B.L.E. of Greater Boston, Inc.

225 Best Jobs™ for Baby Boomers

Part of JIST's Best Jobs™ Series

Michael Farr and Laurence Shatkin, Ph.D.

Also in JIST's Best Jobs Series

- *Best Jobs for the 21st Century*
- *200 Best Jobs for College Graduates*
- *300 Best Jobs Without a Four-Year Degree*
- *250 Best Jobs Through Apprenticeships*
- *50 Best Jobs for Your Personality*
- *40 Best Fields for Your Career*
- *250 Best-Paying Jobs*

JIST Works
America's Career Publisher

225 Best Jobs for Baby Boomers

© 2007 by JIST Publishing, Inc.

Published by JIST Works, an imprint of JIST Publishing, Inc.
8902 Otis Avenue
Indianapolis, IN 46216-1033

Phone: 1-800-648-JIST   Fax: 1-800-JIST-FAX
E-mail: info@jist.com   Web site: www.jist.com

Some Other Books by the Authors

Michael Farr
The Quick Resume & Cover Letter Book
Getting the Job You Really Want
The Very Quick Job Search
Overnight Career Choice

Laurence Shatkin
90-Minute College Major Matcher

Quantity discounts are available for JIST products. Have future editions of JIST books automatically delivered to you on publication through our convenient standing order program. Please call 1-800-648-JIST or visit www.jist.com for a free catalog and more information.

Visit www.jist.com for information on JIST, free job search information, book excerpts, and ordering information on our many products. For free information on 14,000 job titles, visit www.careeroink.com.

Acquisitions Editor: Susan Pines
Development Editor: Stephanie Koutek
Cover and Interior Designer: Aleata Howard

Interior Layout: Carolyn J. Newland
Proofreader: Paula Lowell
Indexer: Kelly D. Henthorne

Printed in the United States of America

11 10 09 08 07 06   9 8 7 6 5 4 3 2 1

Library of Congress Cataloging-in-Publication Data

Farr, J. Michael.
   225 best jobs for baby boomers / Michael Farr and Laurence Shatkin.
       p. cm. — (JIST's best jobs series)
   Includes index.
   ISBN-13: 978-1-59357-325-6 (alk. paper)
   ISBN-10: 1-59357-325-1 (alk. paper)
   1. Vocational guidance—United States. 2. Baby boom generation—Employment—United States.
   3. Employment forecasting—United States. 4. Occupations—United States. I. Shatkin, Laurence.
   II. Title. III. Title: Two hundred twenty-five best jobs for baby boomers. IV. Series.
   HF5382.5.U5F365 2000
   331.7020973—dc22

                                                              2006011526

We have been careful to provide accurate information throughout this book, but it is possible that errors and omissions have been introduced. Please consider this in making any career plans or other important decisions. Trust your own judgment above all else and in all things.

ISBN-13: 978-1-59357-325-6
ISBN-10: 1-59357-325-1

This Is a Big Book, But It Is Very Easy to Use

Bob Dylan has often been called the voice of the baby boom generation, and in his song "Forever Young" he included this blessing on his listeners: "May your hands always be busy." This wish reflects a widespread boomer attitude: We intend to be fully productive through late middle age and to continue working longer than any previous generation has—even after formal retirement.

Yes, but working at what? That's where this book can help. *225 Best Jobs for Baby Boomers* focuses on the jobs that have a large percentage of baby-boomer workers and that promise a lot of mployment and good earnings. So it can help you identify jobs that may be especially appealing at this stage in your life. Here's how to get the most out of this book:

- If you are thinking of changing careers but don't have a specific career goal in mind, look at the lists in Part II to narrow down your thinking—for example, the lists of the best jobs associated with an interest field or with a personality type that fits you. When you find a job that you want to know more about, read the job's description in Part III (where they are arranged alphabetically). Decide whether the job's work tasks, skills, and other characteristics match your preferences and abilities.

- Another strategy for focusing on a career goal is to read the suggestions in Part I for making the most of your work experience. What you learn there about using your skills and knowledge can help you identify especially promising jobs listed in Part II and better evaluate the jobs you read about in Part III.

- If you want to stay in your present career but would prefer a part-time schedule or self-employment—perhaps as a route to retirement—look at the lists in Part II of best jobs for part-time or self-employed workers and see whether your present occupation, or one in the same field, is listed.

- If you just want to advance in your present career, see whether it appears in Part II among the 225 best jobs for baby boomers and the best jobs for people in your age bracket. Also, read the discussion in Part I of why now may be a good time to change careers. Though you may not be convinced of the need to change now, you may be tempted or forced to consider a change in the near future. It's always good to have a Plan B.

(continued)

(continued)

Credits and Acknowledgments: While the authors created this book, it is based on the work of many others. The occupational information is based on data obtained from the U.S. Department of Labor and the U.S. Census Bureau. These sources provide the most authoritative occupational information available. The job titles and their related descriptions are from the O*NET database, which was developed by researchers and developers under the direction of the U.S. Department of Labor. They, in turn, were assisted by thousands of employers who provided details on the nature of work in the many thousands of job samplings used in the database's development. We used the most recent version of the O*NET database, release 8.0. We appreciate and thank the staff of the U.S. Department of Labor for their efforts and expertise in providing such a rich source of data.

Table of Contents

Summary of Major Sections

Introduction. A short overview to help you better understand and use the book. *Starts on page 1.*

Part I: It's Never Too Late to Change Your Career. Part I is an overview of what career change means to baby boomers. It covers the reasons why boomers think about changing their work or work arrangements and what options they most often consider, including working after retirement. *Starts on page 11.*

Part II: The Best Jobs Lists: Jobs with a High Percentage of Baby Boomers. Very useful for exploring career options! The 79 lists in Part II show you the 225 jobs that employ a high percentage of over-45 workers and that offer the best combination of earnings, projected growth, and number of openings. Specialized lists show you which of these 225 jobs are outstanding in terms of these three economic factors; which jobs are linked to the major interest fields and personality types; and which jobs have several other characteristics, such as employing a large percentage of women, employing a large percentage of people age 65 or over, or requiring only a small amount of physical strength. *Starts on page 23.*

Part III: Descriptions of the Best Jobs for Baby Boomers. This part provides a brief but information-packed description of each of the jobs that met our criteria for a high percentage of baby boomers plus high pay, fast growth, or many openings. Each description contains information on earnings, projected growth, job duties, skills, related job titles, related knowledge and courses, and many other details. The descriptions are in alphabetical order. This structure makes it easy to look up a job that you've identified from Part II and that you want to learn more about. *Starts on page 145.*

Detailed Table of Contents

Introduction

The Baby-Boom Generation

In 1946 the United States began an era of unprecedented prosperity, and along with that economic boom came a period of high birth rates that lasted through 1964. This baby boom produced a major chunk of our current population, including both authors of this book. As this book goes to press, the oldest baby boomers have reached age 60 while the youngest are a bit past 40.

The jobs included in this book are those with a high percentage of workers age 45 or older. We chose this set of ages partly to match the brackets that the Census Bureau uses to report data and partly because this book is about planning for the future. Some baby boomers are younger than 45, but they will soon be at that age and need to plan for it. And although today's 65-year-olds were born before the baby boom, the trends they have established can provide some insights for today's 60-year-olds.

Where the Information Came From

The information we used in creating this book came mostly from databases created by the U.S. Department of Labor and the U.S. Census Bureau:

- We started with the jobs included in the Department of Labor's O*NET (Occupational Information Network) database, which is now the primary source of detailed information on occupations. The Labor Department updates the O*NET on a regular basis, and we used the most recent one available—O*NET release 8.

- Because we wanted to include earnings, growth, number of openings, and other data not in the O*NET, we cross-referenced information on earnings developed by the U.S. Bureau of Labor Statistics (BLS) and the U.S. Census Bureau. This information on earnings is the most reliable data we could obtain. For data on earnings, projected growth, and number of openings, the BLS uses a slightly different set of job titles than the O*NET uses, so we had to match similar titles. Data about part-time workers, age of workers, and the male-female breakdown of workers was derived from the Census Bureau, which also uses a slightly different set of job titles. By linking the BLS and

Census data to the O*NET job titles in this book, we tied information about growth, earnings, and characteristics of workers to all the job titles in this book.

Of course, information in a database format can be boring and even confusing, so we did many things to help make the data useful and present it to you in a form that is easy to understand.

How the Best Jobs for Baby Boomers Were Selected

Here is the procedure we followed to select the 225 jobs we included in this book:

1. We began by creating our own database from the O*NET and the Census Bureau and other sources to include the information that we wanted. This database covered about 900 job titles for which a reasonably complete set of information was available.

2. From this set of occupations, we extracted the jobs with a high percentage of baby boomers—specifically, the jobs for which 40% of the workforce is age 45 or older. This left us with 427 jobs.

3. We created three lists that ranked these 427 jobs based on three major criteria: median annual earnings, projected growth through 2012, and number of job openings projected per year.

4. We then added the numerical ranks for each job from all three lists to calculate its overall score.

5. To emphasize jobs that tend to pay more, are likely to grow more rapidly, and have more job openings, we selected the 225 job titles with the best numerical scores for our final list. These jobs are the focus of this book.

For example, Management Analysts has the best combined score for earnings, growth, and number of job openings, so Management Analysts is listed first in our "225 Best Jobs For Baby Boomers" list even though it is not the best-paying job (which is a tie between several medical specializations such as Surgeons and Psychiatrists), the fastest-growing job (which is Social and Human Service Assistants), or the job with the most openings (which is Janitors and Cleaners, Except Maids and Housekeeping Cleaners).

Understand the Limits of the Data in This Book

In this book we use the most reliable and up-to-date information available on earnings, projected growth, number of openings, and other topics. The earnings data came from the U.S. Department of Labor's Bureau of Labor Statistics. As you look at the figures, keep in mind that they are estimates. They give you a general idea about the number of workers employed, annual earnings, rate of job growth, and annual job openings.

Understand that a problem with such data is that it describes an average. Just as there is no precisely average person, there is no such thing as a statistically average example of a particular job. We say this because data, while helpful, can also be misleading.

Take, for example, the yearly earnings information in this book. This is highly reliable data obtained from a very large U.S. working population sample by the Bureau of Labor Statistics. It tells us the average annual pay received as of November 2004 by people in various job titles (actually, it is the median annual pay, which means that half earned more and half less).

This sounds great, except that half of all people in that occupation earned less than that amount. For example, people who are new to the occupation or with only a few years of work experience often earn much less than the average amount. People who live in rural areas or who work for smaller employers typically earn less than those who do similar work in cities (where the cost of living is higher) or for bigger employers. People in certain areas of the country earn less than those in others. Other factors also influence how much you are likely to earn in a given job in your area. For example, Arbitrators, Mediators, and Conciliators in the Detroit metropolitan area have median earnings of $84,130, probably because much of industry in that region is unionized, whereas in the Dallas metropolitan area Arbitrators, Mediators, and Conciliators average less than half that figure—only $35,410.

Also keep in mind that the figures for job growth and number of openings are projections by labor economists—their best guesses about what we can expect between now and 2012. They are not guarantees. A major economic downturn, war, or technological breakthrough could change the actual outcome.

Finally, don't forget that the job market consists of both job openings and job-*seekers*. The figures on job growth and openings don't tell you how many people will be competing with you to be hired. The Department of Labor does not publish figures on the supply of job candidates, so we are unable to tell you about the level of competition you can expect. Competition is an important issue that you should research for any tentative career goal. In some cases, the *Occupational Outlook Handbook* provides informative statements. You should speak to people who educate or train tomorrow's workers; they probably have a good idea of how many graduates find rewarding employment and how quickly. People in the workforce also can provide insights into this issue. Use your critical thinking skills to evaluate what people tell you. For example, educators or trainers may be trying to recruit you, whereas people in the workforce may be trying to discourage you from competing. Get a variety of opinions to balance out possible biases.

So, in reviewing the information in this book, please understand the limitations of the data. You need to use common sense in career decision making as in most other things in life. We hope that, using that approach, you find the information helpful and interesting.

The Data Complexities

For those of you who like details, we present some of the complexities inherent in our sources of information and what we did to make sense of them here. You don't need to know this to use the book, so jump to the next section of the Introduction if you are bored with details.

Earnings, Growth, and Number of Openings

We include information on earnings, projected growth, and number of job openings for each job throughout this book.

Earnings

The employment security agency of each state gathers information on earnings for various jobs and forwards it to the U.S. Bureau of Labor Statistics. This information is organized in standardized ways by a BLS program called Occupational Employment Statistics, or OES. To keep the earnings for the various jobs and regions comparable, the OES screens out certain types of earnings and includes others, so the OES earnings we use in this book represent straight-time gross pay exclusive of premium pay. More specifically, the OES earnings include the job's base rate; cost-of-living allowances; guaranteed pay; hazardous-duty pay; incentive pay, including commissions and production bonuses; on-call pay; and tips but do not include back pay, jury duty pay, overtime pay, severance pay, shift differentials, non-production bonuses, or tuition reimbursements. Also, self-employed workers are not included in the estimates, and they can be a significant segment in certain occupations. When data on earnings for an occupation is highly unreliable, OES does not report a figure, which meant that we reluctantly had to exclude from this book a few occupations such as Musicians and Singers. The median earnings for all workers in all occupations were $29,070 in November 2004.

The OES earnings data uses a system of job titles called the Standard Occupational Classification system, or SOC. We cross-referenced these titles to the O*NET job titles we use in this book so we can rank the jobs by their earnings and include earnings information in the job descriptions. In some cases, an SOC title cross-references to more than one O*NET job title. For example, the O*NET has separate information for Housekeeping Supervisors and Janitorial Supervisors, but the SOC reports earnings for a single occupation called First-Line Supervisors/Managers of Housekeeping and Janitorial Workers. Therefore you may notice that the salary we report for Housekeeping Supervisors ($30,050) is identical to the salary we report for Janitorial Supervisors. In reality there probably is a difference, but this is the best information that is available.

Projected Growth and Number of Job Openings

This information comes from the Office of Occupational Statistics and Employment Projections, a program within the Bureau of Labor Statistics that develops information about projected trends in the nation's labor market for the next ten years. The most recent projections available cover the years from 2002 to 2012. The projections are based on information about people moving into and out of occupations. The BLS uses data from various sources in projecting the growth and number of openings for each job title—some data comes from the Census Bureau's Current Population Survey and some comes from an OES survey. The projections assume that there will be no major war, depression, or other economic upheaval.

Like the earnings figures, the figures on projected growth and job openings are reported according to the SOC classification, so again you will find that some of the SOC jobs crosswalk to more than one O*NET job. To continue the example we used earlier, SOC reports growth (16.2%) and openings (28,000) for one occupation called First-Line Supervisors/Managers of Housekeeping and Janitorial Workers, but in this book we report these figures separately for the occupation Housekeeping Supervisors and for the occupation Janitorial Supervisors. When you see Housekeeping Supervisors with 16.2% projected growth and 28,000 projected job openings and Janitorial Supervisors with the same two numbers, you should realize that the 16.2% rate of projected growth represents the *average* of these two occupations—one may actually experience higher growth than the other—and that these two occupations will *share* the 28,000 projected openings.

While salary figures are fairly straightforward, you may not know what to make of job-growth figures. For example, is projected growth of 15% good or bad? You should keep in mind that the average (mean) growth projected for all occupations by the Bureau of Labor Statistics is 14.8%. One-quarter of the occupations have a growth projection of 4.7% or lower. Growth of 12.4% is the median, meaning that half of the occupations have more, half less. Only one-quarter of the occupations have growth projected at more than 19.4%.

Remember, however, that the jobs in this book were selected as "best" partly on the basis of high growth, so their mean growth is an impressive 15.8%. Among these 225 outstanding jobs, the job ranked 56th by projected growth has a figure of 19.7%, the jobs ranked 112th and 113th (the median) have a projected growth of 16.1%, and the job ranked 168th has a projected growth of 9.8%.

Perhaps you're wondering why we present figures on both job growth *and* number of openings. Aren't these two ways of saying the same thing? Actually, you need to know both. Consider the occupation Geographers, which is projected to grow at the outstanding rate of 19.5%. There should be lots of opportunities in such a fast-growing job, right? Not exactly. This is a tiny occupation, with only about 1,000 people currently employed, so even though it is growing rapidly, it will not create many new jobs (fewer than 500 per year, to be exact). Now consider Executive Secretaries and Administrative Assistants. This occupation is growing at the anemic rate of 8.7%, largely because office automation has eliminated the need for many of these workers. Nevertheless, this is a huge occupation that employs over 1.5 million workers, so even though its growth rate is unimpressive, it is expected to take on 210,000 new workers each year. That's why we base our selection of the best jobs on both of these economic indicators and why you should pay attention to both when you scan our lists of best jobs.

How This Book Is Organized

The information about job options for baby boomers in this book moves from the general to the highly specific.

Part I. It's Never Too Late to Change Your Career

Part I is an overview of the new expectations that we baby boomers bring to career change—why we think about changing our type of work or the terms under which we work and what choices are open to us, such as part-time work, work that lets us use our skills and knowledge in new work roles, and post-retirement work.

Part II. The Best Jobs Lists: Jobs with a High Percentage of Baby Boomers

For many people, the 79 lists in Part II are the most interesting section of the book. Here you can see titles of jobs that have a high percentage of workers age 45 or more and the best combination of high salaries, fast growth, and plentiful job openings. You can see which jobs are best in terms of each of these factors combined or considered separately. The list of high-performers is broken out further according to the interest fields and several other features of the jobs. Look in the Table of Contents for a complete list of lists. Although there are a lot of lists, they are not difficult to understand because they have clear titles and are organized into groupings of related lists.

People who prefer to think about careers in terms of personality types will want to browse the lists that show the best jobs for baby boomers with Realistic, Investigative, Artistic, Social, Enterprising, and Conventional personality types. On the other hand, some people think first in terms of interest fields, and these people will prefer the lists that show the best jobs for boomers using the interest categories of the *New Guide for Occupational Exploration*.

We suggest that you use the lists that make the most sense for you. Following are the names of each group of lists along with short comments on each group. You will find additional information in a brief introduction provided at the beginning of each group of lists in Part III.

Best Jobs for Baby Boomers Overall: Lists of Jobs with the Highest Pay, Fastest Growth, and Most Openings

This group has four lists, and they are the ones that most people want to see first. The first list presents all 225 jobs that are included in this book (all with more than 40% of workers 45 years or older) in order of their combined scores for earnings, growth, and number of job openings. These jobs are used in the more-specialized lists that follow and in the descriptions in Part III. Three more lists in this group present specialized lists of jobs for baby boomers: the 100 best-paying jobs for baby boomers, the 100 fastest-growing jobs for baby boomers, and the 100 jobs for baby boomers with the most openings.

Best Jobs Lists for Baby Boomers by Demographic

This group of lists recognizes the diversity within the baby boomer generation by presenting interesting information for a variety of types of workers based on data from the U.S. Census Bureau. The lists are arranged into groups for workers age 45–54, workers age 55–64, workers age 65 and over, part-time workers, self-employed workers, women, and men. We created five lists for each group, basing the last four on the information in the first list:

- The jobs having the highest percentage of people of each type
- The 25 jobs with the best combined scores for earnings, growth, and number of openings
- The 25 jobs with the highest earnings
- The 25 jobs with the highest growth rates
- The 25 jobs with the largest number of openings

Best Jobs Lists Based on Levels of Education, Training, and Experience

We created separate lists for each level of education and training as defined by the U.S. Department of Labor. We put each of the 225 job titles into one of the lists based on the education, training, and experience required for entry. Jobs within these lists are presented in order of their total combined scores for earnings, growth, and number of openings. The lists include jobs in these groupings:

- Short-term on-the-job training
- Moderate-term on-the-job training
- Long-term on-the-job training
- Work experience in a related job
- Postsecondary vocational training
- Associate degree
- Bachelor's degree
- Work experience plus degree
- Master's degree
- Doctoral degree
- First professional degree

Best Jobs Lists Based on Interests

These lists organize the 225 jobs into groups based on interests. Within each list, jobs are presented in order of their combined scores for earnings, growth, and number of openings. Here are the 16 interest areas used in these lists: Agriculture and Natural Resources; Architecture and Construction; Arts and Communication; Business and Administration; Education and Training; Finance and Insurance; Government and Public Administration; Health Science; Hospitality, Tourism, and Recreation; Human Service; Information Technology; Law and Public Safety; Manufacturing; Retail and Wholesale Sales and Service; Scientific Research, Engineering, and Mathematics; and Transportation, Distribution, and Logistics.

Best Jobs Lists Based on Personality Types

These lists organize the 225 jobs into six personality types, which are described in the introduction to the lists: Realistic, Investigative, Artistic, Social, Enterprising, and Conventional. The jobs within each list are presented in order of their combined scores for earnings, growth, and number of openings.

Best Jobs Based on Some Age-Sensitive Abilities

These lists identify jobs from the full set of 225 that require only a small amount of certain abilities that diminish in some people as they age. The jobs within each list are presented in order of their combined scores for earnings, growth, and number of openings.

Part III: Descriptions of the Best Jobs for Baby Boomers

This part describes each of the best jobs for baby boomers, using a format that is informative yet compact and easy to read. The descriptions contain statistics such as earnings and projected percent of growth; lists such as major work tasks, skills, and related job titles; and key descriptors such as personality type and interest field. Because the jobs in this section are arranged in alphabetical order, you can easily find a job that you've identified from Part II and that you want to learn more about.

We used the most current information from a variety of government sources to create the descriptions. Although we've tried to make the descriptions easy to understand, the sample that follows—with an explanation of each of its parts—may help you better understand and use the descriptions.

Here are some details on each of the major parts of the job descriptions you will find in Part III:

- **Job Title**—This is the job title for the job as defined by the U.S. Department of Labor and used in its O*NET database.

Job Title

Administrative Services Managers

Data Elements

- Education/Training Required: Work experience plus degree
- Annual Earnings: $62,300
- Growth: 19.8%
- Annual Job Openings: 40,000
- Self-Employed: 0.2%
- Part-Time: 4.6%

Age Bracket	Percentage of Workers
45–54 Years Old	42.0%
55–64 Years Old	12.3%
65 or Older	4.9%

Summary Description and Tasks

Plan, direct, or coordinate supportive services of an organization, such as recordkeeping, mail distribution, telephone operator/receptionist, and other office support services. May oversee facilities planning and maintenance and custodial operations. Monitor the facility to ensure that it remains safe, secure, and well-maintained. Direct or coordinate the supportive services department of a business, agency, or organization. Set goals and deadlines for the department. Prepare and review operational reports and schedules to ensure accuracy and efficiency. Analyze internal processes and recommend and implement procedural or policy changes to improve operations, such as supply changes or the disposal of records. Acquire, distribute, and store supplies. Plan, administer, and control budgets for contracts, equipment, and supplies. Oversee construction and renovation projects to improve efficiency and to ensure that facilities meet environmental, health, and security standards and comply with government regulations. Hire and terminate clerical and administrative personnel. Oversee the maintenance and repair of machinery, equipment, and electrical and mechanical systems. Manage leasing of facility space. **SKILLS**—Management of Personnel Resources; Service Orientation; Coordination; Management of Financial Resources; Monitoring; Social Perceptiveness; Speaking; Programming.

Skills

GOE—Interest Area: 04. Business and Administration. **Work Group:** 04.02. Managerial Work in Business Detail. **Other Jobs in This Work Group:** First-Line Supervisors, Administrative Support; First-Line Supervisors, Customer Service; Housekeeping Supervisors; Janitorial Supervisors; Meeting and Convention Planners. **PERSONALITY TYPE:** Enterprising. Enterprising occupations frequently involve starting up and carrying out projects. These occupations can involve leading people and making many decisions. They sometimes require risk taking and often deal with business.

GOE Information

Personality Type

EDUCATION/TRAINING PROGRAM(S) —Business Administration/Management; Business/Commerce, General; Medical Staff Services Technology/Technician; Medical/Health Management and Clinical Assistant/Specialist; Public Administration; Purchasing, Procurement/Acquisitions and Contracts Management; Transportation/Transportation Management.

Education/Training Program(s)

WORK ENVIRONMENT—Contaminants; sitting; sounds, noise levels are distracting or uncomfortable; indoors; very hot or cold.

Work Environment

- **Data Elements**—The information comes from various U.S. Department of Labor and Census Bureau databases, as explained elsewhere in this Introduction.

- **Summary Description and Tasks**—The bold sentences provide a summary description of the occupation. It is followed by a listing of tasks that are generally performed by people who work in this job. This information comes from the O*NET database but where necessary has been edited to avoid exceeding 2,200 characters.

- **Skills:** The O*NET database provides data on many skills; we decided to list only those that were most important for each job rather than list pages of unhelpful details. For each job, we identified any skill with a rating that was higher than the average rating for that skill for all jobs. If there were more than eight, we included only those eight with the highest ratings, and we present them from highest to lowest score (that is, in terms of by how much its score exceeds the average score). We include up to 10 skills if scores were tied for eighth place. If no skill has a rating higher than the average for all jobs, we say "None met the criteria." Each listed skill is followed by a brief description of that skill.

- **GOE Information:** This information cross-references the Guide for Occupational Exploration (or the GOE), a system developed by the U.S. Department of Labor that organizes jobs based on interests. We use the groups from the *New Guide for Occupational Exploration*, as published by JIST. This book uses a set of interest areas based on the 16 career clusters developed by the U.S. Department of Education and used in a variety of career information systems. The description includes the major Interest Area the job fits into, its more-specific Work Group, and a list of related O*NET job titles that are in this same GOE Work Group. This information will help you identify other job titles that have similar interests or require similar skills. You can find more information on the GOE and its Interest Areas in the introduction to the lists of jobs based on interests in Part II.

- **Personality Type:** The O*NET database assigns each job to its most closely related personality type. Our job descriptions include the name of the related personality type as well as a brief definition of this personality type. You can find more information on the personality types in the introduction to the lists of jobs based on personality types in Part II.

- **Education/Training Program(s):** This part of the job description provides the name of the educational or training program or programs for the job. It will help you identify sources of formal or informal training for a job that interests you. To get this information, we used a crosswalk created by the National Crosswalk Service Center to connect information in the Classification of Instructional Programs (CIP) to the O*NET job titles we use in this book. We made various changes to connect the O*NET job titles to the education or training programs related to them and also modified the names of some education and training programs so they would be more easily understood.

- **Work Environment:** This entry in the job description mentions aspects of the work setting that some people may want to avoid, such as exposure to loud noises or the necessity of standing for long periods of time.

Getting all the information we used in the job descriptions was not a simple process, and it is not always perfect. Even so, we used the best and most recent sources of data we could find, and we think that our efforts will be helpful to many people.

It's Never Too Late to Change Your Career

This part of the book explains why right now might be an ideal time for you to change your career. You'll look at various kinds of career changes that baby boomers like you are considering: moving into a new occupation, continuing the same occupation on a part-time basis, or working during retirement. You'll see how to make the most of your previous work experience.

When Is the Right Time to Make a Career Move?

We baby boomers may not consider ourselves "the greatest generation," but we certainly are the biggest generation. In a democratic society, that means we usually get our way. Throughout our lives we have changed many of the rules that American society used to play by, and now we're changing the rules about what a career means.

We are the first generation to popularize the notion that work is not a curse but rather something that can be fulfilling. Of course, not all of us have been able to work in highly fulfilling jobs. Many of us have plugged away at jobs that were tedious, stressful, draining, or even dangerous in order to bring home a steady paycheck, medical benefits, and savings for retirement. Those of us with family members to support may have felt particularly shackled to work that lacked intrinsic satisfactions.

But now the chances are good that you are better able than at any time previously to choose work that *will* be fulfilling. Here are some reasons this may be the best time in your life for moving into a new career:

◎ You may be under less financial pressure than before. Perhaps your nest has emptied out and your kids are now more or less self-supporting. Or perhaps you are eligible for retirement from your present job. Whatever the reason, you may now be able to consider working for less pay than you did in the past and therefore may be able to consider jobs that have other rewarding aspects. A survey by Merrill Lynch found that more than half of baby boomers who say they will continue working after retirement plan to do so in a different line of work.

⊙ You may have no choice but to seek a new career because your old one has reached a dead end. Perhaps you have been downsized or expect to be soon, and you are in an industry that offers few job opportunities. Perhaps you are no longer physically able to do your present job well. Or perhaps you have simply reached the point where you can no longer tolerate the negative aspects of your present job. Now is your chance to make a virtue of necessity and find a career with job openings and real satisfactions.

⊙ You may be able to consider part-time work for a change. Perhaps you don't need the income of a full-time job, or a 40-hour week has become too physically draining. You may even be forced into part-time work because of some other time-consuming commitment, such as care for an elderly relative. If you're lucky, you may actually earn a better hourly rate as a part-timer than you did in the same occupation as a full-time worker! Or you may make the switch to part-time work by moving into a *new* field where part-time work is a more common arrangement. You may even consider a new field that would be daunting to hold down or hard to enter on a full-time basis but that is acceptable to you and to employers part-time.

⊙ You may feel something has signaled you that it's time for a change. Sometimes the death of a parent, spouse, or friend; a spell of ill health; a divorce; a disaster on the evening news; or simply turning a certain age causes people to recognize that they are stuck in a rut and it's time to find more meaning in what they do with their remaining time and energy. Turn a midlife crisis into an opportunity to make your life better.

⊙ At this time of your life, you may be relocating to be near family members (e.g., grandchildren or an aging parent) or because an empty nest means you no longer need a big house in a good school district. The move may sever your ties with your old career, but it may also open opportunities for new kinds of work. You may want to take advantage of a "snowbird" work arrangement that allows you to work for the same employer in different locations at different times of the year.

⊙ Your network of contacts is probably the best it has ever been, and networking can be very important for breaking into a new career. Through networking, you can learn about the pluses and minuses of various careers you might consider and, once you have decided on a career goal, about job openings. Even if you have lost touch with many of your contacts, the Internet makes it easier than ever before to track down old friends and acquaintances and get in touch with them.

⊙ You have a track record of work experience that you can show to prospective employers. Even if you want to move into a career that's very different from your past experiences, workplace traits such as reading and writing ability, commitment to quality, ability to work well in a team, and initiative are transferable anywhere. You merely need to package yourself so these traits are conspicuous to employers. For pointers on doing this, see *The Over-40 Job Search Guide* by Gail Geary, JD (JIST Works).

⊙ You probably understand your abilities and your likes and dislikes better than at any previous time in your life, so you are more capable than ever before of making a wise career decision. When you find a job in this book that looks promising and investigate it further, you can compare it to the experiences you have had in the past and know whether it is consistent with your interests, skills, abilities, and other work-related preferences.

- Economic and cultural trends also make this a good time to consider a new career. By now you should be aware that the traditional bond of loyalty between a company and its employees has largely faded away. For workers age 45 to 54, the average job tenure fell from 9.5 years in 1983 to 7.7 years in 2004. Most employers do not hesitate to cut the jobs of long-time workers who can be replaced with cheaper hires or a computer; neither should you feel that your job is a lifetime commitment. Globalization and technology may threaten your present job, but they are also creating many new job openings in the occupations listed in this book and are facilitating creative work arrangements, such as telecommuting, that are particularly attractive to baby boomers.

- Finally, if you decide to pursue a career that's new to you, you can worry less about what you are committing yourself to than a youngster might. You're (probably) not signing on for a 30-year hitch! Now is your chance to try something that you might not have dared to tackle in the past. If the new job doesn't work out, you can bounce back on the basis of your resume of other successful work experiences.

In spite of all of these factors, right now may not be the ideal time for you to make a career move. But keep these factors in mind and keep your eyes open, because the right time for you may occur sooner than you think. You may encounter a layoff, your spouse's retirement, or an opportunity to work part-time and may suddenly have a pressing reason to consider a new career—maybe one of the jobs in this book. Why not make it a career that you will find really fulfilling?

Of course, personal fulfillment is not the only reason people work, even people in our idealistic generation. According to the AARP, about one-third of us believe that money is the only reason we keep working—and there's nothing wrong with that. Money has meaning beyond the material goods it can buy. Most working baby boomers equate money with independence, and the overwhelming majority of us do not want to depend on our children during retirement. Therefore, one of the important factors that qualifies a job to be listed among the 225 best jobs for baby boomers is a good salary, and many of the lists in Part II are ordered by the average amount of income the jobs pay. Don't be reluctant to browse the lists of the best-paying jobs; on the other hand, don't let income be the only factor you consider in planning your next career move.

How Can I Make the Most of My Work Experience?

As you contemplate changing your job, you should try to make the most of your previous work experience. The most obvious way to do this is to find another position in the same occupation you have worked in until now. But let's assume that this is not an option, because you probably wouldn't be reading this book if you just wanted to go on doing what you've been doing. Perhaps there are no more jobs in your field, or they don't pay well enough, or they would require you to move to a location where you don't want to live. Or perhaps you are unhappy with your present occupation and want to find something more rewarding. How can you leverage your previous work experience in a *different* occupation?

The Skills-Based Approach

You acquired many skills during your education and even more during your years in the workforce. You probably have also acquired skills through activities you have done at home or on a volunteer basis. Now is the time to take stock of those skills, both to help you think about career options and to help you put together an effective resume when you settle on a career goal.

A useful exercise is to take a sheet of lined paper and draw two lines down the page to divide it into three columns. At the top of the left column, write "Major Achievements"; at the top of the middle column, write "Specific Tasks Involved"; and at the top of the right column, write "Skill(s) I Demonstrated."

- To populate the left column, think of your top achievements in school, on the job, at home, and in your leisure activities. You don't have to be as specific as you would be on a resume—for example, you could write either "Was a good salesperson" or "Sold $1,500,000 of widgets in the first quarter of 2004."

- After you have written an achievement in the left column, take several lines of the middle column to name the specific tasks you performed to accomplish the achievement. To continue the example of selling, you might list "Contacted prospects to discuss their needs," "Attended sales meetings," "Computed shipping costs," "Negotiated prices," and so forth.

- To populate the right column, think about the skill(s) that were required for each of these tasks. You may find it useful to draw from this taxonomy of skills, the same one that is used in the O*NET database of the U.S. Department of Labor (and therefore in the job descriptions in Part III of this book):

Basic Content Skills

Reading Comprehension	Understanding written sentences and paragraphs in work-related documents.
Active Listening	Giving full attention to what other people are saying, taking time to understand the points being made, asking questions as appropriate, and not interrupting at inappropriate times.
Writing	Communicating effectively in writing as appropriate for the needs of the audience.
Speaking	Talking to others to convey information effectively.
Mathematics	Using mathematics to solve problems.

Basic Process Skills

Science	Using scientific rules and methods to solve problems.
Critical Thinking	Using logic and reasoning to identify the strengths and weaknesses of alternative solutions, conclusions, or approaches to problems.
Active Learning	Understanding the implications of new information for both current and future problem-solving and decision-making.
Learning Strategies	Selecting and using training/instructional methods and procedures appropriate for the situation when learning or teaching new things.
Monitoring	Monitoring/assessing your performance or that of other individuals or organizations to make improvements or take corrective action.

Social Skills

Social Perceptiveness	Being aware of others' reactions and understanding why they react as they do.
Coordination	Adjusting actions in relation to others' actions.
Persuasion	Persuading others to change their minds or behavior.
Negotiation	Bringing others together and trying to reconcile differences.
Instructing	Teaching others how to do something.
Service Orientation	Actively looking for ways to help people.

Technical and Problem-Solving Skills

Complex Problem Solving	Identifying complex problems and reviewing related information to develop and evaluate options and implement solutions.
Operations Analysis	Analyzing needs and product requirements to create a design.
Technology Design	Generating or adapting equipment and technology to serve user needs.
Equipment Selection	Determining the kind of tools and equipment needed to do a job.
Installation	Installing equipment, machines, wiring, or programs to meet specifications.
Programming	Writing computer programs for various purposes.
Operation Monitoring	Watching gauges, dials, or other indicators to make sure a machine is working properly.

(continued)

(continued)

Operation and Control	Controlling operations of equipment or systems.
Equipment Maintenance	Performing routine maintenance on equipment and determining when and what kind of maintenance is needed.
Troubleshooting	Determining causes of operating errors and deciding what to do about them.
Repairing	Repairing machines or systems by using the needed tools.
Quality Control Analysis	Conducting tests and inspections of products, services, or processes to evaluate quality or performance.

Systems Skills

Judgment and Decision Making	Considering the relative costs and benefits of potential actions to choose the most appropriate one.
Systems Analysis	Determining how a system should work and how changes in conditions, operations, and the environment will affect outcomes.
Systems Evaluation	Identifying measures or indicators of system performance and the actions needed to improve or correct performance relative to the goals of the system.

Resource Management Skills

Time Management	Managing one's own time and the time of others.
Management of Financial Resources	Determining how money will be spent to get the work done and accounting for these expenditures.
Management of Material Resources	Obtaining and seeing to the appropriate use of equipment, facilities, and materials needed to do certain work.
Management of Personnel Resources	Motivating, developing, and directing people as they work; identifying the best people for the job.

You probably will notice that certain skills appear several times in the right column. Circle or underline these; they are your top skills.

If you find this process too tedious, you may want to use the O*NET Skills Profiler at http://www.acinet.org/acinet/skills_home.asp to identify your top skills. Or if you find it hard to populate the middle and right columns, you might ask a friend to help you. Sometimes other people can more easily make generalizations about you than you can by yourself.

When you find interesting jobs in the lists in Part II of this book, look at the top skills that are listed for the jobs in the descriptions in Part III. See how these skills compare with the top skills you have listed on your worksheet.

The Knowledge-Based Approach

Over the years you have worked in your occupation, you have acquired a broad knowledge of your industry and probably some expertise in your particular specialization. You know common problems that workers deal with, shortcuts and resources that help get the job done, important markets, how the cycle of seasons affects business, the regulatory or infrastructure environment, major competitors, and emerging issues. You also have acquired personal contacts in the industry, in the businesses and industries that buy from and sell to your industry, and perhaps in the schools that train tomorrow's workforce. You can "speak the language" that all of these contacts understand.

So consider several ways that you might leverage this knowledge and these contacts. Here are just a few, starting with the most obvious and moving toward some you may not have thought about:

- Instead of being a "doer," you can become a *manager*. With the right organizational and people skills, you can coordinate people and resources in your field. You may need to get some additional education to prepare for this transition, or you may be able to get your employer to give you a trial assignment with a managerial task so you can demonstrate that you already have the skills. You'll notice many managerial jobs in the lists in Part II of this book.

- Instead of being on your employer's payroll, you can become a *consultant* or *freelance worker*. This work arrangement can give you more flexible hours, more variety, more opportunities to travel, more opportunities to work at home, and more recognition. Of course, your income may lose some predictability, and you will need many of the same organizational skills as a manager, plus marketing skills to acquire clients.

- You can *teach* the subject. If you relate well to young people, you may consider teaching in high school or even lower grades. Of course, a teaching license requires a college degree with certain course work and often passing an exam. Teaching the subject in college usually requires a master's degree, but to teach a vocational subject at the postsecondary level, you may need no more than extensive work experience. Note that Teachers, Postsecondary, is ranked second among the best jobs for baby boomers—it's a hot field! You may also find work as a *trainer* in a business setting.

- Every industry needs skilled workers, so you can *recruit* workers for your field. As a recruiter, you can leverage your knowledge of job requirements in the industry and perhaps your contacts in "feeder" schools or other established sources of new hires.

- You can work in *sales*. For example, if you have been a teacher and know the education market well, your expertise can help you land a job selling textbooks or other educational resources. Several sales jobs appear in this book.

- You can work as a *buyer* in your industry, either of raw materials, finished goods, or services. This job allows you to use knowledge about matters such as who the sellers are, what forces affect the market, and what contributes to quality in goods and services.

- You can work as a *broker* or *agent* who brings the buyers and sellers together. This applies to a lot more than just real estate. For example, consider the agents who work in show business. Some of them are former actors who leverage their knowledge of who does the hiring and what the employers are looking for. What business deals might you arrange in your industry?

- You can work as an *investment analyst* in the industry and leverage your knowledge of which companies or commodities are likely to gain or lose value.

- Because you know what determines quality or value in your field, and perhaps legal requirements for work outputs, you can become an *inspector* or *appraiser*. For example, after experience as a construction worker, you may be able to become a building inspector. Work in the arts may qualify you to become an art appraiser.

- If you have a flair for words, you can work as a *writer* about the industry. Every industry has trade publications and technical manuals. Assemble a portfolio of your best writing to show employers or consulting clients what you know and can do.

- You may become a *representative* or *advocate* for the workers in your industry. In some unionized trades, the union officials often rise from the rank and file. Professional associations, including lobbying groups, sometimes fill vacancies in their paid staff with members who have been active volunteers.

- In many of the work roles listed here, you can function as an *entrepreneur* rather than try to get hired by an existing business. For example, to become a broker of some kind, you may create your own brokerage business. To teach an occupation, you may set up your own school (or, in the arts, a studio). You may set up a business that buys, sells, or repairs a type of product that you're familiar with.

Of course, if your industry is shrinking fast, you may want to avoid the knowledge-based approach. After people stopped driving buggies, there wasn't much point in trying to sell buggies, repair them, write about them, or teach people how to drive them. On the other hand, even though the shoe manufacturing industry in the United States is only a tiny fraction of what it once was, there is still a need for buyers and sellers of shoes, managers of shoe stores, repairers of high-priced shoes, and technicians to fashion orthotic inserts for shoes. And a few specialty shoe manufacturers are still in business on these shores.

What About Retirement?

If you are planning to retire soon, or if you are retired already, you probably are reading this book because you intend to do more than go fishing, hit the road in an RV, or look after the grandchildren. In fact, poll after poll has shown that the majority of baby boomers intend to continue working after retirement—either working part-time or cycling between the workplace and leisure. Boomers surveyed for studies by MetLife and Merrill Lynch have identified several motivators for staying in the workforce after retirement, listed here roughly in descending order of importance:

- To stay mentally active
- To stay physically active
- To stay involved with other people
- To keep health insurance
- To face new challenges
- To have a sense of purpose or identity
- To earn income
- To improve the quality of life in their community

It's a good thing that we baby boomers want to stay in the workforce longer than our parents' generation has, because the economy of the United States is going to need us. Unless immigration increases drastically, there simply will not be enough skilled younger workers to fill the jobs that we boomers now hold.

In fact, some industries are already feeling the pinch. A few years ago, when oil prices were low, energy companies pushed senior staff into early retirement; now, as business has picked up, they are changing long-standing policies to encourage workers to stay past retirement. Better known is the shortage of nurses. Many baby-boomer nurses have dropped out of this physically demanding occupation just as their parents are reaching the age when they need a nurse's care. On any given day, there are nearly 100,000 vacant nursing positions in long-term care facilities. Many such facilities, as well as hospitals, are offering premium pay to tempt retired nurses back into the workforce, whether on a full- or part-time basis. In fact, nursing is one of the few careers in which part-time workers average a higher hourly wage than full-timers. (Many of the others are also in health care.)

Here is a listing of occupations that are expected to be most affected by baby-boomer retirements during the years 2003–2008 (based on data from *Monthly Labor Review*, July 2000). Employers of these workers may be particularly receptive to creating new work arrangements to keep their boomer employees from disappearing or to recruit boomers who have been working in other occupations:

Occupation	Number of Employees Needed to Replace Baby Boomer Retirees 2003–2008
Teachers, Elementary School	237,000
Registered Nurses	188,000
Administrators, Education and Related Fields	101,000
Administrators and Officials, Public Administration	81,000
Financial Managers	58,000
Lawyers	57,000
Social Workers	54,000
Teachers Aides	52,000

(continued)

(continued)

Occupation	Number of Employees Needed to Replace Baby Boomer Retirees 2003–2008
Plumbers, Pipefitters, and Steamfitters	36,000
Postal Clerks, Except Mail Carriers	30,000
Psychologists	26,000
Industrial Engineers	21,000
Teachers, Special Education	19,000
Supervisors, Police and Detectives	17,000
Management Analysts	16,000
Airline Pilots and Navigators	14,000
Personnel and Labor Relations Managers	13,000
Eligibility Clerks, Social Welfare	9,000
Photographers	5,000

You can see from the list of motivators ("to stay mentally active" and so on) that employers are going to need to offer more than just good wages to attract retirees to keep working. Certainly flexible hours and various fringe benefits will also be desirable, but many of us baby boomers are seeking personal fulfillment from our post-retirement work. In particular, we boomers have a greater interest than previous generations in doing post-retirement work that will improve the quality of life in our communities—and doing this as paid work, not as volunteering. The 2005 MetLife study found that 60 percent of leading-edge baby boomers (those age 50–59) cited at least one of the following reasons for working in retirement:

- Helping to improve the quality of life
- Helping the poor, the elderly, and other people in need
- Working with children and young people

Only 34 percent of people age 60–70 felt the same way. The MetLife study also found that 58 percent of the leading-edge boomers intend to work in one of these fields:

- Education
- Health care
- Helping those in need
- Working with youth
- Civic activism
- Arts and culture
- The environment

In Part II, you can identify some of the best jobs in these fields by looking at the introduction to the section called "Best Jobs Lists for Baby Boomers Based on Interests." Look for the table that matches these fields with the *Guide for Occupational Exploration* interest areas.

What Fringe Benefits Should I Look For?

At this point in your life, you probably have a lot of experience with fringe benefits as components of your compensation package. You should give some thought to what fringe benefits you may get from your next job.

If it is a regular full-time job, consider negotiating for benefits at the same time you negotiate your salary. In situations where employers lack flexibility on salary, they may be willing to make some concessions on benefits such as vacation time. If you are a retiree whose health care costs are covered by Medicare or a retirement package from a previous employer, you may want to throw this fact into your salary negotiations, asking for higher pay because you will not need health care benefits. At the same time, if you take on any new benefits, you should check to be sure that they do not jeopardize your existing retiree benefits.

Part-time jobs often lack fringe benefits, so if you are in a strong enough position to negotiate your hourly rate for a part-time job, be sure to point out that you need a better hourly rate than a full-time worker to cover the cost of health insurance, retirement savings, and so forth. This is also advisable if you seek temporary full-time work as an independent contractor.

You may be able to get fringe benefits while doing part-time or temporary work by being an employee of a temporary help agency or consulting agency; nowadays these cover a wider variety of jobs than the clerical and nursing positions that used to be their main focus.

Self-employment is an attractive work arrangement for some people late in their careers, but it requires you to have the discipline to set aside money for the benefits that an employer typically provides—unless, of course, you are a retiree who already receives some of these benefits as part of a retirement plan or Medicare.

The core lesson here is that in any work arrangement, even a traditional job, you need to pay close attention to what fringe benefits are available and not be shy about negotiating for the best deal possible.

Will I Face Age Discrimination?

A survey by AARP found that more than two-thirds of working baby boomers believe that age discrimination occurs in the workplace, and job placement specialists confirm that age discrimination is a reality despite laws that are intended to prevent it. Discrimination certainly is a factor in the amount of time that it takes an unemployed baby boomer to find another job—typically a month longer than younger workers.

That's one reason why this book is so valuable. The 225 best jobs listed in Part II have been selected partly because their employment is fast-growing and partly because they will create a large number of job openings. If you are concerned about age discrimination, look in particular at the job lists that are ordered by job growth and openings; these lists may help you identify jobs whose employers are hungry for skilled workers and are more likely to set aside their prejudices and hire you. Also pay attention to the lists of jobs with high percentages of workers age 45–54, workers age 55–64, and workers age 65 and over. You may get a warmer welcome to an occupation with a lot of workers in your age bracket as opposed to an occupation in which you would often be the oldest person in the room.

Time to Make Plans

The important ideas for you to take away from this part are that this stage of your life can be an excellent time for you to change the type of work you do—or the arrangements under which you do it—and that you have a lot of options to choose from. So now is the right time to start evaluating the various options and planning your move.

The lists in Part II and the job descriptions in Part III will help you consider some of the most promising job options in the labor market.

PART II

The Best Jobs Lists: Jobs with a High Percentage of Baby Boomers

This part contains a lot of interesting lists, and it's a good place for you to start using the book. Here are some suggestions for using the lists to explore career options:

⊚ The table of contents at the beginning of this book presents a complete listing of the list titles in this section. You can browse the lists or use the table of contents to find those that interest you most.

⊚ We gave the lists clear titles, so most require little explanation. We provide comments for each group of lists.

⊚ As you review the lists, one or more of the jobs may appeal to you enough that you want to seek additional information. As this happens, mark that job (or, if someone else will be using this book, write it on a separate sheet of paper) so that you can look up the description of the job in Part III.

⊚ Keep in mind that all jobs in these lists meet our basic criteria for being included in this book. All lists, therefore, emphasize occupations with high pay, high growth, or large numbers of openings. These measures are easily quantified and are often presented in lists of best jobs in the newspapers and other media. While earnings, growth, and openings are important, there are other factors to consider in your career planning. For example, location, liking the people you work with, having an opportunity to serve others, and enjoying your work are a few of the many factors that may define the ideal job for you. These measures are difficult or impossible to quantify and thus are not used in this book, so you will need to consider the importance of these issues yourself.

⊚ All data used to create these lists comes from the U.S. Department of Labor and the Census Bureau. The earnings figures are based on the average annual pay received by full-time workers. Because the earnings represent the national averages, actual pay rates can vary greatly by location, amount of previous work experience, and other factors.

Some Details on the Lists

The sources of the information we used in constructing these lists are presented in this book's introduction. Here are some additional details on how we created the lists:

- **We excluded some jobs for which very little information is available.** In the full list of 1,167 jobs that are described in the U.S. Department of Labor's O*NET database, 212 have no information beyond a definition and, in some cases, a list of tasks. These are either catch-all titles (such as "Financial Specialists, All Other") that make the O*NET as comprehensive as possible or dummy occupations that help the O*NET match up better with occupational information from other government agencies. Census Bureau data is available for some of them, but no O*NET data is available for them, so we dropped them from consideration. We also reluctantly excluded seven jobs because no annual wage information is available for them: Actors; Biologists; Dancers; Human Resources Managers; Hunters and Trappers; Musicians, Instrumental; and Singers.

- **We excluded some jobs that are shrinking and that offer very few opportunities.** Among the 948 jobs for which we have both O*NET and wage information, nine are expected to employ fewer than 500 workers per year and to shrink rather than grow in workforce size: Bridge and Lock Tenders; Fabric Menders, Except Garment; Marine Architects; Marine Engineers; Marine Engineers and Naval Architects; Mathematicians; Mining and Geological Engineers, Including Mining Safety Engineers; Nuclear Power Reactor Operators; and Radio Operators. These jobs can't be considered "best jobs," so we excluded them from consideration for this book.

- **We collapsed a number of specialized postsecondary education jobs into one title.** The government database we used for the job titles and descriptions included 38 job titles for postsecondary educators, yet the data source we used for growth and number of openings provided data only for the more general job of Teachers, Postsecondary. To make our lists more useful, we included only one listing—Teachers, Postsecondary—rather than separate listings for each specialized postsecondary education job. We did, however, include descriptions for all the specific postsecondary teaching jobs in Part III (except two for which no detailed information is available). Should you wonder, here are the more specialized titles: Agricultural Sciences Teachers, Postsecondary; Anthropology and Archeology Teachers, Postsecondary; Architecture Teachers, Postsecondary; Area, Ethnic, and Cultural Studies Teachers, Postsecondary; Art, Drama, and Music Teachers, Postsecondary; Atmospheric, Earth, Marine, and Space Sciences Teachers, Postsecondary; Biological Science Teachers, Postsecondary; Business Teachers, Postsecondary; Chemistry Teachers, Postsecondary; Communications Teachers, Postsecondary; Computer Science Teachers, Postsecondary; Criminal Justice and Law Enforcement Teachers, Postsecondary; Economics Teachers, Postsecondary; Education Teachers, Postsecondary; Engineering Teachers, Postsecondary; English Language and Literature Teachers, Postsecondary; Environmental Science Teachers, Postsecondary; Foreign Language and Literature Teachers, Postsecondary; Forestry and Conservation Science Teachers, Postsecondary; Geography Teachers, Postsecondary; Graduate Teaching Assistants; Health Specialties Teachers, Postsecondary; History Teachers, Postsecondary; Home Economics Teachers, Postsecondary; Law Teachers, Postsecondary;

Library Science Teachers, Postsecondary; Mathematical Science Teachers, Postsecondary; Nursing Instructors and Teachers, Postsecondary; Philosophy and Religion Teachers, Postsecondary; Physics Teachers, Postsecondary; Political Science Teachers, Postsecondary; Psychology Teachers, Postsecondary; Recreation and Fitness Studies Teachers, Postsecondary; Social Work Teachers, Postsecondary; Sociology Teachers, Postsecondary; Vocational Education Teachers, Postsecondary.

◎ Some jobs have the same scores for one or more data elements. For example, in the category of jobs with the most openings, two jobs (Clergy and Real Estate Sales Agents) are expected to have the same number of job openings per year, 34,000. Therefore we ordered these two jobs alphabetically, and their order has no other significance. There was no way to avoid these ties, so simply understand that the difference of several positions on a list may not mean as much as it seems.

◎ Some jobs share certain data elements. For example, in Part III you will find separate descriptions of the jobs Clinical Psychologists, Counseling Psychologists, and School Psychologists—so you will also find these as three separate jobs on the lists here in Part II. However, the U.S. Department of Labor provides data on earnings, job growth, and job openings only for the *single combined* job called Clinical, Counseling, and School Psychologists, which means that on these lists we have to print the same information for all three jobs. That can be misleading if you don't understand that these jobs share data. The earnings figure of $56,360 represents the *average* for the three jobs; probably there are differences in their earnings, but we don't have separate data. The figure of 24.4% for their job growth is also an *average*. It's especially important to understand that the figure of 17,000 job openings represents the *total number of job openings for the three jobs*. They share this figure—each job is projected to have *some fraction* of 17,000 job openings, but we don't know exactly how many. To remind you about how to read these figures, we identify all the jobs that share data in footnotes after each list that contains such jobs.

Best Jobs Overall for Baby Boomers: Lists of Jobs with the Highest Pay, Fastest Growth, and Most Openings

The four lists that follow are the most important lists in this book. To create these lists, we ranked 427 major jobs with more than 40 percent of baby boomers in the workforce according to a combination of their earnings, growth, and openings. We then selected the 225 jobs with the best combined scores for use in this book. (The process for ranking the jobs is explained in more detail in the introduction.)

The first list presents all 225 best jobs according to these combined scores for pay, growth, and number of openings. Three additional lists present the 100 jobs with the best scores for each of three measures: annual earnings, projected percentage growth through 2014, and number of annual openings. Descriptions for all the jobs in these lists are included in Part III.

The 225 Best Jobs for Baby Boomers—Jobs with the Best Combination of Pay, Growth, and Openings

This is the list that most people want to see first. It includes the 225 jobs with a high percentage of baby boomers that have the best overall combined ratings for earnings, projected growth, and number of openings. (The section in the introduction called "How the Best Jobs for Baby Boomers Were Selected" explains in detail how we rated jobs to assemble this list.)

You'll notice a wide variety of jobs on the list. Among the top 20 are jobs in health care, education, finance, business management, and law.

Management Analysts was the occupation with the best combined score, and it is on the top of the list. The other occupations follow in descending order based on their combined scores. Many jobs had tied scores and are simply listed one after another, so there are often only very small or even no differences between the scores of jobs that are near each other on the list. All other job lists in this book use this list as their source. You can find descriptions for each of these jobs in Part III, beginning on page 145.

The 225 Best Jobs Overall for Baby Boomers

Job	Annual Earnings	Percent Growth	Annual Openings
1. Management Analysts	$64,560	30.4%	78,000
2. Teachers, Postsecondary	$54,406	38.1%	216,000
3. Logisticians	$59,460	27.5%	162,000
4. General and Operations Managers	$79,300	18.4%	260,000
5. Registered Nurses	$53,640	27.3%	215,000
6. Anesthesiologists	more than $145,600	19.5%	38,000
7. Internists, General	more than $145,600	19.5%	38,000
8. Obstetricians and Gynecologists	more than $145,600	19.5%	38,000
9. Psychiatrists	more than $145,600	19.5%	38,000
10. Surgeons	more than $145,600	19.5%	38,000
11. Family and General Practitioners	$136,170	19.5%	38,000
12. Pediatricians, General	$135,450	19.5%	38,000
13. Medical and Health Services Managers	$68,320	29.3%	33,000
14. Financial Managers, Branch or Department	$83,780	18.3%	71,000
15. Treasurers, Controllers, and Chief Financial Officers	$83,780	18.3%	71,000
16. Chief Executives	$141,820	16.7%	63,000
17. Government Service Executives	$141,820	16.7%	63,000
18. Private Sector Executives	$141,820	16.7%	63,000

The 225 Best Jobs Overall for Baby Boomers

Job	Annual Earnings	Percent Growth	Annual Openings
19. Pharmacists	$87,160	30.1%	23,000
20. Lawyers	$97,420	17.0%	53,000
21. Education Administrators, Elementary and Secondary School	$74,610	20.7%	31,000
22. Administrative Services Managers	$62,300	19.8%	40,000
23. Sales Representatives, Agricultural	$59,390	19.3%	44,000
24. Sales Representatives, Chemical and Pharmaceutical	$59,390	19.3%	44,000
25. Sales Representatives, Electrical/Electronic	$59,390	19.3%	44,000
26. Sales Representatives, Instruments	$59,390	19.3%	44,000
27. Sales Representatives, Mechanical Equipment and Supplies	$59,390	19.3%	44,000
28. Sales Representatives, Medical	$59,390	19.3%	44,000
29. Personal Financial Advisors	$62,450	34.6%	18,000
30. Special Education Teachers, Secondary School	$46,300	30.0%	59,000
31. Special Education Teachers, Middle School	$45,000	30.0%	59,000
32. Training and Development Managers	$70,430	19.4%	21,000
33. Special Education Teachers, Preschool, Kindergarten, and Elementary School	$44,330	30.0%	59,000
34. Compensation and Benefits Managers	$67,040	19.4%	21,000
35. Sales Representatives, Wholesale and Manufacturing, Except Technical and Scientific Products	$46,090	19.1%	160,000
36. Construction Managers	$70,770	12.0%	47,000
37. Public Relations Managers	$73,960	23.4%	10,000
38. Clinical Psychologists	$56,360	24.4%	17,000
39. Counseling Psychologists	$56,360	24.4%	17,000
40. School Psychologists	$56,360	24.4%	17,000
41. Secondary School Teachers, Except Special and Vocational Education	$46,120	18.2%	118,000
42. Training and Development Specialists	$45,370	27.9%	35,000
43. Storage and Distribution Managers	$67,300	19.7%	13,000
44. Transportation Managers	$67,300	19.7%	13,000
45. First-Line Supervisors and Manager/Supervisors— Construction Trades Workers	$50,980	14.1%	67,000
46. First-Line Supervisors and Manager/Supervisors— Extractive Workers	$50,980	14.1%	67,000
47. Instructional Coordinators	$50,060	25.4%	18,000
48. Social and Community Service Managers	$48,330	27.7%	19,000

(continued)

(continued)

The 225 Best Jobs Overall for Baby Boomers

Job	Annual Earnings	Percent Growth	Annual Openings
49. First-Line Supervisors/Managers of Mechanics, Installers, and Repairers	$51,000	15.4%	42,000
50. Cost Estimators	$50,920	18.6%	25,000
51. Speech-Language Pathologists	$53,790	27.2%	10,000
52. Compensation, Benefits, and Job Analysis Specialists	$48,720	28.0%	15,000
53. Employment Interviewers, Private or Public Employment Service	$41,190	27.3%	29,000
54. Personnel Recruiters	$41,190	27.3%	29,000
55. Elementary School Teachers, Except Special Education	$43,660	15.2%	183,000
56. Licensed Practical and Licensed Vocational Nurses	$34,650	20.2%	105,000
57. Airline Pilots, Copilots, and Flight Engineers	$135,430	18.5%	6,000
58. First-Line Supervisors/Managers of Non-Retail Sales Workers	$60,300	6.8%	72,000
59. Tractor-Trailer Truck Drivers	$33,870	19.0%	299,000
60. Truck Drivers, Heavy	$33,870	19.0%	299,000
61. Refractory Materials Repairers, Except Brickmasons	$39,610	16.3%	155,000
62. Child, Family, and School Social Workers	$35,010	23.2%	45,000
63. First-Line Supervisors/Managers of Police and Detectives	$65,020	15.3%	14,000
64. Medical and Clinical Laboratory Technologists	$46,710	19.3%	21,000
65. Technical Writers	$54,390	27.1%	6,000
66. Veterinarians	$68,280	25.1%	4,000
67. Forest Fire Fighting and Prevention Supervisors	$59,760	18.7%	8,000
68. Municipal Fire Fighting and Prevention Supervisors	$59,760	18.7%	8,000
69. Architects, Except Landscape and Naval	$61,430	17.3%	8,000
70. Self-Enrichment Education Teachers	$31,530	40.1%	39,000
71. Medical and Public Health Social Workers	$40,780	28.6%	18,000
72. Environmental Scientists and Specialists, Including Health	$51,950	23.7%	6,000
73. Educational, Vocational, and School Counselors	$46,160	15.0%	32,000
74. Engineering Managers	$99,000	9.2%	16,000
75. Legal Secretaries	$37,390	18.8%	39,000
76. Chiropractors	$67,940	23.3%	3,000
77. Industrial Engineers	$66,080	10.6%	16,000
78. Caption Writers	$45,460	16.1%	23,000
79. Copy Writers	$45,460	16.1%	23,000
80. Creative Writers	$45,460	16.1%	23,000

The 225 Best Jobs Overall for Baby Boomers

Job	Annual Earnings	Percent Growth	Annual Openings
81. Poets and Lyricists	$45,460	16.1%	23,000
82. Industrial Production Managers	$74,100	7.9%	18,000
83. First-Line Supervisors/Managers of Production and Operating Workers	$45,230	9.5%	66,000
84. Purchasing Agents, Except Wholesale, Retail, and Farm Products	$48,360	11.2%	29,000
85. Mental Health and Substance Abuse Social Workers	$34,310	34.5%	17,000
86. Electronics Engineers, Except Computer	$76,810	9.4%	11,000
87. Middle School Teachers, Except Special and Vocational Education	$44,180	9.0%	69,000
88. Multi-Media Artists and Animators	$49,900	15.8%	12,000
89. Social and Human Service Assistants	$24,730	48.7%	63,000
90. Security Guards	$20,520	31.9%	228,000
91. Civil Engineers	$65,280	8.0%	17,000
92. Adult Literacy, Remedial Education, and GED Teachers and Instructors	$39,730	20.4%	14,000
93. Maintenance and Repair Workers, General	$30,930	16.3%	155,000
94. Budget Analysts	$57,190	14.0%	8,000
95. Property, Real Estate, and Community Association Managers	$41,540	12.8%	35,000
96. Clergy	$37,870	15.5%	34,000
97. Art Directors	$63,750	11.4%	8,000
98. Truck Drivers, Light or Delivery Services	$24,420	23.2%	219,000
99. Education Administrators, Preschool and Child Care Center/Program	$36,080	32.0%	9,000
100. Personal and Home Care Aides	$17,020	40.5%	154,000
101. Coroners	$48,530	9.8%	20,000
102. Environmental Compliance Inspectors	$48,530	9.8%	20,000
103. Equal Opportunity Representatives and Officers	$48,530	9.8%	20,000
104. Government Property Inspectors and Investigators	$48,530	9.8%	20,000
105. Licensing Examiners and Inspectors	$48,530	9.8%	20,000
106. Pressure Vessel Inspectors	$48,530	9.8%	20,000
107. Optometrists	$88,290	17.1%	2,000
108. Insurance Sales Agents	$42,030	8.4%	52,000
109. Appraisers, Real Estate	$43,790	17.6%	11,000
110. Assessors	$43,790	17.6%	11,000
111. Mental Health Counselors	$33,400	26.7%	13,000

(continued)

(continued)

The 225 Best Jobs Overall for Baby Boomers

Job	Annual Earnings	Percent Growth	Annual Openings
112. First-Line Supervisors, Administrative Support	$41,850	6.6%	140,000
113. First-Line Supervisors, Customer Service	$41,850	6.6%	140,000
114. Teacher Assistants	$19,760	23.0%	259,000
115. Health Educators	$39,670	21.9%	8,000
116. Executive Secretaries and Administrative Assistants	$35,550	8.7%	210,000
117. Landscape Architects	$54,290	22.2%	2,000
118. Dietitians and Nutritionists	$44,370	17.8%	8,000
119. Audiologists	$53,040	29.0%	1,000
120. Hydrologists	$60,880	21.0%	1,000
121. Bus and Truck Mechanics and Diesel Engine Specialists	$36,150	14.2%	28,000
122. First-Line Supervisors/Managers of Correctional Officers	$48,070	19.0%	4,000
123. Medical and Clinical Laboratory Technicians	$31,440	19.4%	21,000
124. Rehabilitation Counselors	$27,900	33.8%	19,000
125. Directors, Religious Activities and Education	$30,720	24.1%	16,000
126. Librarians	$46,940	10.1%	15,000
127. First-Line Supervisors/Managers of Retail Sales Workers	$32,410	9.1%	251,000
128. Janitors and Cleaners, Except Maids and Housekeeping Cleaners	$19,110	18.3%	454,000
129. Medical Secretaries	$27,030	17.2%	50,000
130. Private Detectives and Investigators	$32,510	25.3%	9,000
131. Agricultural Crop Farm Managers	$50,720	5.1%	25,000
132. Fish Hatchery Managers	$50,720	5.1%	25,000
133. Nursery and Greenhouse Managers	$50,720	5.1%	25,000
134. Substance Abuse and Behavioral Disorder Counselors	$32,630	23.3%	10,000
135. Probation Officers and Correctional Treatment Specialists	$39,760	14.7%	15,000
136. Air Traffic Controllers	$102,390	12.6%	2,000
137. Aircraft Body and Bonded Structure Repairers	$45,910	11.0%	12,000
138. Aircraft Engine Specialists	$45,910	11.0%	12,000
139. Airframe-and-Power-Plant Mechanics	$45,910	11.0%	12,000
140. Bus Drivers, Transit and Intercity	$30,670	15.2%	33,000
141. Emergency Management Specialists	$45,670	28.2%	2,000
142. Construction and Building Inspectors	$43,940	13.8%	10,000
143. Podiatrists	$97,290	15.0%	1,000
144. Purchasing Managers	$74,300	4.8%	9,000
145. Economists	$72,370	13.4%	2,000

The 225 Best Jobs Overall for Baby Boomers

Job	Annual Earnings	Percent Growth	Annual Openings
146. Bus Drivers, School	$23,670	16.7%	76,000
147. Vocational Education Teachers, Secondary School	$46,650	9.0%	12,000
148. Geographers	$61,520	19.5%	fewer than 500
149. Housekeeping Supervisors	$30,050	16.2%	28,000
150. Janitorial Supervisors	$30,050	16.2%	28,000
151. Oral and Maxillofacial Surgeons	more than $145,600	4.1%	7,000
152. Orthodontists	more than $145,600	4.1%	7,000
153. Prosthodontists	more than $145,600	4.1%	7,000
154. Geologists	$70,180	11.5%	2,000
155. Marriage and Family Therapists	$40,440	22.4%	3,000
156. Commercial Pilots	$55,360	14.9%	2,000
157. Electrical Engineers	$72,770	2.5%	11,000
158. Fire-Prevention and Protection Engineers	$64,320	7.9%	4,000
159. Industrial Safety and Health Engineers	$64,320	7.9%	4,000
160. Product Safety Engineers	$64,320	7.9%	4,000
161. Dentists, General	$122,430	4.1%	7,000
162. Operations Research Analysts	$60,230	6.2%	6,000
163. Library Assistants, Clerical	$21,050	21.5%	27,000
164. Gaming Supervisors	$41,080	15.7%	6,000
165. Taxi Drivers and Chauffeurs	$19,790	21.7%	28,000
166. Electrical and Electronics Repairers, Commercial and Industrial Equipment	$43,180	10.3%	10,000
167. Machinists	$34,090	8.2%	30,000
168. Water and Liquid Waste Treatment Plant and System Operators	$34,850	16.0%	9,000
169. Judges, Magistrate Judges, and Magistrates	$97,260	8.7%	2,000
170. Industrial-Organizational Psychologists	$74,060	16.0%	fewer than 500
171. Demonstrators and Product Promoters	$20,490	17.0%	38,000
172. Cartoonists	$41,240	16.5%	4,000
173. Painters and Illustrators	$41,240	16.5%	4,000
174. Sculptors	$41,240	16.5%	4,000
175. Sketch Artists	$41,240	16.5%	4,000
176. Central Office and PBX Installers and Repairers	$50,270	–0.6%	23,000
177. Communication Equipment Mechanics, Installers, and Repairers	$50,270	–0.6%	23,000
178. Frame Wirers, Central Office	$50,270	–0.6%	23,000
179. Station Installers and Repairers, Telephone	$50,270	–0.6%	23,000

(continued)

(continued)

The 225 Best Jobs Overall for Baby Boomers

Job	Annual Earnings	Percent Growth	Annual Openings
180. Telecommunications Facility Examiners	$50,270	–0.6%	23,000
181. Tax Preparers	$26,130	23.2%	11,000
182. Mobile Heavy Equipment Mechanics, Except Engines	$38,630	9.6%	12,000
183. Real Estate Sales Agents	$36,950	5.7%	34,000
184. Real Estate Brokers	$56,970	2.4%	11,000
185. Composers	$34,800	13.5%	8,000
186. Music Arrangers and Orchestrators	$34,800	13.5%	8,000
187. Music Directors	$34,800	13.5%	8,000
188. Curators	$43,920	17.0%	2,000
189. Wholesale and Retail Buyers, Except Farm Products	$42,190	4.3%	24,000
190. Aviation Inspectors	$47,920	7.7%	5,000
191. Freight Inspectors	$47,920	7.7%	5,000
192. Maids and Housekeeping Cleaners	$17,000	9.2%	352,000
193. Marine Cargo Inspectors	$47,920	7.7%	5,000
194. Motor Vehicle Inspectors	$47,920	7.7%	5,000
195. Public Transportation Inspectors	$47,920	7.7%	5,000
196. Railroad Inspectors	$47,920	7.7%	5,000
197. Industrial Machinery Mechanics	$39,310	5.5%	19,000
198. Physicists	$87,480	6.9%	1,000
199. Laundry and Drycleaning Machine Operators and Tenders, Except Pressing	$17,350	12.3%	47,000
200. Precision Dyers	$17,350	12.3%	47,000
201. Spotters, Dry Cleaning	$17,350	12.3%	47,000
202. Medical Equipment Repairers	$38,590	14.8%	4,000
203. Subway and Streetcar Operators	$47,560	13.2%	2,000
204. First-Line Supervisors and Manager/Supervisors— Agricultural Crop Workers	$36,040	11.4%	6,000
205. First-Line Supervisors and Manager/Supervisors— Animal Care Workers, Except Livestock	$36,040	11.4%	6,000
206. First-Line Supervisors and Manager/Supervisors— Animal Husbandry Workers	$36,040	11.4%	6,000
207. First-Line Supervisors and Manager/Supervisors— Fishery Workers	$36,040	11.4%	6,000
208. First-Line Supervisors and Manager/Supervisors— Horticultural Workers	$36,040	11.4%	6,000
209. First-Line Supervisors and Manager/Supervisors— Logging Workers	$36,040	11.4%	6,000

The 225 Best Jobs Overall for Baby Boomers

Job	Annual Earnings	Percent Growth	Annual Openings
210. Postal Service Mail Carriers	$45,880	–0.5%	20,000
211. Sociologists	$56,790	13.4%	fewer than 500
212. Electrical and Electronic Inspectors and Testers	$28,630	4.7%	87,000
213. Materials Inspectors	$28,630	4.7%	87,000
214. Mechanical Inspectors	$28,630	4.7%	87,000
215. Precision Devices Inspectors and Testers	$28,630	4.7%	87,000
216. Production Inspectors, Testers, Graders, Sorters, Samplers, Weighers	$28,630	4.7%	87,000
217. Locksmiths and Safe Repairers	$30,580	21.0%	3,000
218. Court Clerks	$28,980	12.3%	14,000
219. License Clerks	$28,980	12.3%	14,000
220. Municipal Clerks	$28,980	12.3%	14,000
221. Arbitrators, Mediators, and Conciliators	$53,690	13.7%	fewer than 500
222. Lodging Managers	$39,100	6.6%	10,000
223. Crossing Guards	$19,710	16.5%	19,000
224. Farmers and Ranchers	$38,600	–20.6%	118,000
225. Bookkeeping, Accounting, and Auditing Clerks	$29,040	3.0%	274,000

Jobs 6, 7, 8, 9, 10, 11, and 12 share 38,000 openings. Jobs 14 and 15 share 71,000 openings. Jobs 16, 17, and 18 share 63,000 openings. Jobs 23, 24, 25, 26, 27, and 28 share 44,000 openings. Jobs 30, 31, and 33 share 59,000 openings. Jobs 32 and 34 share 21,000 openings. Jobs 38, 39, and 40 share 17,000 openings. Jobs 43 and 44 share 13,000 openings. Jobs 45 and 46 share 67,000 openings. Jobs 53 and 54 share 29,000 openings. Jobs 59 and 60 share 299,000 openings. Jobs 67 and 68 share 8,000 openings. Jobs 78, 79, 80, and 81 share 23,000 openings. Jobs 101, 102, 103, 104, 105, and 106 share 20,000 openings. Jobs 109 and 110 share 11,000 openings. Jobs 112 and 113 share 140,000 openings. Jobs 131, 132, and 133 share 25,000 openings. Jobs 137, 138, and 139 share 12,000 openings. Jobs 149 and 150 share 28,000 openings. Jobs 151, 152, 153, and 161 share 7,000 openings. Jobs 158, 159, and 160 share 4,000 openings. Jobs 172, 173, 174, and 175 share 4,000 openings. Jobs 176, 177, 178, 179, and 180 share 23,000 openings. Jobs 185, 186, and 187 share 8,000 openings. Jobs 190, 191, 193, 194, 195, and 196 share 5,000 openings. Jobs 199, 200, and 201 share 47,000 openings. Jobs 204, 205, 206, 207, 208, and 209 share 6,000 openings. Jobs 212, 213, 214, 215, and 216 share 87,000 openings. Jobs 218, 219, and 220 share 14,000 openings.

The 100 Best-Paying Jobs for Baby Boomers

Of the 225 jobs that met our criteria for this book, this list shows the 100 with the highest median earnings. *(Median earnings* means that half of all workers in these jobs earn more than that amount and half earn less. The median annual wage for all occupations in the workforce is $29,070.) This is a popular list for obvious reasons.

It shouldn't be a big surprise that most of the highest-paying jobs require advanced levels of education, training, and experience. For example, many of the 20 jobs with the highest earnings require a professional degree, and others, such as Chief Executives and Engineering Managers, require extensive training and experience. Although the top 20 jobs may not appeal to you for a variety of reasons, you are likely to find others that will among the top 100 jobs with the highest earnings. Keep in mind that the earnings reflect the national average for all workers in the occupation. This is an important consideration, because starting pay in the job is usually a lot less than the pay that workers can earn with several years of experience. Earnings also vary significantly by region of the country, so actual pay in your area could be substantially different.

The 100 Best-Paying Jobs for Baby Boomers

Job	Annual Earnings
1. Anesthesiologists	more than $145,600
2. Internists, General	more than $145,600
3. Obstetricians and Gynecologists	more than $145,600
4. Oral and Maxillofacial Surgeons	more than $145,600
5. Orthodontists	more than $145,600
6. Prosthodontists	more than $145,600
7. Psychiatrists	more than $145,600
8. Surgeons	more than $145,600
9. Chief Executives	$141,820
10. Government Service Executives	$141,820
11. Private Sector Executives	$141,820
12. Family and General Practitioners	$136,170
13. Pediatricians, General	$135,450
14. Airline Pilots, Copilots, and Flight Engineers	$135,430
15. Dentists, General	$122,430
16. Air Traffic Controllers	$102,390
17. Engineering Managers	$99,000
18. Lawyers	$97,420
19. Podiatrists	$97,290
20. Judges, Magistrate Judges, and Magistrates	$97,260
21. Optometrists	$88,290
22. Physicists	$87,480
23. Pharmacists	$87,160
24. Financial Managers, Branch or Department	$83,780
25. Treasurers, Controllers, and Chief Financial Officers	$83,780
26. General and Operations Managers	$79,300
27. Electronics Engineers, Except Computer	$76,810
28. Education Administrators, Elementary and Secondary School	$74,610
29. Purchasing Managers	$74,300
30. Industrial Production Managers	$74,100

The 100 Best-Paying Jobs for Baby Boomers

Job	Annual Earnings
31. Industrial-Organizational Psychologists	$74,060
32. Public Relations Managers	$73,960
33. Electrical Engineers	$72,770
34. Economists	$72,370
35. Construction Managers	$70,770
36. Training and Development Managers	$70,430
37. Geologists	$70,180
38. Medical and Health Services Managers	$68,320
39. Veterinarians	$68,280
40. Chiropractors	$67,940
41. Storage and Distribution Managers	$67,300
42. Transportation Managers	$67,300
43. Compensation and Benefits Managers	$67,040
44. Industrial Engineers	$66,080
45. Civil Engineers	$65,280
46. First-Line Supervisors/Managers of Police and Detectives	$65,020
47. Management Analysts	$64,560
48. Fire-Prevention and Protection Engineers	$64,320
49. Industrial Safety and Health Engineers	$64,320
50. Product Safety Engineers	$64,320
51. Art Directors	$63,750
52. Personal Financial Advisors	$62,450
53. Administrative Services Managers	$62,300
54. Geographers	$61,520
55. Architects, Except Landscape and Naval	$61,430
56. Hydrologists	$60,880
57. First-Line Supervisors/Managers of Non-Retail Sales Workers	$60,300
58. Operations Research Analysts	$60,230
59. Forest Fire Fighting and Prevention Supervisors	$59,760
60. Municipal Fire Fighting and Prevention Supervisors	$59,760
61. Logisticians	$59,460
62. Sales Representatives, Agricultural	$59,390
63. Sales Representatives, Chemical and Pharmaceutical	$59,390
64. Sales Representatives, Electrical/Electronic	$59,390
65. Sales Representatives, Instruments	$59,390
66. Sales Representatives, Mechanical Equipment and Supplies	$59,390

(continued)

(continued)

The 100 Best-Paying Jobs for Baby Boomers

Job	Annual Earnings
67. Sales Representatives, Medical	$59,390
68. Budget Analysts	$57,190
69. Real Estate Brokers	$56,970
70. Sociologists	$56,790
71. Clinical Psychologists	$56,360
72. Counseling Psychologists	$56,360
73. School Psychologists	$56,360
74. Commercial Pilots	$55,360
75. Teachers, Postsecondary	$54,406
76. Technical Writers	$54,390
77. Landscape Architects	$54,290
78. Speech-Language Pathologists	$53,790
79. Arbitrators, Mediators, and Conciliators	$53,690
80. Registered Nurses	$53,640
81. Audiologists	$53,040
82. Environmental Scientists and Specialists, Including Health	$51,950
83. First-Line Supervisors/Managers of Mechanics, Installers, and Repairers	$51,000
84. First-Line Supervisors and Manager/Supervisors—Construction Trades Workers	$50,980
85. First-Line Supervisors and Manager/Supervisors—Extractive Workers	$50,980
86. Cost Estimators	$50,920
87. Agricultural Crop Farm Managers	$50,720
88. Fish Hatchery Managers	$50,720
89. Nursery and Greenhouse Managers	$50,720
90. Central Office and PBX Installers and Repairers	$50,270
91. Communication Equipment Mechanics, Installers, and Repairers	$50,270
92. Frame Wirers, Central Office	$50,270
93. Station Installers and Repairers, Telephone	$50,270
94. Telecommunications Facility Examiners	$50,270
95. Instructional Coordinators	$50,060
96. Multi-Media Artists and Animators	$49,900
97. Compensation, Benefits, and Job Analysis Specialists	$48,720
98. Coroners	$48,530
99. Environmental Compliance Inspectors	$48,530
100. Equal Opportunity Representatives and Officers	$48,530

The 100 Fastest-Growing Jobs for Baby Boomers

Of the 225 jobs that met our criteria for this book, this list shows the 100 that are projected to have the highest percentage increase in the number of people employed through 2014. (The average growth rate for *all* occupations in the workforce is 14.8 percent.)

Jobs in the education and health care fields dominate the 20 fastest-growing jobs. Social and Human Service Assistants is the job with the highest growth rate—the number employed is projected to grow almost by half during this time. You can find a wide range of rapidly growing jobs in a variety of fields and at different levels of training and education among the jobs in this list.

The 100 Fastest-Growing Jobs for Baby Boomers

Job	Percent Growth
1. Social and Human Service Assistants	48.7%
2. Personal and Home Care Aides	40.5%
3. Self-Enrichment Education Teachers	40.1%
4. Teachers, Postsecondary	38.1%
5. Personal Financial Advisors	34.6%
6. Mental Health and Substance Abuse Social Workers	34.5%
7. Rehabilitation Counselors	33.8%
8. Education Administrators, Preschool and Child Care Center/Program	32.0%
9. Security Guards	31.9%
10. Management Analysts	30.4%
11. Pharmacists	30.1%
12. Special Education Teachers, Middle School	30.0%
13. Special Education Teachers, Preschool, Kindergarten, and Elementary School	30.0%
14. Special Education Teachers, Secondary School	30.0%
15. Medical and Health Services Managers	29.3%
16. Audiologists	29.0%
17. Medical and Public Health Social Workers	28.6%
18. Emergency Management Specialists	28.2%
19. Compensation, Benefits, and Job Analysis Specialists	28.0%
20. Training and Development Specialists	27.9%
21. Social and Community Service Managers	27.7%
22. Logisticians	27.5%
23. Employment Interviewers, Private or Public Employment Service	27.3%
24. Personnel Recruiters	27.3%

(continued)

(continued)

The 100 Fastest-Growing Jobs for Baby Boomers

Job	Percent Growth
25. Registered Nurses	27.3%
26. Speech-Language Pathologists	27.2%
27. Technical Writers	27.1%
28. Mental Health Counselors	26.7%
29. Instructional Coordinators	25.4%
30. Private Detectives and Investigators	25.3%
31. Veterinarians	25.1%
32. Clinical Psychologists	24.4%
33. Counseling Psychologists	24.4%
34. School Psychologists	24.4%
35. Directors, Religious Activities and Education	24.1%
36. Environmental Scientists and Specialists, Including Health	23.7%
37. Public Relations Managers	23.4%
38. Chiropractors	23.3%
39. Substance Abuse and Behavioral Disorder Counselors	23.3%
40. Child, Family, and School Social Workers	23.2%
41. Tax Preparers	23.2%
42. Truck Drivers, Light or Delivery Services	23.2%
43. Teacher Assistants	23.0%
44. Marriage and Family Therapists	22.4%
45. Landscape Architects	22.2%
46. Health Educators	21.9%
47. Taxi Drivers and Chauffeurs	21.7%
48. Library Assistants, Clerical	21.5%
49. Hydrologists	21.0%
50. Locksmiths and Safe Repairers	21.0%
51. Education Administrators, Elementary and Secondary School	20.7%
52 Adult Literacy, Remedial Education, and GED Teachers and Instructors	20.4%
53. Licensed Practical and Licensed Vocational Nurses	20.2%
54. Administrative Services Managers	19.8%
55. Storage and Distribution Managers	19.7%
56. Transportation Managers	19.7%
57. Anesthesiologists	19.5%
58. Family and General Practitioners	19.5%
59. Geographers	19.5%
60. Internists, General	19.5%
61. Obstetricians and Gynecologists	19.5%
62. Pediatricians, General	19.5%

The 100 Fastest-Growing Jobs for Baby Boomers

Job	Percent Growth
63. Psychiatrists	19.5%
64. Surgeons	19.5%
65. Compensation and Benefits Managers	19.4%
66. Medical and Clinical Laboratory Technicians	19.4%
67. Training and Development Managers	19.4%
68. Medical and Clinical Laboratory Technologists	19.3%
69. Sales Representatives, Agricultural	19.3%
70. Sales Representatives, Chemical and Pharmaceutical	19.3%
71. Sales Representatives, Electrical/Electronic	19.3%
72. Sales Representatives, Instruments	19.3%
73. Sales Representatives, Mechanical Equipment and Supplies	19.3%
74. Sales Representatives, Medical	19.3%
75. Sales Representatives, Wholesale and Manufacturing, Except Technical and Scientific Products	19.1%
76. First-Line Supervisors/Managers of Correctional Officers	19.0%
77. Tractor-Trailer Truck Drivers	19.0%
78. Truck Drivers, Heavy	19.0%
79. Legal Secretaries	18.8%
80. Forest Fire Fighting and Prevention Supervisors	18.7%
81. Municipal Fire Fighting and Prevention Supervisors	18.7%
82. Cost Estimators	18.6%
83. Airline Pilots, Copilots, and Flight Engineers	18.5%
84. General and Operations Managers	18.4%
85. Financial Managers, Branch or Department	18.3%
86. Janitors and Cleaners, Except Maids and Housekeeping Cleaners	18.3%
87. Treasurers, Controllers, and Chief Financial Officers	18.3%
88. Secondary School Teachers, Except Special and Vocational Education	18.2%
89. Dietitians and Nutritionists	17.8%
90. Appraisers, Real Estate	17.6%
91. Assessors	17.6%
92. Architects, Except Landscape and Naval	17.3%
93. Medical Secretaries	17.2%
94. Optometrists	17.1%
95. Curators	17.0%
96. Demonstrators and Product Promoters	17.0%
97. Lawyers	17.0%
98. Bus Drivers, School	16.7%
99. Chief Executives	16.7%
100. Government Service Executives	16.7%

The 100 Jobs for Baby Boomers with the Most Openings

Of the 225 jobs that met our criteria for this book, this list shows the 100 jobs that are projected to have the largest number of job openings per year.

Jobs with many openings present several advantages that may be attractive to baby boomers. Because there are many openings, these jobs can be easier to obtain and age discrimination may be less of a barrier. If part-time work is your goal, the odds of achieving that work arrangement are better when there are more openings. Though some of these jobs have average or below-average pay, some also pay quite well.

It is interesting to note that high technology does not play a large role among most of the top 20 jobs on this list. Therefore it is not really true that nowadays you must master high-tech skills to be employable. In fact, most of these jobs have so many openings precisely because they require hands-on work and workers cannot be replaced by technology. Most of these jobs also require on-site work, sometimes in-person work, and therefore cannot be exported overseas.

The 100 Jobs for Baby Boomers with the Most Openings

Job	Annual Openings
1. Janitors and Cleaners, Except Maids and Housekeeping Cleaners	454,000
2. Maids and Housekeeping Cleaners	352,000
3. Tractor-Trailer Truck Drivers	299,000
4. Truck Drivers, Heavy	299,000
5. Bookkeeping, Accounting, and Auditing Clerks	274,000
6. General and Operations Managers	260,000
7. Teacher Assistants	259,000
8. First-Line Supervisors/Managers of Retail Sales Workers	251,000
9. Security Guards	228,000
10. Truck Drivers, Light or Delivery Services	219,000
11. Teachers, Postsecondary	216,000
12. Registered Nurses	215,000
13. Executive Secretaries and Administrative Assistants	210,000
14. Elementary School Teachers, Except Special Education	183,000
15. Logisticians	162,000
16. Sales Representatives, Wholesale and Manufacturing, Except Technical and Scientific Products	160,000
17. Maintenance and Repair Workers, General	155,000
18. Refractory Materials Repairers, Except Brickmasons	155,000

The 100 Jobs for Baby Boomers with the Most Openings

Job	Annual Openings
19. Personal and Home Care Aides	154,000
20. First-Line Supervisors, Administrative Support	140,000
21. First-Line Supervisors, Customer Service	140,000
22. Farmers and Ranchers	118,000
23. Secondary School Teachers, Except Special and Vocational Education	118,000
24. Licensed Practical and Licensed Vocational Nurses	105,000
25. Electrical and Electronic Inspectors and Testers	87,000
26. Materials Inspectors	87,000
27. Mechanical Inspectors	87,000
28. Precision Devices Inspectors and Testers	87,000
29. Production Inspectors, Testers, Graders, Sorters, Samplers, Weighers	87,000
30. Management Analysts	78,000
31. Bus Drivers, School	76,000
32. First-Line Supervisors/Managers of Non-Retail Sales Workers	72,000
33. Financial Managers, Branch or Department	71,000
34. Treasurers, Controllers, and Chief Financial Officers	71,000
35. Middle School Teachers, Except Special and Vocational Education	69,000
36. First-Line Supervisors and Manager/Supervisors—Construction Trades Workers	67,000
37. First-Line Supervisors and Manager/Supervisors—Extractive Workers	67,000
38. First-Line Supervisors/Managers of Production and Operating Workers	66,000
39. Chief Executives	63,000
40. Government Service Executives	63,000
41. Private Sector Executives	63,000
42. Social and Human Service Assistants	63,000
43. Special Education Teachers, Middle School	59,000
44. Special Education Teachers, Preschool, Kindergarten, and Elementary School	59,000
45. Special Education Teachers, Secondary School	59,000
46. Lawyers	53,000
47. Insurance Sales Agents	52,000
48. Medical Secretaries	50,000
49. Construction Managers	47,000
50. Laundry and Drycleaning Machine Operators and Tenders, Except Pressing	47,000
51. Precision Dyers	47,000
52. Spotters, Dry Cleaning	47,000
53. Child, Family, and School Social Workers	45,000

(continued)

(continued)

The 100 Jobs for Baby Boomers with the Most Openings

Job	Annual Openings
54. Sales Representatives, Agricultural	44,000
55. Sales Representatives, Chemical and Pharmaceutical	44,000
56. Sales Representatives, Electrical/Electronic	44,000
57. Sales Representatives, Instruments	44,000
58. Sales Representatives, Mechanical Equipment and Supplies	44,000
59. Sales Representatives, Medical	44,000
60. First-Line Supervisors/Managers of Mechanics, Installers, and Repairers	42,000
61. Administrative Services Managers	40,000
62. Legal Secretaries	39,000
63. Self-Enrichment Education Teachers	39,000
64. Anesthesiologists	38,000
65. Demonstrators and Product Promoters	38,000
66. Family and General Practitioners	38,000
67. Internists, General	38,000
68. Obstetricians and Gynecologists	38,000
69. Pediatricians, General	38,000
70. Psychiatrists	38,000
71. Surgeons	38,000
72. Property, Real Estate, and Community Association Managers	35,000
73. Training and Development Specialists	35,000
74. Clergy	34,000
75. Real Estate Sales Agents	34,000
76. Bus Drivers, Transit and Intercity	33,000
77. Medical and Health Services Managers	33,000
78. Educational, Vocational, and School Counselors	32,000
79. Education Administrators, Elementary and Secondary School	31,000
80. Machinists	30,000
81. Employment Interviewers, Private or Public Employment Service	29,000
82. Personnel Recruiters	29,000
83. Purchasing Agents, Except Wholesale, Retail, and Farm Products	29,000
84. Bus and Truck Mechanics and Diesel Engine Specialists	28,000
85. Housekeeping Supervisors	28,000
86. Janitorial Supervisors	28,000
87. Taxi Drivers and Chauffeurs	28,000
88. Library Assistants, Clerical	27,000
89. Agricultural Crop Farm Managers	25,000
90. Cost Estimators	25,000
91. Fish Hatchery Managers	25,000

The 100 Jobs for Baby Boomers with the Most Openings

Job	Annual Openings
92. Nursery and Greenhouse Managers	25,000
93. Wholesale and Retail Buyers, Except Farm Products	24,000
94. Caption Writers	23,000
95. Central Office and PBX Installers and Repairers	23,000
96. Communication Equipment Mechanics, Installers, and Repairers	23,000
97. Copy Writers	23,000
98. Creative Writers	23,000
99. Frame Wirers, Central Office	23,000
100. Pharmacists	23,000

Jobs 3 and 4 share 299,000 openings. Jobs 33 and 34 share 71,000 openings. Jobs 36 and 37 share 67,000 openings. Jobs 39, 40, and 41 share 63,000 openings. Jobs 43, 44, and 45 share 59,000 openings. Jobs 54, 55, 56, 57, 58, and 59 share 44,000 openings. Jobs 64, 66, 67, 68, 69, 70, and 71 share 38,000 openings. Jobs 94, 97, and 98 share 23,000 openings with another job not on this list. Jobs 95, 96, and 99 share 23,000 openings with two other jobs not on this list.

Best Jobs Lists for Baby Boomers by Demographic

The 225 jobs in this book were selected on the basis of a demographic statistic: They all have a large proportion of baby boomers in the workforce. We thought it also would be useful for you to see lists that highlight other demographic characteristics: jobs with a high percentage of workers in more-specific age brackets, working part-time, self-employed, and male or female.

All of the lists in this section were created by using a similar process. We began with all 225 best jobs for baby boomers and sorted those jobs in order of the primary criterion for each set of lists. Then, we selected the jobs with the highest percentage of workers fitting the primary criterion and listed them along with their earnings, growth, and number of openings data. (For example, we sorted all 225 jobs based on the percentage of workers age 45 to 54 and then selected the jobs with more than 30 percent of these workers for inclusion in the first list for this group.) From the list of jobs with a high percentage of each type of worker, we created four more-specialized lists:

- ◉ 25 Best Jobs Overall (jobs with the best combined score for earnings, growth rate, and number of openings)
- ◉ 25 Best-Paying Jobs
- ◉ 25 Fastest-Growing Jobs
- ◉ 25 Jobs with the Most Openings

Again, each of these four lists includes only jobs from among those with the highest percentages of different types of workers. The same basic process was used to create all the lists in this section. The lists are interesting, and we hope you find them helpful.

Best Jobs for Baby Boomers by Age

The term "baby boomers" is used to lump together all the people born between 1946 and 1964, but this is not a homogeneous group. Demographers customarily divide the group into "older boomers," born between 1946 and 1955, and "younger boomers," born between 1956 and 1964. The older boomers entered the workforce in the late 1960s and early 1970s, an era of relative economic prosperity, whereas the younger boomers started their careers during a much less stable era. Consequently, the work experiences of the two groups have been different. The younger group also is less well educated, contains more immigrants, and is accustomed to changing jobs frequently—on average, they did so 10 times during their first 20 years in the workforce. Therefore we decided that it would be interesting to include lists in this section that show what sorts of jobs have a high representation of workers in certain age brackets *within* the larger category of baby boomers.

Unfortunately, the available data did not allow us to break down this generation into "older boomers" and "younger boomers." Instead, we needed to use the age brackets 45–54, 55–64, and 65 and over when compiling lists of best jobs. But we still think you will find the contrasts informative.

Best Jobs with the Highest Percentage of Workers Age 45–54

From our list of 225 jobs used in this book, this list contains jobs with the highest percentage (more than 30 percent) of workers age 45 to 54, presented in order of the percentage of these workers in each job. Historically, most workers in this age bracket have been in their peak earning years, and in fact the weighted average wage for the jobs in this list is $44,767, compared to $33,636 and $40,813 in the two higher age brackets.

Best Jobs for Baby Boomers with the Highest Percentage of Workers Age 45–54

Job	Percent Age 45–54	Annual Earnings	Percent Growth	Annual Openings
1. Forest Fire Fighting and Prevention Supervisors	57.1%	$59,760	18.7%	8,000
2. Municipal Fire Fighting and Prevention Supervisors	57.1%	$59,760	18.7%	8,000
3. Aviation Inspectors	54.3%	$47,920	7.7%	5,000
4. Freight Inspectors	54.3%	$47,920	7.7%	5,000
5. Marine Cargo Inspectors	54.3%	$47,920	7.7%	5,000

Best Jobs for Baby Boomers with the Highest Percentage of Workers Age 45–54

Job	Percent Age 45–54	Annual Earnings	Percent Growth	Annual Openings
6. Motor Vehicle Inspectors	54.3%	$47,920	7.7%	5,000
7. Public Transportation Inspectors	54.3%	$47,920	7.7%	5,000
8. Railroad Inspectors	54.3%	$47,920	7.7%	5,000
9. Sociologists	50.0%	$56,790	13.4%	fewer than 500
10. Electrical and Electronics Repairers, Commercial and Industrial Equipment	45.5%	$43,180	10.3%	10,000
11. Public Relations Managers	43.5%	$73,960	23.4%	10,000
12. Administrative Services Managers	42.0%	$62,300	19.8%	40,000
13. Instructional Coordinators	41.8%	$50,060	25.4%	18,000
14. First-Line Supervisors/Managers of Police and Detectives	41.7%	$65,020	15.3%	14,000
15. Coroners	40.5%	$48,530	9.8%	20,000
16. Environmental Compliance Inspectors	40.5%	$48,530	9.8%	20,000
17. Equal Opportunity Representatives and Officers	40.5%	$48,530	9.8%	20,000
18. Government Property Inspectors and Investigators	40.5%	$48,530	9.8%	20,000
19. Licensing Examiners and Inspectors	40.5%	$48,530	9.8%	20,000
20. Pressure Vessel Inspectors	40.5%	$48,530	9.8%	20,000
21. Medical and Health Services Managers	39.6%	$68,320	29.3%	33,000
22. Librarians	38.1%	$46,940	10.1%	15,000
23. Engineering Managers	37.7%	$99,000	9.2%	16,000
24. Postal Service Mail Carriers	37.5%	$45,880	–0.5%	20,000
25. Chief Executives	36.2%	$141,820	16.7%	63,000
26. Government Service Executives	36.2%	$141,820	16.7%	63,000
27. Private Sector Executives	36.2%	$141,820	16.7%	63,000
28. Education Administrators, Elementary and Secondary School	36.0%	$74,610	20.7%	31,000
29. Education Administrators, Preschool and Child Care Center/Program	36.0%	$36,080	32.0%	9,000
30. Purchasing Managers	35.5%	$74,300	4.8%	9,000
31. Mobile Heavy Equipment Mechanics, Except Engines	35.0%	$38,630	9.6%	12,000
32. Operations Research Analysts	34.7%	$60,230	6.2%	6,000
33. Technical Writers	34.5%	$54,390	27.1%	6,000
34. Speech-Language Pathologists	34.4%	$53,790	27.2%	10,000

(continued)

(continued)

Best Jobs for Baby Boomers with the Highest Percentage of Workers Age 45–54

Job	Percent Age 45–54	Annual Earnings	Percent Growth	Annual Openings
35. Industrial Production Managers	33.3%	$74,100	7.9%	18,000
36. Clinical Psychologists	33.0%	$56,360	24.4%	17,000
37. Counseling Psychologists	33.0%	$56,360	24.4%	17,000
38. Educational Psychologists	33.0%	$56,360	24.4%	17,000
39. Industrial-Organizational Psychologists	33.0%	$74,060	16.0%	fewer than 500
40. Dietitians and Nutritionists	32.9%	$44,370	17.8%	8,000
41. Chiropractors	32.9%	$67,940	23.3%	3,000
42. Airline Pilots, Copilots, and Flight Engineers	32.8%	$135,430	18.5%	6,000
43. Commercial Pilots	32.8%	$55,360	14.9%	2,000
44. First-Line Supervisors/Managers of Mechanics, Installers, and Repairers	32.6%	$51,000	15.4%	42,000
45. Construction and Building Inspectors	32.6%	$43,940	13.8%	10,000
46. Bus Drivers, School	32.4%	$23,670	16.7%	76,000
47. Bus Drivers, Transit and Intercity	32.4%	$30,670	15.2%	33,000
48. Economists	32.4%	$72,370	13.4%	2,000
49. First-Line Supervisors/Managers of Correctional Officers	32.3%	$48,070	19.0%	4,000
50. Budget Analysts	32.1%	$57,190	14.0%	8,000
51. Industrial Machinery Mechanics	32.0%	$39,310	5.5%	19,000
52. Refractory Materials Repairers, Except Brickmasons	32.0%	$39,610	16.3%	155,000
53. Compensation and Benefits Managers	31.9%	$67,040	19.4%	21,000
54. Training and Development Managers	31.9%	$70,430	19.4%	21,000
55. Air Traffic Controllers	31.6%	$102,390	12.6%	2,000
56. Clergy	31.5%	$37,870	15.5%	34,000
57. Registered Nurses	31.3%	$53,640	27.3%	215,000
58. Water and Liquid Waste Treatment Plant and System Operators	31.1%	$34,850	16.0%	9,000
59. Appraisers, Real Estate	31.1%	$43,790	17.6%	11,000
60. Assessors	31.1%	$43,790	17.6%	11,000
61. Secondary School Teachers, Except Special and Vocational Education	31.0%	$46,120	18.2%	118,000
62. Vocational Education Teachers, Secondary School	31.0%	$46,650	9.0%	12,000
63. Special Education Teachers, Middle School	30.8%	$45,000	30.0%	59,000

Best Jobs for Baby Boomers with the Highest Percentage of Workers Age 45–54

Job	Percent Age 45–54	Annual Earnings	Percent Growth	Annual Openings
64. Special Education Teachers, Preschool, Kindergarten, and Elementary School	30.8%	$44,330	30.0%	59,000
65. Special Education Teachers, Secondary School	30.8%	$46,300	30.0%	59,000
66. First-Line Supervisors and Manager/ Supervisors—Agricultural Crop Workers	30.8%	$36,040	11.4%	6,000
67. First-Line Supervisors and Manager/ Supervisors—Animal Care Workers, Except Livestock	30.8%	$36,040	11.4%	6,000
68. First-Line Supervisors and Manager/ Supervisors—Animal Husbandry Workers	30.8%	$36,040	11.4%	6,000
69. First-Line Supervisors and Manager/ Supervisors—Fishery Workers	30.8%	$36,040	11.4%	6,000
70. First-Line Supervisors and Manager/ Supervisors—Horticultural Workers	30.8%	$36,040	11.4%	6,000
71. First-Line Supervisors and Manager/ Supervisors—Logging Workers	30.8%	$36,040	11.4%	6,000
72. Emergency Management Specialists	30.7%	$45,670	28.2%	2,000
73. Licensed Practical and Licensed Vocational Nurses	30.5%	$34,650	20.2%	105,000
74. Locksmiths and Safe Repairers	30.4%	$30,580	21.0%	3,000
75. Construction Managers	30.3%	$70,770	12.0%	47,000
76. Housekeeping Supervisors	30.1%	$30,050	16.2%	28,000
77. Janitorial Supervisors	30.1%	$30,050	16.2%	28,000
78. First-Line Supervisors, Administrative Support	30.1%	$41,850	6.6%	140,000
79. First-Line Supervisors, Customer Service	30.1%	$41,850	6.6%	140,000
80. General and Operations Managers	30.1%	$79,300	18.4%	260,000
81. Electrical Engineers	30.0%	$72,770	2.5%	11,000
82. Electronics Engineers, Except Computer	30.0%	$76,810	9.4%	11,000

Jobs 1 and 2 share 8,000 openings. Jobs 3, 4, 5, 6, 7, and 8 share 5,000 openings. Jobs 15, 16, 17, 18, 19, and 20 share 20,000 openings. Jobs 25, 26, and 27 share 63,000 openings. Jobs 36, 37, and 38 share 17,000 openings. Jobs 53 and 54 share 21,000 openings. Jobs 59 and 60 share 11,000 openings. Jobs 63, 64, and 65 share 59,000 openings. Jobs 66, 67, 68, 69, 70, and 71 share 6,000 openings. Jobs 76 and 77 share 28,000 openings. Jobs 78 and 79 share 140,000 openings.

The jobs in the following four lists are derived from the preceding list of the jobs with the highest percentage of workers age 45–54.

Best Jobs Overall for Baby Boomers Age 45–54

Job	Percent Age 45–54	Annual Earnings	Percent Growth	Annual Openings
1. General and Operations Managers	30.1%	$79,300	18.4%	260,000
2. Chief Executives	36.2%	$141,820	16.7%	63,000
3. Government Service Executives	36.2%	$141,820	16.7%	63,000
4. Private Sector Executives	36.2%	$141,820	16.7%	63,000
5. Medical and Health Services Managers	39.6%	$68,320	29.3%	33,000
6. Registered Nurses	31.3%	$53,640	27.3%	215,000
7. Education Administrators, Elementary and Secondary School	36.0%	$74,610	20.7%	31,000
8. Administrative Services Managers	42.0%	$62,300	19.8%	40,000
9. Training and Development Managers	31.9%	$70,430	19.4%	21,000
10. Compensation and Benefits Managers	31.9%	$67,040	19.4%	21,000
11. Special Education Teachers, Secondary School	30.8%	$46,300	30.0%	59,000
12. Special Education Teachers, Middle School	30.8%	$45,000	30.0%	59,000
13. Special Education Teachers, Preschool, Kindergarten, and Elementary School	30.8%	$44,330	30.0%	59,000
14. Clinical Psychologists	33.0%	$56,360	24.4%	17,000
15. Counseling Psychologists	33.0%	$56,360	24.4%	17,000
16. Educational Psychologists	33.0%	$56,360	24.4%	17,000
17. Public Relations Managers	43.5%	$73,960	23.4%	10,000
18. Instructional Coordinators	41.8%	$50,060	25.4%	18,000
19. Construction Managers	30.3%	$70,770	12.0%	47,000
20. Secondary School Teachers, Except Special and Vocational Education	31.0%	$46,120	18.2%	118,000
21. Airline Pilots, Copilots, and Flight Engineers	32.8%	$135,430	18.5%	6,000
22. Speech-Language Pathologists	34.4%	$53,790	27.2%	10,000
23. First-Line Supervisors/Managers of Mechanics, Installers, and Repairers	32.6%	$51,000	15.4%	42,000
24. Technical Writers	34.5%	$54,390	27.1%	6,000
25. Forest Fire Fighting and Prevention Supervisors	57.1%	$59,760	18.7%	8,000

Jobs 2, 3, and 4 share 63,000 openings. Jobs 9 and 10 share 21,000 openings. Jobs 11, 12, and 13 share 59,000 openings. Jobs 14, 15, and 16 share 17,000 openings. Job 25 shares 8,000 openings with another job not on this list.

Best-Paying Jobs for Baby Boomers Age 45–54

Job	Percent Age 45–54	Annual Earnings	Percent Growth	Annual Openings
1. Chief Executives	36.2%	$141,820	16.7%	63,000
2. Government Service Executives	36.2%	$141,820	16.7%	63,000
3. Private Sector Executives	36.2%	$141,820	16.7%	63,000
4. Airline Pilots, Copilots, and Flight Engineers	32.8%	$135,430	18.5%	6,000
5. Air Traffic Controllers	31.6%	$102,390	12.6%	2,000
6. Engineering Managers	37.7%	$99,000	9.2%	16,000
7. General and Operations Managers	30.1%	$79,300	18.4%	260,000
8. Electronics Engineers, Except Computer	30.0%	$76,810	9.4%	11,000
9. Education Administrators, Elementary and Secondary School	36.0%	$74,610	20.7%	31,000
10. Purchasing Managers	35.5%	$74,300	4.8%	9,000
11. Industrial Production Managers	33.3%	$74,100	7.9%	18,000
12. Industrial-Organizational Psychologists	33.0%	$74,060	16.0%	fewer than 500
13. Public Relations Managers	43.5%	$73,960	23.4%	10,000
14. Electrical Engineers	30.0%	$72,770	2.5%	11,000
15. Economists	32.4%	$72,370	13.4%	2,000
16. Construction Managers	30.3%	$70,770	12.0%	47,000
17. Training and Development Managers	31.9%	$70,430	19.4%	21,000
18. Medical and Health Services Managers	39.6%	$68,320	29.3%	33,000
19. Chiropractors	32.9%	$67,940	23.3%	3,000
20. Compensation and Benefits Managers	31.9%	$67,040	19.4%	21,000
21. First-Line Supervisors/Managers of Police and Detectives	41.7%	$65,020	15.3%	14,000
22. Administrative Services Managers	42.0%	$62,300	19.8%	40,000
23. Operations Research Analysts	34.7%	$60,230	6.2%	6,000
24. Forest Fire Fighting and Prevention Supervisors	57.1%	$59,760	18.7%	8,000
25. Municipal Fire Fighting and Prevention Supervisors	57.1%	$59,760	18.7%	8,000

Jobs 1, 2, and 3 share 63,000 openings. Jobs 17 and 20 share 21,000 openings.

Fastest-Growing Jobs for Baby Boomers Age 45–54

Job	Percent Age 45–54	Annual Earnings	Percent Growth	Annual Openings
1. Education Administrators, Preschool and Child Care Center/Program	36.0%	$36,080	32.0%	9,000
2. Special Education Teachers, Middle School	30.8%	$45,000	30.0%	59,000
3. Special Education Teachers, Preschool, Kindergarten, and Elementary School	30.8%	$44,330	30.0%	59,000
4. Special Education Teachers, Secondary School	30.8%	$46,300	30.0%	59,000
5. Medical and Health Services Managers	39.6%	$68,320	29.3%	33,000
6. Emergency Management Specialists	30.7%	$45,670	28.2%	2,000
7. Registered Nurses	31.3%	$53,640	27.3%	215,000
8. Speech-Language Pathologists	34.4%	$53,790	27.2%	10,000
9. Technical Writers	34.5%	$54,390	27.1%	6,000
10. Instructional Coordinators	41.8%	$50,060	25.4%	18,000
11. Clinical Psychologists	33.0%	$56,360	24.4%	17,000
12. Counseling Psychologists	33.0%	$56,360	24.4%	17,000
13. Educational Psychologists	33.0%	$56,360	24.4%	17,000
14. Public Relations Managers	43.5%	$73,960	23.4%	10,000
15. Chiropractors	32.9%	$67,940	23.3%	3,000
16. Locksmiths and Safe Repairers	30.4%	$30,580	21.0%	3,000
17. Education Administrators, Elementary and Secondary School	36.0%	$74,610	20.7%	31,000
18. Licensed Practical and Licensed Vocational Nurses	30.5%	$34,650	20.2%	105,000
19. Administrative Services Managers	42.0%	$62,300	19.8%	40,000
20. Compensation and Benefits Managers	31.9%	$67,040	19.4%	21,000
21. Training and Development Managers	31.9%	$70,430	19.4%	21,000
22. First-Line Supervisors/Managers of Correctional Officers	32.3%	$48,070	19.0%	4,000
23. Forest Fire Fighting and Prevention Supervisors	57.1%	$59,760	18.7%	8,000
24. Municipal Fire Fighting and Prevention Supervisors	57.1%	$59,760	18.7%	8,000
25. Airline Pilots, Copilots, and Flight Engineers	32.8%	$135,430	18.5%	6,000

Jobs 2, 3, and 4 share 59,000 openings. Jobs 11, 12, and 13 share 17,000 openings. Jobs 20 and 21 share 21,000 openings. Jobs 23 and 24 share 8,000 openings.

Jobs for Baby Boomers Age 45–54 with the Most Openings

Job	Percent Age 45–54	Annual Earnings	Percent Growth	Annual Openings
1. General and Operations Managers	30.1%	$79,300	18.4%	260,000
2. Registered Nurses	31.3%	$53,640	27.3%	215,000
3. Refractory Materials Repairers, Except Brickmasons	32.0%	$39,610	16.3%	155,000
4. First-Line Supervisors, Administrative Support	30.1%	$41,850	6.6%	140,000
5. First-Line Supervisors, Customer Service	30.1%	$41,850	6.6%	140,000
6. Secondary School Teachers, Except Special and Vocational Education	31.0%	$46,120	18.2%	118,000
7. Licensed Practical and Licensed Vocational Nurses	30.5%	$34,650	20.2%	105,000
8. Bus Drivers, School	32.4%	$23,670	16.7%	76,000
9. Chief Executives	36.2%	$141,820	16.7%	63,000
10. Government Service Executives	36.2%	$141,820	16.7%	63,000
11. Private Sector Executives	36.2%	$141,820	16.7%	63,000
12. Special Education Teachers, Middle School	30.8%	$45,000	30.0%	59,000
13. Special Education Teachers, Preschool, Kindergarten, and Elementary School	30.8%	$44,330	30.0%	59,000
14. Special Education Teachers, Secondary School	30.8%	$46,300	30.0%	59,000
15. Construction Managers	30.3%	$70,770	12.0%	47,000
16. First-Line Supervisors/Managers of Mechanics, Installers, and Repairers	32.6%	$51,000	15.4%	42,000
17. Administrative Services Managers	42.0%	$62,300	19.8%	40,000
18. Clergy	31.5%	$37,870	15.5%	34,000
19. Bus Drivers, Transit and Intercity	32.4%	$30,670	15.2%	33,000
20. Medical and Health Services Managers	39.6%	$68,320	29.3%	33,000
21. Education Administrators, Elementary and Secondary School	36.0%	$74,610	20.7%	31,000
22. Housekeeping Supervisors	30.1%	$30,050	16.2%	28,000
23. Janitorial Supervisors	30.1%	$30,050	16.2%	28,000
24. Compensation and Benefits Managers	31.9%	$67,040	19.4%	21,000
25. Training and Development Managers	31.9%	$70,430	19.4%	21,000

Jobs 4 and 5 share 140,000 openings. Jobs 9, 10, and 11 share 63,000 openings. Jobs 12, 13, and 14 share 59,000 openings. Jobs 22 and 23 share 28,000 openings. Jobs 24 and 25 share 21,000 openings.

Best Jobs with the Highest Percentage of Workers Age 55–64

Whereas the four previous lists show jobs with more than 30 percent of workers in a certain age bracket, this group of four lists sets the cutoff at 15 percent—because the age bracket 55 to 64, which contains a mixture of "older boomers" and pre-boomers, holds fewer American workers than the group on which the previous list is based. Although most of the "older boomers" are not yet eligible for retirement, most of them are probably starting to make plans for it.

Best Jobs for Baby Boomers with the Highest Percentage of Workers Age 55–64

Job	Percent Age 55–64	Annual Earnings	Percent Growth	Annual Openings
1. Physicists	33.3%	$87,480	6.9%	1,000
2. Arbitrators, Mediators, and Conciliators	30.5%	$53,690	13.7%	fewer than 500
3. Judges, Magistrate Judges, and Magistrates	30.5%	$97,260	8.7%	2,000
4. Librarians	25.3%	$46,940	10.1%	15,000
5. Farmers and Ranchers	24.4%	$38,600	−20.6%	118,000
6. Clinical Psychologists	23.8%	$56,360	24.4%	17,000
7. Counseling Psychologists	23.8%	$56,360	24.4%	17,000
8. Educational Psychologists	23.8%	$56,360	24.4%	17,000
9. Industrial-Organizational Psychologists	23.8%	$74,060	16.0%	fewer than 500
10. Real Estate Brokers	23.5%	$56,970	2.4%	11,000
11. Real Estate Sales Agents	23.5%	$36,950	5.7%	34,000
12. Audiologists	23.1%	$53,040	29.0%	1,000
13. Education Administrators, Elementary and Secondary School	22.7%	$74,610	20.7%	31,000
14. Education Administrators, Preschool and Child Care Center/Program	22.7%	$36,080	32.0%	9,000
15. Tax Preparers	22.0%	$26,130	23.2%	11,000
16. Directors, Religious Activities and Education	20.7%	$30,720	24.1%	16,000
17. Management Analysts	20.7%	$64,560	30.4%	78,000
18. Taxi Drivers and Chauffeurs	20.6%	$19,790	21.7%	28,000
19. Property, Real Estate, and Community Association Managers	20.6%	$41,540	12.8%	35,000
20. Clergy	20.5%	$37,870	15.5%	34,000
21. Private Detectives and Investigators	20.3%	$32,510	25.3%	9,000
22. Chief Executives	20.3%	$141,820	16.7%	63,000
23. Government Service Executives	20.3%	$141,820	16.7%	63,000
24. Private Sector Executives	20.3%	$141,820	16.7%	63,000
25. Bus Drivers, School	20.1%	$23,670	16.7%	76,000
26. Bus Drivers, Transit and Intercity	20.1%	$30,670	15.2%	33,000

Best Jobs for Baby Boomers with the Highest Percentage of Workers Age 55–64

Job	Percent Age 55–64	Annual Earnings	Percent Growth	Annual Openings
27. Social and Community Service Managers	19.9%	$48,330	27.7%	19,000
28. Dentists, General	19.7%	$122,430	4.1%	7,000
29. Oral and Maxillofacial Surgeons	19.7%	more than $145,600	4.1%	7,000
30. Orthodontists	19.7%	more than $145,600	4.1%	7,000
31. Prosthodontists	19.7%	more than $145,600	4.1%	7,000
32. Postsecondary Teachers	19.0%	$54,406	38.1%	216,000
33. First-Line Supervisors and Manager/ Supervisors—Agricultural Crop Workers	18.5%	$36,040	11.4%	6,000
34. First-Line Supervisors and Manager/ Supervisors—Animal Care Workers, Except Livestock	18.5%	$36,040	11.4%	6,000
35. First-Line Supervisors and Manager/ Supervisors—Animal Husbandry Workers	18.5%	$36,040	11.4%	6,000
36. First-Line Supervisors and Manager/ Supervisors—Fishery Workers	18.5%	$36,040	11.4%	6,000
37. First-Line Supervisors and Manager/ Supervisors—Horticultural Workers	18.5%	$36,040	11.4%	6,000
38. First-Line Supervisors and Manager/ Supervisors—Logging Workers	18.5%	$36,040	11.4%	6,000
39. Subway and Streetcar Operators	18.2%	$47,560	13.2%	2,000
40. Emergency Management Specialists	18.1%	$45,670	28.2%	2,000
41. Water and Liquid Waste Treatment Plant and System Operators	18.0%	$34,850	16.0%	9,000
42. Instructional Coordinators	17.9%	$50,060	25.4%	18,000
43. Construction and Building Inspectors	17.9%	$43,940	13.8%	10,000
44. Economists	17.6%	$72,370	13.4%	2,000
45. Lodging Managers	17.5%	$39,100	6.6%	10,000
46. Compensation and Benefits Managers	17.5%	$67,040	19.4%	21,000
47. Training and Development Managers	17.5%	$70,430	19.4%	21,000
48. Agricultural Crop Farm Managers	17.5%	$50,720	5.1%	25,000
49. Fish Hatchery Managers	17.5%	$50,720	5.1%	25,000
50. Nursery and Greenhouse Managers	17.5%	$50,720	5.1%	25,000
51. Laundry and Drycleaning Machine Operators and Tenders, Except Pressing	17.1%	$17,350	12.3%	47,000
52. Precision Dyers	17.1%	$17,350	12.3%	47,000
53. Spotters, Dry Cleaning	17.1%	$17,350	12.3%	47,000
54. Personal and Home Care Aides	17.0%	$17,020	40.5%	154,000

(continued)

(continued)

Best Jobs for Baby Boomers with the Highest Percentage of Workers Age 55–64

Job	Percent Age 55–64	Annual Earnings	Percent Growth	Annual Openings
55. Art Directors	17.0%	$63,750	11.4%	8,000
56. Multi-Media Artists and Animators	17.0%	$49,900	15.8%	12,000
57. Cartoonists	17.0%	$41,240	16.5%	4,000
58. Painters and Illustrators	17.0%	$41,240	16.5%	4,000
59. Sculptors	17.0%	$41,240	16.5%	4,000
60. Sketch Artists	17.0%	$41,240	16.5%	4,000
61. Housekeeping Supervisors	16.9%	$30,050	16.2%	28,000
62. Janitorial Supervisors	16.9%	$30,050	16.2%	28,000
63. Lawyers	16.8%	$97,420	17.0%	53,000
64. Bookkeeping, Accounting, and Auditing Clerks	16.6%	$29,040	3.0%	274,000
65. Caption Writers	16.3%	$45,460	16.1%	23,000
66. Copy Writers	16.3%	$45,460	16.1%	23,000
67. Creative Writers	16.3%	$45,460	16.1%	23,000
68. Poets and Lyricists	16.3%	$45,460	16.1%	23,000
69. Executive Secretaries and Administrative Assistants	16.3%	$35,550	8.7%	210,000
70. Legal Secretaries	16.3%	$37,390	18.8%	39,000
71. Medical Secretaries	16.3%	$27,030	17.2%	50,000
72. Janitors and Cleaners, Except Maids and Housekeeping Cleaners	16.2%	$19,110	18.3%	454,000
73. Personal Financial Advisors	16.2%	$62,450	34.6%	18,000
74. Curators	16.1%	$43,920	17.0%	2,000
75. First-Line Supervisors/Managers of Correctional Officers	16.1%	$48,070	19.0%	4,000
76. Postal Service Mail Carriers	16.1%	$45,880	–0.5%	20,000
77. Pharmacists	15.9%	$87,160	30.1%	23,000
78. Special Education Teachers, Middle School	15.9%	$45,000	30.0%	59,000
79. Special Education Teachers, Preschool, Kindergarten, and Elementary School	15.9%	$44,330	30.0%	59,000
80. Special Education Teachers, Secondary School	15.9%	$46,300	30.0%	59,000
81. Insurance Sales Agents	15.9%	$42,030	8.4%	52,000
82. Security Guards	15.9%	$20,520	31.9%	228,000
83. Secondary School Teachers, Except Special and Vocational Education	15.7%	$46,120	18.2%	118,000
84. Vocational Education Teachers, Secondary School	15.7%	$46,650	9.0%	12,000

Best Jobs for Baby Boomers with the Highest Percentage of Workers Age 55–64

Job	Percent Age 55–64	Annual Earnings	Percent Growth	Annual Openings
85. Airline Pilots, Copilots, and Flight Engineers	15.5%	$135,430	18.5%	6,000
86. Commercial Pilots	15.5%	$55,360	14.9%	2,000
87. First-Line Supervisors/Managers of Non-Retail Sales Workers	15.5%	$60,300	6.8%	72,000
88. Purchasing Managers	15.4%	$74,300	4.8%	9,000
89. Veterinarians	15.3%	$68,280	25.1%	4,000
90. Aviation Inspectors	15.2%	$47,920	7.7%	5,000
91. Freight Inspectors	15.2%	$47,920	7.7%	5,000
92. Marine Cargo Inspectors	15.2%	$47,920	7.7%	5,000
93. Motor Vehicle Inspectors	15.2%	$47,920	7.7%	5,000
94. Public Transportation Inspectors	15.2%	$47,920	7.7%	5,000
95. Railroad Inspectors	15.2%	$47,920	7.7%	5,000
96. First-Line Supervisors, Administrative Support	15.2%	$41,850	6.6%	140,000
97. First-Line Supervisors, Customer Service	15.2%	$41,850	6.6%	140,000
98. Appraisers, Real Estate	15.1%	$43,790	17.6%	11,000
99. Assessors	15.1%	$43,790	17.6%	11,000
100. Coroners	15.1%	$48,530	9.8%	20,000
101. Environmental Compliance Inspectors	15.1%	$48,530	9.8%	20,000
102. Equal Opportunity Representatives and Officers	15.1%	$48,530	9.8%	20,000
103. Government Property Inspectors and Investigators	15.1%	$48,530	9.8%	20,000
104. Licensing Examiners and Inspectors	15.1%	$48,530	9.8%	20,000
105. Pressure Vessel Inspectors	15.1%	$48,530	9.8%	20,000
106. Electrical and Electronic Inspectors and Testers	15.0%	$28,630	4.7%	87,000
107. Materials Inspectors	15.0%	$28,630	4.7%	87,000
108. Mechanical Inspectors	15.0%	$28,630	4.7%	87,000
109. Precision Devices Inspectors and Testers	15.0%	$28,630	4.7%	87,000
110. Production Inspectors, Testers, Graders, Sorters, Samplers, Weighers	15.0%	$28,630	4.7%	87,000
111. First-Line Supervisors/Managers of Mechanics, Installers, and Repairers	15.0%	$51,000	15.4%	42,000

Jobs 6, 7, and 8 share 17,000 openings. Jobs 22, 23, and 24 share 63,000 openings. Jobs 28, 29, 30, and 31 share 7,000 openings. Jobs 33, 34, 35, 36, 37, and 38 share 6,000 openings. Jobs 46 and 47 share 21,000 openings. Jobs 48, 49, and 50 share 25,000 openings. Jobs 51, 52, and 53 share 47,000 openings. Jobs 57, 58, 59, and 60 share 4,000 openings. Jobs 61 and 62 share 28,000 openings. Jobs 65, 66, 67, and 68 share 23,000 openings. Jobs 78, 79, and 80 share 59,000 openings. Jobs 90, 191, 92, 93, 94, and 95 share 5,000 openings. Jobs 96 and 97 share 140,000 openings. Jobs 98 and 99 share 11,000 openings. Jobs 100, 101, 102, 103, 104, and 105 share 20,000 openings. Jobs 106, 107, 108, 109, and 110 share 87,000 openings.

The jobs in the following four lists are derived from the preceding list of the jobs with the highest percentage of workers age 55–64.

Best Jobs Overall for Baby Boomers Age 55–64

Job	Percent Age 55–64	Annual Earnings	Percent Growth	Annual Openings
1. Postsecondary Teachers	19.0%	$54,406	38.1%	216,000
2. Management Analysts	20.7%	$64,560	30.4%	78,000
3. Chief Executives	20.3%	$141,820	16.7%	63,000
4. Government Service Executives	20.3%	$141,820	16.7%	63,000
5. Private Sector Executives	20.3%	$141,820	16.7%	63,000
6. Pharmacists	15.9%	$87,160	30.1%	23,000
7. Lawyers	16.8%	$97,420	17.0%	53,000
8. Education Administrators, Elementary and Secondary School	22.7%	$74,610	20.7%	31,000
9. Personal Financial Advisors	16.2%	$62,450	34.6%	18,000
10. Special Education Teachers, Secondary School	15.9%	$46,300	30.0%	59,000
11. Training and Development Managers	17.5%	$70,430	19.4%	21,000
12. Compensation and Benefits Managers	17.5%	$67,040	19.4%	21,000
13. Special Education Teachers, Middle School	15.9%	$45,000	30.0%	59,000
14. Special Education Teachers, Preschool, Kindergarten, and Elementary School	15.9%	$44,330	30.0%	59,000
15. Secondary School Teachers, Except Special and Vocational Education	15.7%	$46,120	18.2%	118,000
16. Clinical Psychologists	23.8%	$56,360	24.4%	17,000
17. Counseling Psychologists	23.8%	$56,360	24.4%	17,000
18. Educational Psychologists	23.8%	$56,360	24.4%	17,000
19. Instructional Coordinators	17.9%	$50,060	25.4%	18,000
20. Security Guards	15.9%	$20,520	31.9%	228,000
21. Social and Community Service Managers	19.9%	$48,330	27.7%	19,000
22. First-Line Supervisors/Managers of Mechanics, Installers, and Repairers	15.0%	$51,000	15.4%	42,000
23. Airline Pilots, Copilots, and Flight Engineers	15.5%	$135,430	18.5%	6,000
24. Personal and Home Care Aides	17.0%	$17,020	40.5%	154,000
25. Veterinarians	15.3%	$68,280	25.1%	4,000

Jobs 3, 4, and 5 share 63,000 openings. Jobs 10, 13, and 14 share 59,000 openings. Jobs 11 and 12 share 21,000 openings. Jobs 16, 17, and 18 share 17,000 openings.

Best-Paying Jobs for Baby Boomers Age 55–64

Job	Percent Age 55–64	Annual Earnings	Percent Growth	Annual Openings
1. Oral and Maxillofacial Surgeons	19.7% ..more than	$145,600	4.1%	7,000
2. Orthodontists	19.7% ..more than	$145,600	4.1%	7,000
3. Prosthodontists	19.7% ..more than	$145,600	4.1%	7,000
4. Chief Executives	20.3%	$141,820	16.7%	63,000
5. Government Service Executives	20.3%	$141,820	16.7%	63,000
6. Private Sector Executives	20.3%	$141,820	16.7%	63,000
7. Airline Pilots, Copilots, and Flight Engineers	15.5%	$135,430	18.5%	6,000
8. Dentists, General	19.7%	$122,430	4.1%	7,000
9. Lawyers	16.8%	$97,420	17.0%	53,000
10. Judges, Magistrate Judges, and Magistrates	30.5%	$97,260	8.7%	2,000
11. Physicists	33.3%	$87,480	6.9%	1,000
12. Pharmacists	15.9%	$87,160	30.1%	23,000
13. Education Administrators, Elementary and Secondary School	22.7%	$74,610	20.7%	31,000
14. Purchasing Managers	15.4%	$74,300	4.8%	9,000
15. Industrial-Organizational Psychologists	23.8%	$74,060	16.0%	fewer than 500
16. Economists	17.6%	$72,370	13.4%	2,000
17. Training and Development Managers	17.5%	$70,430	19.4%	21,000
18. Veterinarians	15.3%	$68,280	25.1%	4,000
19. Compensation and Benefits Managers	17.5%	$67,040	19.4%	21,000
20. Management Analysts	20.7%	$64,560	30.4%	78,000
21. Art Directors	17.0%	$63,750	11.4%	8,000
22. Personal Financial Advisors	16.2%	$62,450	34.6%	18,000
23. First-Line Supervisors/Managers of Non-Retail Sales Workers	15.5%	$60,300	6.8%	72,000
24. Real Estate Brokers	23.5%	$56,970	2.4%	11,000
25. Clinical Psychologists	23.8%	$56,360	24.4%	17,000

Jobs 1, 2, 3, and 8 share 7,000 openings. Jobs 4, 5, and 6 share 63,000 openings. Jobs 17 and 19 share 21,000 openings. Job 25 shares 17,000 openings with two other jobs not on this list.

Fastest-Growing Jobs for Baby Boomers Age 55–64

Job	Percent Age 55–64	Annual Earnings	Percent Growth	Annual Openings
1. Personal and Home Care Aides	17.0%	$17,020	40.5%	154,000
2. Postsecondary Teachers	19.0%	$54,406	38.1%	216,000
3. Personal Financial Advisors	16.2%	$62,450	34.6%	18,000
4. Education Administrators, Preschool and Child Care Center/Program	22.7%	$36,080	32.0%	9,000
5. Security Guards	15.9%	$20,520	31.9%	228,000
6. Management Analysts	20.7%	$64,560	30.4%	78,000
7. Pharmacists	15.9%	$87,160	30.1%	23,000
8. Special Education Teachers, Middle School	15.9%	$45,000	30.0%	59,000
9. Special Education Teachers, Preschool, Kindergarten, and Elementary School	15.9%	$44,330	30.0%	59,000
10. Special Education Teachers, Secondary School	15.9%	$46,300	30.0%	59,000
11. Audiologists	23.1%	$53,040	29.0%	1,000
12. Emergency Management Specialists	18.1%	$45,670	28.2%	2,000
13. Social and Community Service Managers	19.9%	$48,330	27.7%	19,000
14. Instructional Coordinators	17.9%	$50,060	25.4%	18,000
15. Private Detectives and Investigators	20.3%	$32,510	25.3%	9,000
16. Veterinarians	15.3%	$68,280	25.1%	4,000
17. Clinical Psychologists	23.8%	$56,360	24.4%	17,000
18. Counseling Psychologists	23.8%	$56,360	24.4%	17,000
19. Educational Psychologists	23.8%	$56,360	24.4%	17,000
20. Directors, Religious Activities and Education	20.7%	$30,720	24.1%	16,000
21. Tax Preparers	22.0%	$26,130	23.2%	11,000
22. Taxi Drivers and Chauffeurs	20.6%	$19,790	21.7%	28,000
23. Education Administrators, Elementary and Secondary School	22.7%	$74,610	20.7%	31,000
24. Compensation and Benefits Managers	17.5%	$67,040	19.4%	21,000
25. Training and Development Managers	17.5%	$70,430	19.4%	21,000

Jobs 8, 9, and 10 share 59,000 openings. Jobs 17, 18, and 19 share 17,000 openings. Jobs 24 and 25 share 21,000 openings.

Jobs for Baby Boomers Age 55–64 with the Most Openings

Job	Percent Age 55–64	Annual Earnings	Percent Growth	Annual Openings
1. Janitors and Cleaners, Except Maids and Housekeeping Cleaners	16.2%	$19,110	18.3%	454,000
2. Bookkeeping, Accounting, and Auditing Clerks	16.6%	$29,040	3.0%	274,000
3. Security Guards	15.9%	$20,520	31.9%	228,000
4. Postsecondary Teachers	19.0%	$54,406	38.1%	216,000
5. Executive Secretaries and Administrative Assistants	16.3%	$35,550	8.7%	210,000
6. Personal and Home Care Aides	17.0%	$17,020	40.5%	154,000
7. First-Line Supervisors, Administrative Support	15.2%	$41,850	6.6%	140,000
8. First-Line Supervisors, Customer Service	15.2%	$41,850	6.6%	140,000
9. Farmers and Ranchers	24.4%	$38,600	–20.6%	118,000
10. Secondary School Teachers, Except Special and Vocational Education	15.7%	$46,120	18.2%	118,000
11. Electrical and Electronic Inspectors and Testers	15.0%	$28,630	4.7%	87,000
12. Materials Inspectors	15.0%	$28,630	4.7%	87,000
13. Mechanical Inspectors	15.0%	$28,630	4.7%	87,000
14. Precision Devices Inspectors and Testers	15.0%	$28,630	4.7%	87,000
15. Production Inspectors, Testers, Graders, Sorters, Samplers, Weighers	15.0%	$28,630	4.7%	87,000
16. Management Analysts	20.7%	$64,560	30.4%	78,000
17. Bus Drivers, School	20.1%	$23,670	16.7%	76,000
18. First-Line Supervisors/Managers of Non-Retail Sales Workers	15.5%	$60,300	6.8%	72,000
19. Chief Executives	20.3%	$141,820	16.7%	63,000
20. Government Service Executives	20.3%	$141,820	16.7%	63,000
21. Private Sector Executives	20.3%	$141,820	16.7%	63,000
22. Special Education Teachers, Middle School	15.9%	$45,000	30.0%	59,000
23. Special Education Teachers, Preschool, Kindergarten, and Elementary School	15.9%	$44,330	30.0%	59,000
24. Special Education Teachers, Secondary School	15.9%	$46,300	30.0%	59,000
25. Lawyers	16.8%	$97,420	17.0%	53,000

Jobs 7 and 8 share 140,000 openings. Jobs 11, 12, 13, 14, and 15 share 87,000 openings. Jobs 20, 21, and 22 share 63,000 openings. Jobs 22, 23, and 24 share 59,000 openings.

Best Jobs with a High Percentage of Workers Age 65 and Over

Because many workers retire around age 65, those who stay in the workforce at this age or beyond are a relatively small group. Therefore, any of the 225 best jobs that has a workforce with only 5 percent or more of people 65 and over can be considered to have a relatively high concentration of these senior workers. The first list is ordered by percentage of these workers in each job.

These "Eisenhower Generation" workers are actually too old to be baby boomers, but the oldest of the boomers will enter this age bracket in just a few years and therefore may be interested in the experiences of an older cohort. All of these workers are eligible for Social Security, and some of them (such as teachers and government workers) are eligible to retire on nice pensions. So if an occupation has a large percentage of age-65-plus workers, it may be keeping people in the workforce because of unusual rewards or because the amount of preparation required for entry is high and workers want to recoup that investment. Physical demands of these jobs are typically low. Some of these would make good jobs to continue in or enter after retirement, particularly if they allow for part-time work or self-employment.

Best Jobs for Baby Boomers with the Highest Percentage of Workers Age 65 and Over

Job	Percent Age 65 and Over	Annual Earnings	Percent Growth	Annual Openings
1. Crossing Guards	25.0%	$19,710	16.5%	19,000
2. Farmers and Ranchers	24.4%	$38,600	–20.6%	118,000
3. Demonstrators and Product Promoters	20.5%	$20,490	17.0%	38,000
4. Tax Preparers	13.2%	$26,130	23.2%	11,000
5. Agricultural Crop Farm Managers	12.6%	$50,720	5.1%	25,000
6. Fish Hatchery Managers	12.6%	$50,720	5.1%	25,000
7. Nursery and Greenhouse Managers	12.6%	$50,720	5.1%	25,000
8. Clergy	12.2%	$37,870	15.5%	34,000
9. Arbitrators, Mediators, and Conciliators	11.9%	$53,690	13.7%	fewer than 500
10. Judges, Magistrate Judges, and Magistrates	11.9%	$97,260	8.7%	2,000
11. Property, Real Estate, and Community Association Managers	11.5%	$41,540	12.8%	35,000
12. Physicists	11.1%	$87,480	6.9%	1,000
13. Composers	10.6%	$34,800	13.5%	8,000
14. Music Arrangers and Orchestrators	10.6%	$34,800	13.5%	8,000
15. Music Directors	10.6%	$34,800	13.5%	8,000
16. Taxi Drivers and Chauffeurs	10.5%	$19,790	21.7%	28,000
17. Real Estate Brokers	9.9%	$56,970	2.4%	11,000
18. Real Estate Sales Agents	9.9%	$36,950	5.7%	34,000
19. Bus Drivers, School	9.5%	$23,670	16.7%	76,000

Best Jobs for Baby Boomers with the Highest Percentage of Workers Age 65 and Over

Job	Percent Age 65 and Over	Annual Earnings	Percent Growth	Annual Openings
20. Bus Drivers, Transit and Intercity	9.5%	$30,670	15.2%	33,000
21. Lodging Managers	9.4%	$39,100	6.6%	10,000
22. Appraisers, Real Estate	9.2%	$43,790	17.6%	11,000
23. Assessors	9.2%	$43,790	17.6%	11,000
24. Podiatrists	9.1%	$97,290	15.0%	1,000
25. Security Guards	8.5%	$20,520	31.9%	228,000
26. Personal and Home Care Aides	8.4%	$17,020	40.5%	154,000
27. Optometrists	8.1%	$88,290	17.1%	2,000
28. Medical Equipment Repairers	8.1%	$38,590	14.8%	4,000
29. Clinical Psychologists	7.6%	$56,360	24.4%	17,000
30. Counseling Psychologists	7.6%	$56,360	24.4%	17,000
31. Educational Psychologists	7.6%	$56,360	24.4%	17,000
32. Industrial-Organizational Psychologists	7.6%	$74,060	16.0%	fewer than 500
33. Caption Writers	7.4%	$45,460	16.1%	23,000
34. Copy Writers	7.4%	$45,460	16.1%	23,000
35. Creative Writers	7.4%	$45,460	16.1%	23,000
36. Poets and Lyricists	7.4%	$45,460	16.1%	23,000
37. Cost Estimators	7.0%	$50,920	18.6%	25,000
38. Veterinarians	6.8%	$68,280	25.1%	4,000
39. Management Analysts	6.8%	$64,560	30.4%	78,000
40. Geographers	6.7%	$61,520	19.5%	fewer than 500
41. Bookkeeping, Accounting, and Auditing Clerks	6.6%	$29,040	3.0%	274,000
42. Pharmacists	6.5%	$87,160	30.1%	23,000
43. Dentists, General	6.4%	$122,430	4.1%	7,000
44. Oral and Maxillofacial Surgeons	6.4%	more than $145,600	4.1%	7,000
45. Orthodontists	6.4%	more than $145,600	4.1%	7,000
46. Prosthodontists	6.4%	more than $145,600	4.1%	7,000
47. Construction and Building Inspectors	6.3%	$43,940	13.8%	10,000
48. Janitors and Cleaners, Except Maids and Housekeeping Cleaners	6.1%	$19,110	18.3%	454,000
49. Logisticians	5.9%	$59,460	27.5%	162,000
50. Art Directors	5.7%	$63,750	11.4%	8,000
51. Multi-Media Artists and Animators	5.7%	$49,900	15.8%	12,000
52. Cartoonists	5.7%	$41,240	16.5%	4,000
53. Painters and Illustrators	5.7%	$41,240	16.5%	4,000

(continued)

(continued)

Best Jobs for Baby Boomers with the Highest Percentage of Workers Age 65 and Over

Job	Percent Age 65 and Over	Annual Earnings	Percent Growth	Annual Openings
54. Sculptors	5.7%	$41,240	16.5%	4,000
55. Sketch Artists	5.7%	$41,240	16.5%	4,000
56. Postsecondary Teachers	5.5%	$54,406	38.1%	216,000
57. Maintenance and Repair Workers, General	5.5%	$30,930	16.3%	155,000
58. Insurance Sales Agents	5.4%	$42,030	8.4%	52,000
59. Anesthesiologists	5.4%	more than $145,600	19.5%	38,000
60. Family and General Practitioners	5.4%	$136,170	19.5%	38,000
61. Internists, General	5.4%	more than $145,600	19.5%	38,000
62. Obstetricians and Gynecologists	5.4%	more than $145,600	19.5%	38,000
63. Pediatricians, General	5.4%	$135,450	19.5%	38,000
64. Psychiatrists	5.4%	more than $145,600	19.5%	38,000
65. Surgeons	5.4%	more than $145,600	19.5%	38,000
66. Air Traffic Controllers	5.3%	$102,390	12.6%	2,000
67. Chief Executives	5.3%	$141,820	16.7%	63,000
68. Government Service Executives	5.3%	$141,820	16.7%	63,000
69. Private Sector Executives	5.3%	$141,820	16.7%	63,000
70. Laundry and Drycleaning Machine Operators and Tenders, Except Pressing	5.2%	$17,350	12.3%	47,000
71. Precision Dyers	5.2%	$17,350	12.3%	47,000
72. Spotters, Dry Cleaning	5.2%	$17,350	12.3%	47,000
73. Library Assistants, Clerical	5.2%	$21,050	21.5%	27,000
74. Adult Literacy, Remedial Education, and GED Teachers and Instructors	5.1%	$39,730	20.4%	14,000
75. Self-Enrichment Education Teachers	5.1%	$31,530	40.1%	39,000
76. Lawyers	5.0%	$97,420	17.0%	53,000

Jobs 5, 6, and 7 share 25,000 openings. Jobs 13, 14, and 15 share 8,000 openings. Jobs 22 and 23 share 11,000 openings. Jobs 29, 30, and 31 share 17,000 openings. Jobs 33, 34, 35, and 36 share 23,000 openings. Jobs 43, 44, 45, and 46 share 7,000 openings. Jobs 52, 53, 54, and 55 share 4,000 openings. Jobs 59, 60, 61, 62, 63, 64, and 65 share 38,000 openings. Jobs 67, 68, and 69 share 63,000 openings. Jobs 70, 71, and 72 share 47,000 openings.

The jobs in the following four lists are derived from the preceding list of the jobs with the highest percentage of workers age 65 and over.

Best Jobs Overall for Baby Boomers Age 65 and Over

Job	Percent Age 65 and Over	Annual Earnings	Percent Growth	Annual Openings
1. Anesthesiologists	5.4% more than	$145,600	19.5%	38,000
2. Internists, General	5.4% more than	$145,600	19.5%	38,000
3. Obstetricians and Gynecologists	5.4% more than	$145,600	19.5%	38,000
4. Psychiatrists	5.4% more than	$145,600	19.5%	38,000
5. Surgeons	5.4% more than	$145,600	19.5%	38,000
6. Management Analysts	6.8%	$64,560	30.4%	78,000
7. Logisticians	5.9%	$59,460	27.5%	162,000
8. Postsecondary Teachers	5.5%	$54,406	38.1%	216,000
9. Family and General Practitioners	5.4%	$136,170	19.5%	38,000
10. Pediatricians, General	5.4%	$135,450	19.5%	38,000
11. Chief Executives	5.3%	$141,820	16.7%	63,000
12. Government Service Executives	5.3%	$141,820	16.7%	63,000
13. Private Sector Executives	5.3%	$141,820	16.7%	63,000
14. Lawyers	5.0%	$97,420	17.0%	53,000
15. Pharmacists	6.5%	$87,160	30.1%	23,000
16. Security Guards	8.5%	$20,520	31.9%	228,000
17. Clinical Psychologists	7.6%	$56,360	24.4%	17,000
18. Counseling Psychologists	7.6%	$56,360	24.4%	17,000
19. Educational Psychologists	7.6%	$56,360	24.4%	17,000
20. Self-Enrichment Education Teachers	5.1%	$31,530	40.1%	39,000
21. Personal and Home Care Aides	8.4%	$17,020	40.5%	154,000
22. Cost Estimators	7.0%	$50,920	18.6%	25,000
23. Veterinarians	6.8%	$68,280	25.1%	4,000
24. Janitors and Cleaners, Except Maids and Housekeeping Cleaners	6.1%	$19,110	18.3%	454,000
25. Bus Drivers, School	9.5%	$23,670	16.7%	76,000

Jobs 1, 2, 3, 4, 5, 9, and 10 share 38,000 openings. Jobs 11, 12, and 13 share 63,000 openings. Jobs 17, 18, and 19 share 17,000 openings.

Best-Paying Jobs for Baby Boomers Age 65 and Over

Job	Percent Age 65 and Over	Annual Earnings	Percent Growth	Annual Openings
1. Anesthesiologists	5.4% ..more than	$145,600	19.5%	38,000
2. Internists, General	5.4% ..more than	$145,600	19.5%	38,000
3. Obstetricians and Gynecologists	6.4% ..more than	$145,600	19.5%	38,000
4. Oral and Maxillofacial Surgeons	6.4% ..more than	$145,600	4.1%	7,000
5. Orthodontists	6.4% ..more than	$145,600	4.1%	7,000
6. Prosthodontists	6.4% ..more than	$145,600	4.1%	7,000
7. Psychiatrists	5.4% ..more than	$145,600	19.5%	38,000
8. Surgeons	5.4% ..more than	$145,600	19.5%	38,000
9. Chief Executives	5.3%	$141,820	16.7%	63,000
10. Government Service Executives	5.3%	$141,820	16.7%	63,000
11. Private Sector Executives	5.3%	$141,820	16.7%	63,000
12. Family and General Practitioners	5.4%	$136,170	19.5%	38,000
13. Pediatricians, General	5.4%	$135,450	19.5%	38,000
14. Dentists, General	6.4%	$122,430	4.1%	7,000
15. Air Traffic Controllers	5.3%	$102,390	12.6%	2,000
16. Lawyers	5.0%	$97,420	17.0%	53,000
17. Podiatrists	9.1%	$97,290	15.0%	1,000
18. Judges, Magistrate Judges, and Magistrates	11.9%	$97,260	8.7%	2,000
19. Optometrists	8.1%	$88,290	17.1%	2,000
20. Physicists	11.1%	$87,480	6.9%	1,000
21. Pharmacists	6.5%	$87,160	30.1%	23,000
22. Industrial-Organizational Psychologists	7.6%	$74,060	16.0%	fewer than 500
23. Veterinarians	6.8%	$68,280	25.1%	4,000
24. Management Analysts	6.8%	$64,560	30.4%	78,000
25. Art Directors	5.7%	$63,750	11.4%	8,000

Jobs 1, 2, 3, 7, 8, 12, and 13 share 38,000 openings. Jobs 4, 5, 6, and 14 share 7,000 openings. Jobs 9, 10, and 11 share 63,000 openings.

Fastest-Growing Jobs for Baby Boomers Age 65 and Over

Job	Percent Age 65 and Over	Annual Earnings	Percent Growth	Annual Openings
1. Personal and Home Care Aides	8.4%	$17,020	40.5%	154,000
2. Self-Enrichment Education Teachers	5.1%	$31,530	40.1%	39,000
3. Postsecondary Teachers	5.5%	$54,406	38.1%	216,000
4. Security Guards	8.5%	$20,520	31.9%	228,000
5. Management Analysts	6.8%	$64,560	30.4%	78,000
6. Pharmacists	6.5%	$87,160	30.1%	23,000
7. Logisticians	5.9%	$59,460	27.5%	162,000
8. Veterinarians	6.8%	$68,280	25.1%	4,000
9. Clinical Psychologists	7.6%	$56,360	24.4%	17,000
10. Counseling Psychologists	7.6%	$56,360	24.4%	17,000
11. Educational Psychologists	7.6%	$56,360	24.4%	17,000
12. Tax Preparers	13.2%	$26,130	23.2%	11,000
13. Taxi Drivers and Chauffeurs	10.5%	$19,790	21.7%	28,000
14. Library Assistants, Clerical	5.2%	$21,050	21.5%	27,000
15. Adult Literacy, Remedial Education, and GED Teachers and Instructors	5.1%	$39,730	20.4%	14,000
16. Anesthesiologists	5.4%	more than $145,600	19.5%	38,000
17. Family and General Practitioners	5.4%	$136,170	19.5%	38,000
18. Internists, General	5.4%	more than $145,600	19.5%	38,000
19. Obstetricians and Gynecologists	5.4%	more than $145,600	19.5%	38,000
20. Pediatricians, General	5.4%	$135,450	19.5%	38,000
21. Psychiatrists	5.4%	more than $145,600	19.5%	38,000
22. Surgeons	5.4%	more than $145,600	19.5%	38,000
23. Geographers	6.7%	$61,520	19.5%	fewer than 500
24. Cost Estimators	7.0%	$50,920	18.6%	25,000
25. Janitors and Cleaners, Except Maids and Housekeeping Cleaners	6.1%	$19,110	18.3%	454,000

Jobs 9, 10, and 11 share 17,000 openings. Jobs 16, 17, 18, 19, 20, 21, and 22 share 38,000 openings.

Jobs for Baby Boomers Age 65 and Over with the Most Openings

Job	Percent Age 65 and Over	Annual Earnings	Percent Growth	Annual Openings
1. Janitors and Cleaners, Except Maids and Housekeeping Cleaners	6.1%	$19,110	18.3%	454,000
2. Bookkeeping, Accounting, and Auditing Clerks	6.6%	$29,040	3.0%	274,000
3. Security Guards	8.5%	$20,520	31.9%	228,000
4. Postsecondary Teachers	5.5%	$54,406	38.1%	216,000
5. Logisticians	5.9%	$59,460	27.5%	162,000
6. Maintenance and Repair Workers, General	5.5%	$30,930	16.3%	155,000
7. Personal and Home Care Aides	8.4%	$17,020	40.5%	154,000
8. Farmers and Ranchers	24.4%	$38,600	−20.6%	118,000
9. Management Analysts	6.8%	$64,560	30.4%	78,000
10. Bus Drivers, School	9.5%	$23,670	16.7%	76,000
11. Chief Executives	5.3%	$141,820	16.7%	63,000
12. Government Service Executives	5.3%	$141,820	16.7%	63,000
13. Private Sector Executives	5.3%	$141,820	16.7%	63,000
14. Lawyers	5.0%	$97,420	17.0%	53,000
15. Insurance Sales Agents	5.4%	$42,030	8.4%	52,000
16. Laundry and Drycleaning Machine Operators and Tenders, Except Pressing	5.2%	$17,350	12.3%	47,000
17. Precision Dyers	5.2%	$17,350	12.3%	47,000
18. Spotters, Dry Cleaning	5.2%	$17,350	12.3%	47,000
19. Self-Enrichment Education Teachers	5.1%	$31,530	40.1%	39,000
20. Anesthesiologists	5.4% more than	$145,600	19.5%	38,000
21. Family and General Practitioners	5.4%	$136,170	19.5%	38,000
22. Internists, General	5.4% more than	$145,600	19.5%	38,000
23. Obstetricians and Gynecologists	5.4% more than	$145,600	19.5%	38,000
24. Pediatricians, General	5.4%	$135,450	19.5%	38,000
25. Demonstrators and Product Promoters	20.5%	$20,490	17.0%	38,000

Jobs 11, 12, and 13 share 63,000 openings. Jobs 16, 17, and 18 share 47,000 openings. Jobs 20, 21, 22, 23, and 24 share 38,000 openings with each other and with two jobs not on this list.

Best Jobs for Baby Boomers with a High Percentage of Part-Time Workers

Part-time work may be very appealing to you at this stage of your life. According to AARP, about 11 percent of workers age 45 and older are presently working on this schedule and more than half intend to switch to part-time work after retirement. A part-time job can keep you physically, mentally, and socially active and perhaps allow you to experiment with a new work role without the commitment and energy drain of a 40-hour work week. Even if your sense of identity is strongly linked to the work you have done for many years and you are reluctant to make a clean break, you may be willing to cut back on your work hours and stay on as a part-timer.

Social Security, a pension, or a 401(k) (or some combination of these) may cover a major fraction of your income needs, and Medicare or a retirement medical plan may provide health care benefits that previously had been affordable only through a full-time job. Thus part-time work may be financially feasible for the first time since you were a teenager, even though you will be paid for fewer hours and probably at a somewhat lower hourly rate (on average, roughly 60 cents on the dollar). On the other hand, in a few occupations (many of which are in the health care field), part-time workers on average earn a higher hourly wage than full-time workers. This may be partly because the part-timers in these fields tend to have good skills credentials and partly because much of the part-time work is on higher-paid late-night shifts.

Look over the list of the jobs with high percentages (more than 15 percent) of part-time workers and you will find some interesting things. For example, many of the top twenty are connected to education either directly (e.g., Teacher Assistants) or indirectly (e.g., Crossing Guards), which leads one to think that the rhythms of the school day create many opportunities for people to work less than full time. In some cases, people work part time because they want the freedom of time this arrangement can provide, but others may do so because they can't find full-time employment in their field of choice. These folks may work in other full- or part-time jobs to make ends meet. If you want to work part time now or in the future, these lists will help you identify jobs that are more likely to provide that opportunity. If you want full-time work, the lists may also help you identify jobs for which such opportunities are more difficult to find. In either case, it's good information to know in advance.

Best Jobs for Baby Boomers with the Highest Percentage of Part-Time Workers

Job	Percent Part-Time Workers	Annual Earnings	Percent Growth	Annual Openings
1. Crossing Guards	75.6%	$19,710	16.5%	19,000
2. Demonstrators and Product Promoters	52.5%	$20,490	17.0%	38,000
3. Library Assistants, Clerical	50.4%	$21,050	21.5%	27,000
4. Teacher Assistants	41.1%	$19,760	23.0%	259,000
5. Self-Enrichment Education Teachers	41.0%	$31,530	40.1%	39,000
6. Adult Literacy, Remedial Education, and GED Teachers and Instructors	41.0%	$39,730	20.4%	14,000
7. Composers	39.5%	$34,800	13.5%	8,000

(continued)

(continued)

Best Jobs for Baby Boomers with the Highest Percentage of Part-Time Workers

Job	Percent Part-Time Workers	Annual Earnings	Percent Growth	Annual Openings
8. Music Arrangers and Orchestrators	39.5%	$34,800	13.5%	8,000
9. Music Directors	39.5%	$34,800	13.5%	8,000
10. Bus Drivers, Transit and Intercity	35.6%	$30,670	15.2%	33,000
11. Bus Drivers, School	35.6%	$23,670	16.7%	76,000
12. Personal and Home Care Aides	34.0%	$17,020	40.5%	154,000
13. Maids and Housekeeping Cleaners	31.9%	$17,000	9.2%	352,000
14. Directors, Religious Activities and Education	28.2%	$30,720	24.1%	16,000
15. Speech-Language Pathologists	28.1%	$53,790	27.2%	10,000
16. Teachers, Postsecondary	27.7%	$54,406	38.1%	216,000
17. Clinical Psychologists	27.2%	$56,360	24.4%	17,000
18. Counseling Psychologists	27.2%	$56,360	24.4%	17,000
19. School Psychologists	27.2%	$56,360	24.4%	17,000
20. Industrial-Organizational Psychologists	27.2%	$74,060	16.0%	fewer than 500
21. Optometrists	25.1%	$88,290	17.1%	2,000
22. Bookkeeping, Accounting, and Auditing Clerks	25.0%	$29,040	3.0%	274,000
23. Dietitians and Nutritionists	24.3%	$44,370	17.8%	8,000
24. Caption Writers	24.2%	$45,460	16.1%	23,000
25. Copy Writers	24.2%	$45,460	16.1%	23,000
26. Creative Writers	24.2%	$45,460	16.1%	23,000
27. Poets and Lyricists	24.2%	$45,460	16.1%	23,000
28. Art Directors	23.1%	$63,750	11.4%	8,000
29. Cartoonists	23.1%	$41,240	16.5%	4,000
30. Painters and Illustrators	23.1%	$41,240	16.5%	4,000
31. Sculptors	23.1%	$41,240	16.5%	4,000
32. Sketch Artists	23.1%	$41,240	16.5%	4,000
33. Librarians	23.1%	$46,940	10.1%	15,000
34. Audiologists	22.7%	$53,040	29.0%	1,000
35. Dentists, General	22.3%	$122,430	4.1%	7,000
36. Oral and Maxillofacial Surgeons	22.3%	more than $145,600	4.1%	7,000
37. Orthodontists	22.3%	more than $145,600	4.1%	7,000
38. Prosthodontists	22.3%	more than $145,600	4.1%	7,000
39. Chiropractors	22.2%	$67,940	23.3%	3,000
40. Registered Nurses	22.0%	$53,640	27.3%	215,000

Best Jobs for Baby Boomers with the Highest Percentage of Part-Time Workers

Job	Percent Part-Time Workers	Annual Earnings	Percent Growth	Annual Openings
41. Janitors and Cleaners, Except Maids and Housekeeping Cleaners	21.7%	$19,110	18.3%	454,000
42. Tax Preparers	20.3%	$26,130	23.2%	11,000
43. Multi-Media Artists and Animators	20.0%	$49,900	15.8%	12,000
44. Licensed Practical and Licensed Vocational Nurses	19.1%	$34,650	20.2%	105,000
45. Wholesale and Retail Buyers, Except Farm Products	18.1%	$42,190	4.3%	24,000
46. Farmers and Ranchers	17.7%	$38,600	–20.6%	118,000
47. Executive Secretaries and Administrative Assistants	17.5%	$35,550	8.7%	210,000
48. Legal Secretaries	17.5%	$37,390	18.8%	39,000
49. Medical Secretaries	17.5%	$27,030	17.2%	50,000
50. Taxi Drivers and Chauffeurs	17.3%	$19,790	21.7%	28,000
51. Truck Drivers, Light or Delivery Services	17.3%	$24,420	23.2%	219,000
52. Pharmacists	17.3%	$87,160	30.1%	23,000
53. Laundry and Drycleaning Machine Operators and Tenders, Except Pressing	16.9%	$17,350	12.3%	47,000
54. Precision Dyers	16.9%	$17,350	12.3%	47,000
55. Spotters, Dry Cleaning	16.9%	$17,350	12.3%	47,000
56. Geographers	16.8%	$61,520	19.5%	fewer than 500
57. Instructional Coordinators	16.5%	$50,060	25.4%	18,000
58. Medical and Clinical Laboratory Technicians	16.0%	$31,440	19.4%	21,000
59. Medical and Clinical Laboratory Technologists	16.0%	$46,710	19.3%	21,000
60. Podiatrists	15.6%	$97,290	15.0%	1,000
61. Property, Real Estate, and Community Association Managers	15.3%	$41,540	12.8%	35,000
62. Gaming Supervisors	15.2%	$41,080	15.7%	6,000
63. Security Guards	15.1%	$20,520	31.9%	228,000

Jobs 7, 8, and 9 share 8,000 openings. Jobs 17, 18, and 19 share 17,000 openings. Jobs 24, 25, 26, and 27 share 23,000 openings. Jobs 29, 30, 31, and 32 share 4,000 openings. Jobs 35, 36, 37, and 38 share 7,000 openings. Jobs 53, 54, and 55 share 47,000 openings.

The jobs in the following four lists are derived from the preceding list of the jobs with the highest percentage of part-time workers.

Best Jobs Overall for Baby Boomers Working Part Time

Job	Percent Part-Time Workers	Annual Earnings	Percent Growth	Annual Openings
1. Teachers, Postsecondary	27.7%	$54,406	38.1%	216,000
2. Registered Nurses	22.0%	$53,640	27.3%	215,000
3. Pharmacists	17.3%	$87,160	30.1%	23,000
4. Clinical Psychologists	27.2%	$56,360	24.4%	17,000
5. Counseling Psychologists	27.2%	$56,360	24.4%	17,000
6. School Psychologists	27.2%	$56,360	24.4%	17,000
7. Instructional Coordinators	16.5%	$50,060	25.4%	18,000
8. Security Guards	15.1%	$20,520	31.9%	228,000
9. Self-Enrichment Education Teachers	41.0%	$31,530	40.1%	39,000
10. Speech-Language Pathologists	28.1%	$53,790	27.2%	10,000
11. Truck Drivers, Light or Delivery Services	17.3%	$24,420	23.2%	219,000
12. Personal and Home Care Aides	34.0%	$17,020	40.5%	154,000
13. Licensed Practical and Licensed Vocational Nurses	19.1%	$34,650	20.2%	105,000
14. Medical and Clinical Laboratory Technologists	16.0%	$46,710	19.3%	21,000
15. Teacher Assistants	41.1%	$19,760	23.0%	259,000
16. Legal Secretaries	17.5%	$37,390	18.8%	39,000
17. Chiropractors	22.2%	$67,940	23.3%	3,000
18. Audiologists	22.7%	$53,040	29.0%	1,000
19. Janitors and Cleaners, Except Maids and Housekeeping Cleaners	21.7%	$19,110	18.3%	454,000
20. Caption Writers	24.2%	$45,460	16.1%	23,000
21. Copy Writers	24.2%	$45,460	16.1%	23,000
22. Creative Writers	24.2%	$45,460	16.1%	23,000
23. Poets and Lyricists	24.2%	$45,460	16.1%	23,000
24. Medical Secretaries	17.5%	$27,030	17.2%	50,000
25. Optometrists	25.1%	$88,290	17.1%	2,000

Jobs 4, 5, and 6 share 17,000 openings. Jobs 20, 21, 22, and 23 share 23,000 openings.

Best-Paying Jobs for Baby Boomers Working Part Time

Job	Percent Part-Time Workers	Annual Earnings	Percent Growth	Annual Openings
1. Oral and Maxillofacial Surgeons	22.3% ..more than	$145,600	4.1%	7,000
2. Orthodontists	22.3% ..more than	$145,600	4.1%	7,000
3. Prosthodontists	22.3% ..more than	$145,600	4.1%	7,000
4. Dentists, General	22.3%	$122,430	4.1%	7,000
5. Podiatrists	15.6%	$97,290	15.0%	1,000
6. Optometrists	25.1%	$88,290	17.1%	2,000
7. Pharmacists	17.3%	$87,160	30.1%	23,000
8. Industrial-Organizational Psychologists	27.2%	$74,060	16.0%	..fewer than 500
9. Chiropractors	22.2%	$67,940	23.3%	3,000
10. Art Directors	23.1%	$63,750	11.4%	8,000
11. Geographers	16.8%	$61,520	19.5%	..fewer than 500
12. Clinical Psychologists	27.2%	$56,360	24.4%	17,000
13. Counseling Psychologists	27.2%	$56,360	24.4%	17,000
14. School Psychologists	27.2%	$56,360	24.4%	17,000
15. Teachers, Postsecondary	27.7%	$54,406	38.1%	216,000
16. Speech-Language Pathologists	28.1%	$53,790	27.2%	10,000
17. Registered Nurses	22.0%	$53,640	27.3%	215,000
18. Audiologists	22.7%	$53,040	29.0%	1,000
19. Instructional Coordinators	16.5%	$50,060	25.4%	18,000
20. Multi-Media Artists and Animators	20.0%	$49,900	15.8%	12,000
21. Librarians	23.1%	$46,940	10.1%	15,000
22. Medical and Clinical Laboratory Technologists	16.0%	$46,710	19.3%	21,000
23. Caption Writers	24.2%	$45,460	16.1%	23,000
24. Copy Writers	24.2%	$45,460	16.1%	23,000
25. Creative Writers	24.2%	$45,460	16.1%	23,000

Jobs 1, 2, 3, and 4 share 7,000 openings. Jobs 12, 13, and 14 share 17,000 openings. Jobs 23, 24, and 25 share 23,000 openings with each other and with another job not on this list.

Fastest-Growing Jobs for Baby Boomers Working Part Time

Job	Percent Part-Time Workers	Annual Earnings	Percent Growth	Annual Openings
1. Personal and Home Care Aides	34.0%	$17,020	40.5%	154,000
2. Self-Enrichment Education Teachers	41.0%	$31,530	40.1%	39,000
3. Teachers, Postsecondary	27.7%	$54,406	38.1%	216,000
4. Security Guards	15.1%	$20,520	31.9%	228,000
5. Pharmacists	17.3%	$87,160	30.1%	23,000
6. Audiologists	22.7%	$53,040	29.0%	1,000
7. Registered Nurses	22.0%	$53,640	27.3%	215,000
8. Speech-Language Pathologists	28.1%	$53,790	27.2%	10,000
9. Instructional Coordinators	16.5%	$50,060	25.4%	18,000
10. Clinical Psychologists	27.2%	$56,360	24.4%	17,000
11. Counseling Psychologists	27.2%	$56,360	24.4%	17,000
12. School Psychologists	27.2%	$56,360	24.4%	17,000
13. Directors, Religious Activities and Education	28.2%	$30,720	24.1%	16,000
14. Chiropractors	22.2%	$67,940	23.3%	3,000
15. Tax Preparers	20.3%	$26,130	23.2%	11,000
16. Truck Drivers, Light or Delivery Services	17.3%	$24,420	23.2%	219,000
17. Teacher Assistants	41.1%	$19,760	23.0%	259,000
18. Taxi Drivers and Chauffeurs	17.3%	$19,790	21.7%	28,000
19. Library Assistants, Clerical	50.4%	$21,050	21.5%	27,000
20. Adult Literacy, Remedial Education, and GED Teachers and Instructors	41.0%	$39,730	20.4%	14,000
21. Licensed Practical and Licensed Vocational Nurses	19.1%	$34,650	20.2%	105,000
22. Geographers	16.8%	$61,520	19.5%	fewer than 500
23. Medical and Clinical Laboratory Technicians	16.0%	$31,440	19.4%	21,000
24. Medical and Clinical Laboratory Technologists	16.0%	$46,710	19.3%	21,000
25. Legal Secretaries	17.5%	$37,390	18.8%	39,000

Jobs 10, 11, and 12 share 17,000 openings.

Jobs for Baby Boomers Working Part Time with the Most Openings

Job	Percent Part-Time Workers	Annual Earnings	Percent Growth	Annual Openings
1. Janitors and Cleaners, Except Maids and Housekeeping Cleaners	21.7%	$19,110	18.3%	454,000
2. Maids and Housekeeping Cleaners	31.9%	$17,000	9.2%	352,000
3. Bookkeeping, Accounting, and Auditing Clerks	25.0%	$29,040	3.0%	274,000
4. Teacher Assistants	41.1%	$19,760	23.0%	259,000
5. Security Guards	15.1%	$20,520	31.9%	228,000
6. Truck Drivers, Light or Delivery Services	17.3%	$24,420	23.2%	219,000
7. Teachers, Postsecondary	27.7%	$54,406	38.1%	216,000
8. Registered Nurses	22.0%	$53,640	27.3%	215,000
9. Executive Secretaries and Administrative Assistants	17.5%	$35,550	8.7%	210,000
10. Personal and Home Care Aides	34.0%	$17,020	40.5%	154,000
11. Farmers and Ranchers	17.7%	$38,600	–20.6%	118,000
12. Licensed Practical and Licensed Vocational Nurses	19.1%	$34,650	20.2%	105,000
13. Bus Drivers, School	35.6%	$23,670	16.7%	76,000
14. Medical Secretaries	17.5%	$27,030	17.2%	50,000
15. Laundry and Drycleaning Machine Operators and Tenders, Except Pressing	16.9%	$17,350	12.3%	47,000
16. Precision Dyers	16.9%	$17,350	12.3%	47,000
17. Spotters, Dry Cleaning	16.9%	$17,350	12.3%	47,000
18. Legal Secretaries	17.5%	$37,390	18.8%	39,000
19. Self-Enrichment Education Teachers	41.0%	$31,530	40.1%	39,000
20. Demonstrators and Product Promoters	52.5%	$20,490	17.0%	38,000
21. Property, Real Estate, and Community Association Managers	15.3%	$41,540	12.8%	35,000
22. Bus Drivers, Transit and Intercity	35.6%	$30,670	15.2%	33,000
23. Taxi Drivers and Chauffeurs	17.3%	$19,790	21.7%	28,000
24. Library Assistants, Clerical	50.4%	$21,050	21.5%	27,000
25. Wholesale and Retail Buyers, Except Farm Products	18.1%	$42,190	4.3%	24,000

Jobs 15, 16, and 17 share 47,000 openings.

Best Jobs for Baby Boomers with a High Percentage of Self-Employed Workers

More than 10 percent of the workforce is self-employed, but in the baby-boomer-and-older workforce the fraction is about 15 percent. Furthermore, roughly 15 percent of boomers expect to start their own business after retirement from their current job, according to a study by Merrill Lynch. So there's a good chance you are considering self-employment as an option at this stage of your life.

Although you may think of the self-employed as having similar jobs, they actually work in an enormous range of situations, fields, and work environments that you may not have considered.

Among the self-employed are people who own small or large businesses; professionals such as lawyers, psychologists, and medical doctors; part-time workers; people working on a contract basis for one or more employers; people running home consulting companies or other home-based businesses; and people in many other situations. They may go to the same office every day, as an attorney might; visit multiple employers during the course of a week; or do most of their work from home. Some work part time, others full time, some as a way to have fun, some so they can spend time with their grandchildren or go back to school.

The point is that there is an enormous range of situations, and one of them could make sense for you now or in the future.

The following list contains jobs in which more than 25 percent of the workers are self-employed.

Best Jobs for Baby Boomers with the Highest Percentage of Self-Employed Workers

Job	Percent Self-Employed Workers	Annual Earnings	Percent Growth	Annual Openings
1. Farmers and Ranchers	99.3%	$38,600	–20.6%	118,000
2. Caption Writers	67.9%	$45,460	16.1%	23,000
3. Poets and Lyricists	67.9%	$45,460	16.1%	23,000
4. Creative Writers	67.9%	$45,460	16.1%	23,000
5. Copy Writers	67.9%	$45,460	16.1%	23,000
6. Real Estate Brokers	59.1%	$56,970	2.4%	11,000
7. Real Estate Sales Agents	59.0%	$36,950	5.7%	34,000
8. Chiropractors	58.5%	$67,940	23.3%	3,000
9. Sculptors	55.5%	$41,240	16.5%	4,000
10. Sketch Artists	55.5%	$41,240	16.5%	4,000
11. Painters and Illustrators	55.5%	$41,240	16.5%	4,000

Best Jobs for Baby Boomers with the Highest Percentage of Self-Employed Workers

Job	Percent Self-Employed Workers	Annual Earnings	Percent Growth	Annual Openings
12. Cartoonists	55.5%	$41,240	16.5%	4,000
13. Art Directors	53.6%	$63,750	11.4%	8,000
14. Multi-Media Artists and Animators	53.5%	$49,900	15.8%	12,000
15. Lodging Managers	50.3%	$39,100	6.6%	10,000
16. Construction Managers	46.9%	$70,770	12.0%	47,000
17. Property, Real Estate, and Community Association Managers	46.0%	$41,540	12.8%	35,000
18. First-Line Supervisors/Managers of Non-Retail Sales Workers	44.7%	$60,300	6.8%	72,000
19. Podiatrists	44.4%	$97,290	15.0%	1,000
20. Demonstrators and Product Promoters	42.1%	$20,490	17.0%	38,000
21. Dentists, General	39.9%	$122,430	4.1%	7,000
22. Prosthodontists	39.9%	more than $145,600	4.1%	7,000
23. Orthodontists	39.9%	more than $145,600	4.1%	7,000
24. Oral and Maxillofacial Surgeons	39.9%	more than $145,600	4.1%	7,000
25. Music Arrangers and Orchestrators	39.3%	$34,800	13.5%	8,000
26. Composers	39.3%	$34,800	13.5%	8,000
27. Music Directors	39.3%	$34,800	13.5%	8,000
28. Personal Financial Advisors	37.7%	$62,450	34.6%	18,000
29. Appraisers, Real Estate	34.8%	$43,790	17.6%	11,000
30. Assessors	34.8%	$43,790	17.6%	11,000
31. Private Detectives and Investigators	34.7%	$32,510	25.3%	9,000
32. Gaming Supervisors	33.8%	$41,080	15.7%	6,000
33. First-Line Supervisors/Managers of Retail Sales Workers	33.0%	$32,410	9.1%	251,000
34. Management Analysts	29.8%	$64,560	30.4%	78,000
35. Optometrists	29.2%	$88,290	17.1%	2,000
36. Veterinarians	27.7%	$68,280	25.1%	4,000
37. Lawyers	26.8%	$97,420	17.0%	53,000
38. Industrial-Organizational Psychologists	26.8%	$74,060	16.0%	fewer than 500
39. Tax Preparers	26.2%	$26,130	23.2%	11,000
40. Insurance Sales Agents	26.2%	$42,030	8.4%	52,000
41. School Psychologists	25.4%	$56,360	24.4%	17,000
42. Counseling Psychologists	25.4%	$56,360	24.4%	17,000
43. Clinical Psychologists	25.4%	$56,360	24.4%	17,000

Jobs 2, 3, 4, and 5 share 23,000 openings. Jobs 9, 10, 11, and 12 share 4,000 openings. Jobs 21, 22, 23, and 24 share 7,000 openings. Jobs 25, 26, and 27 share 8,000 openings. Jobs 29 and 30 share 11,000 openings. Jobs 41, 42, and 43 share 17,000 openings.

The jobs in the following four lists are derived from the preceding list of the jobs with the highest percentage of self-employed workers.

Best Jobs Overall for Self-Employed Baby Boomers

Job	Percent Self-Employed Workers	Annual Earnings	Percent Growth	Annual Openings
1. Management Analysts	29.8%	$64,560	30.4%	78,000
2. Lawyers	26.8%	$97,420	17.0%	53,000
3. Personal Financial Advisors	37.7%	$62,450	34.6%	18,000
4. Clinical Psychologists	25.4%	$56,360	24.4%	17,000
5. Counseling Psychologists	25.4%	$56,360	24.4%	17,000
6. School Psychologists	25.4%	$56,360	24.4%	17,000
7. Construction Managers	46.9%	$70,770	12.0%	47,000
8. Veterinarians	27.7%	$68,280	25.1%	4,000
9. Caption Writers	67.9%	$45,460	16.1%	23,000
10. Copy Writers	67.9%	$45,460	16.1%	23,000
11. Creative Writers	67.9%	$45,460	16.1%	23,000
12. Poets and Lyricists	67.9%	$45,460	16.1%	23,000
13. First-Line Supervisors/Managers of Non-Retail Sales Workers	44.7%	$60,300	6.8%	72,000
14. Appraisers, Real Estate	34.8%	$43,790	17.6%	11,000
15. Assessors	34.8%	$43,790	17.6%	11,000
16. Chiropractors	58.5%	$67,940	23.3%	3,000
17. Optometrists	29.2%	$88,290	17.1%	2,000
18. Multi-Media Artists and Animators	53.5%	$49,900	15.8%	12,000
19. Demonstrators and Product Promoters	42.1%	$20,490	17.0%	38,000
20. Insurance Sales Agents	26.2%	$42,030	8.4%	52,000
21. Property, Real Estate, and Community Association Managers	46.0%	$41,540	12.8%	35,000
22. Private Detectives and Investigators	34.7%	$32,510	25.3%	9,000
23. Oral and Maxillofacial Surgeons	39.9%	more than $145,600	4.1%	7,000
24. Orthodontists	39.9%	more than $145,600	4.1%	7,000
25. Prosthodontists	39.9%	more than $145,600	4.1%	7,000

Jobs 4, 5, and 6 share 17,000 openings. Jobs 9, 10, 11, and 12 share 23,000 openings. Jobs 14 and 15 share 11,000 openings. Jobs 23, 24, and 25 share 7,000 openings with each other and with another job not on this list.

Best-Paying Jobs for Self-Employed Baby Boomers

Job	Percent Self-Employed Workers	Annual Earnings	Percent Growth	Annual Openings
1. Oral and Maxillofacial Surgeons	39.9%	more than $145,600	4.1%	7,000
2. Orthodontists	39.9%	more than $145,600	4.1%	7,000
3. Prosthodontists	39.9%	more than $145,600	4.1%	7,000
4. Dentists, General	39.9%	$122,430	4.1%	7,000
5. Lawyers	26.8%	$97,420	17.0%	53,000
6. Podiatrists	44.4%	$97,290	15.0%	1,000
7. Optometrists	29.2%	$88,290	17.1%	2,000
8. Industrial-Organizational Psychologists	26.8%	$74,060	16.0%	fewer than 500
9. Construction Managers	46.9%	$70,770	12.0%	47,000
10. Veterinarians	27.7%	$68,280	25.1%	4,000
11. Chiropractors	58.5%	$67,940	23.3%	3,000
12. Management Analysts	29.8%	$64,560	30.4%	78,000
13. Art Directors	53.6%	$63,750	11.4%	8,000
14. Personal Financial Advisors	37.7%	$62,450	34.6%	18,000
15. First-Line Supervisors/Managers of Non-Retail Sales Workers	44.7%	$60,300	6.8%	72,000
16. Real Estate Brokers	59.1%	$56,970	2.4%	11,000
17. Clinical Psychologists	25.4%	$56,360	24.4%	17,000
18. Counseling Psychologists	25.4%	$56,360	24.4%	17,000
19. School Psychologists	25.4%	$56,360	24.4%	17,000
20. Multi-Media Artists and Animators	53.5%	$49,900	15.8%	12,000
21. Caption Writers	67.9%	$45,460	16.1%	23,000
22. Copy Writers	67.9%	$45,460	16.1%	23,000
23. Creative Writers	67.9%	$45,460	16.1%	23,000
24. Poets and Lyricists	67.9%	$45,460	16.1%	23,000
25. Appraisers, Real Estate	34.8%	$43,790	17.6%	11,000

Jobs 1, 2, 3, and 4 share 7,000 openings. Jobs 17, 18, and 19 share 17,000 openings. Jobs 21, 22, 23, and 24 share 23,000 openings. Job 25 shares 11,000 openings with another job not on this list.

Fastest-Growing Jobs for Self-Employed Baby Boomers

Job	Percent Self-Employed Workers	Annual Earnings	Percent Growth	Annual Openings
1. Personal Financial Advisors	37.7%	$62,450	34.6%	18,000
2. Management Analysts	29.8%	$64,560	30.4%	78,000
3. Private Detectives and Investigators	34.7%	$32,510	25.3%	9,000
4. Veterinarians	27.7%	$68,280	25.1%	4,000
5. Clinical Psychologists	25.4%	$56,360	24.4%	17,000
6. Counseling Psychologists	25.4%	$56,360	24.4%	17,000
7. School Psychologists	25.4%	$56,360	24.4%	17,000
8. Chiropractors	58.5%	$67,940	23.3%	3,000
9. Tax Preparers	26.2%	$26,130	23.2%	11,000
10. Appraisers, Real Estate	34.8%	$43,790	17.6%	11,000
11. Assessors	34.8%	$43,790	17.6%	11,000
12. Optometrists	29.2%	$88,290	17.1%	2,000
13. Demonstrators and Product Promoters	42.1%	$20,490	17.0%	38,000
14. Lawyers	26.8%	$97,420	17.0%	53,000
15. Cartoonists	55.5%	$41,240	16.5%	4,000
16. Painters and Illustrators	55.5%	$41,240	16.5%	4,000
17. Sculptors	55.5%	$41,240	16.5%	4,000
18. Sketch Artists	55.5%	$41,240	16.5%	4,000
19. Caption Writers	67.9%	$45,460	16.1%	23,000
20. Copy Writers	67.9%	$45,460	16.1%	23,000
21. Creative Writers	67.9%	$45,460	16.1%	23,000
22. Poets and Lyricists	67.9%	$45,460	16.1%	23,000
23. Industrial-Organizational Psychologists	26.8%	$74,060	16.0%	fewer than 500
24. Multi-Media Artists and Animators	53.5%	$49,900	15.8%	12,000
25. Gaming Supervisors	33.8%	$41,080	15.7%	6,000

Jobs 5, 6, and 7 share 17,000 openings. Jobs 10 and 11 share 11,000 openings. Jobs 15, 16, 17, and 18 share 4,000 openings. Jobs 19, 20, 21, and 22 share 23,000 openings.

Jobs for Self-Employed Baby Boomers with the Most Openings

Job	Percent Self-Employed Workers	Annual Earnings	Percent Growth	Annual Openings
1. First-Line Supervisors/Managers of Retail Sales Workers	33.0%	$32,410	9.1%	251,000
2. Farmers and Ranchers	99.3%	$38,600	–20.6%	118,000
3. Management Analysts	29.8%	$64,560	30.4%	78,000
4. First-Line Supervisors/Managers of Non-Retail Sales Workers	44.7%	$60,300	6.8%	72,000
5. Lawyers	26.8%	$97,420	17.0%	53,000
6. Insurance Sales Agents	26.2%	$42,030	8.4%	52,000
7. Construction Managers	46.9%	$70,770	12.0%	47,000
8. Demonstrators and Product Promoters	42.1%	$20,490	17.0%	38,000
9. Property, Real Estate, and Community Association Managers	46.0%	$41,540	12.8%	35,000
10. Real Estate Sales Agents	59.0%	$36,950	5.7%	34,000
11. Caption Writers	67.9%	$45,460	16.1%	23,000
12. Copy Writers	67.9%	$45,460	16.1%	23,000
13. Creative Writers	67.9%	$45,460	16.1%	23,000
14. Poets and Lyricists	67.9%	$45,460	16.1%	23,000
15. Personal Financial Advisors	37.7%	$62,450	34.6%	18,000
16. Clinical Psychologists	25.4%	$56,360	24.4%	17,000
17. Counseling Psychologists	25.4%	$56,360	24.4%	17,000
18. School Psychologists	25.4%	$56,360	24.4%	17,000
19. Multi-Media Artists and Animators	53.5%	$49,900	15.8%	12,000
20. Appraisers, Real Estate	34.8%	$43,790	17.6%	11,000
21. Assessors	34.8%	$43,790	17.6%	11,000
22. Real Estate Brokers	59.1%	$56,970	2.4%	11,000
23. Tax Preparers	26.2%	$26,130	23.2%	11,000
24. Lodging Managers	50.3%	$39,100	6.6%	10,000
25. Private Detectives and Investigators	34.7%	$32,510	25.3%	9,000

Jobs 11, 12, 13, and 14 share 23,000 openings. Jobs 16, 17, and 18 share 17,000 openings. Jobs 20 and 21 share 11,000 openings.

Best Jobs for Baby Boomers Employing a High Percentage of Women

We found it interesting to look at what kinds of jobs have a high percentage of male or female baby boomers. We're not saying that men or women workers should consider these jobs over others, but it is interesting information to know.

In some cases, the lists can give you ideas for jobs to consider that you might otherwise overlook. For example, perhaps women should consider some jobs that traditionally have high percentages of men in them. Older boomers might consider some jobs typically held by younger ones. Although these are not obvious ways of using these lists, the lists may give you some good ideas on jobs to consider.

To create the four lists that follow, we sorted the 225 best jobs for baby boomers according to the percentages of women and men in the workforce. We knew we would create some controversy when we first included the best jobs lists with high percentages (more than 66 percent) of men and women. But these lists are not meant to restrict women or men from considering job options; one reason for including these lists is exactly the opposite. We hope the lists will help people see possibilities that they might not otherwise have considered.

The fact is that jobs with high percentages of women or high percentages of men offer good opportunities for both men and women if they want to do one of these jobs. So we suggest that women browse the lists of jobs that employ high percentages of men and that men browse the lists of jobs with high percentages of women. There are jobs among both lists that pay well, and women or men who are interested in them and who have or can obtain the necessary education and training should consider them.

An interesting and unfortunate tidbit to bring up at your next party is that in the jobs listed here with the highest percentage of women, the weighted average earnings are $36,108, compared to $53,708 in the jobs with the highest percentage of men. But earnings don't tell the whole story. We computed the average growth and job openings of the jobs with the highest percentage of women and found statistics of 17.0% growth and 71,833 openings, compared to 14.0% growth and 43,021 openings for the jobs with the highest percentage of men. This discrepancy reinforces the idea that men have had more problems than women in adapting to an economy dominated by service and information-based jobs. Many women may simply be better prepared for these jobs, possessing more appropriate skills for the jobs that are now growing rapidly and have more job openings.

Female baby boomers have participated in the workforce more than any previous generation of women; in 2000, 80% of them were employed. They also have postponed childbearing longer than mothers of the previous and following generations, which may encourage them—and their husbands—to postpone retirement longer, because they achieve an empty nest at a later age. Boomer women are also better educated than their mothers, another factor associated with staying in the workforce longer. At the same time, more elderly women are poor, with less in savings and pension plans than men, so many continue working because they need the income.

Best Jobs for Baby Boomers Employing the Highest Percentage of Women

Job	Percent Women	Annual Earnings	Percent Growth	Annual Openings
1. Executive Secretaries and Administrative Assistants	96.5%	$35,550	8.7%	210,000
2. Legal Secretaries	96.5%	$37,390	18.8%	39,000
3. Medical Secretaries	96.5%	$27,030	17.2%	50,000
4. Speech-Language Pathologists	95.1%	$53,790	27.2%	10,000
5. Licensed Practical and Licensed Vocational Nurses	93.0%	$34,650	20.2%	105,000
6. Registered Nurses	92.4%	$53,640	27.3%	215,000
7. Teacher Assistants	91.6%	$19,760	23.0%	259,000
8. Dietitians and Nutritionists	90.5%	$44,370	17.8%	8,000
9. Bookkeeping, Accounting, and Auditing Clerks	89.4%	$29,040	3.0%	274,000
10. Maids and Housekeeping Cleaners	87.6%	$17,000	9.2%	352,000
11. Personal and Home Care Aides	87.3%	$17,020	40.5%	154,000
12. Special Education Teachers, Middle School	86.6%	$45,000	30.0%	59,000
13. Special Education Teachers, Preschool, Kindergarten, and Elementary School	86.6%	$44,330	30.0%	59,000
14. Special Education Teachers, Secondary School	86.6%	$46,300	30.0%	59,000
15. Librarians	82.6%	$46,940	10.1%	15,000
16. Library Assistants, Clerical	81.9%	$21,050	21.5%	27,000
17. Elementary School Teachers, Except Special Education	79.0%	$43,660	15.2%	183,000
18. Middle School Teachers, Except Special and Vocational Education	79.0%	$44,180	9.0%	69,000
19. Child, Family, and School Social Workers	78.5%	$35,010	23.2%	45,000
20. Medical and Public Health Social Workers	78.5%	$40,780	28.6%	18,000
21. Mental Health and Substance Abuse Social Workers	78.5%	$34,310	34.5%	17,000
22. Court Clerks	78.2%	$28,980	12.3%	14,000
23. License Clerks	78.2%	$28,980	12.3%	14,000
24. Municipal Clerks	78.2%	$28,980	12.3%	14,000
25. Demonstrators and Product Promoters	77.4%	$20,490	17.0%	38,000
26. Audiologists	76.7%	$53,040	29.0%	1,000
27. Medical and Clinical Laboratory Technicians	73.9%	$31,440	19.4%	21,000
28. Medical and Clinical Laboratory Technologists	73.9%	$46,710	19.3%	21,000

(continued)

(continued)

Best Jobs for Baby Boomers Employing the Highest Percentage of Women

Job	Percent Women	Annual Earnings	Percent Growth	Annual Openings
29. Medical and Health Services Managers	68.7%	$68,320	29.3%	33,000
30. First-Line Supervisors, Administrative Support	67.6%	$41,850	6.6%	140,000
31. First-Line Supervisors, Customer Service	67.6%	$41,850	6.6%	140,000
32. Adult Literacy, Remedial Education, and GED Teachers and Instructors	66.8%	$39,730	20.4%	14,000
33. Self-Enrichment Education Teachers	66.8%	$31,530	40.1%	39,000
34. Compensation, Benefits, and Job Analysis Specialists	66.7%	$48,720	28.0%	15,000
35. Employment Interviewers, Private or Public Employment Service	66.7%	$41,190	27.3%	29,000
36. Personnel Recruiters	66.7%	$41,190	27.3%	29,000
37. Training and Development Specialists	66.7%	$45,370	27.9%	35,000
38. Educational, Vocational, and School Counselors	66.4%	$46,160	15.0%	32,000
39. Marriage and Family Therapists	66.4%	$40,440	22.4%	3,000
40. Mental Health Counselors	66.4%	$33,400	26.7%	13,000
41. Rehabilitation Counselors	66.4%	$27,900	33.8%	19,000
42. Substance Abuse and Behavioral Disorder Counselors	66.4%	$32,630	23.3%	10,000

Jobs 12, 13, and 14 share 59,000 openings. Jobs 22, 23, and 24 share 14,000 openings. Jobs 30 and 31 share 140,000 openings. Jobs 35 and 36 share 29,000 openings.

The jobs in the following four lists are derived from the preceding list of the jobs employing the highest percentage of women.

Best Jobs Overall for Baby Boomers Employing a High Percentage of Women

Job	Percent Women	Annual Earnings	Percent Growth	Annual Openings
1. Registered Nurses	92.4%	$53,640	27.3%	215,000
2. Special Education Teachers, Secondary School	86.6%	$46,300	30.0%	59,000
3. Special Education Teachers, Middle School	86.6%	$45,000	30.0%	59,000
4. Medical and Health Services Managers	68.7%	$68,320	29.3%	33,000
5. Special Education Teachers, Preschool, Kindergarten, and Elementary School	86.6%	$44,330	30.0%	59,000
6. Training and Development Specialists	66.7%	$45,370	27.9%	35,000
7. Compensation, Benefits, and Job Analysis Specialists	66.7%	$48,720	28.0%	15,000
8. Personal and Home Care Aides	87.3%	$17,020	40.5%	154,000
9. Self-Enrichment Education Teachers	66.8%	$31,530	40.1%	39,000
10. Elementary School Teachers, Except Special Education	79.0%	$43,660	15.2%	183,000
11. Employment Interviewers, Private or Public Employment Service	66.7%	$41,190	27.3%	29,000
12. Personnel Recruiters	66.7%	$41,190	27.3%	29,000
13. Audiologists	76.7%	$53,040	29.0%	1,000
14. Speech-Language Pathologists	95.1%	$53,790	27.2%	10,000
15. Medical and Clinical Laboratory Technologists	73.9%	$46,710	19.3%	21,000
16. Medical and Public Health Social Workers	78.5%	$40,780	28.6%	18,000
17. Child, Family, and School Social Workers	78.5%	$35,010	23.2%	45,000
18. Licensed Practical and Licensed Vocational Nurses	93.0%	$34,650	20.2%	105,000
19. Mental Health and Substance Abuse Social Workers	78.5%	$34,310	34.5%	17,000
20. Educational, Vocational, and School Counselors	66.4%	$46,160	15.0%	32,000
21. Middle School Teachers, Except Special and Vocational Education	79.0%	$44,180	9.0%	69,000
22. Teacher Assistants	91.6%	$19,760	23.0%	259,000
23. First-Line Supervisors, Administrative Support	67.6%	$41,850	6.6%	140,000
24. First-Line Supervisors, Customer Service	67.6%	$41,850	6.6%	140,000
25. Legal Secretaries	96.5%	$37,390	18.8%	39,000

Jobs 2, 3, and 5 share 59,000 openings. Jobs 11 and 12 share 29,000 openings. Jobs 23 and 24 share 140,000 openings.

Best-Paying Jobs for Baby Boomers Employing a High Percentage of Women

Job	Percent Women	Annual Earnings	Percent Growth	Annual Openings
1. Medical and Health Services Managers	68.7%	$68,320	29.3%	33,000
2. Speech-Language Pathologists	95.1%	$53,790	27.2%	10,000
3. Registered Nurses	92.4%	$53,640	27.3%	215,000
4. Audiologists	76.7%	$53,040	29.0%	1,000
5. Compensation, Benefits, and Job Analysis Specialists	66.7%	$48,720	28.0%	15,000
6. Librarians	82.6%	$46,940	10.1%	15,000
7. Medical and Clinical Laboratory Technologists	73.9%	$46,710	19.3%	21,000
8. Special Education Teachers, Secondary School	86.6%	$46,300	30.0%	59,000
9. Educational, Vocational, and School Counselors	66.4%	$46,160	15.0%	32,000
10. Training and Development Specialists	66.7%	$45,370	27.9%	35,000
11. Special Education Teachers, Middle School	86.6%	$45,000	30.0%	59,000
12. Dietitians and Nutritionists	90.5%	$44,370	17.8%	8,000
13. Special Education Teachers, Preschool, Kindergarten, and Elementary School	86.6%	$44,330	30.0%	59,000
14. Middle School Teachers, Except Special and Vocational Education	79.0%	$44,180	9.0%	69,000
15. Elementary School Teachers, Except Special Education	79.0%	$43,660	15.2%	183,000
16. First-Line Supervisors, Administrative Support	67.6%	$41,850	6.6%	140,000
17. First-Line Supervisors, Customer Service	67.6%	$41,850	6.6%	140,000
18. Employment Interviewers, Private or Public Employment Service	66.7%	$41,190	27.3%	29,000
19. Personnel Recruiters	66.7%	$41,190	27.3%	29,000
20. Medical and Public Health Social Workers	78.5%	$40,780	28.6%	18,000
21. Marriage and Family Therapists	66.4%	$40,440	22.4%	3,000
22. Adult Literacy, Remedial Education, and GED Teachers and Instructors	66.8%	$39,730	20.4%	14,000
23. Legal Secretaries	96.5%	$37,390	18.8%	39,000
24. Executive Secretaries and Administrative Assistants	96.5%	$35,550	8.7%	210,000
25. Child, Family, and School Social Workers	78.5%	$35,010	23.2%	45,000

Jobs 8, 11, and 13 share 59,000 openings. Jobs 16 and 17 share 140,000 openings. Jobs 18 and 19 share 29,000 openings.

Fastest-Growing Jobs for Baby Boomers Employing a High Percentage of Women

Job	Percent Women	Annual Earnings	Percent Growth	Annual Openings
1. Personal and Home Care Aides	87.3%	$17,020	40.5%	154,000
2. Self-Enrichment Education Teachers	66.8%	$31,530	40.1%	39,000
3. Mental Health and Substance Abuse Social Workers	78.5%	$34,310	34.5%	17,000
4. Rehabilitation Counselors	66.4%	$27,900	33.8%	19,000
5. Special Education Teachers, Middle School	86.6%	$45,000	30.0%	59,000
6. Special Education Teachers, Preschool, Kindergarten, and Elementary School	86.6%	$44,330	30.0%	59,000
7. Special Education Teachers, Secondary School	86.6%	$46,300	30.0%	59,000
8. Medical and Health Services Managers	68.7%	$68,320	29.3%	33,000
9. Audiologists	76.7%	$53,040	29.0%	1,000
10. Medical and Public Health Social Workers	78.5%	$40,780	28.6%	18,000
11. Compensation, Benefits, and Job Analysis Specialists	66.7%	$48,720	28.0%	15,000
12. Training and Development Specialists	66.7%	$45,370	27.9%	35,000
13. Employment Interviewers, Private or Public Employment Service	66.7%	$41,190	27.3%	29,000
14. Personnel Recruiters	66.7%	$41,190	27.3%	29,000
15. Registered Nurses	92.4%	$53,640	27.3%	215,000
16. Speech-Language Pathologists	95.1%	$53,790	27.2%	10,000
17. Mental Health Counselors	66.4%	$33,400	26.7%	13,000
18. Substance Abuse and Behavioral Disorder Counselors	66.4%	$32,630	23.3%	10,000
19. Child, Family, and School Social Workers	78.5%	$35,010	23.2%	45,000
20. Teacher Assistants	91.6%	$19,760	23.0%	259,000
21. Marriage and Family Therapists	66.4%	$40,440	22.4%	3,000
22. Library Assistants, Clerical	81.9%	$21,050	21.5%	27,000
23. Adult Literacy, Remedial Education, and GED Teachers and Instructors	66.8%	$39,730	20.4%	14,000
24. Licensed Practical and Licensed Vocational Nurses	93.0%	$34,650	20.2%	105,000
25. Medical and Clinical Laboratory Technicians	73.9%	$31,440	19.4%	21,000

Jobs 5, 6, and 7 share 59,000 openings. Job 13 shares 29,000 openings with another job not on this list.

Jobs for Baby Boomers with the Most Openings Employing a High Percentage of Women

Job	Percent Women	Annual Earnings	Percent Growth	Annual Openings
1. Maids and Housekeeping Cleaners	87.6%	$17,000	9.2%	352,000
2. Bookkeeping, Accounting, and Auditing Clerks	89.4%	$29,040	3.0%	274,000
3. Teacher Assistants	91.6%	$19,760	23.0%	259,000
4. Registered Nurses	92.4%	$53,640	27.3%	215,000
5. Executive Secretaries and Administrative Assistants	96.5%	$35,550	8.7%	210,000
6. Elementary School Teachers, Except Special Education	79.0%	$43,660	15.2%	183,000
7. Personal and Home Care Aides	87.3%	$17,020	40.5%	154,000
8. First-Line Supervisors, Administrative Support	67.6%	$41,850	6.6%	140,000
9. First-Line Supervisors, Customer Service	67.6%	$41,850	6.6%	140,000
10. Licensed Practical and Licensed Vocational Nurses	93.0%	$34,650	20.2%	105,000
11. Middle School Teachers, Except Special and Vocational Education	79.0%	$44,180	9.0%	69,000
12. Special Education Teachers, Middle School	86.6%	$45,000	30.0%	59,000
13. Special Education Teachers, Preschool, Kindergarten, and Elementary School	86.6%	$44,330	30.0%	59,000
14. Special Education Teachers, Secondary School	86.6%	$46,300	30.0%	59,000
15. Medical Secretaries	96.5%	$27,030	17.2%	50,000
16. Child, Family, and School Social Workers	78.5%	$35,010	23.2%	45,000
17. Legal Secretaries	96.5%	$37,390	18.8%	39,000
18. Self-Enrichment Education Teachers	66.8%	$31,530	40.1%	39,000
19. Demonstrators and Product Promoters	77.4%	$20,490	17.0%	38,000
20. Training and Development Specialists	66.7%	$45,370	27.9%	35,000
21. Medical and Health Services Managers	68.7%	$68,320	29.3%	33,000
22. Educational, Vocational, and School Counselors	66.4%	$46,160	15.0%	32,000
23. Employment Interviewers, Private or Public Employment Service	66.7%	$41,190	27.3%	29,000
24. Personnel Recruiters	66.7%	$41,190	27.3%	29,000
25. Library Assistants, Clerical	81.9%	$21,050	21.5%	27,000

Jobs 8 and 9 share 140,000 openings. Jobs 12, 13, and 14 share 59,000 openings. Jobs 23 and 24 share 29,000 openings.

Best Jobs for Baby Boomers Employing a High Percentage of Men

If you have not already read the intro to the previous group of lists, best jobs for baby boomers with high percentages of women, consider doing so. Much of the content there applies to these lists as well.

We did not include these groups of lists with the assumption that men should consider jobs with high percentages of men or that women should consider jobs with high percentages of women. Instead, these lists are here because we think they are interesting and perhaps helpful in considering nontraditional career options. For example, some men would do very well in and enjoy some of the jobs with high percentages of women but may not have considered them seriously. In a similar way, some women would very much enjoy and do well in some jobs that traditionally have been held by high percentages of men. We hope that these lists help you consider options that you simply did not seriously consider because of gender stereotypes.

In the jobs on the following lists, more than 66 percent of the workers are men.

Best Jobs for Baby Boomers Employing the Highest Percentage of Men

Job	Percent Men	Annual Earnings	Percent Growth	Annual Openings
1. Mobile Heavy Equipment Mechanics, Except Engines	99.0%	$38,630	9.6%	12,000
2. Bus and Truck Mechanics and Diesel Engine Specialists	98.8%	$36,150	14.2%	28,000
3. First-Line Supervisors and Manager/ Supervisors—Construction Trades Workers	97.2%	$50,980	14.1%	67,000
4. First-Line Supervisors and Manager/ Supervisors—Extractive Workers	97.2%	$50,980	14.1%	67,000
5. Forest Fire Fighting and Prevention Supervisors	97.1%	$59,760	18.7%	8,000
6. Municipal Fire Fighting and Prevention Supervisors	97.1%	$59,760	18.7%	8,000
7. Industrial Machinery Mechanics	96.2%	$39,310	5.5%	19,000
8. Refractory Materials Repairers, Except Brickmasons	96.2%	$39,610	16.3%	155,000
9. Airline Pilots, Copilots, and Flight Engineers	96.0%	$135,430	18.5%	6,000
10. Commercial Pilots	96.0%	$55,360	14.9%	2,000
11. Maintenance and Repair Workers, General	95.9%	$30,930	16.3%	155,000
12. Aircraft Body and Bonded Structure Repairers	95.1%	$45,910	11.0%	12,000

(continued)

(continued)

Best Jobs for Baby Boomers Employing the Highest Percentage of Men

Job	Percent Men	Annual Earnings	Percent Growth	Annual Openings
13. Aircraft Engine Specialists	95.1%	$45,910	11.0%	12,000
14. Airframe-and-Power-Plant Mechanics	95.1%	$45,910	11.0%	12,000
15. Machinists	94.7%	$34,090	8.2%	30,000
16. Water and Liquid Waste Treatment Plant and System Operators	94.6%	$34,850	16.0%	9,000
17. Electrical and Electronics Repairers, Commercial and Industrial Equipment	94.1%	$43,180	10.3%	10,000
18. Tractor-Trailer Truck Drivers	94.1%	$33,870	19.0%	299,000
19. Truck Drivers, Heavy	94.1%	$33,870	19.0%	299,000
20. Truck Drivers, Light or Delivery Services	94.1%	$24,420	23.2%	219,000
21. Engineering Managers	93.4%	$99,000	9.2%	16,000
22. Construction Managers	93.2%	$70,770	12.0%	47,000
23. Locksmiths and Safe Repairers	93.0%	$30,580	21.0%	3,000
24. First-Line Supervisors/Managers of Mechanics, Installers, and Repairers	91.8%	$51,000	15.4%	42,000
25. Electrical Engineers	91.3%	$72,770	2.5%	11,000
26. Electronics Engineers, Except Computer	91.3%	$76,810	9.4%	11,000
27. Subway and Streetcar Operators	91.1%	$47,560	13.2%	2,000
28. Construction and Building Inspectors	90.2%	$43,940	13.8%	10,000
29. Civil Engineers	89.9%	$65,280	8.0%	17,000
30. Cost Estimators	88.0%	$50,920	18.6%	25,000
31. Medical Equipment Repairers	87.9%	$38,590	14.8%	4,000
32. First-Line Supervisors/Managers of Police and Detectives	87.2%	$65,020	15.3%	14,000
33. Central Office and PBX Installers and Repairers	87.0%	$50,270	−0.6%	23,000
34. Communication Equipment Mechanics, Installers, and Repairers	87.0%	$50,270	−0.6%	23,000
35. Frame Wirers, Central Office	87.0%	$50,270	−0.6%	23,000
36. Station Installers and Repairers, Telephone	87.0%	$50,270	−0.6%	23,000
37. Telecommunications Facility Examiners	87.0%	$50,270	−0.6%	23,000
38. Taxi Drivers and Chauffeurs	86.7%	$19,790	21.7%	28,000
39. Physicists	86.1%	$87,480	6.9%	1,000
40. Clergy	85.7%	$37,870	15.5%	34,000
41. Agricultural Crop Farm Managers	85.5%	$50,720	5.1%	25,000
42. Fish Hatchery Managers	85.5%	$50,720	5.1%	25,000
43. Nursery and Greenhouse Managers	85.5%	$50,720	5.1%	25,000

Best Jobs for Baby Boomers Employing the Highest Percentage of Men

Job	Percent Men	Annual Earnings	Percent Growth	Annual Openings
44. Farmers and Ranchers	85.4%	$38,600	–20.6%	118,000
45. First-Line Supervisors and Manager/ Supervisors—Agricultural Crop Workers	84.4%	$36,040	11.4%	6,000
46. First-Line Supervisors and Manager/ Supervisors—Animal Care Workers, Except Livestock	84.4%	$36,040	11.4%	6,000
47. First-Line Supervisors and Manager/ Supervisors—Animal Husbandry Workers	84.4%	$36,040	11.4%	6,000
48. First-Line Supervisors and Manager/ Supervisors—Fishery Workers	84.4%	$36,040	11.4%	6,000
49. First-Line Supervisors and Manager/ Supervisors—Horticultural Workers	84.4%	$36,040	11.4%	6,000
50. First-Line Supervisors and Manager/ Supervisors—Logging Workers	84.4%	$36,040	11.4%	6,000
51. Podiatrists	84.3%	$97,290	15.0%	1,000
52. Aviation Inspectors	83.8%	$47,920	7.7%	5,000
53. Freight Inspectors	83.8%	$47,920	7.7%	5,000
54. Marine Cargo Inspectors	83.8%	$47,920	7.7%	5,000
55. Motor Vehicle Inspectors	83.8%	$47,920	7.7%	5,000
56. Public Transportation Inspectors	83.8%	$47,920	7.7%	5,000
57. Railroad Inspectors	83.8%	$47,920	7.7%	5,000
58. Industrial Engineers	83.4%	$66,080	10.6%	16,000
59. Industrial Production Managers	83.4%	$74,100	7.9%	18,000
60. Fire-Prevention and Protection Engineers	83.4%	$64,320	7.9%	4,000
61. Industrial Safety and Health Engineers	83.4%	$64,320	7.9%	4,000
62. Product Safety Engineers	83.4%	$64,320	7.9%	4,000
63. Storage and Distribution Managers	82.9%	$67,300	19.7%	13,000
64. Transportation Managers	82.9%	$67,300	19.7%	13,000
65. Dentists, General	82.1%	$122,430	4.1%	7,000
66. Oral and Maxillofacial Surgeons	82.1%	more than $145,600	4.1%	7,000
67. Orthodontists	82.1%	more than $145,600	4.1%	7,000
68. Prosthodontists	82.1%	more than $145,600	4.1%	7,000
69. Air Traffic Controllers	81.6%	$102,390	12.6%	2,000
70. Chief Executives	81.2%	$141,820	16.7%	63,000
71. Government Service Executives	81.2%	$141,820	16.7%	63,000
72. Private Sector Executives	81.2%	$141,820	16.7%	63,000
73. Architects, Except Landscape and Naval	79.7%	$61,430	17.3%	8,000

(continued)

(continued)

Best Jobs for Baby Boomers Employing the Highest Percentage of Men

Job	Percent Men	Annual Earnings	Percent Growth	Annual Openings
74. Landscape Architects	79.7%	$54,290	22.2%	2,000
75. First-Line Supervisors/Managers of Production and Operating Workers	79.1%	$45,230	9.5%	66,000
76. Security Guards	79.0%	$20,520	31.9%	228,000
77. Chiropractors	77.8%	$67,940	23.3%	3,000
78. Environmental Scientists and Specialists, Including Health	75.9%	$51,950	23.7%	6,000
79. Geologists	75.9%	$70,180	11.5%	2,000
80. Hydrologists	75.9%	$60,880	21.0%	1,000
81. First-Line Supervisors/Managers of Correctional Officers	74.3%	$48,070	19.0%	4,000
82. Sales Representatives, Agricultural	73.9%	$59,390	19.3%	44,000
83. Sales Representatives, Chemical and Pharmaceutical	73.9%	$59,390	19.3%	44,000
84. Sales Representatives, Electrical/Electronic	73.9%	$59,390	19.3%	44,000
85. Sales Representatives, Instruments	73.9%	$59,390	19.3%	44,000
86. Sales Representatives, Mechanical Equipment and Supplies	73.9%	$59,390	19.3%	44,000
87. Sales Representatives, Medical	73.9%	$59,390	19.3%	44,000
88. Sales Representatives, Wholesale and Manufacturing, Except Technical and Scientific Products	73.9%	$46,090	19.1%	160,000
89. General and Operations Managers	73.7%	$79,300	18.4%	260,000
90. Anesthesiologists	73.2%	more than $145,600	19.5%	38,000
91. Family and General Practitioners	73.2%	$136,170	19.5%	38,000
92. Internists, General	73.2%	more than $145,600	19.5%	38,000
93. Obstetricians and Gynecologists	73.2%	more than $145,600	19.5%	38,000
94. Pediatricians, General	73.2%	$135,450	19.5%	38,000
95. Psychiatrists	73.2%	more than $145,600	19.5%	38,000
96. Surgeons	73.2%	more than $145,600	19.5%	38,000
97. Optometrists	72.4%	$88,290	17.1%	2,000
98. Lawyers	71.3%	$97,420	17.0%	53,000
99. Janitors and Cleaners, Except Maids and Housekeeping Cleaners	70.1%	$19,110	18.3%	454,000
100. Economists	69.4%	$72,370	13.4%	2,000
101. Personal Financial Advisors	68.4%	$62,450	34.6%	18,000
102. First-Line Supervisors/Managers of Non-Retail Sales Workers	67.3%	$60,300	6.8%	72,000

Best Jobs for Baby Boomers Employing the Highest Percentage of Men

Job	Percent Men	Annual Earnings	Percent Growth	Annual Openings
103. Appraisers, Real Estate	66.7%	$43,790	17.6%	11,000
104. Assessors	66.7%	$43,790	17.6%	11,000
105. Postal Service Mail Carriers	66.5%	$45,880	–0.5%	20,000

Jobs 3 and 4 share 67,000 openings. Jobs 5 and 6 share 8,000 openings. Jobs 12, 13, and 14 share 12,000 openings. Jobs 18 and 19 share 299,000 openings. Jobs 33, 34, 35, 36, and 37 share 23,000 openings. Jobs 41, 42, and 43 share 25,000 openings. Jobs 45, 46, 47, 48, 49, and 50 share 6,000 openings. Jobs 52, 53, 54, 55, 56, and 57 share 5,000 openings. Jobs 60, 61, and 62 share 4,000 openings. Jobs 63 and 64 share 13,000 openings. Jobs 65, 66, 67, and 68 share 7,000 openings. Jobs 70, 71, and 72 share 63,000 openings. Jobs 82, 83, 84, 85, 86, and 87 share 44,000 openings. Jobs 90, 91, 92, 93, 94, 95, and 96 share 38,000 openings. Jobs 103 and 104 share 11,000 openings.

The jobs in the following four lists are derived from the preceding list of the jobs employing the highest percentage of men.

Best Jobs Overall for Baby Boomers Employing a High Percentage of Men

Job	Percent Men	Annual Earnings	Percent Growth	Annual Openings
1. Anesthesiologists	73.2%	more than $145,600	19.5%	38,000
2. Internists, General	73.2%	more than $145,600	19.5%	38,000
3. Obstetricians and Gynecologists	73.2%	more than $145,600	19.5%	38,000
4. Psychiatrists	73.2%	more than $145,600	19.5%	38,000
5. Surgeons	73.2%	more than $145,600	19.5%	38,000
6. Family and General Practitioners	73.2%	$136,170	19.5%	38,000
7. Pediatricians, General	73.2%	$135,450	19.5%	38,000
8. General and Operations Managers	73.7%	$79,300	18.4%	260,000
9. Chief Executives	81.2%	$141,820	16.7%	63,000
10. Government Service Executives	81.2%	$141,820	16.7%	63,000
11. Private Sector Executives	81.2%	$141,820	16.7%	63,000
12. Lawyers	71.3%	$97,420	17.0%	53,000
13. Sales Representatives, Agricultural	73.9%	$59,390	19.3%	44,000
14. Sales Representatives, Chemical and Pharmaceutical	73.9%	$59,390	19.3%	44,000
15. Sales Representatives, Electrical/Electronic	73.9%	$59,390	19.3%	44,000
16. Sales Representatives, Instruments	73.9%	$59,390	19.3%	44,000
17. Sales Representatives, Mechanical Equipment and Supplies	73.9%	$59,390	19.3%	44,000

(continued)

(continued)

Best Jobs Overall for Baby Boomers
Employing a High Percentage of Men

Job	Percent Men	Annual Earnings	Percent Growth	Annual Openings
18. Sales Representatives, Medical	73.9%	$59,390	19.3%	44,000
19. Personal Financial Advisors	68.4%	$62,450	34.6%	18,000
20. Storage and Distribution Managers	82.9%	$67,300	19.7%	13,000
21. Transportation Managers	82.9%	$67,300	19.7%	13,000
22. Construction Managers	93.2%	$70,770	12.0%	47,000
23. Sales Representatives, Wholesale and Manufacturing, Except Technical and Scientific Products	73.9%	$46,090	19.1%	160,000
24. Security Guards	79.0%	$20,520	31.9%	228,000
25. Truck Drivers, Light or Delivery Services	94.1%	$24,420	23.2%	219,000

Jobs 1, 2, 3, 4, 5, 6, and 7 share 38,000 openings. Jobs 9, 10, and 11 share 63,000 openings. Jobs 13, 14, 15, 16, 17, and 18 share 44,000 openings. Jobs 20 and 21 share 13,000 openings.

Best-Paying Jobs for Baby Boomers
Employing a High Percentage of Men

Job	Percent Men	Annual Earnings	Percent Growth	Annual Openings
1. Anesthesiologists	73.2%	more than $145,600	19.5%	38,000
2. Internists, General	73.2%	more than $145,600	19.5%	38,000
3. Obstetricians and Gynecologists	73.2%	more than $145,600	19.5%	38,000
4. Oral and Maxillofacial Surgeons	82.1%	more than $145,600	4.1%	7,000
5. Orthodontists	82.1%	more than $145,600	4.1%	7,000
6. Prosthodontists	82.1%	more than $145,600	4.1%	7,000
7. Psychiatrists	73.2%	more than $145,600	19.5%	38,000
8. Surgeons	73.2%	more than $145,600	19.5%	38,000
9. Chief Executives	81.2%	$141,820	16.7%	63,000
10. Government Service Executives	81.2%	$141,820	16.7%	63,000
11. Private Sector Executives	81.2%	$141,820	16.7%	63,000
12. Family and General Practitioners	73.2%	$136,170	19.5%	38,000
13. Pediatricians, General	73.2%	$135,450	19.5%	38,000
14. Airline Pilots, Copilots, and Flight Engineers	96.0%	$135,430	18.5%	6,000
15. Dentists, General	82.1%	$122,430	4.1%	7,000
16. Air Traffic Controllers	81.6%	$102,390	12.6%	2,000

Best-Paying Jobs for Baby Boomers Employing a High Percentage of Men

Job	Percent Men	Annual Earnings	Percent Growth	Annual Openings
17. Engineering Managers	93.4%	$99,000	9.2%	16,000
18. Lawyers	71.3%	$97,420	17.0%	53,000
19. Podiatrists	84.3%	$97,290	15.0%	1,000
20. Optometrists	72.4%	$88,290	17.1%	2,000
21. Physicists	86.1%	$87,480	6.9%	1,000
22. General and Operations Managers	73.7%	$79,300	18.4%	260,000
23. Electronics Engineers, Except Computer	91.3%	$76,810	9.4%	11,000
24. Industrial Production Managers	83.4%	$74,100	7.9%	18,000
25. Electrical Engineers	91.3%	$72,770	2.5%	11,000

Jobs 1, 2, 3, 7, 8, 12, and 13 share 38,000 openings. Jobs 4, 5, 6, and 15 share 7,000 openings. Jobs 9, 10, and 11 share 63,000 openings.

Fastest-Growing Jobs for Baby Boomers Employing a High Percentage of Men

Job	Percent Men	Annual Earnings	Percent Growth	Annual Openings
1. Personal Financial Advisors	68.4%	$62,450	34.6%	18,000
2. Security Guards	79.0%	$20,520	31.9%	228,000
3. Environmental Scientists and Specialists, Including Health	75.9%	$51,950	23.7%	6,000
4. Chiropractors	77.8%	$67,940	23.3%	3,000
5. Truck Drivers, Light or Delivery Services	94.1%	$24,420	23.2%	219,000
6. Landscape Architects	79.7%	$54,290	22.2%	2,000
7. Taxi Drivers and Chauffeurs	86.7%	$19,790	21.7%	28,000
8. Hydrologists	75.9%	$60,880	21.0%	1,000
9. Locksmiths and Safe Repairers	93.0%	$30,580	21.0%	3,000
10. Storage and Distribution Managers	82.9%	$67,300	19.7%	13,000
11. Transportation Managers	82.9%	$67,300	19.7%	13,000
12. Anesthesiologists	73.2%	more than $145,600	19.5%	38,000
13. Family and General Practitioners	73.2%	$136,170	19.5%	38,000
14. Internists, General	73.2%	more than $145,600	19.5%	38,000
15. Obstetricians and Gynecologists	73.2%	more than $145,600	19.5%	38,000
16. Pediatricians, General	73.2%	$135,450	19.5%	38,000
17. Psychiatrists	73.2%	more than $145,600	19.5%	38,000

(continued)

(continued)

Fastest-Growing Jobs for Baby Boomers Employing a High Percentage of Men

Job	Percent Men	Annual Earnings	Percent Growth	Annual Openings
18. Surgeons	73.2% ....more than	$145,600	19.5%	38,000
19. Sales Representatives, Agricultural	73.9%	$59,390	19.3%	44,000
20. Sales Representatives, Chemical and Pharmaceutical	73.9%	$59,390	19.3%	44,000
21. Sales Representatives, Electrical/Electronic	73.9%	$59,390	19.3%	44,000
22. Sales Representatives, Instruments	73.9%	$59,390	19.3%	44,000
23. Sales Representatives, Mechanical Equipment and Supplies	73.9%	$59,390	19.3%	44,000
24. Sales Representatives, Medical	73.9%	$59,390	19.3%	44,000
25. Sales Representatives, Wholesale and Manufacturing, Except Technical and Scientific Products	73.9%	$46,090	19.1%	160,000

Jobs 10 and 11 share 13,000 openings. Jobs 12, 13, 14, 15, 16, 17, and 18 share 38,000 openings. Jobs 19, 20, 21, 22, 23, and 24 share 44,000 openings.

Jobs for Baby Boomers with the Most Openings Employing a High Percentage of Men

Job	Percent Men	Annual Earnings	Percent Growth	Annual Openings
1. Janitors and Cleaners, Except Maids and Housekeeping Cleaners	70.1%	$19,110	18.3%	454,000
2. Tractor-Trailer Truck Drivers	94.1%	$33,870	19.0%	299,000
3. Truck Drivers, Heavy	94.1%	$33,870	19.0%	299,000
4. General and Operations Managers	73.7%	$79,300	18.4%	260,000
5. Security Guards	79.0%	$20,520	31.9%	228,000
6. Truck Drivers, Light or Delivery Services	94.1%	$24,420	23.2%	219,000
7. Sales Representatives, Wholesale and Manufacturing, Except Technical and Scientific Products	73.9%	$46,090	19.1%	160,000
8. Maintenance and Repair Workers, General	95.9%	$30,930	16.3%	155,000
9. Refractory Materials Repairers, Except Brickmasons	96.2%	$39,610	16.3%	155,000
10. Farmers and Ranchers	85.4%	$38,600	−20.6%	118,000

Jobs for Baby Boomers with the Most Openings Employing a High Percentage of Men

Job	Percent Men	Annual Earnings	Percent Growth	Annual Openings
11. First-Line Supervisors/Managers of Non-Retail Sales Workers	67.3%	$60,300	6.8%	72,000
12. First-Line Supervisors and Manager/Supervisors—Construction Trades Workers	97.2%	$50,980	14.1%	67,000
13. First-Line Supervisors and Manager/Supervisors—Extractive Workers	97.2%	$50,980	14.1%	67,000
14. First-Line Supervisors/Managers of Production and Operating Workers	79.1%	$45,230	9.5%	66,000
15. Chief Executives	81.2%	$141,820	16.7%	63,000
16. Government Service Executives	81.2%	$141,820	16.7%	63,000
17. Private Sector Executives	81.2%	$141,820	16.7%	63,000
18. Lawyers	71.3%	$97,420	17.0%	53,000
19. Construction Managers	93.2%	$70,770	12.0%	47,000
20. Sales Representatives, Agricultural	73.9%	$59,390	19.3%	44,000
21. Sales Representatives, Chemical and Pharmaceutical	73.9%	$59,390	19.3%	44,000
22. Sales Representatives, Electrical/Electronic	73.9%	$59,390	19.3%	44,000
23. Sales Representatives, Instruments	73.9%	$59,390	19.3%	44,000
24. Sales Representatives, Mechanical Equipment and Supplies	73.9%	$59,390	19.3%	44,000
25. Sales Representatives, Medical	73.9%	$59,390	19.3%	44,000

Jobs 2 and 3 share 299,000 openings. Jobs 12 and 13 share 67,000 openings. Jobs 15, 16, and 17 share 63,000 openings. Jobs 20, 21, 22, 23, 24, and 25 share 44,000 openings.

Best Jobs Lists for Baby Boomers Based on Levels of Education and Experience

The lists in this section organize the 225 best jobs into groups based on the education or training typically required for entry. Unlike many of the previous sections, here we do not include separate lists for highest pay, growth, or number of openings. Instead, we provide one list that includes all the occupations in our database that fit into each of the education levels and ranks them by their combined score for earnings, growth, and number of openings.

These lists can help you identify a job with higher earnings or a more promising outlook but with a similar level of education to the job you now hold. For example, you will find Cost Estimators and Creative Writers in the same level of education, yet Cost Estimators pays significantly better than Creative Writers, is projected to grow more rapidly, and has significantly more job openings per year. Comparisons like this can help you leverage your present skills and experience into jobs that might provide better long-term career opportunities.

You can also use these lists to explore possible job options if you were to get additional training, education, or work experience. For example, you can use these lists to identify occupations that offer high potential and then (in Part III) look into the specific education or training required to get the jobs that interest you most.

The lists can also help you when you plan your further education. For example, you might be thinking about entering a particular training program or returning to college in a certain major because you believe it will lead to a high-paying job, but the lists may help you identify a job that interests you more and offers even better potential for the same general educational requirements.

We include *all* levels of education here (see the following bulleted list), even those requiring many years of study, because we assume that you may want to consider more education or training no matter how old you are. According to the Census Bureau, in October 2003 some 835,000 people age 45–54 were enrolled in college—that's 2.0% of the population in that age bracket—and 249,000 were enrolled in the sixth year of college or higher. Of those age 55 and over, 269,000 (0.4%) were enrolled in college, 106,000 in the sixth year or higher. Perhaps some of the jobs on the lists below will inspire you to join these adult learners, either in college or in a training program.

The following definitions are used by the federal government to classify jobs based on the minimum level of education or training typically required for entry into a job:

- **Short-term on-the-job training:** It is possible to work in these occupations and achieve an average level of performance within a few days or weeks through on-the-job training.

- **Moderate-term on-the-job training:** Occupations that require this type of training can be performed adequately after a 1- to 12-month period of combined on-the-job and informal training. Typically, untrained workers begin by observing experienced workers performing tasks and are gradually moved into progressively more difficult assignments.

- **Long-term on-the-job training:** This type of training requires more than 12 months of on-the-job training or combined work experience and formal classroom instruction. This includes occupations that use formal apprenticeships for training workers that may take up to four years. It also includes intensive occupation-specific employer-sponsored training like police academies. Furthermore, it includes occupations that require natural talent that must be developed over many years.

- **Work experience in a related occupation:** This type of job requires a worker to have experience—usually several years of experience—in a related occupation (such as police detectives, who are selected based on their experience as police patrol officers).

- **Postsecondary vocational training:** This training requirement can vary in length; training usually lasts from a few months up to one year. In a few instances, there may be as many as four years of training.

- **Associate degree:** The associate degree usually requires 60 to 63 semester hours to complete. A normal course load for a full-time student each semester is 15 hours. This means that it typically takes two years to complete an associate degree.

- **Bachelor's degree:** A bachelor's degree usually requires 120 to 130 semester hours to complete. A full-time student usually takes four to five years to complete a bachelor's degree, depending on the complexity of courses. Traditionally, people have thought of the bachelor's degree as a four-year degree. There are some bachelor's degrees—like the Bachelor of Architecture—that are considered a first professional degree and take five or more years to complete.

- **Work experience plus degree:** Some jobs require work experience in a related job in addition to a degree. For example, almost all managers have worked in a related job before being promoted into a management position. Most of the jobs in this group require a four-year bachelor's degree, although some require an associate degree or a master's degree.

- **Master's degree:** This degree usually requires 33 to 60 semester hours beyond the bachelor's degree. The academic master's degrees—such as a Master of Arts in Political Science—usually require 33 to 36 hours. A first professional degree at the master's level—such as a Master of Social Work—requires almost two years of full-time work.

- **Doctoral degree:** The doctoral degree prepares students for careers that consist primarily of theory development, research, and/or college teaching. This type of degree is typically the Doctor of Philosophy (Ph.D.) or Doctor of Education (Ed.D.). Normally, a requirement for a doctoral degree is the completion of a master's degree plus an additional two to three years of full-time coursework and a one- to two-semester research project and paper called the dissertation. It usually takes four to five years beyond the bachelor's degree to complete a doctoral degree.

- **First professional degree:** Some professional degrees require three or more years of full-time academic study beyond the bachelor's degree. A professional degree prepares students for a specific profession. It uses theory and research to teach practical applications in a professional occupation. Examples of this type of degree are Doctor of Medicine (M.D.) for physicians, Doctor of Ministry (D.Min.) for clergy, and Juris Doctor (J.D.) for attorneys.

Another Warning About the Data

We warned you in the introduction to use caution in interpreting the data we use, and we want to do it again here. The occupational data we use is the most accurate available anywhere, but it has limitations. For example, a four-year degree in accounting, finance, or a related area is typically required for entry into the accounting profession. But some people working as accountants don't have such a degree, and others have much more education than the "minimum" required for entry.

In a similar way, people with a graduate degree will typically earn considerably more than someone with an associate or bachelor's degree. However, some people with an associate degree earn considerably more than the average for those with higher levels of education.

So as you browse the lists that follow, please use them as a way to be encouraged rather than discouraged. Education and training are very important for success in the labor market, but so are ability, drive, initiative, and, yes, luck.

Having said this, we encourage you to get as much education and training as you can. It is not too late for you to go back to school, and there are also many other ways to learn, such as workshops, adult education programs, certification programs, employer training, professional conferences, Internet training, reading related books and magazines, and so forth. Upgrading your computer skills—and other technical skills—is particularly important in our rapidly changing workplace, and you avoid doing so at your peril, especially if you want to be able to compete with younger workers.

Best Jobs for Baby Boomers Requiring Short-Term On-the-Job Training

Job	Annual Earnings	Percent Growth	Annual Openings
1. Truck Drivers, Light or Delivery Services	$24,420	23.2%	219,000
2. Security Guards	$20,520	31.9%	228,000
3. Teacher Assistants	$19,760	23.0%	259,000
4. Janitors and Cleaners, Except Maids and Housekeeping Cleaners	$19,110	18.3%	454,000
5. Personal and Home Care Aides	$17,020	40.5%	154,000
6. Bus Drivers, School	$23,670	16.7%	76,000
7. Library Assistants, Clerical	$21,050	21.5%	27,000
8. Taxi Drivers and Chauffeurs	$19,790	21.7%	28,000
9. Court Clerks	$28,980	12.3%	14,000
10. License Clerks	$28,980	12.3%	14,000
11. Municipal Clerks	$28,980	12.3%	14,000
12. Postal Service Mail Carriers	$45,880	–0.5%	20,000
13. Maids and Housekeeping Cleaners	$17,000	9.2%	352,000
14. Crossing Guards	$19,710	16.5%	19,000

Jobs 9, 10, and 11 share 14,000 openings.

Best Jobs for Baby Boomers Requiring Moderate-Term On-the-Job Training

Job	Annual Earnings	Percent Growth	Annual Openings
1. Sales Representatives, Agricultural	$59,390	19.3%	44,000
2. Sales Representatives, Chemical and Pharmaceutical	$59,390	19.3%	44,000
3. Sales Representatives, Electrical/Electronic	$59,390	19.3%	44,000
4. Sales Representatives, Instruments	$59,390	19.3%	44,000
5. Sales Representatives, Mechanical Equipment and Supplies	$59,390	19.3%	44,000
6. Sales Representatives, Medical	$59,390	19.3%	44,000
7. Sales Representatives, Wholesale and Manufacturing, Except Technical and Scientific Products	$46,090	19.1%	160,000
8. Tractor-Trailer Truck Drivers	$33,870	19.0%	299,000
9. Truck Drivers, Heavy	$33,870	19.0%	299,000
10. Refractory Materials Repairers, Except Brickmasons	$39,610	16.3%	155,000
11. Maintenance and Repair Workers, General	$30,930	16.3%	155,000
12. Executive Secretaries and Administrative Assistants	$35,550	8.7%	210,000
13. Social and Human Service Assistants	$24,730	48.7%	63,000
14. Locksmiths and Safe Repairers	$30,580	21.0%	3,000
15. Bookkeeping, Accounting, and Auditing Clerks	$29,040	3.0%	274,000
16. Electrical and Electronic Inspectors and Testers	$28,630	4.7%	87,000
17. Materials Inspectors	$28,630	4.7%	87,000
18. Mechanical Inspectors	$28,630	4.7%	87,000
19. Precision Devices Inspectors and Testers	$28,630	4.7%	87,000
20. Production Inspectors, Testers, Graders, Sorters, Samplers, Weighers	$28,630	4.7%	87,000
21. Caption Writers	$45,460	16.1%	23,000
22. Tax Preparers	$26,130	23.2%	11,000
23. Subway and Streetcar Operators	$47,560	13.2%	2,000
24. Bus Drivers, Transit and Intercity	$30,670	15.2%	33,000
25. Laundry and Drycleaning Machine Operators and Tenders, Except Pressing	$17,350	12.3%	47,000
26. Precision Dyers	$17,350	12.3%	47,000
27. Spotters, Dry Cleaning	$17,350	12.3%	47,000
28. Demonstrators and Product Promoters	$20,490	17.0%	38,000

Jobs 1, 2, 3, 4, 5, and 6 share 44,000 openings. Jobs 8 and 9 share 299,000 openings. Jobs 16, 17, 18, 19, and 20 share 87,000 openings. Job 21 shares 23,000 openings with three other jobs not on this list. Jobs 25, 26, and 27 share 47,000 openings.

Best Jobs for Baby Boomers
Requiring Long-Term On-the-Job Training

Job	Annual Earnings	Percent Growth	Annual Openings
1. Central Office and PBX Installers and Repairers	$50,270	–0.6%	23,000
2. Communication Equipment Mechanics, Installers, and Repairers	$50,270	–0.6%	23,000
3. Frame Wirers, Central Office	$50,270	–0.6%	23,000
4. Station Installers and Repairers, Telephone	$50,270	–0.6%	23,000
5. Telecommunications Facility Examiners	$50,270	–0.6%	23,000
6. Environmental Compliance Inspectors	$48,530	9.8%	20,000
7. Equal Opportunity Representatives and Officers	$48,530	9.8%	20,000
8. Government Property Inspectors and Investigators	$48,530	9.8%	20,000
9. Licensing Examiners and Inspectors	$48,530	9.8%	20,000
10. Pressure Vessel Inspectors	$48,530	9.8%	20,000
11. Air Traffic Controllers	$102,390	12.6%	2,000
12. Cartoonists	$41,240	16.5%	4,000
13. Painters and Illustrators	$41,240	16.5%	4,000
14. Sculptors	$41,240	16.5%	4,000
15. Sketch Artists	$41,240	16.5%	4,000
16. Machinists	$34,090	8.2%	30,000
17. Farmers and Ranchers	$38,600	–20.6%	118,000
18. Water and Liquid Waste Treatment Plant and System Operators	$34,850	16.0%	9,000
19. Industrial Machinery Mechanics	$39,310	5.5%	19,000

Jobs 1, 2, 4, 5, and 6 share 23,000 openings. Jobs 6, 7, 8, 9, and 10 share 20,000 openings. Jobs 12, 13, 14, and 15 share 4,000 openings.

Best Jobs for Baby Boomers
Requiring Work Experience in a Related Occupation

Job	Annual Earnings	Percent Growth	Annual Openings
1. Storage and Distribution Managers	$67,300	19.7%	13,000
2. Transportation Managers	$67,300	19.7%	13,000
3. First-Line Supervisors and Manager/Supervisors— Construction Trades Workers	$50,980	14.1%	67,000
4. First-Line Supervisors and Manager/Supervisors— Extractive Workers	$50,980	14.1%	67,000

Best Jobs for Baby Boomers
Requiring Work Experience in a Related Occupation

Job	Annual Earnings	Percent Growth	Annual Openings
5. First-Line Supervisors/Managers of Mechanics, Installers, and Repairers	$51,000	15.4%	42,000
6. Cost Estimators	$50,920	18.6%	25,000
7. First-Line Supervisors/Managers of Police and Detectives	$65,020	15.3%	14,000
8. Forest Fire Fighting and Prevention Supervisors	$59,760	18.7%	8,000
9. Municipal Fire Fighting and Prevention Supervisors	$59,760	18.7%	8,000
10. First-Line Supervisors/Managers of Non-Retail Sales Workers	$60,300	6.8%	72,000
11. Purchasing Agents, Except Wholesale, Retail, and Farm Products	$48,360	11.2%	29,000
12. Self-Enrichment Education Teachers	$31,530	40.1%	39,000
13. Coroners	$48,530	9.8%	20,000
14. First-Line Supervisors/Managers of Production and Operating Workers	$45,230	9.5%	66,000
15. First-Line Supervisors/Managers of Correctional Officers	$48,070	19.0%	4,000
16. First-Line Supervisors/Managers of Retail Sales Workers	$32,410	9.1%	251,000
17. Housekeeping Supervisors	$30,050	16.2%	28,000
18. Janitorial Supervisors	$30,050	16.2%	28,000
19. Private Detectives and Investigators	$32,510	25.3%	9,000
20. Emergency Management Specialists	$45,670	28.2%	2,000
21. First-Line Supervisors, Administrative Support	$41,850	6.6%	140,000
22. First-Line Supervisors, Customer Service	$41,850	6.6%	140,000
23. Real Estate Brokers	$56,970	2.4%	11,000
24. Construction and Building Inspectors	$43,940	13.8%	10,000
25. Aviation Inspectors	$47,920	7.7%	5,000
26. Freight Inspectors	$47,920	7.7%	5,000
27. Marine Cargo Inspectors	$47,920	7.7%	5,000
28. Motor Vehicle Inspectors	$47,920	7.7%	5,000
29. Public Transportation Inspectors	$47,920	7.7%	5,000
30. Railroad Inspectors	$47,920	7.7%	5,000
31. Gaming Supervisors	$41,080	15.7%	6,000
32. Wholesale and Retail Buyers, Except Farm Products	$42,190	4.3%	24,000
33. Lodging Managers	$39,100	6.6%	10,000

Jobs 1 and 2 share 13,000 openings. Jobs 3 and 4 share 67,000 openings. Jobs 8 and 9 share 8,000 openings. Job 13 shares 20,000 openings with five other jobs not on this list. Jobs 17 and 18 share 28,000 openings. Jobs 21 and 22 share 140,000 openings. Jobs 25, 26, 27, 28, 29, and 30 share 5,000 openings.

Best Jobs for Baby Boomers Requiring Postsecondary Vocational Training

Job	Annual Earnings	Percent Growth	Annual Openings
1. Legal Secretaries	$37,390	18.8%	39,000
2. Licensed Practical and Licensed Vocational Nurses	$34,650	20.2%	105,000
3. Aircraft Body and Bonded Structure Repairers	$45,910	11.0%	12,000
4. Aircraft Engine Specialists	$45,910	11.0%	12,000
5. Airframe-and-Power-Plant Mechanics	$45,910	11.0%	12,000
6. Appraisers, Real Estate	$43,790	17.6%	11,000
7. Assessors	$43,790	17.6%	11,000
8. Medical Secretaries	$27,030	17.2%	50,000
9. Commercial Pilots	$55,360	14.9%	2,000
10. Bus and Truck Mechanics and Diesel Engine Specialists	$36,150	14.2%	28,000
11. Mobile Heavy Equipment Mechanics, Except Engines	$38,630	9.6%	12,000
12. Real Estate Sales Agents	$36,950	5.7%	34,000
13. Electrical and Electronics Repairers, Commercial and Industrial Equipment	$43,180	10.3%	10,000

Jobs 3, 4, and 5 share 12,000 openings. Jobs 6 and 7 share 11,000 openings.

Best Jobs for Baby Boomers Requiring an Associate Degree

Job	Annual Earnings	Percent Growth	Annual Openings
1. First-Line Supervisors and Manager/Supervisors—Agricultural Crop Workers	$36,040	11.4%	6,000
2. First-Line Supervisors and Manager/Supervisors—Animal Care Workers, Except Livestock	$36,040	11.4%	6,000
3. First-Line Supervisors and Manager/Supervisors—Animal Husbandry Workers	$36,040	11.4%	6,000
4. First-Line Supervisors and Manager/Supervisors—Fishery Workers	$36,040	11.4%	6,000
5. First-Line Supervisors and Manager/Supervisors—Horticultural Workers	$36,040	11.4%	6,000
6. Medical and Clinical Laboratory Technicians	$31,440	19.4%	21,000
7. Medical Equipment Repairers	$38,590	14.8%	4,000

Jobs 1, 2, 3, 4, and 5 share 6,000 openings with each other and with another job not on this list.

Best Jobs for Baby Boomers Requiring a Bachelor's Degree

Job	Annual Earnings	Percent Growth	Annual Openings
1. Logisticians	$59,460	27.5%	162,000
2. Special Education Teachers, Secondary School	$46,300	30.0%	59,000
3. Personal Financial Advisors	$62,450	34.6%	18,000
4. Special Education Teachers, Middle School	$45,000	30.0%	59,000
5. Special Education Teachers, Preschool, Kindergarten, and Elementary School	$44,330	30.0%	59,000
6. Construction Managers	$70,770	12.0%	47,000
7. Secondary School Teachers, Except Special and Vocational Education	$46,120	18.2%	118,000
8. Training and Development Specialists	$45,370	27.9%	35,000
9. Social and Community Service Managers	$48,330	27.7%	19,000
10. Compensation, Benefits, and Job Analysis Specialists	$48,720	28.0%	15,000
11. Airline Pilots, Copilots, and Flight Engineers	$135,430	18.5%	6,000
12. Medical and Clinical Laboratory Technologists	$46,710	19.3%	21,000
13. Employment Interviewers, Private or Public Employment Service	$41,190	27.3%	29,000
14. Personnel Recruiters	$41,190	27.3%	29,000
15. Elementary School Teachers, Except Special Education	$43,660	15.2%	183,000
16. Copy Writers	$45,460	16.1%	23,000
17. Creative Writers	$45,460	16.1%	23,000
18. Industrial Production Managers	$74,100	7.9%	18,000
19. Poets and Lyricists	$45,460	16.1%	23,000
20. Medical and Public Health Social Workers	$40,780	28.6%	18,000
21. Industrial Engineers	$66,080	10.6%	16,000
22. Technical Writers	$54,390	27.1%	6,000
23. Child, Family, and School Social Workers	$35,010	23.2%	45,000
24. Architects, Except Landscape and Naval	$61,430	17.3%	8,000
25. Electronics Engineers, Except Computer	$76,810	9.4%	11,000
26. Civil Engineers	$65,280	8.0%	17,000
27. Middle School Teachers, Except Special and Vocational Education	$44,180	9.0%	69,000
28. Multi-Media Artists and Animators	$49,900	15.8%	12,000
29. Landscape Architects	$54,290	22.2%	2,000
30. Property, Real Estate, and Community Association Managers	$41,540	12.8%	35,000
31. Budget Analysts	$57,190	14.0%	8,000
32. Electrical Engineers	$72,770	2.5%	11,000

(continued)

(continued)

Best Jobs for Baby Boomers Requiring a Bachelor's Degree

Job	Annual Earnings	Percent Growth	Annual Openings
33. Insurance Sales Agents	$42,030	8.4%	52,000
34. Directors, Religious Activities and Education	$30,720	24.1%	16,000
35. Dietitians and Nutritionists	$44,370	17.8%	8,000
36. Adult Literacy, Remedial Education, and GED Teachers and Instructors	$39,730	20.4%	14,000
37. Fire-Prevention and Protection Engineers	$64,320	7.9%	4,000
38. Industrial Safety and Health Engineers	$64,320	7.9%	4,000
39. Product Safety Engineers	$64,320	7.9%	4,000
40. Probation Officers and Correctional Treatment Specialists	$39,760	14.7%	15,000
41. First-Line Supervisors and Manager/Supervisors—Logging Workers	$36,040	11.4%	6,000

Jobs 2, 4, and 5 share 59,000 openings. Jobs 13 and 14 share 29,000 openings. Jobs 16, 17, and 19 share 23,000 openings with each other and with another job not on this list. Jobs 37, 38, and 39 share 4,000 openings. Job 41 shares 6,000 openings with five other jobs not on this list.

Best Jobs for Baby Boomers Requiring Work Experience Plus Degree

Job	Annual Earnings	Percent Growth	Annual Openings
1. Chief Executives	$141,820	16.7%	63,000
2. Government Service Executives	$141,820	16.7%	63,000
3. Private Sector Executives	$141,820	16.7%	63,000
4. General and Operations Managers	$79,300	18.4%	260,000
5. Financial Managers, Branch or Department	$83,780	18.3%	71,000
6. Management Analysts	$64,560	30.4%	78,000
7. Treasurers, Controllers, and Chief Financial Officers	$83,780	18.3%	71,000
8. Education Administrators, Elementary and Secondary School	$74,610	20.7%	31,000
9. Medical and Health Services Managers	$68,320	29.3%	33,000
10. Administrative Services Managers	$62,300	19.8%	40,000
11. Public Relations Managers	$73,960	23.4%	10,000
12. Training and Development Managers	$70,430	19.4%	21,000
13. Compensation and Benefits Managers	$67,040	19.4%	21,000
14. Engineering Managers	$99,000	9.2%	16,000
15. Education Administrators, Preschool and Child Care Center/Program	$36,080	32.0%	9,000
16. Judges, Magistrate Judges, and Magistrates	$97,260	8.7%	2,000
17. Agricultural Crop Farm Managers	$50,720	5.1%	25,000

Best Jobs for Baby Boomers Requiring Work Experience Plus Degree

Job	Annual Earnings	Percent Growth	Annual Openings
18. Fish Hatchery Managers	$50,720	5.1%	25,000
19. Nursery and Greenhouse Managers	$50,720	5.1%	25,000
20. Purchasing Managers	$74,300	4.8%	9,000
21. Art Directors	$63,750	11.4%	8,000
22. Arbitrators, Mediators, and Conciliators	$53,690	13.7%	fewer than 500
23. Vocational Education Teachers, Secondary School	$46,650	9.0%	12,000
24. Composers	$34,800	13.5%	8,000
25. Music Arrangers and Orchestrators	$34,800	13.5%	8,000

Jobs 1, 2, and 3 share 63,000 openings. Jobs 5 and 7 share 71,000 openings. Jobs 12 and 13 share 21,000 openings. Jobs 17, 18, and 19 share 25,000 openings. Jobs 24 and 25 share 8,000 openings with each other and with another job not on this list.

Best Jobs for Baby Boomers Requiring a Master's Degree

Job	Annual Earnings	Percent Growth	Annual Openings
1. Teachers, Postsecondary	$54,406	38.1%	216,000
2. Speech-Language Pathologists	$53,790	27.2%	10,000
3. Instructional Coordinators	$50,060	25.4%	18,000
4. Mental Health and Substance Abuse Social Workers	$34,310	34.5%	17,000
5. Rehabilitation Counselors	$27,900	33.8%	19,000
6. Environmental Scientists and Specialists, Including Health	$51,950	23.7%	6,000
7. Audiologists	$53,040	29.0%	1,000
8. Educational, Vocational, and School Counselors	$46,160	15.0%	32,000
9. Mental Health Counselors	$33,400	26.7%	13,000
10. Economists	$72,370	13.4%	2,000
11. Hydrologists	$60,880	21.0%	1,000
12. Industrial-Organizational Psychologists	$74,060	16.0%	fewer than 500
13. Geographers	$61,520	19.5%	fewer than 500
14. Geologists	$70,180	11.5%	2,000
15. Health Educators	$39,670	21.9%	8,000
16. Substance Abuse and Behavioral Disorder Counselors	$32,630	23.3%	10,000
17. Librarians	$46,940	10.1%	15,000
18. Marriage and Family Therapists	$40,440	22.4%	3,000
19. Operations Research Analysts	$60,230	6.2%	6,000
20. Curators	$43,920	17.0%	2,000
21. Music Directors	$34,800	13.5%	8,000
22. Sociologists	$56,790	13.4%	fewer than 500

Job 21 shares 8,000 openings with two other jobs not on this list.

Best Jobs for Baby Boomers Requiring a Doctoral Degree

Job	Annual Earnings	Percent Growth	Annual Openings
1. Clinical Psychologists	$56,360	24.4%	17,000
2. Counseling Psychologists	$56,360	24.4%	17,000
3. School Psychologists	$56,360	24.4%	17,000
4. Physicists	$87,480	6.9%	1,000

Jobs 1, 2, and 3 share 17,000 openings.

Best Jobs for Baby Boomers Requiring a First Professional Degree

Job	Annual Earnings	Percent Growth	Annual Openings
1. Anesthesiologists	more than $145,600	19.5%	38,000
2. Internists, General	more than $145,600	19.5%	38,000
3. Obstetricians and Gynecologists	more than $145,600	19.5%	38,000
4. Psychiatrists	more than $145,600	19.5%	38,000
5. Surgeons	more than $145,600	19.5%	38,000
6. Family and General Practitioners	$136,170	19.5%	38,000
7. Pediatricians, General	$135,450	19.5%	38,000
8. Lawyers	$97,420	17.0%	53,000
9. Pharmacists	$87,160	30.1%	23,000
10. Oral and Maxillofacial Surgeons	more than $145,600	4.1%	7,000
11. Orthodontists	more than $145,600	4.1%	7,000
12. Prosthodontists	more than $145,600	4.1%	7,000
13. Veterinarians	$68,280	25.1%	4,000
14. Chiropractors	$67,940	23.3%	3,000
15. Dentists, General	$122,430	4.1%	7,000
16. Clergy	$37,870	15.5%	34,000
17. Optometrists	$88,290	17.1%	2,000
18. Podiatrists	$97,290	15.0%	1,000

Jobs 1, 2, 3, 4, 5, 6, and 7 share 38,000 openings. Jobs 10, 11, 12, and 15 share 7,000 openings.

Best Jobs Lists for Baby Boomers Based on Interests

This group of lists organizes the 225 best jobs into 16 interest areas. You can use these lists to quickly identify jobs based on your interests.

Find the interest area or areas that are most appealing to you. Then review the jobs in those areas to identify jobs you want to explore in more detail and look up their descriptions in Part III. You can also review interest areas where you have had past experience, education, or training to see if other jobs in those areas would meet your current requirements.

Within each interest area, jobs are listed in order of their combined scores based on earnings, growth, and number of openings.

Note: The 16 interest areas used in these lists are those used in the *New Guide for Occupational Exploration,* Fourth Edition, published by JIST. The original GOE was developed by the U.S. Department of Labor as an intuitive way to assist in career exploration. The 16 interest areas used in the *New GOE* are based on the 16 career clusters that were developed by the U.S. Department of Education's Office of Vocational and Adult Education around 1999 and that presently are being used by many states to organize their career-oriented programs and career information.

Descriptions for the 16 Interest Areas

Brief descriptions for the 16 interest areas we use in the lists follow. The descriptions are from the *New Guide for Occupational Exploration,* Fourth Edition. Some of them refer to jobs (as examples) that aren't included in this book.

Also note that we put each of the 225 best jobs into only one interest area list, the one it fit into best. However, many jobs could be included in more than one list, so consider reviewing a variety of these interest areas to find jobs that you might otherwise overlook.

It is interesting to note that one of the interest areas defined below, Information Technology, accounts for *none* of the 225 jobs that met the criteria for this book. This field is so new and is growing so fast that the jobs tend to be dominated by young workers. In addition, many of the comparatively small number of baby boomers who took jobs in this interest area in the 1960s and 1970s have moved into management or some other field, willingly or otherwise.

- Agriculture and Natural Resources: *An interest in working with plants, animals, forests, or mineral resources for agriculture, horticulture, conservation, extraction, and other purposes.* You can satisfy this interest by working in farming, landscaping, forestry, fishing, mining, and related fields. You may like doing physical work outdoors, such as on a farm or ranch, in a forest, or on a drilling rig. If you have scientific curiosity, you could study plants and animals or analyze biological or rock samples in a lab. If you have management ability, you could own, operate, or manage a fish hatchery, a landscaping business, or a greenhouse.

Shelton State Libraries
Shelton State Community College

○ Architecture and Construction: *An interest in designing, assembling, and maintaining components of buildings and other structures.* You may want to be part of the team of architects, drafters, and others who design buildings and render the plans. If construction interests you, you can find fulfillment in the many building projects that are being undertaken at all times. If you like to organize and plan, you can find careers in managing these projects. Or you can play a more direct role in putting up and finishing buildings by doing jobs such as plumbing, carpentry, masonry, painting, or roofing, either as a skilled craftsworker or as a helper. You can prepare the building site by operating heavy equipment or install, maintain, and repair vital building equipment and systems such as electricity and heating.

○ Arts and Communication: *An interest in creatively expressing feelings or ideas, in communicating news or information, or in performing.* You can satisfy this interest in creative, verbal, or performing activities. For example, if you enjoy literature, perhaps writing or editing would appeal to you. Journalism and public relations are other fields for people who like to use their writing or speaking skills. Do you prefer to work in the performing arts? If so, you could direct or perform in drama, music, or dance. If you especially enjoy the visual arts, you could create paintings, sculpture, or ceramics or design products or visual displays. A flair for technology might lead you to specialize in photography, broadcast production, or dispatching.

○ Business and Administration: *An interest in making a business organization or function run smoothly.* You can satisfy this interest by working in a position of leadership or by specializing in a function that contributes to the overall effort in a business, a nonprofit organization, or a government agency. If you especially enjoy working with people, you may find fulfillment from working in human resources. An interest in numbers may lead you to consider accounting, finance, budgeting, billing, or financial record-keeping. A job as an administrative assistant may interest you if you like a variety of work in a busy environment. If you are good with details and word processing, you may enjoy a job as a secretary or data entry keyer. Or perhaps you would do well as the manager of a business.

○ Education and Training: *An interest in helping people learn.* You can satisfy this interest by teaching students, who may be preschoolers, retirees, or any age in between. You may specialize in a particular academic field or work with learners of a particular age, with a particular interest, or with a particular learning problem. Working in a library or museum may give you an opportunity to expand people's understanding of the world.

○ Finance and Insurance: *An interest in helping businesses and people be assured of a financially secure future.* You can satisfy this interest by working in a financial or insurance business in a leadership or support role. If you like gathering and analyzing information, you may find fulfillment as an insurance adjuster or financial analyst. Or you may deal with information at the clerical level as a banking or insurance clerk or in person-to-person situations providing customer service. Another way to interact with people is to sell financial or insurance services that will meet their needs.

○ Government and Public Administration: *An interest in helping a government agency serve the needs of the public.* You can satisfy this interest by working in a position of leadership or by specializing in a function that contributes to the role of government. You may help protect the public by working as an inspector or examiner to enforce standards. If you enjoy using clerical skills, you may work as a clerk in a law court or government office. Or perhaps you prefer the top-down perspective of a government executive or urban planner.

◎ Health Science: *An interest in helping people and animals be healthy.* You can satisfy this interest by working in a health care team as a doctor, therapist, or nurse. You might specialize in one of the many different parts of the body (such as the teeth or eyes) or in one of the many different types of care. Or you may wish to be a generalist who deals with the whole patient. If you like technology, you might find satisfaction working with X rays or new methods of diagnosis. You might work with healthy people, helping them eat right. If you enjoy working with animals, you might care for them and keep them healthy.

◎ Hospitality, Tourism, and Recreation: *An interest in catering to the personal wishes and needs of others so that they may enjoy a clean environment, good food and drink, comfortable lodging away from home, and recreation.* You can satisfy this interest by providing services for the convenience, care, and pampering of others in hotels, restaurants, airplanes, beauty parlors, and so on. You may wish to use your love of cooking as a chef. If you like working with people, you may wish to provide personal services by being a travel guide, a flight attendant, a concierge, a hairdresser, or a waiter. You may wish to work in cleaning and building services if you like a clean environment. If you enjoy sports or games, you may work for an athletic team or casino.

◎ Human Service: *An interest in improving people's social, mental, emotional, or spiritual well-being.* You can satisfy this interest as a counselor, social worker, or religious worker who helps people sort out their complicated lives or solve personal problems. You may work as a caretaker for very young people or the elderly. Or you may interview people to help identify the social services they need.

◎ Information Technology: *An interest in designing, developing, managing, and supporting information systems.* You can satisfy this interest by working with hardware, software, multimedia, or integrated systems. If you like to use your organizational skills, you might work as an administrator of a system or database. Or you can solve complex problems as a software engineer or systems analyst. If you enjoy getting your hands on the hardware, you might find work servicing computers, peripherals, and information-intense machines such as cash registers and ATMs.

◎ Law and Public Safety: *An interest in upholding people's rights or in protecting people and property by using authority, inspecting, or investigating.* You can satisfy this interest by working in law, law enforcement, fire fighting, the military, and related fields. For example, if you enjoy mental challenge and intrigue, you could investigate crimes or fires for a living. If you enjoy working with verbal skills and research skills, you may want to defend citizens in court or research deeds, wills, and other legal documents. If you want to help people in critical situations, you may want to fight fires, work as a police officer, or become a paramedic. Or, if you want more routine work in public safety, perhaps a job in guarding, patrolling, or inspecting would appeal to you. If you have management ability, you could seek a leadership position in law enforcement and the protective services. Work in the military gives you a chance to use technical and leadership skills while serving your country.

- Manufacturing: *An interest in processing materials into intermediate or final products or maintaining and repairing products by using machines or hand tools.* You can satisfy this interest by working in one of many industries that mass-produce goods or by working for a utility that distributes electric power or other resources. You may enjoy manual work, using your hands or hand tools in highly skilled jobs such as assembling engines or electronic equipment. If you enjoy making machines run efficiently or fixing them when they break down, you could seek a job installing or repairing such devices as copiers, aircraft engines, cars, or watches. Perhaps you prefer to set up or operate machines that are used to manufacture products made of food, glass, or paper. You may enjoy cutting and grinding metal and plastic parts to desired shapes and measurements. Or you may wish to operate equipment in systems that provide water and process wastewater. You may like inspecting, sorting, counting, or weighing products. Another option is to work with your hands and machinery to move boxes and freight in a warehouse. If leadership appeals to you, you could manage people engaged in production and repair.

- Retail and Wholesale Sales and Service: *An interest in bringing others to a particular point of view by personal persuasion and by sales and promotional techniques.* You can satisfy this interest in a variety of jobs that involve persuasion and selling. If you like using knowledge of science, you may enjoy selling pharmaceutical, medical, or electronic products or services. Real estate offers several kinds of sales jobs as well. If you like speaking on the phone, you could work as a telemarketer. Or you may enjoy selling apparel and other merchandise in a retail setting. If you prefer to help people, you may want a job in customer service.

- Scientific Research, Engineering, and Mathematics: *An interest in discovering, collecting, and analyzing information about the natural world; in applying scientific research findings to problems in medicine, the life sciences, human behavior, and the natural sciences; in imagining and manipulating quantitative data; and in applying technology to manufacturing, transportation, and other economic activities.* You can satisfy this interest by working with the knowledge and processes of the sciences. You may enjoy researching and developing new knowledge in mathematics, or perhaps solving problems in the physical, life, or social sciences would appeal to you. You may wish to study engineering and help create new machines, processes, and structures. If you want to work with scientific equipment and procedures, you could seek a job in a research or testing laboratory.

- Transportation, Distribution, and Logistics: *An interest in operations that move people or materials.* You can satisfy this interest by managing a transportation service, by helping vehicles keep on their assigned schedules and routes, or by driving or piloting a vehicle. If you enjoy taking responsibility, perhaps managing a rail line would appeal to you. If you work well with details and can take pressure on the job, you might consider being an air traffic controller. Or would you rather get out on the highway, on the water, or up in the air? If so, then you could drive a truck from state to state, be employed on a ship, or fly a crop duster over a cornfield. If you prefer to stay closer to home, you could drive a delivery van, taxi, or school bus. You can use your physical strength to load freight and arrange it so it gets to its destination in one piece.

In Part I, we referred to a study that found that 58 percent of leading-edge baby boomers are attracted to seven particular areas of work that contribute to improving their communities. These areas of work are listed below, along with the GOE interest fields that most closely correspond to them. You may find that this table helps you choose which of the following lists to study in detail.

Area of Work	Corresponding Interest Field
Education	Education and Training
Health care	Health Science
Helping those in need	Human Service
Working with youth	Education and Training *or* Human Service
Civic activism	Government and Public Administration
Arts and culture	Arts and Communication
The environment	Agriculture and Natural Resources

Best Jobs for Baby Boomers Interested in Agriculture and Natural Resources

Job	Annual Earnings	Percent Growth	Annual Openings
1. First-Line Supervisors and Manager/Supervisors—Extractive Workers	$50,980	14.1%	67,000
2. Agricultural Crop Farm Managers	$50,720	5.1%	25,000
3. Fish Hatchery Managers	$50,720	5.1%	25,000
4. Nursery and Greenhouse Managers	$50,720	5.1%	25,000
5. First-Line Supervisors and Manager/Supervisors—Agricultural Crop Workers	$36,040	11.4%	6,000
6. First-Line Supervisors and Manager/Supervisors—Animal Husbandry Workers	$36,040	11.4%	6,000
7. First-Line Supervisors and Manager/Supervisors—Fishery Workers	$36,040	11.4%	6,000
8. First-Line Supervisors and Manager/Supervisors—Horticultural Workers	$36,040	11.4%	6,000
9. First-Line Supervisors and Manager/Supervisors—Logging Workers	$36,040	11.4%	6,000
10. Farmers and Ranchers	$38,600	–20.6%	118,000

Job 1 shares 67,000 openings with another job not on this list. Jobs 2, 3, and 4 share 25,000 openings. Jobs 5, 6, 7, 8, and 9 share 6,000 openings with each other and with another job not on this list.

Best Jobs for Baby Boomers Interested in Architecture and Construction

Job	Annual Earnings	Percent Growth	Annual Openings
1. Construction Managers	$70,770	12.0%	47,000
2. First-Line Supervisors and Manager/Supervisors— Construction Trades Workers	$50,980	14.1%	67,000
3. Architects, Except Landscape and Naval	$61,430	17.3%	8,000
4. Refractory Materials Repairers, Except Brickmasons	$39,610	16.3%	155,000
5. Landscape Architects	$54,290	22.2%	2,000
6. Maintenance and Repair Workers, General	$30,930	16.3%	155,000
7. Central Office and PBX Installers and Repairers	$50,270	–0.6%	23,000
8. Communication Equipment Mechanics, Installers, and Repairers	$50,270	–0.6%	23,000
9. Frame Wirers, Central Office	$50,270	–0.6%	23,000
10. Station Installers and Repairers, Telephone	$50,270	–0.6%	23,000
11. Telecommunications Facility Examiners	$50,270	–0.6%	23,000
12. Construction and Building Inspectors	$43,940	13.8%	10,000

Job 2 shares 67,000 openings with another job not on this list. Jobs 7, 8, 9, 10, and 11 share 23,000 openings.

Best Jobs for Baby Boomers Interested in Arts and Communication

Job	Annual Earnings	Percent Growth	Annual Openings
1. Public Relations Managers	$73,960	23.4%	10,000
2. Caption Writers	$45,460	16.1%	23,000
3. Copy Writers	$45,460	16.1%	23,000
4. Creative Writers	$45,460	16.1%	23,000
5. Poets and Lyricists	$45,460	16.1%	23,000
6. Technical Writers	$54,390	27.1%	6,000
7. Multi-Media Artists and Animators	$49,900	15.8%	12,000
8. Cartoonists	$41,240	16.5%	4,000
9. Painters and Illustrators	$41,240	16.5%	4,000
10. Sculptors	$41,240	16.5%	4,000
11. Sketch Artists	$41,240	16.5%	4,000
12. Art Directors	$63,750	11.4%	8,000
13. Air Traffic Controllers	$102,390	12.6%	2,000
14. Composers	$34,800	13.5%	8,000
15. Music Arrangers and Orchestrators	$34,800	13.5%	8,000
16. Music Directors	$34,800	13.5%	8,000

Jobs 2, 3, 4, and 5 share 23,000 openings. Jobs 8, 9, 10, and 11 share 4,000 openings. Jobs 14, 15, and 16 share 8,000 openings.

Best Jobs for Baby Boomers Interested in Business and Administration

Job	Annual Earnings	Percent Growth	Annual Openings
1. Management Analysts	$64,560	30.4%	78,000
2. General and Operations Managers	$79,300	18.4%	260,000
3. Logisticians	$59,460	27.5%	162,000
4. Chief Executives	$141,820	16.7%	63,000
5. Private Sector Executives	$141,820	16.7%	63,000
6. Administrative Services Managers	$62,300	19.8%	40,000
7. Training and Development Specialists	$45,370	27.9%	35,000
8. Training and Development Managers	$70,430	19.4%	21,000
9. Compensation and Benefits Managers	$67,040	19.4%	21,000
10. Compensation, Benefits, and Job Analysis Specialists	$48,720	28.0%	15,000
11. Employment Interviewers, Private or Public Employment Service	$41,190	27.3%	29,000
12. Personnel Recruiters	$41,190	27.3%	29,000
13. First-Line Supervisors, Administrative Support	$41,850	6.6%	140,000
14. First-Line Supervisors, Customer Service	$41,850	6.6%	140,000
15. Executive Secretaries and Administrative Assistants	$35,550	8.7%	210,000
16. Legal Secretaries	$37,390	18.8%	39,000
17. Bookkeeping, Accounting, and Auditing Clerks	$29,040	3.0%	274,000
18. Medical Secretaries	$27,030	17.2%	50,000
19. Budget Analysts	$57,190	14.0%	8,000
20. Housekeeping Supervisors	$30,050	16.2%	28,000
21. Janitorial Supervisors	$30,050	16.2%	28,000
22. Tax Preparers	$26,130	23.2%	11,000
23. Operations Research Analysts	$60,230	6.2%	6,000

Jobs 4 and 5 share 63,000 openings with another job not on this list. Jobs 8 and 9 share 21,000 openings. Jobs 11 and 12 share 29,000 openings. Jobs 13 and 14 share 140,000 openings. Job 21 shares 28,000 openings with another job not on this list.

Best Jobs for Baby Boomers Interested in Education and Training

Job	Annual Earnings	Percent Growth	Annual Openings
1. Teachers, Postsecondary	$54,406	38.1%	216,000
2. Special Education Teachers, Secondary School	$46,300	30.0%	59,000
3. Special Education Teachers, Middle School	$45,000	30.0%	59,000
4. Special Education Teachers, Preschool, Kindergarten, and Elementary School	$44,330	30.0%	59,000

(continued)

(continued)

Best Jobs for Baby Boomers Interested in Education and Training

Job	Annual Earnings	Percent Growth	Annual Openings
5. Education Administrators, Elementary and Secondary School	$74,610	20.7%	31,000
6. Instructional Coordinators	$50,060	25.4%	18,000
7. Secondary School Teachers, Except Special and Vocational Education	$46,120	18.2%	118,000
8. Self-Enrichment Education Teachers	$31,530	40.1%	39,000
9. Teacher Assistants	$19,760	23.0%	259,000
10. Elementary School Teachers, Except Special Education	$43,660	15.2%	183,000
11. Educational, Vocational, and School Counselors	$46,160	15.0%	32,000
12. Middle School Teachers, Except Special and Vocational Education	$44,180	9.0%	69,000
13. Librarians	$46,940	10.1%	15,000
14. Education Administrators, Preschool and Child Care Center/Program	$36,080	32.0%	9,000
15. Vocational Education Teachers, Secondary School	$46,650	9.0%	12,000
16. Library Assistants, Clerical	$21,050	21.5%	27,000
17. Adult Literacy, Remedial Education, and GED Teachers and Instructors	$39,730	20.4%	14,000
18. Health Educators	$39,670	21.9%	8,000
19. Curators	$43,920	17.0%	2,000

Jobs 2, 3, and 4 share 59,000 openings.

Best Jobs for Baby Boomers Interested in Finance and Insurance

Job	Annual Earnings	Percent Growth	Annual Openings
1. Financial Managers, Branch or Department	$83,780	18.3%	71,000
2. Treasurers, Controllers, and Chief Financial Officers	$83,780	18.3%	71,000
3. Personal Financial Advisors	$62,450	34.6%	18,000
4. Cost Estimators	$50,920	18.6%	25,000
5. Appraisers, Real Estate	$43,790	17.6%	11,000
6. Assessors	$43,790	17.6%	11,000
7. Insurance Sales Agents	$42,030	8.4%	52,000

Jobs 1 and 2 share 71,000 openings. Jobs 5 and 6 share 11,000 openings.

Best Jobs for Baby Boomers Interested in Government and Public Administration

Job	Annual Earnings	Percent Growth	Annual Openings
1. Government Service Executives	$141,820	16.7%	63,000
2. Environmental Compliance Inspectors	$48,530	9.8%	20,000
3. Equal Opportunity Representatives and Officers	$48,530	9.8%	20,000
4. Government Property Inspectors and Investigators	$48,530	9.8%	20,000
5. Licensing Examiners and Inspectors	$48,530	9.8%	20,000
6. Pressure Vessel Inspectors	$48,530	9.8%	20,000
7. Social and Community Service Managers	$48,330	27.7%	19,000
8. Court Clerks	$28,980	12.3%	14,000
9. License Clerks	$28,980	12.3%	14,000
10. Municipal Clerks	$28,980	12.3%	14,000
11. Aviation Inspectors	$47,920	7.7%	5,000
12. Marine Cargo Inspectors	$47,920	7.7%	5,000
13. Motor Vehicle Inspectors	$47,920	7.7%	5,000
14. Railroad Inspectors	$47,920	7.7%	5,000
15. Mechanical Inspectors	$28,630	4.7%	87,000

Job 1 shares 63,000 openings with two other jobs not on this list. Jobs 2, 3, 4, 5, and 6 share 20,000 openings with each other and with another job not on this list. Jobs 8, 9, and 10 share 14,000 openings. Jobs 11, 12, 13, and 14 share 5,000 openings with each other and with two other jobs not on this list. Job 15 shares 87,000 openings with four other jobs not on this list.

Best Jobs for Baby Boomers Interested in Health Science

Job	Annual Earnings	Percent Growth	Annual Openings
1. Anesthesiologists	more than $145,600	19.5%	38,000
2. Internists, General	more than $145,600	19.5%	38,000
3. Obstetricians and Gynecologists	more than $145,600	19.5%	38,000
4. Psychiatrists	more than $145,600	19.5%	38,000
5. Surgeons	more than $145,600	19.5%	38,000
6. Family and General Practitioners	$136,170	19.5%	38,000
7. Pediatricians, General	$135,450	19.5%	38,000
8. Registered Nurses	$53,640	27.3%	215,000
9. Pharmacists	$87,160	30.1%	23,000
10. Medical and Health Services Managers	$68,320	29.3%	33,000
11. Licensed Practical and Licensed Vocational Nurses	$34,650	20.2%	105,000
12. Speech-Language Pathologists	$53,790	27.2%	10,000

(continued)

(continued)

Best Jobs for Baby Boomers Interested in Health Science

Job	Annual Earnings	Percent Growth	Annual Openings
13. Oral and Maxillofacial Surgeons	more than $145,600	4.1%	7,000
14. Orthodontists	more than $145,600	4.1%	7,000
15. Prosthodontists	more than $145,600	4.1%	7,000
16. Veterinarians	$68,280	25.1%	4,000
17. Chiropractors	$67,940	23.3%	3,000
18. Audiologists	$53,040	29.0%	1,000
19. Dentists, General	$122,430	4.1%	7,000
20. Medical and Clinical Laboratory Technologists	$46,710	19.3%	21,000
21. Medical and Clinical Laboratory Technicians	$31,440	19.4%	21,000
22. Optometrists	$88,290	17.1%	2,000
23. Coroners	$48,530	9.8%	20,000
24. Dietitians and Nutritionists	$44,370	17.8%	8,000
25. Podiatrists	$97,290	15.0%	1,000
26. First-Line Supervisors and Manager/Supervisors— Animal Care Workers, Except Livestock	$36,040	11.4%	6,000

Jobs 1, 2, 3, 4, 5, 6, and 7 share 38,000 openings. Jobs 13, 14, 15, and 20 share 7,000 openings. Job 23 shares 20,000 openings with five other jobs not on this list. Job 26 shares 6,000 openings with five other jobs not on this list.

Best Jobs for Baby Boomers Interested in Hospitality, Tourism, and Recreation

Job	Annual Earnings	Percent Growth	Annual Openings
1. Janitors and Cleaners, Except Maids and Housekeeping Cleaners	$19,110	18.3%	454,000
2. Gaming Supervisors	$41,080	15.7%	6,000
3. Lodging Managers	$39,100	6.6%	10,000
4. Maids and Housekeeping Cleaners	$17,000	9.2%	352,000

Best Jobs for Baby Boomers Interested in Human Service

Job	Annual Earnings	Percent Growth	Annual Openings
1. Medical and Public Health Social Workers	$40,780	28.6%	18,000
2. Clinical Psychologists	$56,360	24.4%	17,000
3. Counseling Psychologists	$56,360	24.4%	17,000
4. Social and Human Service Assistants	$24,730	48.7%	63,000
5. Personal and Home Care Aides	$17,020	40.5%	154,000
6. Mental Health and Substance Abuse Social Workers	$34,310	34.5%	17,000
7. Child, Family, and School Social Workers	$35,010	23.2%	45,000
8. Rehabilitation Counselors	$27,900	33.8%	19,000
9. Clergy	$37,870	15.5%	34,000
10. Mental Health Counselors	$33,400	26.7%	13,000
11. Directors, Religious Activities and Education	$30,720	24.1%	16,000
12. Marriage and Family Therapists	$40,440	22.4%	3,000
13. Probation Officers and Correctional Treatment Specialists	$39,760	14.7%	15,000
14. Substance Abuse and Behavioral Disorder Counselors	$32,630	23.3%	10,000

Jobs 2 and 3 share 17,000 openings with each other and with another job not on this list.

Best Jobs for Baby Boomers Interested in Law and Public Safety

Job	Annual Earnings	Percent Growth	Annual Openings
1. Lawyers	$97,420	17.0%	53,000
2. Security Guards	$20,520	31.9%	228,000
3. Forest Fire Fighting and Prevention Supervisors	$59,760	18.7%	8,000
4. Municipal Fire Fighting and Prevention Supervisors	$59,760	18.7%	8,000
5. First-Line Supervisors/Managers of Police and Detectives	$65,020	15.3%	14,000
6. Private Detectives and Investigators	$32,510	25.3%	9,000
7. Emergency Management Specialists	$45,670	28.2%	2,000
8. First-Line Supervisors/Managers of Correctional Officers	$48,070	19.0%	4,000
9. Crossing Guards	$19,710	16.5%	19,000
10. Judges, Magistrate Judges, and Magistrates	$97,260	8.7%	2,000
11. Arbitrators, Mediators, and Conciliators	$53,690	13.7%	fewer than 500

Jobs 3 and 4 share 8,000 openings.

Best Jobs for Baby Boomers Interested in Manufacturing

Job	Annual Earnings	Percent Growth	Annual Openings
1. First-Line Supervisors/Managers of Mechanics, Installers, and Repairers	$51,000	15.4%	42,000
2. First-Line Supervisors/Managers of Production and Operating Workers	$45,230	9.5%	66,000
3. Aircraft Body and Bonded Structure Repairers	$45,910	11.0%	12,000
4. Aircraft Engine Specialists	$45,910	11.0%	12,000
5. Airframe-and-Power-Plant Mechanics	$45,910	11.0%	12,000
6. Bus and Truck Mechanics and Diesel Engine Specialists	$36,150	14.2%	28,000
7. Industrial Production Managers	$74,100	7.9%	18,000
8. Laundry and Drycleaning Machine Operators and Tenders, Except Pressing	$17,350	12.3%	47,000
9. Precision Dyers	$17,350	12.3%	47,000
10. Spotters, Dry Cleaning	$17,350	12.3%	47,000
11. Water and Liquid Waste Treatment Plant and System Operators	$34,850	16.0%	9,000
12. Electrical and Electronic Inspectors and Testers	$28,630	4.7%	87,000
13. Materials Inspectors	$28,630	4.7%	87,000
14. Precision Devices Inspectors and Testers	$28,630	4.7%	87,000
15. Production Inspectors, Testers, Graders, Sorters, Samplers, Weighers	$28,630	4.7%	87,000
16. Medical Equipment Repairers	$38,590	14.8%	4,000
17. Locksmiths and Safe Repairers	$30,580	21.0%	3,000
18. Mobile Heavy Equipment Mechanics, Except Engines	$38,630	9.6%	12,000
19. Electrical and Electronics Repairers, Commercial and Industrial Equipment	$43,180	10.3%	10,000
20. Industrial Machinery Mechanics	$39,310	5.5%	19,000
21. Machinists	$34,090	8.2%	30,000

Jobs 3, 4, and 5 share 12,000 openings. Jobs 8, 9, and 10 share 47,000 openings. Jobs 12, 13, 14, and 15 share 87,000 openings with each other and with another job not on this list.

Best Jobs for Baby Boomers Interested in Retail and Wholesale Sales and Service

Job	Annual Earnings	Percent Growth	Annual Openings
1. Sales Representatives, Agricultural	$59,390	19.3%	44,000
2. Sales Representatives, Chemical and Pharmaceutical	$59,390	19.3%	44,000
3. Sales Representatives, Electrical/Electronic	$59,390	19.3%	44,000
4. Sales Representatives, Instruments	$59,390	19.3%	44,000
5. Sales Representatives, Mechanical Equipment and Supplies	$59,390	19.3%	44,000
6. Sales Representatives, Medical	$59,390	19.3%	44,000
7. First-Line Supervisors/Managers of Non-Retail Sales Workers	$60,300	6.8%	72,000
8. Sales Representatives, Wholesale and Manufacturing, Except Technical and Scientific Products	$46,090	19.1%	160,000
9. First-Line Supervisors/Managers of Retail Sales Workers	$32,410	9.1%	251,000
10. Purchasing Managers	$74,300	4.8%	9,000
11. Property, Real Estate, and Community Association Managers	$41,540	12.8%	35,000
12. Purchasing Agents, Except Wholesale, Retail, and Farm Products	$48,360	11.2%	29,000
13. Demonstrators and Product Promoters	$20,490	17.0%	38,000
14. Real Estate Sales Agents	$36,950	5.7%	34,000
15. Real Estate Brokers	$56,970	2.4%	11,000
16. Wholesale and Retail Buyers, Except Farm Products	$42,190	4.3%	24,000

Jobs 1, 2, 3, 4, 5, and 6 share 44,000 openings.

Best Jobs for Baby Boomers Interested in Scientific Research, Engineering, and Mathematics

Job	Annual Earnings	Percent Growth	Annual Openings
1. Engineering Managers	$99,000	9.2%	16,000
2. Electronics Engineers, Except Computer	$76,810	9.4%	11,000
3. School Psychologists	$56,360	24.4%	17,000
4. Industrial Engineers	$66,080	10.6%	16,000
5. Civil Engineers	$65,280	8.0%	17,000
6. Economists	$72,370	13.4%	2,000

(continued)

(continued)

Best Jobs for Baby Boomers
Interested in Scientific Research, Engineering, and Mathematics

Job	Annual Earnings	Percent Growth	Annual Openings
7. Industrial-Organizational Psychologists	$74,060	16.0%	fewer than 500
8. Environmental Scientists and Specialists, Including Health	$51,950	23.7%	6,000
9. Geologists	$70,180	11.5%	2,000
10. Electrical Engineers	$72,770	2.5%	11,000
11. Hydrologists	$60,880	21.0%	1,000
12. Fire-Prevention and Protection Engineers	$64,320	7.9%	4,000
13. Industrial Safety and Health Engineers	$64,320	7.9%	4,000
14. Product Safety Engineers	$64,320	7.9%	4,000
15. Physicists	$87,480	6.9%	1,000
16. Geographers	$61,520	19.5%	fewer than 500
17. Sociologists	$56,790	13.4%	fewer than 500

Jobs 12, 13, and 14 share 4,000 openings.

Best Jobs for Baby Boomers
Interested in Transportation, Distribution, and Logistics

Job	Annual Earnings	Percent Growth	Annual Openings
1. Storage and Distribution Managers	$67,300	19.7%	13,000
2. Transportation Managers	$67,300	19.7%	13,000
3. Tractor-Trailer Truck Drivers	$33,870	19.0%	299,000
4. Truck Drivers, Heavy	$33,870	19.0%	299,000
5. Truck Drivers, Light or Delivery Services	$24,420	23.2%	219,000
6. Airline Pilots, Copilots, and Flight Engineers	$135,430	18.5%	6,000
7. Taxi Drivers and Chauffeurs	$19,790	21.7%	28,000
8. Bus Drivers, School	$23,670	16.7%	76,000
9. Bus Drivers, Transit and Intercity	$30,670	15.2%	33,000
10. Commercial Pilots	$55,360	14.9%	2,000
11. Freight Inspectors	$47,920	7.7%	5,000
12. Public Transportation Inspectors	$47,920	7.7%	5,000
13. Postal Service Mail Carriers	$45,880	−0.5%	20,000
14. Subway and Streetcar Operators	$47,560	13.2%	2,000

Jobs 1 and 2 share 13,000 openings. Jobs 3 and 4 share 299,000 openings. Jobs 11 and 12 share 5,000 openings with each other and with four other jobs not on this list.

Best Jobs Lists Based on Personality Types

These lists organize the 225 best jobs into groups matching six personality types. The personality types are Realistic, Investigative, Artistic, Social, Enterprising, and Conventional. This system was developed by John L. Holland and is used in the *Self Directed Search (SDS)* and other career assessment inventories and information systems.

If you have used one of these career inventories or systems, the lists will help you identify jobs that most closely match these personality types. Even if you have not used one of these systems, the concept of personality types and the jobs that are related to them can help you identify jobs that most closely match the type of person you are.

We've ranked the jobs within each personality type based on their combined scores for earnings, growth, and annual job openings. As in the job lists for education levels, only one list for each personality type is given below. Note that each job is listed in the one personality type it most closely matches, even though it might also fit into others. (The only exception is Teachers, Postsecondary, which is included in several lists because the various postsecondary teaching occupations fall into several personality types. A footnote lists the specific postsecondary teaching occupations for each personality type.) Consider reviewing the jobs for more than one personality type so you don't overlook possible jobs that would interest you. Also, note that we did not have data to crosswalk 10 of the 225 best jobs to their related personality type, so some of the jobs do not appear on the lists in this section.

Following are brief descriptions for each of the six personality types used in the lists. Select the two or three descriptions that most closely resemble you and then use the lists to identify jobs that best fit these personality types.

Descriptions of the Six Personality Types

- **Realistic:** These occupations frequently involve work activities that include practical, hands-on problems and solutions. They often deal with plants, animals, and real-world materials like wood, tools, and machinery. Many of the occupations require working outside and do not involve a lot of paperwork or working closely with others.

- **Investigative:** These occupations frequently involve working with ideas and require an extensive amount of thinking. These occupations can involve searching for facts and figuring out problems mentally.

- **Artistic:** These occupations frequently involve working with forms, designs, and patterns. They often require self-expression, and the work can be done without following a clear set of rules.

- **Social:** These occupations frequently involve working with, communicating with, and teaching people. These occupations often involve helping or providing service to others.

- **Enterprising:** These occupations frequently involve starting up and carrying out projects. These occupations can involve leading people and making many decisions. They sometimes require risk taking and often deal with business.

- **Conventional:** These occupations frequently involve following set procedures and routines. These occupations can include working with data and details more than with ideas. Usually there is a clear line of authority to follow.

Best Jobs for Baby Boomers with a Realistic Personality Type

Job	Annual Earnings	Percent Growth	Annual Openings
1. Refractory Materials Repairers, Except Brickmasons	$39,610	16.3%	155,000
2. Tractor-Trailer Truck Drivers	$33,870	19.0%	299,000
3. Truck Drivers, Heavy	$33,870	19.0%	299,000
4. Forest Fire Fighting and Prevention Supervisors	$59,760	18.7%	8,000
5. Municipal Fire Fighting and Prevention Supervisors	$59,760	18.7%	8,000
6. Airline Pilots, Copilots, and Flight Engineers	$135,430	18.5%	6,000
7. Truck Drivers, Light or Delivery Services	$24,420	23.2%	219,000
8. Maintenance and Repair Workers, General	$30,930	16.3%	155,000
9. Janitors and Cleaners, Except Maids and Housekeeping Cleaners	$19,110	18.3%	454,000
10. Bus and Truck Mechanics and Diesel Engine Specialists	$36,150	14.2%	28,000
11. Medical and Clinical Laboratory Technicians	$31,440	19.4%	21,000
12. Civil Engineers	$65,280	8.0%	17,000
13. Taxi Drivers and Chauffeurs	$19,790	21.7%	28,000
14. Bus Drivers, School	$23,670	16.7%	76,000
15. Bus Drivers, Transit and Intercity	$30,670	15.2%	33,000
16. Commercial Pilots	$55,360	14.9%	2,000
17. Pressure Vessel Inspectors	$48,530	9.8%	20,000
18. Central Office and PBX Installers and Repairers	$50,270	−0.6%	23,000
19. Communication Equipment Mechanics, Installers, and Repairers	$50,270	−0.6%	23,000
20. Frame Wirers, Central Office	$50,270	−0.6%	23,000
21. Station Installers and Repairers, Telephone	$50,270	−0.6%	23,000
22. Telecommunications Facility Examiners	$50,270	−0.6%	23,000
23. Aircraft Body and Bonded Structure Repairers	$45,910	11.0%	12,000
24. Aircraft Engine Specialists	$45,910	11.0%	12,000
25. Airframe-and-Power-Plant Mechanics	$45,910	11.0%	12,000
26. Water and Liquid Waste Treatment Plant and System Operators	$34,850	16.0%	9,000
27. Farmers and Ranchers	$38,600	−20.6%	118,000

Best Jobs for Baby Boomers with a Realistic Personality Type

Job	Annual Earnings	Percent Growth	Annual Openings
28. Laundry and Drycleaning Machine Operators and Tenders, Except Pressing	$17,350	12.3%	47,000
29. Precision Dyers	$17,350	12.3%	47,000
30. Spotters, Dry Cleaning	$17,350	12.3%	47,000
31. Subway and Streetcar Operators	$47,560	13.2%	2,000
32. Electrical and Electronics Repairers, Commercial and Industrial Equipment	$43,180	10.3%	10,000
33. Machinists	$34,090	8.2%	30,000
34. Maids and Housekeeping Cleaners	$17,000	9.2%	352,000
35. Mobile Heavy Equipment Mechanics, Except Engines	$38,630	9.6%	12,000
36. Electrical and Electronic Inspectors and Testers	$28,630	4.7%	87,000
37. Materials Inspectors	$28,630	4.7%	87,000
38. Mechanical Inspectors	$28,630	4.7%	87,000
39. Precision Devices Inspectors and Testers	$28,630	4.7%	87,000
40. Production Inspectors, Testers, Graders, Sorters, Samplers, Weighers	$28,630	4.7%	87,000
41. First-Line Supervisors and Manager/Supervisors— Animal Care Workers, Except Livestock	$36,040	11.4%	6,000
42. First-Line Supervisors and Manager/Supervisors— Fishery Workers	$36,040	11.4%	6,000
43. First-Line Supervisors and Manager/Supervisors— Horticultural Workers	$36,040	11.4%	6,000
44. First-Line Supervisors and Manager/Supervisors— Logging Workers	$36,040	11.4%	6,000
45. Locksmiths and Safe Repairers	$30,580	21.0%	3,000
46. Medical Equipment Repairers	$38,590	14.8%	4,000
47. Industrial Machinery Mechanics	$39,310	5.5%	19,000
48. Aviation Inspectors	$47,920	7.7%	5,000
49. Motor Vehicle Inspectors	$47,920	7.7%	5,000
50. Railroad Inspectors	$47,920	7.7%	5,000

Jobs 2 and 3 share 299,000 openings. Jobs 4 and 5 share 8,000 openings. Job 17 shares 20,000 openings with five other jobs not on this list. Jobs 18, 19, 20, 21, and 22 share 23,000 openings. Jobs 23, 24, and 25 share 12,000 openings. Jobs 28, 29, and 30 share 47,000 openings. Jobs 36, 37, 38, 39, and 40 share 87,000 openings. Jobs 41, 42, 43, and 44 share 6,000 openings with each other and with two other jobs not on this list.

Best Jobs for Baby Boomers with an Investigative Personality Type

Job	Annual Earnings	Percent Growth	Annual Openings
1. Anesthesiologists	more than $145,600	19.5%	38,000
2. Internists, General	more than $145,600	19.5%	38,000
3. Obstetricians and Gynecologists	more than $145,600	19.5%	38,000
4. Psychiatrists	more than $145,600	19.5%	38,000
5. Surgeons	more than $145,600	19.5%	38,000
6. Family and General Practitioners	$136,170	19.5%	38,000
7. Pediatricians, General	$135,450	19.5%	38,000
8. Pharmacists	$87,160	30.1%	23,000
9. Teachers, Postsecondary	$54,406	38.1%	216,000
10. Clinical Psychologists	$56,360	24.4%	17,000
11. School Psychologists	$56,360	24.4%	17,000
12. Veterinarians	$68,280	25.1%	4,000
13. Compensation, Benefits, and Job Analysis Specialists	$48,720	28.0%	15,000
14. Oral and Maxillofacial Surgeons	more than $145,600	4.1%	7,000
15. Orthodontists	more than $145,600	4.1%	7,000
16. Prosthodontists	more than $145,600	4.1%	7,000
17. Chiropractors	$67,940	23.3%	3,000
18. Electronics Engineers, Except Computer	$76,810	9.4%	11,000
19. Environmental Scientists and Specialists, Including Health	$51,950	23.7%	6,000
20. Optometrists	$88,290	17.1%	2,000
21. Dentists, General	$122,430	4.1%	7,000
22. Medical and Clinical Laboratory Technologists	$46,710	19.3%	21,000
23. Hydrologists	$60,880	21.0%	1,000
24. Coroners	$48,530	9.8%	20,000
25. Environmental Compliance Inspectors	$48,530	9.8%	20,000
26. Economists	$72,370	13.4%	2,000
27. Electrical Engineers	$72,770	2.5%	11,000
28. Geographers	$61,520	19.5%	fewer than 500
29. Industrial-Organizational Psychologists	$74,060	16.0%	fewer than 500
30. Geologists	$70,180	11.5%	2,000
31. Dietitians and Nutritionists	$44,370	17.8%	8,000
32. Fire-Prevention and Protection Engineers	$64,320	7.9%	4,000
33. Industrial Safety and Health Engineers	$64,320	7.9%	4,000

Best Jobs for Baby Boomers with an Investigative Personality Type

Job	Annual Earnings	Percent Growth	Annual Openings
34. Product Safety Engineers	$64,320	7.9%	4,000
35. Physicists	$87,480	6.9%	1,000
36. Operations Research Analysts	$60,230	6.2%	6,000
37. Sociologists	$56,790	13.4%	fewer than 500

Jobs 1, 2, 3, 4, 5, 6, and 7 share 38,000 openings. Jobs 10 and 11 share 17,000 openings with each other and with another job not on this list. Jobs 14, 15, 16, and 21 share 7,000 openings. Jobs 24 and 25 share 20,000 openings with each other and with four other jobs not on this list. Jobs 32, 33, and 34 share 4,000 openings.

Teachers, Postsecondary, is listed here because the following jobs are associated with the Investigative personality type: Agricultural Sciences Teachers, Postsecondary; Biological Science Teachers, Postsecondary; Chemistry Teachers, Postsecondary; Computer Science Teachers, Postsecondary; Engineering Teachers, Postsecondary; Forestry and Conservation Science Teachers, Postsecondary; Health Specialties Teachers, Postsecondary; Mathematical Science Teachers, Postsecondary; and Physics Teachers, Postsecondary.

Best Jobs for Baby Boomers with an Artistic Personality Type

Job	Annual Earnings	Percent Growth	Annual Openings
1. Teachers, Postsecondary	$54,406	38.1%	216,000
2. Architects, Except Landscape and Naval	$61,430	17.3%	8,000
3. Technical Writers	$54,390	27.1%	6,000
4. Caption Writers	$45,460	16.1%	23,000
5. Copy Writers	$45,460	16.1%	23,000
6. Creative Writers	$45,460	16.1%	23,000
7. Poets and Lyricists	$45,460	16.1%	23,000
8. Art Directors	$63,750	11.4%	8,000
9. Landscape Architects	$54,290	22.2%	2,000
10. Librarians	$46,940	10.1%	15,000
11. Cartoonists	$41,240	16.5%	4,000
12. Painters and Illustrators	$41,240	16.5%	4,000
13. Sculptors	$41,240	16.5%	4,000
14. Sketch Artists	$41,240	16.5%	4,000
15. Curators	$43,920	17.0%	2,000
16. Composers	$34,800	13.5%	8,000
17. Music Arrangers and Orchestrators	$34,800	13.5%	8,000
18. Music Directors	$34,800	13.5%	8,000

Jobs 4, 5, 6, and 7 share 23,000 openings. Jobs 11, 12, 13, and 14 share 4,000 openings. Jobs 16, 17, and 18 share 8,000 openings.

Teachers, Postsecondary, is listed here because the following jobs are associated with the Artistic personality type: Art, Drama, and Music Teachers, Postsecondary; English Language and Literature Teachers, Postsecondary; and Foreign Language and Literature Teachers, Postsecondary.

Best Jobs for Baby Boomers with a Social Personality Type

Job	Annual Earnings	Percent Growth	Annual Openings
1. Teachers, Postsecondary	$54,406	38.1%	216,000
2. Registered Nurses	$53,640	27.3%	215,000
3. Personal Financial Advisors	$62,450	34.6%	18,000
4. Special Education Teachers, Secondary School	$46,300	30.0%	59,000
5. Special Education Teachers, Middle School	$45,000	30.0%	59,000
6. Special Education Teachers, Preschool, Kindergarten, and Elementary School	$44,330	30.0%	59,000
7. Security Guards	$20,520	31.9%	228,000
8. Social and Human Service Assistants	$24,730	48.7%	63,000
9. Training and Development Specialists	$45,370	27.9%	35,000
10. Personal and Home Care Aides	$17,020	40.5%	154,000
11. Education Administrators, Elementary and Secondary School	$74,610	20.7%	31,000
12. Social and Community Service Managers	$48,330	27.7%	19,000
13. Self-Enrichment Education Teachers	$31,530	40.1%	39,000
14. Counseling Psychologists	$56,360	24.4%	17,000
15. Secondary School Teachers, Except Special and Vocational Education	$46,120	18.2%	118,000
16. Instructional Coordinators	$50,060	25.4%	18,000
17. Employment Interviewers, Private or Public Employment Service	$41,190	27.3%	29,000
18. Audiologists	$53,040	29.0%	1,000
19. Elementary School Teachers, Except Special Education	$43,660	15.2%	183,000
20. Speech-Language Pathologists	$53,790	27.2%	10,000
21. Medical and Public Health Social Workers	$40,780	28.6%	18,000
22. Mental Health and Substance Abuse Social Workers	$34,310	34.5%	17,000
23. Teacher Assistants	$19,760	23.0%	259,000
24. Child, Family, and School Social Workers	$35,010	23.2%	45,000
25. Educational, Vocational, and School Counselors	$46,160	15.0%	32,000
26. Licensed Practical and Licensed Vocational Nurses	$34,650	20.2%	105,000
27. Middle School Teachers, Except Special and Vocational Education	$44,180	9.0%	69,000
28. Equal Opportunity Representatives and Officers	$48,530	9.8%	20,000
29. Education Administrators, Preschool and Child Care Center/Program	$36,080	32.0%	9,000
30. Podiatrists	$97,290	15.0%	1,000
31. Clergy	$37,870	15.5%	34,000

Best Jobs for Baby Boomers with a Social Personality Type

Job	Annual Earnings	Percent Growth	Annual Openings
32. Mental Health Counselors	$33,400	26.7%	13,000
33. Adult Literacy, Remedial Education, and GED Teachers and Instructors	$39,730	20.4%	14,000
34. Vocational Education Teachers, Secondary School	$46,650	9.0%	12,000
35. Directors, Religious Activities and Education	$30,720	24.1%	16,000
36. Health Educators	$39,670	21.9%	8,000
37. Probation Officers and Correctional Treatment Specialists	$39,760	14.7%	15,000
38. Substance Abuse and Behavioral Disorder Counselors	$32,630	23.3%	10,000
39. Crossing Guards	$19,710	16.5%	19,000

Jobs 4, 5, and 6 share 59,000 openings. Job 14 shares 17,000 openings with two other jobs not on this list. Job 17 shares 29,000 openings with another job not on this list. Job 28 shares 20,000 openings with five other jobs not on this list.

Teachers, Postsecondary, is listed here because the following jobs are associated with the Social personality type: Anthropology and Archeology Teachers, Postsecondary; Area, Ethnic, and Cultural Studies Teachers, Postsecondary; Economics Teachers, Postsecondary; History Teachers, Postsecondary; Nursing Instructors and Teachers, Postsecondary; Political Science Teachers, Postsecondary; Psychology Teachers, Postsecondary; and Sociology Teachers, Postsecondary.

Best Jobs for Baby Boomers with an Enterprising Personality Type

Job	Annual Earnings	Percent Growth	Annual Openings
1. First-Line Supervisors/Managers of Retail Sales Workers	$32,410	9.1%	251,000
2. Sales Representatives, Wholesale and Manufacturing, Except Technical and Scientific Products	$46,090	19.1%	160,000
3. First-Line Supervisors, Administrative Support	$41,850	6.6%	140,000
4. First-Line Supervisors, Customer Service	$41,850	6.6%	140,000
5. Management Analysts	$64,560	30.4%	78,000
6. First-Line Supervisors/Managers of Non-Retail Sales Workers	$60,300	6.8%	72,000
7. Financial Managers, Branch or Department	$83,780	18.3%	71,000
8. Treasurers, Controllers, and Chief Financial Officers	$83,780	18.3%	71,000
9. First-Line Supervisors and Manager/Supervisors— Construction Trades Workers	$50,980	14.1%	67,000
10. First-Line Supervisors and Manager/Supervisors— Extractive Workers	$50,980	14.1%	67,000
11. First-Line Supervisors/Managers of Production and Operating Workers	$45,230	9.5%	66,000

(continued)

(continued)

Best Jobs for Baby Boomers with an Enterprising Personality Type

Job	Annual Earnings	Percent Growth	Annual Openings
12. Government Service Executives	$141,820	16.7%	63,000
13. Private Sector Executives	$141,820	16.7%	63,000
14. Lawyers	$97,420	17.0%	53,000
15. Insurance Sales Agents	$42,030	8.4%	52,000
16. Construction Managers	$70,770	12.0%	47,000
17. Sales Representatives, Agricultural	$59,390	19.3%	44,000
18. Sales Representatives, Chemical and Pharmaceutical	$59,390	19.3%	44,000
19. Sales Representatives, Electrical/Electronic	$59,390	19.3%	44,000
20. Sales Representatives, Instruments	$59,390	19.3%	44,000
21. Sales Representatives, Mechanical Equipment and Supplies	$59,390	19.3%	44,000
22. Sales Representatives, Medical	$59,390	19.3%	44,000
23. First-Line Supervisors/Managers of Mechanics, Installers, and Repairers	$51,000	15.4%	42,000
24. Administrative Services Managers	$62,300	19.8%	40,000
25. Demonstrators and Product Promoters	$20,490	17.0%	38,000
26. Property, Real Estate, and Community Association Managers	$41,540	12.8%	35,000
27. Real Estate Sales Agents	$36,950	5.7%	34,000
28. Medical and Health Services Managers	$68,320	29.3%	33,000
29. Personnel Recruiters	$41,190	27.3%	29,000
30. Purchasing Agents, Except Wholesale, Retail, and Farm Products	$48,360	11.2%	29,000
31. Housekeeping Supervisors	$30,050	16.2%	28,000
32. Janitorial Supervisors	$30,050	16.2%	28,000
33. Agricultural Crop Farm Managers	$50,720	5.1%	25,000
34. Fish Hatchery Managers	$50,720	5.1%	25,000
35. Nursery and Greenhouse Managers	$50,720	5.1%	25,000
36. Wholesale and Retail Buyers, Except Farm Products	$42,190	4.3%	24,000
37. Compensation and Benefits Managers	$67,040	19.4%	21,000
38. Training and Development Managers	$70,430	19.4%	21,000
39. Government Property Inspectors and Investigators	$48,530	9.8%	20,000
40. Industrial Production Managers	$74,100	7.9%	18,000
41. Engineering Managers	$99,000	9.2%	16,000
42. Industrial Engineers	$66,080	10.6%	16,000
43. First-Line Supervisors/Managers of Police and Detectives	$65,020	15.3%	14,000

Best Jobs for Baby Boomers with an Enterprising Personality Type

Job	Annual Earnings	Percent Growth	Annual Openings
44. Storage and Distribution Managers	$67,300	19.7%	13,000
45. Transportation Managers	$67,300	19.7%	13,000
46. Appraisers, Real Estate	$43,790	17.6%	11,000
47. Lodging Managers	$39,100	6.6%	10,000
48. Private Detectives and Investigators	$32,510	25.3%	9,000
49. Purchasing Managers	$74,300	4.8%	9,000
50. First-Line Supervisors and Manager/Supervisors—Agricultural Crop Workers	$36,040	11.4%	6,000
51. First-Line Supervisors and Manager/Supervisors—Animal Husbandry Workers	$36,040	11.4%	6,000
52. Gaming Supervisors	$41,080	15.7%	6,000
53. Public Transportation Inspectors	$47,920	7.7%	5,000
54. Judges, Magistrate Judges, and Magistrates	$97,260	8.7%	2,000
55. Arbitrators, Mediators, and Conciliators	$53,690	13.7%	fewer than 500

Jobs 3 and 4 share 140,000 openings. Jobs 7 and 8 share 71,000 openings. Jobs 9 and 10 share 67,000 openings. Jobs 12 and 13 share 63,000 openings with each other and with another job not on this list. Jobs 17, 18, 19, 20, and 21 share 44,000 openings with each other and with another job not on this list. Job 29 shares 29,000 openings with another job not on this list. Jobs 31 and 32 share 28,000 openings. Jobs 33, 34, and 35 share 25,000 openings. Jobs 37 and 38 share 21,000 openings. Job 39 shares 20,000 openings with five other jobs not on this list. Jobs 44 and 45 share 13,000 openings. Job 46 shares 11,000 openings with another job not on this list. Jobs 50 and 51 share 6,000 openings with each other and with four other jobs not on this list. Job 53 shares 5,000 openings with five other jobs not on this list.

Best Jobs for Baby Boomers with a Conventional Personality Type

Job	Annual Earnings	Percent Growth	Annual Openings
1. Bookkeeping, Accounting, and Auditing Clerks	$29,040	3.0%	274,000
2. Executive Secretaries and Administrative Assistants	$35,550	8.7%	210,000
3. Medical Secretaries	$27,030	17.2%	50,000
4. Legal Secretaries	$37,390	18.8%	39,000
5. Library Assistants, Clerical	$21,050	21.5%	27,000
6. Cost Estimators	$50,920	18.6%	25,000
7. Licensing Examiners and Inspectors	$48,530	9.8%	20,000
8. Postal Service Mail Carriers	$45,880	–0.5%	20,000
9. Court Clerks	$28,980	12.3%	14,000
10. License Clerks	$28,980	12.3%	14,000
11. Municipal Clerks	$28,980	12.3%	14,000

(continued)

(continued)

Best Jobs for Baby Boomers with a Conventional Personality Type

Job	Annual Earnings	Percent Growth	Annual Openings
12. Assessors	$43,790	17.6%	11,000
13. Tax Preparers	$26,130	23.2%	11,000
14. Construction and Building Inspectors	$43,940	13.8%	10,000
15. Budget Analysts	$57,190	14.0%	8,000
16. Freight Inspectors	$47,920	7.7%	5,000
17. Marine Cargo Inspectors	$47,920	7.7%	5,000
18. Air Traffic Controllers	$102,390	12.6%	2,000

Job 7 shares 20,000 openings with five other jobs not on this list. Jobs 9, 10, and 11 share 14,000 openings. Job 12 shares 11,000 openings with another job not on this list. Jobs 16 and 17 share 5,000 openings with four other jobs not on this list.

Best Jobs Based on Some Age-Sensitive Abilities

If your physical and sensory abilities are as good as when you were 21 (or better!), you can skip the following lists. But as you are growing older, some of your physical or sensory abilities may be diminishing, even though on the whole you are still fit for many years of fulfilling and productive work. You may notice that you like to have the television turned up louder than anyone else in the household. Perhaps it takes you a while to remember the name of the actor who played Han Solo. Or maybe your back "goes out" on occasion. Minor problems such as these should not keep you out of the workforce, but you may want to choose a job where they are less likely to hamper your performance. That's why we put together the following set of lists based on five abilities that diminish in some people as they advance in years.

It is true that the Americans with Disabilities Act ensures that you cannot be discriminated against for hiring, compensation, or promotion on the basis of physical or sensory disability as long as you are able to perform the essential functions of a job, perhaps with the help of certain reasonable accommodations. On the other hand, employers are not expected to provide personal-use items such as glasses or hearing aids, and some disabilities are not easily accommodated on the job and interfere with essential work functions. For example, an air traffic controller who cannot react quickly to what appears on the control screen and a janitor who cannot lift a drum of floor wax will be unlikely to win an employment discrimination lawsuit if they lose their jobs. More important, if your abilities are poorly suited to a job, you probably would not be very satisfied by the work.

That's why the following set of lists may be useful to you if you have some (but not a severe) loss of one or more of these abilities:

- Physical Strength
- Hearing Sensitivity
- Memorization Ability
- Fast Reaction Time
- Night Vision

Each of these lists focuses on one of these physical or sensory abilities and contains a subset of the 225 best jobs that require a comparatively low level of the ability. (The level we use is what statisticians call the "first quartile," meaning that three-quarters of all the jobs in the O*NET database require more.)

Note that within each list the jobs are not ordered by the amount to which they require this particular ability. Instead they are ordered by their combined scores based on earnings, growth, and number of openings. The assumption is that because these jobs require only a low level of the ability, you meet the threshold requirement for the ability and can focus on the comparative rewards of these jobs rather than on this physical or sensory requirement. (Six of the 225 best jobs do not appear on any of the following lists because ratings on physical abilities are not available for these jobs.)

In addition, when you look up any job in Part III, you may want to make note of other factors that may be listed under "Work Environment" so that you will be aware if the job requires (for example) a lot of standing, crouching, climbing, or exposure to loud noises. At this stage of your life, you may have less tolerance than you used to for certain working conditions.

Best Jobs for Baby Boomers That Require Only a Small Amount of Physical Strength

The first list in this set features jobs that require only a small amount of physical strength. We ranked jobs on the basis of their combined ratings in the O*NET database on two abilities: *dynamic strength,* which is defined as "the ability to exert muscle force repeatedly or continuously over time—this involves muscular endurance and resistance to muscle fatigue"; and *explosive strength,* which is defined as "the ability to use short bursts of muscle force to propel oneself (as in jumping or sprinting) or to throw an object."

The good news about physical strength is that it is related to usage; as long as you continue to use it, it will not diminish with age as rapidly as it would if you were less active. Nevertheless, many of us baby boomers have lived sedentary lifestyles and might not adjust well now to a job as, say, a truck driver. So another piece of good news is that as the American economy has moved increasingly toward service jobs, there are more good jobs than ever that do not require a lot of physical effort. The jobs on the following list require only a small amount of physical strength. They are ordered by their combined scores for earnings, job growth, and openings.

Best Jobs for Baby Boomers
That Require Only a Small Amount of Physical Strength

Job	Annual Earnings	Percent Growth	Annual Openings
1. Pharmacists	$87,160	30.1%	23,000
2. Teachers, Postsecondary	$54,406	38.1%	216,000
3. Medical and Health Services Managers	$68,320	29.3%	33,000
4. General and Operations Managers	$79,300	18.4%	260,000
5. Government Service Executives	$141,820	16.7%	63,000
6. Lawyers	$97,420	17.0%	53,000
7. Personal Financial Advisors	$62,450	34.6%	18,000
8. Administrative Services Managers	$62,300	19.8%	40,000
9. Sales Representatives, Chemical and Pharmaceutical	$59,390	19.3%	44,000
10. Sales Representatives, Electrical/Electronic	$59,390	19.3%	44,000
11. Sales Representatives, Instruments	$59,390	19.3%	44,000
12. Sales Representatives, Mechanical Equipment and Supplies	$59,390	19.3%	44,000
13. Sales Representatives, Medical	$59,390	19.3%	44,000
14. Training and Development Managers	$70,430	19.4%	21,000
15. Compensation and Benefits Managers	$67,040	19.4%	21,000
16. Training and Development Specialists	$45,370	27.9%	35,000
17. Construction Managers	$70,770	12.0%	47,000
18. Public Relations Managers	$73,960	23.4%	10,000
19. Counseling Psychologists	$56,360	24.4%	17,000
20. School Psychologists	$56,360	24.4%	17,000
21. Transportation Managers	$67,300	19.7%	13,000
22. Self-Enrichment Education Teachers	$31,530	40.1%	39,000
23. Social and Community Service Managers	$48,330	27.7%	19,000
24. Instructional Coordinators	$50,060	25.4%	18,000
25. Compensation, Benefits, and Job Analysis Specialists	$48,720	28.0%	15,000
26. Employment Interviewers, Private or Public Employment Service	$41,190	27.3%	29,000
27. Personnel Recruiters	$41,190	27.3%	29,000
28. Child, Family, and School Social Workers	$35,010	23.2%	45,000
29. Teacher Assistants	$19,760	23.0%	259,000
30. First-Line Supervisors/Managers of Non-Retail Sales Workers	$60,300	6.8%	72,000
31. Speech-Language Pathologists	$53,790	27.2%	10,000
32. Cost Estimators	$50,920	18.6%	25,000
33. Engineering Managers	$99,000	9.2%	16,000

Best Jobs for Baby Boomers
That Require Only a Small Amount of Physical Strength

Job	Annual Earnings	Percent Growth	Annual Openings
34. Technical Writers	$54,390	27.1%	6,000
35. Legal Secretaries	$37,390	18.8%	39,000
36. Optometrists	$88,290	17.1%	2,000
37. Architects, Except Landscape and Naval	$61,430	17.3%	8,000
38. Industrial Engineers	$66,080	10.6%	16,000
39. Audiologists	$53,040	29.0%	1,000
40. Electronics Engineers, Except Computer	$76,810	9.4%	11,000
41. Educational, Vocational, and School Counselors	$46,160	15.0%	32,000
42. Copy Writers	$45,460	16.1%	23,000
43. Geographers	$61,520	19.5%	fewer than 500
44. Medical Secretaries	$27,030	17.2%	50,000
45. Adult Literacy, Remedial Education, and GED Teachers and Instructors	$39,730	20.4%	14,000
46. Directors, Religious Activities and Education	$30,720	24.1%	16,000
47. Medical and Clinical Laboratory Technicians	$31,440	19.4%	21,000
48. Mental Health Counselors	$33,400	26.7%	13,000
49. Landscape Architects	$54,290	22.2%	2,000
50. Insurance Sales Agents	$42,030	8.4%	52,000
51. Property, Real Estate, and Community Association Managers	$41,540	12.8%	35,000
52. Industrial-Organizational Psychologists	$74,060	16.0%	fewer than 500
53. Clergy	$37,870	15.5%	34,000
54. Purchasing Agents, Except Wholesale, Retail, and Farm Products	$48,360	11.2%	29,000
55. Economists	$72,370	13.4%	2,000
56. Art Directors	$63,750	11.4%	8,000
57. Executive Secretaries and Administrative Assistants	$35,550	8.7%	210,000
58. Budget Analysts	$57,190	14.0%	8,000
59. Electrical Engineers	$72,770	2.5%	11,000
60. Orthodontists	more than $145,600	4.1%	7,000
61. Prosthodontists	more than $145,600	4.1%	7,000
62. Multi-Media Artists and Animators	$49,900	15.8%	12,000
63. Health Educators	$39,670	21.9%	8,000
64. Appraisers, Real Estate	$43,790	17.6%	11,000
65. Pressure Vessel Inspectors	$48,530	9.8%	20,000

(continued)

(continued)

Best Jobs for Baby Boomers
That Require Only a Small Amount of Physical Strength

Job	Annual Earnings	Percent Growth	Annual Openings
66. Geologists	$70,180	11.5%	2,000
67. Tax Preparers	$26,130	23.2%	11,000
68. Dietitians and Nutritionists	$44,370	17.8%	8,000
69. Physicists	$87,480	6.9%	1,000
70. Bookkeeping, Accounting, and Auditing Clerks	$29,040	3.0%	274,000
71. Librarians	$46,940	10.1%	15,000
72. Industrial Safety and Health Engineers	$64,320	7.9%	4,000
73. Real Estate Brokers	$56,970	2.4%	11,000
74. Real Estate Sales Agents	$36,950	5.7%	34,000
75. Sociologists	$56,790	13.4%	fewer than 500
76. Operations Research Analysts	$60,230	6.2%	6,000
77. Arbitrators, Mediators, and Conciliators	$53,690	13.7%	fewer than 500
78. Cartoonists	$41,240	16.5%	4,000
79. Sketch Artists	$41,240	16.5%	4,000
80. Court Clerks	$28,980	12.3%	14,000
81. Municipal Clerks	$28,980	12.3%	14,000
82. Composers	$34,800	13.5%	8,000
83. Music Arrangers and Orchestrators	$34,800	13.5%	8,000
84. Public Transportation Inspectors	$47,920	7.7%	5,000
85. Lodging Managers	$39,100	6.6%	10,000

Job 5 shares 63,000 openings with two other jobs not on this list. Jobs 9, 10, 11, 12, and 13 share 44,000 openings with each other and with another job not on this list. Jobs 14 and 15 share 21,000 openings. Jobs 19 and 20 share 17,000 openings with each other and with another job not on this list. Job 21 shares 13,000 openings with another job not on this list. Jobs 26 and 27 share 29,000 openings. Job 42 shares 23,000 openings with three other jobs not on this list. Jobs 60 and 61 share 7,000 openings with each other and with two other jobs not on this list. Job 64 shares 11,000 openings with another job not on this list. Job 65 shares 20,000 openings with five other jobs not on this list. Job 72 shares 4,000 openings with two other jobs not on this list. Jobs 78 and 79 share 4,000 openings with each other and with two other jobs not on this list. Jobs 80 and 81 share 14,000 openings with each other and with another job not on this list. Jobs 82 and 83 share 8,000 openings with each other and with another job not on this list. Job 84 shares 5,000 openings with five other jobs not on this list.

Best Jobs for Baby Boomers That Require Only a Small Amount of Hearing Sensitivity

According to the National Institutes of Health, about one in five people has some loss of hearing due to nerve damage by age 55. In some cases this is brought on simply by age, but in other cases it is aggravated by long exposure to environmental noise, such as a noisy workplace or too much high-volume music (a preference that we baby boomers invented).

The jobs on the following list require only a small amount of hearing sensitivity. They are ordered by their combined scores for income, growth, and job openings.

Best Jobs for Baby Boomers That Require Only a Small Amount of Hearing Sensitivity

Job	Annual Earnings	Percent Growth	Annual Openings
1. Management Analysts	$64,560	30.4%	78,000
2. Psychiatrists	more than $145,600	19.5%	38,000
3. Pharmacists	$87,160	30.1%	23,000
4. Education Administrators, Elementary and Secondary School	$74,610	20.7%	31,000
5. Personal Financial Advisors	$62,450	34.6%	18,000
6. Sales Representatives, Agricultural	$59,390	19.3%	44,000
7. Sales Representatives, Instruments	$59,390	19.3%	44,000
8. Sales Representatives, Mechanical Equipment and Supplies	$59,390	19.3%	44,000
9. Sales Representatives, Medical	$59,390	19.3%	44,000
10. Construction Managers	$70,770	12.0%	47,000
11. Employment Interviewers, Private or Public Employment Service	$41,190	27.3%	29,000
12. Self-Enrichment Education Teachers	$31,530	40.1%	39,000
13. Child, Family, and School Social Workers	$35,010	23.2%	45,000
14. First-Line Supervisors/Managers of Non-Retail Sales Workers	$60,300	6.8%	72,000
15. Architects, Except Landscape and Naval	$61,430	17.3%	8,000
16. Technical Writers	$54,390	27.1%	6,000
17. Legal Secretaries	$37,390	18.8%	39,000
18. Educational, Vocational, and School Counselors	$46,160	15.0%	32,000
19. Industrial Engineers	$66,080	10.6%	16,000
20. Copy Writers	$45,460	16.1%	23,000
21. Creative Writers	$45,460	16.1%	23,000
22. Hydrologists	$60,880	21.0%	1,000
23. Directors, Religious Activities and Education	$30,720	24.1%	16,000
24. Purchasing Agents, Except Wholesale, Retail, and Farm Products	$48,360	11.2%	29,000
25. Appraisers, Real Estate	$43,790	17.6%	11,000
26. Mental Health Counselors	$33,400	26.7%	13,000
27. Clergy	$37,870	15.5%	34,000

(continued)

(continued)

Best Jobs for Baby Boomers
That Require Only a Small Amount of Hearing Sensitivity

Job	Annual Earnings	Percent Growth	Annual Openings
28. Executive Secretaries and Administrative Assistants	$35,550	8.7%	210,000
29. Industrial-Organizational Psychologists	$74,060	16.0%	fewer than 500
30. Health Educators	$39,670	21.9%	8,000
31. Oral and Maxillofacial Surgeons	more than $145,600	4.1%	7,000
32. Orthodontists	more than $145,600	4.1%	7,000
33. Prosthodontists	more than $145,600	4.1%	7,000
34. Substance Abuse and Behavioral Disorder Counselors	$32,630	23.3%	10,000
35. Precision Dyers	$17,350	12.3%	47,000
36. Nursery and Greenhouse Managers	$50,720	5.1%	25,000
37. Geologists	$70,180	11.5%	2,000
38. Fire-Prevention and Protection Engineers	$64,320	7.9%	4,000
39. Product Safety Engineers	$64,320	7.9%	4,000
40. Probation Officers and Correctional Treatment Specialists	$39,760	14.7%	15,000
41. Cartoonists	$41,240	16.5%	4,000
42. Painters and Illustrators	$41,240	16.5%	4,000
43. Sculptors	$41,240	16.5%	4,000
44. Wholesale and Retail Buyers, Except Farm Products	$42,190	4.3%	24,000
45. Bookkeeping, Accounting, and Auditing Clerks	$29,040	3.0%	274,000
46. Operations Research Analysts	$60,230	6.2%	6,000
47. Gaming Supervisors	$41,080	15.7%	6,000
48. Real Estate Brokers	$56,970	2.4%	11,000
49. Sociologists	$56,790	13.4%	fewer than 500
50. Court Clerks	$28,980	12.3%	14,000
51. Municipal Clerks	$28,980	12.3%	14,000
52. Marine Cargo Inspectors	$47,920	7.7%	5,000
53. Lodging Managers	$39,100	6.6%	10,000

Job 2 shares 38,000 openings with six other jobs not on this list. Jobs 6, 7, 8, and 9 share 44,000 openings with each other and with two other jobs not on this list. Job 11 shares 29,000 openings with another job not on this list. Jobs 20 and 21 share 23,000 openings with each other and with two other jobs not on this list. Job 25 shares 11,000 openings with another job not on this list. Jobs 31, 32, 33 share 7,000 openings with each other and with another job not on this list. Job 35 shares 47,000 openings with two other jobs not on this list. Job 36 shares 25,000 openings with two other jobs not on this list. Jobs 38 and 39 share 4,000 openings with each other and with another job not on this list. Jobs 41, 42, and 43 share 4,000 openings with each other and with another job not on this list. Jobs 50 and 51 share 14,000 openings with each other and with another job not on this list. Job 52 shares 5,000 openings with five other jobs not on this list.

Best Jobs for Baby Boomers That Require Only a Small Amount of Memorization Ability

The relationship between aging and memory loss is complex and not well understood, but many baby boomers have encountered "senior moments." Sometimes we find that we can remember all of the lyrics to "My Girl" or "Dancing Queen" but have a tough time remembering the number of our new cell phone and how to use all of its functions. Fortunately, many good jobs for baby boomers require only a small ability to memorize, and they are listed here, ordered by their combined scores for income, growth, and job openings.

Best Jobs for Baby Boomers That Require Only a Small Amount of Memorization Ability

Job	Annual Earnings	Percent Growth	Annual Openings
1. First-Line Supervisors/Managers of Non-Retail Sales Workers	$60,300	6.8%	72,000
2. Refractory Materials Repairers, Except Brickmasons	$39,610	16.3%	155,000
3. Technical Writers	$54,390	27.1%	6,000
4. Personal and Home Care Aides	$17,020	40.5%	154,000
5. Copy Writers	$45,460	16.1%	23,000
6. Clergy	$37,870	15.5%	34,000
7. Housekeeping Supervisors	$30,050	16.2%	28,000
8. Central Office and PBX Installers and Repairers	$50,270	–0.6%	23,000
9. Communication Equipment Mechanics, Installers, and Repairers	$50,270	–0.6%	23,000
10. Frame Wirers, Central Office	$50,270	–0.6%	23,000
11. Station Installers and Repairers, Telephone	$50,270	–0.6%	23,000
12. Telecommunications Facility Examiners	$50,270	–0.6%	23,000
13. Precision Dyers	$17,350	12.3%	47,000
14. Pressure Vessel Inspectors	$48,530	9.8%	20,000
15. Spotters, Dry Cleaning	$17,350	12.3%	47,000
16. Orthodontists	more than $145,600	4.1%	7,000
17. Prosthodontists	more than $145,600	4.1%	7,000
18. Maids and Housekeeping Cleaners	$17,000	9.2%	352,000
19. Operations Research Analysts	$60,230	6.2%	6,000
20. Tax Preparers	$26,130	23.2%	11,000
21. Sculptors	$41,240	16.5%	4,000
22. Sketch Artists	$41,240	16.5%	4,000
23. License Clerks	$28,980	12.3%	14,000

(continued)

(continued)

Best Jobs for Baby Boomers That Require Only a Small Amount of Memorization Ability			
Job	Annual Earnings	Percent Growth	Annual Openings
24. Motor Vehicle Inspectors	$47,920	7.7%	5,000
25. Public Transportation Inspectors	$47,920	7.7%	5,000
26. Railroad Inspectors	$47,920	7.7%	5,000
27. Postal Service Mail Carriers	$45,880	–0.5%	20,000

Job 5 shares 23,000 openings with three other jobs not on this list. Job 7 shares 28,000 openings with another job not on this list. Jobs 8, 9, 10, 11, and 12 share 23,000 openings. Jobs 13 and 15 share 47,000 openings with each other and with another job not on this list. Job 14 shares 20,000 openings with five other jobs not on this list. Jobs 16 and 17 share 7,000 openings with each other and with two other jobs not on this list. Jobs 21 and 22 share 4,000 openings with each other and with two other jobs not on this list. Job 23 shares 14,000 openings with two other jobs not on this list. Jobs 24, 25, and 26 share 5,000 openings with each other and with three other jobs not on this list.

Best Jobs for Baby Boomers That Require Only a Low Speed of Reaction

Research has shown that people's reaction time improves from infancy until the late 20s and then begins to decline slowly, although the rate of decline varies widely. Sometimes a baby boomer's work experience can compensate for slower reaction time. For example, an experienced bus driver may anticipate a hazard on the highway and not have to react to it suddenly. Nevertheless, at this stage of your life you may want a job in which lives and property do not depend on the speed of your reflexes. All of the jobs on the following list require only a low speed of reaction. They are ordered by their combined scores for income, growth, and job openings.

Best Jobs for Baby Boomers That Require Only a Low Speed of Reaction			
Job	Annual Earnings	Percent Growth	Annual Openings
1. Teachers, Postsecondary	$54,406	38.1%	216,000
2. Pharmacists	$87,160	30.1%	23,000
3. General and Operations Managers	$79,300	18.4%	260,000
4. Medical and Health Services Managers	$68,320	29.3%	33,000
5. Lawyers	$97,420	17.0%	53,000
6. Administrative Services Managers	$62,300	19.8%	40,000
7. Special Education Teachers, Preschool, Kindergarten, and Elementary School	$44,330	30.0%	59,000
8. Sales Representatives, Chemical and Pharmaceutical	$59,390	19.3%	44,000

Best Jobs for Baby Boomers
That Require Only a Low Speed of Reaction

Job	Annual Earnings	Percent Growth	Annual Openings
9. Sales Representatives, Electrical/Electronic	$59,390	19.3%	44,000
10. Sales Representatives, Instruments	$59,390	19.3%	44,000
11. Sales Representatives, Mechanical Equipment and Supplies	$59,390	19.3%	44,000
12. Training and Development Managers	$70,430	19.4%	21,000
13. Training and Development Specialists	$45,370	27.9%	35,000
14. Compensation and Benefits Managers	$67,040	19.4%	21,000
15. Public Relations Managers	$73,960	23.4%	10,000
16. Counseling Psychologists	$56,360	24.4%	17,000
17. School Psychologists	$56,360	24.4%	17,000
18. Social and Human Service Assistants	$24,730	48.7%	63,000
19. Secondary School Teachers, Except Special and Vocational Education	$46,120	18.2%	118,000
20. Social and Community Service Managers	$48,330	27.7%	19,000
21. Compensation, Benefits, and Job Analysis Specialists	$48,720	28.0%	15,000
22. Transportation Managers	$67,300	19.7%	13,000
23. Instructional Coordinators	$50,060	25.4%	18,000
24. Self-Enrichment Education Teachers	$31,530	40.1%	39,000
25. Employment Interviewers, Private or Public Employment Service	$41,190	27.3%	29,000
26. Personnel Recruiters	$41,190	27.3%	29,000
27. Speech-Language Pathologists	$53,790	27.2%	10,000
28. Chiropractors	$67,940	23.3%	3,000
29. Child, Family, and School Social Workers	$35,010	23.2%	45,000
30. Elementary School Teachers, Except Special Education	$43,660	15.2%	183,000
31. Technical Writers	$54,390	27.1%	6,000
32. Geographers	$61,520	19.5%	fewer than 500
33. Architects, Except Landscape and Naval	$61,430	17.3%	8,000
34. Legal Secretaries	$37,390	18.8%	39,000
35. Middle School Teachers, Except Special and Vocational Education	$44,180	9.0%	69,000
36. Educational, Vocational, and School Counselors	$46,160	15.0%	32,000
37. Copy Writers	$45,460	16.1%	23,000
38. Education Administrators, Preschool and Child Care Center/Program	$36,080	32.0%	9,000
39. Industrial-Organizational Psychologists	$74,060	16.0%	fewer than 500

(continued)

(continued)

Best Jobs for Baby Boomers
That Require Only a Low Speed of Reaction

Job	Annual Earnings	Percent Growth	Annual Openings
40. Purchasing Agents, Except Wholesale, Retail, and Farm Products	$48,360	11.2%	29,000
41. Medical Secretaries	$27,030	17.2%	50,000
42. Adult Literacy, Remedial Education, and GED Teachers and Instructors	$39,730	20.4%	14,000
43. Directors, Religious Activities and Education	$30,720	24.1%	16,000
44. Insurance Sales Agents	$42,030	8.4%	52,000
45. Library Assistants, Clerical	$21,050	21.5%	27,000
46. Electrical Engineers	$72,770	2.5%	11,000
47. Art Directors	$63,750	11.4%	8,000
48. Property, Real Estate, and Community Association Managers	$41,540	12.8%	35,000
49. Executive Secretaries and Administrative Assistants	$35,550	8.7%	210,000
50. Multi-Media Artists and Animators	$49,900	15.8%	12,000
51. Budget Analysts	$57,190	14.0%	8,000
52. Assessors	$43,790	17.6%	11,000
53. Dietitians and Nutritionists	$44,370	17.8%	8,000
54. Bookkeeping, Accounting, and Auditing Clerks	$29,040	3.0%	274,000
55. Librarians	$46,940	10.1%	15,000
56. Real Estate Brokers	$56,970	2.4%	11,000
57. Operations Research Analysts	$60,230	6.2%	6,000
58. Sociologists	$56,790	13.4%	fewer than 500
59. Wholesale and Retail Buyers, Except Farm Products	$42,190	4.3%	24,000
60. Real Estate Sales Agents	$36,950	5.7%	34,000
61. Arbitrators, Mediators, and Conciliators	$53,690	13.7%	fewer than 500
62. Curators	$43,920	17.0%	2,000
63. Cartoonists	$41,240	16.5%	4,000
64. Painters and Illustrators	$41,240	16.5%	4,000
65. Sculptors	$41,240	16.5%	4,000
66. Court Clerks	$28,980	12.3%	14,000
67. Municipal Clerks	$28,980	12.3%	14,000
68. Music Arrangers and Orchestrators	$34,800	13.5%	8,000
69. Lodging Managers	$39,100	6.6%	10,000

Job 7 shares 59,000 openings with two other jobs not on this list. Jobs 8, 9, 10, and 11 share 44,000 openings with each other and with two other jobs not on this list. Jobs 12 and 14 share 21,000 openings. Jobs 16 and 17 share 17,000 openings with each other and with another job not on this list. Job 22 shares 13,000 openings with another job not on this list. Jobs 25 and 26 share 29,000 openings. Job 37 shares 23,000 openings with three other jobs not on this list. Job 52 shares 11,000 openings with another job not on this list. Jobs 63, 64, and 65 share 4,000 openings with each other and with another job not on this list. Jobs 66 and 67 share 14,000 openings with each other and with another job not on this list. Job 68 shares 8,000 openings with two other jobs not on this list.

Best Jobs for Baby Boomers That Require Only a Small Level of Night Vision

With age, the rate at which people's eyes adjust to the dark tends to slow down. Cataracts can also diminish night vision. Fortunately, only a few jobs require above-average night vision, and the jobs on the following list require only a small level of this ability. They are ordered by their combined scores for earnings, growth, and job openings.

Best Jobs for Baby Boomers That Require Only a Small Level of Night Vision			
Job	Annual Earnings	Percent Growth	Annual Openings
1. Pharmacists	$87,160	30.1%	23,000
2. Medical and Health Services Managers	$68,320	29.3%	33,000
3. Registered Nurses	$53,640	27.3%	215,000
4. Anesthesiologists	more than $145,600	19.5%	38,000
5. Psychiatrists	more than $145,600	19.5%	38,000
6. Education Administrators, Elementary and Secondary School	$74,610	20.7%	31,000
7. Lawyers	$97,420	17.0%	53,000
8. Special Education Teachers, Secondary School	$46,300	30.0%	59,000
9. Special Education Teachers, Middle School	$45,000	30.0%	59,000
10. Special Education Teachers, Preschool, Kindergarten, and Elementary School	$44,330	30.0%	59,000
11. Administrative Services Managers	$62,300	19.8%	40,000
12. Sales Representatives, Chemical and Pharmaceutical	$59,390	19.3%	44,000
13. Sales Representatives, Electrical/Electronic	$59,390	19.3%	44,000
14. Sales Representatives, Mechanical Equipment and Supplies	$59,390	19.3%	44,000
15. Compensation and Benefits Managers	$67,040	19.4%	21,000
16. Public Relations Managers	$73,960	23.4%	10,000
17. School Psychologists	$56,360	24.4%	17,000
18. Storage and Distribution Managers	$67,300	19.7%	13,000
19. Instructional Coordinators	$50,060	25.4%	18,000
20. Secondary School Teachers, Except Special and Vocational Education	$46,120	18.2%	118,000
21. Employment Interviewers, Private or Public Employment Service	$41,190	27.3%	29,000
22. Personnel Recruiters	$41,190	27.3%	29,000
23. Compensation, Benefits, and Job Analysis Specialists	$48,720	28.0%	15,000

(continued)

(continued)

Best Jobs for Baby Boomers
That Require Only a Small Level of Night Vision

Job	Annual Earnings	Percent Growth	Annual Openings
24. Veterinarians	$68,280	25.1%	4,000
25. First-Line Supervisors/Managers of Non-Retail Sales Workers	$60,300	6.8%	72,000
26. Medical and Public Health Social Workers	$40,780	28.6%	18,000
27. Speech-Language Pathologists	$53,790	27.2%	10,000
28. Cost Estimators	$50,920	18.6%	25,000
29. Elementary School Teachers, Except Special Education	$43,660	15.2%	183,000
30. Mental Health and Substance Abuse Social Workers	$34,310	34.5%	17,000
31. Chiropractors	$67,940	23.3%	3,000
32. Industrial Production Managers	$74,100	7.9%	18,000
33. Technical Writers	$54,390	27.1%	6,000
34. Industrial Engineers	$66,080	10.6%	16,000
35. Electronics Engineers, Except Computer	$76,810	9.4%	11,000
36. Educational, Vocational, and School Counselors	$46,160	15.0%	32,000
37. Audiologists	$53,040	29.0%	1,000
38. Civil Engineers	$65,280	8.0%	17,000
39. Middle School Teachers, Except Special and Vocational Education	$44,180	9.0%	69,000
40. Education Administrators, Preschool and Child Care Center/Program	$36,080	32.0%	9,000
41. Architects, Except Landscape and Naval	$61,430	17.3%	8,000
42. Copy Writers	$45,460	16.1%	23,000
43. Purchasing Agents, Except Wholesale, Retail, and Farm Products	$48,360	11.2%	29,000
44. Geographers	$61,520	19.5%	fewer than 500
45. Executive Secretaries and Administrative Assistants	$35,550	8.7%	210,000
46. Medical Secretaries	$27,030	17.2%	50,000
47. Mental Health Counselors	$33,400	26.7%	13,000
48. Adult Literacy, Remedial Education, and GED Teachers and Instructors	$39,730	20.4%	14,000
49. Directors, Religious Activities and Education	$30,720	24.1%	16,000
50. First-Line Supervisors/Managers of Retail Sales Workers	$32,410	9.1%	251,000
51. Landscape Architects	$54,290	22.2%	2,000
52. Insurance Sales Agents	$42,030	8.4%	52,000
53. Art Directors	$63,750	11.4%	8,000

Best Jobs for Baby Boomers
That Require Only a Small Level of Night Vision

Job	Annual Earnings	Percent Growth	Annual Openings
54. Multi-Media Artists and Animators	$49,900	15.8%	12,000
55. Budget Analysts	$57,190	14.0%	8,000
56. Electrical Engineers	$72,770	2.5%	11,000
57. Oral and Maxillofacial Surgeons	more than $145,600	4.1%	7,000
58. Judges, Magistrate Judges, and Magistrates	$97,260	8.7%	2,000
59. Precision Dyers	$17,350	12.3%	47,000
60. Substance Abuse and Behavioral Disorder Counselors	$32,630	23.3%	10,000
61. Frame Wirers, Central Office	$50,270	–0.6%	23,000
62. Bookkeeping, Accounting, and Auditing Clerks	$29,040	3.0%	274,000
63. Dietitians and Nutritionists	$44,370	17.8%	8,000
64. Tax Preparers	$26,130	23.2%	11,000
65. Industrial Safety and Health Engineers	$64,320	7.9%	4,000
66. Product Safety Engineers	$64,320	7.9%	4,000
67. Vocational Education Teachers, Secondary School	$46,650	9.0%	12,000
68. Wholesale and Retail Buyers, Except Farm Products	$42,190	4.3%	24,000
69. Sociologists	$56,790	13.4%	fewer than 500
70. Operations Research Analysts	$60,230	6.2%	6,000
71. Sculptors	$41,240	16.5%	4,000
72. Court Clerks	$28,980	12.3%	14,000
73. Municipal Clerks	$28,980	12.3%	14,000
74. Composers	$34,800	13.5%	8,000
75. Music Arrangers and Orchestrators	$34,800	13.5%	8,000
76. Lodging Managers	$39,100	6.6%	10,000

Jobs 4 and 5 share 38,000 openings with each other and with four other jobs not on this list. Jobs 8, 9, and 10 share 59,000 openings. Jobs 12, 13, and 14 share 44,000 openings with each other and with three other jobs not on this list. Job 15 shares 21,000 openings with another job not on this list. Job 17 shares 17,000 openings with two other jobs not on this list. Job 18 shares 13,000 openings with another job not on this list. Jobs 21 and 22 share 29,000 openings. Job 42 shares 23,000 openings with three other jobs not on this list. Job 57 shares 7,000 openings with three other jobs not on this list. Job 59 shares 47,000 openings with two other jobs not on this list. Job 61 shares 23,000 openings with four other jobs not on this list. Jobs 65 and 66 share 4,000 openings with each other and with another job not on this list. Job 71 shares 4,000 openings with three other jobs not on this list. Jobs 72 and 73 share 14,000 openings with each other and with another job not on this list. Jobs 74 and 75 share 8,000 openings with each other and with another job not on this list.

PART III

Descriptions of the Best Jobs for Baby Boomers

This part provides descriptions for all the jobs included in one or more of the lists in Part II. The Introduction gives more details on how to use and interpret the job descriptions, but here is some additional information:

- Job descriptions are arranged in alphabetical order by job title. This approach allows you to find a description quickly if you know its correct title from one of the lists in Part II.

- If you are using this section to browse for interesting options, we suggest you begin with the Table of Contents. Part II features many interesting lists that will help you identify job titles to explore in more detail. If you have not browsed the lists in Part II, consider spending some time there. The lists are interesting and will help you identify job titles you can find described in the material that follows. The job titles in Part III are also listed in the Table of Contents.

- We include descriptions for the many specific jobs that we included under the single job title of Postsecondary Teachers in the lists in Part II. These more-specific job titles are also cross-referenced under the Postsecondary Teachers job title in Part II and include Agricultural Sciences Teachers, Postsecondary; Anthropology and Archeology Teachers, Postsecondary; Architecture Teachers, Postsecondary; Area, Ethnic, and Cultural Studies Teachers, Postsecondary; Art, Drama, and Music Teachers, Postsecondary; Atmospheric, Earth, Marine, and Space Sciences Teachers, Postsecondary; Biological Science Teachers, Postsecondary; Business Teachers, Postsecondary; Chemistry Teachers, Postsecondary; Communications Teachers, Postsecondary; Computer Science Teachers, Postsecondary; Criminal Justice and Law Enforcement Teachers, Postsecondary; Economics Teachers, Postsecondary; Education Teachers, Postsecondary; Engineering Teachers, Postsecondary; English Language and Literature Teachers, Postsecondary; Environmental Science Teachers, Postsecondary; Foreign Language and Literature Teachers, Postsecondary; Forestry and Conservation Science Teachers, Postsecondary; Geography Teachers, Postsecondary; Graduate Teaching Assistants; Health Specialties Teachers, Postsecondary; History Teachers, Postsecondary; Home Economics Teachers, Postsecondary; Law Teachers, Postsecondary; Library Science Teachers, Postsecondary;

Mathematical Science Teachers, Postsecondary; Nursing Instructors and Teachers, Postsecondary; Philosophy and Religion Teachers, Postsecondary; Physics Teachers, Postsecondary; Political Science Teachers, Postsecondary; Psychology Teachers, Postsecondary; Recreation and Fitness Studies Teachers, Postsecondary; Social Work Teachers, Postsecondary; Sociology Teachers, Postsecondary; and Vocational Education Teachers, Postsecondary.

Administrative Services Managers

- ◎ Education/Training Required: Work experience plus degree
- ◎ Annual Earnings: $62,300
- ◎ Growth: 19.8%
- ◎ Annual Job Openings: 40,000
- ◎ Self-Employed: 0.2%
- ◎ Part-Time: 4.6%

Age Bracket	Percentage of Workers
45–54 Years Old	42.0%
55–64 Years Old	12.3%
65 or Older	4.9%

Plan, direct, or coordinate supportive services of an organization, such as recordkeeping, mail distribution, telephone operator/receptionist, and other office support services. May oversee facilities planning and maintenance and custodial operations. Monitor the facility to ensure that it remains safe, secure, and well-maintained. Direct or coordinate the supportive services department of a business, agency, or organization. Set goals and deadlines for the department. Prepare and review operational reports and schedules to ensure accuracy and efficiency. Analyze internal processes and recommend and implement procedural or policy changes to improve operations, such as supply changes or the disposal of records. Acquire, distribute, and store supplies. Plan, administer, and control budgets for contracts, equipment, and supplies. Oversee construction and renovation projects to improve efficiency and to ensure that facilities meet environmental, health, and security standards and comply with government regulations. Hire and terminate clerical and administrative personnel. Oversee the maintenance and repair of machinery, equipment, and electrical and mechanical systems. Manage leasing of facility space. **SKILLS**—Management of Personnel Resources; Service Orientation; Coordination; Management of Financial Resources; Monitoring; Social Perceptiveness; Speaking; Programming.

GOE—Interest Area: 04. Business and Administration. **Work Group:** 04.02. Managerial Work in Business Detail. **Other Jobs in This Work Group:** First-Line Supervisors, Administrative Support; First-Line Supervisors, Customer Service; Housekeeping Supervisors; Janitorial Supervisors; Meeting and Convention Planners. **PERSONALITY TYPE:** Enterprising. Enterprising occupations frequently involve starting up and carrying out projects. These occupations can involve leading people and making many decisions. They sometimes require risk taking and often deal with business.

EDUCATION/TRAINING PROGRAM(S)—Business Administration/Management; Business/Commerce, General; Medical Staff Services Technology/Technician; Medical/Health Management and Clinical Assistant/Specialist; Public Administration; Purchasing, Procurement/Acquisitions and Contracts Management; Transportation/Transportation Management.

WORK ENVIRONMENT—Contaminants; sitting; sounds, noise levels are distracting or uncomfortable; indoors; very hot or cold.

Adult Literacy, Remedial Education, and GED Teachers and Instructors

- Education/Training Required: Bachelor's degree
- Annual Earnings: $39,730
- Growth: 20.4%
- Annual Job Openings: 14,000
- Self-Employed: 19.5%
- Part-Time: 41.0%

Age Bracket	Percentage of Workers
45–54 Years Old	22.4%
55–64 Years Old	14.8%
65 or Older	5.1%

Teach or instruct out-of-school youths and adults in remedial education classes, preparatory classes for the General Educational Development test, literacy, or English as a Second Language. Teaching may or may not take place in a traditional educational institution. Adapt teaching methods and instructional materials to meet students' varying needs, abilities, and interests. Observe and evaluate students' work to determine progress and make suggestions for improvement. Plan and conduct activities for a balanced program of instruction, demonstration, and work time that provides students with opportunities to observe, question, and investigate. Instruct students individually and in groups, using various teaching methods such as lectures, discussions, and demonstrations. Maintain accurate and complete student records as required by laws or administrative policies. Prepare materials and classrooms for class activities. Establish clear objectives for all lessons, units, and projects and communicate those objectives to students. Conduct classes, workshops, and demonstrations to teach principles, techniques, or methods in subjects such as basic English language skills, life skills, and workforce entry skills. Prepare students for further education by encouraging them to explore learning opportunities and to persevere with challenging tasks. Establish and enforce rules for behavior and procedures for maintaining order among the students for whom they are responsible. Provide information, guidance, and preparation for the General Equivalency Diploma (GED) examination. Assign and grade class work and homework. Observe students to determine qualifications, limitations, abilities, interests, and other individual characteristics. Register, orient, and assess new students according to standards and procedures. Prepare and implement remedial programs for students requiring extra help. Prepare and administer written, oral, and performance tests and issue grades in accordance with performance. Use computers, audiovisual aids, and other equipment and materials to supplement presentations. Prepare objectives and outlines for courses of study, following curriculum guidelines or requirements of states and schools. Guide and counsel students with adjustment and/or academic problems or special academic interests. Enforce administration policies and rules governing students. **SKILLS**—Instructing; Social Perceptiveness; Learning Strategies; Service Orientation; Persuasion; Speaking; Monitoring; Active Listening.

GOE—Interest Area: 05. Education and Training. **Work Group:** 05.03. Postsecondary and Adult Teaching and Instructing. **Other Jobs in This Work Group:** Agricultural Sciences Teachers, Postsecondary; Anthropology and

Archeology Teachers, Postsecondary; Architecture Teachers, Postsecondary; Area, Ethnic, and Cultural Studies Teachers, Postsecondary; Art, Drama, and Music Teachers, Postsecondary; Atmospheric, Earth, Marine, and Space Sciences Teachers, Postsecondary; Biological Science Teachers, Postsecondary; Business Teachers, Postsecondary; Chemistry Teachers, Postsecondary; Communications Teachers, Postsecondary; Computer Science Teachers, Postsecondary; Criminal Justice and Law Enforcement Teachers, Postsecondary; Economics Teachers, Postsecondary; Education Teachers, Postsecondary; Engineering Teachers, Postsecondary; English Language and Literature Teachers, Postsecondary; Environmental Science Teachers, Postsecondary; Farm and Home Management Advisors; Foreign Language and Literature Teachers, Postsecondary; Forestry and Conservation Science Teachers, Postsecondary; Geography Teachers, Postsecondary; Graduate Teaching Assistants; Health Specialties Teachers, Postsecondary; History Teachers, Postsecondary; Home Economics Teachers, Postsecondary; Law Teachers, Postsecondary; Library Science Teachers, Postsecondary; Mathematical Science Teachers, Postsecondary; Nursing Instructors and Teachers, Postsecondary; Philosophy and Religion Teachers, Postsecondary; Physics Teachers, Postsecondary; Political Science Teachers, Postsecondary; Psychology Teachers, Postsecondary; Recreation and Fitness Studies Teachers, Postsecondary; Self-Enrichment Education Teachers; Social Work Teachers, Postsecondary; Sociology Teachers, Postsecondary; Vocational Education Teachers, Postsecondary. **PERSONALITY TYPE:** Social. Social occupations frequently involve working with, communicating with, and teaching people. These occupations often involve helping or providing service to others.

EDUCATION/TRAINING PROGRAM(S)— Adult and Continuing Education and Teaching; Adult Literacy Tutor/Instructor; Bilingual and Multilingual Education; Multicultural Education; Teaching English as a Second or Foreign Language/ESL Language Instructor.

WORK ENVIRONMENT—Physical proximity to others; sounds, noise levels are distracting or uncomfortable; sitting; indoors; contaminants.

Agricultural Crop Farm Managers

- Education/Training Required: Work experience plus degree
- Annual Earnings: $50,720
- Growth: 5.1%
- Annual Job Openings: 25,000
- Self-Employed: 0.9%
- Part-Time: 9.2%

The job openings listed here are shared with Fish Hatchery Managers and Nursery and Greenhouse Managers.

Age Bracket	Percentage of Workers
45–54 Years Old	29.6%
55–64 Years Old	17.5%
65 or Older	12.6%

Direct and coordinate, through subordinate supervisory personnel, activities of workers engaged in agricultural crop production for corporations, cooperatives, or other owners. Directs and coordinates worker activities, such as planting, irrigation, chemical application, harvesting, grading, payroll, and recordkeeping. Contracts with farmers or independent owners for raising of crops or for management of crop production. Coordinates growing activities with those of engineering, equipment maintenance, packing houses, and other related departments. Analyzes market conditions to determine acreage allocations. Confers with purchasers and arranges for sale of crops. Records information such as production, farm management practices, and parent stock, and prepares financial and operational reports. Determines procedural changes in drying, grading, storage, and shipment for greater efficiency and accuracy. Analyzes soil to determine type and quantity of fertilizer required for maximum production. Inspects equipment to ensure proper functioning. Inspects orchards and fields to determine maturity dates of crops or to estimate potential crop damage from weather. Plans and directs development and production of hybrid plant varieties with high yield or disease- and insect-resistant characteristics. Purchases machinery, equipment, and supplies, such as tractors, seed, fertilizer, and chemicals. Hires, discharges, transfers, and promotes workers; enforces safety regulations; and interprets policies. Negotiates with bank officials to obtain credit from bank. Evaluates financial statements and makes budget proposals. **SKILLS**—Management of Financial Resources; Management of Personnel Resources; Negotiation; Management of Material Resources; Coordination; Systems Analysis; Writing; Speaking; Systems Evaluation.

GOE—**Interest Area:** 01. Agriculture and Natural Resources. **Work Group:** 01.01. Managerial Work in Agriculture and Natural Resources. **Other Jobs in This Work Group:** Farmers and Ranchers; First-Line Supervisors and Manager/Supervisors—Agricultural Crop Workers; First-Line Supervisors and Manager/ Supervisors—Animal Husbandry Workers; First-Line Supervisors and Manager/Supervisors —Extractive Workers; First-Line Supervisors and Manager/Supervisors—Fishery Workers; First-Line Supervisors and Manager/Supervisors —Horticultural Workers; First-Line Supervisors and Manager/Supervisors—Landscaping Workers; First-Line Supervisors and Manager/ Supervisors—Logging Workers; Fish Hatchery Managers; Lawn Service Managers; Nursery and Greenhouse Managers; Park Naturalists; Purchasing Agents and Buyers, Farm Products. **PERSONALITY TYPE:** Enterprising. Enterprising occupations frequently involve starting up and carrying out projects. These occupations can involve leading people and making many decisions. They sometimes require risk taking and often deal with business.

EDUCATION/TRAINING PROGRAM(S)— Agribusiness/Agricultural Business Operations; Agricultural Animal Breeding; Agricultural Business and Management, General; Agricultural Business and Management, Other; Agricultural Production Operations, General; Agricultural Production Operations, Other; Agronomy and Crop Science; Animal Nutrition; Animal Sciences, General; Animal/Livestock Husbandry and Production; Crop Production; Dairy Husbandry and Production; Dairy Science; Farm/Farm and Ranch Management; others.

WORK ENVIRONMENT—Outdoors; standing; minor burns, cuts, bites, or stings; hazardous equipment; sitting.

Agricultural Sciences Teachers, Postsecondary

- Education/Training Required: Master's degree
- Annual Earnings: $70,610
- Growth: 38.1%
- Annual Job Openings: 216,000
- Self-Employed: 0.3%
- Part-Time: 27.7%

The job openings listed here are shared with all other postsecondary teaching occupations.

Age Bracket	Percentage of Workers
45–54 Years Old	22.8%
55–64 Years Old	19.0%
65 or Older	5.5%

Teach courses in the agricultural sciences. Includes teachers of agronomy, dairy sciences, fisheries management, horticultural sciences, poultry sciences, range management, and agricultural soil conservation. Prepare course materials such as syllabi, homework assignments, and handouts. Evaluate and grade students' class work, laboratory work, assignments, and papers. Keep abreast of developments in their field by reading current literature, talking with colleagues, and participating in professional conferences. Prepare and deliver lectures to undergraduate and/or graduate students on topics such as crop production, plant genetics, and soil chemistry. Initiate, facilitate, and moderate classroom discussions. Conduct research in a particular field of knowledge and publish findings in professional journals, books, and/or electronic media. Supervise laboratory sessions and fieldwork and coordinate laboratory operations. Supervise undergraduate and/or graduate teaching, internship, and research work. Compile, administer, and grade examinations or assign this work to others. Advise students on academic and vocational curricula and on career issues. Plan, evaluate, and revise curricula, course content, and course materials and methods of instruction. Maintain student attendance records, grades, and other required records. Write grant proposals to procure external research funding. Collaborate with colleagues to address teaching and research issues. Maintain regularly scheduled office hours in order to advise and assist students. Participate in student recruitment, registration, and placement activities. Select and obtain materials and supplies such as textbooks and laboratory equipment. Act as advisers to student organizations. Participate in campus and community events. Serve on academic or administrative committees that deal with institutional policies, departmental matters, and academic issues. Provide professional consulting services to government and/or industry. Perform administrative duties such as serving as department head. **SKILLS**—Science; Instructing; Writing; Management of Financial Resources; Active Learning; Learning Strategies; Reading Comprehension; Persuasion.

GOE—Interest Area: 05. Education and Training. **Work Group:** 05.03. Postsecondary and Adult Teaching and Instructing. **Other Jobs in This Work Group:** Adult Literacy, Remedial Education, and GED Teachers and Instructors; Anthropology and Archeology Teachers, Postsecondary; Architecture Teachers, Postsecondary; Area, Ethnic, and Cultural Studies Teachers, Postsecondary; Art, Drama, and Music Teachers, Postsecondary; Atmospheric, Earth, Marine, and Space Sciences Teachers, Postsecondary; Biological Science Teachers, Postsecondary; Business Teachers,

Postsecondary; Chemistry Teachers, Post-secondary; Communications Teachers, Postsecondary; Computer Science Teachers, Postsecondary; Criminal Justice and Law Enforcement Teachers, Postsecondary; Economics Teachers, Postsecondary; Education Teachers, Postsecondary; Engineering Teachers, Postsecondary; English Language and Literature Teachers, Postsecondary; Environmental Science Teachers, Postsecondary; Farm and Home Management Advisors; Foreign Language and Literature Teachers, Postsecondary; Forestry and Conservation Science Teachers, Postsecondary; Geography Teachers, Postsecondary; Graduate Teaching Assistants; Health Specialties Teachers, Postsecondary; History Teachers, Postsecondary; Home Economics Teachers, Postsecondary; Law Teachers, Postsecondary; Library Science Teachers, Postsecondary; Mathematical Science Teachers, Postsecondary; Nursing Instructors and Teachers, Postsecondary; Philosophy and Religion Teachers, Postsecondary; Physics Teachers, Postsecondary; Political Science Teachers, Postsecondary; Psychology Teachers, Postsecondary; Recreation and Fitness Studies Teachers, Postsecondary; Self-Enrichment Education Teachers; Social Work Teachers, Postsecondary; Sociology Teachers, Post-secondary; Vocational Education Teachers, Postsecondary. **PERSONALITY TYPE:** Investigative. Investigative occupations frequently involve working with ideas and require an extensive amount of thinking. These occupations can involve searching for facts and figuring out problems mentally.

EDUCATION/TRAINING PROGRAM(S)— Agribusiness/Agricultural Business Operations; Agricultural and Food Products Processing, General; Agricultural and Horticultural Plant Breeding; Agricultural Animal Breeding;

Agricultural Business and Management, General; Agricultural Business and Management, Other; Agricultural Economics; Agricultural Mechanization, General; Agricultural Mechanization, Other; Agricultural Power Machinery Operation; Agricultural Production Operations, General; Agricultural Production Operations, Other; others.

WORK ENVIRONMENT—Sitting; very hot or cold; outdoors, under cover; contaminants; indoors, not environmentally controlled; in an enclosed vehicle or equipment.

Air Traffic Controllers

- Education/Training Required: Long-term on-the-job training
- Annual Earnings: $102,390
- Growth: 12.6%
- Annual Job Openings: 2,000
- Self-Employed: 0%
- Part-Time: 3.6%

Age Bracket	Percentage of Workers
45–54 Years Old	31.6%
55–64 Years Old	13.2%
65 or Older	5.3%

Control air traffic on and within vicinity of airport and movement of air traffic between altitude sectors and control centers according to established procedures and policies. Authorize, regulate, and control commercial airline flights according to government or company regulations to expedite and ensure flight safety. Monitor aircraft within a specific airspace, using radar, computer equipment, and visual refer-

ences. Monitor and direct the movement of aircraft within an assigned air space and on the ground at airports to minimize delays and maximize safety. Organize flight plans and traffic management plans to prepare for planes about to enter assigned airspace. Provide flight path changes or directions to emergency landing fields for pilots traveling in bad weather or in emergency situations. Compile information about flights from flight plans, pilot reports, radar, and observations. Relay to control centers such air traffic information as courses, altitudes, and expected arrival times. Transfer control of departing flights to traffic control centers and accept control of arriving flights. Complete daily activity reports and keep records of messages from aircraft. Initiate and coordinate searches for missing aircraft. Inspect, adjust, and control radio equipment and airport lights. Review records and reports for clarity and completeness and maintain records and reports as required under federal law. Alert airport emergency services in cases of emergency and when aircraft are experiencing difficulties. Analyze factors such as weather reports, fuel requirements, and maps in order to determine air routes. Check conditions and traffic at different altitudes in response to pilots' requests for altitude changes. Conduct pre-flight briefings on weather conditions, suggested routes, altitudes, indications of turbulence, and other flight safety information. Contact pilots by radio to provide meteorological, navigational, and other information. Determine the timing and procedures for flight vector changes. Direct ground traffic, including taxiing aircraft, maintenance and baggage vehicles, and airport workers. Direct pilots to runways when space is available or direct them to maintain a traffic pattern until there is space for them to land. Inform pilots about nearby planes as well as potentially hazardous conditions such as weather, speed and direction of wind, and visibility problems. Issue landing and takeoff authorizations and instructions. **SKILLS**— Operation and Control; Operation Monitoring; Active Listening; Coordination; Critical Thinking; Systems Analysis; Active Learning; Troubleshooting; Judgment and Decision Making.

GOE—Interest Area: 03. Arts and Communication. **Work Group:** 03.10. Communications Technology. **Other Jobs in This Work Group:** Airfield Operations Specialists; Central Office Operators; Directory Assistance Operators; Dispatchers, Except Police, Fire, and Ambulance; Police, Fire, and Ambulance Dispatchers. **PERSONALITY TYPE:** Conventional. Conventional occupations frequently involve following set procedures and routines. These occupations can include working with data and details more than with ideas. Usually there is a clear line of authority to follow.

EDUCATION/TRAINING PROGRAM(S)— Air Traffic Controller.

WORK ENVIRONMENT—Sitting; indoors; sounds, noise levels are distracting or uncomfortable; using hands on objects, tools, or controls; extremely bright or inadequate lighting.

Aircraft Body and Bonded Structure Repairers

- ◉ Education/Training Required: Postsecondary vocational training
- ◉ Annual Earnings: $45,910
- ◉ Growth: 11.0%
- ◉ Annual Job Openings: 12,000
- ◉ Self-Employed: 1.0%
- ◉ Part-Time: 1.2%

The job openings listed here are shared with Aircraft Engine Specialists and Airframe-and-Power-Plant Mechanics.

Age Bracket	Percentage of Workers
45–54 Years Old	29.7%
55–64 Years Old	10.9%
65 or Older	0.8%

Repair body or structure of aircraft according to specifications. Locates and marks dimension and reference lines on defective or replacement part, using templates, scribes, compass, and steel rule. Trims and shapes replacement section to specified size and fits and secures section in place, using adhesives, hand tools, and power tools. Cleans, strips, primes, and sands structural surfaces and materials prior to bonding. Spreads plastic film over area to be repaired to prevent damage to surrounding area. Cures bonded structure, using portable or stationary curing equipment. Reinstalls repaired or replacement parts for subsequent riveting or welding, using clamps and wrenches. Repairs or fabricates defective section or part, using metal fabricating machines, saws, brakes, shears, and grinders. Reads work orders, blueprints, and specifications or examines sample or damaged part or structure to determine repair or fabrication procedures and sequence of operations. Communicates with other workers to fit and align heavy parts or expedite processing of repair parts. Removes or cuts out defective part or drills holes to gain access to internal defect or damage, using drill and punch. **SKILLS—** Installation; Repairing; Equipment Maintenance; Equipment Selection; Mathematics; Operation Monitoring; Operation and Control; Troubleshooting.

GOE—Interest Area: 13. Manufacturing. **Work Group:** 13.14. Vehicle and Facility Mechanical Work. **Other Jobs in This Work Group:** Aircraft Engine Specialists; Aircraft Rigging Assemblers; Aircraft Structure Assemblers, Precision; Aircraft Systems Assemblers, Precision; Airframe-and-Power-Plant Mechanics; Automotive Body and Related Repairers; Automotive Glass Installers and Repairers; Automotive Master Mechanics; Automotive Specialty Technicians; Bus and Truck Mechanics and Diesel Engine Specialists; Farm Equipment Mechanics; Fiberglass Laminators and Fabricators; Mobile Heavy Equipment Mechanics, Except Engines; Motorboat Mechanics; Motorcycle Mechanics; Outdoor Power Equipment and Other Small Engine Mechanics; Rail Car Repairers; Recreational Vehicle Service Technicians; Tire Repairers and Changers. **PERSONALITY TYPE:** Realistic. Realistic occupations frequently involve work activities that include practical, hands-on problems and solutions. They often deal with plants, animals, and real-world materials like wood, tools, and machinery. Many of the occupations require working outside and do not involve a lot of paperwork or working closely with others.

EDUCATION/TRAINING PROGRAM(S)— Agricultural Mechanics and Equipment/Machine Technology; Airframe Mechanics and Aircraft Maintenance Technology/Technician.

WORK ENVIRONMENT—Hazardous equipment; minor burns, cuts, bites, or stings; standing; climbing ladders, scaffolds, or poles; using hands on objects, tools, or controls.

Aircraft Engine Specialists

◎ Education/Training Required: Postsecondary vocational training

◎ Annual Earnings: $45,910

◎ Growth: 11.0%

◎ Annual Job Openings: 12,000

◎ Self-Employed: 1.0%

◎ Part-Time: 1.2%

The job openings listed here are shared with Aircraft Body and Bonded Structure Repairers and Airframe-and-Power-Plant Mechanics.

Age Bracket	Percentage of Workers
45–54 Years Old	29.7%
55–64 Years Old	10.9%
65 or Older	0.8%

Repair and maintain the operating condition of aircraft engines. Includes helicopter engine mechanics. Replaces or repairs worn, defective, or damaged components, using hand tools, gauges, and testing equipment. Tests engine operation, using test equipment such as ignition analyzer, compression checker, distributor timer, and ammeter, to identify malfunction. Listens to operating engine to detect and diagnose malfunctions, such as sticking or burned valves. Reassembles engine and installs engine in aircraft. Disassembles and inspects engine parts, such as turbine blades and cylinders, for wear, warping, cracks, and leaks. Removes engine from aircraft, using hoist or forklift truck. Services, repairs, and rebuilds aircraft structures, such as wings, fuselage, rigging, and surface and hydraulic controls, using hand or power tools and equipment. Adjusts, repairs, or replaces electrical wiring system and aircraft accessories. Reads and interprets manufacturers' maintenance manuals, service bulletins, and other specifications to determine feasibility and methods of repair. Services and maintains aircraft and related apparatus by performing activities such as flushing crankcase, cleaning screens, and lubricating moving parts. **SKILLS**—Equipment Maintenance; Repairing; Installation; Troubleshooting; Operation Monitoring; Quality Control Analysis; Judgment and Decision Making; Systems Analysis.

GOE—Interest Area: 13. Manufacturing. **Work Group:** 13.14. Vehicle and Facility Mechanical Work. **Other Jobs in This Work Group:** Aircraft Body and Bonded Structure Repairers; Aircraft Rigging Assemblers; Aircraft Structure Assemblers, Precision; Aircraft Systems Assemblers, Precision; Airframe-and-Power-Plant Mechanics; Automotive Body and Related Repairers; Automotive Glass Installers and Repairers; Automotive Master Mechanics; Automotive Specialty Technicians; Bus and Truck Mechanics and Diesel Engine Specialists; Farm Equipment Mechanics; Fiberglass Laminators and Fabricators; Mobile Heavy Equipment Mechanics, Except Engines; Motorboat Mechanics; Motorcycle Mechanics; Outdoor Power Equipment and Other Small Engine Mechanics; Rail Car Repairers; Recreational Vehicle Service Technicians; Tire Repairers and Changers. **PERSONALITY TYPE:** Realistic. Realistic occupations frequently involve work activities that include practical, hands-on problems and solutions. They often deal with plants, animals, and real-world materials like wood, tools, and machinery. Many of the occupations require working outside and do not involve a lot of paperwork or working closely with others.

EDUCATION/TRAINING PROGRAM(S)— Agricultural Mechanics and Equipment/Machine Technology; Aircraft Powerplant Technology/Technician.

WORK ENVIRONMENT—Hazardous equipment; minor burns, cuts, bites, or stings; hazardous conditions; outdoors; standing.

Airframe-and-Power-Plant Mechanics

- Education/Training Required: Postsecondary vocational training
- Annual Earnings: $45,910
- Growth: 11.0%
- Annual Job Openings: 12,000
- Self-Employed: 1.0%
- Part-Time: 1.2%

The job openings listed here are shared with Aircraft Body and Bonded Structure Repairers and Aircraft Engine Specialists.

Age Bracket	Percentage of Workers
45–54 Years Old	29.7%
55–64 Years Old	10.9%
65 or Older	0.8%

Inspect, test, repair, maintain, and service aircraft. Adjusts, aligns, and calibrates aircraft systems, using hand tools, gauges, and test equipment. Examines and inspects engines or other components for cracks, breaks, or leaks. Disassembles and inspects parts for wear, warping, or other defects. Assembles and installs elec-

trical, plumbing, mechanical, hydraulic, and structural components and accessories, using hand tools and power tools. Services and maintains aircraft systems by performing tasks such as flushing crankcase, cleaning screens, greasing moving parts, and checking brakes. Repairs, replaces, and rebuilds aircraft structures, functional components, and parts such as wings and fuselage, rigging, and hydraulic units. Tests engine and system operations, using testing equipment, and listens to engine sounds to detect and diagnose malfunctions. Removes engine from aircraft or installs engine, using hoist or forklift truck. Modifies aircraft structures, space vehicles, systems, or components, following drawings, engineering orders, and technical publications. Reads and interprets aircraft maintenance manuals and specifications to determine feasibility and method of repairing or replacing malfunctioning or damaged components. **SKILLS—**Equipment Maintenance; Installation; Repairing; Troubleshooting; Operation Monitoring; Quality Control Analysis; Science; Equipment Selection.

GOE—Interest Area: 13. Manufacturing. **Work Group:** 13.14. Vehicle and Facility Mechanical Work. **Other Jobs in This Work Group:** Aircraft Body and Bonded Structure Repairers; Aircraft Engine Specialists; Aircraft Rigging Assemblers; Aircraft Structure Assemblers, Precision; Aircraft Systems Assemblers, Precision; Automotive Body and Related Repairers; Automotive Glass Installers and Repairers; Automotive Master Mechanics; Automotive Specialty Technicians; Bus and Truck Mechanics and Diesel Engine Specialists; Farm Equipment Mechanics; Fiberglass Laminators and Fabricators; Mobile Heavy Equipment Mechanics, Except Engines; Motorboat Mechanics; Motorcycle Mechanics; Outdoor Power Equipment and Other Small Engine Mechanics; Rail Car Repairers;

Recreational Vehicle Service Technicians; Tire Repairers and Changers. **PERSONALITY TYPE**: Realistic. Realistic occupations frequently involve work activities that include practical, hands-on problems and solutions. They often deal with plants, animals, and real-world materials like wood, tools, and machinery. Many of the occupations require working outside and do not involve a lot of paperwork or working closely with others.

EDUCATION/TRAINING PROGRAM(S)— Agricultural Mechanics and Equipment/ Machine Technology; Aircraft Powerplant Technology/Technician; Airframe Mechanics and Aircraft Maintenance Technology/ Technician.

WORK ENVIRONMENT—Hazardous equipment; common protective or safety equipment; spend time bending or twisting the body; spend time kneeling, crouching, stooping, or crawling; very hot or cold.

Airline Pilots, Copilots, and Flight Engineers

- Education/Training Required: Bachelor's degree
- Annual Earnings: $135,430
- Growth: 18.5%
- Annual Job Openings: 6,000
- Self-Employed: 0%
- Part-Time: 12.9%

Age Bracket	Percentage of Workers
45–54 Years Old	32.8%
55–64 Years Old	15.5%
65 or Older	2.6%

Pilot and navigate the flight of multi-engine aircraft in regularly scheduled service for the transport of passengers and cargo. Requires Federal Air Transport rating and certification in specific aircraft type used. Brief crews about flight details such as destinations, duties, and responsibilities. Check passenger and cargo distributions and fuel amounts to ensure that weight and balance specifications are met. Choose routes, altitudes, and speeds that will provide the fastest, safest, and smoothest flights. Confer with flight dispatchers and weather forecasters to keep abreast of flight conditions. Contact control towers for takeoff clearances, arrival instructions, and other information, using radio equipment. Coordinate flight activities with ground crews and air-traffic control and inform crew members of flight and test procedures. Direct activities of aircraft crews during flights. File instrument flight plans with air traffic control to ensure that flights are coordinated with other air traffic. Inspect aircraft for defects and malfunctions according to pre-flight checklists. Make announcements regarding flights, using public address systems. Monitor engine operation, fuel consumption, and functioning of aircraft systems during flights. Monitor gauges, warning devices, and control panels to verify aircraft performance and to regulate engine speed. Order changes in fuel supplies, loads, routes, or schedules to ensure safety of flights. Plan and formulate flight activities and test schedules and prepare flight evaluation reports. Respond to and report in-flight emergencies and malfunctions. Start engines, operate controls, and pilot airplanes to transport passengers, mail, or freight while adhering to flight plans, regulations, and procedures. Steer aircraft along planned routes with the assistance of autopilot and flight management computers. Work as part of a flight team with other crew members, especially during takeoffs and landings. Conduct in-flight tests and evaluations at specified altitudes and in all types of weather in order to determine the receptivity and other characteristics of equipment and systems. Evaluate other pilots or pilot-license applicants for proficiency. Instruct other pilots and student pilots in aircraft operations and the principles of flight. Load smaller aircraft, handling passenger luggage and supervising refueling. **SKILLS**—Operation and Control; Operation Monitoring; Instructing; Science; Coordination; Systems Evaluation; Systems Analysis; Judgment and Decision Making.

GOE—Interest Area: 16. Transportation, Distribution, and Logistics. **Work Group:** 16.02. Air Vehicle Operation. **Other Jobs in This Work Group:** Commercial Pilots. **PERSONALITY TYPE:** Realistic. Realistic occupations frequently involve work activities that include practical, hands-on problems and solutions. They often deal with plants, animals, and real-world materials like wood, tools, and machinery. Many of the occupations require working outside and do not involve a lot of paperwork or working closely with others.

EDUCATION/TRAINING PROGRAM(S)—Airline/Commercial/Professional Pilot and Flight Crew; Flight Instructor.

WORK ENVIRONMENT—High places; sitting; hazardous equipment; exposed to whole body vibration; outdoors.

Anesthesiologists

- Education/Training Required: First professional degree
- Annual Earnings: more than $145,600
- Growth: 19.5%
- Annual Job Openings: 38,000
- Self-Employed: 16.9%
- Part-Time: 8.1%

The job openings listed here are shared with Family and General Practitioners; Internists, General; Obstetricians and Gynecologists; Pediatricians, General; Psychiatrists; and Surgeons.

Age Bracket	Percentage of Workers
45–54 Years Old	29.3%
55–64 Years Old	13.4%
65 or Older	5.4%

Administer anesthetics during surgery or other medical procedures. Administer anesthetic or sedation during medical procedures, using local, intravenous, spinal, or caudal methods. Confer with other medical professionals to determine type and method of anesthetic or sedation to render patient insensible to pain. Coordinate administration of anesthetics with surgeons during operation. Decide when patients have recovered or stabilized enough to be sent to another room or ward or to be sent home following outpatient surgery. Examine patient, obtain medical history, and use diagnostic tests to determine risk during surgical, obstetrical, and other medical procedures. Monitor patient before, during, and after anesthesia and counteract adverse reactions or complications. Record type and amount of anesthesia and patient condition throughout procedure. Conduct medical research to aid in controlling and curing disease, to investigate new medications, and to develop and test new medical techniques. Coordinate and direct work of nurses, medical technicians, and other health care providers. Diagnose illnesses, using examinations, tests and reports. Inform students and staff of types and methods of anesthesia administration, signs of complications, and emergency methods to counteract reactions. Manage anesthesiological services, coordinating them with other medical activities and formulating plans and procedures. Order laboratory tests, X rays, and other diagnostic procedures. Position patient on operating table to maximize patient comfort and surgical accessibility. Provide and maintain life support and airway management and help prepare patients for emergency surgery. Provide medical care and consultation in many settings, prescribing medication and treatment and referring patients for surgery. Instruct individuals and groups on ways to preserve health and prevent disease. Schedule and maintain use of surgical suite, including operating, wash-up, and waiting rooms and anesthetic and sterilizing equipment. **SKILLS**—Operation Monitoring; Judgment and Decision Making; Reading Comprehension; Systems Evaluation; Systems Analysis; Critical Thinking; Coordination; Instructing; Operation and Control.

GOE—Interest Area: 08. Health Science. **Work Group:** 08.02. Medicine and Surgery. **Other Jobs in This Work Group:** Family and General Practitioners; Internists, General; Medical Assistants; Medical Transcriptionists; Obstetricians and Gynecologists; Pediatricians, General; Pharmacists; Pharmacy Aides; Pharmacy Technicians; Physician Assistants; Psychiatrists; Registered Nurses; Surgeons; Surgical Technologists. **PERSONALITY TYPE:** Investigative. Investigative occupations frequently involve working with ideas and require an extensive amount of thinking. These occupations can involve searching for facts and figuring out problems mentally.

EDUCATION/TRAINING PROGRAM(S)—Anesthesiology; Critical Care Anesthesiology.

WORK ENVIRONMENT—Common protective or safety equipment; disease or infections; indoors; standing; hazardous conditions; spend time bending or twisting the body.

Anthropology and Archeology Teachers, Postsecondary

- ⊚ Education/Training Required: Master's degree
- ⊚ Annual Earnings: $60,190
- ⊚ Growth: 38.1%
- ⊚ Annual Job Openings: 216,000
- ⊚ Self-Employed: 0.3%
- ⊚ Part-Time: 27.7%

The job openings listed here are shared with all other postsecondary teaching occupations.

Age Bracket	Percentage of Workers
45–54 Years Old	22.8%
55–64 Years Old	19.0%
65 or Older	5.5%

Teach courses in anthropology or archeology. Conduct research in a particular field of knowledge and publish findings in professional journals, books, and/or electronic media. Keep abreast of developments in their field by reading current literature, talking with colleagues, and participating in professional conferences. Prepare and deliver lectures to undergraduate and/or graduate students on topics such as research methods, urban anthropology, and language and culture. Evaluate and grade students' class work, assignments, and papers. Initiate, facilitate, and moderate classroom discussions. Write grant proposals to procure external research funding. Supervise undergraduate and/or graduate teaching, internship, and research work. Prepare course materials such as syllabi, homework assignments, and handouts. Compile, administer, and grade examinations or assign this work to others. Supervise students' laboratory work or fieldwork. Plan, evaluate, and revise curricula, course content, and course materials and methods of instruction. Advise students on academic and vocational curricula, career issues, and laboratory and field research. Maintain student attendance records, grades, and other required records. Maintain regularly scheduled office hours in order to advise and assist students. Collaborate with colleagues to address teaching and research issues. Compile bibliographies of specialized materials for outside reading assignments. Perform administrative duties such as serving as department head. Select and obtain materials and supplies such as textbooks and laboratory equipment. Serve on academic or administrative committees that deal with institutional policies, departmental matters, and academic issues. Participate in student recruitment, registration, and placement activities. **SKILLS**—Instructing; Writing; Critical Thinking; Active Learning; Reading Comprehension; Science; Learning Strategies; Active Listening.

GOE—Interest Area: 05. Education and Training. **Work Group:** 05.03. Postsecondary and Adult Teaching and Instructing. **Other Jobs in This Work Group:** Adult Literacy, Remedial Education, and GED Teachers and Instructors; Agricultural Sciences Teachers, Postsecondary; Architecture Teachers, Postsecondary; Area, Ethnic, and Cultural Studies Teachers, Postsecondary; Art, Drama, and Music Teachers, Postsecondary; Atmospheric, Earth, Marine, and Space Sciences Teachers, Postsecondary; Biological Science Teachers, Postsecondary; Business Teachers, Postsecondary; Chemistry Teachers, Postsecondary; Communications Teachers, Postsecondary; Computer Science Teachers, Postsecondary; Criminal Justice and Law Enforcement Teachers, Postsecondary; Economics Teachers, Postsecondary; Education Teachers, Postsecondary; Engineering Teachers, Postsecondary; English Language and Literature Teachers, Postsecondary; Environmental Science Teachers, Postsecondary; Farm and Home Management Advisors; Foreign Language and Literature Teachers, Postsecondary; Forestry and Conservation Science Teachers, Postsecondary; Geography Teachers, Postsecondary; Graduate Teaching Assistants; Health Specialties Teachers, Postsecondary; History Teachers, Postsecondary; Home Economics Teachers, Postsecondary; Law Teachers, Postsecondary; Library Science Teachers, Postsecondary; Mathematical Science Teachers, Postsecondary; Nursing Instructors and Teachers, Postsecondary; Philosophy and Religion Teachers, Postsecondary; Physics Teachers, Postsecondary; Political Science Teachers, Postsecondary; Psychology Teachers, Postsecondary; Recreation and Fitness Studies Teachers, Postsecondary; Self-Enrichment Education Teachers; Social Work Teachers, Postsecondary; Sociology Teachers, Postsecondary; Vocational Education Teachers, Postsecondary. **PERSONALITY TYPE:** Social. Social occupations frequently involve working with, communicating with, and teaching people. These occupations often involve helping or providing service to others.

EDUCATION/TRAINING PROGRAM(S)— Anthropology; Archeology; Physical Anthropology; Social Science Teacher Education.

WORK ENVIRONMENT—Sitting; indoors; contaminants; physical proximity to others; sounds, noise levels are distracting or uncomfortable.

Appraisers, Real Estate

- Education/Training Required: Postsecondary vocational training
- Annual Earnings: $43,790
- Growth: 17.6%
- Annual Job Openings: 11,000
- Self-Employed: 34.8%
- Part-Time: 8.9%

The job openings listed here are shared with Assessors.

Age Bracket	Percentage of Workers
45–54 Years Old	31.1%
55–64 Years Old	15.1%
65 or Older	9.2%

Appraise real property to determine its value for purchase, sales, investment, mortgage, or loan purposes. Compute final estimation of property values, taking into account such factors as depreciation, replacement costs, value comparisons of similar properties, and income potential. Draw land diagrams that will be used in appraisal reports to support findings. Estimate building replacement costs, using building valuation manuals and professional cost estimators. Evaluate land and neighborhoods where properties are situated, considering locations and trends or impending changes that could influence future values. Examine the type and location of nearby services such as shopping centers, schools, parks, and other neighborhood features in order to evaluate their impact on property values. Inspect properties to evaluate construction, condition, special features, and functional design and to take property measurements. Obtain county land values and sales information about nearby properties in order to aid in establishment of property values. Photograph interiors and exteriors of properties in order to assist in estimating property value, substantiate findings, and complete appraisal reports. Prepare written reports that estimate property values, outline methods by which the estimations were made, and meet appraisal standards. Search public records for transactions such as sales, leases, and assessments. Verify legal descriptions of properties by comparing them to county records. Check building codes and zoning bylaws in order to determine any effects on the properties being appraised. Examine income records and operating costs of income properties. Interview persons familiar with properties and immediate surroundings, such as contractors, homeowners, and realtors, in order to obtain pertinent information. Testify in court as to the value of a piece of real estate property. **SKILLS**—Writing; Mathematics; Management of Personnel Resources; Speaking; Systems Analysis; Reading Comprehension; Time Management; Active Listening.

GOE—Interest Area: 06. Finance and Insurance. **Work Group:** 06.02. Finance/Insurance Investigation and Analysis. **Other Jobs in This Work Group:** Assessors; Claims Examiners, Property and Casualty Insurance; Cost Estimators; Credit Analysts; Financial Analysts; Insurance Adjusters, Examiners, and Investigators; Insurance Appraisers, Auto Damage; Insurance Underwriters; Loan Counselors; Loan Officers; Market Research Analysts; Survey Researchers. **PERSONALITY TYPE:** Enterprising. Enterprising occupations frequently involve starting up and carrying out projects. These occupations can involve leading people and making many decisions. They sometimes require risk taking and often deal with business.

EDUCATION/TRAINING PROGRAM(S)— Real Estate.

WORK ENVIRONMENT—Sitting; outdoors; walking and running; standing; spend time bending or twisting the body.

Arbitrators, Mediators, and Conciliators

- Education/Training Required: Work experience plus degree
- Annual Earnings: $53,690
- Growth: 13.7%
- Annual Job Openings: fewer than 500
- Self-Employed: 11.2%
- Part-Time: 6.2%

Age Bracket	Percentage of Workers
45–54 Years Old	27.1%
55–64 Years Old	30.5%
65 or Older	11.9%

Facilitate negotiation and conflict resolution through dialogue. Resolve conflicts outside of the court system by mutual consent of parties involved. Review and evaluate information from documents such as claim applications, birth or death certificates, and physician or employer records. Set up appointments for parties to meet for mediation. Use mediation techniques to facilitate communication between disputants, to further parties' understanding of different perspectives, and to guide parties toward mutual

agreement. Authorize payment of valid claims. Determine existence and amount of liability according to evidence, laws, and administrative and judicial precedents. Issue subpoenas and administer oaths to prepare for formal hearings. Notify claimants of denied claims and appeal rights. Analyze evidence and apply relevant laws, regulations, policies, and precedents in order to reach conclusions. Arrange and conduct hearings to obtain information and evidence relative to disposition of claims. Conduct initial meetings with disputants to outline the arbitration process, settle procedural matters such as fees, and determine details such as witness numbers and time requirements. Confer with disputants to clarify issues, identify underlying concerns, and develop an understanding of their respective needs and interests. Interview claimants, agents, or witnesses to obtain information about disputed issues. Participate in court proceedings. Prepare settlement agreements for disputants to sign. Recommend acceptance or rejection of compromise settlement offers. Research laws, regulations, policies, and precedent decisions to prepare for hearings. Prepare written opinions and decisions regarding cases. Rule on exceptions, motions, and admissibility of evidence. Conduct studies of appeals procedures in order to ensure adherence to legal requirements and to facilitate disposition of cases. Organize and deliver public presentations about mediation to organizations such as community agencies and schools. **SKILLS—**Judgment and Decision Making; Active Listening; Critical Thinking; Writing; Reading Comprehension; Speaking; Active Learning; Negotiation.

GOE—Interest Area: 12. Law and Public Safety. **Work Group:** 12.02. Legal Practice and Justice Administration. **Other Jobs in This Work Group:** Administrative Law Judges, Adjudicators, and Hearing Officers; Judges,

Magistrate Judges, and Magistrates; Lawyers. **PERSONALITY TYPE:** Enterprising. Enterprising occupations frequently involve starting up and carrying out projects. These occupations can involve leading people and making many decisions. They sometimes require risk taking and often deal with business.

EDUCATION/TRAINING PROGRAM(S)— Law (LL.B., J.D.); Law, Legal Services, and Legal Studies, Other; Legal Studies, General.

WORK ENVIRONMENT—Sitting; indoors.

Architects, Except Landscape and Naval

- Education/Training Required: Bachelor's degree
- Annual Earnings: $61,430
- Growth: 17.3%
- Annual Job Openings: 8,000
- Self-Employed: 21.4%
- Part-Time: 5.5%

Age Bracket	Percentage of Workers
45–54 Years Old	24.4%
55–64 Years Old	12.8%
65 or Older	3.9%

Plan and design structures, such as private residences, office buildings, theaters, factories, and other structural property. Prepare information regarding design, structure specifications, materials, color, equipment, estimated costs, and construction time. Consult with client to determine functional and spatial requirements of structure. Direct activities of workers engaged in

preparing drawings and specification documents. Plan layout of project. Prepare contract documents for building contractors. Prepare scale drawings. Integrate engineering element into unified design. Conduct periodic on-site observation of work during construction to monitor compliance with plans. Administer construction contracts. Represent client in obtaining bids and awarding construction contracts. **SKILLS**—Operations Analysis; Management of Financial Resources; Coordination; Management of Personnel Resources; Complex Problem Solving; Negotiation; Persuasion; Active Listening; Time Management.

GOE—Interest Area: 02. Architecture and Construction. **Work Group:** 02.02. Architectural Design. **Other Jobs in This Work Group:** Landscape Architects. **PERSONALITY TYPE:** Artistic. Artistic occupations frequently involve working with forms, designs, and patterns. They often require self-expression, and the work can be done without following a clear set of rules.

EDUCATION/TRAINING PROGRAM(S)— Architectural History and Criticism; Architecture (BArch, BA/BS, MArch, MA/MS, PhD); Architecture and Related Programs, Other; Environmental Design/Architecture.

WORK ENVIRONMENT—Sitting; physical proximity to others; extremely bright or inadequate lighting; in an enclosed vehicle or equipment; very hot or cold.

Architecture Teachers, Postsecondary

- ◉ Education/Training Required: Master's degree
- ◉ Annual Earnings: $60,400
- ◉ Growth: 38.1%
- ◉ Annual Job Openings: 216,000
- ◉ Self-Employed: 0.3%
- ◉ Part-Time: 27.7%

The job openings listed here are shared with all other postsecondary teaching occupations.

Age Bracket	Percentage of Workers
45–54 Years Old	22.8%
55–64 Years Old	19.0%
65 or Older	5.5%

Teach courses in architecture and architectural design, such as architectural environmental design, interior architecture/design, and landscape architecture. Evaluate and grade students' work, including work performed in design studios. Prepare and deliver lectures to undergraduate and/or graduate students on topics such as architectural design methods, aesthetics and design, and structures and materials. Prepare course materials such as syllabi, homework assignments, and handouts. Initiate, facilitate, and moderate classroom discussions. Plan, evaluate, and revise curricula, course content, and course materials and methods of instruction. Keep abreast of developments in their field by reading current literature, talking with colleagues, and participating in professional conferences. Maintain student attendance records, grades, and other required records. Maintain regularly scheduled office hours in order to advise and assist students. Compile, administer, and grade examinations or assign this work to others. Conduct research in a particular field of knowledge and publish findings in professional journals, books, and/or electronic media. Supervise undergraduate and/or graduate teaching, internship, and research work. Advise students on academic and vocational curricula and on career issues. Collaborate with colleagues to address teaching and research issues. Compile bibliographies of specialized materials for outside reading assignments. Serve on academic or administrative committees that deal with institutional policies, departmental matters, and academic issues. Participate in student recruitment, registration, and placement activities. Select and obtain materials and supplies such as textbooks and laboratory equipment. Write grant proposals to procure external research funding. Provide professional consulting services to government and/or industry. Perform administrative duties such as serving as department head. **SKILLS—** Instructing; Technology Design; Writing; Learning Strategies; Active Learning; Critical Thinking; Operations Analysis; Persuasion.

GOE—Interest Area: 05. Education and Training. **Work Group:** 05.03. Postsecondary and Adult Teaching and Instructing. **Other Jobs in This Work Group:** Adult Literacy, Remedial Education, and GED Teachers and Instructors; Agricultural Sciences Teachers, Postsecondary; Anthropology and Archeology Teachers, Postsecondary; Area, Ethnic, and Cultural Studies Teachers, Postsecondary; Art, Drama, and Music Teachers, Postsecondary; Atmospheric, Earth, Marine, and Space Sciences Teachers, Postsecondary; Biological Science Teachers, Postsecondary; Business Teachers, Postsecondary; Chemistry Teachers, Postsecondary; Communications Teachers, Postsecondary; Computer Science Teachers, Postsecondary; Criminal Justice and Law

Enforcement Teachers, Postsecondary; Economics Teachers, Postsecondary; Education Teachers, Postsecondary; Engineering Teachers, Postsecondary; English Language and Literature Teachers, Postsecondary; Environmental Science Teachers, Postsecondary; Farm and Home Management Advisors; Foreign Language and Literature Teachers, Postsecondary; Forestry and Conservation Science Teachers, Postsecondary; Geography Teachers, Postsecondary; Graduate Teaching Assistants; Health Specialties Teachers, Postsecondary; History Teachers, Postsecondary; Home Economics Teachers, Postsecondary; Law Teachers, Postsecondary; Library Science Teachers, Postsecondary; Mathematical Science Teachers, Postsecondary; Nursing Instructors and Teachers, Postsecondary; Philosophy and Religion Teachers, Postsecondary; Physics Teachers, Postsecondary; Political Science Teachers, Postsecondary; Psychology Teachers, Postsecondary; Recreation and Fitness Studies Teachers, Postsecondary; Self-Enrichment Education Teachers; Social Work Teachers, Postsecondary; Sociology Teachers, Postsecondary; Vocational Education Teachers, Postsecondary. **PERSONALITY TYPE:** No data available.

EDUCATION/TRAINING PROGRAM(S)—

Architectural Engineering; Architecture (BArch, BA/BS, MArch, MA/MS, PhD); City/Urban, Community and Regional Planning; Environmental Design/Architecture; Interior Architecture; Landscape Architecture (BS, BSLA, BLA, MSLA, MLA, PhD); Teacher Education and Professional Development, Specific Subject Areas, Other.

WORK ENVIRONMENT—Physical proximity to others; sitting; extremely bright or inadequate lighting; indoors; sounds, noise levels are distracting or uncomfortable.

Area, Ethnic, and Cultural Studies Teachers, Postsecondary

- Education/Training Required: Master's degree
- Annual Earnings: $55,660
- Growth: 38.1%
- Annual Job Openings: 216,000
- Self-Employed: 0.3%
- Part-Time: 27.7%

The job openings listed here are shared with all other postsecondary teaching occupations.

Age Bracket	Percentage of Workers
45–54 Years Old	22.8%
55–64 Years Old	19.0%
65 or Older	5.5%

Teach courses pertaining to the culture and development of an area (e.g., Latin America), an ethnic group, or any other group (e.g., women's studies, urban affairs). Keep abreast of developments in their field by reading current literature, talking with colleagues, and participating in professional conferences. Conduct research in a particular field of knowledge and publish findings in professional journals, books, and/or electronic media. Evaluate and grade students' class work, assignments, and papers. Prepare course materials such as syllabi, homework assignments, and handouts. Prepare and deliver lectures to undergraduate and/or graduate students on topics such as race and ethnic relations, gender studies, and cross-cultural perspectives. Initiate, facilitate, and moderate classroom discussions. Compile, administer, and grade examinations or assign this work to others. Maintain regularly scheduled office hours in order to advise and assist students. Plan, evaluate, and revise curricula, course content, and course materials and methods of instruction. Maintain student attendance records, grades, and other required records. Advise students on academic and vocational curricula and on career issues. Supervise undergraduate and/or graduate teaching, internship, and research work. Collaborate with colleagues to address teaching and research issues. Select and obtain materials and supplies such as textbooks. Serve on academic or administrative committees that deal with institutional policies, departmental matters, and academic issues. Compile bibliographies of specialized materials for outside reading assignments. Write grant proposals to procure external research funding. Participate in campus and community events. Participate in student recruitment, registration, and placement activities. Act as advisers to student organizations. Incorporate experiential/site visit components into courses. Perform administrative duties such as serving as department head. **SKILLS—**Writing; Instructing; Critical Thinking; Persuasion; Learning Strategies; Active Learning; Social Perceptiveness; Speaking.

GOE—Interest Area: 05. Education and Training. **Work Group:** 05.03. Postsecondary and Adult Teaching and Instructing. **Other Jobs in This Work Group:** Adult Literacy, Remedial Education, and GED Teachers and Instructors; Agricultural Sciences Teachers, Postsecondary; Anthropology and Archeology Teachers, Postsecondary; Architecture Teachers, Postsecondary; Art, Drama, and Music Teachers, Postsecondary; Atmospheric, Earth, Marine, and Space Sciences Teachers, Postsecondary; Biological Science Teachers, Postsecondary; Business Teachers, Postsecondary; Chemistry

Teachers, Postsecondary; Communications Teachers, Postsecondary; Computer Science Teachers, Postsecondary; Criminal Justice and Law Enforcement Teachers, Postsecondary; Economics Teachers, Postsecondary; Education Teachers, Postsecondary; Engineering Teachers, Postsecondary; English Language and Literature Teachers, Postsecondary; Environmental Science Teachers, Postsecondary; Farm and Home Management Advisors; Foreign Language and Literature Teachers, Postsecondary; Forestry and Conservation Science Teachers, Postsecondary; Geography Teachers, Postsecondary; Graduate Teaching Assistants; Health Specialties Teachers, Postsecondary; History Teachers, Postsecondary; Home Economics Teachers, Postsecondary; Law Teachers, Postsecondary; Library Science Teachers, Postsecondary; Mathematical Science Teachers, Postsecondary; Nursing Instructors and Teachers, Postsecondary; Philosophy and Religion Teachers, Postsecondary; Physics Teachers, Postsecondary; Political Science Teachers, Postsecondary; Psychology Teachers, Postsecondary; Recreation and Fitness Studies Teachers, Postsecondary; Self-Enrichment Education Teachers; Social Work Teachers, Postsecondary; Sociology Teachers, Postsecondary; Vocational Education Teachers, Postsecondary. **PERSONALITY TYPE:** Social. Social occupations frequently involve working with, communicating with, and teaching people. These occupations often involve helping or providing service to others.

EDUCATION/TRAINING PROGRAM(S)—African Studies; African-American/Black Studies; American Indian/Native American Studies; American/United States Studies/Civilization; Area Studies, Other; Area, Ethnic, Cultural, and Gender Studies, Other; Asian Studies/Civilization; Asian-American Studies; Balkans Studies; Baltic Studies; Canadian

Studies; Caribbean Studies; Central/Middle and Eastern European Studies; Chinese Studies; Commonwealth Studies; East Asian Studies; Ethnic, Cultural Minority, and Gender Studies, Other; others.

WORK ENVIRONMENT—Sitting; sounds, noise levels are distracting or uncomfortable; indoors; contaminants; extremely bright or inadequate lighting.

Art Directors

- Education/Training Required: Work experience plus degree
- Annual Earnings: $63,750
- Growth: 11.4%
- Annual Job Openings: 8,000
- Self-Employed: 53.6%
- Part-Time: 23.1%

Age Bracket	Percentage of Workers
45–54 Years Old	25.5%
55–64 Years Old	17.0%
65 or Older	5.7%

Formulate design concepts and presentation approaches and direct workers engaged in artwork, layout design, and copy writing for visual communications media, such as magazines, books, newspapers, and packaging. Formulate basic layout design or presentation approach and specify material details, such as style and size of type, photographs, graphics, animation, video, and sound. Review and approve proofs of printed copy and art and copy materials developed by staff members. Manage own accounts and projects, working within budget and scheduling requirements. Confer with creative, art, copy-writing, or production department heads to discuss client requirements and presentation concepts and to coordinate creative activities. Present final layouts to clients for approval. Confer with clients to determine objectives; budget; background information; and presentation approaches, styles, and techniques. Hire, train, and direct staff members who develop design concepts into art layouts or who prepare layouts for printing. Work with creative directors to develop design solutions. Review illustrative material to determine if it conforms to standards and specifications. Attend photo shoots and printing sessions to ensure that the products needed are obtained. Create custom illustrations or other graphic elements. Mark up, paste, and complete layouts and write typography instructions to prepare materials for typesetting or printing. Negotiate with printers and estimators to determine what services will be performed. Conceptualize and help design interfaces for multimedia games, products, and devices. **SKILLS**—Coordination; Negotiation; Persuasion; Service Orientation; Management of Financial Resources; Instructing; Operations Analysis; Time Management.

GOE—Interest Area: 03. Arts and Communication. **Work Group:** 03.01. Managerial Work in Arts and Communication. **Other Jobs in This Work Group:** Agents and Business Managers of Artists, Performers, and Athletes; Producers; Program Directors; Public Relations Managers; Technical Directors/ Managers. **PERSONALITY TYPE:** Artistic. Artistic occupations frequently involve working with forms, designs, and patterns. They often require self-expression, and the work can be done without following a clear set of rules.

EDUCATION/TRAINING PROGRAM(S)— Graphic Design; Intermedia/Multimedia.

WORK ENVIRONMENT—Sitting; sounds, noise levels are distracting or uncomfortable; physical proximity to others; indoors.

Art, Drama, and Music Teachers, Postsecondary

- ◉ Education/Training Required: Master's degree
- ◉ Annual Earnings: $49,740
- ◉ Growth: 38.1%
- ◉ Annual Job Openings: 216,000
- ◉ Self-Employed: 0.3%
- ◉ Part-Time: 27.7%

The job openings listed here are shared with all other postsecondary teaching occupations.

Age Bracket	Percentage of Workers
45–54 Years Old	22.8%
55–64 Years Old	19.0%
65 or Older	5.5%

Teach courses in drama; music; and the arts, including fine and applied art, such as painting and sculpture, or design and crafts. Evaluate and grade students' class work, performances, projects, assignments, and papers. Explain and demonstrate artistic techniques. Prepare students for performances, exams, or assessments. Prepare and deliver lectures to undergraduate and/or graduate students on topics such as acting techniques, fundamentals of music, and art history. Organize performance groups and direct their rehearsals. Prepare course materials such as syllabi, homework assignments, and handouts. Initiate, facilitate, and moderate classroom dis-

cussions. Keep abreast of developments in their field by reading current literature, talking with colleagues, and participating in professional conferences. Advise students on academic and vocational curricula and on career issues. Maintain student attendance records, grades, and other required records. Conduct research in a particular field of knowledge and publish findings in professional journals, books, and/or electronic media. Supervise undergraduate and/or graduate teaching, internship, and research work. Plan, evaluate, and revise curricula, course content, and course materials and methods of instruction. Maintain regularly scheduled office hours in order to advise and assist students. Compile, administer, and grade examinations or assign this work to others. Participate in student recruitment, registration, and placement activities. Select and obtain materials and supplies such as textbooks and performance pieces. Collaborate with colleagues to address teaching and research issues. Serve on academic or administrative committees that deal with institutional policies, departmental matters, and academic issues. Participate in campus and community events. Keep students informed of community events such as plays and concerts. Compile bibliographies of specialized materials for outside reading assignments. Display students' work in schools, galleries, and exhibitions. Perform administrative duties such as serving as department head. **SKILLS**—Instructing; Social Perceptiveness; Learning Strategies; Persuasion; Speaking; Active Listening; Critical Thinking; Active Learning.

GOE—Interest Area: 05. Education and Training. **Work Group:** 05.03. Postsecondary and Adult Teaching and Instructing. **Other Jobs in This Work Group:** Adult Literacy, Remedial Education, and GED Teachers and Instructors; Agricultural Sciences Teachers, Postsecondary;

Anthropology and Archeology Teachers, Postsecondary; Architecture Teachers, Postsecondary; Area, Ethnic, and Cultural Studies Teachers, Postsecondary; Atmospheric, Earth, Marine, and Space Sciences Teachers, Postsecondary; Biological Science Teachers, Postsecondary; Business Teachers, Postsecondary; Chemistry Teachers, Postsecondary; Communications Teachers, Postsecondary; Computer Science Teachers, Postsecondary; Criminal Justice and Law Enforcement Teachers, Postsecondary; Economics Teachers, Postsecondary; Education Teachers, Postsecondary; Engineering Teachers, Postsecondary; English Language and Literature Teachers, Postsecondary; Environmental Science Teachers, Postsecondary; Farm and Home Management Advisors; Foreign Language and Literature Teachers, Postsecondary; Forestry and Conservation Science Teachers, Postsecondary; Geography Teachers, Postsecondary; Graduate Teaching Assistants; Health Specialties Teachers, Postsecondary; History Teachers, Postsecondary; Home Economics Teachers, Postsecondary; Law Teachers, Postsecondary; Library Science Teachers, Postsecondary; Mathematical Science Teachers, Postsecondary; Nursing Instructors and Teachers, Postsecondary; Philosophy and Religion Teachers, Postsecondary; Physics Teachers, Postsecondary; Political Science Teachers, Postsecondary; Psychology Teachers, Postsecondary; Recreation and Fitness Studies Teachers, Postsecondary; Self-Enrichment Education Teachers; Social Work Teachers, Postsecondary; Sociology Teachers, Postsecondary; Vocational Education Teachers, Postsecondary. **PERSONALITY TYPE:** Artistic. Artistic occupations frequently involve working with forms, designs, and patterns. They often require self-expression, and the work can be done without following a clear set of rules.

EDUCATION/TRAINING PROGRAM(S)—
Art History, Criticism, and Conservation; Art/Art Studies, General; Arts Management; Ceramic Arts and Ceramics; Cinematography and Film/Video Production; Commercial Photography; Conducting; Crafts/Craft Design, Folk Art and Artisanry; Dance, General; Design and Applied Arts, Other; Design and Visual Communications, General; Directing and Theatrical Production; Drama and Dramatics/Theatre Arts, General; Dramatic/Theatre Arts and Stagecraft, Other; Fashion/Apparel Design; others.

WORK ENVIRONMENT—Sitting; physical proximity to others; sounds, noise levels are distracting or uncomfortable; indoors; extremely bright or inadequate lighting.

Assessors

- Education/Training Required: Postsecondary vocational training
- Annual Earnings: $43,790
- Growth: 17.6%
- Annual Job Openings: 11,000
- Self-Employed: 34.8%
- Part-Time: 8.9%

The job openings listed here are shared with Appraisers, Real Estate.

Age Bracket	Percentage of Workers
45–54 Years Old	31.1%
55–64 Years Old	15.1%
65 or Older	9.2%

Appraise real and personal property to determine its fair value. May assess taxes in accordance with prescribed schedules. Determine taxability and value of properties, using methods such as field inspection, structural measurement, calculation, sales analysis, market trend studies, and income and expense analysis. Inspect new construction and major improvements to existing structures in order to determine values. Explain assessed values to property owners and defend appealed assessments at public hearings. Inspect properties, considering factors such as market value, location, and building or replacement costs to determine appraisal value. Prepare and maintain current data on each parcel assessed, including maps of boundaries, inventories of land and structures, property characteristics, and any applicable exemptions. Identify the ownership of each piece of taxable property. Conduct regular reviews of property within jurisdictions in order to determine changes in property due to construction or demolition. Complete and maintain assessment rolls that show the assessed values and status of all property in a municipality. Issue notices of assessments and taxes. Review information about transfers of property to ensure its accuracy, checking basic information on buyers, sellers, and sales prices and making corrections as necessary. Maintain familiarity with aspects of local real estate markets. Analyze trends in sales prices, construction costs, and rents in order to assess property values and/or determine the accuracy of assessments. Approve applications for property tax exemptions or deductions. Establish uniform and equitable systems for assessing all classes and kinds of property. Write and submit appraisal and tax reports for public record. Serve on assessment review boards. Hire staff members. Provide sales analyses to be used for equalization of school aid. Calculate tax bills for properties by multiplying assessed values by jurisdiction tax rates. **SKILLS**—Social Perceptiveness; Persuasion; Negotiation; Mathematics; Active Listening; Speaking; Service Orientation; Instructing.

GOE—Interest Area: 06. Finance and Insurance. **Work Group:** 06.02. Finance/Insurance Investigation and Analysis. **Other Jobs in This Work Group:** Appraisers, Real Estate; Claims Examiners, Property and Casualty Insurance; Cost Estimators; Credit Analysts; Financial Analysts; Insurance Adjusters, Examiners, and Investigators; Insurance Appraisers, Auto Damage; Insurance Underwriters; Loan Counselors; Loan Officers; Market Research Analysts; Survey Researchers. **PERSONALITY TYPE:** Conventional. Conventional occupations frequently involve following set procedures and routines. These occupations can include working with data and details more than with ideas. Usually there is a clear line of authority to follow.

EDUCATION/TRAINING PROGRAM(S)— Real Estate.

WORK ENVIRONMENT—In an enclosed vehicle or equipment; outdoors; very hot or cold; physical proximity to others; sitting.

Atmospheric, Earth, Marine, and Space Sciences Teachers, Postsecondary

- Education/Training Required: Master's degree
- Annual Earnings: $65,250
- Growth: 38.1%
- Annual Job Openings: 216,000
- Self-Employed: 0.3%
- Part-Time: 27.7%

The job openings listed here are shared with all other postsecondary teaching occupations.

Age Bracket	Percentage of Workers
45–54 Years Old	22.8%
55–64 Years Old	19.0%
65 or Older	5.5%

Teach courses in the physical sciences, except chemistry and physics. Conduct research in a particular field of knowledge and publish findings in professional journals, books, and/or electronic media. Write grant proposals to procure external research funding. Keep abreast of developments in their field by reading current literature, talking with colleagues, and participating in professional conferences. Supervise undergraduate and/or graduate teaching, internship, and research work. Prepare and deliver lectures to undergraduate and/or graduate students on topics such as structural geology, micrometeorology, and atmospheric thermodynamics. Supervise laboratory work and fieldwork. Evaluate and grade students' class work, assignments, and papers. Prepare course materials such as syllabi, homework assignments, and handouts. Collaborate with colleagues to address teaching and research issues. Compile, administer, and grade examinations or assign this work to others. Plan, evaluate, and revise curricula, course content, and course materials and methods of instruction. Initiate, facilitate, and moderate classroom discussions. Maintain regularly scheduled office hours in order to advise and assist students. Advise students on academic and vocational curricula and on career issues. Maintain student attendance records, grades, and other required records. Participate in student recruitment, registration, and placement activities. Perform administrative duties such as serving as department head. Select and obtain materials and supplies such as textbooks and laboratory equipment. Serve on academic or administrative committees that deal with institutional policies, departmental matters, and academic issues. Compile bibliographies of specialized materials for outside reading assignments. **SKILLS**—Science; Instructing; Programming; Active Learning; Management of Financial Resources; Complex Problem Solving; Writing; Mathematics.

GOE—Interest Area: 05. Education and Training. **Work Group:** 05.03. Postsecondary and Adult Teaching and Instructing. **Other Jobs in This Work Group:** Adult Literacy, Remedial Education, and GED Teachers and Instructors; Agricultural Sciences Teachers, Postsecondary; Anthropology and Archeology Teachers, Postsecondary; Architecture Teachers, Postsecondary; Area, Ethnic, and Cultural Studies Teachers, Postsecondary; Art, Drama, and Music Teachers, Postsecondary; Biological Science Teachers, Postsecondary; Business Teachers, Postsecondary; Chemistry Teachers, Postsecondary; Communications Teachers, Postsecondary; Computer Science Teachers, Postsecondary; Criminal Justice and Law Enforcement Teachers, Postsecondary; Economics Teachers, Postsecondary; Education Teachers, Postsecondary; Engineering Teachers, Postsecondary; English Language and Literature Teachers, Postsecondary; Environmental Science Teachers, Postsecondary; Farm and Home Management Advisors; Foreign Language and Literature Teachers, Postsecondary; Forestry and Conservation Science Teachers, Postsecondary; Geography Teachers, Postsecondary; Graduate Teaching Assistants; Health Specialties Teachers, Postsecondary; History Teachers, Postsecondary; Home Economics Teachers, Postsecondary; Law Teachers, Postsecondary; Library Science Teachers, Postsecondary; Mathematical Science Teachers, Postsecondary; Nursing Instructors and Teachers, Postsecondary; Philosophy and Religion Teachers, Postsecondary; Physics

Teachers, Postsecondary; Political Science Teachers, Postsecondary; Psychology Teachers, Postsecondary; Recreation and Fitness Studies Teachers, Postsecondary; Self-Enrichment Education Teachers; Social Work Teachers, Postsecondary; Sociology Teachers, Postsecondary; Vocational Education Teachers, Postsecondary. **PERSONALITY TYPE:** No data available.

EDUCATION/TRAINING PROGRAM(S)— Acoustics; Astronomy; Astrophysics; Atmospheric Chemistry and Climatology; Atmospheric Physics and Dynamics; Atmospheric Sciences and Meteorology, General; Atmospheric Sciences and Meteorology, Other; Atomic/Molecular Physics; Elementary Particle Physics; Geochemistry; Geochemistry and Petrology; Geological and Earth Sciences/Geosciences, Other; Geology/Earth Science, General; Geophysics and Seismology; Hydrology and Water Resources Science; Meteorology; Nuclear Physics; others.

WORK ENVIRONMENT—Sitting; indoors; sounds, noise levels are distracting or uncomfortable; very hot or cold; extremely bright or inadequate lighting.

Audiologists

- ◎ Education/Training Required: Master's degree
- ◎ Annual Earnings: $53,040
- ◎ Growth: 29.0%
- ◎ Annual Job Openings: 1,000
- ◎ Self-Employed: 7.1%
- ◎ Part-Time: 22.7%

Age Bracket	Percentage of Workers
45–54 Years Old	23.1%
55–64 Years Old	23.1%
65 or Older	close to 0%

Assess and treat persons with hearing and related disorders. May fit hearing aids and provide auditory training. May perform research related to hearing problems. Educate and supervise audiology students and health care personnel. Fit and tune cochlear implants, providing rehabilitation for adjustment to listening with implant amplification systems. Instruct clients, parents, teachers, or employers in how to avoid behavior patterns that lead to miscommunication. Participate in conferences or training to update or share knowledge of new hearing or speech disorder treatment methods or technologies. Measure noise levels in workplaces and conduct hearing protection programs in industry, schools, and communities. Work with multi-disciplinary teams to assess and rehabilitate recipients of implanted hearing devices. Administer hearing or speech/language evaluations, tests, or examinations to patients to collect information on type and degree of impairment, using specialized instruments and electronic equipment. Counsel and instruct clients in techniques to improve hearing or speech impairment, including sign language or lip-reading. Evaluate hearing and speech/language disorders to determine diagnoses and courses of treatment. Examine and clean patients' ear canals. Fit and dispense assistive devices, such as hearing aids. Maintain client records at all stages, including initial evaluation and discharge. Monitor clients' progress and discharge them from treatment when goals have been attained. Plan and conduct treatment programs for clients' hearing or speech problems, consulting with physicians, nurses, psychologists, and other health care personnel as necessary. Recommend assistive devices according to clients' needs or nature of impairments. Refer clients to additional medical or educational services if needed. Advise educators or other medical staff on speech or hearing topics. Conduct or direct research on hearing or speech topics and report findings to help in the development of procedures, technology, or treatments. Develop and supervise hearing screening programs. **SKILLS**—Instructing; Management of Personnel Resources; Writing; Management of Financial Resources; Learning Strategies; Speaking; Service Orientation; Reading Comprehension; Social Perceptiveness; Technology Design.

GOE—Interest Area: 08. Health Science. **Work Group:** 08.07. Medical Therapy. **Other Jobs in This Work Group:** Massage Therapists; Occupational Therapist Aides; Occupational Therapist Assistants; Occupational Therapists; Physical Therapist Aides; Physical Therapist Assistants; Physical Therapists; Radiation Therapists; Recreational Therapists; Respiratory Therapists; Respiratory Therapy Technicians; Speech-Language Pathologists. **PERSONALITY TYPE:** Social. Social occupations frequently involve working with, communicating with, and teaching people. These occupations often involve helping or providing service to others.

EDUCATION/TRAINING PROGRAM(S)— Audiology/Audiologist and Hearing Sciences; Audiology/Audiologist and Speech-Language Pathology/Pathologist; Communication Disorders Sciences and Services, Other; Communication Disorders, General.

WORK ENVIRONMENT—Sitting; indoors.

Aviation Inspectors

- Education/Training Required: Work experience in a related occupation
- Annual Earnings: $47,920
- Growth: 7.7%
- Annual Job Openings: 5,000
- Self-Employed: 0.4%
- Part-Time: 3.2%

The job openings listed here are shared with Freight Inspectors, Marine Cargo Inspectors, Motor Vehicle Inspectors, Public Transportation Inspectors, and Railroad Inspectors.

Age Bracket	Percentage of Workers
45–54 Years Old	54.3%
55–64 Years Old	15.2%
65 or Older	2.2%

Inspect aircraft, maintenance procedures, air navigational aids, air traffic controls, and communications equipment to ensure conformance with federal safety regulations. Analyze training programs and conduct oral and written examinations to ensure the competency of persons operating, installing, and repairing aircraft equipment. Approve or deny issuance of certificates of airworthiness. Conduct flight test programs to test equipment, instruments, and systems under a variety of conditions, using both manual and automatic controls. Examine landing gear, tires, and exteriors of fuselage, wings, and engines for evidence of damage or corrosion and to determine whether repairs are needed. Examine maintenance records and flight logs to determine if service and maintenance checks and overhauls were performed at prescribed intervals. Inspect new, repaired, or modified aircraft to identify damage or defects and to assess airworthiness and conformance to standards, using checklists, hand tools, and test instruments. Inspect work of aircraft mechanics performing maintenance, modification, or repair and overhaul of aircraft and aircraft mechanical systems in order to ensure adherence to standards and procedures. Prepare and maintain detailed repair, inspection, investigation, and certification records and reports. Recommend replacement, repair, or modification of aircraft equipment. Start aircraft and observe gauges, meters, and other instruments to detect evidence of malfunctions. Examine aircraft access plates and doors for security. Investigate air accidents and complaints to determine causes. Issue pilots' licenses to individuals meeting standards. Observe flight activities of pilots to assess flying skills and to ensure conformance to flight and safety regulations. Recommend changes in rules, policies, standards, and regulations based on knowledge of operating conditions, aircraft improvements, and other factors. Schedule and coordinate in-flight testing programs with ground crews and air traffic control to ensure availability of ground tracking, equipment monitoring, and related services. **SKILLS**—Operation Monitoring; Quality Control Analysis; Science; Systems Analysis; Systems Evaluation; Writing; Critical Thinking; Reading Comprehension; Troubleshooting.

GOE—Interest Area: 07. Government and Public Administration. **Work Group:** 07.03. Regulations Enforcement. **Other Jobs in This Work Group:** Agricultural Inspectors; Child Support, Missing Persons, and Unemployment Insurance Fraud Investigators; Environmental Compliance Inspectors; Equal Opportunity Representatives and Officers; Financial Examiners; Fire Inspectors; Fish and Game Wardens; Forest Fire Inspectors and Prevention Specialists; Government Property Inspectors and Investigators; Immigration and Customs

Inspectors; Licensing Examiners and Inspectors; Marine Cargo Inspectors; Mechanical Inspectors; Motor Vehicle Inspectors; Nuclear Monitoring Technicians; Occupational Health and Safety Specialists; Pressure Vessel Inspectors; Railroad Inspectors; Tax Examiners, Collectors, and Revenue Agents. **PERSONALITY TYPE:** Realistic. Realistic occupations frequently involve work activities that include practical, hands-on problems and solutions. They often deal with plants, animals, and real-world materials like wood, tools, and machinery. Many of the occupations require working outside and do not involve a lot of paperwork or working closely with others.

EDUCATION/TRAINING PROGRAM(S)— No data available.

WORK ENVIRONMENT—Outdoors; sounds, noise levels are distracting or uncomfortable; standing; hazardous equipment; walking and running.

Biological Science Teachers, Postsecondary

- Education/Training Required: Master's degree
- Annual Earnings: $63,750
- Growth: 38.1%
- Annual Job Openings: 216,000
- Self-Employed: 0.3%
- Part-Time: 27.7%

The job openings listed here are shared with all other postsecondary teaching occupations.

Age Bracket	Percentage of Workers
45–54 Years Old	22.8%
55–64 Years Old	19.0%
65 or Older	5.5%

Teach courses in biological sciences. Prepare and deliver lectures to undergraduate and/or graduate students on topics such as molecular biology, marine biology, and botany. Evaluate and grade students' class work, laboratory work, assignments, and papers. Prepare course materials such as syllabi, homework assignments, and handouts. Compile, administer, and grade examinations or assign this work to others. Supervise students' laboratory work. Keep abreast of developments in their field by reading current literature, talking with colleagues, and participating in professional conferences. Maintain student attendance records, grades, and other required records. Initiate, facilitate, and moderate classroom discussions. Plan, evaluate, and revise curricula, course content, and course materials and methods of instruction. Advise students on academic and vocational curricula and on career issues. Maintain regularly scheduled office hours in order to advise and assist students. Supervise undergraduate and/or graduate teaching, internship, and research work. Select and obtain materials and supplies such as textbooks and laboratory equipment. Collaborate with colleagues to address teaching and research issues. Conduct research in a particular field of knowledge and publish findings in professional journals, books, and/or electronic media. Serve on academic or administrative committees that deal with institutional policies, departmental matters, and academic issues. Participate in student recruitment, registration, and placement activities. Write grant proposals to procure external research funding. Perform administrative duties such as serving as depart-ment head. **SKILLS**—Science; Instructing; Learning Strategies; Writing; Active Learning; Reading Comprehension; Critical Thinking; Speaking.

GOE—Interest Area: 05. Education and Training. **Work Group:** 05.03. Postsecondary and Adult Teaching and Instructing. **Other Jobs in This Work Group:** Adult Literacy, Remedial Education, and GED Teachers and Instructors; Agricultural Sciences Teachers, Postsecondary; Anthropology and Archeology Teachers, Postsecondary; Architecture Teachers, Postsecondary; Area, Ethnic, and Cultural Studies Teachers, Postsecondary; Art, Drama, and Music Teachers, Postsecondary; Atmospheric, Earth, Marine, and Space Sciences Teachers, Postsecondary; Business Teachers, Postsecondary; Chemistry Teachers, Postsecondary; Communications Teachers, Postsecondary; Computer Science Teachers, Postsecondary; Criminal Justice and Law Enforcement Teachers, Postsecondary; Economics Teachers, Postsecondary; Education Teachers, Postsecondary; Engineering Teachers, Postsecondary; English Language and Literature Teachers, Postsecondary; Environmental Science Teachers, Postsecondary; Farm and Home Management Advisors; Foreign Language and Literature Teachers, Postsecondary; Forestry and Conservation Science Teachers, Postsecondary; Geography Teachers, Postsecondary; Graduate Teaching Assistants; Health Specialties Teachers, Postsecondary; History Teachers, Postsecondary; Home Economics Teachers, Postsecondary; Law Teachers, Postsecondary; Library Science Teachers, Postsecondary; Mathematical Science Teachers, Postsecondary; Nursing Instructors and Teachers, Postsecondary; Philosophy and Religion Teachers, Postsecondary; Physics Teachers, Postsecondary; Political Science Teachers, Postsecondary; Psychology Teachers,

Postsecondary; Recreation and Fitness Studies Teachers, Postsecondary; Self-Enrichment Education Teachers; Social Work Teachers, Postsecondary; Sociology Teachers, Postsecondary; Vocational Education Teachers, Postsecondary. **PERSONALITY TYPE:** Investigative. Investigative occupations frequently involve working with ideas and require an extensive amount of thinking. These occupations can involve searching for facts and figuring out problems mentally.

EDUCATION/TRAINING PROGRAM(S)— Anatomy; Animal Physiology; Biochemistry; Biological and Biomedical Sciences, Other; Biology/Biological Sciences, General; Biometry/ Biometrics; Biophysics; Biotechnology; Botany/Plant Biology; Cell/Cellular Biology and Histology; Ecology; Ecology, Evolution, and Systematics, Other; Entomology; Evolutionary Biology; Immunology; Marine Biology and Biological Oceanography; Microbiology, General; Molecular Biology; Neuroscience; Nutrition Sciences; Parasitology; Pathology/ Exper. Pathology; others.

WORK ENVIRONMENT—Contaminants; physical proximity to others; sitting; hazardous conditions; indoors.

Bookkeeping, Accounting, and Auditing Clerks

- Education/Training Required: Moderate-term on-the-job training
- Annual Earnings: $29,040
- Growth: 3.0%
- Annual Job Openings: 274,000
- Self-Employed: 7.9%
- Part-Time: 25.0%

Age Bracket	Percentage of Workers
45–54 Years Old	26.5%
55–64 Years Old	16.6%
65 or Older	6.6%

Compute, classify, and record numerical data to keep financial records complete. Perform any combination of routine calculating, posting, and verifying duties to obtain primary financial data for use in maintaining accounting records. May also check the accuracy of figures, calculations, and postings pertaining to business transactions recorded by other workers. Check figures, postings, and documents for correct entry, mathematical accuracy, and proper codes. Operate computers programmed with accounting software to record, store, and analyze information. Comply with federal, state, and company policies, procedures, and regulations. Debit, credit, and total accounts on computer spreadsheets and databases, using specialized accounting software. Classify, record, and summarize numerical and financial data in order to compile and keep financial records, using journals and ledgers or computers. Calculate, prepare, and issue bills, invoices, account statements, and other financial statements according to established procedures. Compile statistical, financial, accounting, or auditing reports and tables pertaining to such matters as cash receipts, expenditures, accounts payable and receivable, and profits and losses. Code documents according to company procedures. Access computerized financial information to answer general questions as well as those related to specific accounts. Operate 10-key calculators, typewriters, and copy machines to perform calculations and produce documents. Reconcile or note and report discrepancies found in records. Perform financial calculations such as amounts due, interest charges, balances, discounts, equity, and principal. Perform general office duties such as filing, answering telephones, and handling routine correspondence. Prepare bank deposits by compiling data from cashiers; verifying and balancing receipts; and sending cash, checks, or other forms of payment to banks. Receive, record, and bank cash, checks, and vouchers. Calculate and prepare checks for utilities, taxes, and other payments. Compare computer printouts to manually maintained journals in order to determine if they match. Reconcile records of bank transactions. Prepare trial balances of books. Monitor status of loans and accounts to ensure that payments are up to date. Transfer details from separate journals to general ledgers and/or data processing sheets. Compile budget data and documents, based on estimated revenues and expenses and previous budgets. **SKILLS**—Management of Financial Resources; Time Management; Instructing; Negotiation; Active Learning; Critical Thinking; Mathematics; Learning Strategies.

GOE—**Interest Area:** 04. Business and Administration. **Work Group:** 04.06. Mathematical Clerical Support. **Other Jobs in This Work Group:** Billing, Cost, and Rate Clerks; Brokerage Clerks; Payroll and Timekeeping Clerks; Statement Clerks; Tax Preparers. **PERSONALITY TYPE:** Conventional. Conventional occupations frequently involve following set procedures and routines. These occupations can include working with data and details more than with ideas. Usually there is a clear line of authority to follow.

EDUCATION/TRAINING PROGRAM(S)— Accounting and Related Services, Other; Accounting Technology/Technician and Bookkeeping.

WORK ENVIRONMENT—Sitting; physical proximity to others; sounds, noise levels are distracting or uncomfortable; contaminants.

Budget Analysts

- Education/Training Required: Bachelor's degree
- Annual Earnings: $57,190
- Growth: 14.0%
- Annual Job Openings: 8,000
- Self-Employed: 0%
- Part-Time: 4.7%

Age Bracket	Percentage of Workers
45–54 Years Old	32.1%
55–64 Years Old	14.3%
65 or Older	less than 1.3%

Examine budget estimates for completeness, accuracy, and conformance with procedures and regulations. Analyze budgeting and accounting reports for the purpose of maintaining expenditure controls. Analyze monthly department budgeting and accounting reports to maintain expenditure controls. Direct the preparation of regular and special budget reports. Consult with managers to ensure that budget adjustments are made in accordance with program changes. Match appropriations for specific programs with appropriations for broader programs, including items for emergency funds. Provide advice and technical assistance with cost analysis, fiscal allocation, and budget preparation. Summarize budgets and submit recommendations for the approval or disapproval of funds requests. Seek new ways to improve efficiency and increase profits. Review operating budgets to analyze trends affecting budget needs. Examine budget estimates for completeness, accuracy, and conformance with procedures and regulations. Perform cost-benefits analyses to compare operating programs, review financial requests, and explore alternative financing methods. Interpret budget directives and establish policies for carrying out directives. Compile and analyze accounting records and other data to determine the financial resources required to implement a program. Testify before examining and fund-granting authorities, clarifying and promoting the proposed budgets. **SKILLS**—Management of Financial Resources; Operations Analysis; Mathematics; Service Orientation; Active Learning; Negotiation; Time Management; Monitoring.

GOE—Interest Area: 04. Business and Administration. **Work Group:** 04.05. Accounting, Auditing, and Analytical Support. **Other Jobs in This Work Group:** Accountants; Auditors; Industrial Engineering Technicians; Logisticians; Management Analysts; Operations Research Analysts. **PERSONALITY TYPE:** Conventional. Conventional occupations frequently involve following set procedures and routines. These occupations can include working with data and details more than with ideas. Usually there is a clear line of authority to follow.

EDUCATION/TRAINING PROGRAM(S)— Accounting; Finance, General.

WORK ENVIRONMENT—Sitting; indoors; physical proximity to others.

Bus and Truck Mechanics and Diesel Engine Specialists

- Education/Training Required: Postsecondary vocational training
- Annual Earnings: $36,150
- Growth: 14.2%
- Annual Job Openings: 28,000
- Self-Employed: 3.9%
- Part-Time: 2.5%

Age Bracket	Percentage of Workers
45–54 Years Old	26.3%
55–64 Years Old	13.3%
65 or Older	2.7%

Diagnose, adjust, repair, or overhaul trucks, buses, and all types of diesel engines. Includes mechanics working primarily with automobile diesel engines. Use hand tools such as screwdrivers, pliers, wrenches, pressure gauges, and precision instruments, as well as power tools such as pneumatic wrenches, lathes, welding equipment, and jacks and hoists. Inspect brake systems, steering mechanisms, wheel bearings, and other important parts to ensure that they are in proper operating condition. Perform routine maintenance such as changing oil, checking batteries, and lubricating equipment and machinery. Adjust and reline brakes, align wheels, tighten bolts and screws, and reassemble equipment. Raise trucks, buses, and heavy parts or equipment, using hydraulic jacks or hoists. Test drive trucks and buses to diagnose malfunctions or to ensure that they are working properly. Inspect, test, and listen to defective equipment to diagnose malfunctions, using test instruments such as handheld computers, motor analyzers, chassis charts, and pressure gauges. Examine and adjust protective guards, loose bolts, and specified safety devices. Inspect and verify dimensions and clearances of parts to ensure conformance to factory specifications. Specialize in repairing and maintaining parts of the engine, such as fuel injection systems. Attach test instruments to equipment and read dials and gauges in order to diagnose malfunctions. Rewire ignition systems, lights, and instrument panels. Recondition and replace parts, pistons, bearings, gears, and valves. Repair and adjust seats, doors, and windows and install and repair accessories. Inspect, repair, and maintain automotive and mechanical equipment and machinery such as pumps and compressors. Disassemble and overhaul internal combustion engines, pumps, generators, transmissions, clutches, and differential units. Rebuild gas and/or diesel engines. Align front ends and suspension systems. **SKILLS**—Equipment Maintenance; Repairing; Troubleshooting; Installation; Learning Strategies; Technology Design; Instructing; Science; Social Perceptiveness; Coordination.

GOE—Interest Area: 13. Manufacturing. **Work Group:** 13.14. Vehicle and Facility Mechanical Work. **Other Jobs in This Work Group:** Aircraft Body and Bonded Structure Repairers; Aircraft Engine Specialists; Aircraft Rigging Assemblers; Aircraft Structure Assemblers, Precision; Aircraft Systems Assemblers, Precision; Airframe-and-Power-Plant Mechanics; Automotive Body and Related Repairers; Automotive Glass Installers and Repairers; Automotive Master Mechanics; Automotive Specialty Technicians; Farm Equipment Mechanics; Fiberglass Laminators and Fabricators; Mobile Heavy Equipment Mechanics, Except Engines; Motorboat Mechanics; Motorcycle Mechanics; Outdoor Power Equipment and Other Small Engine Mechanics; Rail Car Repairers; Recreational Vehicle Service Technicians; Tire Repairers and Changers. **PERSONALITY TYPE:** Realistic. Realistic occupations frequently involve work activities that include practical, hands-on problems and solutions. They often deal with plants, animals, and real-world materials like wood, tools, and machinery. Many of the occupations require working outside and do not involve a lot of paperwork or working closely with others.

EDUCATION/TRAINING PROGRAM(S)—Diesel Mechanics Technology/Technician; Medium/Heavy Vehicle and Truck Technology/Technician.

WORK ENVIRONMENT—Contaminants; extremely bright or inadequate lighting; sounds, noise levels are distracting or uncomfortable; indoors, not environmentally controlled; very hot or cold; hazardous conditions.

Bus Drivers, School

- Education/Training Required: Short-term on-the-job training
- Annual Earnings: $23,670
- Growth: 16.7%
- Annual Job Openings: 76,000
- Self-Employed: 0.7%
- Part-Time: 35.6%

Age Bracket	Percentage of Workers
45–54 Years Old	32.4%
55–64 Years Old	20.1%
65 or Older	9.5%

Transport students or special clients, such as the elderly or persons with disabilities. Ensure adherence to safety rules. May assist passengers in boarding or exiting. Drive gasoline, diesel, or electrically powered multi-passenger vehicles to transport students between neighborhoods, schools, and school activities. Check the condition of a vehicle's tires, brakes, windshield wipers, lights, oil, fuel, water, and safety equipment to ensure that everything is in working order. Comply with traffic regulations in order to operate vehicles in a safe and courteous manner. Follow safety rules as students are boarding and exiting buses and as they cross streets near bus stops. Pick up and drop off students at regularly scheduled neighborhood locations, following strict time schedules. Read maps and follow written and verbal geographic directions. Regulate heating, lighting, and ventilation systems for passenger comfort. Escort small children across roads and highways. Keep bus interiors clean for passengers. Maintain knowledge of first-aid procedures. Maintain order among pupils during trips in order to ensure safety. Make minor repairs to vehicles. Prepare and submit reports that may include the number of passengers or trips, hours worked, mileage, fuel consumption, and/or fares received. Report any bus malfunctions or needed repairs. Report delays, accidents, or other traffic and transportation situations, using telephones or mobile two-way radios. **SKILLS**—Repairing; Operation and Control; Operation Monitoring; Equipment Maintenance.

GOE—Interest Area: 16. Transportation, Distribution, and Logistics. **Work Group:** 16.06. Other Services Requiring Driving. **Other Jobs in This Work Group:** Ambulance Drivers and Attendants, Except Emergency Medical Technicians; Bus Drivers, Transit and Intercity; Couriers and Messengers; Driver/Sales Workers; Parking Lot Attendants; Postal Service Mail Carriers; Taxi Drivers and Chauffeurs. **PERSONALITY TYPE:** Realistic. Realistic occupations frequently involve work activities that include practical, hands-on problems and solutions. They often deal with plants, animals, and real-world materials like wood, tools, and machinery. Many of the occupations require working outside and do not involve a lot of paperwork or working closely with others.

EDUCATION/TRAINING PROGRAM(S)—Truck and Bus Driver/Commercial Vehicle Operation.

WORK ENVIRONMENT—Sitting; sounds, noise levels are distracting or uncomfortable; outdoors; extremely bright or inadequate lighting; spend time making repetitive motions.

Bus Drivers, Transit and Intercity

- Education/Training Required: Moderate-term on-the-job training
- Annual Earnings: $30,670
- Growth: 15.2%
- Annual Job Openings: 33,000
- Self-Employed: 0.7%
- Part-Time: 35.6%

Age Bracket	Percentage of Workers
45–54 Years Old	32.4%
55–64 Years Old	20.1%
65 or Older	9.5%

Drive bus or motor coach, including regular route operations, charters, and private carriage. May assist passengers with baggage. May collect fares or tickets. Inspect vehicles and check gas, oil, and water levels prior to departure. Drive vehicles over specified routes or to specified destinations according to time schedules in order to transport passengers, complying with traffic regulations. Park vehicles at loading areas so that passengers can board. Assist passengers with baggage and collect tickets or cash fares. Report delays or accidents. Advise passengers to be seated and orderly while on vehicles. Regulate heating, lighting, and ventilating systems for passenger comfort. Load and unload baggage in baggage compartments. Record cash receipts and ticket fares. Make minor repairs to vehicle and change tires. **SKILLS**—Social Perceptiveness; Equipment Maintenance; Troubleshooting; Operation and Control; Negotiation; Operation Monitoring; Instructing; Service Orientation.

GOE—Interest Area: 16. Transportation, Distribution, and Logistics. **Work Group:** 16.06. Other Services Requiring Driving. **Other Jobs in This Work Group:** Ambulance Drivers and Attendants, Except Emergency Medical Technicians; Bus Drivers, School; Couriers and Messengers; Driver/Sales Workers; Parking Lot Attendants; Postal Service Mail Carriers; Taxi Drivers and Chauffeurs. **PERSONALITY TYPE:** Realistic. Realistic occupations frequently involve work activities that include practical, hands-on problems and solutions. They often deal with plants, animals, and real-world materials like wood, tools, and machinery. Many of the occupations require working outside and do not involve a lot of paperwork or working closely with others.

EDUCATION/TRAINING PROGRAM(S)—Truck and Bus Driver/Commercial Vehicle Operation.

WORK ENVIRONMENT—In an enclosed vehicle or equipment; sounds, noise levels are distracting or uncomfortable; contaminants; sitting; physical proximity to others.

Business Teachers, Postsecondary

- Education/Training Required: Master's degree
- Annual Earnings: $58,230
- Growth: 38.1%
- Annual Job Openings: 216,000
- Self-Employed: 0.3%
- Part-Time: 27.7%

The job openings listed here are shared with all other postsecondary teaching occupations.

Age Bracket	Percentage of Workers
45–54 Years Old	22.8%
55–64 Years Old	19.0%
65 or Older	5.5%

Teach courses in business administration and management, such as accounting, finance, human resources, labor relations, marketing, and operations research. Prepare and deliver lectures to undergraduate and/or graduate students on topics such as financial accounting, principles of marketing, and operations management.

Evaluate and grade students' class work, assignments, and papers. Compile, administer, and grade examinations or assign this work to others. Prepare course materials such as syllabi, homework assignments, and handouts. Maintain student attendance records, grades, and other required records. Initiate, facilitate, and moderate classroom discussions. Plan, evaluate, and revise curricula, course content, and course materials and methods of instruction. Maintain regularly scheduled office hours in order to advise and assist students. Keep abreast of developments in their field by reading current literature, talking with colleagues, and participating in professional organizations and conferences. Advise students on academic and vocational curricula and on career issues. Select and obtain materials and supplies such as textbooks. Collaborate with colleagues to address teaching and research issues. Collaborate with members of the business community to improve programs, to develop new programs, and to provide student access to learning opportunities such as internships. Participate in student recruitment, registration, and placement activities. Serve on academic or administrative committees that deal with institutional policies, departmental matters, and academic issues. Participate in campus and community events. Compile bibliographies of specialized materials for outside reading assignments. Perform administrative duties such as serving as department head. Supervise undergraduate and/or graduate teaching, internship, and research work. Conduct research in a particular field of knowledge and publish findings in professional journals, books, and/or electronic media. Act as advisers to student organizations. **SKILLS**—Instructing; Learning Strategies; Writing; Active Learning; Monitoring; Social Perceptiveness; Persuasion; Time Management.

GOE—Interest Area: 05. Education and Training. **Work Group:** 05.03. Postsecondary and Adult Teaching and Instructing. **Other Jobs in This Work Group:** Adult Literacy, Remedial Education, and GED Teachers and Instructors; Agricultural Sciences Teachers, Postsecondary; Anthropology and Archeology Teachers, Postsecondary; Architecture Teachers, Postsecondary; Area, Ethnic, and Cultural Studies Teachers, Postsecondary; Art, Drama, and Music Teachers, Postsecondary; Atmospheric, Earth, Marine, and Space Sciences Teachers, Postsecondary; Biological Science Teachers, Postsecondary; Chemistry Teachers, Postsecondary; Communications Teachers, Postsecondary; Computer Science Teachers, Postsecondary; Criminal Justice and Law Enforcement Teachers, Postsecondary; Economics Teachers, Postsecondary; Education Teachers, Postsecondary; Engineering Teachers, Postsecondary; English Language and Literature Teachers, Postsecondary; Environmental Science Teachers, Postsecondary; Farm and Home Management Advisors; Foreign Language and Literature Teachers, Postsecondary; Forestry and Conservation Science Teachers, Postsecondary; Geography Teachers, Postsecondary; Graduate Teaching Assistants; Health Specialties Teachers, Postsecondary; History Teachers, Postsecondary; Home Economics Teachers, Postsecondary; Law Teachers, Postsecondary; Library Science Teachers, Postsecondary; Mathematical Science Teachers, Postsecondary; Nursing Instructors and Teachers, Postsecondary; Philosophy and Religion Teachers, Postsecondary; Physics Teachers, Postsecondary; Political Science Teachers, Postsecondary; Psychology Teachers, Postsecondary; Recreation and Fitness Studies Teachers, Postsecondary; Self-Enrichment Education Teachers; Social Work Teachers, Postsecondary; Sociology Teachers, Postsecondary; Vocational Education Teachers,

Postsecondary. **PERSONALITY TYPE:** No data available.

EDUCATION/TRAINING PROGRAM(S)— Accounting; Actuarial Science; Business Administration/Management; Business Statistics; Business Teacher Education; Business/Commerce, General; Business/Corporate Communications; Entrepreneurship/Entrepreneurial Studies; Finance, General; Financial Planning and Services; Franchising and Franchise Operations; Human Resources Management/Personnel Administration, General; Insurance; International Business/Trade/Commerce; International Finance; International Marketing; Investments and Securities; others.

WORK ENVIRONMENT—Sitting; indoors; physical proximity to others; sounds, noise levels are distracting or uncomfortable.

Caption Writers

- Education/Training Required: Moderate-term on-the-job training
- Annual Earnings: $45,460
- Growth: 16.1%
- Annual Job Openings: 23,000
- Self-Employed: 67.9%
- Part-Time: 24.2%

The job openings listed here are shared with Copy Writers, Creative Writers, and Poets and Lyricists.

Age Bracket	Percentage of Workers
45–54 Years Old	24.7%
55–64 Years Old	16.3%
65 or Older	7.4%

Write caption phrases of dialogue for hearing-impaired and foreign language–speaking viewers of movie or television productions. Writes captions to describe music and background noises. Watches production and reviews captions simultaneously to determine which caption phrases require editing. Enters commands to synchronize captions with dialogue and place on the screen. Translates foreign-language dialogue into English-language captions or English-dialogue into foreign-language captions. Operates computerized captioning system for movies or television productions for hearing-impaired and foreign language–speaking viewers. Oversees encoding of captions to master tape of television production. Discusses captions with directors or producers of movie and television productions. Edits translations for correctness of grammar, punctuation, and clarity of expression. **SKILLS**—Writing; Reading Comprehension; Operation and Control.

GOE—Interest Area: 03. Arts and Communication. **Work Group:** 03.03. News, Broadcasting, and Public Relations. **Other Jobs in This Work Group:** Broadcast News Analysts; Interpreters and Translators; Public Relations Specialists; Reporters and Correspondents. **PERSONALITY TYPE:** Artistic. Artistic occupations frequently involve working with forms, designs, and patterns. They often require self-expression, and the work can be done without following a clear set of rules.

EDUCATION/TRAINING PROGRAM(S)— Communications Studies/Speech Communication and Rhetoric; English Composition; Journalism; Mass Communications/Media Studies.

WORK ENVIRONMENT—Sitting; indoors; spend time making repetitive motions; extremely bright or inadequate lighting.

Cartoonists

- Education/Training Required: Long-term on-the-job training
- Annual Earnings: $41,240
- Growth: 16.5%
- Annual Job Openings: 4,000
- Self-Employed: 55.5%
- Part-Time: 23.1%

The job openings listed here are shared with Painters and Illustrators, Sculptors, and Sketch Artists.

Age Bracket	Percentage of Workers
45–54 Years Old	25.5%
55–64 Years Old	17.0%
65 or Older	5.7%

Create original artwork by using any of a wide variety of mediums and techniques, such as painting and sculpture. Sketches and submits cartoon or animation for approval. Develops personal ideas for cartoons, comic strips, or animations or reads written material to develop ideas. Makes changes and corrections to cartoon, comic strip, or animation as necessary. Creates and prepares sketches and model drawings of characters, providing details from memory, live models, manufactured products, or reference material. Renders sequential drawings of characters or other subject material that, when photographed and projected at specific speed, becomes animated. Develops color patterns and moods and paints background layouts to dramatize action for animated cartoon scenes. Discusses ideas for cartoons, comic strips, or animations with editor or publisher's representative. Labels each section with designated colors when colors are used. **SKILLS**—Operations Analysis.

GOE—Interest Area: 03. Arts and Communication. **Work Group:** 03.04. Studio Art. **Other Jobs in This Work Group:** Craft Artists; Painters and Illustrators; Potters; Sculptors; Sketch Artists. **PERSONALITY TYPE:** Artistic. Artistic occupations frequently involve working with forms, designs, and patterns. They often require self-expression, and the work can be done without following a clear set of rules.

EDUCATION/TRAINING PROGRAM(S)— Art/Art Studies, General; Drawing.

WORK ENVIRONMENT—Sitting; indoors; spend time making repetitive motions; spend time bending or twisting the body.

Central Office and PBX Installers and Repairers

- Education/Training Required: Long-term on-the-job training
- Annual Earnings: $50,270
- Growth: –0.6%
- Annual Job Openings: 23,000
- Self-Employed: 4.6%
- Part-Time: 1.7%

The job openings listed here are shared with Communication Equipment Mechanics, Installers, and Repairers; Frame Wirers, Central Office; Station Installers and Repairers, Telephone; and Telecommunications Facility Examiners.

Age Bracket	Percentage of Workers
45–54 Years Old	29.5%
55–64 Years Old	9.6%
65 or Older	1.2%

Test, analyze, and repair telephone or telegraph circuits and equipment at a central office location, using test meters and hand tools. Analyze and repair defects in communications equipment on customers' premises, using circuit diagrams, polarity probes, meters, and a telephone test set. May install equipment. Tests circuits and components of malfunctioning telecommunication equipment to isolate source of malfunction, using test instruments and circuit diagrams. Analyzes test readings, computer printouts, and trouble reports to determine method of repair. Tests and adjusts installed equipment to ensure circuit continuity and operational performance, using test instruments. Connects wires to equipment, using hand tools, soldering iron, or wire wrap gun. Installs preassembled or partially assembled switching equipment, switchboards, wiring frames, and power apparatus according to floor plans. Retests repaired equipment to ensure that malfunction has been corrected. Repairs or replaces defective components, such as switches, relays, amplifiers, and circuit boards, using hand tools and soldering iron. Removes and remakes connections on wire distributing frame to change circuit layout, following diagrams. Routes cables and trunklines from entry points to specified equipment, following diagrams. Enters codes to correct programming of electronic switching systems. **SKILLS**—Repairing; Installation; Troubleshooting; Technology Design; Operation Monitoring; Science; Equipment Maintenance; Quality Control Analysis.

GOE—Interest Area: 02. Architecture and Construction. **Work Group:** 02.05. Systems and Equipment Installation, Maintenance, and Repair. **Other Jobs in This Work Group:** Communication Equipment Mechanics, Installers, and Repairers; Electric Meter Installers and Repairers; Electrical and Electronics Repairers, Powerhouse, Substation, and Relay; Electrical Power-Line Installers and Repairers; Elevator Installers and Repairers;

Frame Wirers, Central Office; Heating and Air Conditioning Mechanics; Home Appliance Installers; Maintenance and Repair Workers, General; Meter Mechanics; Refrigeration Mechanics; Station Installers and Repairers, Telephone; Telecommunications Facility Examiners; Telecommunications Line Installers and Repairers. **PERSONALITY TYPE:** Realistic. Realistic occupations frequently involve work activities that include practical, hands-on problems and solutions. They often deal with plants, animals, and real-world materials like wood, tools, and machinery. Many of the occupations require working outside and do not involve a lot of paperwork or working closely with others.

EDUCATION/TRAINING PROGRAM(S)— Communications Systems Installation and Repair Technology.

WORK ENVIRONMENT—Sitting; standing; hazardous equipment; spend time kneeling, crouching, stooping, or crawling; hazardous conditions.

Chemistry Teachers, Postsecondary

- Education/Training Required: Master's degree
- Annual Earnings: $57,340
- Growth: 38.1%
- Annual Job Openings: 216,000
- Self-Employed: 0.3%
- Part-Time: 27.7%

The job openings listed here are shared with all other postsecondary teaching occupations.

Age Bracket	Percentage of Workers
45–54 Years Old	22.8%
55–64 Years Old	19.0%
65 or Older	5.5%

Teach courses pertaining to the chemical and physical properties and compositional changes of substances. Work may include instruction in the methods of qualitative and quantitative chemical analysis. Includes both teachers primarily engaged in teaching and those who do a combination of both teaching and research. Prepare and deliver lectures to undergraduate and/or graduate students on topics such as organic chemistry, analytical chemistry, and chemical separation. Supervise students' laboratory work. Evaluate and grade students' class work, laboratory performance, assignments, and papers. Compile, administer, and grade examinations or assign this work to others. Maintain student attendance records, grades, and other required records. Prepare course materials such as syllabi, homework assignments, and handouts. Maintain regularly scheduled office hours in order to advise and assist students. Plan, evaluate, and revise curricula, course content, and course materials and methods of instruction. Supervise undergraduate and/or graduate teaching, internship, and research work. Keep abreast of developments in their field by reading current literature, talking with colleagues, and participating in professional conferences. Initiate, facilitate, and moderate classroom discussions. Select and obtain materials and supplies such as textbooks and laboratory equipment. Conduct research in a particular field of knowledge and publish findings in professional journals, books, and/or electronic media. Advise students on academic and vocational curricula and on career issues. Collaborate with colleagues to address teaching and research issues. Serve on academic or administrative committees that deal with institutional policies, departmental matters, and academic issues. Write grant proposals to procure external research funding. Participate in student recruitment, registration, and placement activities. Prepare and submit required reports related to instruction. Perform administrative duties such as serving as a department head. **SKILLS**—Science; Instructing; Active Learning; Learning Strategies; Mathematics; Reading Comprehension; Writing; Critical Thinking.

GOE—Interest Area: 05. Education and Training. **Work Group:** 05.03. Postsecondary and Adult Teaching and Instructing. **Other Jobs in This Work Group:** Adult Literacy, Remedial Education, and GED Teachers and Instructors; Agricultural Sciences Teachers, Postsecondary; Anthropology and Archeology Teachers, Postsecondary; Architecture Teachers, Postsecondary; Area, Ethnic, and Cultural Studies Teachers, Postsecondary; Art, Drama, and Music Teachers, Postsecondary; Atmospheric, Earth, Marine, and Space Sciences Teachers, Postsecondary; Biological Science Teachers, Postsecondary; Business Teachers, Postsecondary; Communications Teachers, Postsecondary; Computer Science Teachers, Postsecondary; Criminal Justice and Law Enforcement Teachers, Postsecondary; Economics Teachers, Postsecondary; Education Teachers, Postsecondary; Engineering Teachers, Postsecondary; English Language and Literature Teachers, Postsecondary; Environmental Science Teachers, Postsecondary; Farm and Home Management Advisors; Foreign Language and Literature Teachers, Postsecondary; Forestry and Conservation Science Teachers, Postsecondary; Geography Teachers, Postsecondary; Graduate Teaching Assistants; Health Specialties Teachers, Postsecondary; History Teachers, Postsecondary; Home Economics Teachers, Postsecondary; Law

Teachers, Postsecondary; Library Science Teachers, Postsecondary; Mathematical Science Teachers, Postsecondary; Nursing Instructors and Teachers, Postsecondary; Philosophy and Religion Teachers, Postsecondary; Physics Teachers, Postsecondary; Political Science Teachers, Postsecondary; Psychology Teachers, Postsecondary; Recreation and Fitness Studies Teachers, Postsecondary; Self-Enrichment Education Teachers; Social Work Teachers, Postsecondary; Sociology Teachers, Postsecondary; Vocational Education Teachers, Postsecondary. **PERSONALITY TYPE:** Investigative. Investigative occupations frequently involve working with ideas and require an extensive amount of thinking. These occupations can involve searching for facts and figuring out problems mentally.

EDUCATION/TRAINING PROGRAM(S)— Analytical Chemistry; Chemical Physics; Chemistry, General; Chemistry, Other; Geochemistry; Inorganic Chemistry; Organic Chemistry; Physical and Theoretical Chemistry; Polymer Chemistry.

WORK ENVIRONMENT—Hazardous conditions; contaminants; sitting; indoors; physical proximity to others.

Chief Executives

- Education/Training Required: Work experience plus degree
- Annual Earnings: $141,820
- Growth: 16.7%
- Annual Job Openings: 63,000
- Self-Employed: 14.6%
- Part-Time: 5.3%

The job openings listed here are shared with Government Service Executives and Private Sector Executives.

Age Bracket	Percentage of Workers
45–54 Years Old	36.2%
55–64 Years Old	20.3%
65 or Older	5.3%

Determine and formulate policies and provide the overall direction of companies or private and public sector organizations within the guidelines set up by a board of directors or similar governing body. Plan, direct, or coordinate operational activities at the highest level of management with the help of subordinate executives and staff managers. Analyze operations to evaluate performance of a company and its staff in meeting objectives and to determine areas of potential cost reduction, program improvement, or policy change. Appoint department heads or managers and assign or delegate responsibilities to them. Confer with board members, organization officials, and staff members to discuss issues, coordinate activities, and resolve problems. Coordinate the development and implementation of budgetary control systems, record-keeping systems, and other administrative control processes. Direct and coordinate an organization's financial and budget activities in order to fund operations, maximize investments, and increase efficiency. Direct human resources activities, including the approval of human resource plans and activities, the selection of directors and other high-level staff, and the establishment and organization of major departments. Direct, plan, and implement policies, objectives, and activities of organizations or businesses in order to ensure continuing operations, to maximize returns on investments, and to increase productivity. Establish departmental responsibilities and coordinate functions among departments and sites. Implement corrective action plans to solve organizational or departmental problems. Prepare and present reports concerning activities, expenses, budgets, government statutes and rulings, and other items affecting businesses or program services. Preside over or serve on boards of directors, management committees, or other governing boards. Represent organizations and promote their objectives at official functions or delegate representatives to do so. Serve as liaisons between organizations, shareholders, and outside organizations. Administer programs for selection of sites, construction of buildings, and provision of equipment and supplies. Attend and participate in meetings of municipal councils and council committees. Deliver speeches, write articles, and present information at meetings or conventions in order to promote services, exchange ideas, and accomplish objectives. Direct and conduct studies and research on issues affecting areas of responsibility. **SKILLS**—No data available.

GOE—**Interest Area:** 04. Business and Administration. **Work Group:** 04.01. Managerial Work in General Business. **Other Jobs in This Work Group:** Compensation and Benefits Managers; General and Operations Managers; Human Resources Managers; Private Sector Executives; Training and Development Managers. **PERSONALITY TYPE:** No data available.

EDUCATION/TRAINING PROGRAM(S)—Business Administration/Management; Business/Commerce, General; Entrepreneurship/Entrepreneurial Studies; International Business/Trade/Commerce; Public Administration; Public Administration and Services, Other; Public Policy Analysis; Transportation/Transportation Management.

WORK ENVIRONMENT—No data available.

Child, Family, and School Social Workers

- Education/Training Required: Bachelor's degree
- Annual Earnings: $35,010
- Growth: 23.2%
- Annual Job Openings: 45,000
- Self-Employed: 1.7%
- Part-Time: 8.7%

Age Bracket	Percentage of Workers
45–54 Years Old	26.4%
55–64 Years Old	12.9%
65 or Older	1.9%

Provide social services and assistance to improve the social and psychological functioning of children and their families and to maximize the family well-being and the academic functioning of children. May assist single parents, arrange adoptions, and find foster homes for abandoned or abused children. In schools, they address such problems as teenage pregnancy, misbehavior, and truancy. May also advise teachers on how to deal with problem children. Interview clients individually, in families, or in groups, assessing their situations, capabilities, and problems, to determine what services are required to meet their needs. Counsel individuals, groups, families, or communities regarding issues including mental health, poverty, unemployment, substance abuse, physical abuse, rehabilitation, social adjustment, child care, and/or medical care. Maintain case history records and prepare reports. Counsel students whose behavior, school progress, or mental or physical impairment indicate a need for assistance, diagnosing students' problems and arranging for needed services. Consult with parents, teachers, and other school personnel to determine causes of problems such as truancy and misbehavior and to implement solutions. Counsel parents with child-rearing problems, interviewing the child and family to determine whether further action is required. Develop and review service plans in consultation with clients and perform follow-ups assessing the quantity and quality of services provided. Collect supplementary information needed to assist client, such as employment records, medical records, or school reports. Address legal issues, such as child abuse and discipline, assisting with hearings and providing testimony to inform custody arrangements. Provide, find, or arrange for support services, such as child care, homemaker service, prenatal care, substance abuse treatment, job training, counseling, or parenting classes, to prevent more serious problems from developing. Refer clients to community resources for services such as job placement, debt counseling, legal aid, housing, medical treatment, or financial assistance and provide concrete information, such as where to go and how to apply. Arrange for medical, psychiatric, and other tests that may disclose causes of difficulties and indicate remedial measures. Work in child and adolescent residential institutions. Administer welfare programs. Evaluate personal characteristics and home conditions of foster home or adoption applicants. Serve as liaisons between students, homes, schools, family services, child guidance clinics, courts, protective services, doctors, and other contacts to help children who face problems such as disabilities, abuse, or poverty. **SKILLS**—Social Perceptiveness; Service Orientation; Learning Strategies; Negotiation; Speaking; Monitoring; Active Listening; Writing; Persuasion; Instructing.

GOE—Interest Area: 10. Human Service. **Work Group:** 10.01. Counseling and Social Work. **Other Jobs in This Work Group:** Clinical Psychologists; Counseling Psychologists; Marriage and Family Therapists; Medical and Public Health Social Workers; Mental Health and Substance Abuse Social Workers; Mental Health Counselors; Probation Officers and Correctional Treatment Specialists; Rehabilitation Counselors; Residential Advisors; Social and Human Service Assistants; Substance Abuse and Behavioral Disorder Counselors. **PERSONALITY TYPE:** Social. Social occupations frequently involve working with, communicating with, and teaching people. These occupations often involve helping or providing service to others.

EDUCATION/TRAINING PROGRAM(S)—Juvenile Corrections; Social Work; Youth Services/Administration.

WORK ENVIRONMENT—Sitting; in an enclosed vehicle or equipment; sounds, noise levels are distracting or uncomfortable; physical proximity to others; outdoors.

Chiropractors

- Education/Training Required: First professional degree
- Annual Earnings: $67,940
- Growth: 23.3%
- Annual Job Openings: 3,000
- Self-Employed: 58.5%
- Part-Time: 22.2%

Age Bracket	Percentage of Workers
45–54 Years Old	32.9%
55–64 Years Old	12.9%
65 or Older	1.4%

Adjust spinal column and other articulations of the body to correct abnormalities of the human body believed to be caused by interference with the nervous system. Examine patient to determine nature and extent of disorder. Manipulate spine or other involved area. May utilize supplementary measures, such as exercise, rest, water, light, heat, and nutritional therapy. Perform a series of manual adjustments to the spine, or other articulations of the body, in order to correct the musculoskeletal system. Evaluate the functioning of the neuromuscularskeletal system and the spine, using systems of chiropractic diagnosis. Diagnose health problems by reviewing patients' health and medical histories; questioning, observing, and examining patients; and interpreting X rays. Maintain accurate case histories of patients. Advise patients about recommended courses of treatment. Obtain and record patients' medical histories. Analyze X rays in order to locate the sources of patients' difficulties and to rule out fractures or diseases as sources of problems. Counsel patients about nutrition, exercise, sleeping habits, stress management, and other matters. Arrange for diagnostic X rays to be taken. Consult with and refer patients to appropriate health practitioners when necessary. Suggest and apply the use of supports such as straps, tapes, bandages, and braces if necessary. **SKILLS**—Social Perceptiveness; Persuasion; Service Orientation; Management of Financial Resources; Science; Reading Comprehension; Instructing; Critical Thinking.

GOE—**Interest Area:** 08. Health Science. **Work Group:** 08.04. Health Specialties. **Other Jobs in This Work Group:** Optometrists; Podiatrists. **PERSONALITY TYPE:** Investigative. Investigative occupations frequently involve working with ideas and require an extensive amount of thinking. These occupations can involve searching for facts and figuring out problems mentally.

EDUCATION/TRAINING PROGRAM(S)—Chiropractic (DC).

WORK ENVIRONMENT—Physical proximity to others; disease or infections; indoors; exposed to radiation; standing.

Civil Engineers

- Education/Training Required: Bachelor's degree
- Annual Earnings: $65,280
- Growth: 8.0%
- Annual Job Openings: 17,000
- Self-Employed: 6.7%
- Part-Time: 3.3%

Age Bracket	Percentage of Workers
45–54 Years Old	28.1%
55–64 Years Old	13.7%
65 or Older	4.3%

Perform engineering duties in planning, designing, and overseeing construction and maintenance of building structures and facilities, such as roads, railroads, airports, bridges, harbors, channels, dams, irrigation projects, pipelines, power plants, water and sewage systems, and waste disposal units. Includes architectural, structural, traffic, ocean, and geo-technical engineers. Analyze survey reports, maps, drawings, blueprints, aerial photography, and other topographical or geologic data to plan projects. Plan and design transportation or hydraulic systems and structures, following construction and government standards and using design software and drawing tools. Compute load and grade requirements, water flow rates, and material stress factors to determine design specifications. Inspect project sites to monitor progress and ensure conformance to design specifications and safety or sanitation standards. Direct construction, operations, and maintenance activities at project site. Direct or participate in surveying to lay out installations and establish reference points, grades, and elevations to guide construction. Estimate quantities and cost of materials, equipment, or labor to determine project feasibility. Prepare or present public reports, such as bid proposals, deeds, environmental impact statements, and property and right-of-way descriptions. Test soils and materials to determine the adequacy and strength of foundations, concrete, asphalt, or steel. Provide technical advice regarding design, construction, or program modifications and structural repairs to industrial and managerial personnel. **SKILLS**— Science; Coordination; Negotiation; Persuasion; Mathematics; Instructing; Operations Analysis; Complex Problem Solving.

GOE—**Interest Area:** 15. Scientific Research, Engineering, and Mathematics. **Work Group:** 15.07. Research and Design Engineering. **Other Jobs in This Work Group:** Aerospace Engineers; Biomedical Engineers; Chemical Engineers; Computer Hardware Engineers; Electrical Engineers; Electronics Engineers, Except Computer; Marine Architects; Marine Engineers; Materials Engineers; Mechanical Engineers; Nuclear Engineers. **PERSONALITY TYPE:** Realistic. Realistic occupations frequently involve work activities that include practical, hands-on problems and solutions. They often deal with plants, animals, and real-world materials like wood, tools, and machinery. Many of the occupations require working outside and do not involve a lot of paperwork or working closely with others.

EDUCATION/TRAINING PROGRAM(S)— Civil Engineering, General; Civil Engineering, Other; Transportation and Highway Engineering; Water Resources Engineering.

WORK ENVIRONMENT—In an enclosed vehicle or equipment; sitting; outdoors; very hot or cold; contaminants.

Clergy

- Education/Training Required: First professional degree
- Annual Earnings: $37,870
- Growth: 15.5%
- Annual Job Openings: 34,000
- Self-Employed: 0.3%
- Part-Time: 9.4%

Age Bracket	Percentage of Workers
45–54 Years Old	31.5%
55–64 Years Old	20.5%
65 or Older	12.2%

Conduct religious worship and perform other spiritual functions associated with beliefs and practices of religious faith or denomination. Provide spiritual and moral guidance and assistance to members. Administer religious rites or ordinances. Study and interpret religious laws, doctrines, and/or traditions. Counsel individuals and groups concerning their spiritual, emotional, and personal needs. Organize and lead regular religious services. Conduct special ceremonies such as weddings, funerals, and confirmations. Instruct people who seek conversion to a particular faith. Pray and promote spirituality. Prepare and deliver sermons and other talks. Prepare people for participation in religious ceremonies. Read from sacred texts such as the

Bible, Torah, or Koran. Collaborate with committees and individuals to address financial and administrative issues pertaining to congregations. Devise ways in which congregation membership can be expanded. Organize and engage in interfaith, community, civic, educational, and recreational activities sponsored by or related to their religion. Participate in fundraising activities to support congregation activities and facilities. Perform administrative duties such as overseeing building management, ordering supplies, contracting for services and repairs, and supervising the work of staff members and volunteers. Plan and lead religious education programs for their congregations. Refer people to community support services, psychologists, and/or doctors as necessary. Respond to requests for assistance during emergencies or crises. Share information about religious issues by writing articles, giving speeches, or teaching. Train leaders of church, community, and youth groups. Visit people in homes, hospitals, and prisons to provide them with comfort and support. **SKILLS**—Service Orientation; Social Perceptiveness; Speaking; Writing; Active Listening; Reading Comprehension; Learning Strategies; Persuasion.

GOE—Interest Area: 10. Human Service. **Work Group:** 10.02. Religious Work. **Other Jobs in This Work Group:** Directors, Religious Activities and Education. **PERSONALITY TYPE:** Social. Social occupations frequently involve working with, communicating with, and teaching people. These occupations often involve helping or providing service to others.

EDUCATION/TRAINING PROGRAM(S)— Clinical Pastoral Counseling/Patient Counseling; Divinity/Ministry (BD, MDiv.); Pastoral Counseling and Specialized Ministries, Other; Pastoral Studies/Counseling; Pre-

Theology/Pre-Ministerial Studies; Rabbinical Studies (M.H.L./Rav); Theological and Ministerial Studies, Other; Theological Studies and Religious Vocations, Other; Theology/Theological Studies; Youth Ministry.

WORK ENVIRONMENT—Standing; sitting; indoors; outdoors; walking and running.

Clinical Psychologists

- Education/Training Required: Doctoral degree
- Annual Earnings: $56,360
- Growth: 24.4%
- Annual Job Openings: 17,000
- Self-Employed: 25.4%
- Part-Time: 27.2%

The job openings listed here are shared with School Psychologists and Counseling Psychologists.

Age Bracket	Percentage of Workers
45–54 Years Old	33.0%
55–64 Years Old	23.8%
65 or Older	7.6%

Diagnose or evaluate mental and emotional disorders of individuals through observation, interview, and psychological tests and formulate and administer programs of treatment. Consult reference material such as textbooks, manuals, and journals in order to identify symptoms, to make diagnoses, and to develop approaches to treatment. Counsel individuals and groups regarding problems such as stress, substance abuse, and family situations in order to modify behavior and/or to improve personal, social, and vocational adjustment. Develop and implement individual treatment plans, specifying type, frequency, intensity, and duration of therapy. Discuss the treatment of problems with clients. Evaluate the effectiveness of counseling or treatments and the accuracy and completeness of diagnoses and then modify plans and diagnoses as necessary. Identify psychological, emotional, or behavioral issues and diagnose disorders, using information obtained from interviews, tests, records, and reference materials. Interact with clients to assist them in gaining insight, defining goals, and planning action to achieve effective personal, social, educational, and vocational development and adjustment. Observe individuals at play, in group interactions, or in other contexts to detect indications of mental deficiency, abnormal behavior, or maladjustment. Obtain and study medical, psychological, social, and family histories by interviewing individuals, couples, or families and by reviewing records. Provide occupational, educational, and other information to individuals so that they can make educational and vocational plans. Select, administer, score, and interpret psychological tests in order to obtain information on individuals' intelligence, achievements, interests, and personalities. Utilize a variety of treatment methods such as psychotherapy, hypnosis, behavior modification, stress reduction therapy, psychodrama, and play therapy. Maintain current knowledge of relevant research. Plan, supervise, and conduct psychological research and write papers describing research results. Refer clients to other specialists, institutions, or support services as necessary. Write reports on clients and maintain required paperwork. Develop, direct, and participate in training programs for staff and students. **SKILLS**—Social Perceptiveness; Active Listening; Systems Evaluation; Persuasion; Systems Analysis; Reading Comprehension; Speaking; Science; Complex Problem Solving.

GOE—Interest Area: 10. Human Service. **Work Group:** 10.01. Counseling and Social Work. **Other Jobs in This Work Group:** Child, Family, and School Social Workers; Counseling Psychologists; Marriage and Family Therapists; Medical and Public Health Social Workers; Mental Health and Substance Abuse Social Workers; Mental Health Counselors; Probation Officers and Correctional Treatment Specialists; Rehabilitation Counselors; Residential Advisors; Social and Human Service Assistants; Substance Abuse and Behavioral Disorder Counselors. **PERSONALITY TYPE:** Investigative. Investigative occupations frequently involve working with ideas and require an extensive amount of thinking. These occupations can involve searching for facts and figuring out problems mentally.

EDUCATION/TRAINING PROGRAM(S)— Clinical Child Psychology; Clinical Psychology; Counseling Psychology; Developmental and Child Psychology; Psychoanalysis and Psychotherapy; Psychology, General; School Psychology.

WORK ENVIRONMENT—Sitting; indoors; disease or infections.

Commercial Pilots

- Education/Training Required: Postsecondary vocational training
- Annual Earnings: $55,360
- Growth: 14.9%
- Annual Job Openings: 2,000
- Self-Employed: 11.2%
- Part-Time: 12.9%

Age Bracket	Percentage of Workers
45–54 Years Old	32.8%
55–64 Years Old	15.5%
65 or Older	2.6%

Pilot and navigate the flight of small fixed or rotary winged aircraft, primarily for the transport of cargo and passengers. Requires Commercial Rating. Check aircraft prior to flights to ensure that the engines, controls, instruments, and other systems are functioning properly. Check baggage or cargo to ensure that it has been loaded correctly. Choose routes, altitudes, and speeds that will provide the fastest, safest, and smoothest flights. Consider airport altitudes, outside temperatures, plane weights, and wind speeds and directions in order to calculate the speed needed to become airborne. Contact control towers for takeoff clearances, arrival instructions, and other information, using radio equipment. Coordinate flight activities with ground crews and air-traffic control and inform crew members of flight and test procedures. File instrument flight plans with air traffic control so that flights can be coordinated with other air traffic. Monitor engine operation, fuel consumption, and functioning of aircraft systems during flights. Obtain and review data such as load weights, fuel supplies, weather conditions, and flight schedules in order to determine flight plans and to see if changes might be necessary. Order changes in fuel supplies, loads, routes, or schedules to ensure safety of flights. Plan and formulate flight activities and test schedules and prepare flight evaluation reports. Plan flights, following government and company regulations, using aeronautical charts and navigation instruments. Request changes in altitudes or routes as circumstances dictate. Start engines; operate controls; and pilot airplanes to transport passengers, mail, or freight while adhering to flight plans, regulations, and procedures. Use instrumentation to pilot aircraft when visibility is poor. Check the flight performance of new and experimental planes. Conduct in-flight tests and evaluations at specified altitudes and in all types of weather in order to determine the receptivity and other characteristics of equipment and systems. Co-pilot aircraft or perform captain's duties if required. Fly with other pilots or pilot-license applicants to evaluate their proficiency. Instruct other pilots and student pilots in aircraft operations. Perform minor aircraft maintenance and repair work or arrange for major maintenance. **SKILLS**—Operation and Control; Operation Monitoring; Instructing; Science; Coordination; Systems Evaluation; Systems Analysis; Judgment and Decision Making.

GOE—Interest Area: 16. Transportation, Distribution, and Logistics. **Work Group:** 16.02. Air Vehicle Operation. **Other Jobs in This Work Group:** Airline Pilots, Copilots, and Flight Engineers. **PERSONALITY TYPE:** Realistic. Realistic occupations frequently involve work activities that include practical, hands-on problems and solutions. They often deal with plants, animals, and real-world materials like wood, tools, and machinery. Many of the occupations require working outside and do not involve a lot of paperwork or working closely with others.

EDUCATION/TRAINING PROGRAM(S)— Airline/Commercial/Professional Pilot and Flight Crew; Flight Instructor.

WORK ENVIRONMENT—High places; sitting; hazardous equipment; exposed to whole body vibration; outdoors.

Communication Equipment Mechanics, Installers, and Repairers

- Education/Training Required: Long-term on-the-job training
- Annual Earnings: $50,270
- Growth: –0.6%
- Annual Job Openings: 23,000
- Self-Employed: 4.6%
- Part-Time: 1.7%

The job openings listed here are shared with Central Office and PBX Installers and Repairers; Frame Wirers, Central Office; Station Installers and Repairers, Telephone; and Telecommunications Facility Examiners.

Age Bracket	Percentage of Workers
45–54 Years Old	29.5%
55–64 Years Old	9.6%
65 or Older	1.2%

Install, maintain, test, and repair communication cables and equipment. Examines and tests malfunctioning equipment to determine defects, using blueprints and electrical measuring instruments. Tests installed equipment for conformance to specifications, using test equipment. Assembles and installs communication equipment, such as data communication lines and equipment, computer systems, and antennas and towers, using hand tools. Repairs, replaces, or adjusts defective components. Disassembles equipment to adjust, repair, or replace parts, using hand tools. Evaluates quality of performance of installed equipment by observance and using test equipment. Digs holes or trenches. Answers customers' inquiries or complaints.

Cleans and maintains tools, test equipment, and motor vehicle. Communicates with base, using telephone or two-way radio to receive instructions or technical advice or to report unauthorized use of equipment. Demonstrates equipment and instructs customer in use of equipment. Determines viability of site through observation and discusses site location and construction requirements with customer. Measures distance from landmarks to identify exact installation site. Climbs poles and ladders; constructs pole, roof mounts, or reinforcements; and mixes concrete to enable equipment installation. Plans layout and installation of data communications equipment. Reviews work orders, building permits, manufacturer's instructions, and ordinances to move, change, install, repair, or remove communication equipment. Adjusts or modifies equipment in accordance with customer request or to enhance performance of equipment. Performs routine maintenance on equipment, which includes adjustment, repair, and painting. Measures, cuts, splices, connects, solders, and installs wires and cables. **SKILLS—**Repairing; Installation; Troubleshooting; Equipment Maintenance; Technology Design; Quality Control Analysis; Operation Monitoring; Operation and Control.

GOE—Interest Area: 02. Architecture and Construction. **Work Group:** 02.05. Systems and Equipment Installation, Maintenance, and Repair. **Other Jobs in This Work Group:** Central Office and PBX Installers and Repairers; Electric Meter Installers and Repairers; Electrical and Electronics Repairers, Powerhouse, Substation, and Relay; Electrical Power-Line Installers and Repairers; Elevator Installers and Repairers; Frame Wirers, Central Office; Heating and Air Conditioning Mechanics; Home Appliance Installers; Maintenance and Repair Workers, General; Meter Mechanics;

Refrigeration Mechanics; Station Installers and Repairers, Telephone; Telecommunications Facility Examiners; Telecommunications Line Installers and Repairers. **PERSONALITY TYPE:** Realistic. Realistic occupations frequently involve work activities that include practical, hands-on problems and solutions. They often deal with plants, animals, and real-world materials like wood, tools, and machinery. Many of the occupations require working outside and do not involve a lot of paperwork or working closely with others.

EDUCATION/TRAINING PROGRAM(S)— Communications Systems Installation and Repair Technology.

WORK ENVIRONMENT—Hazardous conditions; outdoors; high places; climbing ladders, scaffolds, or poles; common protective or safety equipment.

Communications Teachers, Postsecondary

- Education/Training Required: Master's degree
- Annual Earnings: $50,610
- Growth: 38.1%
- Annual Job Openings: 216,000
- Self-Employed: 0.3%
- Part-Time: 27.7%

The job openings listed here are shared with all other postsecondary teaching occupations.

Age Bracket	Percentage of Workers
45–54 Years Old	22.8%
55–64 Years Old	19.0%
65 or Older	5.5%

Teach courses in communications, such as organizational communications, public relations, radio/television broadcasting, and journalism. Evaluate and grade students' class work, assignments, and papers. Prepare course materials such as syllabi, homework assignments, and handouts. Initiate, facilitate, and moderate classroom discussions. Prepare and deliver lectures to undergraduate and/or graduate students on topics such as public speaking, media criticism, and oral traditions. Compile, administer, and grade examinations or assign this work to others. Maintain student attendance records, grades, and other required records. Plan, evaluate, and revise curricula, course content, and course materials and methods of instruction. Maintain regularly scheduled office hours in order to advise and assist students. Keep abreast of developments in their field by reading current literature, talking with colleagues, and participating in professional conferences. Advise students on academic and vocational curricula and on career issues. Supervise undergraduate and/or graduate teaching, internship, and research work. Select and obtain materials and supplies such as textbooks. Collaborate with colleagues to address teaching and research issues. Conduct research in a particular field of knowledge and publish findings in professional journals, books, and/or electronic media. Participate in student recruitment, registration, and placement activities. Serve on academic or administrative committees that deal with institutional policies, departmental matters, and academic issues. Compile bibliographies of specialized materials for outside reading assignments. Act as advisers to student organizations. Participate in campus and community events. Perform administrative duties such as serving as department head. **SKILLS**—Instructing; Learning Strategies; Persuasion; Writing; Social Perceptiveness; Monitoring; Active Learning; Critical Thinking.

GOE—Interest Area: 05. Education and Training. **Work Group:** 05.03. Postsecondary and Adult Teaching and Instructing. **Other Jobs in This Work Group:** Adult Literacy, Remedial Education, and GED Teachers and Instructors; Agricultural Sciences Teachers, Postsecondary; Anthropology and Archeology Teachers, Postsecondary; Architecture Teachers, Postsecondary; Area, Ethnic, and Cultural Studies Teachers, Postsecondary; Art, Drama, and Music Teachers, Postsecondary; Atmospheric, Earth, Marine, and Space Sciences Teachers, Postsecondary; Biological Science Teachers, Postsecondary; Business Teachers, Postsecondary; Chemistry Teachers, Postsecondary; Computer Science Teachers, Postsecondary; Criminal Justice and Law Enforcement Teachers, Postsecondary; Economics Teachers, Postsecondary; Education Teachers, Postsecondary; Engineering Teachers, Postsecondary; English Language and Literature Teachers, Postsecondary; Environmental Science Teachers, Postsecondary; Farm and Home Management Advisors; Foreign Language and Literature Teachers, Postsecondary; Forestry and Conservation Science Teachers, Postsecondary; Geography Teachers, Postsecondary; Graduate Teaching Assistants; Health Specialties Teachers, Postsecondary; History Teachers, Postsecondary; Home Economics Teachers, Postsecondary; Law Teachers, Postsecondary; Library Science Teachers, Postsecondary; Mathematical Science Teachers, Postsecondary; Nursing Instructors and Teachers, Postsecondary; Philosophy and Religion Teachers, Postsecondary; Physics Teachers, Postsecondary; Political Science Teachers, Postsecondary; Psychology Teachers, Postsecondary; Recreation and Fitness Studies Teachers, Postsecondary; Self-Enrichment Education Teachers; Social Work Teachers, Postsecondary; Sociology Teachers, Postsecondary; Vocational Education Teachers, Postsecondary. **PERSONALITY TYPE:** No data available.

EDUCATION/TRAINING PROGRAM(S)—Advertising; Broadcast Journalism; Communications Studies/Speech Communication and Rhetoric; Communications, Journalism, and Related Fields, Other; Digital Communications and Media/Multimedia; Health Communications; Journalism; Journalism, Other; Mass Communications/Media Studies; Political Communications; Public Relations/Image Management; Radio and Television.

WORK ENVIRONMENT—Sitting; physical proximity to others; indoors; sounds, noise levels are distracting or uncomfortable; extremely bright or inadequate lighting.

Compensation and Benefits Managers

- ◎ Education/Training Required: Work experience plus degree
- ◎ Annual Earnings: $67,040
- ◎ Growth: 19.4%
- ◎ Annual Job Openings: 21,000
- ◎ Self-Employed: 0%
- ◎ Part-Time: 3.7%

The job openings listed here are shared with Training and Development Managers.

Age Bracket	Percentage of Workers
45–54 Years Old	31.9%
55–64 Years Old	17.5%
65 or Older	0.8%

Plan, direct, or coordinate compensation and benefits activities and staff of an organization. Advise management on such matters as equal employment opportunity, sexual harassment and discrimination. Direct preparation and distribution of written and verbal information to inform employees of benefits, compensation, and personnel policies. Administer, direct, and review employee benefit programs, including the integration of benefit programs following mergers and acquisition. Plan and conduct new employee orientations to foster positive attitude toward organizational objectives. Plan, direct, supervise, and coordinate work activities of subordinates and staff relating to employment, compensation, labor relations, and employee relations. Identify and implement benefits to increase the quality of life for employees by working with brokers and researching benefits issues. Design, evaluate, and modify benefits policies to ensure that programs are current, competitive, and in compliance with legal requirements. Analyze compensation policies, government regulations, and prevailing wage rates to develop competitive compensation plan. Formulate policies, procedures, and programs for recruitment, testing, placement, classification, orientation, benefits and compensation, and labor and industrial relations. Mediate between benefits providers and employees, such as by assisting in handling employees' benefits-related questions or taking suggestions. Fulfill all reporting requirements of all relevant government rules and regulations, including the Employee Retirement Income Security Act (ERISA). Maintain records and compile statistical reports concerning personnel-related data such as hires, transfers, performance appraisals, and absenteeism rates. Analyze statistical data and reports to identify and determine causes of personnel problems and develop recommendations for improvement of organization's personnel policies and practices. Develop methods to improve employment policies, processes, and practices and recommend changes to management. Negotiate bargaining agreements. Investigate and report on industrial accidents for insurance carriers. Represent organization at personnel-related hearings and investigations. **SKILLS**—Management of Personnel Resources; Management of Financial Resources; Social Perceptiveness; Management of Material Resources; Time Management; Monitoring; Instructing; Negotiation.

GOE—Interest Area: 04. Business and Administration. **Work Group:** 04.01. Managerial Work in General Business. **Other Jobs in This Work Group:** Chief Executives; General and Operations Managers; Human Resources Managers; Private Sector Executives; Training and Development Managers. **PERSONALITY TYPE:** Enterprising. Enterprising occupations frequently involve starting up and carrying out projects. These occupations can involve leading people and making many decisions. They sometimes require risk taking and often deal with business.

EDUCATION/TRAINING PROGRAM(S)—Human Resources Management/Personnel Administration, General; Labor and Industrial Relations.

WORK ENVIRONMENT—Sitting; indoors; physical proximity to others; sounds, noise levels are distracting or uncomfortable; contaminants.

Compensation, Benefits, and Job Analysis Specialists

- Education/Training Required: Bachelor's degree
- Annual Earnings: $48,720
- Growth: 28.0%
- Annual Job Openings: 15,000
- Self-Employed: 0.8%
- Part-Time: 7.7%

Age Bracket	Percentage of Workers
45–54 Years Old	26.6%
55–64 Years Old	13.4%
65 or Older	1.6%

Conduct programs of compensation and benefits and job analysis for employer. May specialize in specific areas, such as position classification and pension programs. Evaluate job positions, determining classification, exempt or non-exempt status, and salary. Ensure company compliance with federal and state laws, including reporting requirements. Advise managers and employees on state and federal employment regulations, collective agreements, benefit and compensation policies, personnel procedures, and classification programs. Plan, develop, evaluate, improve, and communicate methods and techniques for selecting, promoting, compensating, evaluating, and training workers. Provide advice on the resolution of classification and salary complaints. Prepare occupational classifications, job descriptions, and salary scales. Assist in preparing and maintaining personnel records and handbooks. Prepare reports, such as organization and flow charts and career path reports, to summarize job analysis and evaluation and compensation analysis information. Administer employee insurance, pension, and savings plans, working with insurance brokers and plan carriers. Negotiate collective agreements on behalf of employers or workers and mediate labor disputes and grievances. Develop, implement, administer, and evaluate personnel and labor relations programs, including performance appraisal, affirmative action, and employment equity programs. Perform multifactor data and cost analyses that may be used in areas such as support of collective bargaining agreements. Research employee benefit and health and safety practices and recommend changes or modifications to existing policies. Analyze organizational, occupational, and industrial data to facilitate organizational functions and provide technical information to business, industry, and government. Advise staff of individuals' qualifications. Assess need for and develop job analysis instruments and materials. Review occupational data on Alien Employment Certification Applications to determine the appropriate occupational title and code and provide local offices with information about immigration and occupations. Research job and worker requirements, structural and functional relationships among jobs and occupations, and occupational trends. **SKILLS**—Service Orientation; Persuasion; Negotiation; Coordination; Active Listening; Social Perceptiveness; Judgment and Decision Making; Critical Thinking; Time Management.

GOE—Interest Area: 04. Business and Administration. **Work Group:** 04.03. Human Resources Support. **Other Jobs in This Work Group:** Employment Interviewers, Private or Public Employment Service; Personnel Recruiters; Training and Development Specialists. **PERSONALITY TYPE:** Investigative. Investigative occupations frequently involve working with ideas and require an extensive amount of thinking. These occupations can involve searching for facts and figuring out problems mentally.

EDUCATION/TRAINING PROGRAM(S)— Human Resources Management/Personnel Administration, General; Labor and Industrial Relations.

WORK ENVIRONMENT—Sitting; sounds, noise levels are distracting or uncomfortable; indoors; contaminants; physical proximity to others.

Composers

- ◉ Education/Training Required: Work experience plus degree
- ◉ Annual Earnings: $34,800
- ◉ Growth: 13.5%
- ◉ Annual Job Openings: 8,000
- ◉ Self-Employed: 39.3%
- ◉ Part-Time: 39.5%

The job openings listed here are shared with Music Arrangers and Orchestrators and Music Directors.

Age Bracket	Percentage of Workers
45–54 Years Old	23.5%
55–64 Years Old	11.2%
65 or Older	10.6%

Compose music for orchestra, choral group, or band. Creates original musical form or writes within circumscribed musical form, such as sonata, symphony, or opera. Transcribes or records musical ideas into notes on scored music paper. Develops pattern of harmony, applying knowledge of music theory. Synthesizes ideas for melody of musical scores for choral group or band. Creates musical and tonal structure, applying elements of music theory, such as instrumental and vocal capabilities. Determines basic pattern of melody, applying knowledge of music theory. **SKILLS—**None met the criteria.

GOE—Interest Area: 03. Arts and Communication. **Work Group:** 03.07. Music. **Other Jobs in This Work Group:** Music Arrangers and Orchestrators; Music Directors; Musicians, Instrumental; Singers; Talent Directors. **PERSONALITY TYPE:** Artistic. Artistic occupations frequently involve working with forms, designs, and patterns. They often require self-expression, and the work can be done without following a clear set of rules.

EDUCATION/TRAINING PROGRAM(S)— Conducting; Music Management and Merchandising; Music Performance, General; Music Theory and Composition; Music, Other; Musicology and Ethnomusicology; Religious/Sacred Music; Voice and Opera.

WORK ENVIRONMENT—Sitting; indoors; outdoors.

Computer Science Teachers, Postsecondary

- ◉ Education/Training Required: Master's degree
- ◉ Annual Earnings: $53,520
- ◉ Growth: 38.1%
- ◉ Annual Job Openings: 216,000
- ◉ Self-Employed: 0.3%
- ◉ Part-Time: 27.7%

The job openings listed here are shared with all other postsecondary teaching occupations.

Age Bracket	Percentage of Workers
45–54 Years Old	22.8%
55–64 Years Old	19.0%
65 or Older	5.5%

Teach courses in computer science. May specialize in a field of computer science, such as the design and function of computers or operations and research analysis. Evaluate and grade students' class work, laboratory work, assignments, and papers. Maintain student attendance records, grades, and other required records. Prepare and deliver lectures to undergraduate and/or graduate students on topics such as programming, data structures, and software design. Prepare course materials such as syllabi, homework assignments, and handouts. Compile, administer, and grade examinations or assign this work to others. Keep abreast of developments in their field by reading current literature, talking with colleagues, and participating in professional conferences. Initiate, facilitate, and moderate classroom discussions. Plan, evaluate, and revise curricula, course content, and course materials and methods of instruction. Supervise students' laboratory work. Maintain regularly scheduled office hours in order to advise and assist students. Select and obtain materials and supplies such as textbooks and laboratory equipment. Advise students on academic and vocational curricula and on career issues. Participate in student recruitment, registration, and placement activities. Collaborate with colleagues to address teaching and research issues. Serve on academic or administrative committees that deal with institutional policies, departmental matters, and academic issues. Act as advisers to student organizations. Supervise undergraduate and/or graduate teaching, internship, and research work. Perform administrative duties such as serving as department head. Conduct research in a particular field of knowledge and publish findings in professional journals, books, and/or electronic media. Direct research of other teachers or of graduate students working for advanced academic degrees. **SKILLS—** Instructing; Programming; Learning Strategies; Active Learning; Technology Design; Operations Analysis; Critical Thinking; Complex Problem Solving.

GOE—Interest Area: 05. Education and Training. **Work Group:** 05.03. Postsecondary and Adult Teaching and Instructing. **Other Jobs in This Work Group:** Adult Literacy, Remedial Education, and GED Teachers and Instructors; Agricultural Sciences Teachers, Postsecondary; Anthropology and Archeology Teachers, Postsecondary; Architecture Teachers, Postsecondary; Area, Ethnic, and Cultural Studies Teachers, Postsecondary; Art, Drama, and Music Teachers, Postsecondary; Atmospheric, Earth, Marine, and Space Sciences Teachers, Postsecondary; Biological Science Teachers, Postsecondary; Business Teachers, Postsecondary; Chemistry Teachers, Postsecondary; Communications Teachers, Postsecondary; Criminal Justice and Law Enforcement Teachers, Postsecondary; Economics Teachers, Postsecondary; Education Teachers, Postsecondary; Engineering Teachers, Postsecondary; English Language and Literature Teachers, Postsecondary; Environmental Science Teachers, Postsecondary; Farm and Home Management Advisors; Foreign Language and Literature Teachers, Postsecondary; Forestry and Conservation Science Teachers, Postsecondary; Geography Teachers, Postsecondary; Graduate Teaching Assistants; Health Specialties Teachers, Postsecondary; History Teachers, Postsecondary; Home Economics Teachers, Postsecondary; Law Teachers, Postsecondary; Library Science Teachers, Postsecondary; Mathematical Science

Teachers, Postsecondary; Nursing Instructors and Teachers, Postsecondary; Philosophy and Religion Teachers, Postsecondary; Physics Teachers, Postsecondary; Political Science Teachers, Postsecondary; Psychology Teachers, Postsecondary; Recreation and Fitness Studies Teachers, Postsecondary; Self-Enrichment Education Teachers; Social Work Teachers, Postsecondary; Sociology Teachers, Postsecondary; Vocational Education Teachers, Postsecondary. **PERSONALITY TYPE:** Investigative. Investigative occupations frequently involve working with ideas and require an extensive amount of thinking. These occupations can involve searching for facts and figuring out problems mentally.

EDUCATION/TRAINING PROGRAM(S)— Computer and Information Sciences, General; Computer Programming/Programmer, General; Computer Science; Computer Systems Analysis/Analyst; Information Science/Studies.

WORK ENVIRONMENT—Sitting; physical proximity to others; indoors.

Construction and Building Inspectors

- ◎ Education/Training Required: Work experience in a related occupation
- ◎ Annual Earnings: $43,940
- ◎ Growth: 13.8%
- ◎ Annual Job Openings: 10,000
- ◎ Self-Employed: 8.1%
- ◎ Part-Time: 5.9%

Age Bracket	Percentage of Workers
45–54 Years Old	32.6%
55–64 Years Old	17.9%
65 or Older	6.3%

Inspect structures, using engineering skills to determine structural soundness and compliance with specifications, building codes, and other regulations. Inspections may be general in nature or may be limited to a specific area, such as electrical systems or plumbing. Use survey instruments, metering devices; tape measures; and test equipment, such as concrete strength measurers, to perform inspections. Inspect bridges, dams, highways, buildings, wiring, plumbing, electrical circuits, sewers, heating systems, and foundations during and after construction for structural quality, general safety, and conformance to specifications and codes. Maintain daily logs and supplement inspection records with photographs. Review and interpret plans, blueprints, site layouts, specifications, and construction methods to ensure compliance to legal requirements and safety regulations. Inspect and monitor construction sites to ensure adherence to safety standards, building codes, and specifications. Measure dimensions and verify level, alignment, and elevation of structures and fixtures to ensure compliance to building plans and codes. Issue violation notices and stop-work orders, conferring with owners, violators, and authorities to explain regulations and recommend rectifications. Issue permits for construction, relocation, demolition, and occupancy. Approve and sign plans that meet required specifications. Compute estimates of work completed or of needed renovations or upgrades and approve payment for contractors. Monitor installation of plumbing, wiring, equipment, and appliances to ensure that installation is performed properly and is in compliance with applicable regulations. Examine lifting and conveying devices, such as elevators, escalators, moving sidewalks, lifts and hoists, inclined railways, ski lifts, and amusement rides, to ensure safety and proper functioning. Train, direct, and supervise other construction inspectors. Evaluate premises for cleanliness, including proper garbage disposal and lack of vermin infestation. **SKILLS**— Persuasion; Time Management; Mathematics; Reading Comprehension; Active Learning; Social Perceptiveness; Coordination; Instructing.

GOE—Interest Area: 02. Architecture and Construction. **Work Group:** 02.03. Architecture/Construction Engineering Technologies. **Other Jobs in This Work Group:** Architectural Drafters; Civil Drafters; Electrical Drafters; Surveyors. **PERSONALITY TYPE:** Conventional. Conventional occupations frequently involve following set procedures and routines. These occupations can include working with data and details more than with ideas. Usually there is a clear line of authority to follow.

EDUCATION/TRAINING PROGRAM(S)— Building/Home/Construction Inspection/ Inspector.

WORK ENVIRONMENT—Outdoors; in an enclosed vehicle or equipment; sounds, noise levels are distracting or uncomfortable; very hot or cold; extremely bright or inadequate lighting; contaminants.

Construction Managers

- Education/Training Required: Bachelor's degree
- Annual Earnings: $70,770
- Growth: 12.0%
- Annual Job Openings: 47,000
- Self-Employed: 46.9%
- Part-Time: 3.6%

Age Bracket	Percentage of Workers
45–54 Years Old	30.3%
55–64 Years Old	14.1%
65 or Older	3.5%

Plan, direct, coordinate, or budget, usually through subordinate supervisory personnel, activities concerned with the construction and maintenance of structures, facilities, and systems. Participate in the conceptual development of a construction project and oversee its organization, scheduling, and implementation. Confer with supervisory personnel, owners, contractors, and design professionals to discuss and resolve matters such as work procedures, complaints, and construction problems. Plan, organize, and direct activities concerned with the construction and maintenance of structures, facilities, and systems. Schedule the project in logical steps and budget time required to meet deadlines. Determine labor requirements and dispatch workers to construction sites. Inspect and review projects to monitor compliance with building and safety codes and other regulations. Interpret and explain plans and contract terms to administrative staff, workers, and clients, representing the owner or developer. Prepare contracts and negotiate revisions, changes, and additions to contractual agreements with architects, consultants, clients, suppliers, and subcontractors. Obtain all necessary permits and licenses. Direct and supervise workers. Study job specifications to determine appropriate construction methods. Select, contract, and oversee workers who complete specific pieces of the project, such as painting or plumbing. Requisition supplies and materials to complete construction projects. Prepare and submit budget estimates and progress and cost tracking reports. Develop and implement quality control programs. Take actions to deal with the results of delays, bad weather, or emergencies at construction site. Investigate damage, accidents, or delays at construction sites to ensure that proper procedures are being carried out. Evaluate construction methods and determine cost-effectiveness of plans, using computers. **SKILLS** —Coordination; Troubleshooting; Negotiation; Installation; Repairing; Management of Material Resources; Instructing; Persuasion.

GOE—Interest Area: 02. Architecture and Construction. **Work Group:** 02.01. Managerial Work in Architecture and Construction. **Other Jobs in This Work Group:** First-Line Supervisors and Manager/Supervisors—Construction Trades Workers. **PERSONALITY TYPE:** Enterprising. Enterprising occupations frequently involve starting up and carrying out projects. These occupations can involve leading people and making many decisions. They sometimes require risk taking and often deal with business.

EDUCATION/TRAINING PROGRAM(S)— Business Administration/Management; Business/Commerce, General; Construction Engineering Technology/Technician; Operations Management and Supervision.

WORK ENVIRONMENT—In an enclosed vehicle or equipment; sounds, noise levels are distracting or uncomfortable; contaminants; indoors, not environmentally controlled; very hot or cold; sitting.

Copy Writers

- ◎ Education/Training Required: Bachelor's degree
- ◎ Annual Earnings: $45,460
- ◎ Growth: 16.1%
- ◎ Annual Job Openings: 23,000
- ◎ Self-Employed: 67.9%
- ◎ Part-Time: 24.2%

The job openings listed here are shared with Caption Writers, Creative Writers, and Poets and Lyricists.

Age Bracket	Percentage of Workers
45–54 Years Old	24.7%
55–64 Years Old	16.3%
65 or Older	7.4%

Write advertising copy for use by publication or broadcast media to promote sale of goods and services. Write advertising copy for use by publication, broadcast, or Internet media to promote the sale of goods and services. Present drafts and ideas to clients. Discuss with the client the product, advertising themes and methods, and any changes that should be made in advertising copy. Vary language and tone of messages based on product and medium. Consult with sales, media, and marketing representatives to obtain information on product or service and discuss style and length of advertising copy. Edit or rewrite existing copy as necessary and submit copy for approval by supervisor. Write to customers in their terms and on their level so that the advertiser's sales message is more readily received. Write articles, bulletins, sales letters, speeches, and other related informative, marketing, and promotional material. Invent names for products and write the slogans that appear on packaging, brochures, and other promotional material. Review advertising trends, consumer surveys, and other data regarding marketing of goods and services to determine the best way to promote products. Develop advertising campaigns for a wide range of clients, working with an advertising agency's creative director and art director to determine the best way to present advertising information. Conduct research and interviews to determine which of a product's selling features should be promoted. **SKILLS**—Persuasion; Instructing; Time Management; Negotiation; Coordination; Technology Design; Active Listening; Critical Thinking.

GOE—**Interest Area:** 03. Arts and Communication. **Work Group:** 03.02. Writing and Editing. **Other Jobs in This Work Group:** Creative Writers; Editors; Poets and Lyricists; Technical Writers. **PERSONALITY TYPE:** Artistic. Artistic occupations frequently involve working with forms, designs, and patterns. They often require self-expression, and the work can be done without following a clear set of rules.

EDUCATION/TRAINING PROGRAM(S)— Communications Studies/Speech Communication and Rhetoric; English Composition; Journalism; Mass Communications/Media Studies.

WORK ENVIRONMENT—Sitting; contaminants; indoors; physical proximity to others; sounds, noise levels are distracting or uncomfortable.

Coroners

- Education/Training Required: Work experience in a related occupation
- Annual Earnings: $48,530
- Growth: 9.8%
- Annual Job Openings: 20,000
- Self-Employed: 0.9%
- Part-Time: 5.3%

The job openings listed here are shared with Environmental Compliance Inspectors, Equal Opportunity Representatives and Officers, Government Property Inspectors and Investigators, Licensing Examiners and Inspectors, and Pressure Vessel Inspectors.

Age Bracket	Percentage of Workers
45–54 Years Old	40.5%
55–64 Years Old	15.1%
65 or Older	0.8%

Direct activities such as autopsies, pathological and toxicological analyses, and inquests relating to the investigation of deaths occurring within a legal jurisdiction to determine cause of death or to fix responsibility for accidental, violent, or unexplained deaths. Collect and document any pertinent medical history information. Complete death certificates, including the assignment of a cause and manner of death. Complete reports and forms required to finalize cases. Direct activities of workers who conduct autopsies, perform pathological and toxicological analyses, and prepare documents for permanent records. Inquire into the cause, manner, and circumstances of human deaths and establish the identities of deceased persons. Interview persons present at death scenes to obtain information useful in determining the manner of death. Observe and record the positions and conditions of bodies and of related evidence. Observe, record, and preserve any objects or personal property related to deaths, including objects such as medication containers and suicide notes. Perform medico-legal examinations and autopsies, conducting preliminary examinations of the body in order to identify victims, to locate signs of trauma, and to identify factors that would indicate time of death. Testify at inquests, hearings, and court trials. Arrange for the next of kin to be notified of deaths. Collect wills, burial instructions, and other documentation needed for investigations and for handling of the remains. Confer with officials of public health and law enforcement agencies in order to coordinate interdepartmental activities. Coordinate the release of personal effects to authorized persons and facilitate the disposition of unclaimed corpses and personal effects. Inventory personal effects, such as jewelry or wallets, that are recovered from bodies. Locate and document information regarding the next of kin, including their relationship to the deceased and the status of notification attempts. Provide information concerning the circumstances of death to relatives of the deceased. Remove or supervise removal of bodies from death scenes, using the proper equipment and supplies, and arrange for transportation to morgues. Witness and certify deaths that are the result of a judicial order. Record the disposition of minor children as well as details of arrangements made for their care. **SKILLS**—Science; Reading Comprehension; Speaking; Writing; Critical Thinking; Mathematics; Management of Personnel Resources; Complex Problem Solving.

GOE—Interest Area: 08. Health Science. **Work Group:** 08.01. Managerial Work in Medical and Health Services. **Other Jobs in This Work Group:** First-Line Supervisors and Manager/Supervisors—Animal Care Workers, Except Livestock; Medical and Health Services Managers. **PERSONALITY TYPE:** Investigative. Investigative occupations fre-

quently involve working with ideas and require an extensive amount of thinking. These occupations can involve searching for facts and figuring out problems mentally.

EDUCATION/TRAINING PROGRAM(S)— No data available.

WORK ENVIRONMENT—Disease or infections; common protective or safety equipment; standing; outdoors; contaminants.

Cost Estimators

- Education/Training Required: Work experience in a related occupation
- Annual Earnings: $50,920
- Growth: 18.6%
- Annual Job Openings: 25,000
- Self-Employed: 1.7%
- Part-Time: 5.9%

Age Bracket	Percentage of Workers
45–54 Years Old	25.0%
55–64 Years Old	14.0%
65 or Older	7.0%

Prepare cost estimates for product manufacturing, construction projects, or services to aid management in bidding on or determining price of product or service. May specialize according to particular service performed or type of product manufactured. Analyze blueprints and other documentation to prepare time, cost, materials, and labor estimates. Assess cost-effectiveness of products, projects, or services, tracking actual costs relative to bids as the project develops. Consult with clients, vendors, personnel in other departments, or construction foremen to discuss and formulate estimates and resolve issues. Confer with engineers, architects, owners, contractors, and subcontractors on changes and adjustments to cost estimates. Prepare estimates used by management for purposes such as planning, organizing, and scheduling work. Prepare estimates for use in selecting vendors or subcontractors. Review material and labor requirements to decide whether it is more cost-effective to produce or purchase components. Prepare cost and expenditure statements and other necessary documentation at regular intervals for the duration of the project. Prepare and maintain a directory of suppliers, contractors, and subcontractors. Set up cost-monitoring and -reporting systems and procedures. Establish and maintain tendering process and conduct negotiations. Conduct special studies to develop and establish standard hour and related cost data or to effect cost reduction. Visit site and record information about access, drainage and topography, and availability of services such as water and electricity. **SKILLS**—Negotiation; Management of Financial Resources; Management of Personnel Resources; Coordination; Mathematics; Active Listening; Persuasion; Time Management.

GOE—Interest Area: 06. Finance and Insurance. **Work Group:** 06.02. Finance/Insurance Investigation and Analysis. **Other Jobs in This Work Group:** Appraisers, Real Estate; Assessors; Claims Examiners, Property and Casualty Insurance; Credit Analysts; Financial Analysts; Insurance Adjusters, Examiners, and Investigators; Insurance Appraisers, Auto Damage; Insurance Underwriters; Loan Counselors; Loan Officers; Market Research Analysts; Survey Researchers. **PERSONALITY TYPE:** Conventional. Conventional occupations frequently involve following set procedures and routines. These occupations can include working with data and

details more than with ideas. Usually there is a clear line of authority to follow.

EDUCATION/TRAINING PROGRAM(S)—Business Administration/Management; Business/Commerce, General; Construction Engineering; Construction Engineering Technology/Technician; Manufacturing Engineering; Materials Engineering; Mechanical Engineering.

WORK ENVIRONMENT—Contaminants; very hot or cold; sitting; in an enclosed vehicle or equipment; physical proximity to others.

Counseling Psychologists

- Education/Training Required: Doctoral degree
- Annual Earnings: $56,360
- Growth: 24.4%
- Annual Job Openings: 17,000
- Self-Employed: 25.4%
- Part-Time: 27.2%

The job openings listed here are shared with Clinical Psychologists and School Psychologists.

Age Bracket	Percentage of Workers
45–54 Years Old	33.0%
55–64 Years Old	23.8%
65 or Older	7.6%

Assess and evaluate individuals' problems through the use of case history, interview, and observation and provide individual or group counseling services to assist individuals in achieving more effective personal, social, educational, and vocational development and

adjustment. Advise clients on how they could be helped by counseling. Analyze data such as interview notes, test results, and reference manuals in order to identify symptoms and to diagnose the nature of clients' problems. Collect information about individuals or clients, using interviews, case histories, observational techniques, and other assessment methods. Counsel individuals, groups, or families to help them understand problems, define goals, and develop realistic action plans. Develop therapeutic and treatment plans based on clients' interests, abilities, and needs. Evaluate the results of counseling methods to determine the reliability and validity of treatments. Select, administer, and interpret psychological tests to assess intelligence, aptitudes, abilities, or interests. Consult with other professionals to discuss therapies, treatments, counseling resources, or techniques and to share occupational information. Refer clients to specialists or to other institutions for non-counseling treatment of problems. Conduct research to develop or improve diagnostic or therapeutic counseling techniques. Provide consulting services to schools, social service agencies, and businesses. **SKILLS—** Social Perceptiveness; Active Listening; Learning Strategies; Reading Comprehension; Critical Thinking; Persuasion; Active Learning; Speaking; Science.

GOE—Interest Area: 10. Human Service. **Work Group:** 10.01. Counseling and Social Work. **Other Jobs in This Work Group:** Child, Family, and School Social Workers; Clinical Psychologists; Marriage and Family Therapists; Medical and Public Health Social Workers; Mental Health and Substance Abuse Social Workers; Mental Health Counselors; Probation Officers and Correctional Treatment Specialists; Rehabilitation Counselors; Residential Advisors; Social and Human Service Assistants; Substance Abuse and Behavioral Disorder Counselors. **PERSONALITY TYPE:** Social. Social occupations frequently involve working with, communicating with, and teaching people. These occupations often involve helping or providing service to others.

EDUCATION/TRAINING PROGRAM(S)— Clinical Child Psychology; Clinical Psychology; Counseling Psychology; Developmental and Child Psychology; Psychoanalysis and Psychotherapy; Psychology, General; School Psychology.

WORK ENVIRONMENT—Sitting; indoors; disease or infections.

Court Clerks

- Education/Training Required: Short-term on-the-job training
- Annual Earnings: $28,980
- Growth: 12.3%
- Annual Job Openings: 14,000
- Self-Employed: 2.6%
- Part-Time: 8.3%

The job openings listed here are shared with Municipal Clerks and License Clerks.

Age Bracket	Percentage of Workers
45–54 Years Old	25.8%
55–64 Years Old	13.5%
65 or Older	2.2%

Perform clerical duties in court of law; prepare docket of cases to be called; secure information for judges; and contact witnesses, attorneys, and litigants to obtain information for court. Prepare dockets or calendars of cases to be called, using typewriters or computers. Record case dispositions, court orders, and arrangements made for payment of court fees. Answer inquiries from the general public regarding judicial procedures, court appearances, trial dates, adjournments, outstanding warrants, summonses, subpoenas, witness fees, and payment of fines. Prepare and issue orders of the court, including probation orders, release documentation, sentencing information, and summonses. Prepare documents recording the outcomes of court proceedings. Instruct parties about timing of court appearances. Explain procedures or forms to parties in cases or to the general public. Search files and contact witnesses, attorneys, and litigants in order to obtain information for the court. Follow procedures to secure courtrooms and exhibits such as money, drugs, and weapons. Amend indictments when necessary and endorse indictments with pertinent information. Read charges and related information to the court and, if necessary, record defendants' pleas. Swear in jury members, interpreters, witnesses, and defendants. Collect court fees or fines and record amounts collected. Direct support staff in handling of paperwork processed by clerks' offices. Prepare and mark all applicable court exhibits and evidence. Examine legal documents submitted to courts for adherence to laws or court procedures. Record court proceedings, using recording equipment, or record minutes of court proceedings, using stenotype machines or shorthand. Prepare courtrooms with paper, pens, water, easels, and electronic equipment and ensure that recording equipment is working. Conduct roll calls and poll jurors. Open courts, calling them to order and announcing judges. Meet with judges, lawyers, parole officers, police, and social agency officials in order to coordinate the functions of the court. **SKILLS—**Instructing; Service Orientation; Active Listening; Coordination; Learning Strategies; Writing; Critical Thinking; Time Management.

GOE—Interest Area: 07. Government and Public Administration. **Work Group:** 07.04. Public Administration Clerical Support. **Other Jobs in This Work Group:** Court Reporters; License Clerks; Municipal Clerks. **PERSONALITY TYPE:** Conventional. Conventional occupations frequently involve following set procedures and routines. These occupations can include working with data and details more than with ideas. Usually there is a clear line of authority to follow.

EDUCATION/TRAINING PROGRAM(S)—General Office Occupations and Clerical Services.

WORK ENVIRONMENT—Sitting; physical proximity to others; contaminants; sounds, noise levels are distracting or uncomfortable; extremely bright or inadequate lighting.

Creative Writers

- Education/Training Required: Bachelor's degree
- Annual Earnings: $45,460
- Growth: 16.1%
- Annual Job Openings: 23,000
- Self-Employed: 67.9%
- Part-Time: 24.2%

The job openings listed here are shared with Caption Writers, Copy Writers, and Poets and Lyricists.

Age Bracket	Percentage of Workers
45–54 Years Old	24.7%
55–64 Years Old	16.3%
65 or Older	7.4%

Create original written works, such as plays or prose, for publication or performance. Writes fiction or nonfiction prose work, such as short story, novel, biography, article, descriptive or critical analysis, or essay. Writes play or script for moving pictures or television, based on original ideas or adapted from fictional, historical, or narrative sources. Organizes material for project, plans arrangement or outline, and writes synopsis. Collaborates with other writers on specific projects. Confers with client, publisher, or producer to discuss development changes or revisions. Conducts research to obtain factual information and authentic detail, utilizing sources such as newspaper accounts, diaries, and interviews. Reviews, submits for approval, and revises written material to meet personal standards and satisfy needs of client, publisher, director, or producer. Selects subject or theme for writing project based on personal interest and writing specialty or assignment from publisher, client, producer, or director. Develops factors such as theme, plot, characterization, psychological analysis, historical environment, action, and dialogue to create material. Writes humorous material for publication or performance, such as comedy routines, gags, comedy shows, or scripts for entertainers. **SKILLS**— Writing; Reading Comprehension; Coordination; Critical Thinking; Complex Problem Solving; Social Perceptiveness; Systems Analysis; Monitoring.

GOE—Interest Area: 03. Arts and Communication. **Work Group:** 03.02. Writing and Editing. **Other Jobs in This Work Group:** Copy Writers; Editors; Poets and Lyricists; Technical Writers. **PERSONALITY TYPE:** Artistic. Artistic occupations frequently involve working with forms, designs, and patterns. They often require self-expression, and the work can be done without following a clear set of rules.

EDUCATION/TRAINING PROGRAM(S)— Communications Studies/Speech Communica-

tion and Rhetoric; Creative Writing; English Composition; Family and Consumer Sciences/Human Sciences Communications; Mass Communications/Media Studies; Playwriting and Screenwriting.

WORK ENVIRONMENT—Sitting; indoors.

Criminal Justice and Law Enforcement Teachers, Postsecondary

- Education/Training Required: Master's degree
- Annual Earnings: $49,290
- Growth: 38.1%
- Annual Job Openings: 216,000
- Self-Employed: 0.3%
- Part-Time: 27.7%

The job openings listed here are shared with all other postsecondary teaching occupations.

Age Bracket	Percentage of Workers
45–54 Years Old	22.8%
55–64 Years Old	19.0%
65 or Older	5.5%

Teach courses in criminal justice, corrections, and law enforcement administration. Initiate, facilitate, and moderate classroom discussions. Keep abreast of developments in their field by reading current literature, talking with colleagues, and participating in professional conferences. Evaluate and grade students' class work, assignments, and papers. Compile, administer, and grade examinations or assign this work to others. Prepare and deliver lectures to under-graduate and/or graduate students on topics such as criminal law, defensive policing, and investigation techniques. Prepare course materials such as syllabi, homework assignments, and handouts. Conduct research in a particular field of knowledge and publish findings in professional journals, books, and/or electronic media. Plan, evaluate, and revise curricula, course content, and course materials and methods of instruction. Supervise undergraduate and/or graduate teaching, internship, and research work. Maintain student attendance records, grades, and other required records. Select and obtain materials and supplies such as textbooks. Advise students on academic and vocational curricula and on career issues. Maintain regularly scheduled office hours in order to advise and assist students. Collaborate with colleagues to address teaching and research issues. Write grant proposals to procure external research funding. Serve on academic or administrative committees that deal with institutional policies, departmental matters, and academic issues. Compile bibliographies of specialized materials for outside reading assignments. Participate in student recruitment, registration, and placement activities. Provide professional consulting services to government and/or industry. Perform administrative duties such as serving as department head. **SKILLS**—Instructing; Critical Thinking; Writing; Active Learning; Persuasion; Learning Strategies; Time Management; Reading Comprehension.

GOE—Interest Area: 05. Education and Training. **Work Group:** 05.03. Postsecondary and Adult Teaching and Instructing. **Other Jobs in This Work Group:** Adult Literacy, Remedial Education, and GED Teachers and Instructors; Agricultural Sciences Teachers, Postsecondary; Anthropology and Archeology Teachers, Postsecondary; Architecture Teachers, Postsecondary; Area, Ethnic, and Cultural Studies Teachers, Postsecondary; Art, Drama, and Music Teachers, Postsecondary; Atmospheric, Earth, Marine, and Space Sciences Teachers, Postsecondary; Biological Science Teachers, Postsecondary; Business Teachers, Postsecondary; Chemistry Teachers, Postsecondary; Communications Teachers, Postsecondary; Computer Science Teachers, Postsecondary; Economics Teachers, Postsecondary; Education Teachers, Postsecondary; Engineering Teachers, Postsecondary; English Language and Literature Teachers, Postsecondary; Environmental Science Teachers, Postsecondary; Farm and Home Management Advisors; Foreign Language and Literature Teachers, Postsecondary; Forestry and Conservation Science Teachers, Postsecondary; Geography Teachers, Postsecondary; Graduate Teaching Assistants; Health Specialties Teachers, Postsecondary; History Teachers, Postsecondary; Home Economics Teachers, Postsecondary; Law Teachers, Postsecondary; Library Science Teachers, Postsecondary; Mathematical Science Teachers, Postsecondary; Nursing Instructors and Teachers, Postsecondary; Philosophy and Religion Teachers, Postsecondary; Physics Teachers, Postsecondary; Political Science Teachers, Postsecondary; Psychology Teachers, Postsecondary; Recreation and Fitness Studies Teachers, Postsecondary; Self-Enrichment Education Teachers; Social Work Teachers, Postsecondary; Sociology Teachers, Postsecondary; Vocational Education Teachers, Postsecondary. **PERSONALITY TYPE:** No data available.

EDUCATION/TRAINING PROGRAM(S)—Corrections; Corrections Administration; Corrections and Criminal Justice, Other; Criminal Justice/Law Enforcement Administration; Criminal Justice/Police Science; Criminal Justice/Safety Studies; Criminalistics and Criminal Science; Forensic Science and Technology; Juvenile Corrections; Security and Loss Prevention Services; Teacher Education and Professional Development, Specific Subject Areas, Other.

WORK ENVIRONMENT—Sitting; physical proximity to others; sounds, noise levels are distracting or uncomfortable; indoors; extremely bright or inadequate lighting.

Crossing Guards

- Education/Training Required: Short-term on-the-job training
- Annual Earnings: $19,710
- Growth: 16.5%
- Annual Job Openings: 19,000
- Self-Employed: 0%
- Part-Time: 75.6%

Age Bracket	Percentage of Workers
45–54 Years Old	22.7%
55–64 Years Old	13.6%
65 or Older	25.0%

Guide or control vehicular or pedestrian traffic at such places as streets, schools, railroad crossings, or construction sites. Direct or escort pedestrians across streets, stopping traffic as necessary. Guide or control vehicular or pedestrian traffic at such places as street and railroad crossings and construction sites. Communicate traffic and crossing rules and other information to students and adults. Direct traffic movement or warn of hazards, using signs, flags, lanterns, and hand signals. Inform drivers of detour routes through construction sites. Learn the location and purpose of street traffic signs within assigned patrol areas. Monitor traffic flow to locate safe gaps through which pedestrians can cross streets. Activate railroad warning signal lights, lower crossing gates until trains pass, and raise gates when crossings are clear. Discuss traffic routing plans and control point locations with superiors. Distribute traffic control signs and markers at designated points. Record license numbers of vehicles disregarding traffic signals and report infractions to appropriate authorities. Report unsafe behavior of children to school officials. Stop speeding vehicles to warn drivers of traffic laws. **SKILLS**—None met the criteria.

GOE—Interest Area: 12. Law and Public Safety. **Work Group:** 12.05. Safety and Security. **Other Jobs in This Work Group:** Animal Control Workers; Gaming Surveillance Officers and Gaming Investigators; Lifeguards, Ski Patrol, and Other Recreational Protective Service Workers; Private Detectives and Investigators; Security Guards. **PERSONALITY TYPE:** Social. Social occupations frequently involve working with, communicating with, and teaching people. These occupations often involve helping or providing service to others.

EDUCATION/TRAINING PROGRAM(S)—Protective Services, Other; Security and Loss Prevention Services.

WORK ENVIRONMENT—Outdoors; standing; walking and running; common protective or safety equipment; sounds, noise levels are distracting or uncomfortable.

Curators

- Education/Training Required: Master's degree
- Annual Earnings: $43,920
- Growth: 17.0%
- Annual Job Openings: 2,000
- Self-Employed: 3.4%
- Part-Time: 11.8%

Age Bracket	Percentage of Workers
45–54 Years Old	25.8%
55–64 Years Old	16.1%
65 or Older	3.2%

Administer affairs of museum and conduct research programs. Direct instructional, research, and public service activities of institution. Plan and organize the acquisition, storage, and exhibition of collections and related materials, including the selection of exhibition themes and designs. Develop and maintain an institution's registration, cataloging, and basic record-keeping systems, using computer databases. Provide information from the institution's holdings to other curators and to the public. Inspect premises to assess the need for repairs and to ensure that climate and pest-control issues are addressed. Train and supervise curatorial, fiscal, technical, research, and clerical staff, as well as volunteers or interns. Negotiate and authorize purchase, sale, exchange, or loan of collections. Plan and conduct special research projects in area of interest or expertise. Conduct or organize tours, workshops, and instructional sessions to acquaint individuals with an institution's facilities and materials. Confer with the board of directors to formulate and interpret policies, to determine budget requirements, and to plan overall operations. Attend meetings, conventions, and civic events to promote use of institution's services, to seek financing, and to maintain community alliances. Schedule events and organize details, including refreshment, entertainment, decorations, and the collection of any fees. Write and review grant proposals, journal articles, institutional reports, and publicity materials. Study, examine, and test acquisitions to authenticate their origin, composition, and history and to assess their current value. Arrange insurance coverage for objects on loan or for special exhibits and recommend changes in coverage for the entire collection. **SKILLS**—Management of Financial Resources; Management of Personnel Resources; Time Management; Writing; Persuasion; Service Orientation; Speaking; Negotiation.

GOE—Interest Area: 05. Education and Training. **Work Group:** 05.05. Archival and Museum Services. **Other Jobs in This Work Group:** Archivists; Audio-Visual Collections Specialists; Museum Technicians and Conservators. **PERSONALITY TYPE:** Artistic. Artistic occupations frequently involve working with forms, designs, and patterns. They often require self-expression, and the work can be done without following a clear set of rules.

EDUCATION/TRAINING PROGRAM(S)—Art History, Criticism, and Conservation; Museology/Museum Studies; Public/Applied History and Archival Administration.

WORK ENVIRONMENT—Sitting; physical proximity to others; indoors, not environmentally controlled; contaminants; extremely bright or inadequate lighting.

Demonstrators and Product Promoters

- ◉ Education/Training Required: Moderate-term on-the-job training
- ◉ Annual Earnings: $20,490
- ◉ Growth: 17.0%
- ◉ Annual Job Openings: 38,000
- ◉ Self-Employed: 42.1%
- ◉ Part-Time: 52.5%

Age Bracket	Percentage of Workers
45–54 Years Old	9.6%
55–64 Years Old	13.7%
65 or Older	20.5%

Demonstrate merchandise and answer questions for the purpose of creating public interest in buying the product. May sell demonstrated merchandise. Demonstrate and explain products, methods, or services in order to persuade customers to purchase products or utilize services. Identify interested and qualified customers in order to provide them with additional information. Keep areas neat while working and return items to correct locations following demonstrations. Practice demonstrations to ensure that they will run smoothly. Prepare and alter presentation contents to target specific audiences. Provide product information, using lectures, films, charts, and/or slide shows. Provide product samples, coupons, informational brochures, and other incentives to persuade people to buy products. Record and report demonstration-related information such as the number of questions asked by the audience and the number of coupons distributed. Research and investigate products to be presented to prepare for demonstrations. Sell products being promoted and keep records of sales. Set up and arrange displays and demonstration areas to attract the attention of prospective customers. Stock shelves with products. Suggest specific product purchases to meet customers' needs. Transport, assemble, and disassemble materials used in presentations. Visit trade shows, stores, community organizations, and other venues to demonstrate products or services and to answer questions from potential customers. Collect fees or accept donations. Contact businesses and civic establishments to arrange to exhibit and sell merchandise. Develop lists of prospective clients from sources such as newspaper items, company records, local merchants, and customers. Give tours of plants where specific products are made. Instruct customers in alteration of products. Learn about competitors' products and consumers' interests and concerns in order to answer questions and provide more complete information. Recommend product or service improvements to employers. Train demonstrators to present a company's products or services. Wear costumes or signboards and walk in public to promote merchandise, services, or events. Work as part of a team of demonstrators to accommodate large crowds. **SKILLS**—Persuasion; Speaking; Social Perceptiveness; Learning Strategies; Instructing; Writing; Active Learning; Systems Evaluation.

GOE—Interest Area: 14. Retail and Wholesale Sales and Service. **Work Group:** 14.04. Personal Soliciting. **Other Jobs in This Work Group:** Door-To-Door Sales Workers, News and Street Vendors, and Related Workers; Models; Telemarketers. **PERSONALITY TYPE:** Enterprising. Enterprising occupations frequently involve starting up and carrying out projects. These occupations can involve leading people and making many decisions. They sometimes require risk taking and often deal with business.

EDUCATION/TRAINING PROGRAM(S)— Retailing and Retail Operations.

WORK ENVIRONMENT—Outdoors; walking and running; standing; extremely bright or inadequate lighting; very hot or cold; minor burns, cuts, bites, or stings.

Dentists, General

- ◎ Education/Training Required: First professional degree
- ◎ Annual Earnings: $122,430
- ◎ Growth: 4.1%
- ◎ Annual Job Openings: 7,000
- ◎ Self-Employed: 39.9%
- ◎ Part-Time: 22.3%

The job openings listed here are shared with Oral and Maxillofacial Surgeons, Orthodontists, and Prosthodontists.

Age Bracket	Percentage of Workers
45–54 Years Old	28.2%
55–64 Years Old	19.7%
65 or Older	6.4%

Diagnose and treat diseases, injuries, and malformations of teeth and gums and related oral structures. May treat diseases of nerve, pulp, and other dental tissues affecting vitality of teeth. Use masks, gloves, and safety glasses to protect themselves and their patients from infectious diseases. Administer anesthetics to limit the amount of pain experienced by patients during procedures. Examine teeth, gums, and related tissues, using dental instruments, X rays, and other diagnostic equipment, to evaluate dental health, diagnose diseases or abnormalities, and plan appropriate treatments. Formulate plan of treatment for patient's teeth and mouth tissue.

Use air turbine and hand instruments, dental appliances, and surgical implements. Advise and instruct patients regarding preventive dental care, the causes and treatment of dental problems, and oral health care services. Design, make, and fit prosthodontic appliances such as space maintainers, bridges, and dentures or write fabrication instructions or prescriptions for denturists and dental technicians. Diagnose and treat diseases, injuries, and malformations of teeth, gums, and related oral structures and provide preventive and corrective services. Fill pulp chamber and canal with endodontic materials. Write prescriptions for antibiotics and other medications. Analyze and evaluate dental needs to determine changes and trends in patterns of dental disease. Treat exposure of pulp by pulp capping, removal of pulp from pulp chamber, or root canal, using dental instruments. Eliminate irritating margins of fillings and correct occlusions, using dental instruments. Perform oral and periodontal surgery on the jaw or mouth. Remove diseased tissue, using surgical instruments. Apply fluoride and sealants to teeth. Manage business, employing and supervising staff and handling paperwork and insurance claims. Bleach, clean, or polish teeth to restore natural color. Plan, organize, and maintain dental health programs. Produce and evaluate dental health educational materials. **SKILLS**—Science; Management of Financial Resources; Management of Material Resources; Service Orientation; Complex Problem Solving; Persuasion; Equipment Selection; Management of Personnel Resources.

GOE—Interest Area: 08. Health Science. **Work Group:** 08.03. Dentistry. **Other Jobs in This Work Group:** Dental Assistants; Dental Hygienists; Oral and Maxillofacial Surgeons; Orthodontists; Prosthodontists. **PERSONALITY TYPE:** Investigative. Investigative occupa-

D

tions frequently involve working with ideas and require an extensive amount of thinking. These occupations can involve searching for facts and figuring out problems mentally.

EDUCATION/TRAINING PROGRAM(S)—Advanced General Dentistry (Cert, MS, PhD); Dental Public Health and Education (Cert, MS/MPH, PhD/DPH); Dental Public Health Specialty; Dentistry (DDS, DMD); Pediatric Dentistry/Pedodontics (Cert, MS, PhD); Pedodontics Specialty.

WORK ENVIRONMENT—Exposed to radiation; contaminants; physical proximity to others; disease or infections; sitting.

Dietitians and Nutritionists

- Education/Training Required: Bachelor's degree
- Annual Earnings: $44,370
- Growth: 17.8%
- Annual Job Openings: 8,000
- Self-Employed: 6.3%
- Part-Time: 24.3%

Age Bracket	Percentage of Workers
45–54 Years Old	32.9%
55–64 Years Old	8.2%
65 or Older	2.4%

Plan and conduct food service or nutritional programs to assist in the promotion of health and control of disease. May supervise activities of a department providing quantity food services, counsel individuals, or conduct nutritional research. Assess nutritional needs, diet restrictions, and current health plans to develop and implement dietary-care plans and provide nutritional counseling. Consult with physicians and health care personnel to determine nutritional needs and diet restrictions of patient or client. Advise patients and their families on nutritional principles, dietary plans and diet modifications, and food selection and preparation. Counsel individuals and groups on basic rules of good nutrition, healthy eating habits, and nutrition monitoring to improve their quality of life. Monitor food service operations to ensure conformance to nutritional, safety, sanitation, and quality standards. Coordinate recipe development and standardization and develop new menus for independent food service operations. Develop policies for food service or nutritional programs to assist in health promotion and disease control. Inspect meals served for conformance to prescribed diets and standards of palatability and appearance. Develop curriculum and prepare manuals, visual aids, course outlines, and other materials used in teaching. Prepare and administer budgets for food, equipment, and supplies. Purchase food in accordance with health and safety codes. Select, train, and supervise workers who plan, prepare, and serve meals. Manage quantity food service departments or clinical and community nutrition services. Coordinate diet counseling services. Advise food service managers and organizations on sanitation, safety procedures, menu development, budgeting, and planning to assist with the establishment, operation, and evaluation of food service facilities and nutrition programs. Organize, develop, analyze, test, and prepare special meals such as low-fat, low-cholesterol, and chemical-free meals. Plan, conduct, and evaluate dietary, nutritional, and epidemiological research. Plan and conduct training programs in dietetics, nutrition, and institutional management and administration for medical students, health care personnel, and the general public. Make recommendations regarding public policy, such as nutrition labeling, food fortification, and nutrition standards for school programs. **SKILLS**—Instructing; Social Perceptiveness; Learning Strategies; Writing; Science; Persuasion; Service Orientation; Speaking.

GOE—Interest Area: 08. Health Science. **Work Group:** 08.09. Health Protection and Promotion. **Other Jobs in This Work Group:** Athletic Trainers; Dietetic Technicians; Embalmers. **PERSONALITY TYPE:** Investigative. Investigative occupations frequently involve working with ideas and require an extensive amount of thinking. These occupations can involve searching for facts and figuring out problems mentally.

EDUCATION/TRAINING PROGRAM(S)— Clinical Nutrition/Nutritionist (NR); Dietetic and Clinical Nutrition Services, Other; Dietetics/Dietician (RD); Foods, Nutrition, and Related Services, Other; Foods, Nutrition, and Wellness Studies, General; Foodservice Systems Administration/Management; Human Nutrition; Nutrition Sciences.

WORK ENVIRONMENT—Sitting; physical proximity to others; very hot or cold.

Directors, Religious Activities and Education

- Education/Training Required: Bachelor's degree
- Annual Earnings: $30,720
- Growth: 24.1%
- Annual Job Openings: 16,000
- Self-Employed: 0%
- Part-Time: 28.2%

Age Bracket	Percentage of Workers
45–54 Years Old	27.6%
55–64 Years Old	20.7%
65 or Older	3.4%

Direct and coordinate activities of a denominational group to meet religious needs of students. Plan, direct, or coordinate church school programs designed to promote religious education among church membership. May provide counseling and guidance relative to marital, health, financial, and religious problems. Analyze member participation and changes in congregation emphasis to determine needs for religious education. Collaborate with other ministry members to establish goals and objectives for religious education programs and to develop ways to encourage program participation. Confer with clergy members, congregation officials, and congregation organizations to encourage support of and participation in religious education activities. Develop and direct study courses and religious education programs within congregations. Identify and recruit potential volunteer workers. Implement program plans by ordering needed materials, scheduling speakers, reserving space, and handling other administrative details. Locate and distribute resources such as periodicals and curricula in order to enhance the effectiveness of educational programs. Publicize programs through sources such as newsletters, bulletins, and mailings. Schedule special events such as camps, conferences, meetings, seminars, and retreats. Select appropriate curricula and class structures for educational programs. Train and supervise religious education instructional staff. Analyze revenue and program cost data to determine budget priorities. Attend workshops, seminars, and conferences to obtain program ideas, information, and resources. Counsel individuals regarding interpersonal, health, financial, and religious problems. Interpret religious education activities to the public through speaking, leading discussions, and writing articles for local and national publications. Participate in denominational activities aimed at goals such as promoting interfaith understanding or providing aid to new or small congregations. Plan and conduct conferences dealing with the interpretation of religious ideas and convictions. Visit congregation members' homes, or arrange for pastoral visits, in order to provide information and resources regarding religious education programs. **SKILLS**—Management of Financial Resources; Social Perceptiveness; Management of Personnel Resources; Service Orientation; Management of Material Resources; Systems Analysis; Systems Evaluation; Instructing.

GOE—**Interest Area:** 10. Human Service. **Work Group:** 10.02. Religious Work. **Other Jobs in This Work Group:** Clergy. **PERSONALITY TYPE:** Social. Social occupations frequently involve working with, communicating with, and teaching people. These occupations often involve helping or providing service to others.

EDUCATION/TRAINING PROGRAM(S)— Bible/Biblical Studies; Missions/Missionary Studies and Missiology; Religious Education; Youth Ministry.

WORK ENVIRONMENT—Sitting; indoors; walking and running; standing.

Economics Teachers, Postsecondary

- ◎ Education/Training Required: Master's degree
- ◎ Annual Earnings: $68,050
- ◎ Growth: 38.1%
- ◎ Annual Job Openings: 216,000
- ◎ Self-Employed: 0.3%
- ◎ Part-Time: 27.7%

The job openings listed here are shared with all other postsecondary teaching occupations.

Age Bracket	Percentage of Workers
45–54 Years Old	22.8%
55–64 Years Old	19.0%
65 or Older	5.5%

Teach courses in economics. Prepare and deliver lectures to undergraduate and/or graduate students on topics such as econometrics, price theory, and macroeconomics. Prepare course materials such as syllabi, homework assignments, and handouts. Evaluate and grade students' class work, assignments, and papers. Compile, administer, and grade examinations or assign this work to others. Keep abreast of developments in their field by reading current literature, talking with colleagues, and participating in professional conferences. Maintain student attendance records, grades, and other required records. Initiate, facilitate, and moderate classroom discussions. Maintain regularly scheduled office hours in order to advise and assist students. Select and obtain materials and supplies such as textbooks. Plan, evaluate, and revise curricula, course content, and course materials and methods of instruction. Conduct research in a particular field of knowledge and publish findings in professional journals, books, and/or electronic media. Supervise undergraduate and/or graduate teaching, internship, and research work. Advise students on academic and vocational curricula and on career issues. Serve on academic or administrative committees that deal with institutional policies, departmental matters, and academic issues. Collaborate with colleagues to address teaching and research issues. Compile bibliographies of specialized materials for outside reading assignments. Participate in student recruitment, registration, and placement activities. Perform administrative duties such as serving as department head. **SKILLS—**Instructing; Writing; Speaking; Mathematics; Critical Thinking; Reading Comprehension; Learning Strategies; Active Learning.

GOE—Interest Area: 05. Education and Training. **Work Group:** 05.03. Postsecondary and Adult Teaching and Instructing. **Other Jobs in This Work Group:** Adult Literacy, Remedial Education, and GED Teachers and Instructors; Agricultural Sciences Teachers, Postsecondary; Anthropology and Archeology Teachers, Postsecondary; Architecture Teachers, Postsecondary; Area, Ethnic, and Cultural Studies Teachers, Postsecondary; Art, Drama, and Music Teachers, Postsecondary; Atmospheric, Earth, Marine, and Space Sciences Teachers, Postsecondary; Biological Science Teachers, Postsecondary; Business Teachers, Postsecondary; Chemistry Teachers, Postsecondary; Communications Teachers, Postsecondary; Computer Science Teachers, Postsecondary; Criminal Justice and Law Enforcement Teachers, Postsecondary; Education Teachers, Postsecondary; Engineering Teachers, Postsecondary; English Language and Literature Teachers, Postsecondary; Environmental Science Teachers, Postsecondary; Farm and Home Management Advisors; Foreign Language and Literature Teachers, Postsecondary; Forestry and Conservation Science Teachers, Postsecondary; Geography Teachers, Postsecondary; Graduate Teaching Assistants; Health Specialties Teachers, Postsecondary; History Teachers, Postsecondary; Home Economics Teachers, Postsecondary; Law Teachers, Postsecondary; Library Science Teachers, Postsecondary; Mathematical Science Teachers, Postsecondary; Nursing Instructors and Teachers, Postsecondary; Philosophy and Religion Teachers, Postsecondary; Physics Teachers, Postsecondary; Political Science Teachers, Postsecondary; Psychology Teachers, Postsecondary; Recreation and Fitness Studies Teachers, Postsecondary; Self-Enrichment Education Teachers; Social Work Teachers, Postsecondary; Sociology Teachers, Postsecondary; Vocational Education Teachers, Postsecondary. **PERSONALITY TYPE:** Social. Social occupations frequently involve working with, communicating with, and teaching people. These occupations often involve helping or providing service to others.

EDUCATION/TRAINING PROGRAM(S)—Applied Economics; Business/Managerial Economics; Development Economics and International Development; Econometrics and Quantitative Economics; Economics, General; Economics, Other; International Economics; Social Science Teacher Education.

WORK ENVIRONMENT—Sitting; physical proximity to others; sounds, noise levels are distracting or uncomfortable; indoors.

Economists

- ⊚ Education/Training Required: Master's degree
- ⊚ Annual Earnings: $72,370
- ⊚ Growth: 13.4%
- ⊚ Annual Job Openings: 2,000
- ⊚ Self-Employed: 11.5%
- ⊚ Part-Time: 8.3%

Age Bracket	Percentage of Workers
45–54 Years Old	32.4%
55–64 Years Old	17.6%
65 or Older	2.9%

Conduct research, prepare reports, or formulate plans to aid in solution of economic problems arising from production and distribution of goods and services. May collect and process economic and statistical data, using econometric and sampling techniques. Study economic and statistical data in area of specialization, such as finance, labor, or agriculture. Formulate recommendations, policies, or plans to solve economic problems or to interpret markets. Provide advice and consultation on economic relationships to businesses, public and private agencies, and other employers. Supervise research projects and students' study projects. Teach theories, principles, and methods of economics. Testify at regulatory or legislative hearings concerning the estimated effects of changes in legislation or public policy and present recommendations based on cost-benefit analyses. Compile, analyze, and report data to explain economic phenomena and forecast market trends, applying mathematical models and statistical techniques. Develop economic guidelines and standards and prepare points of view used in forecasting trends and formulating economic policy. Forecast production and consumption of renewable resources and supply, consumption, and depletion of non-renewable resources. **SKILLS—** Systems Evaluation; Systems Analysis; Persuasion; Judgment and Decision Making; Complex Problem Solving; Writing; Instructing; Learning Strategies.

GOE—Interest Area: 15. Scientific Research, Engineering, and Mathematics. **Work Group:** 15.04. Social Sciences. **Other Jobs in This Work Group:** Anthropologists; Archeologists; Educational Psychologists; Historians; Industrial-Organizational Psychologists; Political Scientists; Sociologists. **PERSONALITY TYPE:** Investigative. Investigative occupations frequently involve working with ideas and require an extensive amount of thinking. These occupations can involve searching for facts and figuring out problems mentally.

EDUCATION/TRAINING PROGRAM(S)— Agricultural Economics; Applied Economics; Business/Managerial Economics; Development Economics and International Development; Econometrics and Quantitative Economics; Economics, General; Economics, Other; International Economics.

WORK ENVIRONMENT—Sitting; indoors; standing.

Education Administrators, Elementary and Secondary School

- ◎ Education/Training Required: Work experience plus degree
- ◎ Annual Earnings: $74,610
- ◎ Growth: 20.7%
- ◎ Annual Job Openings: 31,000
- ◎ Self-Employed: 3.2%
- ◎ Part-Time: 7.2%

Age Bracket	Percentage of Workers
45–54 Years Old	36.0%
55–64 Years Old	22.7%
65 or Older	3.2%

Plan, direct, or coordinate the academic, clerical, or auxiliary activities of public or private elementary or secondary-level schools. Review and approve new programs, or recommend modifications to existing programs, submitting program proposals for school board approval as necessary. Prepare, maintain, or oversee the preparation/maintenance of attendance, activity, planning, or personnel reports and records. Confer with parents and staff to discuss educational activities, policies, and student behavioral or learning problems. Prepare and submit budget requests and recommendations or grant proposals to solicit program funding. Direct and coordinate school maintenance services and the use of school facilities. Counsel and provide guidance to students regarding personal, academic, vocational, or behavioral issues. Organize and direct committees of specialists, volunteers, and staff to provide technical and advisory assistance for programs. Teach classes or courses to students. Advocate for new schools to be built or for existing facilities to be repaired or remodeled. Plan and develop instructional methods and content for educational, vocational, or student activity programs. Develop partnerships with businesses, communities, and other organizations to help meet identified educational needs and to provide school-to-work programs. Direct and coordinate activities of teachers, administrators, and support staff at schools, public agencies, and institutions. Evaluate curricula, teaching methods, and programs to determine their effectiveness, efficiency, and utilization and to ensure that school activities comply with federal, state, and local regulations. Set educational standards and goals and help establish policies and procedures to carry them out. Recruit, hire, train, and evaluate primary and supplemental staff. Enforce discipline and attendance rules. Observe teaching methods and examine learning materials in order to evaluate and standardize curricula and teaching techniques and to determine areas where improvement is needed. Establish, coordinate, and oversee particular programs across school districts, such as programs to evaluate student academic achievement. Review and interpret government codes and develop programs to ensure adherence to codes and facility safety, security, and maintenance. **SKILLS—** Management of Personnel Resources; Management of Financial Resources; Learning Strategies; Negotiation; Social Perceptiveness; Persuasion; Monitoring; Service Orientation.

GOE—Interest Area: 05. Education and Training. **Work Group:** 05.01. Managerial Work in Education. **Other Jobs in This Work Group:** Education Administrators, Postsecondary; Education Administrators, Preschool and Child Care Center/Program; Instructional

E

Coordinators. **PERSONALITY TYPE:** Social. Social occupations frequently involve working with, communicating with, and teaching people. These occupations often involve helping or providing service to others.

EDUCATION/TRAINING PROGRAM(S)— Educational Administration and Supervision, Other; Educational Leadership and Administration, General; Educational, Instructional, and Curriculum Supervision; Elementary and Middle School Administration/Principalship; Secondary School Administration/Principalship.

WORK ENVIRONMENT—Sounds, noise levels are distracting or uncomfortable; physical proximity to others; sitting; indoors; very hot or cold.

Education Administrators, Postsecondary

- Education/Training Required: Work experience plus degree
- Annual Earnings: $69,400
- Growth: 25.9%
- Annual Job Openings: 19,000
- Self-Employed: 2.6%
- Part-Time: 7.2%

Age Bracket	Percentage of Workers
45–54 Years Old	36.0%
55–64 Years Old	22.7%
65 or Older	3.2%

Plan, direct, or coordinate research, instructional, student administration and services, and other educational activities at postsecondary institutions, including universities, colleges, and junior and community colleges. Recruit, hire, train, and terminate departmental personnel. Plan, administer, and control budgets; maintain financial records; and produce financial reports. Represent institutions at community and campus events, in meetings with other institution personnel, and during accreditation processes. Participate in faculty and college committee activities. Provide assistance to faculty and staff in duties such as teaching classes, conducting orientation programs, issuing transcripts, and scheduling events. Establish operational policies and procedures and make any necessary modifications based on analysis of operations, demographics, and other research information. Confer with other academic staff to explain and formulate admission requirements and course credit policies. Appoint individuals to faculty positions and evaluate their performance. Direct activities of administrative departments such as admissions, registration, and career services. Develop curricula and recommend curricula revisions and additions. Determine course schedules, and coordinate teaching assignments and room assignments in order to ensure optimum use of buildings and equipment. Consult with government regulatory and licensing agencies in order to ensure the institution's conformance with applicable standards. Direct, coordinate, and evaluate the activities of personnel engaged in administering academic institutions, departments, and/or alumni organizations. Teach courses within their department. Participate in student recruitment, selection, and admission, making admissions recommendations when required to do so. Review student misconduct reports requiring disciplinary action and counsel students regarding such reports. Supervise coaches. Assess and collect tuition and fees. Direct scholarship, fellowship, and loan programs, performing activities such as selecting recipients and distributing aid. Coordinate the production and dissemination of university publications such as course catalogs and class schedules. Review registration statistics and consult with faculty officials to develop registration policies. **SKILLS**— Management of Personnel Resources; Management of Financial Resources; Social Perceptiveness; Persuasion; Service Orientation; Coordination; Negotiation; Monitoring.

GOE—Interest Area: 05. Education and Training. **Work Group:** 05.01. Managerial Work in Education. **Other Jobs in This Work Group:** Education Administrators, Elementary and Secondary School; Education Administrators, Preschool and Child Care Center/Program; Instructional Coordinators. **PERSONALITY TYPE:** Enterprising. Enterprising occupations frequently involve starting up and carrying out projects. These occupations can involve leading people and making many decisions. They sometimes require risk taking and often deal with business.

EDUCATION/TRAINING PROGRAM(S)— Community College Education; Educational Administration and Supervision, Other; Educational Leadership and Administration, General; Educational, Instructional, and Curriculum Supervision; Higher Education/ Higher Education Administration.

WORK ENVIRONMENT—Sitting; indoors; sounds, noise levels are distracting or uncomfortable; physical proximity to others.

Education Administrators, Preschool and Child Care Center/Program

- Education/Training Required: Work experience plus degree
- Annual Earnings: $36,080
- Growth: 32.0%
- Annual Job Openings: 9,000
- Self-Employed: 3.0%
- Part-Time: 7.2%

Age Bracket	Percentage of Workers
45–54 Years Old	36.0%
55–64 Years Old	22.7%
65 or Older	3.2%

Plan, direct, or coordinate the academic and nonacademic activities of preschool and child care centers or programs. Confer with parents and staff to discuss educational activities and policies and students' behavioral or learning problems. Prepare and maintain attendance, activity, planning, accounting, or personnel reports and records for officials and agencies or direct preparation and maintenance activities. Set educational standards and goals and help establish policies, procedures, and programs to carry them out. Monitor students' progress and provide students and teachers with assistance in resolving any problems. Determine allocations of funds for staff, supplies, materials, and equipment and authorize purchases. Recruit, hire, train, and evaluate primary and supplemental staff and recommend personnel actions for programs and services. Direct and coordinate activities of teachers or administrators at daycare

E

centers, schools, public agencies, and/or institutions. Plan, direct, and monitor instructional methods and content of educational, vocational, or student activity programs. Review and interpret government codes and develop procedures to meet codes and to ensure facility safety, security, and maintenance. Determine the scope of educational program offerings and prepare drafts of program schedules and descriptions in order to estimate staffing and facility requirements. Review and evaluate new and current programs to determine their efficiency; effectiveness; and compliance with state, local, and federal regulations; recommend any necessary modifications. Teach classes or courses and/or provide direct care to children. Prepare and submit budget requests or grant proposals to solicit program funding. Write articles, manuals, and other publications and assist in the distribution of promotional literature about programs and facilities. Collect and analyze survey data, regulatory information, and demographic and employment trends in order to forecast enrollment patterns and the need for curriculum changes. Inform businesses, community groups, and governmental agencies about educational needs, available programs, and program policies. Organize and direct committees of specialists, volunteers, and staff to provide technical and advisory assistance for programs. **SKILLS—** Management of Personnel Resources; Management of Financial Resources; Learning Strategies; Social Perceptiveness; Monitoring; Persuasion; Negotiation; Service Orientation.

GOE—Interest Area: 05. Education and Training. **Work Group:** 05.01. Managerial Work in Education. **Other Jobs in This Work Group:** Education Administrators, Elementary and Secondary School; Education Administrators, Postsecondary; Instructional Coordinators. **PERSONALITY TYPE:** Social.

Social occupations frequently involve working with, communicating with, and teaching people. These occupations often involve helping or providing service to others.

EDUCATION/TRAINING PROGRAM(S)— Educational Administration and Supervision, Other; Educational Leadership and Administration, General; Educational, Instructional, and Curriculum Supervision; Elementary and Middle School Administration/Principalship.

WORK ENVIRONMENT—Physical proximity to others; in an enclosed vehicle or equipment; sounds, noise levels are distracting or uncomfortable; sitting; outdoors.

Education Teachers, Postsecondary

- Education/Training Required: Master's degree
- Annual Earnings: $50,410
- Growth: 38.1%
- Annual Job Openings: 216,000
- Self-Employed: 0.3%
- Part-Time: 27.7%

The job openings listed here are shared with all other postsecondary teaching occupations.

Age Bracket	Percentage of Workers
45–54 Years Old	22.8%
55–64 Years Old	19.0%
65 or Older	5.5%

Teach courses pertaining to education, such as counseling, curriculum, guidance, instruction, teacher education, and teaching English as a second language. Prepare course materials such as syllabi, homework assignments, and handouts. Prepare and deliver lectures to undergraduate and/or graduate students on topics such as children's literature, learning and development, and reading instruction. Initiate, facilitate, and moderate classroom discussions. Evaluate and grade students' class work, assignments, and papers. Plan, evaluate, and revise curricula, course content, and course materials and methods of instruction. Supervise students' fieldwork, internship, and research work. Keep abreast of developments in their field by reading current literature, talking with colleagues, and participating in professional conferences. Advise students on academic and vocational curricula and on career issues. Maintain regularly scheduled office hours in order to advise and assist students. Maintain student attendance records, grades, and other required records. Collaborate with colleagues to address teaching and research issues. Compile, administer, and grade examinations or assign this work to others. Conduct research in a particular field of knowledge and publish findings in professional journals, books, and/or electronic media. Select and obtain materials and supplies such as textbooks. Participate in student recruitment, registration, and placement activities. Advise and instruct teachers employed in school systems by providing activities such as in-service seminars. Serve on academic or administrative committees that deal with institutional policies, departmental matters, and academic issues. Compile bibliographies of specialized materials for outside reading assignments. Write grant proposals to procure external research funding. Participate in campus and community events. Perform administrative duties such as serving as department head. Act as advisers to student organizations. **SKILLS—** Instructing; Learning Strategies; Writing; Social Perceptiveness; Persuasion; Service Orientation; Speaking; Active Learning.

GOE—Interest Area: 05. Education and Training. **Work Group:** 05.03. Postsecondary and Adult Teaching and Instructing. **Other Jobs in This Work Group:** Adult Literacy, Remedial Education, and GED Teachers and Instructors; Agricultural Sciences Teachers, Postsecondary; Anthropology and Archeology Teachers, Postsecondary; Architecture Teachers, Postsecondary; Area, Ethnic, and Cultural Studies Teachers, Postsecondary; Art, Drama, and Music Teachers, Postsecondary; Atmospheric, Earth, Marine, and Space Sciences Teachers, Postsecondary; Biological Science Teachers, Postsecondary; Business Teachers, Postsecondary; Chemistry Teachers, Postsecondary; Communications Teachers, Postsecondary; Computer Science Teachers, Postsecondary; Criminal Justice and Law Enforcement Teachers, Postsecondary; Economics Teachers, Postsecondary; Engineering Teachers, Postsecondary; English Language and Literature Teachers, Postsecondary; Environmental Science Teachers, Postsecondary; Farm and Home Management Advisors; Foreign Language and Literature Teachers, Postsecondary; Forestry and Conservation Science Teachers, Postsecondary; Geography Teachers, Postsecondary; Graduate Teaching Assistants; Health Specialties Teachers, Postsecondary; History Teachers, Postsecondary; Home Economics Teachers, Postsecondary; Law Teachers, Postsecondary; Library Science Teachers, Postsecondary; Mathematical Science Teachers, Postsecondary; Nursing Instructors and Teachers, Postsecondary; Philosophy and Religion Teachers, Postsecondary; Physics Teachers, Postsecondary; Political Science Teachers, Postsecondary; Psychology Teachers, Postsecondary; Recreation and Fitness Studies Teachers, Postsecondary; Self-Enrichment Education Teachers; Social Work Teachers, Postsecondary; Sociology Teachers, Postsecondary; Vocational Education Teachers, Post-

E

secondary. **PERSONALITY TYPE:** No data available.

EDUCATION/TRAINING PROGRAM(S)—Agricultural Teacher Education; Art Teacher Education; Biology Teacher Education; Business Teacher Education; Chemistry Teacher Education; Computer Teacher Education; Drama and Dance Teacher Education; Driver and Safety Teacher Education; Education, General; English/Language Arts Teacher Education; Family and Consumer Sciences/Home Economics Teacher Education; Foreign Language Teacher Education; French Language Teacher Education; Geography Teacher Education; others.

WORK ENVIRONMENT—Sitting; physical proximity to others; extremely bright or inadequate lighting; sounds, noise levels are distracting or uncomfortable.

Educational, Vocational, and School Counselors

- Education/Training Required: Master's degree
- Annual Earnings: $46,160
- Growth: 15.0%
- Annual Job Openings: 32,000
- Self-Employed: 4.4%
- Part-Time: 14.6%

Age Bracket	Percentage of Workers
45–54 Years Old	28.0%
55–64 Years Old	13.4%
65 or Older	2.3%

Counsel individuals and provide group educational and vocational guidance services. Counsel students regarding educational issues such as course and program selection, class scheduling, school adjustment, truancy, study habits, and career planning. Counsel individuals to help them understand and overcome personal, social, or behavioral problems affecting their educational or vocational situations. Maintain accurate and complete student records as required by laws, district policies, and administrative regulations. Confer with parents or guardians, teachers, other counselors, and administrators to resolve students' behavioral, academic, and other problems. Provide crisis intervention to students when difficult situations occur at schools. Identify cases involving domestic abuse or other family problems affecting students' development. Meet with parents and guardians to discuss their children's progress and to determine their priorities for their children and their resource needs. Prepare students for later educational experiences by encouraging them to explore learning opportunities and to persevere with challenging tasks. Encourage students and/or parents to seek additional assistance from mental health professionals when necessary. Observe and evaluate students' performance, behavior, social development, and physical health. Enforce all administration policies and rules governing students. Meet with other professionals to discuss individual students' needs and progress. Provide students with information on such topics as college degree programs and admission requirements, financial aid opportunities, trade and technical schools, and apprenticeship programs. Evaluate individuals' abilities, interests, and personality characteristics, using tests, records, interviews, and professional sources. Collaborate with teachers and administrators in the development, evaluation, and revision of school programs. Teach classes and present self-help or information sessions on subjects related to education and career planning. Establish and enforce behavioral rules and procedures to maintain order among students.

Conduct follow-up interviews with counselees to determine if their needs have been met. **SKILLS**—Social Perceptiveness; Service Orientation; Persuasion; Negotiation; Active Listening; Learning Strategies; Coordination; Instructing.

GOE—**Interest Area:** 05. Education and Training. **Work Group:** 05.06. Counseling, Health, and Fitness Education. **Other Jobs in This Work Group:** Fitness Trainers and Aerobics Instructors; Health Educators. **PERSONALITY TYPE:** Social. Social occupations frequently involve working with, communicating with, and teaching people. These occupations often involve helping or providing service to others.

EDUCATION/TRAINING PROGRAM(S)—College Student Counseling and Personnel Services; Counselor Education/School Counseling and Guidance Services.

WORK ENVIRONMENT—Sitting; physical proximity to others; sounds, noise levels are distracting or uncomfortable; indoors.

Electrical and Electronic Inspectors and Testers

- Education/Training Required: Moderate-term on-the-job training
- Annual Earnings: $28,630
- Growth: 4.7%
- Annual Job Openings: 87,000
- Self-Employed: 1.2%
- Part-Time: 5.0%

The job openings listed here are shared with Materials Inspectors; Mechanical Inspectors; Precision Devices Inspectors and Testers; and Production Inspectors, Testers, Graders, Sorters, Samplers, Weighers.

Age Bracket	Percentage of Workers
45–54 Years Old	27.3%
55–64 Years Old	15.0%
65 or Older	2.2%

Inspect and test electrical and electronic systems, such as radar navigational equipment, computer memory units, and television and radio transmitters, using precision measuring instruments. Tests and measures finished products, components, or assemblies for functioning, operation, accuracy, or assembly to verify adherence to functional specifications. Reads dials and meters to verify functioning of equipment according to specifications. Analyzes and interprets blueprints, sample data, and other materials to determine, change, or measure specifications or inspection and testing procedures. Marks items for acceptance or rejection, records test results and inspection data, and compares findings with specifications to ensure conformance to standards. Inspects materials, products, and work in progress for conformance to specifications and adjusts process or assembly equipment to meet standards. Computes and/or calculates sample data and test results. Confers with vendors and others regarding inspection results; recommends corrective procedures; and compiles reports of results, recommendations, and needed repairs. Writes and installs computer programs to control test equipment. Installs, positions, or connects new or replacement parts, components, and instruments. Reviews maintenance records to ensure that plant equipment functions properly. Disassembles defective parts and components. Cleans and maintains test equipment and instruments to ensure proper functioning. Positions or directs other workers to position products, components, or parts for testing. Operates or tends machinery and equipment and uses hand tools. Examines and adjusts or repairs finished products and components or parts. **SKILLS**—Programming; Quality Control Analysis; Installation; Troubleshooting; Operation Monitoring; Repairing; Science; Equipment Maintenance.

GOE—**Interest Area:** 13. Manufacturing. **Work Group:** 13.07. Production Quality Control. **Other Jobs in This Work Group:** Graders and Sorters, Agricultural Products; Materials Inspectors; Precision Devices Inspectors and Testers; Production Inspectors, Testers, Graders, Sorters, Samplers, Weighers. **PERSONALITY TYPE:** Realistic. Realistic occupations frequently involve work activities that include practical, hands-on problems and solutions. They often deal with plants, animals, and real-world materials like wood, tools, and machinery. Many of the occupations require working outside and do not involve a lot of paperwork or working closely with others.

EDUCATION/TRAINING PROGRAM(S)— Quality Control Technology/Technician.

WORK ENVIRONMENT—Common protective or safety equipment; standing; walking and running; hazardous conditions; hazardous equipment.

Electrical and Electronics Repairers, Commercial and Industrial Equipment

- Education/Training Required: Postsecondary vocational training
- Annual Earnings: $43,180
- Growth: 10.3%
- Annual Job Openings: 10,000
- Self-Employed: 0.7%
- Part-Time: 1.2%

Age Bracket	Percentage of Workers
45–54 Years Old	45.5%
55–64 Years Old	less than 4.5%
65 or Older	close to 0%

Repair, test, adjust, or install electronic equipment, such as industrial controls, transmitters, and antennas. Perform scheduled preventive maintenance tasks, such as checking, cleaning, and repairing equipment, to detect and prevent problems. Examine work orders and converse with equipment operators to detect equipment problems and to ascertain whether mechanical or human errors contributed to the problems. Set up and test industrial equipment to ensure that it functions properly. Operate equipment to demonstrate proper use and to analyze malfunctions. Test faulty equipment to diagnose malfunctions, using test equipment and software and applying knowledge of the functional operation of electronic units and systems. Repair and adjust equipment, machines, and defective components, replacing worn parts such as gaskets and seals in watertight electrical equipment. Calibrate testing instruments and installed or repaired equipment to prescribed specifications. Advise management regarding customer satisfaction, product performance, and suggestions for product improvements. Inspect components of industrial equipment for accurate assembly and installation and for defects such as loose connections and frayed wires. Study blueprints, schematics, manuals, and other specifications to determine installation procedures. Maintain equipment logs that record performance problems, repairs, calibrations, and tests. Coordinate efforts with other workers involved in installing and maintaining equipment or components. Maintain inventory of spare parts. Consult with customers, supervisors, and engineers to plan layout of equipment and to resolve problems in system operation and maintenance. Send defective units to the manufacturer or to a specialized repair shop for repair. Install repaired equipment in various settings, such as industrial or military establishments. Determine feasibility of using standardized equipment and develop specifications for equipment required to perform additional functions. Enter information into computer to copy program or to draw, modify, or store schematics, applying knowledge of software package used. Sign overhaul documents for equipment replaced or repaired. Develop or modify industrial electronic devices, circuits, and equipment according to available specifications. **SKILLS**—Installation; Troubleshooting; Repairing; Operation Monitoring; Equipment Maintenance; Systems Analysis; Operation and Control; Coordination.

GOE—Interest Area: 13. Manufacturing. **Work Group:** 13.12. Electrical and Electronic Repair. **Other Jobs in This Work Group:** Avionics Technicians; Battery Repairers; Electric Home Appliance and Power Tool Repairers; Electric Motor and Switch Assemblers and Repairers; Electrical and Electronics Installers and Repairers, Transportation Equipment; Electrical Parts Reconditioners; Electronic Equipment Installers and Repairers, Motor Vehicles; Electronic Home Entertainment Equipment Installers and Repairers; Radio Mechanics; Transformer Repairers. **PERSONALITY TYPE:** Realistic. Realistic occupations frequently involve work activities that include practical, hands-on problems and solutions. They often deal with plants, animals, and real-world materials like wood, tools, and machinery. Many of the occupations require working outside and do not involve a lot of paperwork or working closely with others.

EDUCATION/TRAINING PROGRAM(S)— Computer Installation and Repair Technology/Technician; Industrial Electronics Technology/Technician.

WORK ENVIRONMENT—Cramped work space, awkward positions; hazardous conditions; sounds, noise levels are distracting or uncomfortable; indoors, not environmentally controlled; physical proximity to others.

Electrical Engineers

- Education/Training Required: Bachelor's degree
- Annual Earnings: $72,770
- Growth: 2.5%
- Annual Job Openings: 11,000
- Self-Employed: 3.3%
- Part-Time: 2.4%

Age Bracket	Percentage of Workers
45–54 Years Old	30.0%
55–64 Years Old	11.6%
65 or Older	1.1%

Design, develop, test, or supervise the manufacturing and installation of electrical equipment, components, or systems for commercial, industrial, military, or scientific use. Confer with engineers, customers, and others to discuss existing or potential engineering projects and products. Design, implement, maintain, and improve electrical instruments, equipment, facilities, components, products, and systems for commercial, industrial, and domestic purposes. Operate computer-assisted engineering and design software and equipment to perform engineering tasks. Direct and coordinate manufacturing, construction, installation, maintenance, support, documentation, and testing activities to ensure compliance with specifications, codes, and customer requirements. Perform detailed calculations to compute and establish manufacturing, construction, and installation standards and specifications. Inspect completed installations and observe operations to ensure conformance to design and equipment specifications and compliance with operational and safety standards. Plan and implement research methodology and procedures to apply principles of electrical theory to engineering projects. Prepare specifications for purchase of materials and equipment. Supervise and train project team members as necessary. Investigate and test vendors' and competitors' products. Oversee project production efforts to assure projects are completed satisfactorily, on time, and within budget. Prepare and study technical drawings, specifications of electrical systems, and topographical maps to ensure that installation and operations conform to standards and customer requirements. Investigate customer or public complaints, determine nature and extent of problem, and recommend remedial measures. Plan layout of electric power generating plants and distribution lines and stations. Assist in developing capital project programs for new equipment and major repairs. Develop budgets, estimating labor, material, and construction costs. **SKILLS**—Technology Design; Troubleshooting; Systems Analysis; Science; Systems Evaluation; Complex Problem Solving; Equipment Selection; Management of Material Resources.

GOE—Interest Area: 15. Scientific Research, Engineering, and Mathematics. **Work Group:** 15.07. Research and Design Engineering. **Other Jobs in This Work Group:** Aerospace Engineers; Biomedical Engineers; Chemical Engineers; Civil Engineers; Computer Hardware Engineers; Electronics Engineers, Except Computer; Marine Architects; Marine Engineers; Materials Engineers; Mechanical Engineers; Nuclear Engineers. **PERSONALITY TYPE:** Investigative. Investigative occupations frequently involve working with ideas and require an extensive amount of thinking. These occupations can involve searching for facts and figuring out problems mentally.

EDUCATION/TRAINING PROGRAM(S)— Electrical, Electronics and Communications Engineering.

WORK ENVIRONMENT—Sitting; indoors; sounds, noise levels are distracting or uncomfortable; hazardous conditions; physical proximity to others.

Electronics Engineers, Except Computer

- Education/Training Required: Bachelor's degree
- Annual Earnings: $76,810
- Growth: 9.4%
- Annual Job Openings: 11,000
- Self-Employed: 3.1%
- Part-Time: 2.4%

Age Bracket	Percentage of Workers
45–54 Years Old	30.0%
55–64 Years Old	11.6%
65 or Older	1.1%

Research, design, develop, and test electronic components and systems for commercial, industrial, military, or scientific use, utilizing knowledge of electronic theory and materials properties. Design electronic circuits and components for use in fields such as telecommunications, aerospace guidance and propulsion control, acoustics, or instruments and controls. Design electronic components and software, products, and systems for commercial, industrial, medical, military, and scientific applications. Provide technical support and instruction to staff and customers regarding equipment standards and help solve specific, difficult in-service engineering problems. Operate computer-assisted engineering and design software and equipment to perform engineering tasks. Analyze system requirements, capacity, cost, and customer needs to determine feasibility of project and develop system plan. Confer with engineers, customers, vendors, and others to discuss existing and potential engineering projects or products. Review and evaluate work of others, inside and outside the organization, to ensure effectiveness, technical adequacy, and compatibility in the resolution of complex engineering problems. Determine material and equipment needs and order supplies. Inspect electronic equipment, instruments, products, and systems to ensure conformance to specifications, safety standards, and applicable codes and regulations. Evaluate operational systems, prototypes, and proposals and recommend repair or design modifications based on factors such as environment, service, cost, and system capabilities. Prepare documentation containing information such as confidential descriptions and specifications of proprietary hardware and software, product development and introduction schedules, product costs, and information about product performance weaknesses. Direct and coordinate activities concerned with manufacture, construction, installation, maintenance, operation, and modification of electronic equipment, products, and systems. Develop and perform operational, maintenance, and testing procedures for electronic products, components, equipment, and systems. Plan and develop applications and modifications for electronic properties used in components, products, and systems to improve technical performance. Prepare engineering sketches and specifications for construction, relocation, and installation of equipment, facilities, products, and systems. Plan and implement research, methodology, and procedures to apply principles of electronic theory to engineering projects. **SKILLS**—Troubleshooting; Technology Design; Operations Analysis; Installation; Science; Complex Problem Solving; Equipment Selection; Active Learning; Systems Evaluation.

GOE—Interest Area: 15. Scientific Research, Engineering, and Mathematics. **Work Group:** 15.07. Research and Design Engineering. **Other Jobs in This Work Group:** Aerospace Engineers; Biomedical Engineers; Chemical Engineers;

Civil Engineers; Computer Hardware Engineers; Electrical Engineers; Marine Architects; Marine Engineers; Materials Engineers; Mechanical Engineers; Nuclear Engineers. **PERSONALITY TYPE:** Investigative. Investigative occupations frequently involve working with ideas and require an extensive amount of thinking. These occupations can involve searching for facts and figuring out problems mentally.

EDUCATION/TRAINING PROGRAM(S)— Electrical, Electronics, and Communications Engineering.

WORK ENVIRONMENT—Sitting; sounds, noise levels are distracting or uncomfortable; indoors; contaminants; indoors, not environmentally controlled.

Elementary School Teachers, Except Special Education

- Education/Training Required: Bachelor's degree
- Annual Earnings: $43,660
- Growth: 15.2%
- Annual Job Openings: 183,000
- Self-Employed: 0.1%
- Part-Time: 9.2%

Age Bracket	Percentage of Workers
45–54 Years Old	28.0%
55–64 Years Old	14.5%
65 or Older	2.0%

Teach pupils in public or private schools at the elementary level basic academic, social, and **other formative skills.** Establish and enforce rules for behavior and procedures for maintaining order among the students for whom they are responsible. Observe and evaluate students' performance, behavior, social development, and physical health. Prepare materials and classrooms for class activities. Adapt teaching methods and instructional materials to meet students' varying needs and interests. Plan and conduct activities for a balanced program of instruction, demonstration, and work time that provides students with opportunities to observe, question, and investigate. Instruct students individually and in groups, using various teaching methods such as lectures, discussions, and demonstrations. Establish clear objectives for all lessons, units, and projects and communicate those objectives to students. Assign and grade class work and homework. Read books to entire classes or small groups. Prepare, administer, and grade tests and assignments in order to evaluate students' progress. Confer with parents or guardians, teachers, counselors, and administrators in order to resolve students' behavioral and academic problems. Meet with parents and guardians to discuss their children's progress and to determine their priorities for their children and their resource needs. Maintain accurate and complete student records as required by laws, district policies, and administrative regulations. Prepare students for later grades by encouraging them to explore learning opportunities and to persevere with challenging tasks. Guide and counsel students with adjustment and/or academic problems or special academic interests. Prepare and implement remedial programs for students requiring extra help. Prepare objectives and outlines for courses of study, following curriculum guidelines or requirements of states and schools. Provide a variety of materials and resources for children to explore, manipulate, and use, both in learning activities and in imaginative play. Enforce administration policies and rules governing students. Confer with other staff members to plan and schedule lessons promoting learning, following approved curricula. **SKILLS**—Instructing; Learning Strategies; Social Perceptiveness; Monitoring; Persuasion; Service Orientation; Time Management; Speaking; Negotiation.

GOE—Interest Area: 05. Education and Training. **Work Group:** 05.02. Preschool, Elementary, and Secondary Teaching and Instructing. **Other Jobs in This Work Group:** Kindergarten Teachers, Except Special Education; Middle School Teachers, Except Special and Vocational Education; Preschool Teachers, Except Special Education; Secondary School Teachers, Except Special and Vocational Education; Special Education Teachers, Middle School; Special Education Teachers, Preschool, Kindergarten, and Elementary School; Special Education Teachers, Secondary School; Teacher Assistants; Vocational Education Teachers, Middle School; Vocational Education Teachers, Secondary School. **PERSONALITY TYPE:** Social. Social occupations frequently involve working with, communicating with, and teaching people. These occupations often involve helping or providing service to others.

EDUCATION/TRAINING PROGRAM(S)— Elementary Education and Teaching; Teacher Education, Multiple Levels.

WORK ENVIRONMENT—Physical proximity to others; sounds, noise levels are distracting or uncomfortable; disease or infections; standing; very hot or cold.

Emergency Management Specialists

- Education/Training Required: Work experience in a related occupation
- Annual Earnings: $45,670
- Growth: 28.2%
- Annual Job Openings: 2,000
- Self-Employed: 0%
- Part-Time: 7.4%

Age Bracket	Percentage of Workers
45–54 Years Old	30.7%
55–64 Years Old	18.1%
65 or Older	1.0%

Coordinate disaster response or crisis management activities; provide disaster-preparedness training; and prepare emergency plans and procedures for natural (e.g., hurricanes, floods, earthquakes), wartime, or technological (e.g., nuclear power plant emergencies, hazardous materials spills) disasters or hostage situations. Collaborate with other officials in order to prepare and analyze damage assessments following disasters or emergencies. Conduct surveys to determine the types of emergency-related needs that will need to be addressed in disaster planning or provide technical support to others conducting such surveys. Consult with officials of local and area governments, schools, hospitals, and other institutions in order to determine their needs and capabilities in the event of a natural disaster or other emergency. Coordinate disaster response or crisis management activities such as ordering evacuations, opening public shelters, and implementing special needs plans and programs. Design and administer emer-

E

gency/disaster-preparedness training courses that teach people how to effectively respond to major emergencies and disasters. Develop and maintain liaisons with municipalities, county departments, and similar entities in order to facilitate plan development, response effort coordination, and exchanges of personnel and equipment. Develop and perform tests and evaluations of emergency management plans in accordance with state and federal regulations. Inspect facilities and equipment such as emergency management centers and communications equipment in order to determine their operational and functional capabilities in emergency situations. Keep informed of activities or changes that could affect the likelihood of an emergency as well as those that could affect response efforts and details of plan implementation. Keep informed of federal, state, and local regulations affecting emergency plans and ensure that plans adhere to these regulations. Maintain and update all resource materials associated with emergency-preparedness plans. Prepare emergency situation status reports that describe response and recovery efforts, needs, and preliminary damage assessments. Prepare plans that outline operating procedures to be used in response to disasters/emergencies such as hurricanes, nuclear accidents, and terrorist attacks and in recovery from these events. Propose alteration of emergency response procedures based on regulatory changes, technological changes, or knowledge gained from outcomes of previous emergency situations. **SKILLS**—No data available.

GOE—Interest Area: 12. Law and Public Safety. **Work Group:** 12.01. Managerial Work in Law and Public Safety. **Other Jobs in This Work Group:** First-Line Supervisors/Managers of Correctional Officers; First-Line Supervisors/ Managers of Police and Detectives; Forest Fire

Fighting and Prevention Supervisors; Municipal Fire Fighting and Prevention Supervisors. **PERSONALITY TYPE:** No data available.

EDUCATION/TRAINING PROGRAM(S)— Community Organization and Advocacy; Public Administration.

WORK ENVIRONMENT—No data available.

Employment Interviewers, Private or Public Employment Service

- Education/Training Required: Bachelor's degree
- Annual Earnings: $41,190
- Growth: 27.3%
- Annual Job Openings: 29,000
- Self-Employed: 0.8%
- Part-Time: 7.7%

The job openings listed here are shared with Personnel Recruiters.

Age Bracket	Percentage of Workers
45–54 Years Old	26.6%
55–64 Years Old	13.4%
65 or Older	1.6%

Interview job applicants in employment office and refer them to prospective employers for consideration. Search application files, notify selected applicants of job openings, and refer qualified applicants to prospective employers. Contact employers to verify referral results. Record and evaluate various pertinent data.

Inform applicants of job openings and details such as duties and responsibilities, compensation, benefits, schedules, working conditions, and promotion opportunities. Interview job applicants to match their qualifications with employers' needs, recording and evaluating applicant experience, education, training, and skills. Review employment applications and job orders to match applicants with job requirements, using manual or computerized file searches. Select qualified applicants or refer them to employers according to organization policy. Perform reference and background checks on applicants. Maintain records of applicants not selected for employment. Instruct job applicants in presenting a positive image by providing help with resume writing, personal appearance, and interview techniques. Refer applicants to services such as vocational counseling, literacy or language instruction, transportation assistance, vocational training, and child care. Contact employers to solicit orders for job vacancies, determining their requirements and recording relevant data such as job descriptions. Conduct workshops and demonstrate the use of job listings to assist applicants with skill building. Search for and recruit applicants for open positions through campus job fairs and advertisements. Provide background information on organizations with which interviews are scheduled. Administer assessment tests to identify skill-building needs. Conduct or arrange for skill, intelligence, or psychological testing of applicants and current employees. Hire workers and place them with employers needing temporary help. Evaluate selection and testing techniques by conducting research or follow-up activities and conferring with management and supervisory personnel. **SKILLS**—Social Perceptiveness; Service Orientation; Management of Personnel Resources; Persuasion; Negotiation; Instructing; Speaking; Active Listening.

GOE—Interest Area: 04. Business and Administration. **Work Group:** 04.03. Human Resources Support. **Other Jobs in This Work Group:** Compensation, Benefits, and Job Analysis Specialists; Personnel Recruiters; Training and Development Specialists. **PERSONALITY TYPE:** Social. Social occupations frequently involve working with, communicating with, and teaching people. These occupations often involve helping or providing service to others.

EDUCATION/TRAINING PROGRAM(S)— Human Resources Management/Personnel Administration, General; Labor and Industrial Relations.

WORK ENVIRONMENT—Sitting; physical proximity to others; sounds, noise levels are distracting or uncomfortable; extremely bright or inadequate lighting; indoors.

Engineering Managers

- Education/Training Required: Work experience plus degree
- Annual Earnings: $99,000
- Growth: 9.2%
- Annual Job Openings: 16,000
- Self-Employed: 0.1%
- Part-Time: 1.0%

Age Bracket	Percentage of Workers
45–54 Years Old	37.7%
55–64 Years Old	11.7%
65 or Older	1.3%

E

Plan, direct, or coordinate activities in such fields as architecture and engineering or research and development in these fields. Confer with management, production, and marketing staff to discuss project specifications and procedures. Coordinate and direct projects, making detailed plans to accomplish goals and directing the integration of technical activities. Analyze technology, resource needs, and market demand to plan and assess the feasibility of projects. Plan and direct the installation, testing, operation, maintenance, and repair of facilities and equipment. Direct, review, and approve product design and changes. Recruit employees; assign, direct, and evaluate their work; and oversee the development and maintenance of staff competence. Prepare budgets, bids, and contracts and direct the negotiation of research contracts. Develop and implement policies, standards, and procedures for the engineering and technical work performed in the department, service, laboratory, or firm. Perform administrative functions such as reviewing and writing reports, approving expenditures, enforcing rules, and making decisions about the purchase of materials or services. Review and recommend or approve contracts and cost estimates. Present and explain proposals, reports, and findings to clients. Consult or negotiate with clients to prepare project specifications. Set scientific and technical goals within broad outlines provided by top management. Administer highway planning, construction, and maintenance. Direct the engineering of water control, treatment, and distribution projects. Plan, direct, and coordinate survey work with other staff activities, certifying survey work and writing land legal descriptions. Confer with and report to officials and the public to provide information and solicit support for projects. **SKILLS**—Technology Design; Operations

Analysis; Science; Management of Financial Resources; Installation; Negotiation; Persuasion; Mathematics.

GOE—Interest Area: 15. Scientific Research, Engineering, and Mathematics. **Work Group:** 15.01. Managerial Work in Scientific Research, Engineering, and Mathematics. **Other Jobs in This Work Group:** Natural Sciences Managers. **PERSONALITY TYPE:** Enterprising. Enterprising occupations frequently involve starting up and carrying out projects. These occupations can involve leading people and making many decisions. They sometimes require risk taking and often deal with business.

EDUCATION/TRAINING PROGRAM(S)—Aerospace, Aeronautical, and Astronautical Engineering; Agricultural/Biological Engineering and Bioengineering; Architectural Engineering; Architecture (BArch, BA/BS, MArch, MA/MS, PhD); Biomedical/Medical Engineering; Ceramic Sciences and Engineering; Chemical Engineering; City/Urban, Community, and Regional Planning; Civil Engineering, General; Civil Engineering, Other; Computer Engineering, General; Computer Engineering, Other; Computer Hardware Engineering; Computer Software Engineering; others.

WORK ENVIRONMENT—Indoors, not environmentally controlled; sounds, noise levels are distracting or uncomfortable; extremely bright or inadequate lighting; sitting; very hot or cold; contaminants.

Engineering Teachers, Postsecondary

- Education/Training Required: Master's degree
- Annual Earnings: $74,840
- Growth: 38.1%
- Annual Job Openings: 216,000
- Self-Employed: 0.3%
- Part-Time: 27.7%

The job openings listed here are shared with all other postsecondary teaching occupations.

Age Bracket	Percentage of Workers
45–54 Years Old	22.8%
55–64 Years Old	19.0%
65 or Older	5.5%

Teach courses pertaining to the application of physical laws and principles of engineering for the development of machines, materials, instruments, processes, and services. Includes teachers of subjects such as chemical, civil, electrical, industrial, mechanical, mineral, and petroleum engineering. Includes both teachers primarily engaged in teaching and those who do a combination of both teaching and research. Prepare and deliver lectures to undergraduate and/or graduate students on topics such as mechanics, hydraulics, and robotics. Keep abreast of developments in their field by reading current literature, talking with colleagues, and participating in professional conferences. Supervise undergraduate and/or graduate teaching, internship, and research work. Evaluate and grade students' class work, laboratory work, assignments, and papers. Conduct research in a particular field of knowledge and publish findings in professional journals, books, and/or electronic media. Prepare course materials such as syllabi, homework assignments, and handouts. Compile, administer, and grade examinations or assign this work to others. Write grant proposals to procure external research funding. Supervise students' laboratory work. Initiate, facilitate, and moderate class discussions. Maintain regularly scheduled office hours in order to advise and assist students. Plan, evaluate, and revise curricula, course content, and course materials and methods of instruction. Advise students on academic and vocational curricula and on career issues. Maintain student attendance records, grades, and other required records. Collaborate with colleagues to address teaching and research issues. Select and obtain materials and supplies such as textbooks and laboratory equipment. Participate in student recruitment, registration, and placement activities. Serve on academic or administrative committees that deal with institutional policies, departmental matters, and academic issues. Perform administrative duties such as serving as department head. SKILLS— Science; Programming; Instructing; Active Learning; Critical Thinking; Technology Design; Mathematics; Complex Problem Solving.

GOE—Interest Area: 05. Education and Training. Work Group: 05.03. Postsecondary and Adult Teaching and Instructing. Other Jobs in This Work Group: Adult Literacy, Remedial Education, and GED Teachers and Instructors; Agricultural Sciences Teachers, Postsecondary; Anthropology and Archeology Teachers, Postsecondary; Architecture Teachers, Postsecondary; Area, Ethnic, and Cultural Studies Teachers, Postsecondary; Art, Drama, and Music Teachers, Postsecondary; Atmospheric, Earth, Marine, and Space Sciences Teachers, Postsecondary; Biological Science

Teachers, Postsecondary; Business Teachers, Postsecondary; Chemistry Teachers, Postsecondary; Communications Teachers, Postsecondary; Computer Science Teachers, Postsecondary; Criminal Justice and Law Enforcement Teachers, Postsecondary; Economics Teachers, Postsecondary; Education Teachers, Postsecondary; English Language and Literature Teachers, Postsecondary; Environmental Science Teachers, Postsecondary; Farm and Home Management Advisors; Foreign Language and Literature Teachers, Postsecondary; Forestry and Conservation Science Teachers, Postsecondary; Geography Teachers, Postsecondary; Graduate Teaching Assistants; Health Specialties Teachers, Postsecondary; History Teachers, Postsecondary; Home Economics Teachers, Postsecondary; Law Teachers, Postsecondary; Library Science Teachers, Postsecondary; Mathematical Science Teachers, Postsecondary; Nursing Instructors and Teachers, Postsecondary; Philosophy and Religion Teachers, Postsecondary; Physics Teachers, Postsecondary; Political Science Teachers, Postsecondary; Psychology Teachers, Postsecondary; Recreation and Fitness Studies Teachers, Postsecondary; Self-Enrichment Education Teachers; Social Work Teachers, Postsecondary; Sociology Teachers, Postsecondary; Vocational Education Teachers, Postsecondary. **PERSONALITY TYPE:** Investigative. Investigative occupations frequently involve working with ideas and require an extensive amount of thinking. These occupations can involve searching for facts and figuring out problems mentally.

EDUCATION/TRAINING PROGRAM(S)— Aerospace, Aeronautical, and Astronautical Engineering; Agricultural/Biological Engineering and Bioengineering; Architectural Engineering; Biomedical/Medical Engineering; Ceramic Sciences and Engineering; Chemical Engineering; Civil Engineering, General; Civil Engineering, Other; Computer Engineering, General; Computer Engineering, Other; Computer Hardware Engineering; Computer Software Engineering; Construction Engineering; Electrical, Electronics, and Communications Engineering; others.

WORK ENVIRONMENT—Sitting; indoors; physical proximity to others; hazardous conditions.

English Language and Literature Teachers, Postsecondary

- ◎ Education/Training Required: Master's degree
- ◎ Annual Earnings: $48,920
- ◎ Growth: 38.1%
- ◎ Annual Job Openings: 216,000
- ◎ Self-Employed: 0.3%
- ◎ Part-Time: 27.7%

The job openings listed here are shared with all other postsecondary teaching occupations.

Age Bracket	Percentage of Workers
45–54 Years Old	22.8%
55–64 Years Old	19.0%
65 or Older	5.5%

Teach courses in English language and literature, including linguistics and comparative literature. Initiate, facilitate, and moderate classroom discussions. Evaluate and grade students' class work, assignments, and papers. Prepare course materials such as syllabi, homework assignments, and handouts. Prepare and deliver lectures to undergraduate and/or graduate students on topics such as poetry, novel structure, and translation and adaptation. Maintain student attendance records, grades, and other required records. Plan, evaluate, and revise curricula, course content, and course materials and methods of instruction. Compile, administer, and grade examinations or assign this work to others. Maintain regularly scheduled office hours in order to advise and assist students. Keep abreast of developments in their field by reading current literature, talking with colleagues, and participating in professional conferences. Select and obtain materials and supplies such as textbooks. Advise students on academic and vocational curricula and on career issues. Conduct research in a particular field of knowledge and publish findings in professional journals, books, and/or electronic media. Collaborate with colleagues to address teaching and research issues. Serve on academic or administrative committees that deal with institutional policies, departmental matters, and academic issues. Participate in campus and community events. Participate in student recruitment, registration, and placement activities. Compile bibliographies of specialized materials for outside reading assignments. Supervise undergraduate and/or graduate teaching, internship, and research work. Provide assistance to students in college writing centers. Perform administrative duties such as serving as department head. Recruit, train, and supervise student writing instructors. Act as advisers to student organizations. **SKILLS**—Instructing; Learning Strategies; Social Perceptiveness; Persuasion; Writing; Active Learning; Critical Thinking; Reading Comprehension.

GOE—**Interest Area:** 05. Education and Training. **Work Group:** 05.03. Postsecondary and Adult Teaching and Instructing. **Other Jobs in This Work Group:** Adult Literacy, Remedial Education, and GED Teachers and Instructors; Agricultural Sciences Teachers, Postsecondary; Anthropology and Archeology Teachers, Postsecondary; Architecture Teachers, Postsecondary; Area, Ethnic, and Cultural Studies Teachers, Postsecondary; Art, Drama, and Music Teachers, Postsecondary; Atmospheric, Earth, Marine, and Space Sciences Teachers, Postsecondary; Biological Science Teachers, Postsecondary; Business Teachers, Postsecondary; Chemistry Teachers, Postsecondary; Communications Teachers, Postsecondary; Computer Science Teachers, Postsecondary; Criminal Justice and Law Enforcement Teachers, Postsecondary; Economics Teachers, Postsecondary; Education Teachers, Postsecondary; Engineering Teachers, Postsecondary; Environmental Science Teachers, Postsecondary; Farm and Home Management Advisors; Foreign Language and Literature Teachers, Postsecondary; Forestry and Conservation Science Teachers, Postsecondary; Geography Teachers, Postsecondary; Graduate Teaching Assistants; Health Specialties Teachers, Postsecondary; History Teachers, Postsecondary; Home Economics Teachers, Postsecondary; Law Teachers, Postsecondary; Library Science Teachers, Postsecondary; Mathematical Science Teachers, Postsecondary; Nursing Instructors and Teachers, Postsecondary; Philosophy and Religion Teachers, Postsecondary; Physics Teachers, Postsecondary; Political Science Teachers, Postsecondary; Psychology Teachers, Postsecondary; Recreation and Fitness Studies Teachers, Postsecondary; Self-Enrichment Education Teachers; Social Work Teachers, Postsecondary; Sociology Teachers, Postsecondary; Vocational Education Teachers, Postsecondary. **PERSONALITY TYPE:** Artistic. Artistic occupations frequently involve working with forms, designs, and patterns. They often require self-expression, and the work can be done without following a clear set of rules.

EDUCATION/TRAINING PROGRAM(S)— American Literature (Canadian); American Literature (United States); Comparative Literature; Creative Writing; English Composition; English Language and Literature, General; English Language and Literature/Letters, Other; English Literature (British and Commonwealth); Technical and Business Writing.

WORK ENVIRONMENT—Physical proximity to others; sitting; indoors; sounds, noise levels are distracting or uncomfortable.

Environmental Compliance Inspectors

- ◎ Education/Training Required: Long-term on-the-job training
- ◎ Annual Earnings: $48,530
- ◎ Growth: 9.8%
- ◎ Annual Job Openings: 20,000
- ◎ Self-Employed: 0.9%
- ◎ Part-Time: 5.3%

The job openings listed here are shared with Coroners, Equal Opportunity Representatives and Officers, Government Property Inspectors and Investigators, Licensing Examiners and Inspectors, and Pressure Vessel Inspectors.

Age Bracket	Percentage of Workers
45–54 Years Old	40.5%
55–64 Years Old	15.1%
65 or Older	0.8%

Inspect and investigate sources of pollution to protect the public and environment and ensure conformance with federal, state, and local regulations and ordinances. Inform health professionals, property owners, and the public about harmful properties and related problems of water pollution and contaminated wastewater. Participate in the development of spill prevention programs and hazardous waste rules and regulations and recommend corrective actions for hazardous waste problems. Prepare data to calculate sewer service charges and capacity fees. Prepare written, oral, tabular, and graphic reports summarizing requirements and regulations, including enforcement and chain of custody documentation. Research and keep informed of pertinent information and developments in areas such as EPA laws and regulations. Respond to questions and inquiries, such as those concerning service charges and capacity fees, or refer them to supervisors. Maintain and repair materials, worksites, and equipment. Analyze and implement state, federal, or local requirements as necessary to maintain approved pretreatment, pollution prevention, and storm water runoff programs. Conduct research on hazardous waste management projects in order to determine the magnitude of problems and treatment or disposal alternatives and costs. Determine the nature of code violations and actions to be taken and issue written notices of violation; participate in enforcement hearings as necessary. Determine sampling locations and methods and collect water or wastewater samples for analysis, preserving samples with appropriate containers and preservation methods. Determine which sites and violation reports to investigate and coordinate compliance and enforcement activities with other government agencies. Examine permits, licenses, applications, and records to ensure compliance with licensing requirements. Inform individuals and groups of pollution control regulations and inspection findings and explain how problems can be corrected. Inspect waste pretreatment, treatment, and disposal facilities and systems for conformance to federal, state, or local regulations. Interview individuals to determine the nature of suspected violations and to obtain evidence of violations. Investigate complaints and suspected violations regarding illegal dumping, pollution, pesticides, product quality, or labeling laws. **SKILLS**—Science; Systems Evaluation; Systems Analysis; Reading Comprehension; Speaking; Negotiation; Critical Thinking; Writing; Judgment and Decision Making.

GOE—**Interest Area:** 07. Government and Public Administration. **Work Group:** 07.03. Regulations Enforcement. **Other Jobs in This Work Group:** Agricultural Inspectors; Aviation Inspectors; Child Support, Missing Persons, and Unemployment Insurance Fraud Investigators; Equal Opportunity Representatives and Officers; Financial Examiners; Fire Inspectors; Fish and Game Wardens; Forest Fire Inspectors and Prevention Specialists; Government Property Inspectors and Investigators; Immigration and Customs Inspectors; Licensing Examiners and Inspectors; Marine Cargo Inspectors; Mechanical Inspectors; Motor Vehicle Inspectors; Nuclear Monitoring Technicians; Occupational Health and Safety Specialists; Pressure Vessel Inspectors; Railroad Inspectors; Tax Examiners, Collectors, and Revenue Agents. **PERSONALITY TYPE:** Investigative. Investigative occupations frequently involve working with ideas and require an extensive amount of thinking. These occupations can involve searching for facts and figuring out problems mentally.

EDUCATION/TRAINING PROGRAM(S)— No data available.

WORK ENVIRONMENT—Contaminants; walking and running; climbing ladders, scaffolds, or poles; disease or infections; hazardous conditions.

Environmental Science Teachers, Postsecondary

- Education/Training Required: Master's degree
- Annual Earnings: $61,490
- Growth: 38.1%
- Annual Job Openings: 216,000
- Self-Employed: 0.3%
- Part-Time: 27.7%

The job openings listed here are shared with all other postsecondary teaching occupations.

Age Bracket	Percentage of Workers
45–54 Years Old	22.8%
55–64 Years Old	19.0%
65 or Older	5.5%

Teach courses in environmental science. Supervise undergraduate and/or graduate teaching, internship, and research work. Conduct research in a particular field of knowledge and publish findings in professional journals, books, and/or electronic media. Keep abreast of developments in their field by reading current literature, talking with colleagues, and participating in professional conferences. Evaluate and grade students' class work, laboratory work, assignments, and papers. Write grant proposals to procure external research funding. Supervise students' laboratory work and fieldwork. Prepare course materials such as syllabi, homework assignments, and handouts. Plan, evaluate, and revise curricula, course content, and course materials and methods of instruction. Initiate, facilitate, and moderate classroom discussions. Compile, administer, and grade examinations or assign this work to others. Advise students on academic and vocational curricula and on career issues. Prepare and deliver lectures to undergraduate and/or graduate students on topics such as hazardous waste management, industrial safety, and environmental toxicology. Maintain student attendance records, grades, and other required records. Select and obtain materials and supplies such as textbooks and laboratory equipment. Maintain regularly scheduled office hours in order to advise and assist students. Collaborate with colleagues to address teaching and research issues. Perform administrative duties such as serving as department head. Participate in student recruitment, registration, and placement activities. Provide professional consulting services to government and/or industry. Serve on academic or administrative committees that deal with institutional policies, departmental matters, and academic issues. Compile bibliographies of specialized materials for outside reading assignments. **SKILLS**—Science; Instructing; Writing; Critical Thinking; Reading Comprehension; Active Learning; Learning Strategies; Management of Financial Resources.

GOE—**Interest Area:** 05. Education and Training. **Work Group:** 05.03. Postsecondary and Adult Teaching and Instructing. **Other Jobs in This Work Group:** Adult Literacy, Remedial Education, and GED Teachers and Instructors; Agricultural Sciences Teachers, Postsecondary; Anthropology and Archeology Teachers, Postsecondary; Architecture Teachers, Postsecondary; Area, Ethnic, and Cultural Studies Teachers, Postsecondary; Art, Drama, and Music Teachers, Postsecondary; Atmospheric, Earth, Marine, and Space Sciences Teachers, Postsecondary; Biological Science Teachers, Postsecondary; Business Teachers, Postsecondary; Chemistry Teachers, Postsecondary; Communications Teachers, Postsecondary; Computer Science Teachers, Postsecondary; Criminal Justice and Law Enforcement Teachers, Postsecondary; Economics Teachers, Postsecondary; Education Teachers, Postsecondary; Engineering Teachers, Postsecondary; English Language and Literature Teachers, Postsecondary; Farm and Home Management Advisors; Foreign Language and Literature Teachers, Postsecondary; Forestry and Conservation Science Teachers, Postsecondary; Geography Teachers, Postsecondary; Graduate Teaching Assistants; Health Specialties Teachers, Postsecondary; History Teachers, Postsecondary; Home Economics Teachers, Postsecondary; Law Teachers, Postsecondary; Library Science Teachers, Postsecondary; Mathematical Science Teachers, Postsecondary; Nursing Instructors and Teachers, Postsecondary; Philosophy and Religion Teachers, Postsecondary; Physics Teachers, Postsecondary; Political Science Teachers, Postsecondary; Psychology Teachers, Postsecondary; Recreation and Fitness Studies Teachers, Postsecondary; Self-Enrichment Education Teachers; Social Work Teachers, Postsecondary; Sociology Teachers, Postsecondary; Vocational Education Teachers, Postsecondary. **PERSONALITY TYPE:** No data available.

EDUCATION/TRAINING PROGRAM(S)— Environmental Science; Environmental Studies; Science Teacher Education/General Science Teacher Education.

WORK ENVIRONMENT—Sitting; very hot or cold; outdoors; sounds, noise levels are distracting or uncomfortable; contaminants.

Environmental Scientists and Specialists, Including Health

- Education/Training Required: Master's degree
- Annual Earnings: $51,950
- Growth: 23.7%
- Annual Job Openings: 6,000
- Self-Employed: 2.9%
- Part-Time: 7.7%

Age Bracket	Percentage of Workers
45–54 Years Old	29.4%
55–64 Years Old	11.8%
65 or Older	2.4%

Conduct research or perform investigation for the purpose of identifying, abating, or eliminating sources of pollutants or hazards that affect either the environment or the health of the population. Utilizing knowledge of various scientific disciplines, may collect, synthesize, study, report, and take action based on data derived from measurements or observations of air, food, soil, water, and other sources. Conduct environmental audits and inspections and investigations of violations. Evaluate violations or problems discovered during inspections in order to determine appropriate regulatory actions or to provide advice on the development and prosecution of regulatory cases. Communicate scientific and technical information through oral briefings, written documents, workshops, conferences, and public hearings. Review and implement environmental technical standards, guidelines, policies, and formal regulations that meet all appropriate requirements. Provide technical guidance, support, and oversight to environmental programs, industry, and the public. Provide advice on proper standards and regulations and the development of policies, strategies, and codes of practice for environmental management. Analyze data to determine validity, quality, and scientific significance and to interpret correlations between human activities and environmental effects. Collect, synthesize, and analyze data derived from pollution emission measurements, atmospheric monitoring, meteorological and mineralogical information, and soil or water samples. Determine data collection methods to be employed in research projects and surveys. Prepare charts or graphs from data samples and provide summary information on the environmental relevance of the data. Develop the technical portions of legal documents, administrative orders, or consent decrees. Investigate and report on accidents affecting the environment. Monitor environmental impacts of development activities. Supervise environmental technologists and technicians. Develop programs designed to obtain the most productive, non-damaging use of land. Research sources of pollution to determine their effects on the environment and to develop theories or methods of pollution abatement or control. Monitor effects of pollution and land degradation and recommend means of prevention or control. Design and direct studies to obtain technical environmental information about planned projects. Conduct applied research on topics such as waste control and treatment and pollution control methods. **SKILLS**—Service Orientation; Science; Coordination; Negotiation; Reading Comprehension; Persuasion; Active Learning; Social Perceptiveness.

GOE—Interest Area: 15. Scientific Research, Engineering, and Mathematics. **Work Group:** 15.03. Life Sciences. **Other Jobs in This Work**

E

Group: Biochemists; Biologists; Biophysicists; Epidemiologists; Medical Scientists, Except Epidemiologists; Microbiologists. **PERSONALITY TYPE:** Investigative. Investigative occupations frequently involve working with ideas and require an extensive amount of thinking. These occupations can involve searching for facts and figuring out problems mentally.

EDUCATION/TRAINING PROGRAM(S)— Environmental Science; Environmental Studies.

WORK ENVIRONMENT—Very hot or cold; in an enclosed vehicle or equipment; sitting; contaminants; sounds, noise levels are distracting or uncomfortable.

Equal Opportunity Representatives and Officers

- ◎ Education/Training Required: Long-term on-the-job training
- ◎ Annual Earnings: $48,530
- ◎ Growth: 9.8%
- ◎ Annual Job Openings: 20,000
- ◎ Self-Employed: 0.9%
- ◎ Part-Time: 5.3%

The job openings listed here are shared with Coroners, Environmental Compliance Inspectors, Government Property Inspectors and Investigators, Licensing Examiners and Inspectors, and Pressure Vessel Inspectors.

Age Bracket	Percentage of Workers
45–54 Years Old	40.5%
55–64 Years Old	15.1%
65 or Older	0.8%

Monitor and evaluate compliance with equal opportunity laws, guidelines, and policies to ensure that employment practices and contracting arrangements give equal opportunity without regard to race, religion, color, national origin, sex, age, or disability. Conduct surveys and evaluate findings in order to determine if systematic discrimination exists. Counsel newly hired members of minority and disadvantaged groups, informing them about details of civil rights laws. Interpret civil rights laws and equal opportunity regulations for individuals and employers. Investigate employment practices and alleged violations of laws in order to document and correct discriminatory factors. Meet with persons involved in equal opportunity complaints in order to verify case information and to arbitrate and settle disputes. Prepare reports of selection, survey, and other statistics and recommendations for corrective action. Provide information, technical assistance, and training to supervisors, managers, and employees on topics such as employee supervision, hiring, grievance procedures, and staff development. Review company contracts to determine actions required to meet governmental equal opportunity provisions. Study equal opportunity complaints in order to clarify issues. Act as liaisons between minority placement agencies and employers or between job search committees and other equal opportunity administrators. Consult with community representatives to develop technical assistance agreements in accordance with governmental regulations. Coordinate, monitor, and revise complaint procedures to ensure timely processing and review of complaints. Develop guidelines for non-discriminatory employment practices and monitor their implementation and impact. Meet with job search committees or coordinators to explain the role of the equal opportunity coordinator, to provide resources for advertising, and to explain expectations for future contacts. Participate in the recruitment of employees through job fairs, career days, and advertising plans. Verify that all job descriptions are submitted for review and approval and that descriptions meet regulatory standards. **SKILLS**—Negotiation; Writing; Speaking; Persuasion; Systems Analysis; Reading Comprehension; Systems Evaluation; Active Listening.

GOE—Interest Area: 07. Government and Public Administration. **Work Group:** 07.03. Regulations Enforcement. **Other Jobs in This Work Group:** Agricultural Inspectors; Aviation Inspectors; Child Support, Missing Persons, and Unemployment Insurance Fraud Investigators; Environmental Compliance Inspectors; Financial Examiners; Fire Inspectors; Fish and Game Wardens; Forest Fire Inspectors and Prevention Specialists; Government Property Inspectors and Investigators; Immigration and Customs Inspectors; Licensing Examiners and Inspectors; Marine Cargo Inspectors; Mechanical Inspectors; Motor Vehicle Inspectors; Nuclear Monitoring Technicians; Occupational Health and Safety Specialists; Pressure Vessel Inspectors; Railroad Inspectors; Tax Examiners, Collectors, and Revenue Agents. **PERSONALITY TYPE:** Social. Social occupations frequently involve working with, communicating with, and teaching people. These occupations often involve helping or providing service to others.

EDUCATION/TRAINING PROGRAM(S)— No data available.

WORK ENVIRONMENT—Sitting; walking and running; indoors; standing; extremely bright or inadequate lighting.

Executive Secretaries and Administrative Assistants

- Education/Training Required: Moderate-term on-the-job training
- Annual Earnings: $35,550
- Growth: 8.7%
- Annual Job Openings: 210,000
- Self-Employed: 1.6%
- Part-Time: 17.5%

Age Bracket	Percentage of Workers
45–54 Years Old	28.6%
55–64 Years Old	16.3%
65 or Older	3.2%

Provide high-level administrative support by conducting research; preparing statistical reports; handling information requests; and performing clerical functions such as preparing correspondence, receiving visitors, arranging conference calls, and scheduling meetings. May also train and supervise lower-level clerical staff. Manage and maintain executives' schedules. Prepare invoices, reports, memos, letters, financial statements, and other documents, using word processing, spreadsheet, database, and/or presentation software. Read and analyze incoming memos, submissions, and reports in order to determine their significance and plan their distribution. Open, sort, and distribute incoming correspondence, including faxes and e-mail. File and retrieve corporate documents, records, and reports. Greet visitors and determine whether they should be given access to specific individuals. Prepare responses to correspondence containing routine inquiries. Perform general office duties such as ordering supplies, maintaining

E

records management systems, and performing basic bookkeeping work. Prepare agendas and make arrangements for committee, board, and other meetings. Make travel arrangements for executives. Conduct research, compile data, and prepare papers for consideration and presentation by executives, committees, and boards of directors. Compile, transcribe, and distribute minutes of meetings. Attend meetings in order to record minutes. Coordinate and direct office services, such as records and budget preparation, personnel, and housekeeping, in order to aid executives. Meet with individuals, special interest groups, and others on behalf of executives, committees, and boards of directors. Set up and oversee administrative policies and procedures for offices and/or organizations. Supervise and train other clerical staff. Review operating practices and procedures in order to determine whether improvements can be made in areas such as workflow, reporting procedures, or expenditures. Interpret administrative and operating policies and procedures for employees. **SKILLS**—Active Listening; Time Management; Writing; Speaking; Instructing; Management of Financial Resources; Service Orientation; Management of Material Resources.

GOE—**Interest Area:** 04. Business and Administration. **Work Group:** 04.04. Secretarial Support. **Other Jobs in This Work Group:** Legal Secretaries; Medical Secretaries; Secretaries, Except Legal, Medical, and Executive. **PERSONALITY TYPE:** Conventional. Conventional occupations frequently involve following set procedures and routines. These occupations can include working with data and details more than with ideas. Usually there is a clear line of authority to follow.

EDUCATION/TRAINING PROGRAM(S)— Administrative Assistant and Secretarial Science, General; Executive Assistant/Executive Secretary; Medical Administrative/Executive Assistant and Medical Secretary .

WORK ENVIRONMENT—Sitting; sounds, noise levels are distracting or uncomfortable; physical proximity to others.

Family and General Practitioners

- Education/Training Required: First professional degree
- Annual Earnings: $136,170
- Growth: 19.5%
- Annual Job Openings: 38,000
- Self-Employed: 16.9%
- Part-Time: 8.1%

The job openings listed here are shared with Anesthesiologists; Internists, General; Obstetricians and Gynecologists; Pediatricians, General; Psychiatrists; and Surgeons.

Age Bracket	Percentage of Workers
45–54 Years Old	29.3%
55–64 Years Old	13.4%
65 or Older	5.4%

Diagnose, treat, and help prevent diseases and injuries that commonly occur in the general population. Advise patients and community members concerning diet, activity, hygiene, and disease prevention. Collect, record, and maintain patient information, such as medical history, reports, and examination results. Explain procedures and discuss test results or prescribed treatments with patients. Monitor the patients' conditions and progress and re-evaluate treatments as necessary. Order, perform, and interpret tests and analyze records, reports, and examination information to diagnose patients' condition. Prescribe or administer treatment, therapy, medication, vaccination, and other specialized medical care to treat or prevent illness, disease, or injury. Refer patients to medical specialists or other practitioners when necessary. Conduct research to study anatomy and develop or test medications, treatments, or procedures to prevent or control disease or injury. Coordinate work with nurses, social workers, rehabilitation therapists, pharmacists, psychologists, and other health care providers. Deliver babies. Direct and coordinate activities of nurses, students, assistants, specialists, therapists, and other medical staff. Operate on patients to remove, repair, or improve functioning of diseased or injured body parts and systems. Plan, implement, or administer health programs or standards in hospital, business, or community for information, prevention, or treatment of injury or illness. Prepare reports for government or management of birth, death, and disease statistics; workforce evaluations; or medical status of individuals. **SKILLS**—Science; Systems Evaluation; Reading Comprehension; Active Learning; Judgment and Decision Making; Management of Personnel Resources; Systems Analysis; Social Perceptiveness.

GOE—Interest Area: 08. Health Science. **Work Group:** 08.02. Medicine and Surgery. **Other Jobs in This Work Group:** Anesthesiologists; Internists, General; Medical Assistants; Medical Transcriptionists; Obstetricians and Gynecologists; Pediatricians, General; Pharmacists; Pharmacy Aides; Pharmacy Technicians; Physician Assistants; Psychiatrists; Registered Nurses; Surgeons; Surgical Technologists. **PERSONALITY TYPE:** Investigative. Investigative occupations frequently involve working with ideas and require an extensive amount of thinking. These occupations can involve searching for facts and figuring out problems mentally.

EDUCATION/TRAINING PROGRAM(S)—Family Medicine; Medicine (MD); Osteopathic Medicine/Osteopathy (DO).

WORK ENVIRONMENT—Disease or infections; common protective or safety equipment; walking and running; spend time bending or twisting the body; indoors; standing.

Farmers and Ranchers

- Education/Training Required: Long-term on-the-job training
- Annual Earnings: $38,600
- Growth: –20.6%
- Annual Job Openings: 118,000
- Self-Employed: 99.3%
- Part-Time: 17.7%

Age Bracket	Percentage of Workers
45–54 Years Old	21.9%
55–64 Years Old	24.4%
65 or Older	24.4%

On an ownership or rental basis, operate farms, ranches, greenhouses, nurseries, timber tracts, or other agricultural production establishments that produce crops, horticultural specialties, livestock, poultry, finfish, shellfish, or animal specialties. May plant, cultivate, harvest, perform post-harvest activities for, and market crops and livestock; may hire, train, and supervise farm workers or supervise a farm labor contractor; may prepare cost, production, and other records. May maintain and operate machinery and perform physical work. Assist in animal births and care for newborn livestock. Breed and raise stock such as cattle, poultry, and honeybees, using recognized breeding practices to ensure continued improvement in stock. Clean and disinfect buildings and yards and remove manure. Clean and sanitize milking equipment, storage tanks, collection cups, and cows' udders or ensure that procedures are followed to maintain sanitary conditions for handling of milk. Clean, grade, and package crops for marketing. Control the spread of disease and parasites in herds by using vaccination and medication and by separating sick animals. Destroy diseased or superfluous crops. Determine types and quantities of crops or livestock to be raised, according to factors such as market conditions, federal program availability, and soil conditions. Evaluate product marketing alternatives and then promote and market farm products, acting as the sales agent for livestock and crops. Harvest crops and collect specialty products such as royal jelly, wax, pollen, and honey from bee colonies. Install and shift irrigation systems to irrigate fields evenly or according to crop need. Maintain pastures or grazing lands to ensure that animals have enough feed, employing pasture-conservation measures such as arranging rotational grazing. Milk cows, using milking machinery. Monitor crops as they grow in order to ensure that they are growing properly and are free from diseases and contaminants. Negotiate and arrange with buyers for the sale, storage, and shipment of crops. Perform crop production duties such as planning, tilling, planting, fertilizing, cultivating, spraying, and harvesting. Plan crop activities based on factors such as crop maturity and weather conditions. Purchase and store livestock feed. Remove lower-quality or older animals from herds and purchase other livestock to replace culled animals. Select and purchase supplies and equipment such as seed, fertilizers, and farm machinery. Select animals for market and provide transportation of livestock to market. Set up and operate farm machinery to cultivate, harvest, and haul crops.

SKILLS—Management of Financial Resources; Management of Personnel Resources; Installation; Management of Material Resources; Equipment Selection; Operation and Control; Equipment Maintenance; Repairing.

GOE—**Interest Area:** 01. Agriculture and Natural Resources. **Work Group:** 01.01. Managerial Work in Agriculture and Natural Resources. **Other Jobs in This Work Group:** Agricultural Crop Farm Managers; First-Line Supervisors and Manager/Supervisors—Agricultural Crop Workers; First-Line Supervisors and Manager/Supervisors—Animal Husbandry Workers; First-Line Supervisors and Manager/Supervisors—Extractive Workers; First-Line Supervisors and Manager/Supervisors—Fishery Workers; First-Line Supervisors and Manager/Supervisors—Horticultural Workers; First-Line Supervisors and Manager/Supervisors—Landscaping Workers; First-Line Supervisors and Manager/Supervisors—Logging Workers; Fish Hatchery Managers; Lawn Service Managers; Nursery and Greenhouse Managers; Park Naturalists; Purchasing Agents and Buyers, Farm Products. **PERSONALITY TYPE:** Realistic. Realistic occupations frequently involve work activities that include practical, hands-on problems and solutions. They often deal with plants, animals, and real-world materials like wood, tools, and machinery. Many of the occupations require working outside and do not involve a lot of paperwork or working closely with others.

EDUCATION/TRAINING PROGRAM(S)—Agribusiness/Agricultural Business Operations; Agricultural Animal Breeding; Agricultural Business and Management, General; Agricultural Production Operations, General; Agricultural Production Operations, Other;

Agronomy and Crop Science; Animal Nutrition; Animal Sciences, General; Animal/Livestock Husbandry and Production; Aquaculture; Crop Production; Dairy Husbandry and Production; Dairy Science; Farm/Farm and Ranch Management; Greenhouse Operations and Management; Horticultural Science; others.

WORK ENVIRONMENT—Outdoors; minor burns, cuts, bites, or stings; hazardous equipment; standing; using hands on objects, tools, or controls.

Financial Managers, Branch or Department

- Education/Training Required: Work experience plus degree
- Annual Earnings: $83,780
- Growth: 18.3%
- Annual Job Openings: 71,000
- Self-Employed: 3.1%
- Part-Time: 4.8%

The job openings listed here are shared with Chief Financial Officers, Controllers, and Treasurers.

Age Bracket	Percentage of Workers
45–54 Years Old	26.6%
55–64 Years Old	13.4%
65 or Older	1.8%

Direct and coordinate financial activities of workers in a branch, office, or department of an establishment, such as branch bank, brokerage firm, risk and insurance department, or credit department. Prepare operational and risk reports for management analysis. Communicate with stockholders and other investors to provide information and to raise capital. Direct floor operations of brokerage firm engaged in buying and selling securities at exchange. Direct insurance negotiations, select insurance brokers and carriers, and place insurance. Establish and maintain relationships with individual and business customers and provide assistance with problems these customers may encounter. Examine, evaluate, and process loan applications. Monitor order flow and transactions that brokerage firm executes on the floor of exchange. Recruit staff members and oversee training programs. Review collection reports to determine the status of collections and the amounts of outstanding balances. Review reports of securities transactions and price lists in order to analyze market conditions. Submit delinquent accounts to attorneys or outside agencies for collection. Analyze and classify risks and investments to determine their potential impacts on companies. Approve or reject, or coordinate the approval and rejection of, lines of credit and commercial, real estate, and personal loans. Develop and analyze information to assess the current and future financial status of firms. Establish procedures for custody and control of assets, records, loan collateral, and securities in order to ensure safekeeping. Evaluate data pertaining to costs in order to plan budgets. Evaluate financial reporting systems, accounting and collection procedures, and investment activities and make recommendations for changes to procedures, operating systems, budgets, and other financial control functions. Network within communities to find and attract new business. Oversee the flow of cash and financial instruments. Plan, direct, and coordinate risk and insurance programs of establishments to control risks and losses. Plan, direct, and coordinate the activities of workers in branches, offices, or departments of such establishments as branch banks, brokerage firms, risk and insurance departments, or credit departments. Prepare financial and regulatory reports required by laws, regulations, and boards of directors. **SKILLS**—Management of Financial Resources; Management of Personnel Resources; Systems Analysis; Systems Evaluation; Judgment and Decision Making; Writing; Monitoring; Negotiation.

GOE—Interest Area: 06. Finance and Insurance. **Work Group:** 06.01. Managerial Work in Finance and Insurance. **Other Jobs in This Work Group:** Treasurers, Controllers, and Chief Financial Officers. **PERSONALITY TYPE:** Enterprising. Enterprising occupations frequently involve starting up and carrying out projects. These occupations can involve leading people and making many decisions. They sometimes require risk taking and often deal with business.

EDUCATION/TRAINING PROGRAM(S)— Accounting and Finance; Credit Management; Finance and Financial Management Services, Other; Finance, General; International Finance; Public Finance.

WORK ENVIRONMENT—Sitting; indoors; walking and running; standing.

Fire-Prevention and Protection Engineers

- ◎ Education/Training Required: Bachelor's degree
- ◎ Annual Earnings: $64,320
- ◎ Growth: 7.9%
- ◎ Annual Job Openings: 4,000
- ◎ Self-Employed: 1.6%
- ◎ Part-Time: 1.5%

The job openings listed here are shared with Industrial Safety and Health Engineers and Product Safety Engineers.

Age Bracket	Percentage of Workers
45–54 Years Old	23.3%
55–64 Years Old	14.4%
65 or Older	2.8%

Research causes of fires, determine fire protection methods, and design or recommend materials or equipment such as structural components or fire-detection equipment to assist organizations in safeguarding life and property against fire, explosion, and related hazards. Advise architects, builders, and other construction personnel on fire-prevention equipment and techniques and on fire code and standard interpretation and compliance. Conduct research on fire retardants and the fire safety of materials and devices. Consult with authorities to discuss safety regulations and to recommend changes as necessary. Design fire-detection equipment, alarm systems, and fire-extinguishing devices and systems. Determine causes of fires and ways in which they could have been prevented. Direct the purchase, modification, installation, maintenance, and operation of fire-protection systems. Inspect buildings or building designs to determine fire-protection system requirements and potential problems in areas such as water supplies, exit locations, and construction materials. Study the relationships between ignition sources and materials to determine how fires start. Attend workshops, seminars, or conferences to present or obtain information regarding fire prevention and protection. Develop plans for the prevention of destruction by fire, wind, and water. Develop training materials and conduct training sessions on fire protection. Evaluate fire department performance and the laws and regulations affecting fire prevention or fire safety. Prepare and write reports detailing specific fire-prevention and protection issues such as work performed and proposed review schedules. **SKILLS—** Technology Design; Instructing; Operations Analysis; Systems Evaluation; Science; Systems Analysis; Speaking; Active Learning; Quality Control Analysis.

GOE—Interest Area: 15. Scientific Research, Engineering, and Mathematics. **Work Group:** 15.08. Industrial and Safety Engineering. **Other Jobs in This Work Group:** Industrial Engineers; Industrial Safety and Health Engineers; Product Safety Engineers. **PERSONALITY TYPE:** Investigative. Investigative occupations frequently involve working with ideas and require an extensive amount of thinking. These occupations can involve searching for facts and figuring out problems mentally.

EDUCATION/TRAINING PROGRAM(S)— Environmental/Environmental Health Engineering.

WORK ENVIRONMENT—Sitting; specialized protective or safety equipment; climbing ladders, scaffolds, or poles; walking and running; spend time kneeling, crouching, stooping, or crawling.

First-Line Supervisors and Manager/Supervisors— Agricultural Crop Workers

- Education/Training Required: Associate degree
- Annual Earnings: $36,040
- Growth: 11.4%
- Annual Job Openings: 6,000
- Self-Employed: 0.9%
- Part-Time: 6.1%

The job openings listed here are shared with First-Line Supervisors and Manager/Supervisors—Animal Care Workers, Except Livestock; First-Line Supervisors and Manager/Supervisors—Animal Husbandry Workers; First-Line Supervisors and Manager/Supervisors— Fishery Workers; First-Line Supervisors and Manager/Supervisors—Horticultural Workers; and First-Line Supervisors and Manager/Supervisors— Logging Workers.

Age Bracket	Percentage of Workers
45–54 Years Old	30.8%
55–64 Years Old	18.5%
65 or Older	3.1%

Directly supervise and coordinate activities of agricultural crop workers. Manager/supervisors are generally found in smaller establishments, where they perform both supervisory and management functions, such as accounting, marketing, and personnel work, and may also engage in the same agricultural work as the workers they supervise. Assigns duties, such as tilling soil, planting, irrigating, storing crops, and maintaining machines, and assigns fields or rows to workers. Determines number and kind of workers needed to perform required work and schedules activities. Observes workers to detect inefficient and unsafe work procedures or identify problems and initiates actions to correct improper procedure or solve problem. Issues farm implements and machinery, ladders, or containers to workers and collects them at end of workday. Investigates grievances and settles disputes to maintain harmony among workers. Opens gate to permit entry of water into ditches or pipes and signals worker to start flow of water to irrigate fields. Drives and operates farm machinery, such as trucks, tractors, or self-propelled harvesters, to transport workers or cultivate and harvest fields. Requisitions and purchases farm supplies, such as insecticides, machine parts or lubricants, and tools. Confers with manager to evaluate weather and soil conditions and to develop and revise plans and procedures. Prepares time, payroll, and production reports, such as farm conditions, amount of yield, machinery breakdowns, and labor problems. Directs or assists in adjustment, repair, and maintenance of farm machinery and equipment. Trains workers in methods of fieldwork and safety regulations and briefs them on identifying characteristic of insects and diseases. Contracts with seasonal workers and farmers to provide employment and arranges for transportation, equipment, and living quarters. Recruits, hires, and discharges workers. Inspects crops and fields to determine maturity, yield, infestation, or work requirements, such as cultivating, spraying, weeding, or harvesting. **SKILLS—**Management of Personnel Resources; Management of Material Resources; Equipment Maintenance; Coordination; Repairing; Time Management; Instructing; Management of Financial Resources.

GOE—Interest Area: 01. Agriculture and Natural Resources. **Work Group:** 01.01. Managerial Work in Agriculture and Natural Resources. **Other Jobs in This Work Group:** Agricultural Crop Farm Managers; Farmers and Ranchers; First-Line Supervisors and Manager/Supervisors—Animal Husbandry Workers; First-Line Supervisors and Manager/Supervisors—Extractive Workers; First-Line Supervisors and Manager/Supervisors—Fishery Workers; First-Line Supervisors and Manager/Supervisors—Horticultural Workers; First-Line Supervisors and Manager/Supervisors—Landscaping Workers; First-Line Supervisors and Manager/Supervisors—Logging Workers; Fish Hatchery Managers; Lawn Service Managers; Nursery and Greenhouse Managers; Park Naturalists; Purchasing Agents and Buyers, Farm Products. **PERSONALITY TYPE:** Enterprising. Enterprising occupations frequently involve starting up and carrying out projects. These occupations can involve leading people and making many decisions. They sometimes require risk taking and often deal with business.

EDUCATION/TRAINING PROGRAM(S)—Agricultural Business and Management, Other; Agricultural Production Operations, General; Agricultural Production Operations, Other; Agriculture, Agricultural Operations, and Related Sciences, Other; Agronomy and Crop Science; Crop Production; Farm/Farm and Ranch Management; Plant Sciences, General.

WORK ENVIRONMENT—Outdoors; hazardous equipment; standing; minor burns, cuts, bites, or stings; contaminants; walking and running.

First-Line Supervisors and Manager/Supervisors— Animal Care Workers, Except Livestock

- Education/Training Required: Associate degree
- Annual Earnings: $36,040
- Growth: 11.4%
- Annual Job Openings: 6,000
- Self-Employed: 0.9%
- Part-Time: 6.1%

The job openings listed here are shared with First-Line Supervisors and Manager/Supervisors—Agricultural Crop Workers; First-Line Supervisors and Manager/Supervisors—Animal Husbandry Workers; First-Line Supervisors and Manager/Supervisors— Fishery Workers; First-Line Supervisors and Manager/Supervisors—Horticultural Workers; and First-Line Supervisors and Manager/Supervisors— Logging Workers.

Age Bracket	Percentage of Workers
45–54 Years Old	30.8%
55–64 Years Old	18.5%
65 or Older	3.1%

Directly supervise and coordinate activities of animal care workers. Manager/supervisors are generally found in smaller establishments, where they perform both supervisory and management functions, such as accounting, marketing, and personnel work, and may also engage in the same animal care work as the workers they supervise. Assigns workers to tasks such as feeding and treatment of animals and cleaning and maintenance of animal quarters.

Establishes work schedule and procedures of animal care. Monitors animal care, inspects facilities to identify problems, and discusses solutions with workers. Trains workers in animal care procedures, maintenance duties, and safety precautions. Plans budget and arranges for purchase of animals, feed, or supplies. Prepares reports concerning activity of facility, employees' time records, and animal treatment. Delivers lectures to public to stimulate interest in animals and communicate humane philosophy to public. Operates euthanasia equipment to destroy animals. Investigates complaints of animal neglect or cruelty and follows up on complaints appearing to justify prosecution. Observes and examines animals to detect signs of illness and determine need of services from veterinarian. Directs and assists workers in maintenance and repair of facilities. **SKILLS**—Management of Financial Resources; Management of Personnel Resources; Instructing; Management of Material Resources; Systems Evaluation; Systems Analysis; Writing; Speaking; Time Management.

GOE—Interest Area: 08. Health Science. **Work Group:** 08.01. Managerial Work in Medical and Health Services. **Other Jobs in This Work Group:** Coroners; Medical and Health Services Managers. **PERSONALITY TYPE:** Realistic. Realistic occupations frequently involve work activities that include practical, hands-on problems and solutions. They often deal with plants, animals, and real-world materials like wood, tools, and machinery. Many of the occupations require working outside and do not involve a lot of paperwork or working closely with others.

EDUCATION/TRAINING PROGRAM(S)— Poultry Science.

WORK ENVIRONMENT—Minor burns, cuts, bites, or stings; outdoors; standing; disease or infections; walking and running; spend time kneeling, crouching, stooping, or crawling.

First-Line Supervisors and Manager/Supervisors— Animal Husbandry Workers

- Education/Training Required: Associate degree
- Annual Earnings: $36,040
- Growth: 11.4%
- Annual Job Openings: 6,000
- Self-Employed: 16.9%
- Part-Time: 6.1%

The job openings listed here are shared with First-Line Supervisors and Manager/Supervisors—Agricultural Crop Workers; First-Line Supervisors and Manager/Supervisors—Animal Care Workers, Except Livestock; First-Line Supervisors and Manager/Supervisors—Fishery Workers; First-Line Supervisors and Manager/Supervisors—Horticultural Workers; and First-Line Supervisors and Manager/Supervisors—Logging Workers.

Age Bracket	Percentage of Workers
45–54 Years Old	30.8%
55–64 Years Old	18.5%
65 or Older	3.1%

Directly supervise and coordinate activities of animal husbandry workers. Manager/supervisors are generally found in smaller establishments, where they perform both supervisory and management functions, such as accounting, marketing, and personnel work, and may also engage in the same animal husbandry work as the workers they supervise. Assigns workers to tasks such as feeding and treating animals, cleaning quarters, transferring animals, and maintaining facilities. Notifies veterinarian and manager of serious illnesses or injuries to animals. Monitors eggs and adjusts incubator thermometer and gauges to ascertain hatching progress and maintain specified conditions. Treats animal illness or injury, following experience or instructions of veterinarian. Inseminates livestock artificially to produce desired offspring and to demonstrate techniques to farmers. Transports or arranges for transport of animals, equipment, food, animal feed, and other supplies to and from worksite. Requisitions equipment, materials, and supplies. Prepares animal condition, production, feed consumption, and worker attendance reports. Trains workers in animal care, artificial insemination techniques, egg candling and sorting, and transfer of animals. Observes animals, such as cattle, sheep, poultry, or game animals, for signs of illness, injury, nervousness, or unnatural behavior. Plans and prepares work schedules. Recruits, hires, and pays workers. Confers with manager to discuss and ascertain production requirements, condition of equipment and supplies, and work schedules. Inspects buildings, fences, fields or range, supplies, and equipment to determine work to be done. Studies feed, weight, health, genetic, or milk production records to determine feed formula and rations or breeding schedule. Oversees animal care, maintenance, breeding, or packing and transfer activities to ensure work is done correctly and to identify and solve problems. **SKILLS**—Management of Personnel Resources; Management of Material Resources; Systems Evaluation; Instructing; Systems Analysis; Time Management; Coordination; Equipment Selection.

GOE—Interest Area: 01. Agriculture and Natural Resources. **Work Group:** 01.01. Managerial Work in Agriculture and Natural Resources. **Other Jobs in This Work Group:**

Agricultural Crop Farm Managers; Farmers and Ranchers; First-Line Supervisors and Manager/Supervisors—Agricultural Crop Workers; First-Line Supervisors and Manager/Supervisors—Extractive Workers; First-Line Supervisors and Manager/Supervisors—Fishery Workers; First-Line Supervisors and Manager/Supervisors—Horticultural Workers; First-Line Supervisors and Manager/Supervisors—Landscaping Workers; First-Line Supervisors and Manager/Supervisors—Logging Workers; Fish Hatchery Managers; Lawn Service Managers; Nursery and Greenhouse Managers; Park Naturalists; Purchasing Agents and Buyers, Farm Products. **PERSONALITY TYPE:** Enterprising. Enterprising occupations frequently involve starting up and carrying out projects. These occupations can involve leading people and making many decisions. They sometimes require risk taking and often deal with business.

EDUCATION/TRAINING PROGRAM(S)— Agricultural Animal Breeding; Agriculture, Agricultural Operations, and Related Sciences, Other; Animal Nutrition; Animal Sciences, General; Livestock Management; Poultry Science.

WORK ENVIRONMENT—Outdoors; walking and running; very hot or cold; standing; contaminants.

First-Line Supervisors and Manager/Supervisors—Construction Trades Workers

- Education/Training Required: Work experience in a related occupation
- Annual Earnings: $50,980
- Growth: 14.1%
- Annual Job Openings: 67,000
- Self-Employed: 20.1%
- Part-Time: 2.1%

The job openings listed here are shared with First-Line Supervisors and Manager/Supervisors—Extractive Workers.

Age Bracket	Percentage of Workers
45–54 Years Old	27.9%
55–64 Years Old	11.8%
65 or Older	1.8%

Directly supervise and coordinate activities of construction trades workers and their helpers. Manager/supervisors are generally found in smaller establishments, where they perform both supervisory and management functions, such as accounting, marketing, and personnel work, and may also engage in the same construction trades work as the workers they supervise. Suggests and initiates personnel actions, such as promotions, transfers, and hires. Analyzes and resolves worker problems and recommends motivational plans. Examines and inspects work progress, equipment, and construction sites to verify safety and ensure that specifications are met. Estimates material and worker requirements to complete job. Reads specifications, such as blueprints and data, to determine construction requirements. Analyzes and plans installation and construction of equipment and structures. Locates, measures, and marks location and placement of structures and equipment. Records information, such as personnel, production, and operational data, on specified forms and reports. Trains workers in construction methods and operation of equipment. Recommends measures to improve production methods and equipment performance to increase efficiency and safety. Assists workers engaged in construction activities, using hand tools and equipment. Supervises and coordinates activities of construction trades workers. Directs and leads workers engaged in construction activities. Assigns work to employees, using material and worker requirements data. Confers with staff and workers to ensure production and personnel problems are resolved. **SKILLS—** Management of Personnel Resources; Management of Material Resources; Installation; Systems Evaluation; Systems Analysis; Time Management; Persuasion; Instructing; Quality Control Analysis.

GOE—Interest Area: 02. Architecture and Construction. **Work Group:** 02.01. Managerial Work in Architecture and Construction. **Other Jobs in This Work Group:** Construction Managers. **PERSONALITY TYPE:** Enterprising. Enterprising occupations frequently involve starting up and carrying out projects. These occupations can involve leading people and making many decisions. They sometimes require risk taking and often deal with business.

EDUCATION/TRAINING PROGRAM(S)— Building/Construction Finishing, Management, and Inspection, Other; Building/Construction Site Management/Manager; Building/

Construction Trades, Other; Building/Home/Construction Inspection/Inspector; Building/Property Maintenance and Management; Carpentry/Carpenter; Concrete Finishing/Concrete Finisher; Drywall Installation/Drywaller; Electrical and Power Transmission Installation/Installer, General; Electrical and Power Transmission Installers, Other; Electrician; Glazier; Lineworker; others.

WORK ENVIRONMENT—Outdoors; common protective or safety equipment; hazardous equipment; high places; climbing ladders, scaffolds, or poles.

First-Line Supervisors and Manager/Supervisors—Extractive Workers

- Education/Training Required: Work experience in a related occupation
- Annual Earnings: $50,980
- Growth: 14.1%
- Annual Job Openings: 67,000
- Self-Employed: 20.1%
- Part-Time: 2.1%

The job openings listed here are shared with First-Line Supervisors and Manager/Supervisors—Construction Trades Workers.

Age Bracket	Percentage of Workers
45–54 Years Old	27.9%
55–64 Years Old	11.8%
65 or Older	1.8%

Directly supervise and coordinate activities of extractive workers and their helpers. Manager/supervisors are generally found in smaller establishments, where they perform both supervisory and management functions, such as accounting, marketing, and personnel work, and may also engage in the same extractive work as the workers they supervise. Supervises and coordinates activities of workers engaged in the extraction of geological materials. Directs and leads workers engaged in extraction of geological materials. Assigns work to employees, using material and worker requirements data. Confers with staff and workers to ensure production personnel problems are resolved. Analyzes and resolves worker problems and recommends motivational plans. Analyzes and plans extraction process of geological materials. Trains workers in construction methods and operation of equipment. Examines and inspects equipment, site, and materials to verify specifications are met. Recommends measures to improve production methods and equipment performance to increase efficiency and safety. Suggests and initiates personnel actions, such as promotions, transfers, and hires. Records information such as personnel, production, and operational data on specified forms. Assists workers engaged in extraction activities, using hand tools and equipment. Locates, measures, and marks materials and site location, using measuring and marking equipment. Orders materials, supplies, and repair of equipment and machinery. **SKILLS**—Management of Personnel Resources; Management of Material Resources; Instructing; Systems Evaluation; Systems Analysis; Coordination; Operation Monitoring; Social Perceptiveness.

GOE—Interest Area: 01. Agriculture and Natural Resources. **Work Group:** 01.01.

Managerial Work in Agriculture and Natural Resources. **Other Jobs in This Work Group:** Agricultural Crop Farm Managers; Farmers and Ranchers; First-Line Supervisors and Manager/Supervisors—Agricultural Crop Workers; First-Line Supervisors and Manager/Supervisors—Animal Husbandry Workers; First-Line Supervisors and Manager/Supervisors—Fishery Workers; First-Line Supervisors and Manager/Supervisors—Horticultural Workers; First-Line Supervisors and Manager/Supervisors—Landscaping Workers; First-Line Supervisors and Manager/Supervisors—Logging Workers; Fish Hatchery Managers; Lawn Service Managers; Nursery and Greenhouse Managers; Park Naturalists; Purchasing Agents and Buyers, Farm Products. **PERSONALITY TYPE:** Enterprising. Enterprising occupations frequently involve starting up and carrying out projects. These occupations can involve leading people and making many decisions. They sometimes require risk taking and often deal with business.

EDUCATION/TRAINING PROGRAM(S)— Blasting/Blaster; Well Drilling/Driller.

WORK ENVIRONMENT—Common protective or safety equipment; outdoors; standing; hazardous equipment; specialized protective or safety equipment.

First-Line Supervisors and Manager/Supervisors—Fishery Workers

- Education/Training Required: Associate degree
- Annual Earnings: $36,040
- Growth: 11.4%
- Annual Job Openings: 6,000
- Self-Employed: 16.9%
- Part-Time: 6.1%

The job openings listed here are shared with First-Line Supervisors and Manager/Supervisors—Agricultural Crop Workers; First-Line Supervisors and Manager/Supervisors—Animal Care Workers, Except Livestock; First-Line Supervisors and Manager/Supervisors—Animal Husbandry Workers; First-Line Supervisors and Manager/Supervisors—Horticultural Workers; and First-Line Supervisors and Manager/Supervisors—Logging Workers.

Age Bracket	Percentage of Workers
45–54 Years Old	30.8%
55–64 Years Old	18.5%
65 or Older	3.1%

Directly supervise and coordinate activities of fishery workers. Manager/supervisors are generally found in smaller establishments, where they perform both supervisory and management functions, such as accounting, marketing, and personnel work, and may also engage in the same fishery work as the workers they supervise. Assigns workers to duties such as fertilizing and incubating spawn; feeding and transferring fish; and planting, cultivating, and harvesting shellfish beds. Oversees worker activities, such as treatment and rearing of fingerlings, maintenance of equipment, and harvesting of fish or shellfish. Directs workers to correct deviations or problems, such as disease, quality of seed distribution, or adequacy of cultivation. Plans work schedules according to availability of personnel and equipment, tidal levels, feeding schedules, or need for transfer or harvest. Observes fish and beds or ponds to detect diseases, determine quality of fish, or determine completeness of harvesting. Records number and type of fish or shellfish reared and harvested and keeps workers' time records. Confers with manager to determine time and place of seed planting and cultivating, feeding, or harvesting of fish or shellfish. Trains workers in spawning, rearing, cultivating, and harvesting methods and use of equipment. **SKILLS**—Management of Personnel Resources; Instructing; Systems Analysis; Time Management; Management of Material Resources; Coordination; Systems Evaluation; Learning Strategies; Equipment Maintenance.

GOE—Interest Area: 01. Agriculture and Natural Resources. **Work Group:** 01.01. Managerial Work in Agriculture and Natural Resources. **Other Jobs in This Work Group:** Agricultural Crop Farm Managers; Farmers and Ranchers; First-Line Supervisors and Manager/Supervisors—Agricultural Crop Workers; First-Line Supervisors and Manager/Supervisors—Animal Husbandry Workers; First-Line Supervisors and Manager/Supervisors—Extractive Workers; First-Line Supervisors and Manager/Supervisors—Horticultural Workers; First-Line Supervisors and Manager/Supervisors—Landscaping Workers; First-Line Supervisors and Manager/Supervisors—Logging Workers; Fish Hatchery Managers; Lawn Service Managers; Nursery and Greenhouse Managers; Park Naturalists; Purchasing Agents and Buyers, Farm Products. **PERSONALITY TYPE:**

Realistic. Realistic occupations frequently involve work activities that include practical, hands-on problems and solutions. They often deal with plants, animals, and real-world materials like wood, tools, and machinery. Many of the occupations require working outside and do not involve a lot of paperwork or working closely with others.

EDUCATION/TRAINING PROGRAM(S)— Agricultural Business and Management, Other; Aquaculture; Fishing and Fisheries Sciences and Management.

WORK ENVIRONMENT—Outdoors; walking and running; sitting; standing; extremely bright or inadequate lighting.

First-Line Supervisors and Manager/Supervisors— Horticultural Workers

- Education/Training Required: Associate degree
- Annual Earnings: $36,040
- Growth: 11.4%
- Annual Job Openings: 6,000
- Self-Employed: 16.9%
- Part-Time: 6.1%

The job openings listed here are shared with First-Line Supervisors and Manager/Supervisors—Agricultural Crop Workers; First-Line Supervisors and Manager/Supervisors—Animal Care Workers, Except Livestock; First-Line Supervisors and Manager/Supervisors—Animal Husbandry Workers; First-Line Supervisors and Manager/Supervisors—Fishery Workers; and First-Line Supervisors and Manager/Supervisors—Logging Workers.

Age Bracket	Percentage of Workers
45–54 Years Old	30.8%
55–64 Years Old	18.5%
65 or Older	3.1%

Directly supervise and coordinate activities of horticultural workers. Manager/supervisors are generally found in smaller establishments, where they perform both supervisory and management functions, such as accounting, marketing, and personnel work, and may also engage in the same horticultural work as the workers they supervise. Assigns workers to duties such as cultivation, harvesting, maintenance, grading and packing products, or altering greenhouse environmental conditions. Estimates work-hour requirements to plant, cultivate, or harvest and prepares work schedule. Confers with management to report conditions; plan planting and harvesting schedules; and discuss changes in fertilizer, herbicides, or cultivating techniques. Drives and operates heavy machinery, such as dump truck, tractor, or growth-media tiller, to transport materials and supplies. Maintains records of employees' hours worked and work completed. Prepares and submits written or oral reports of personnel actions, such as performance evaluations, hires, promotions, and discipline. Trains employees in horticultural techniques, such as transplanting and weeding, shearing and harvesting trees, and grading and packing flowers. Inspects facilities to determine maintenance needs, such as malfunctioning environmental-control system, clogged sprinklers, or missing glass panes in greenhouse. Observes plants, flowers, shrubs, and trees in greenhouses, cold frames, or fields to ascertain condition. Reads inventory records, customer orders, and shipping schedules to ascertain day's activities. Reviews employees' work to ascertain quality and quantity of work performed.

SKILLS—Management of Personnel Resources; Management of Material Resources; Instructing; Coordination; Operation Monitoring; Troubleshooting; Repairing; Time Management.

GOE—**Interest Area:** 01. Agriculture and Natural Resources. **Work Group:** 01.01. Managerial Work in Agriculture and Natural Resources. **Other Jobs in This Work Group:** Agricultural Crop Farm Managers; Farmers and Ranchers; First-Line Supervisors and Manager/Supervisors—Agricultural Crop Workers; First-Line Supervisors and Manager/Supervisors—Animal Husbandry Workers; First-Line Supervisors and Manager/Supervisors—Extractive Workers; First-Line Supervisors and Manager/Supervisors—Fishery Workers; First-Line Supervisors and Manager/Supervisors—Landscaping Workers; First-Line Supervisors and Manager/Supervisors—Logging Workers; Fish Hatchery Managers; Lawn Service Managers; Nursery and Greenhouse Managers; Park Naturalists; Purchasing Agents and Buyers, Farm Products. **PERSONALITY TYPE:** Realistic. Realistic occupations frequently involve work activities that include practical, hands-on problems and solutions. They often deal with plants, animals, and real-world materials like wood, tools, and machinery. Many of the occupations require working outside and do not involve a lot of paperwork or working closely with others.

EDUCATION/TRAINING PROGRAM(S)— Agricultural Business and Management, Other; Agricultural Production Operations, General; Agricultural Production Operations, Other; Plant Sciences, General.

WORK ENVIRONMENT—Outdoors; very hot or cold; standing; minor burns, cuts, bites, or stings; walking and running.

First-Line Supervisors and Manager/Supervisors— Logging Workers

- Education/Training Required: Bachelor's degree
- Annual Earnings: $36,040
- Growth: 11.4%
- Annual Job Openings: 6,000
- Self-Employed: 16.9%
- Part-Time: 6.1%

The job openings listed here are shared with First-Line Supervisors and Manager/Supervisors—Agricultural Crop Workers; First-Line Supervisors and Manager/Supervisors—Animal Care Workers, Except Livestock; First-Line Supervisors and Manager/Supervisors—Animal Husbandry Workers; First-Line Supervisors and Manager/Supervisors—Fishery Workers; and First-Line Supervisors and Manager/Supervisors—Horticultural Workers.

Age Bracket	Percentage of Workers
45–54 Years Old	30.8%
55–64 Years Old	18.5%
65 or Older	3.1%

Directly supervise and coordinate activities of logging workers. Manager/supervisors are generally found in smaller establishments, where they perform both supervisory and management functions, such as accounting, marketing, and personnel work, and may also engage in the same logging work as the workers they supervise. Assign to workers duties such as trees to be cut; cutting sequences and specifications; and loading of trucks, railcars, or rafts. Change logging operations or methods to eliminate unsafe conditions. Communicate with forestry personnel regarding forest harvesting and forest management plans, procedures, and schedules. Determine logging operation methods, crew sizes, and equipment requirements, conferring with mill, company, and forestry officials as necessary. Monitor logging operations to identify and solve problems; improve work methods; and ensure compliance with safety, company, and government regulations. Monitor workers to ensure that safety regulations are followed, warning or disciplining those who violate safety regulations. Plan and schedule logging operations such as felling and bucking trees and grading, sorting, yarding, or loading logs. Schedule work crews, equipment, and transportation for several different work locations. Supervise and coordinate the activities of workers engaged in logging operations and silvicultural operations. Train workers in tree felling and bucking, operation of tractors and loading machines, yarding and loading techniques, and safety regulations. Coordinate dismantling, moving, and setting up equipment at new work sites. Coordinate the selection and movement of logs from storage areas according to transportation schedules or production requirements. Prepare production and personnel time records for management. SKILLS—Management of Personnel Resources; Management of Material Resources; Instructing; Time Management; Coordination; Systems Analysis; Systems Evaluation; Operation and Control.

GOE—Interest Area: 01. Agriculture and Natural Resources. Work Group: 01.01. Managerial Work in Agriculture and Natural Resources. Other Jobs in This Work Group: Agricultural Crop Farm Managers; Farmers and Ranchers; First-Line Supervisors and Manager/Supervisors—Agricultural Crop Workers; First-Line Supervisors and Manager/Supervisors—Animal Husbandry Workers; First-Line Super-visors and Manager/Supervisors—Extractive Workers; First-Line Supervisors and Manager/Supervisors—Fishery Workers; First-Line Supervisors and Manager/Supervisors—Horticultural Workers; First-Line Supervisors and Manager/Supervisors—Landscaping Workers; Fish Hatchery Managers; Lawn Service Managers; Nursery and Greenhouse Managers; Park Naturalists; Purchasing Agents and Buyers, Farm Products. PERSONALITY TYPE: Realistic. Realistic occupations frequently involve work activities that include practical, hands-on problems and solutions. They often deal with plants, animals, and real-world materials like wood, tools, and machinery. Many of the occupations require working outside and do not involve a lot of paperwork or working closely with others.

EDUCATION/TRAINING PROGRAM(S)—Agricultural Business and Management, Other; Farm/Farm and Ranch Management.

WORK ENVIRONMENT—Outdoors; hazardous equipment; minor burns, cuts, bites, or stings; standing; very hot or cold.

First-Line Supervisors, Administrative Support

- Education/Training Required: Work experience in a related occupation
- Annual Earnings: $41,850
- Growth: 6.6%
- Annual Job Openings: 140,000
- Self-Employed: 0.9%
- Part-Time: 6.7%

The job openings listed here are shared with First-Line Supervisors, Customer Service.

Age Bracket	Percentage of Workers
45–54 Years Old	30.1%
55–64 Years Old	15.2%
65 or Older	2.1%

Supervise and coordinate activities of workers involved in providing administrative support. Supervises and coordinates activities of workers engaged in clerical or administrative support activities. Plans, prepares, and revises work schedules and duty assignments according to budget allotments, customer needs, problems, workloads, and statistical forecasts. Verifies completeness and accuracy of subordinates' work, computations, and records. Interviews, selects, and discharges employees. Oversees, coordinates, or performs activities associated with shipping, receiving, distribution, and transportation. Evaluates subordinate job performance and conformance to regulations and recommends appropriate personnel action. Consults with supervisor and other personnel to resolve problems such as equipment performance, output quality, and work schedules. Trains employees in work and safety procedures and company policies. Computes figures such as balances, totals, and commissions. Analyzes financial activities of establishment or department and assists in planning budget. Inspects equipment for defects and notifies maintenance personnel or outside service contractors for repairs. Plans layout of stockroom, warehouse, or other storage areas, considering turnover, size, weight, and related factors pertaining to items stored. Compiles reports and information required by management or governmental agencies. Identifies and resolves discrepancies or errors. Maintains records of such matters as inventory, personnel, orders, supplies, and machine maintenance. Examines procedures and recommends changes to save time, labor, and other costs and to improve quality control and operating efficiency. Participates in work of subordinates to facilitate productivity or overcome difficult aspects of work. Requisitions supplies. Reviews records and reports pertaining to such activities as production, operation, payroll, customer accounts, and shipping. **SKILLS**—Management of Personnel Resources; Management of Financial Resources; Management of Material Resources; Social Perceptiveness; Systems Evaluation; Time Management; Systems Analysis; Monitoring.

GOE—Interest Area: 04. Business and Administration. **Work Group:** 04.02. Managerial Work in Business Detail. **Other Jobs in This Work Group:** Administrative Services Managers; First-Line Supervisors, Customer Service; Housekeeping Supervisors; Janitorial Supervisors; Meeting and Convention Planners. **PERSONALITY TYPE:** Enterprising. Enterprising occupations frequently involve starting up and carrying out projects. These occupations can involve leading people and making many decisions. They sometimes require risk taking and often deal with business.

EDUCATION/TRAINING PROGRAM(S)—Agricultural Business Technology; Medical Staff Services Technolgy/ Technician; Medical/Health Management and Clinical Assistant/Specialist; Office Management and Supervision.

WORK ENVIRONMENT—Sitting; indoors; walking and running; standing.

First-Line Supervisors, Customer Service

- ◎ Education/Training Required: Work experience in a related occupation
- ◎ Annual Earnings: $41,850
- ◎ Growth: 6.6%
- ◎ Annual Job Openings: 140,000
- ◎ Self-Employed: 0.9%
- ◎ Part-Time: 6.7%

The job openings listed here are shared with First-Line Supervisors, Administrative Support.

Age Bracket	Percentage of Workers
45–54 Years Old	30.1%
55–64 Years Old	15.2%
65 or Older	2.1%

Supervise and coordinate activities of workers involved in providing customer service. Supervises and coordinates activities of workers engaged in customer service activities. Plans, prepares, and devises work schedules according to budgets and workloads. Observes and evaluates workers' performance. Issues instructions and assigns duties to workers. Trains and instructs employees. Hires and discharges workers. Communicates with other departments and management to resolve problems and expedite work. Interprets and communicates work procedures and company policies to staff. Helps workers in resolving problems and completing work. Resolves complaints and answers questions of customers regarding services and procedures. Reviews and checks work of subordinates such as reports, records, and applications for accuracy and content and corrects errors. Prepares, maintains, and submits reports and records, such as budgets and operational and personnel reports. Makes recommendations to management concerning staff and improvement of procedures. Plans and develops improved procedures. Requisitions or purchases supplies. **SKILLS—** Management of Personnel Resources; Management of Financial Resources; Service Orientation; Social Perceptiveness; Systems Evaluation; Coordination; Time Management; Learning Strategies.

GOE—Interest Area: 04. Business and Administration. **Work Group:** 04.02. Managerial Work in Business Detail. **Other Jobs in This Work Group:** Administrative Services Managers; First-Line Supervisors, Administrative Support; Housekeeping Supervisors; Janitorial Supervisors; Meeting and Convention Planners. **PERSONALITY TYPE:** Enterprising. Enterprising occupations frequently involve starting up and carrying out projects. These occupations can involve leading people and making many decisions. They sometimes require risk taking and often deal with business.

EDUCATION/TRAINING PROGRAM(S)— Customer Service Management.

WORK ENVIRONMENT—Sitting; walking and running; indoors; standing.

First-Line Supervisors/Managers of Correctional Officers

- Education/Training Required: Work experience in a related occupation
- Annual Earnings: $48,070
- Growth: 19.0%
- Annual Job Openings: 4,000
- Self-Employed: 0%
- Part-Time: 1.4%

Age Bracket	Percentage of Workers
45–54 Years Old	32.3%
55–64 Years Old	16.1%
65 or Older	close to 0%

Supervise and coordinate activities of correctional officers and jailers. Complete administrative paperwork and supervise the preparation and maintenance of records, forms, and reports. Conduct roll calls of correctional officers. Develop work and security procedures. Instruct employees and provide on-the-job training. Maintain knowledge of, comply with, and enforce all institutional policies, rules, procedures, and regulations. Maintain order, discipline, and security within assigned areas in accordance with relevant rules, regulations, policies, and laws. Monitor behavior of subordinates to ensure alert, courteous, and professional behavior toward inmates, parolees, fellow employees, visitors, and the public. Read and review offender information to identify issues that require special attention. Respond to emergencies such as escapes. Restrain, secure, and control offenders, using chemical agents, firearms, and other weapons of force as necessary. Set up employee work schedules. Supervise and direct the work of correctional officers to ensure the safe custody, discipline, and welfare of inmates. Supervise and perform searches of inmates and their quarters to locate contraband items. Supervise activities such as searches, shakedowns, riot control, and institutional tours. Take, receive, and check periodic inmate counts. Carry injured offenders or employees to safety and provide emergency first aid when necessary. Convey correctional officers' and inmates' complaints to superiors. Examine incoming and outgoing mail to ensure conformance with regulations. Rate behavior of inmates, promoting acceptable attitudes and behaviors to those with low ratings. Resolve problems between inmates. Supervise and provide security for offenders performing tasks such as construction, maintenance, laundry, food service, and other industrial or agricultural operations. Transfer and transport offenders on foot or by driving vehicles such as trailers, vans, and buses. **SKILLS**—No data available.

GOE—Interest Area: 12. Law and Public Safety. **Work Group:** 12.01. Managerial Work in Law and Public Safety. **Other Jobs in This Work Group:** Emergency Management Specialists; First-Line Supervisors/Managers of Police and Detectives; Forest Fire Fighting and Prevention Supervisors; Municipal Fire Fighting and Prevention Supervisors. **PERSONALITY TYPE:** No data available.

EDUCATION/TRAINING PROGRAM(S)— Corrections; Corrections Administration.

WORK ENVIRONMENT—No data available.

First-Line Supervisors/Managers of Mechanics, Installers, and Repairers

- ⊚ Education/Training Required: Work experience in a related occupation
- ⊚ Annual Earnings: $51,000
- ⊚ Growth: 15.4%
- ⊚ Annual Job Openings: 42,000
- ⊚ Self-Employed: 0.1%
- ⊚ Part-Time: 1.3%

Age Bracket	Percentage of Workers
45–54 Years Old	32.6%
55–64 Years Old	15.0%
65 or Older	1.8%

Supervise and coordinate the activities of mechanics, installers, and repairers. Determine schedules, sequences, and assignments for work activities, based on work priority, quantity of equipment and skill of personnel. Patrol and monitor work areas and examine tools and equipment in order to detect unsafe conditions or violations of procedures or safety rules. Monitor employees' work levels and review work performance. Examine objects, systems, or facilities and analyze information to determine needed installations, services, or repairs. Participate in budget preparation and administration, coordinating purchasing and documentation and monitoring departmental expenditures. Counsel employees about work-related issues and assist employees to correct job-skill deficiencies. Requisition materials and supplies, such as tools, equipment, and replacement parts. Compute estimates and actual costs of factors such as materials, labor, and outside contractors. Interpret specifications, blueprints, and job orders in order to construct templates and lay out reference points for workers. Conduct or arrange for worker training in safety, repair, and maintenance techniques; operational procedures; and equipment use. Investigate accidents and injuries and prepare reports of findings. Confer with personnel, such as management, engineering, quality control, customer, and union workers' representatives, in order to coordinate work activities, resolve employee grievances, and identify and review resource needs. Recommend or initiate personnel actions, such as hires, promotions, transfers, discharges, and disciplinary measures. Perform skilled repair and maintenance operations, using equipment such as hand and power tools, hydraulic presses and shears, and welding equipment. Compile operational and personnel records, such as time and production records, inventory data, repair and maintenance statistics, and test results. Develop, implement, and evaluate maintenance policies and procedures. Monitor tool inventories and the condition and maintenance of shops in order to ensure adequate working conditions. Inspect, test, and measure completed work, using devices such as hand tools and gauges to verify conformance to standards and repair requirements. **SKILLS**—Management of Personnel Resources; Installation; Repairing; Management of Material Resources; Management of Financial Resources; Equipment Maintenance; Negotiation; Troubleshooting.

GOE—Interest Area: 13. Manufacturing. **Work Group:** 13.01. Managerial Work in Manufacturing. **Other Jobs in This Work Group:** First-Line Supervisors/Managers of Helpers, Laborers, and Material Movers, Hand; First-Line Supervisors/Managers of Production and Operating Workers; Industrial Production Managers. **PERSONALITY TYPE:** Enterprising. Enterprising occupations frequently involve starting up and carrying out projects. These occupations can involve leading people and making many decisions. They sometimes require risk taking and often deal with business.

EDUCATION/TRAINING PROGRAM(S)— Operations Management and Supervision.

WORK ENVIRONMENT—Contaminants; outdoors; indoors, not environmentally controlled; very hot or cold; in an enclosed vehicle or equipment.

First-Line Supervisors/Managers of Non-Retail Sales Workers

- Education/Training Required: Work experience in a related occupation
- Annual Earnings: $60,300
- Growth: 6.8%
- Annual Job Openings: 72,000
- Self-Employed: 44.7%
- Part-Time: 5.7%

Age Bracket	Percentage of Workers
45–54 Years Old	25.6%
55–64 Years Old	15.5%
65 or Older	3.5%

Directly supervise and coordinate activities of sales workers other than retail sales workers. May perform duties such as budgeting, accounting, and personnel work in addition to

supervisory duties. Analyze details of sales territories to assess their growth potential and to set quotas. Direct and supervise employees engaged in sales, inventory-taking, reconciling cash receipts, or performing specific services such as pumping gasoline for customers. Hire, train, and evaluate personnel. Inventory stock and reorder when inventories drop to specified levels. Keep records pertaining to purchases, sales, and requisitions. Listen to and resolve customer complaints regarding services, products, or personnel. Monitor sales staff performance to ensure that goals are met. Plan and prepare work schedules and assign employees to specific duties. Prepare sales and inventory reports for management and budget departments. Provide staff with assistance in performing difficult or complicated duties. Attend company meetings to exchange product information and coordinate work activities with other departments. Confer with company officials to develop methods and procedures to increase sales, expand markets, and promote business. Coordinate sales promotion activities and prepare merchandise displays and advertising copy. Examine merchandise to ensure correct pricing and display and ensure that it functions as advertised. Examine products purchased for resale or received for storage to determine product condition. Formulate pricing policies on merchandise according to profitability requirements. Prepare rental or lease agreements, specifying charges and payment procedures for use of machinery, tools, or other items. Visit retailers and sales representatives to promote products and gather information. **SKILLS—**Management of Personnel Resources; Management of Material Resources; Management of Financial Resources; Systems Evaluation; Systems Analysis; Negotiation; Social Perceptiveness; Coordination.

GOE—**Interest Area:** 14. Retail and Wholesale Sales and Service. **Work Group:** 14.01. Managerial Work in Retail/Wholesale Sales and Service. **Other Jobs in This Work Group:** Advertising and Promotions Managers; First-Line Supervisors/Managers of Retail Sales Workers; Funeral Directors; Marketing Managers; Property, Real Estate, and Community Association Managers; Purchasing Managers; Sales Managers. **PERSONALITY TYPE:** Enterprising. Enterprising occupations frequently involve starting up and carrying out projects. These occupations can involve leading people and making many decisions. They sometimes require risk taking and often deal with business.

EDUCATION/TRAINING PROGRAM(S)— Business, Management, Marketing, and Related Support Services; General Merchandising, Sales, and Related Marketing Operations, Other; Special Products Marketing Operations; Specialized Merchandising, Sales, and Related Marketing Operations, Other.

WORK ENVIRONMENT—Walking and running; standing; sitting.

First-Line Supervisors/Managers of Police and Detectives

- Education/Training Required: Work experience in a related occupation
- Annual Earnings: $65,020
- Growth: 15.3%
- Annual Job Openings: 14,000
- Self-Employed: 0%
- Part-Time: 1.4%

Age Bracket	Percentage of Workers
45–54 Years Old	41.7%
55–64 Years Old	10.2%
65 or Older	2.4%

Supervise and coordinate activities of members of police force. Explain police operations to subordinates to assist them in performing their job duties. Inform personnel of changes in regulations and policies, implications of new or amended laws, and new techniques of police work. Supervise and coordinate the investigation of criminal cases, offering guidance and expertise to investigators and ensuring that procedures are conducted in accordance with laws and regulations. Investigate and resolve personnel problems within organization and charges of misconduct against staff. Train staff in proper police work procedures. Maintain logs prepare reports; and direct the preparation, handling, and maintenance of departmental records. Monitor and evaluate the job performance of subordinates and authorize promotions and transfers. Direct collection, preparation, and handling of evidence and personal property of prisoners. Develop, implement, and revise departmental policies and procedures. Conduct raids and order detention of witnesses and suspects for questioning. Prepare work schedules and assign duties to subordinates. Discipline staff for violation of department rules and regulations. Cooperate with court personnel and officials from other law enforcement agencies and testify in court as necessary. Review contents of written orders to ensure adherence to legal requirements. Inspect facilities, supplies, vehicles, and equipment to ensure conformance to standards. Prepare news releases and respond to police correspondence. Requisition and issue equipment and supplies. Meet with civic, educational, and community groups to develop community programs and events and to discuss law enforcement subjects. Direct release or transfer of prisoners. Prepare budgets and manage expenditures of department funds. **SKILLS**— Management of Personnel Resources; Persuasion; Negotiation; Social Perceptiveness; Service Orientation; Monitoring; Instructing; Learning Strategies.

GOE—Interest Area: 12. Law and Public Safety. **Work Group:** 12.01. Managerial Work in Law and Public Safety. **Other Jobs in This Work Group:** Emergency Management Specialists; First-Line Supervisors/Managers of Correctional Officers; Forest Fire Fighting and Prevention Supervisors; Municipal Fire Fighting and Prevention Supervisors. **PERSONALITY TYPE:** Enterprising. Enterprising occupations frequently involve starting up and carrying out projects. These occupations can involve leading people and making many decisions. They sometimes require risk taking and often deal with business.

EDUCATION/TRAINING PROGRAM(S)— Corrections; Criminal Justice/Law Enforcement Administration; Criminal Justice/Safety Studies.

WORK ENVIRONMENT—Very hot or cold; in an enclosed vehicle or equipment; outdoors; extremely bright or inadequate lighting; hazardous equipment.

First-Line Supervisors/Managers of Production and Operating Workers

- Education/Training Required: Work experience in a related occupation
- Annual Earnings: $45,230
- Growth: 9.5%
- Annual Job Openings: 66,000
- Self-Employed: 2.2%
- Part-Time: 1.9%

Age Bracket	Percentage of Workers
45–54 Years Old	29.7%
55–64 Years Old	14.5%
65 or Older	2.1%

Supervise and coordinate the activities of production and operating workers, such as inspectors, precision workers, machine setters and operators, assemblers, fabricators, and plant and system operators. Calculate labor and equipment requirements and production specifications, using standard formulas. Confer with management or subordinates to resolve worker problems, complaints, or grievances. Confer with other supervisors to coordinate operations and activities within or between departments. Demonstrate equipment operations and work and safety procedures to new employees or assign employees to experienced workers for training. Direct and coordinate the activities of employees engaged in the production or processing of goods, such as inspectors, machine setters, and fabricators. Inspect materials, products, or equipment to detect defects or malfunctions. Interpret specifications, blueprints, job orders, and company policies and procedures for workers. Maintain operations data such as time, production, and cost records and prepare management reports of production results. Observe work and monitor gauges, dials, and other indicators to ensure that operators conform to production or processing standards. Plan and establish work schedules, assignments, and production sequences to meet production goals. Recommend or implement measures to motivate employees and to improve production methods, equipment performance, product quality, or efficiency. Requisition materials, supplies, equipment parts, or repair services. Determine standards, budgets, production goals, and rates, based on company policies, equipment and labor availability, and workloads. Enforce safety and sanitation regulations. Plan and develop new products and production processes. Read and analyze charts, work orders, production schedules, and other records and reports in order to determine production requirements and to evaluate current production estimates and outputs. Recommend personnel actions such as hirings and promotions. Set up and adjust machines and equipment. **SKILLS—** Management of Personnel Resources; Management of Material Resources; Systems Analysis; Negotiation; Coordination; Operation Monitoring; Social Perceptiveness; Systems Evaluation.

GOE—Interest Area: 13. Manufacturing. **Work Group:** 13.01. Managerial Work in Manufacturing. **Other Jobs in This Work Group:** First-Line Supervisors/Managers of Helpers, Laborers, and Material Movers, Hand; First-Line Supervisors/Managers of Mechanics, Installers, and Repairers; Industrial Production Managers. **PERSONALITY TYPE:** Enterprising. Enterprising occupations frequently involve starting up and carrying out projects.

These occupations can involve leading people and making many decisions. They sometimes require risk taking and often deal with business.

EDUCATION/TRAINING PROGRAM(S)— Operations Management and Supervision.

WORK ENVIRONMENT—Walking and running; sitting; indoors; hazardous equipment; standing.

First-Line Supervisors/Managers of Retail Sales Workers

- Education/Training Required: Work experience in a related occupation
- Annual Earnings: $32,410
- Growth: 9.1%
- Annual Job Openings: 251,000
- Self-Employed: 33.0%
- Part-Time: 7.3%

Age Bracket	Percentage of Workers
45–54 Years Old	23.0%
55–64 Years Old	13.1%
65 or Older	4.2%

Directly supervise sales workers in a retail establishment or department. Duties may include management functions, such as purchasing, budgeting, accounting, and personnel work, in addition to supervisory duties. Provide customer service by greeting and assisting customers and responding to customer inquiries and complaints. Monitor sales activities to ensure that customers receive satisfactory service and quality goods. Assign employees to specific duties. Direct and supervise employees engaged in sales, inventory-taking, reconciling cash receipts, or performing services for customers. Inventory stock and reorder when inventory drops to a specified level. Keep records of purchases, sales, and requisitions. Enforce safety, health, and security rules. Examine products purchased for resale or received for storage to assess the condition of each product or item. Hire, train, and evaluate personnel in sales or marketing establishments, promoting or firing workers when appropriate. Perform work activities of subordinates, such as cleaning and organizing shelves and displays and selling merchandise. Establish and implement policies, goals, objectives, and procedures for their department. Instruct staff on how to handle difficult and complicated sales. Formulate pricing policies for merchandise according to profitability requirements. Estimate consumer demand and determine the types and amounts of goods to be sold. Examine merchandise to ensure that it is correctly priced and displayed and that it functions as advertised. Plan and prepare work schedules and keep records of employees' work schedules and time cards. Review inventory and sales records to prepare reports for management and budget departments. Plan and coordinate advertising campaigns and sales promotions and prepare merchandise displays and advertising copy. Confer with company officials to develop methods and procedures to increase sales, expand markets, and promote business. Establish credit policies and operating procedures. Plan budgets and authorize payments and merchandise returns. **SKILLS**—Management of Personnel Resources; Persuasion; Instructing; Management of Financial Resources; Social Perceptiveness; Service Orientation; Time Management; Monitoring.

GOE—Interest Area: 14. Retail and Wholesale Sales and Service. **Work Group:** 14.01. Managerial Work in Retail/Wholesale Sales and Service. **Other Jobs in This Work Group:** Advertising and Promotions Managers; First-Line Supervisors/Managers of Non-Retail Sales Workers; Funeral Directors; Marketing Managers; Property, Real Estate, and Community Association Managers; Purchasing Managers; Sales Managers. **PERSONALITY TYPE:** Enterprising. Enterprising occupations frequently involve starting up and carrying out projects. These occupations can involve leading people and making many decisions. They sometimes require risk taking and often deal with business.

EDUCATION/TRAINING PROGRAM(S)— Business, Management, Marketing, and Related Support Services; Consumer Merchandising/Retailing Management; E-Commerce/Electronic Commerce; Floriculture/Floristry Operations and Management; Retailing and Retail Operations; Selling Skills and Sales Operations; Special Products Marketing Operations; Specialized Merchandising, Sales, and Related Marketing Operations, Other.

WORK ENVIRONMENT—Physical proximity to others; walking and running; standing; hazardous equipment; indoors.

Fish Hatchery Managers

- ◉ Education/Training Required: Work experience plus degree
- ◉ Annual Earnings: $50,720
- ◉ Growth: 5.1%
- ◉ Annual Job Openings: 25,000
- ◉ Self-Employed: 0.9%
- ◉ Part-Time: 9.2%

The job openings listed here are shared with Agricultural Crop Farm Managers and Nursery and Greenhouse Managers.

Age Bracket	Percentage of Workers
45–54 Years Old	29.6%
55–64 Years Old	17.5%
65 or Older	12.6%

Direct and coordinate, through subordinate supervisory personnel, activities of workers engaged in fish hatchery production for corporations, cooperatives, or other owners. Determines, administers, and executes policies relating to administration, standards of hatchery operations, and facility maintenance. Oversees trapping and spawning of fish, egg incubation, and fry rearing, applying knowledge of management and fish culturing techniques. Oversees movement of mature fish to lakes, ponds, streams, or commercial tanks. Collects information regarding techniques for collecting, fertilizing, incubating spawn, and treatment of spawn and fry. Accounts for and dispenses funds. Prepares reports required by state and federal laws. Prepares budget reports. Confers with biologists and other fishery personnel to obtain data concerning fish habits, food, and environmental requirements. Approves employment and discharge of employees, signs payrolls, and performs personnel duties. **SKILLS**—Management of Financial Resources; Management of Personnel Resources; Management of Material Resources; Science; Writing; Time Management; Systems Analysis; Reading Comprehension.

GOE—Interest Area: 01. Agriculture and Natural Resources. **Work Group:** 01.01. Managerial Work in Agriculture and Natural Resources. **Other Jobs in This Work Group:** Agricultural Crop Farm Managers; Farmers and Ranchers; First-Line Supervisors and Manager/Supervisors—Agricultural Crop Workers; First-Line Supervisors and Manager/Supervisors—Animal Husbandry Workers; First-Line Supervisors and Manager/Supervisors—Extractive Workers; First-Line Supervisors and Manager/Supervisors—Fishery Workers; First-Line Supervisors and Manager/Supervisors—Horticultural Workers; First-Line Supervisors and Manager/Supervisors—Landscaping Workers; First-Line Supervisors and Manager/Supervisors—Logging Workers; Lawn Service Managers; Nursery and Greenhouse Managers; Park Naturalists; Purchasing Agents and Buyers, Farm Products. **PERSONALITY TYPE:** Enterprising. Enterprising occupations frequently involve starting up and carrying out projects. These occupations can involve leading people and making many decisions. They sometimes require risk taking and often deal with business.

EDUCATION/TRAINING PROGRAM(S)— Agribusiness/Agricultural Business Operations; Agricultural Business and Management, General; Agricultural Business and Management, Other; Agricultural Production Operations, General; Agricultural Production Operations, Other; Animal/Livestock Husbandry and Production; Crop Production; Farm/Farm and Ranch Management.

WORK ENVIRONMENT—Outdoors; sitting; minor burns, cuts, bites, or stings; standing; extremely bright or inadequate lighting; contaminants.

Foreign Language and Literature Teachers, Postsecondary

- Education/Training Required: Master's degree
- Annual Earnings: $49,120
- Growth: 38.1%
- Annual Job Openings: 216,000
- Self-Employed: 0.3%
- Part-Time: 27.7%

The job openings listed here are shared with all other postsecondary teaching occupations.

Age Bracket	Percentage of Workers
45–54 Years Old	22.8%
55–64 Years Old	19.0%
65 or Older	5.5%

Teach courses in foreign (i.e., other than English) languages and literature. Evaluate and grade students' class work, assignments, and papers. Prepare course materials such as syllabi, homework assignments, and handouts. Initiate, facilitate, and moderate classroom discussions. Maintain student attendance records, grades, and other required records. Compile, administer, and grade examinations or assign this work to others. Plan, evaluate, and revise curricula, course content, and course materials and methods of instruction. Prepare and deliver lectures to undergraduate and/or graduate students on topics such as how to speak and write a foreign language and the cultural aspects of areas where a particular language is used. Maintain regularly scheduled office hours in order to advise and assist students. Select and obtain materials and supplies such as textbooks. Keep abreast of developments in their field by reading current literature, talking with colleagues, and participating in professional organizations and activities. Advise students on academic and vocational curricula and on career issues. Conduct research in a particular field of knowledge and publish findings in scholarly journals, books, and/or electronic media. Collaborate with colleagues to address teaching and research issues. Serve on academic or administrative committees that deal with institutional policies, departmental matters, and academic issues. Participate in student recruitment, registration, and placement activities. Compile bibliographies of specialized materials for outside reading assignments. Participate in campus and community events. Act as advisers to student organizations. Perform administrative duties such as serving as department head. Supervise undergraduate and/or graduate teaching, internship, and research work. **SKILLS**—Instructing; Learning Strategies; Social Perceptiveness; Persuasion; Critical Thinking; Reading Comprehension; Writing; Speaking.

GOE—Interest Area: 05. Education and Training. **Work Group:** 05.03. Postsecondary and Adult Teaching and Instructing. **Other Jobs in This Work Group:** Adult Literacy, Remedial Education, and GED Teachers and Instructors; Agricultural Sciences Teachers, Postsecondary; Anthropology and Archeology Teachers, Postsecondary; Architecture Teachers, Postsecondary; Area, Ethnic, and Cultural Studies Teachers, Postsecondary; Art, Drama, and Music Teachers, Postsecondary; Atmospheric, Earth,

Marine, and Space Sciences Teachers, Postsecondary; Biological Science Teachers, Postsecondary; Business Teachers, Postsecondary; Chemistry Teachers, Postsecondary; Communications Teachers, Postsecondary; Computer Science Teachers, Postsecondary; Criminal Justice and Law Enforcement Teachers, Postsecondary; Economics Teachers, Postsecondary; Education Teachers, Postsecondary; Engineering Teachers, Postsecondary; English Language and Literature Teachers, Postsecondary; Environmental Science Teachers, Postsecondary; Farm and Home Management Advisors; Forestry and Conservation Science Teachers, Postsecondary; Geography Teachers, Postsecondary; Graduate Teaching Assistants; Health Specialties Teachers, Postsecondary; History Teachers, Postsecondary; Home Economics Teachers, Postsecondary; Law Teachers, Postsecondary; Library Science Teachers, Postsecondary; Mathematical Science Teachers, Postsecondary; Nursing Instructors and Teachers, Postsecondary; Philosophy and Religion Teachers, Postsecondary; Physics Teachers, Postsecondary; Political Science Teachers, Postsecondary; Psychology Teachers, Postsecondary; Recreation and Fitness Studies Teachers, Postsecondary; Self-Enrichment Education Teachers; Social Work Teachers, Postsecondary; Sociology Teachers, Postsecondary; Vocational Education Teachers, Postsecondary. **PERSONALITY TYPE:** Artistic. Artistic occupations frequently involve working with forms, designs, and patterns. They often require self-expression, and the work can be done without following a clear set of rules.

EDUCATION/TRAINING PROGRAM(S)—

African Languages, Literatures, and Linguistics; Albanian Language and Literature; American Indian/Native American Languages, Literatures, and Linguistics; Ancient Near Eastern and Biblical Languages, Literatures, and Linguistics; Ancient/Classical Greek Language and Literature; Arabic Language and Literature; others.

WORK ENVIRONMENT—Sitting; physical proximity to others; sounds, noise levels are distracting or uncomfortable; indoors.

Forest Fire Fighting and Prevention Supervisors

- Education/Training Required: Work experience in a related occupation
- Annual Earnings: $59,760
- Growth: 18.7%
- Annual Job Openings: 8,000
- Self-Employed: 0%
- Part-Time: 0.1%

The job openings listed here are shared with Municipal Fire Fighting and Prevention Supervisors.

Age Bracket	Percentage of Workers
45–54 Years Old	57.1%
55–64 Years Old	4.8%
65 or Older	2.4%

Supervise fire fighters who control and suppress fires in forests or vacant public land. Communicate fire details to superiors, subordinates, and interagency dispatch centers, using two-way radios. Direct investigations of suspected arsons in wildfires, working closely with other investigating agencies. Direct the loading of fire suppression equipment into aircraft and the parachuting of equipment to crews on the ground. Evaluate size, location, and condition of forest fires in order to request and dispatch crews and position equipment so fires can be contained safely and effectively. Identify staff training and development needs in order to ensure that appropriate training can be arranged. Maintain fire suppression equipment in good condition, checking equipment periodically in order to ensure that it is ready for use. Maintain knowledge of forest fire laws and fire prevention techniques and tactics. Monitor prescribed burns to ensure that they are conducted safely and effectively. Observe fires and crews from air to determine fire-fighting force requirements and to note changing conditions that will affect fire-fighting efforts. Operate wildland fire engines and hoselays. Perform administrative duties such as compiling and maintaining records, completing forms, preparing reports, and composing correspondence. Recruit and hire forest fire-fighting personnel. Review and evaluate employee performance. Schedule employee work assignments and set work priorities. Serve as working leader of an engine, hand, helicopter, or prescribed fire crew of three or more firefighters. Train workers in such skills as parachute jumping, fire suppression, aerial observation, and radio communication, both in the classroom and on the job. Appraise damage caused by fires in order to prepare damage reports. Direct and supervise prescribed burn projects and prepare post-burn reports analyzing burn conditions and results. Drive crew carriers in order to transport firefighters to fire sites. Educate the public about forest fire prevention by participating in activities such as exhibits and presentations and by distributing promotional materials. Inspect all stations, uniforms, equipment, and recreation areas in order to ensure compliance with safety standards, taking corrective action as necessary. **SKILLS**—Management of Personnel Resources; Management of Material Resources; Systems Evaluation; Systems Analysis; Service

Orientation; Coordination; Instructing; Judgment and Decision Making.

GOE—Interest Area: 12. Law and Public Safety. **Work Group:** 12.01. Managerial Work in Law and Public Safety. **Other Jobs in This Work Group:** Emergency Management Specialists; First-Line Supervisors/Managers of Correctional Officers; First-Line Supervisors/Managers of Police and Detectives; Municipal Fire Fighting and Prevention Supervisors. **PERSONALITY TYPE:** Realistic. Realistic occupations frequently involve work activities that include practical, hands-on problems and solutions. They often deal with plants, animals, and real-world materials like wood, tools, and machinery. Many of the occupations require working outside and do not involve a lot of paperwork or working closely with others.

EDUCATION/TRAINING PROGRAM(S)—Fire Protection and Safety Technology/Technician; Fire Services Administration.

WORK ENVIRONMENT—Specialized protective or safety equipment; common protective or safety equipment; outdoors; very hot or cold; minor burns, cuts, bites, or stings.

Forestry and Conservation Science Teachers, Postsecondary

- ◎ Education/Training Required: Master's degree
- ◎ Annual Earnings: $64,120
- ◎ Growth: 38.1%
- ◎ Annual Job Openings: 216,000
- ◎ Self-Employed: 0.3%
- ◎ Part-Time: 27.7%

The job openings listed here are shared with all other postsecondary teaching occupations.

Age Bracket	Percentage of Workers
45–54 Years Old	22.8%
55–64 Years Old	19.0%
65 or Older	5.5%

Teach courses in environmental and conservation science. Conduct research in a particular field of knowledge and publish findings in books, professional journals, and/or electronic media. Keep abreast of developments in their field by reading current literature, talking with colleagues, and participating in professional conferences. Prepare and deliver lectures to undergraduate and/or graduate students on topics such as forest resource policy, forest pathology, and mapping. Evaluate and grade students' class work, assignments, and papers. Write grant proposals to procure external research funding. Supervise undergraduate and/or graduate teaching, internship, and research work. Plan, evaluate, and revise curricula, course content, and course materials and methods of instruction. Prepare course materials such as syllabi, home-work assignments, and handouts. Compile, administer, and grade examinations or assign this work to others. Advise students on academic and vocational curricula and on career issues. Initiate, facilitate, and moderate classroom discussions. Supervise students' laboratory work and/or fieldwork. Maintain student attendance records, grades, and other required records. Collaborate with colleagues to address teaching and research issues. Maintain regularly scheduled office hours in order to advise and assist students. Select and obtain materials and supplies such as textbooks and laboratory equipment. Participate in student recruitment, registration, and placement activities. Serve on academic or administrative committees that deal with institutional policies, departmental matters, and academic issues. Provide professional consulting services to government and/or industry. Perform administrative duties such as serving as department head. **SKILLS**—Science; Instructing; Management of Financial Resources; Management of Personnel Resources; Writing; Active Learning; Learning Strategies; Critical Thinking; Time Management.

GOE—Interest Area: 05. Education and Training. **Work Group:** 05.03. Postsecondary and Adult Teaching and Instructing. **Other Jobs in This Work Group:** Adult Literacy, Remedial Education, and GED Teachers and Instructors; Agricultural Sciences Teachers, Postsecondary; Anthropology and Archeology Teachers, Postsecondary; Architecture Teachers, Postsecondary; Area, Ethnic, and Cultural Studies Teachers, Postsecondary; Art, Drama, and Music Teachers, Postsecondary; Atmospheric, Earth, Marine, and Space Sciences Teachers, Postsecondary; Biological Science Teachers, Postsecondary; Business Teachers, Postsecondary; Chemistry Teachers, Postsecondary; Communications Teachers, Postsecondary;

Computer Science Teachers, Postsecondary; Criminal Justice and Law Enforcement Teachers, Postsecondary; Economics Teachers, Postsecondary; Education Teachers, Postsecondary; Engineering Teachers, Postsecondary; English Language and Literature Teachers, Postsecondary; Environmental Science Teachers, Postsecondary; Farm and Home Management Advisors; Foreign Language and Literature Teachers, Postsecondary; Geography Teachers, Postsecondary; Graduate Teaching Assistants; Health Specialties Teachers, Postsecondary; History Teachers, Postsecondary; Home Economics Teachers, Postsecondary; Law Teachers, Postsecondary; Library Science Teachers, Postsecondary; Mathematical Science Teachers, Postsecondary; Nursing Instructors and Teachers, Postsecondary; Philosophy and Religion Teachers, Postsecondary; Physics Teachers, Postsecondary; Political Science Teachers, Postsecondary; Psychology Teachers, Postsecondary; Recreation and Fitness Studies Teachers, Postsecondary; Self-Enrichment Education Teachers; Social Work Teachers, Postsecondary; Sociology Teachers, Postsecondary; Vocational Education Teachers, Postsecondary. **PERSONALITY TYPE:** Investigative. Investigative occupations frequently involve working with ideas and require an extensive amount of thinking. These occupations can involve searching for facts and figuring out problems mentally.

EDUCATION/TRAINING PROGRAM(S)— Science Teacher Education/General Science Teacher Education.

WORK ENVIRONMENT—Sitting; indoors, not environmentally controlled; very hot or cold; outdoors; in an enclosed vehicle or equipment.

Frame Wirers, Central Office

- Education/Training Required: Long-term on-the-job training
- Annual Earnings: $50,270
- Growth: –0.6%
- Annual Job Openings: 23,000
- Self-Employed: 4.6%
- Part-Time: 1.7%

The job openings listed here are shared with Central Office and PBX Installers and Repairers; Communication Equipment Mechanics, Installers, and Repairers; Station Installers and Repairers, Telephone; and Telecommunications Facility Examiners.

Age Bracket	Percentage of Workers
45–54 Years Old	29.5%
55–64 Years Old	9.6%
65 or Older	1.2%

Connect wires from telephone lines and cables to distributing frames in telephone company central office, using soldering iron and other hand tools. Solders connections, following diagram or oral instructions. Strings distributing frames with connecting wires. Tests circuit connections, using voltmeter or ammeter. Assists in locating and correcting malfunction in wiring on distributing frame. Lubricates moving switch parts. Cleans switches and replaces contact points, using vacuum hose, solvents, and hand tools. Removes and remakes connections to change circuit layouts. **SKILLS—**Installation; Repairing; Troubleshooting; Quality Control Analysis; Operation Monitoring; Equipment Maintenance.

GOE—**Interest Area:** 02. Architecture and Construction. **Work Group:** 02.05. Systems and Equipment Installation, Maintenance, and Repair. **Other Jobs in This Work Group:** Central Office and PBX Installers and Repairers; Communication Equipment Mechanics, Installers, and Repairers; Electric Meter Installers and Repairers; Electrical and Electronics Repairers, Powerhouse, Substation, and Relay; Electrical Power-Line Installers and Repairers; Elevator Installers and Repairers; Heating and Air Conditioning Mechanics; Home Appliance Installers; Maintenance and Repair Workers, General; Meter Mechanics; Refrigeration Mechanics; Station Installers and Repairers, Telephone; Telecommunications Facility Examiners; Telecommunications Line Installers and Repairers. **PERSONALITY TYPE:** Realistic. Realistic occupations frequently involve work activities that include practical, hands-on problems and solutions. They often deal with plants, animals, and real-world materials like wood, tools, and machinery. Many of the occupations require working outside and do not involve a lot of paperwork or working closely with others.

EDUCATION/TRAINING PROGRAM(S)— Communications Systems Installation and Repair Technology.

WORK ENVIRONMENT—Climbing ladders, scaffolds, or poles; hazardous conditions; standing; common protective or safety equipment; spend time kneeling, crouching, stooping, or crawling.

Freight Inspectors

- Education/Training Required: Work experience in a related occupation
- Annual Earnings: $47,920
- Growth: 7.7%
- Annual Job Openings: 5,000
- Self-Employed: 0.4%
- Part-Time: 3.2%

The job openings listed here are shared with Aviation Inspectors, Marine Cargo Inspectors, Motor Vehicle Inspectors, Public Transportation Inspectors, and Railroad Inspectors.

Age Bracket	Percentage of Workers
45–54 Years Old	54.3%
55–64 Years Old	15.2%
65 or Older	2.2%

Inspect freight for proper storage according to specifications. Inspects shipment to ascertain that freight is securely braced and blocked. Observes loading of freight to ensure that crews comply with procedures. Monitors temperature and humidity of freight storage area. Records freight condition and handling and notifies crews to reload freight or insert additional bracing or packing. Measures height and width of loads that will pass over bridges or through tunnels. Notifies workers of special treatment required for shipments. Prepares and submits report after trip. Posts warning signs on vehicles containing explosives or inflammatory or radioactive materials. **SKILLS—**Systems Analysis.

GOE—**Interest Area:** 16. Transportation, Distribution, and Logistics. **Work Group:** 16.07. Transportation Support Work. **Other Jobs in This Work Group:** Bridge and Lock

Tenders; Cargo and Freight Agents; Cleaners of Vehicles and Equipment; Public Transportation Inspectors; Railroad Yard Workers; Stevedores, Except Equipment Operators; Traffic Technicians; Train Crew Members. **PERSONALITY TYPE:** Conventional. Conventional occupations frequently involve following set procedures and routines. These occupations can include working with data and details more than with ideas. Usually there is a clear line of authority to follow.

EDUCATION/TRAINING PROGRAM(S)— No data available.

WORK ENVIRONMENT—Outdoors; standing; climbing ladders, scaffolds, or poles; walking and running; spend time bending or twisting the body.

Gaming Supervisors

- ◎ Education/Training Required: Work experience in a related occupation
- ◎ Annual Earnings: $41,080
- ◎ Growth: 15.7%
- ◎ Annual Job Openings: 6,000
- ◎ Self-Employed: 33.8%
- ◎ Part-Time: 15.2%

Age Bracket	Percentage of Workers
45–54 Years Old	25.2%
55–64 Years Old	13.0%
65 or Older	4.6%

Supervise gaming operations and personnel in an assigned area. Circulate among tables and observe operations. Ensure that stations and games are covered for each shift. May explain and interpret operating rules of house to patrons. May plan and organize activities and create friendly atmosphere for guests in hotels/casinos. May adjust service complaints. Monitor game operations to ensure that house rules are followed; that tribal, state, and federal regulations are adhered to; and that employees provide prompt and courteous service. Observe gamblers' behavior for signs of cheating such as marking, switching, or counting cards; notify security staff of suspected cheating. Maintain familiarity with the games at a facility and with strategies and tricks used by cheaters at such games. Perform paperwork required for monetary transactions. Resolve customer and employee complaints. Greet customers and ask about the quality of service they are receiving. Establish and maintain banks and table limits for each game. Monitor stations and games and move dealers from game to game to ensure adequate staffing. Report customer-related incidents occurring in gaming areas to supervisors. Explain and interpret house rules, such as game rules and betting limits, for patrons. Supervise the distribution of complimentary meals, hotel rooms, discounts, and other items given to players based on length of play and amount bet. Evaluate workers' performance and prepare written performance evaluations. Monitor patrons for signs of compulsive gambling, offering assistance if necessary. Record, issue receipts for, and pay off bets. Monitor and verify the counting, wrapping, weighing, and distribution of currency and coins. Direct workers compiling summary sheets for each race or event to record amounts wagered and amounts to be paid to winners. Determine how many gaming tables to open each day and schedule staff accordingly. Establish policies on types of gambling offered, odds, and extension of credit. Interview, hire, and train workers. Provide fire protection and first-aid assistance when necessary. Review operational expenses, budget estimates, betting accounts, and collection reports for accuracy. **SKILLS**—Instructing; Management of Personnel Resources; Social Perceptiveness; Service Orientation; Monitoring; Critical Thinking; Learning Strategies; Persuasion.

GOE—**Interest Area:** 09. Hospitality, Tourism, and Recreation. **Work Group:** 09.01. Managerial Work in Hospitality and Tourism. **Other Jobs in This Work Group:** First-Line Supervisors/Managers of Food Preparation and Serving Workers; First-Line Supervisors/Managers of Personal Service Workers; Food Service Managers; Gaming Managers; Lodging Managers. **PERSONALITY TYPE:** Enterprising. Enterprising occupations frequently involve starting up and carrying out projects. These occupations can involve leading people and making many decisions. They sometimes require risk taking and often deal with business.

EDUCATION/TRAINING PROGRAM(S)— No data available.

WORK ENVIRONMENT—Sounds, noise levels are distracting or uncomfortable; physical proximity to others; contaminants; extremely bright or inadequate lighting; standing.

General and Operations Managers

- ◎ Education/Training Required: Work experience plus degree
- ◎ Annual Earnings: $79,300
- ◎ Growth: 18.4%
- ◎ Annual Job Openings: 260,000
- ◎ Self-Employed: 0.7%
- ◎ Part-Time: 2.6%

Age Bracket	Percentage of Workers
45–54 Years Old	30.1%
55–64 Years Old	12.1%
65 or Older	2.4%

Plan, direct, or coordinate the operations of companies or public and private sector organizations. Duties and responsibilities include formulating policies, managing daily operations, and planning the use of materials and human resources, but are too diverse and general in nature to be classified in any one functional area of management or administration, such as personnel, purchasing, or administrative services. Includes owners and managers who head small business establishments whose duties are primarily managerial. Direct and coordinate activities of businesses or departments concerned with the production, pricing, sales, and/or distribution of products. Manage staff, preparing work schedules and assigning specific duties. Review financial statements, sales and activity reports, and other performance data to measure productivity and goal achievement and to determine areas needing cost reduction and program improvement. Establish and implement departmental policies, goals, objectives, and procedures, conferring with board members, organization officials, and staff members as necessary. Determine staffing requirements and interview, hire, and train new employees or oversee those personnel processes. Monitor businesses and agencies to ensure that they efficiently and effectively provide needed services while staying within budgetary limits. Oversee activities directly related to making products or providing services. Direct and coordinate organization's financial and budget activities to fund operations, maximize investments, and increase efficiency. Determine goods and services to be sold and set prices and credit terms based on forecasts of customer demand. Manage the movement of goods into and out of production facilities. Locate, select, and procure merchandise for resale, representing management in purchase negotiations. Perform sales floor work such as greeting and assisting customers, stocking shelves, and taking inventory. Develop and implement product marketing strategies, including advertising campaigns and sales promotions. Plan and direct activities such as sales promotions, coordinating with other department heads as required. Direct non-merchandising departments of businesses, such as advertising and purchasing. **SKILLS**—Management of Financial Resources; Management of Personnel Resources; Management of Material Resources; Negotiation; Monitoring; Persuasion; Coordination; Social Perceptiveness.

GOE—Interest Area: 04. Business and Administration. **Work Group:** 04.01. Managerial Work in General Business. **Other Jobs in This Work Group:** Chief Executives; Compensation and Benefits Managers; Human Resources Managers; Private Sector Executives; Training and Development Managers. **PERSONALITY TYPE:** No data available.

EDUCATION/TRAINING PROGRAM(S)—Business Administration/Management; Entrepreneurship/Entrepreneurial Studies; International Business/Trade/Commerce; Public Administration.

WORK ENVIRONMENT—Sounds, noise levels are distracting or uncomfortable; sitting; indoors, not environmentally controlled; physical proximity to others; walking and running.

Geographers

- Education/Training Required: Master's degree
- Annual Earnings: $61,520
- Growth: 19.5%
- Annual Job Openings: fewer than 500
- Self-Employed: 3.7%
- Part-Time: 16.8%

Age Bracket	Percentage of Workers
45–54 Years Old	24.4%
55–64 Years Old	13.3%
65 or Older	6.7%

Study nature and use of areas of earth's surface, relating and interpreting interactions of physical and cultural phenomena. Conduct research on physical aspects of a region, including land forms, climates, soils, plants, and animals, and conduct research on the spatial implications of human activities within a given area, including social characteristics, economic activities, and political organization, as well as researching interdependence between regions at scales ranging from local to global. Create and modify maps, graphs, and/or diagrams, using geographical information software and related equipment and principles of cartography such as coordinate systems, longitude, latitude, elevation, topography, and map scales. Write and present reports of research findings. Develop, operate, and maintain geographical information (GIS) computer systems, including hardware, software, plotters, digitizers, printers, and video cameras. Locate and obtain existing geographic information databases. Analyze geographic distributions of physical and cultural phenomena on local, regional, continental, and/or global scales. Teach geography. Gather and compile geographic data from sources including censuses, field observations, satellite imagery, aerial photographs, and existing maps. Conduct fieldwork at outdoor sites. Study the economic, political, and cultural characteristics of a specific region's population. Provide consulting services in fields including resource development and management, business location and market area analysis, environmental hazards, regional cultural history, and urban social planning. Collect data on physical characteristics of specified areas, such as geological formations, climates, and vegetation, using surveying or meteorological equipment. Provide geographical information systems support to the private and public sectors. **SKILLS**—Programming; Science; Complex Problem Solving; Writing; Instructing; Critical Thinking; Reading Comprehension; Management of Financial Resources.

GOE—Interest Area: 15. Scientific Research, Engineering, and Mathematics. **Work Group:** 15.02. Physical Sciences. **Other Jobs in This Work Group:** Astronomers; Atmospheric and Space Scientists; Chemists; Geologists; Hydrologists; Materials Scientists; Physicists. **PERSONALITY TYPE:** Investigative. Investigative occupations frequently involve working with ideas and require an extensive amount of thinking. These occupations can involve searching for facts and figuring out problems mentally.

EDUCATION/TRAINING PROGRAM(S)— Geography.

WORK ENVIRONMENT—Sitting; indoors; very hot or cold; outdoors; physical proximity to others.

Geography Teachers, Postsecondary

- Education/Training Required: Master's degree
- Annual Earnings: $57,370
- Growth: 38.1%
- Annual Job Openings: 216,000
- Self-Employed: 0.3%
- Part-Time: 27.7%

The job openings listed here are shared with all other postsecondary teaching occupations.

Age Bracket	Percentage of Workers
45–54 Years Old	22.8%
55–64 Years Old	19.0%
65 or Older	5.5%

Teach courses in geography. Prepare and deliver lectures to undergraduate and/or graduate students on topics such as urbanization, environmental systems, and cultural geography. Evaluate and grade students' class work, assignments, and papers. Compile, administer, and grade examinations or assign this work to others. Initiate, facilitate, and moderate classroom discussions. Maintain student attendance records, grades, and other required records. Prepare course materials such as syllabi, homework assignments, and handouts. Keep abreast of developments in their field by reading current literature, talking with colleagues, and participating in professional conferences. Supervise undergraduate and/or graduate teaching, internship, and research work. Plan, evaluate, and revise curricula, course content, and course materials and methods of instruction. Maintain regularly scheduled office hours in order to advise and assist students. Supervise students' laboratory work and fieldwork. Conduct research in a particular field of knowledge and publish findings in professional journals, books, and/or electronic media. Collaborate with colleagues to address teaching and research issues. Select and obtain materials and supplies such as textbooks. Advise students on academic and vocational curricula and on career issues. Serve on academic or administrative committees that deal with institutional policies, departmental matters, and academic issues. Participate in student recruitment, registration, and placement activities. Participate in campus and community events. Compile bibliographies of specialized materials for outside reading assignments. Perform administrative duties such as serving as department head. Write grant proposals to procure external research funding. Maintain geographic information systems laboratories, performing duties such as updating software. Perform spatial analysis and modeling, using geographic information system techniques. **SKILLS**—Instructing; Learning Strategies; Writing; Science; Active Learning; Critical Thinking; Reading Comprehension; Speaking.

GOE—Interest Area: 05. Education and Training. **Work Group:** 05.03. Postsecondary and Adult Teaching and Instructing. **Other Jobs in This Work Group:** Adult Literacy, Remedial Education, and GED Teachers and Instructors; Agricultural Sciences Teachers, Postsecondary; Anthropology and Archeology Teachers, Postsecondary; Architecture Teachers, Postsecondary; Area, Ethnic, and Cultural Studies Teachers, Postsecondary; Art, Drama, and Music Teachers, Postsecondary; Atmospheric, Earth, Marine, and Space Sciences Teachers, Postsecondary; Biological Science Teachers, Postsecondary; Business Teachers, Postsecondary; Chemistry Teachers, Postsecondary; Communications Teachers, Postsecondary; Computer Science Teachers, Postsecondary; Criminal Justice and Law Enforcement Teachers, Postsecondary; Economics Teachers, Postsecondary; Education Teachers, Postsecondary; Engineering Teachers, Postsecondary; English Language and Literature Teachers, Postsecondary; Environmental Science Teachers, Postsecondary; Farm and Home Management Advisors; Foreign Language and Literature Teachers, Postsecondary; Forestry and Conservation Science Teachers, Postsecondary; Graduate Teaching Assistants; Health Specialties Teachers, Postsecondary; History Teachers, Postsecondary; Home Economics Teachers, Postsecondary; Law Teachers, Postsecondary; Library Science Teachers, Postsecondary; Mathematical Science Teachers, Postsecondary; Nursing Instructors and Teachers, Postsecondary; Philosophy and Religion Teachers, Postsecondary; Physics Teachers, Postsecondary; Political Science Teachers, Postsecondary; Psychology Teachers, Postsecondary; Recreation and Fitness Studies Teachers, Postsecondary; Self-Enrichment Education Teachers; Social Work Teachers, Postsecondary; Sociology Teachers, Postsecondary; Vocational Education Teachers, Postsecondary. **PERSONALITY TYPE:** No data available.

EDUCATION/TRAINING PROGRAM(S)—Geography; Geography Teacher Education.

WORK ENVIRONMENT—Sitting; indoors; physical proximity to others.

Geologists

- ◎ Education/Training Required: Master's degree
- ◎ Annual Earnings: $70,180
- ◎ Growth: 11.5%
- ◎ Annual Job Openings: 2,000
- ◎ Self-Employed: 2.7%
- ◎ Part-Time: 7.7%

Age Bracket	Percentage of Workers
45–54 Years Old	29.4%
55–64 Years Old	11.8%
65 or Older	2.4%

Study composition, structure, and history of the earth's crust; examine rocks, minerals, and fossil remains to identify and determine the sequence of processes affecting the development of the earth; apply knowledge of chemistry, physics, biology, and mathematics to explain these phenomena and to help locate mineral and petroleum deposits and underground water resources; prepare geologic reports and maps; and interpret research data to recommend further action for study. Analyze and interpret geological, geochemical, and geophysical information from sources such as survey data, well logs, boreholes, and aerial photos. Plan and conduct geological, geochemical, and geophysical field studies and surveys; sample collection; and drilling and testing programs used to collect data for research and/or application. Investigate the composition, structure, and history of the Earth's crust through the collection, examination, measurement, and classification of soils, minerals, rocks, and fossil remains. Prepare geological maps, cross-sectional diagrams, charts, and reports concerning mineral extraction, land use, and resource management, using results of fieldwork and laboratory research. Locate and estimate probable natural gas, oil, and mineral ore deposits and underground water resources, using aerial photographs, charts, and research and survey results. Assess ground and surface water movement in order to provide advice regarding issues such as waste management, route and site selection, and the restoration of contaminated sites. Identify risks for natural disasters such as mudslides, earthquakes, and volcanic eruptions and provide advice on ways in which potential damage can be mitigated. Conduct geological and geophysical studies to provide information for use in regional development, site selection, and the development of public works projects. Inspect construction projects in order to analyze engineering problems, applying geological knowledge and using test equipment and drilling machinery. Advise construction firms and government agencies on dam and road construction, foundation design, and land use and resource management. **SKILLS**—Science; Management of Financial Resources; Time Management; Active Learning; Coordination; Critical Thinking; Persuasion; Negotiation.

GOE—Interest Area: 15. Scientific Research, Engineering, and Mathematics. **Work Group:** 15.02. Physical Sciences. **Other Jobs in This Work Group:** Astronomers; Atmospheric and Space Scientists; Chemists; Geographers; Hydrologists; Materials Scientists; Physicists. **PERSONALITY TYPE:** Investigative. Investigative occupations frequently involve working with ideas and require an extensive amount of thinking. These occupations can involve searching for facts and figuring out problems mentally.

EDUCATION/TRAINING PROGRAM(S)—Geochemistry; Geochemistry and Petrology;

Geological and Earth Sciences/Geosciences, Other; Geology/Earth Science, General; Geophysics and Seismology; Oceanography, Chemical and Physical; Paleontology.

WORK ENVIRONMENT—Sitting; very hot or cold; extremely bright or inadequate lighting; contaminants; hazardous conditions.

Government Property Inspectors and Investigators

- Education/Training Required: Long-term on-the-job training
- Annual Earnings: $48,530
- Growth: 9.8%
- Annual Job Openings: 20,000
- Self-Employed: 0.9%
- Part-Time: 5.3%

The job openings listed here are shared with Coroners, Environmental Compliance Inspectors, Equal Opportunity Representatives and Officers, Licensing Examiners and Inspectors, and Pressure Vessel Inspectors.

Age Bracket	Percentage of Workers
45–54 Years Old	40.5%
55–64 Years Old	15.1%
65 or Older	0.8%

Investigate or inspect government property to ensure compliance with contract agreements and government regulations. Collect, identify, evaluate, and preserve case evidence. Examine records, reports, and documents in order to establish facts and detect discrepancies. Inspect government-owned equipment and materials in the possession of private contractors in order to ensure compliance with contracts and regulations and to prevent misuse. Inspect manufactured or processed products to ensure compliance with contract specifications and legal requirements. Locate and interview plaintiffs, witnesses, or representatives of business or government in order to gather facts relevant to inspections or alleged violations. Prepare correspondence, reports of inspections or investigations, and recommendations for action. Recommend legal or administrative action to protect government property. Submit samples of products to government laboratories for testing as required. Coordinate with and assist law enforcement agencies in matters of mutual concern. Investigate applications for special licenses or permits as well as alleged license or permit violations. Testify in court or at administrative proceedings concerning investigation findings. Monitor investigations of suspected offenders to ensure that they are conducted in accordance with constitutional requirements. **SKILLS**—Systems Analysis; Negotiation; Speaking; Judgment and Decision Making; Reading Comprehension; Writing; Systems Evaluation; Critical Thinking.

GOE—Interest Area: 07. Government and Public Administration. **Work Group:** 07.03. Regulations Enforcement. **Other Jobs in This Work Group:** Agricultural Inspectors; Aviation Inspectors; Child Support, Missing Persons, and Unemployment Insurance Fraud Investigators; Environmental Compliance Inspectors; Equal Opportunity Representatives and Officers; Financial Examiners; Fire Inspectors; Fish and Game Wardens; Forest Fire Inspectors and Prevention Specialists; Immigration and Customs Inspectors; Licensing Examiners and Inspectors; Marine Cargo Inspectors; Mechanical Inspectors; Motor Vehicle

Inspectors; Nuclear Monitoring Technicians; Occupational Health and Safety Specialists; Pressure Vessel Inspectors; Railroad Inspectors; Tax Examiners, Collectors, and Revenue Agents. **PERSONALITY TYPE:** Enterprising. Enterprising occupations frequently involve starting up and carrying out projects. These occupations can involve leading people and making many decisions. They sometimes require risk taking and often deal with business.

EDUCATION/TRAINING PROGRAM(S)— No data available.

WORK ENVIRONMENT—Walking and running; standing; sitting; extremely bright or inadequate lighting; very hot or cold.

Government Service Executives

- ◎ Education/Training Required: Work experience plus degree
- ◎ Annual Earnings: $141,820
- ◎ Growth: 16.7%
- ◎ Annual Job Openings: 63,000
- ◎ Self-Employed: 14.6%
- ◎ Part-Time: 5.3%

The job openings listed here are shared with Government Chief Executives and Private Sector Executives.

Age Bracket	Percentage of Workers
45–54 Years Old	36.2%
55–64 Years Old	20.3%
65 or Older	5.3%

Determine and formulate policies and provide overall direction of federal, state, local, or international government activities. Plan, direct, and coordinate operational activities at the highest level of management with the help of subordinate managers. Directs organization charged with administering and monitoring regulated activities to interpret and clarify laws and ensure compliance with laws. Administers, interprets, and explains policies, rules, regulations, and laws to organizations and individuals under authority of commission or applicable legislation. Develops, plans, organizes, and administers policies and procedures for organization to ensure administrative and operational objectives are met. Directs and coordinates activities of workers in public organization to ensure continuing operations, maximize returns on investments, and increase productivity. Negotiates contracts and agreements with federal and state agencies and other organizations and prepares budget for funding and implementation of programs. Implements corrective action plan to solve problems. Reviews and analyzes legislation, laws, and public policy and recommends changes to promote and support interests of general population as well as special groups. Develops, directs, and coordinates testing, hiring, training, and evaluation of staff personnel. Establishes and maintains comprehensive and current record-keeping system of activities and operational procedures in business office. Testifies in court, before control or review board, or at legislature. Participates in activities to promote business and expand services and provides technical assistance in conducting of conferences, seminars, and workshops. Delivers speeches, writes articles, and presents information for organization at meetings or conventions to promote services, exchange ideas, and accomplish objectives. Plans, promotes, organizes, and coordinates public community service program and maintains cooperative working relationships among public and agency participants. Conducts or directs investigations or hearings to resolve complaints and violations of laws. Prepares, reviews, and submits reports concerning activities, expenses, budget, government statutes and rulings, and other items affecting business or program services. Directs, coordinates, and conducts activities between United States government and foreign entities to provide information to promote international interest and harmony. **SKILLS**—Management of Financial Resources; Systems Analysis; Systems Evaluation; Coordination; Management of Personnel Resources; Judgment and Decision Making; Negotiation; Persuasion.

GOE—Interest Area: 07. Government and Public Administration. **Work Group:** 07.01. Managerial Work in Government and Public Administration. **Other Jobs in This Work Group:** Social and Community Service Managers. **PERSONALITY TYPE:** Enterprising. Enterprising occupations frequently involve starting up and carrying out projects. These occupations can involve leading people and making many decisions. They sometimes require risk taking and often deal with business.

EDUCATION/TRAINING PROGRAM(S)— Public Administration; Public Administration and Services, Other; Public Policy Analysis.

WORK ENVIRONMENT—Sitting; walking and running; indoors; standing.

Graduate Teaching Assistants

- ⊚ Education/Training Required: Master's degree
- ⊚ Annual Earnings: $27,100
- ⊚ Growth: 38.1%
- ⊚ Annual Job Openings: 216,000
- ⊚ Self-Employed: 0.3%
- ⊚ Part-Time: 27.7%

The job openings listed here are shared with all other postsecondary teaching occupations.

Age Bracket	Percentage of Workers
45–54 Years Old	22.8%
55–64 Years Old	19.0%
65 or Older	5.5%

Assist department chairperson, faculty members, or other professional staff members in college or university by performing teaching or teaching-related duties, such as teaching lower-level courses, developing teaching materials, preparing and giving examinations, and grading examinations or papers. Graduate assistants must be enrolled in a graduate school program. Graduate assistants who primarily perform non-teaching duties, such as laboratory research, should be reported in the occupational category related to the work performed. Evaluate and grade examinations, assignments, and papers and record grades. Lead discussion sections, tutorials, and laboratory sections. Teach undergraduate-level courses. Develop teaching materials such as syllabi, visual aids, answer keys, supplementary notes, and course Web sites. Attend lectures given by the instructor whom they are assisting. Complete laboratory projects prior to assigning them to students so that any needed modifications can be made. Copy and distribute classroom materials. Demonstrate use of laboratory equipment and enforce laboratory rules. Inform students of the procedures for completing and submitting class work such as lab reports. Meet with supervisors to discuss students' grades and to complete required grade-related paperwork. Notify instructors of errors or problems with assignments. Order or obtain materials needed for classes. Prepare and proctor examinations. Return assignments to students in accordance with established deadlines. Schedule and maintain regular office hours to meet with students. Arrange for supervisors to conduct teaching observations; meet with supervisors to receive feedback about teaching performance. Assist faculty members or staff with student conferences. Provide assistance to faculty members or staff with laboratory or field research. Provide instructors with assistance in the use of audiovisual equipment. Provide assistance to library staff in maintaining library collections. **SKILLS**—Instructing; Learning Strategies; Speaking; Reading Comprehension; Writing; Science; Critical Thinking; Mathematics.

GOE—**Interest Area:** 05. Education and Training. **Work Group:** 05.03. Postsecondary and Adult Teaching and Instructing. **Other Jobs in This Work Group:** Adult Literacy, Remedial Education, and GED Teachers and Instructors; Agricultural Sciences Teachers, Postsecondary; Anthropology and Archeology Teachers, Postsecondary; Architecture Teachers, Postsecondary; Area, Ethnic, and Cultural Studies Teachers, Postsecondary; Art, Drama, and Music Teachers, Postsecondary; Atmospheric, Earth, Marine, and Space Sciences Teachers, Postsecondary; Biological Science Teachers, Postsecondary; Business Teachers, Postsecondary; Chemistry Teachers, Postsecondary;

Communications Teachers, Postsecondary; Computer Science Teachers, Postsecondary; Criminal Justice and Law Enforcement Teachers, Postsecondary; Economics Teachers, Postsecondary; Education Teachers, Postsecondary; Engineering Teachers, Postsecondary; English Language and Literature Teachers, Postsecondary; Environmental Science Teachers, Postsecondary; Farm and Home Management Advisors; Foreign Language and Literature Teachers, Postsecondary; Forestry and Conservation Science Teachers, Postsecondary; Geography Teachers, Postsecondary; Health Specialties Teachers, Postsecondary; History Teachers, Postsecondary; Home Economics Teachers, Postsecondary; Law Teachers, Postsecondary; Library Science Teachers, Postsecondary; Mathematical Science Teachers, Postsecondary; Nursing Instructors and Teachers, Postsecondary; Philosophy and Religion Teachers, Postsecondary; Physics Teachers, Postsecondary; Political Science Teachers, Postsecondary; Psychology Teachers, Postsecondary; Recreation and Fitness Studies Teachers, Postsecondary; Self-Enrichment Education Teachers; Social Work Teachers, Postsecondary; Sociology Teachers, Postsecondary; Vocational Education Teachers, Postsecondary. **PERSONALITY TYPE:** Social. Social occupations frequently involve working with, communicating with, and teaching people. These occupations often involve helping or providing service to others.

EDUCATION/TRAINING PROGRAM(S)—No data available.

WORK ENVIRONMENT—Indoors; standing; sitting.

Health Educators

- ◉ Education/Training Required: Master's degree
- ◉ Annual Earnings: $39,670
- ◉ Growth: 21.9%
- ◉ Annual Job Openings: 8,000
- ◉ Self-Employed: 0.2%
- ◉ Part-Time: 10.6%

Age Bracket	Percentage of Workers
45–54 Years Old	27.7%
55–64 Years Old	11.4%
65 or Older	2.9%

Promote, maintain, and improve individual and community health by assisting individuals and communities in adopting healthy behaviors. Collect and analyze data to identify community needs prior to planning, implementing, monitoring, and evaluating programs designed to encourage healthy lifestyles, policies, and environments. May also serve as a resource to assist individuals, other professionals, or the community and may administer fiscal resources for health education programs. Collaborate with health specialists and civic groups to determine community health needs and the availability of services and to develop goals for meeting needs. Design and conduct evaluations and diagnostic studies to assess the quality and performance of health education programs. Develop and present health education and promotion programs such as training workshops, conferences, and school or community presentations. Develop operational plans and policies necessary to achieve health education objectives and services. Develop, conduct, or coordinate health needs assessments and other public health surveys. Prepare and distribute health education materials, including reports, bulletins, and visual aids such as films, videotapes, photographs, and posters. Provide guidance to agencies and organizations in the assessment of health education needs and in the development and delivery of health education programs. Provide program information to the public by preparing and presenting press releases, conducting media campaigns, and/or maintaining program-related Web sites. Develop and maintain cooperative working relationships with agencies and organizations interested in public health care. Develop and maintain health education libraries to provide resources for staff and community agencies. Develop, prepare, and coordinate grant applications and grant-related activities to obtain funding for health education programs and related work. Document activities, recording information such as the numbers of applications completed, presentations conducted, and persons assisted. Maintain databases, mailing lists, telephone networks, and other information to facilitate the functioning of health education programs. Supervise professional and technical staff in implementing health programs, objectives, and goals. **SKILLS**—Speaking; Systems Analysis; Coordination; Writing; Systems Evaluation; Persuasion; Active Learning; Complex Problem Solving.

GOE—Interest Area: 05. Education and Training. **Work Group:** 05.06. Counseling, Health, and Fitness Education. **Other Jobs in This Work Group:** Educational, Vocational, and School Counselors; Fitness Trainers and Aerobics Instructors. **PERSONALITY TYPE:** Social. Social occupations frequently involve working with, communicating with, and teaching people. These occupations often involve helping or providing service to others.

EDUCATION/TRAINING PROGRAM(S)— Community Health Services/Liaison/ Counseling; Health Communications; International Public Health/International Health; Maternal and Child Health; Public Health Education and Promotion.

WORK ENVIRONMENT—Sitting; indoors; standing.

Health Specialties Teachers, Postsecondary

- Education/Training Required: Master's degree
- Annual Earnings: $70,310
- Growth: 38.1%
- Annual Job Openings: 216,000
- Self-Employed: 0.3%
- Part-Time: 27.7%

The job openings listed here are shared with all other postsecondary teaching occupations.

Age Bracket	Percentage of Workers
45–54 Years Old	22.8%
55–64 Years Old	19.0%
65 or Older	5.5%

Teach courses in health specialties, such as veterinary medicine, dentistry, pharmacy, therapy, laboratory technology, and public health. Initiate, facilitate, and moderate classroom discussions. Keep abreast of developments in their field by reading current literature, talking with colleagues, and participating in professional conferences. Compile, administer, and grade examinations or assign this work to others. Evaluate and grade students' class work, assignments, and papers. Prepare course materials such as syllabi, homework assignments, and handouts. Prepare and deliver lectures to undergraduate and/or graduate students on topics such as public health, stress management, and worksite health promotion. Plan, evaluate, and revise curricula, course content, and course materials and methods of instruction. Supervise undergraduate and/or graduate teaching, internship, and research work. Conduct research in a particular field of knowledge and publish findings in professional journals, books, and/or electronic media. Collaborate with colleagues to address teaching and research issues. Supervise laboratory sessions. Maintain student attendance records, grades, and other required records. Maintain regularly scheduled office hours in order to advise and assist students. Advise students on academic and vocational curricula and on career issues. Participate in student recruitment, registration, and placement activities. Write grant proposals to procure external research funding. Serve on academic or administrative committees that deal with institutional policies, departmental matters, and academic issues. Select and obtain materials and supplies such as textbooks and laboratory equipment. Act as advisers to student organizations. Perform administrative duties such as serving as department head. **SKILLS—**Science; Instructing; Learning Strategies; Writing; Critical Thinking; Reading Comprehension; Active Learning; Time Management.

GOE—Interest Area: 05. Education and Training. **Work Group:** 05.03. Postsecondary and Adult Teaching and Instructing. **Other Jobs in This Work Group:** Adult Literacy, Remedial Education, and GED Teachers and Instructors; Agricultural Sciences Teachers, Postsecondary; Anthropology and Archeology Teachers,

Postsecondary; Architecture Teachers, Post-secondary; Area, Ethnic, and Cultural Studies Teachers, Postsecondary; Art, Drama, and Music Teachers, Postsecondary; Atmospheric, Earth, Marine, and Space Sciences Teachers, Postsecondary; Biological Science Teachers, Postsecondary; Business Teachers, Postsecondary; Chemistry Teachers, Postsecondary; Communications Teachers, Postsecondary; Computer Science Teachers, Postsecondary; Criminal Justice and Law Enforcement Teachers, Postsecondary; Economics Teachers, Postsecondary; Education Teachers, Postsecondary; Engineering Teachers, Postsecondary; English Language and Literature Teachers, Postsecondary; Environmental Science Teachers, Postsecondary; Farm and Home Management Advisors; Foreign Language and Literature Teachers, Postsecondary; Forestry and Conservation Science Teachers, Postsecondary; Geography Teachers, Postsecondary; Graduate Teaching Assistants; History Teachers, Postsecondary; Home Economics Teachers, Postsecondary; Law Teachers, Postsecondary; Library Science Teachers, Postsecondary; Mathematical Science Teachers, Postsecondary; Nursing Instructors and Teachers, Postsecondary; Philosophy and Religion Teachers, Postsecondary; Physics Teachers, Postsecondary; Political Science Teachers, Postsecondary; Psychology Teachers, Postsecondary; Recreation and Fitness Studies Teachers, Postsecondary; Self-Enrichment Education Teachers; Social Work Teachers, Postsecondary; Sociology Teachers, Postsecondary; Vocational Education Teachers, Postsecondary. **PERSONALITY TYPE:** Investigative. Investigative occupations frequently involve working with ideas and require an extensive amount of thinking. These occupations can involve searching for facts and figuring out problems mentally.

EDUCATION/TRAINING PROGRAM(S)— Allied Health Diagnostic, Intervention, and Treatment Professions, Other; Art Therapy/Therapist; Asian Bodywork Therapy; Audiology/Audiologist and Hearing Sciences; Audiology/Audiologist and Speech-Language Pathology/Pathologist; Biostatistics; Blood Bank Technology Specialist; Cardiovascular Technology/Technologist; Chiropractic (DC); Clinical Laboratory Science/Medical Technology/Technologist; Clinical/Medical Laboratory Technician; others.

WORK ENVIRONMENT—Sitting; indoors; physical proximity to others; contaminants; hazardous conditions.

History Teachers, Postsecondary

- Education/Training Required: Master's degree
- Annual Earnings: $54,310
- Growth: 38.1%
- Annual Job Openings: 216,000
- Self-Employed: 0.3%
- Part-Time: 27.7%

The job openings listed here are shared with all other postsecondary teaching occupations.

Age Bracket	Percentage of Workers
45–54 Years Old	22.8%
55–64 Years Old	19.0%
65 or Older	5.5%

Teach courses in human history and historiography. Prepare and deliver lectures to undergraduate and/or graduate students on topics such as ancient history, postwar civilizations, and the history of third-world countries. Evaluate and grade students' class work, assignments, and papers. Prepare course materials such as syllabi, homework assignments, and handouts. Compile, administer, and grade examinations or assign this work to others. Initiate, facilitate, and moderate classroom discussions. Keep abreast of developments in their field by reading current literature, talking with colleagues, and participating in professional conferences. Maintain student attendance records, grades, and other required records. Plan, evaluate, and revise curricula, course content, and course materials and methods of instruction. Maintain regularly scheduled office hours in order to advise and assist students. Conduct research in a particular field of knowledge and publish findings in professional journals, books, and/or electronic media. Select and obtain materials and supplies such as textbooks. Advise students on academic and vocational curricula and on career issues. Collaborate with colleagues to address teaching and research issues. Serve on academic or administrative committees that deal with institutional policies, departmental matters, and academic issues. Participate in campus and community events. Act as advisers to student organizations. Participate in student recruitment, registration, and placement activities. Compile bibliographies of specialized materials for outside reading assignments. Supervise undergraduate and/or graduate teaching, internship, and research work. Perform administrative duties such as serving as department head. **SKILLS**—Instructing; Writing; Learning Strategies; Persuasion; Critical Thinking; Social Perceptiveness; Reading Comprehension; Speaking; Active Learning.

GOE—Interest Area: 05. Education and Training. **Work Group:** 05.03. Postsecondary and Adult Teaching and Instructing. **Other Jobs in This Work Group:** Adult Literacy, Remedial Education, and GED Teachers and Instructors; Agricultural Sciences Teachers, Postsecondary; Anthropology and Archeology Teachers, Postsecondary; Architecture Teachers, Postsecondary; Area, Ethnic, and Cultural Studies Teachers, Postsecondary; Art, Drama, and Music Teachers, Postsecondary; Atmospheric, Earth, Marine, and Space Sciences Teachers, Postsecondary; Biological Science Teachers, Postsecondary; Business Teachers, Postsecondary; Chemistry Teachers, Postsecondary; Communications Teachers, Postsecondary; Computer Science Teachers, Postsecondary; Criminal Justice and Law Enforcement Teachers, Postsecondary; Economics Teachers, Postsecondary; Education Teachers, Postsecondary; Engineering Teachers, Postsecondary; English Language and Literature Teachers, Postsecondary; Environmental Science Teachers, Postsecondary; Farm and Home Management Advisors; Foreign Language and Literature Teachers, Postsecondary; Forestry and Conservation Science Teachers, Postsecondary; Geography Teachers, Postsecondary; Graduate Teaching Assistants; Health Specialties Teachers, Postsecondary; Home Economics Teachers, Postsecondary; Law Teachers, Postsecondary; Library Science Teachers, Postsecondary; Mathematical Science Teachers, Postsecondary; Nursing Instructors and Teachers, Postsecondary; Philosophy and Religion Teachers, Postsecondary; Physics Teachers, Postsecondary; Political Science Teachers, Postsecondary; Psychology Teachers, Postsecondary; Recreation and Fitness Studies Teachers, Postsecondary; Self-Enrichment Education Teachers; Social Work Teachers, Postsecondary; Sociology Teachers, Postsecondary; Vocational Education Teachers, Postsecondary. **PERSONALITY TYPE:** Social. Social occupations frequently

H

involve working with, communicating with, and teaching people. These occupations often involve helping or providing service to others.

EDUCATION/TRAINING PROGRAM(S)— American History (United States); Asian History; Canadian History; European History; History and Philosophy of Science and Technology; History, General; History, Other; Public/Applied History and Archival Administration.

WORK ENVIRONMENT—Sitting; physical proximity to others; sounds, noise levels are distracting or uncomfortable; indoors.

Home Economics Teachers, Postsecondary

- Education/Training Required: Master's degree
- Annual Earnings: $47,670
- Growth: 38.1%
- Annual Job Openings: 216,000
- Self-Employed: 0.3%
- Part-Time: 27.7%

The job openings listed here are shared with all other postsecondary teaching occupations.

Age Bracket	Percentage of Workers
45–54 Years Old	22.8%
55–64 Years Old	19.0%
65 or Older	5.5%

Teach courses in child care, family relations, finance, nutrition, and related subjects as pertaining to home management. Evaluate and grade students' class work, laboratory work, projects, assignments, and papers. Initiate, facilitate, and moderate classroom discussions. Prepare and deliver lectures to undergraduate and/or graduate students on topics such as food science, nutrition, and child care. Prepare course materials such as syllabi, homework assignments, and handouts. Keep abreast of developments in their field by reading current literature, talking with colleagues, and participating in professional conferences. Maintain student attendance records, grades, and other required records. Plan, evaluate, and revise curricula, course content, and course materials and methods of instruction. Compile, administer, and grade examinations or assign this work to others. Advise students on academic and vocational curricula, and on career issues. Maintain regularly scheduled office hours in order to advise and assist students. Supervise undergraduate and/or graduate teaching, internship, and research work. Select and obtain materials and supplies such as textbooks. Conduct research in a particular field of knowledge and publish findings in professional journals, books, and/or electronic media. Collaborate with colleagues to address teaching and research issues. Act as advisers to student organizations. Participate in student recruitment, registration, and placement activities. Serve on academic or administrative committees that deal with institutional policies, departmental matters, and academic issues. Participate in campus and community events. Compile bibliographies of specialized materials for outside reading assignments. Perform administrative duties such as serving as department head. Write grant proposals to procure external research funding. Provide professional consulting services to government and/or industry. **SKILLS**—Instructing; Learning Strategies; Writing; Social Perceptiveness; Service Orientation; Active Learning; Persuasion; Negotiation.

GOE—**Interest Area:** 05. Education and Training. **Work Group:** 05.03. Postsecondary and Adult Teaching and Instructing. **Other Jobs in This Work Group:** Adult Literacy, Remedial Education, and GED Teachers and Instructors; Agricultural Sciences Teachers, Postsecondary; Anthropology and Archeology Teachers, Postsecondary; Architecture Teachers, Postsecondary; Area, Ethnic, and Cultural Studies Teachers, Postsecondary; Art, Drama, and Music Teachers, Postsecondary; Atmospheric, Earth, Marine, and Space Sciences Teachers, Postsecondary; Biological Science Teachers, Postsecondary; Business Teachers, Postsecondary; Chemistry Teachers, Postsecondary; Communications Teachers, Postsecondary; Computer Science Teachers, Postsecondary; Criminal Justice and Law Enforcement Teachers, Postsecondary; Economics Teachers, Postsecondary; Education Teachers, Postsecondary; Engineering Teachers, Postsecondary; English Language and Literature Teachers, Postsecondary; Environmental Science Teachers, Postsecondary; Farm and Home Management Advisors; Foreign Language and Literature Teachers, Postsecondary; Forestry and Conservation Science Teachers, Postsecondary; Geography Teachers, Postsecondary; Graduate Teaching Assistants; Health Specialties Teachers, Postsecondary; History Teachers, Postsecondary; Law Teachers, Postsecondary; Library Science Teachers, Postsecondary; Mathematical Science Teachers, Postsecondary; Nursing Instructors and Teachers, Postsecondary; Philosophy and Religion Teachers, Postsecondary; Physics Teachers, Postsecondary; Political Science Teachers, Postsecondary; Psychology Teachers, Postsecondary; Recreation and Fitness Studies Teachers, Postsecondary; Self-Enrichment Education Teachers; Social Work Teachers, Postsecondary; Sociology Teachers, Postsecondary; Vocational Education Teachers,

Postsecondary. **PERSONALITY TYPE:** No data available.

EDUCATION/TRAINING PROGRAM(S)— Business Family and Consumer Sciences/Human Sciences; Child Care and Support Services Management; Family and Consumer Sciences/Human Sciences, General; Foodservice Systems Administration/Management; Human Development and Family Studies, General.

WORK ENVIRONMENT—Physical proximity to others; sitting; indoors; sounds, noise levels are distracting or uncomfortable.

Housekeeping Supervisors

- ◎ Education/Training Required: Work experience in a related occupation
- ◎ Annual Earnings: $30,050
- ◎ Growth: 16.2%
- ◎ Annual Job Openings: 28,000
- ◎ Self-Employed: 5.6%
- ◎ Part-Time: 6.6%

The job openings listed here are shared with Janitorial Supervisors.

Age Bracket	Percentage of Workers
45–54 Years Old	30.1%
55–64 Years Old	16.9%
65 or Older	3.0%

Supervise work activities of cleaning personnel to ensure clean, orderly, and attractive rooms in hotels, hospitals, educational institutions, and similar establishments. Assign duties, inspect work, and investigate complaints regarding

housekeeping service and equipment and take corrective action. **May purchase housekeeping supplies and equipment, take periodic inventories, screen applicants, train new employees, and recommend dismissals.** Assigns workers their duties and inspects work for conformance to prescribed standards of cleanliness. Investigates complaints regarding housekeeping service and equipment and takes corrective action. Obtains list of rooms to be cleaned immediately and list of prospective check-outs or discharges to prepare work assignments. Coordinates work activities among departments. Conducts orientation training and in-service training to explain policies and work procedures and to demonstrate use and maintenance of equipment. Inventories stock to ensure adequate supplies. Evaluates records to forecast department personnel requirements. Makes recommendations to improve service and ensure more efficient operation. Prepares reports concerning room occupancy, payroll, and department expenses. Selects and purchases new furnishings. Performs cleaning duties in cases of emergency or staff shortage. Examines building to determine need for repairs or replacement of furniture or equipment and makes recommendations to management. Attends staff meetings to discuss company policies and patrons' complaints. Issues supplies and equipment to workers. Establishes standards and procedures for work of housekeeping staff. Advises manager, desk clerk, or admitting personnel of rooms ready for occupancy. Records data regarding work assignments, personnel actions, and time cards and prepares periodic reports. Screens job applicants; hires new employees; and recommends promotions, transfers, and dismissals. **SKILLS—** Management of Personnel Resources; Time Management; Management of Material Resources; Management of Financial Resources;

Systems Evaluation; Systems Analysis; Coordination; Speaking.

GOE—Interest Area: 04. Business and Administration. **Work Group:** 04.02. Managerial Work in Business Detail. **Other Jobs in This Work Group:** Administrative Services Managers; First-Line Supervisors, Administrative Support; First-Line Supervisors, Customer Service; Janitorial Supervisors; Meeting and Convention Planners. **PERSONALITY TYPE:** Enterprising. Enterprising occupations frequently involve starting up and carrying out projects. These occupations can involve leading people and making many decisions. They sometimes require risk taking and often deal with business.

EDUCATION/TRAINING PROGRAM(S)— No data available.

WORK ENVIRONMENT—Sitting; indoors; walking and running; standing; climbing ladders, scaffolds, or poles.

Hydrologists

- Education/Training Required: Master's degree
- Annual Earnings: $60,880
- Growth: 21.0%
- Annual Job Openings: 1,000
- Self-Employed: 3.0%
- Part-Time: 7.7%

Age Bracket	Percentage of Workers
45–54 Years Old	29.4%
55–64 Years Old	11.8%
65 or Older	2.4%

Research the distribution, circulation, and physical properties of underground and surface waters; study the form and intensity of precipitation, its rate of infiltration into the soil, movement through the earth, and its return to the ocean and atmosphere. Apply research findings to help minimize the environmental impacts of pollution, water-borne diseases, erosion, and sedimentation. Compile and evaluate hydrologic information in order to prepare navigational charts and maps and to predict atmospheric conditions. Conduct research and communicate information to promote the conservation and preservation of water resources. Conduct short-term and long-term climate assessments and study storm occurrences. Design and conduct scientific hydrogeological investigations to ensure that accurate and appropriate information is available for use in water resource management decisions. Evaluate research data in terms of its impact on issues such as soil and water conservation, flood control planning, and water supply forecasting. Investigate properties, origins, and activities of glaciers, ice, snow, and permafrost. Measure and graph phenomena such as lake levels, stream flows, and changes in water volumes. Study and analyze the physical aspects of the Earth in terms of the hydrological components, including atmosphere, hydrosphere, and interior structure. Study and document quantities, distribution, disposition, and development of underground and surface waters. Study public water supply issues, including flood and drought risks, water quality, wastewater, and impacts on wetland habitats. Answer questions and provide technical assistance and information to contractors and/or the public regarding issues such as well drilling, code requirements, hydrology, and geology. Collect and analyze water samples as part of field investigations and/or to validate data from automatic monitors. Coordinate and supervise the work of professional and technical staff, including research assistants, technologists, and technicians. Design civil works associated with hydrographic activities and supervise their construction, installation, and maintenance. Develop or modify methods of conducting hydrologic studies. Draft final reports describing research results, including illustrations, appendices, maps, and other attachments. Evaluate data and provide recommendations regarding the feasibility of municipal projects such as hydroelectric power plants, irrigation systems, flood warning systems, and waste treatment facilities. **SKILLS**—Science; Mathematics; Systems Analysis; Writing; Active Learning; Critical Thinking; Complex Problem Solving; Judgment and Decision Making.

GOE—Interest Area: 15. Scientific Research, Engineering, and Mathematics. **Work Group:** 15.02. Physical Sciences. **Other Jobs in This Work Group:** Astronomers; Atmospheric and Space Scientists; Chemists; Geographers; Geologists; Materials Scientists; Physicists. **PERSONALITY TYPE:** Investigative. Investigative occupations frequently involve working with ideas and require an extensive amount of thinking. These occupations can involve searching for facts and figuring out problems mentally.

EDUCATION/TRAINING PROGRAM(S)—Geology/Earth Science, General; Hydrology and Water Resources Science; Oceanography, Chemical and Physical.

WORK ENVIRONMENT—Outdoors; sitting; very hot or cold; extremely bright or inadequate lighting; standing.

Industrial Engineers

- Education/Training Required: Bachelor's degree
- Annual Earnings: $66,080
- Growth: 10.6%
- Annual Job Openings: 16,000
- Self-Employed: 1.5%
- Part-Time: 1.5%

Age Bracket	Percentage of Workers
45–54 Years Old	23.3%
55–64 Years Old	14.4%
65 or Older	2.8%

Design, develop, test, and evaluate integrated systems for managing industrial production processes, including human work factors, quality control, inventory control, logistics and material flow, cost analysis, and production coordination. Analyze statistical data and product specifications to determine standards and establish quality and reliability objectives of finished product. Develop manufacturing methods, labor utilization standards, and cost analysis systems to promote efficient staff and facility utilization. Recommend methods for improving utilization of personnel, material, and utilities. Plan and establish sequence of operations to fabricate and assemble parts or products and to promote efficient utilization. Apply statistical methods and perform mathematical calculations to determine manufacturing processes, staff requirements, and production standards. Coordinate quality control objectives and activities to resolve production problems, maximize product reliability, and minimize cost. Confer with vendors, staff, and management personnel regarding purchases, procedures, product specifications, manufacturing capabilities, and project status. Draft and design layout of equipment, materials, and workspace to illustrate maximum efficiency, using drafting tools and computer. Review production schedules, engineering specifications, orders, and related information to obtain knowledge of manufacturing methods, procedures, and activities. Communicate with management and user personnel to develop production and design standards. Estimate production cost and effect of product design changes for management review, action, and control. Formulate sampling procedures and designs and develop forms and instructions for recording, evaluating, and reporting quality and reliability data. Record or oversee recording of information to ensure currency of engineering drawings and documentation of production problems. Study operations sequence, material flow, functional statements, organization charts, and project information to determine worker functions and responsibilities. Direct workers engaged in product measurement, inspection, and testing activities to ensure quality control and reliability. Implement methods and procedures for disposition of discrepant material and defective or damaged parts and assess cost and responsibility. **SKILLS**—Equipment Selection; Technology Design; Negotiation; Troubleshooting; Judgment and Decision Making; Active Learning; Persuasion; Complex Problem Solving.

GOE—Interest Area: 15. Scientific Research, Engineering, and Mathematics. **Work Group:** 15.08. Industrial and Safety Engineering. **Other Jobs in This Work Group:** Fire-Prevention and Protection Engineers; Industrial Safety and Health Engineers; Product Safety Engineers. **PERSONALITY TYPE:** Enterprising. Enterprising occupations frequently involve starting up and carrying out projects. These occupations can involve leading people and making many decisions. They sometimes require risk taking and often deal with business.

EDUCATION/TRAINING PROGRAM(S)— Industrial Engineering.

WORK ENVIRONMENT—Sounds, noise levels are distracting or uncomfortable; contaminants; sitting; indoors, not environmentally controlled; hazardous equipment.

Industrial Machinery Mechanics

- ◎ Education/Training Required: Long-term on-the-job training
- ◎ Annual Earnings: $39,310
- ◎ Growth: 5.5%
- ◎ Annual Job Openings: 19,000
- ◎ Self-Employed: 6.3%
- ◎ Part-Time: 2.1%

Age Bracket	Percentage of Workers
45–54 Years Old	32.0%
55–64 Years Old	13.5%
65 or Older	1.3%

Repair, install, adjust, or maintain industrial production and processing machinery or refinery and pipeline distribution systems. Analyze test results, machine error messages, and information obtained from operators in order to diagnose equipment problems. Clean, lubricate, and adjust parts, equipment, and machinery. Disassemble machinery and equipment to remove parts and make repairs. Examine parts for defects such as breakage and excessive wear. Observe and test the operation of machinery and equipment in order to diagnose malfunctions, using voltmeters and other testing devices. Operate newly repaired machinery and equipment to verify the adequacy of repairs. Reassemble equipment after completion of inspections, testing, or repairs. Repair and maintain the operating condition of industrial production and processing machinery and equipment. Repair and replace broken or malfunctioning components of machinery and equipment. Study blueprints and manufacturers' manuals to determine correct installation and operation of machinery. Cut and weld metal to repair broken metal parts, fabricate new parts, and assemble new equipment. Demonstrate equipment functions and features to machine operators. Enter codes and instructions to program computer-controlled machinery. Record parts and materials used and order or requisition new parts and materials as necessary. Record repairs and maintenance performed. **SKILLS—** Repairing; Equipment Maintenance; Troubleshooting; Operation Monitoring; Quality Control Analysis; Installation; Operation and Control; Technology Design.

GOE—Interest Area: 13. Manufacturing. **Work Group:** 13.13. Machinery Repair. **Other Jobs in This Work Group:** Bicycle Repairers; Gas Appliance Repairers; Hand and Portable Power Tool Repairers; Locksmiths and Safe Repairers; Maintenance Workers, Machinery; Mechanical Door Repairers; Millwrights; Signal and Track Switch Repairers; Valve and Regulator Repairers. **PERSONALITY TYPE:** Realistic. Realistic occupations frequently involve work activities that include practical, hands-on problems and solutions. They often deal with plants, animals, and real-world materials like wood, tools, and machinery. Many of the occupations require working outside and do not involve a lot of paperwork or working closely with others.

EDUCATION/TRAINING PROGRAM(S)— Heavy/Industrial Equipment Maintenance Technologies; Industrial Mechanics and Maintenance Technology.

WORK ENVIRONMENT—Hazardous equipment; common protective or safety equipment; sounds, noise levels are distracting or uncomfortable; minor burns, cuts, bites, or stings; standing.

Industrial Production Managers

- Education/Training Required: Bachelor's degree
- Annual Earnings: $74,100
- Growth: 7.9%
- Annual Job Openings: 18,000
- Self-Employed: 1.5%
- Part-Time: 1.8%

Age Bracket	Percentage of Workers
45–54 Years Old	33.3%
55–64 Years Old	11.2%
65 or Older	2.2%

Plan, direct, or coordinate the work activities and resources necessary for manufacturing products in accordance with cost, quality, and quantity specifications. Direct and coordinate production, processing, distribution, and marketing activities of industrial organization. Develop budgets and approve expenditures for supplies, materials, and human resources, ensuring that materials, labor, and equipment are used efficiently to meet production targets. Review processing schedules and production orders to make decisions concerning inventory requirements, staffing requirements, work procedures, and duty assignments, considering budgetary limitations and time constraints. Review operations and confer with technical or administrative staff to resolve production or processing problems. Hire, train, evaluate, and discharge staff and resolve personnel grievances. Initiate and coordinate inventory and cost-control programs. Prepare and maintain production reports and personnel records. Set and monitor product standards, examining samples of raw products or directing testing during processing, to ensure finished products are of prescribed quality. Develop and implement production tracking and quality control systems, analyzing production, quality control, maintenance, and other operational reports, to detect production problems. Review plans and confer with research and support staff to develop new products and processes. Institute employee suggestion or involvement programs. Coordinate and recommend procedures for facility and equipment maintenance or modification, including the replacement of machines. Maintain current knowledge of the quality control field, relying on current literature pertaining to materials use, technological advances, and statistical studies. Negotiate materials prices with suppliers. **SKILLS**—Management of Material Resources; Management of Personnel Resources; Persuasion; Coordination; Systems Evaluation; Monitoring; Operations Analysis; Time Management.

GOE—Interest Area: 13. Manufacturing. **Work Group:** 13.01. Managerial Work in Manufacturing. **Other Jobs in This Work Group:** First-Line Supervisors/Managers of Helpers, Laborers, and Material Movers, Hand; First-Line Supervisors/Managers of Mechanics, Installers, and Repairers; First-Line Supervisors/Managers of Production and Operating Workers. **PERSONALITY TYPE:** Enterprising. Enterprising occupations frequently involve starting up and carrying out projects. These occupations can involve leading people and making many decisions. They sometimes require risk taking and often deal with business.

EDUCATION/TRAINING PROGRAM(S)— Business Administration/Management; Business/Commerce, General; Operations Management and Supervision.

WORK ENVIRONMENT—Sitting; contaminants; sounds, noise levels are distracting or uncomfortable; indoors, not environmentally controlled; physical proximity to others.

Industrial Safety and Health Engineers

- Education/Training Required: Bachelor's degree
- Annual Earnings: $64,320
- Growth: 7.9%
- Annual Job Openings: 4,000
- Self-Employed: 1.6%
- Part-Time: 1.5%

The job openings listed here are shared with Fire-Prevention and Protection Engineers and Product Safety Engineers.

Age Bracket	Percentage of Workers
45–54 Years Old	23.3%
55–64 Years Old	14.4%
65 or Older	2.8%

Plan, implement, and coordinate safety programs requiring application of engineering principles and technology to prevent or correct unsafe environmental working conditions. Investigate industrial accidents, injuries, or occupational diseases to determine causes and preventive measures. Report or review findings from accident investigations, facilities inspections, or environmental testing. Maintain and apply knowledge of current policies, regulations, and industrial processes. Inspect facilities, machinery, and safety equipment in order to identify and correct potential hazards and to ensure safety regulation compliance. Conduct or coordinate worker training in areas such as safety laws and regulations, hazardous condition monitoring, and use of safety equipment. Review employee safety programs to determine their adequacy. Interview employers and employees to obtain information about work environments and workplace incidents. Review plans and specifications for construction of new machinery or equipment in order to determine if all safety requirements have been met. Compile, analyze, and interpret statistical data related to occupational illnesses and accidents. Interpret safety regulations for others interested in industrial safety, such as safety engineers, labor representatives, and safety inspectors. Recommend process and product safety features that will reduce employees' exposure to chemical, physical, and biological work hazards. Conduct or direct testing of air quality, noise, temperature, and/or radiation levels to verify compliance with health and safety regulations. Provide technical advice and guidance to organizations on how to handle health-related problems and make needed changes. Confer with medical professionals to assess health risks and to develop ways to manage health issues and concerns. Install safety devices on machinery or direct device installation. Maintain liaisons with outside organizations, such as fire departments, mutual aid societies, and rescue teams, so that emergency responses can be facilitated. Evaluate adequacy of actions taken to correct health inspection violations. Write and revise safety regulations and codes. Check floors of plants to ensure that they are strong enough to support heavy machinery. Plan and conduct industrial hygiene research. **SKILLS**—Persuasion; Management of Financial Resources; Service Orientation; Science; Negotiation; Systems Analysis; Management of Personnel Resources; Management of Material Resources.

GOE—Interest Area: 15. Scientific Research, Engineering, and Mathematics. **Work Group:** 15.08. Industrial and Safety Engineering. **Other Jobs in This Work Group:** Fire-Prevention and Protection Engineers; Industrial Engineers; Product Safety Engineers. **PERSONALITY TYPE:** Investigative. Investigative occupations frequently involve working with ideas and require an extensive amount of thinking. These occupations can involve searching for facts and figuring out problems mentally.

EDUCATION/TRAINING PROGRAM(S)—Environmental/Environmental Health Engineering.

WORK ENVIRONMENT—Indoors, not environmentally controlled; outdoors; in an enclosed vehicle or equipment; very hot or cold; sounds, noise levels are distracting or uncomfortable.

Industrial-Organizational Psychologists

◉ Education/Training Required: Master's degree

◉ Annual Earnings: $74,060

◉ Growth: 16.0%

◉ Annual Job Openings: fewer than 500

◉ Self-Employed: 26.8%

◉ Part-Time: 27.2%

Age Bracket	Percentage of Workers
45–54 Years Old	33.0%
55–64 Years Old	23.8%
65 or Older	7.6%

Apply principles of psychology to personnel, administration, management, sales, and marketing problems. Activities may include policy planning; employee screening, training, and development; and organizational development and analysis. May work with management to reorganize the work setting to improve worker productivity. Analyze data, using statistical methods and applications, in order to evaluate the outcomes and effectiveness of workplace programs. Analyze job requirements and content in order to establish criteria for classification, selection, training, and other related personnel functions. Conduct research studies of physical work environments, organizational structures, communication systems, group interactions, morale, and motivation in order to assess organizational functioning. Develop and implement employee selection and placement programs. Develop interview techniques, rating scales, and psychological tests used to assess skills, abilities, and interests for the purpose of employee selection, placement, and promotion. Facilitate organizational development and change. Formulate and implement training programs, applying principles of learning and individual differences. Identify training and development needs. Observe and interview workers in order to obtain information about the physical, mental, and educational requirements of jobs as well as information about aspects such as job satisfaction. Study organizational effectiveness, productivity, and efficiency, including the nature of workplace supervision and leadership. Advise management concerning personnel, managerial, and marketing policies and practices and their potential effects on organizational effectiveness and efficiency. Assess employee performance. Counsel workers about job and career-related issues. Participate in mediation and dispute resolution. Study consumers' reactions to new products and package designs and to advertising efforts, using surveys and tests. Write reports on research findings and implications in order to contribute to general knowledge and to suggest potential changes in organizational functioning. **SKILLS**—Systems Evaluation; Management of Personnel Resources; Systems Analysis; Science; Complex Problem Solving; Mathematics; Social Perceptiveness; Writing; Active Learning.

GOE—**Interest Area:** 15. Scientific Research, Engineering, and Mathematics. **Work Group:** 15.04. Social Sciences. **Other Jobs in This Work Group:** Anthropologists; Archeologists; Economists; Educational Psychologists; Historians; Political Scientists; Sociologists. **PERSONALITY TYPE:** Investigative. Investigative occupations frequently involve working with ideas and require an extensive amount of thinking. These occupations can involve searching for facts and figuring out problems mentally.

EDUCATION/TRAINING PROGRAM(S)— Industrial and Organizational Psychology; Psychology, General.

WORK ENVIRONMENT—Sitting; indoors.

Instructional Coordinators

- Education/Training Required: Master's degree
- Annual Earnings: $50,060
- Growth: 25.4%
- Annual Job Openings: 18,000
- Self-Employed: 2.7%
- Part-Time: 16.5%

Age Bracket	Percentage of Workers
45–54 Years Old	41.8%
55–64 Years Old	17.9%
65 or Older	3.0%

Develop instructional material, coordinate educational content, and incorporate current technology in specialized fields that provide guidelines to educators and instructors for developing curricula and conducting courses. Conduct or participate in workshops, committees, and conferences designed to promote the intellectual, social, and physical welfare of students. Plan and conduct teacher training programs and conferences dealing with new classroom procedures, instructional materials and equipment, and teaching aids. Advise teaching and administrative staff in curriculum development, use of materials and equipment, and implementation of state and federal programs and procedures. Recommend, order, or authorize purchase of instructional materials, supplies, equipment, and visual aids designed to meet student educational needs and district standards. Interpret and enforce provisions of state education codes and rules and regulations of state education boards. Confer with members of educational committees and advisory groups to obtain knowledge of subject areas and to relate curriculum materials to specific subjects, individual student needs, and occupational areas. Organize production and design of curriculum materials. Research, evaluate, and prepare recommendations on curricula, instructional methods, and materials for school systems. Observe work of teaching staff in order to evaluate performance and to recommend changes that could strengthen teaching skills. Develop instructional materials to be used by educators and instructors. Prepare grant proposals, budgets, and program policies and goals or assist in their preparation. Develop tests, questionnaires, and procedures that measure the effectiveness of curricula; use these tools to determine whether program objectives are being met. Update the content of educational programs to ensure that students are being trained with equipment and processes that are technologically current. Address public audiences to explain program objectives and to elicit support. Advise and teach students. Prepare or approve manuals, guidelines, and reports on state educational policies and practices for distribution to school districts. Develop classroom-based and distance learning training courses, using needs assessments and skill-level analyses. Inspect instructional equipment to determine if repairs are needed; authorize necessary repairs. **SKILLS**—Learning Strategies; Social Perceptiveness; Management of Financial Resources; Coordination; Time Management; Monitoring; Instructing; Persuasion; Management of Personnel Resources.

GOE—**Interest Area:** 05. Education and Training. **Work Group:** 05.01. Managerial Work in Education. **Other Jobs in This Work Group:** Education Administrators, Elementary and Secondary School; Education Administrators, Postsecondary; Education Administrators, Preschool and Child Care Center/Program. **PERSONALITY TYPE:** Social. Social occupations frequently involve working with, communicating with, and teaching people. These occupations often involve helping or providing service to others.

EDUCATION/TRAINING PROGRAM(S)— Curriculum and Instruction; Educational/Instructional Media Design.

WORK ENVIRONMENT—Sitting; physical proximity to others; in an enclosed vehicle or equipment; indoors; contaminants.

Insurance Sales Agents

- Education/Training Required: Bachelor's degree
- Annual Earnings: $42,030
- Growth: 8.4%
- Annual Job Openings: 52,000
- Self-Employed: 26.2%
- Part-Time: 9.2%

Age Bracket	Percentage of Workers
45–54 Years Old	25.2%
55–64 Years Old	15.9%
65 or Older	5.4%

Sell life, property, casualty, health, automotive, or other types of insurance. May refer clients to independent brokers, work as independent broker, or be employed by an insurance company. Call on policyholders to deliver and explain policy, to analyze insurance program and suggest additions or changes, or to change beneficiaries. Calculate premiums and establish payment method. Customize insurance programs to suit individual customers, often covering a variety of risks. Sell various types of insurance policies to businesses and individuals on behalf of insurance companies, including automobile, fire, life, property, medical, and dental insurance or specialized policies such as marine, farm/crop, and medical malpractice. Interview prospective clients to obtain data about their financial resources and needs and the physical condition of the person or property to be insured and to discuss any existing coverage. Seek out new clients and develop clientele by networking to find new customers and generate lists of prospective clients. Explain features, advantages, and disadvantages of various policies to promote sale of insurance plans. Contact underwriter and submit forms to obtain binder coverage. Ensure that policy requirements are fulfilled, including any necessary medical examinations and the completion of appropriate forms. Confer with clients to obtain and provide information when claims are made on a policy. Perform administrative tasks, such as maintaining records and handling policy renewals. Select company that offers type of coverage requested by client to underwrite policy. Monitor insurance claims to ensure they are settled equitably for both the client and the insurer. Develop marketing strategies to compete with other individuals or companies who sell insurance. Attend meetings, seminars, and programs to learn about new products and services, learn new skills, and receive technical assistance in developing new accounts. Inspect property, examining its general condition, type of construction, age, and other characteristics, to decide if it is a good insurance risk. Install bookkeeping systems and resolve system problems. Plan and oversee incorporation of insurance program into bookkeeping system of company. Explain necessary bookkeeping requirements for customer to implement and provide group insurance program. **SKILLS—** Persuasion; Time Management; Negotiation; Service Orientation; Social Perceptiveness; Judgment and Decision Making; Speaking; Active Listening.

GOE—Interest Area: 06. Finance and Insurance. **Work Group:** 06.05. Finance/Insurance Sales and Support. **Other Jobs in This Work Group:** Advertising Sales Agents; Personal Financial Advisors; Sales Agents, Financial Services; Sales Agents, Securities and Commodities. **PERSONALITY TYPE:** Enterprising. Enterprising occupations frequently involve starting up and carrying out projects. These occupations can involve leading people and making many decisions. They sometimes require risk taking and often deal with business.

EDUCATION/TRAINING PROGRAM(S)— Insurance.

WORK ENVIRONMENT—Sitting; physical proximity to others; in an enclosed vehicle or equipment; extremely bright or inadequate lighting; sounds, noise levels are distracting or uncomfortable.

Internists, General

- ◎ Education/Training Required: First professional degree
- ◎ Annual Earnings: more than $145,600
- ◎ Growth: 19.5%
- ◎ Annual Job Openings: 38,000
- ◎ Self-Employed: 16.9%
- ◎ Part-Time: 8.1%

The job openings listed here are shared with Anesthesiologists; Family and General Practitioners; Obstetricians and Gynecologists; Pediatricians, General; Psychiatrists; and Surgeons.

Age Bracket	Percentage of Workers
45–54 Years Old	29.3%
55–64 Years Old	13.4%
65 or Older	5.4%

Diagnose and provide non-surgical treatment of diseases and injuries of internal organ systems. Provide care mainly for adults who have a wide range of problems associated with the internal organs. Advise patients and community members concerning diet, activity, hygiene, and disease prevention. Analyze records, reports, test results, or examination information to diagnose medical condition of patient. Collect, record, and maintain patient information, such as medical history, reports, and examination results. Make diagnoses when different illnesses occur together or in situations where the diagnosis may be obscure. Explain procedures and discuss test results or prescribed treatments with patients. Immunize patients to protect them from preventable diseases. Manage and treat common health problems, such as infections, influenza, and pneumonia, as well as serious, chronic, and complex illnesses, in adolescents, adults, and the elderly. Monitor patients' conditions and progress and re-evaluate treatments as necessary. Prescribe or administer medication, therapy, and other specialized medical care to treat or prevent illness, disease, or injury. Provide and manage long-term, comprehensive medical care, including diagnosis and non-surgical treatment of diseases, for adult patients in an office or hospital. Refer patient to medical specialist or other practitioner when necessary. Treat internal disorders, such as hypertension; heart disease; diabetes; and problems of the lung, brain, kidney, and gastrointestinal tract. Advise surgeon of a patient's risk status and recommend appropriate intervention to minimize risk. Conduct research to develop or test medications, treatments, or procedures to prevent or control disease or injury. Direct and coordinate activities of nurses, students, assistants, specialists, therapists, and other medical staff. Operate on patients to remove, repair, or improve functioning of diseased or injured body parts and systems. Provide consulting services to other doctors caring for patients with special or difficult problems. Plan, implement, or administer health programs in hospitals, businesses, or communities for prevention and treatment of injuries or illnesses. Prepare government or organizational reports on birth, death, and disease statistics; workforce evaluations; or the medical status of individuals. **SKILLS**—Science; Systems Evaluation; Reading Comprehension; Active Learning; Judgment and Decision Making; Management of Personnel Resources; Systems Analysis; Social Perceptiveness.

GOE—Interest Area: 08. Health Science. **Work Group:** 08.02. Medicine and Surgery. **Other Jobs in This Work Group:** Anesthesiologists; Family and General Practitioners; Medical Assistants; Medical Transcriptionists; Obstetricians and Gynecologists; Pediatricians, General; Pharmacists; Pharmacy Aides; Pharmacy Technicians; Physician Assistants; Psychiatrists; Registered Nurses; Surgeons; Surgical Technologists. **PERSONALITY TYPE:** Investigative. Investigative occupations frequently involve working with ideas and require an extensive amount of thinking. These occupations can involve searching for facts and figuring out problems mentally.

EDUCATION/TRAINING PROGRAM(S)—Cardiology; Critical Care Medicine; Endocrinology and Metabolism; Gastroenterology; Geriatric Medicine; Hematology; Infectious Disease; Internal Medicine; Nephrology; Neurology; Nuclear Medicine; Oncology; Pulmonary Disease; Rheumatology.

WORK ENVIRONMENT—Disease or infections; common protective or safety equipment; walking and running; spend time bending or twisting the body; indoors; standing.

Janitorial Supervisors

- Education/Training Required: Work experience in a related occupation
- Annual Earnings: $30,050
- Growth: 16.2%
- Annual Job Openings: 28,000
- Self-Employed: 5.6%
- Part-Time: 6.6%

The job openings listed here are shared with Housekeeping Supervisors.

Age Bracket	Percentage of Workers
45–54 Years Old	30.1%
55–64 Years Old	16.9%
65 or Older	3.0%

Supervise work activities of janitorial personnel in commercial and industrial establishments. Assign duties, inspect work, and investigate complaints regarding janitorial services and take corrective action. May purchase janitorial supplies and equipment, take periodic inventories, screen applicants, train new employees, and recommend dismissals. Supervises and coordinates activities of workers engaged in janitorial services. Assigns janitorial work to employees, following material and work requirements. Inspects work performed to ensure conformance to specifications and established standards. Records personnel data on specified forms. Recommends personnel actions, such as hires and discharges, to ensure proper staffing. Confers with staff to resolve production and personnel problems. Trains workers in janitorial methods and procedures and proper operation of equipment. Issues janitorial supplies and equipment to workers to ensure quality and timely delivery of services. SKILLS—Management of Personnel Resources; Coordination; Time Management; Social Perceptiveness; Persuasion; Speaking; Management of Material Resources; Negotiation.

GOE—Interest Area: 04. Business and Administration. Work Group: 04.02. Managerial Work in Business Detail. Other Jobs in This Work Group: Administrative Services Managers; First-Line Supervisors, Administrative Support; First-Line Supervisors, Customer Service; Housekeeping Supervisors; Meeting and Convention Planners. PERSONALITY TYPE: Enterprising. Enterprising occupations frequently involve starting up and carrying out projects. These occupations can involve leading people and making many decisions. They sometimes require risk taking and often deal with business.

EDUCATION/TRAINING PROGRAM(S)— No data available.

WORK ENVIRONMENT—Standing; walking and running; spend time bending or twisting the body; outdoors; contaminants; spend time kneeling, crouching, stooping, or crawling.

Janitors and Cleaners, Except Maids and Housekeeping Cleaners

- Education/Training Required: Short-term on-the-job training
- Annual Earnings: $19,110
- Growth: 18.3%
- Annual Job Openings: 454,000
- Self-Employed: 4.7%
- Part-Time: 21.7%

Age Bracket	Percentage of Workers
45–54 Years Old	24.1%
55–64 Years Old	16.2%
65 or Older	6.1%

Keep buildings in clean and orderly condition. Perform heavy cleaning duties, such as cleaning floors, shampooing rugs, washing walls and glass, and removing rubbish. Duties may include tending furnace and boiler, performing routine maintenance activities, notifying management of need for repairs, and cleaning snow or debris from sidewalk. Clean building floors by sweeping, mopping, scrubbing, or vacuuming them. Gather and empty trash. Service, clean, and supply restrooms. Clean and polish furniture and fixtures. Clean windows, glass partitions, and mirrors, using soapy water or other cleaners, sponges, and squeegees. Dust furniture, walls, machines, and equipment. Make adjustments and minor repairs to heating, cooling, ventilating, plumbing, and electrical systems. Mix water and detergents or acids in containers to prepare cleaning solutions according to specifications. Steam-clean or shampoo carpets. Strip, seal, finish, and polish floors. Clean and restore building interiors damaged by fire, smoke, or water, using commercial cleaning equipment. Clean chimneys, flues, and connecting pipes, using power and hand tools. Clean laboratory equipment, such as glassware and metal instruments, using solvents, brushes, rags, and power cleaning equipment. Drive vehicles required to perform or travel to cleaning work, including vans, industrial trucks, or industrial vacuum cleaners. Follow procedures for the use of chemical cleaners and power equipment in order to prevent damage to floors and fixtures. Monitor building security and safety by performing such tasks as locking doors after operating hours and checking electrical appliance use to ensure that hazards are not created. Move heavy furniture, equipment, and supplies, either manually or by using handtrucks. Mow and trim lawns and shrubbery, using mowers and hand and power trimmers, and clear debris from grounds. Notify managers concerning the need for major repairs or additions to building operating systems. Remove snow from sidewalks, driveways, and parking areas, using snowplows, snowblowers, and snow shovels, and spread snow-melting chemicals. Requisition supplies and equipment needed for cleaning and maintenance duties. Set up, arrange, and remove decorations, tables, chairs, ladders, and scaffolding to prepare facilities for events such as banquets and meetings. Spray insecticides and fumigants to prevent insect and rodent infestation. **SKILLS—**Repairing; Equipment Maintenance; Installation; Troubleshooting.

GOE—Interest Area: 09. Hospitality, Tourism, and Recreation. **Work Group:** 09.03. Hospitality and Travel Services. **Other Jobs in This Work Group:** Baggage Porters and Bellhops; Concierges; Flight Attendants; Hotel, Motel, and Resort Desk Clerks; Maids and Housekeeping Cleaners; Reservation and Transportation Ticket Agents; Tour Guides and

Escorts; Transportation Attendants, Except Flight Attendants and Baggage Porters; Travel Agents; Travel Clerks; Travel Guides. **PERSON-ALITY TYPE**: Realistic. Realistic occupations frequently involve work activities that include practical, hands-on problems and solutions. They often deal with plants, animals, and real-world materials like wood, tools, and machinery. Many of the occupations require working outside and do not involve a lot of paperwork or working closely with others.

EDUCATION/TRAINING PROGRAM(S)— No data available.

WORK ENVIRONMENT—Standing; contaminants; very hot or cold; walking and running; hazardous conditions; spend time bending or twisting the body.

Judges, Magistrate Judges, and Magistrates

- ◉ Education/Training Required: Work experience plus degree
- ◉ Annual Earnings: $97,260
- ◉ Growth: 8.7%
- ◉ Annual Job Openings: 2,000
- ◉ Self-Employed: 0%
- ◉ Part-Time: 6.2%

Age Bracket	Percentage of Workers
45–54 Years Old	27.1%
55–64 Years Old	30.5%
65 or Older	11.9%

Arbitrate, advise, adjudicate, or administer justice in a court of law. May sentence defendant in criminal cases according to government statutes. May determine liability of defendant in civil cases. May issue marriage licenses and perform wedding ceremonies. Instruct juries on applicable laws, direct juries to deduce the facts from the evidence presented, and hear their verdicts. Sentence defendants in criminal cases on conviction by jury according to applicable government statutes. Rule on admissibility of evidence and methods of conducting testimony. Preside over hearings and listen to allegations made by plaintiffs to determine whether the evidence supports the charges. Read documents on pleadings and motions to ascertain facts and issues. Interpret and enforce rules of procedure or establish new rules in situations where there are no procedures already established by law. Monitor proceedings to ensure that all applicable rules and procedures are followed. Advise attorneys, juries, litigants, and court personnel regarding conduct, issues, and proceedings. Research legal issues and write opinions on the issues. Conduct preliminary hearings to decide issues such as whether there is reasonable and probable cause to hold defendants in felony cases. Write decisions on cases. Award compensation for damages to litigants in civil cases in relation to findings by juries or by the court. Settle disputes between opposing attorneys. Supervise other judges, court officers, and the court's administrative staff. Impose restrictions upon parties in civil cases until trials can be held. Rule on custody and access disputes and enforce court orders regarding custody and support of children. Grant divorces and divide assets between spouses. Participate in judicial tribunals to help resolve disputes. **SKILLS**—Judgment and Decision Making; Persuasion; Negotiation; Social Perceptiveness; Critical Thinking; Active Listening; Service Orientation; Management of Personnel Resources.

GOE—**Interest Area:** 12. Law and Public Safety. **Work Group:** 12.02. Legal Practice and Justice Administration. **Other Jobs in This Work Group:** Administrative Law Judges, Adjudicators, and Hearing Officers; Arbitrators, Mediators, and Conciliators; Lawyers. **PERSONALITY TYPE:** Enterprising. Enterprising occupations frequently involve starting up and carrying out projects. These occupations can involve leading people and making many decisions. They sometimes require risk taking and often deal with business.

EDUCATION/TRAINING PROGRAM(S)— Law (LL.B., J.D.); Law, Legal Services, and Legal Studies, Other; Legal Studies, General.

WORK ENVIRONMENT—Sitting; physical proximity to others; indoors; sounds, noise levels are distracting or uncomfortable.

Landscape Architects

- ◎ Education/Training Required: Bachelor's degree
- ◎ Annual Earnings: $54,290
- ◎ Growth: 22.2%
- ◎ Annual Job Openings: 2,000
- ◎ Self-Employed: 23.4%
- ◎ Part-Time: 5.5%

Age Bracket	Percentage of Workers
45–54 Years Old	24.4%
55–64 Years Old	12.8%
65 or Older	3.9%

Plan and design land areas for such projects as parks and other recreational facilities; airports; highways; hospitals; schools; land subdivisions; and commercial, industrial, and residential sites. Prepare site plans, specifications, and cost estimates for land development, coordinating arrangement of existing and proposed land features and structures. Confer with clients, engineering personnel, and architects on overall program. Compile and analyze data on conditions such as location, drainage, and location of structures for environmental reports and landscaping plans. Inspect landscape work to ensure compliance with specifications, approve quality of materials and work, and advise client and construction personnel. **SKILLS**—Operations Analysis; Coordination; Management of Financial Resources; Social Perceptiveness; Persuasion; Complex Problem Solving; Time Management; Mathematics; Instructing.

GOE—**Interest Area:** 02. Architecture and Construction. **Work Group:** 02.02. Architectural Design. **Other Jobs in This Work Group:** Architects, Except Landscape and Naval. **PERSONALITY TYPE:** Artistic. Artistic occupations frequently involve working with forms, designs, and patterns. They often require self-expression, and the work can be done without following a clear set of rules.

EDUCATION/TRAINING PROGRAM(S)— Environmental Design/Architecture; Landscape Architecture (BS, BSLA, BLA, MSLA, MLA, PhD).

WORK ENVIRONMENT—Very hot or cold; in an enclosed vehicle or equipment; outdoors; extremely bright or inadequate lighting; sitting.

Laundry and Drycleaning Machine Operators and Tenders, Except Pressing

- ◎ Education/Training Required:
  Moderate-term on-the-job training
- ◎ Annual Earnings: $17,350
- ◎ Growth: 12.3%
- ◎ Annual Job Openings: 47,000
- ◎ Self-Employed: 6.8%
- ◎ Part-Time: 16.9%

The job openings listed here are shared with Precision Dyers and Spotters, Dry Cleaning.

Age Bracket	Percentage of Workers
45–54 Years Old	25.9%
55–64 Years Old	17.1%
65 or Older	5.2%

Operate or tend washing or dry-cleaning machines to wash or dry-clean commercial, industrial, or household articles, such as cloth garments, suede, leather, furs, blankets, draperies, fine linens, rugs, and carpets. Starts washer, dry cleaner, drier, or extractor and turns valves or levers to regulate and monitor cleaning or drying operations. Loads or directs other workers to load articles into washer or dry-cleaning machine. Starts pumps to operate distilling system that drains and reclaims dry-cleaning solvents. Adjusts switches to tend and regulate equipment that fumigates and removes foreign matter from furs. Cleans machine filters and lubricates equipment. Mends and sews articles, using hand stitching, adhesive patch, or power sewing machine. Hangs curtains, drapes, blankets, pants, and other garments on stretch frames to dry and transports items between specified locations. Irons or presses articles, fabrics, and furs, using hand iron or pressing machine. Receives and marks articles for laundry or drycleaning with identifying code number or name, using hand or machine marker. Sorts and counts articles removed from dryer and folds, wraps, or hangs items for airing out, pickup, or delivery. Examines and sorts articles to be cleaned into lots according to color, fabric, dirt content, and cleaning technique required. Pre-soaks, sterilizes, scrubs, spot-cleans, and dries contaminated or stained articles, using neutralizer solutions and portable machines. Washes, dry-cleans, or glazes delicate articles or fur garment linings by hand, using mild detergent or dry-cleaning solutions. Removes or directs other workers to remove items from washer or dry-cleaning machine and into extractor or tumbler. Tends variety of automatic machines that comb and polish furs; clean, sterilize, and fluff feathers and blankets; and roll and package towels. Mixes and adds detergents, dyes, bleach, starch, and other solutions and chemicals to clean, color, dry, or stiffen articles. **SKILLS**—Operation Monitoring; Equipment Maintenance; Operation and Control; Installation.

GOE—Interest Area: 13. Manufacturing. **Work Group:** 13.11. Apparel, Shoes, Leather, and Fabric Care. **Other Jobs in This Work Group:** Custom Tailors; Fabric Menders, Except Garment; Precision Dyers; Pressers, Delicate Fabrics; Pressers, Hand; Shoe and Leather Workers and Repairers; Shop and Alteration Tailors; Spotters, Dry Cleaning; Upholsterers. **PERSONALITY TYPE:** Realistic. Realistic occupations frequently involve work activities that include practical, hands-on problems and solutions. They often deal with plants, animals, and real-world materials like wood, tools, and machinery. Many of the occupations require working outside and do not involve a lot of paperwork or working closely with others.

EDUCATION/TRAINING PROGRAM(S)— No data available.

WORK ENVIRONMENT—Hazardous equipment; very hot or cold; hazardous conditions; contaminants; standing.

Law Teachers, Postsecondary

- ◎ Education/Training Required: First professional degree
- ◎ Annual Earnings: $89,000
- ◎ Growth: 38.1%
- ◎ Annual Job Openings: 216,000
- ◎ Self-Employed: 0.3%
- ◎ Part-Time: 27.7%

The job openings listed here are shared with all other postsecondary teaching occupations.

Age Bracket	Percentage of Workers
45–54 Years Old	22.8%
55–64 Years Old	19.0%
65 or Older	5.5%

Teach courses in law. Evaluate and grade students' class work, assignments, papers, and oral presentations. Compile, administer, and grade examinations or assign this work to others. Prepare and deliver lectures to undergraduate and/or graduate students on topics such as civil procedure, contracts, and torts. Initiate, facilitate, and moderate classroom discussions. Prepare course materials such as syllabi, homework assignments, and handouts. Keep abreast of developments in their field by reading current

literature, talking with colleagues, and participating in professional conferences. Plan, evaluate, and revise curricula, course content, and course materials and methods of instruction. Maintain regularly scheduled office hours in order to advise and assist students. Conduct research in a particular field of knowledge and publish findings in professional journals, books, and/or electronic media. Advise students on academic and vocational curricula, and on career issues. Supervise undergraduate and/or graduate teaching, internship, and research work. Select and obtain materials and supplies such as textbooks. Maintain student attendance records, grades, and other required records. Serve on academic or administrative committees that deal with institutional policies, departmental matters, and academic issues. Perform administrative duties such as serving as department head. Collaborate with colleagues to address teaching and research issues. Participate in student recruitment, registration, and placement activities. Compile bibliographies of specialized materials for outside reading assignments. Participate in campus and community events. Act as advisers to student organizations. Assign cases for students to hear and try. **SKILLS—**Instructing; Critical Thinking; Persuasion; Reading Comprehension; Writing; Speaking; Learning Strategies; Active Listening.

GOE—Interest Area: 05. Education and Training. **Work Group:** 05.03. Postsecondary and Adult Teaching and Instructing. **Other Jobs in This Work Group:** Adult Literacy, Remedial Education, and GED Teachers and Instructors; Agricultural Sciences Teachers, Postsecondary; Anthropology and Archeology Teachers, Postsecondary; Architecture Teachers, Postsecondary; Area, Ethnic, and Cultural Studies Teachers, Postsecondary; Art, Drama, and Music Teachers, Postsecondary; Atmospheric, Earth,

Marine, and Space Sciences Teachers, Postsecondary; Biological Science Teachers, Postsecondary; Business Teachers, Postsecondary; Chemistry Teachers, Postsecondary; Communications Teachers, Postsecondary; Computer Science Teachers, Postsecondary; Criminal Justice and Law Enforcement Teachers, Postsecondary; Economics Teachers, Postsecondary; Education Teachers, Postsecondary; Engineering Teachers, Postsecondary; English Language and Literature Teachers, Postsecondary; Environmental Science Teachers, Postsecondary; Farm and Home Management Advisors; Foreign Language and Literature Teachers, Postsecondary; Forestry and Conservation Science Teachers, Postsecondary; Geography Teachers, Postsecondary; Graduate Teaching Assistants; Health Specialties Teachers, Postsecondary; History Teachers, Postsecondary; Home Economics Teachers, Postsecondary; Library Science Teachers, Postsecondary; Mathematical Science Teachers, Postsecondary; Nursing Instructors and Teachers, Postsecondary; Philosophy and Religion Teachers, Postsecondary; Physics Teachers, Postsecondary; Political Science Teachers, Postsecondary; Psychology Teachers, Postsecondary; Recreation and Fitness Studies Teachers, Postsecondary; Self-Enrichment Education Teachers; Social Work Teachers, Postsecondary; Sociology Teachers, Postsecondary; Vocational Education Teachers, Postsecondary. **PERSONALITY TYPE:** No data available.

EDUCATION/TRAINING PROGRAM(S)— Law (LL.B., J.D.).

WORK ENVIRONMENT—Sitting; indoors; physical proximity to others; sounds, noise levels are distracting or uncomfortable.

Lawyers

- Education/Training Required: First professional degree
- Annual Earnings: $97,420
- Growth: 17.0%
- Annual Job Openings: 53,000
- Self-Employed: 26.8%
- Part-Time: 6.2%

Age Bracket	Percentage of Workers
45–54 Years Old	26.8%
55–64 Years Old	16.8%
65 or Older	5.0%

Represent clients in criminal and civil litigation and other legal proceedings, draw up legal documents, and manage or advise clients on legal transactions. May specialize in a single area or may practice broadly in many areas of law. Advise clients concerning business transactions, claim liability, advisability of prosecuting or defending lawsuits, or legal rights and obligations. Interpret laws, rulings and regulations for individuals and businesses. Analyze the probable outcomes of cases, using knowledge of legal precedents. Present and summarize cases to judges and juries. Evaluate findings and develop strategies and arguments in preparation for presentation of cases. Gather evidence to formulate defense or to initiate legal actions, by such means as interviewing clients and witnesses to ascertain the facts of a case. Represent clients in court or before government agencies. Examine legal data to determine advisability of defending or prosecuting lawsuit. Select jurors, argue motions, meet with judges and question witnesses during the course of a trial. Present evidence to defend clients or prosecute defendants in criminal or civil litigation. Study Constitution, statutes, decisions, regulations, and ordinances of quasi-judicial bodies to determine ramifications for cases. Prepare and draft legal documents, such as wills, deeds, patent applications, mortgages, leases, and contracts. Prepare legal briefs and opinions, and file appeals in state and federal courts of appeal. Negotiate settlements of civil disputes. Confer with colleagues with specialties in appropriate areas of legal issue to establish and verify bases for legal proceedings. Search for and examine public and other legal records to write opinions or establish ownership. Supervise legal assistants. Perform administrative and management functions related to the practice of law. Act as agent, trustee, guardian, or executor for businesses or individuals. Probate wills and represent and advise executors and administrators of estates. Help develop federal and state programs, draft and interpret laws and legislation, and establish enforcement procedures. Work in environmental law, representing public interest groups, waste disposal companies, or construction firms in their dealings with state and federal agencies. **SKILLS**—Persuasion; Negotiation; Critical Thinking; Writing; Social Perceptiveness; Judgment and Decision Making; Time Management; Speaking; Active Learning.

GOE—**Interest Area:** 12. Law and Public Safety. **Work Group:** 12.02. Legal Practice and Justice Administration. **Other Jobs in This Work Group:** Administrative Law Judges, Adjudicators, and Hearing Officers; Arbitrators, Mediators, and Conciliators; Judges, Magistrate Judges, and Magistrates. **PERSONALITY TYPE:** Enterprising. Enterprising occupations frequently involve starting up and carrying out projects. These occupations can involve leading people and making many decisions. They sometimes require risk taking and often deal with business.

EDUCATION/TRAINING PROGRAM(S)—Advanced Legal Research/Studies, General (LL.M., M.C.L., M.L.I., M.S.L., J.S.D./S.J.D.); American/U.S. Law/Legal Studies/Jurisprudence (LL.M., M.C.J., J.S.D./S.J.D.); Banking, Corporate, Finance, and Securities Law (LL.M., J.S.D./S.J.D.); Canadian Law/Legal Studies/ Jurisprudence (LL.M., M.C.J., J.S.D./S.J.D.); Comparative Law (LL.M., M.C.L., J.S.D./ S.J.D.); Energy, Environment, and Natural Resources Law (LL.M., M.S., J.S.D./S.J.D.); Health Law (LL.M., M.J., J.S.D./S.J.D.); others.

WORK ENVIRONMENT—Sitting; indoors; in an enclosed vehicle or equipment.

Legal Secretaries

- Education/Training Required: Postsecondary vocational training
- Annual Earnings: $37,390
- Growth: 18.8%
- Annual Job Openings: 39,000
- Self-Employed: 1.7%
- Part-Time: 17.5%

Age Bracket	Percentage of Workers
45–54 Years Old	28.6%
55–64 Years Old	16.3%
65 or Older	3.2%

Perform secretarial duties utilizing legal terminology, procedures, and documents. Prepare legal papers and correspondence, such as summonses, complaints, motions, and subpoenas. May also assist with legal research. Prepare and process legal documents and papers, such as summonses, subpoenas, complaints, appeals, motions, and pretrial agreements. Mail, fax, or arrange for delivery of legal correspondence to clients, witnesses, and court officials. Receive and place telephone calls. Schedule and make appointments. Make photocopies of correspondence, document, and other printed matter. Organize and maintain law libraries and document and case files. Assist attorneys in collecting information such as employment, medical, and other records. Attend legal meetings, such as client interviews, hearings, or depositions, and take notes. Draft and type office memos. Review legal publications and perform data base searches to identify laws and court decisions relevant to pending cases. Submit articles and information from searches to attorneys for review and approval for use. Complete various forms, such as accident reports, trial and courtroom requests, and applications for clients. **SKILLS**—Writing; Time Management; Social Perceptiveness; Reading Comprehension; Learning Strategies; Negotiation; Active Listening; Persuasion.

GOE—Interest Area: 04. Business and Administration. **Work Group:** 04.04. Secretarial Support. **Other Jobs in This Work Group:** Executive Secretaries and Administrative Assistants; Medical Secretaries; Secretaries, Except Legal, Medical, and Executive. **PERSONALITY TYPE:** Conventional. Conventional occupations frequently involve following set procedures and routines. These occupations can include working with data and details more than with ideas. Usually there is a clear line of authority to follow.

EDUCATION/TRAINING PROGRAM(S)— Legal Administrative Assistant/Secretary.

WORK ENVIRONMENT—Sitting.

Librarians

- Education/Training Required: Master's degree
- Annual Earnings: $46,940
- Growth: 10.1%
- Annual Job Openings: 15,000
- Self-Employed: 0.1%
- Part-Time: 23.1%

Age Bracket	Percentage of Workers
45–54 Years Old	38.1%
55–64 Years Old	25.3%
65 or Older	3.6%

Administer libraries and perform related library services. Work in a variety of settings, including public libraries, schools, colleges and universities, museums, corporations, government agencies, law firms, non-profit organizations, and healthcare providers. Tasks may include selecting, acquiring, cataloguing, classifying, circulating, and maintaining library materials; and furnishing reference, bibliographical, and readers' advisory services. May perform in-depth, strategic research, and synthesize, analyze, edit, and filter information. May set up or work with databases and information systems to catalogue and access information. Search standard reference materials, including on-line sources and the Internet, in order to answer patrons' reference questions. Analyze patrons' requests to determine needed information, and assist in furnishing or locating that information. Teach library patrons to search for information using databases. Keep records of circulation and materials. Supervise budgeting, planning, and personnel activities. Check books in and out of the library. Explain use of library facilities, resources, equipment, and services, and provide information about library policies. Review and evaluate resource material, such as book reviews and catalogs, in order to select and order print, audiovisual, and electronic resources. Code, classify, and catalog books, publications, films, audiovisual aids, and other library materials based on subject matter or standard library classification systems. Locate unusual or unique information in response to specific requests. Direct and train library staff in duties such as receiving, shelving, researching, cataloging, and equipment use. Respond to customer complaints, taking action as necessary. Organize collections of books, publications, documents, audiovisual aids, and other reference materials for convenient access. Develop library policies and procedures. Evaluate materials to determine outdated or unused items to be discarded. Develop information access aids such as indexes and annotated bibliographies, web pages, electronic pathfinders, and on-line tutorials. Plan and deliver client-centered programs and services such as special services for corporate clients, storytelling for children, newsletters, or programs for special groups. Compile lists of books, periodicals, articles, and audiovisual materials on particular subjects. Arrange for interlibrary loans of materials not available in a particular library. Assemble and arrange display materials. Confer with teachers, parents, and community organizations to develop, plan, and conduct programs in reading, viewing, and communication skills. Compile lists of overdue materials, and notify borrowers that their materials are overdue. **SKILLS**—Learning Strategies; Management of Financial Resources; Service Orientation; Instructing; Persuasion; Management of Material Resources; Social Perceptiveness; Monitoring.

GOE—Interest Area: 05. Education and Training. **Work Group:** 05.04. Library Services.

Other Jobs in This Work Group: Library Assistants, Clerical; Library Technicians. **PERSONALITY TYPE:** Artistic. Artistic occupations frequently involve working with forms, designs, and patterns. They often require self-expression, and the work can be done without following a clear set of rules.

EDUCATION/TRAINING PROGRAM(S)— Library Science, Other; Library Science/ Librarianship; School Librarian/School Library Media Specialist.

WORK ENVIRONMENT—Sitting; physical proximity to others; indoors; sounds, noise levels are distracting or uncomfortable; contaminants.

Library Assistants, Clerical

- Education/Training Required: Short-term on-the-job training
- Annual Earnings: $21,050
- Growth: 21.5%
- Annual Job Openings: 27,000
- Self-Employed: 0.1%
- Part-Time: 50.4%

Age Bracket	Percentage of Workers
45–54 Years Old	25.9%
55–64 Years Old	14.7%
65 or Older	5.2%

Compile records, sort and shelve books, and issue and receive library materials such as pictures, cards, slides and microfilm. Locate library materials for loan and replace material in shelving area, stacks, or files according to identification number and title. Register patrons to

permit them to borrow books, periodicals, and other library materials. Lend and collect books, periodicals, videotapes, and other materials at circulation desks. Enter and update patrons' records on computers. Process new materials including books, audiovisual materials, and computer software. Sort books, publications, and other items according to established procedure and return them to shelves, files, or other designated storage areas. Locate library materials for patrons, including books, periodicals, tape cassettes, Braille volumes, and pictures. Instruct patrons on how to use reference sources, card catalogs, and automated information systems. Inspect returned books for condition and due-date status, and compute any applicable fines. Answer routine inquiries, and refer patrons in need of professional assistance to librarians. Maintain records of items received, stored, issued, and returned, and file catalog cards according to system used. Perform clerical activities such as filing, typing, word processing, photocopying and mailing out material, and mail sorting. Provide assistance to librarians in the maintenance of collections of books, periodicals, magazines, newspapers, and audiovisual and other materials. Take action to deal with disruptive or problem patrons. Classify and catalog items according to content and purpose. Register new patrons and issue borrower identification cards that permit patrons to borrow books and other materials. Send out notices and accept fine payments for lost or overdue books. Operate small branch libraries, under the direction of off-site librarian supervisors. Prepare, store, and retrieve classification and catalog information, lecture notes, or other information related to stored documents, using computers. Schedule and supervise clerical workers, volunteers, and student assistants. Operate and maintain audiovisual equipment. Review records, such as microfilm and issue cards, in order to identify titles of overdue materials and delinquent borrowers. Select substitute titles when requested materials are unavailable following criteria such as age, education, and interests. Repair books, using mending tape, paste, and brushes. **SKILLS—** Service Orientation; Reading Comprehension; Instructing; Active Listening; Learning Strategies; Social Perceptiveness; Time Management; Writing.

GOE—Interest Area: 05. Education and Training. **Work Group:** 05.04. Library Services. **Other Jobs in This Work Group:** Librarians; Library Technicians. **PERSONALITY TYPE:** Conventional. Conventional occupations frequently involve following set procedures and routines. These occupations can include working with data and details more than with ideas. Usually there is a clear line of authority to follow.

EDUCATION/TRAINING PROGRAM(S)— Library Assistant.

WORK ENVIRONMENT—Physical proximity to others; sitting; contaminants; sounds, noise levels are distracting or uncomfortable.

Library Science Teachers, Postsecondary

- Education/Training Required: Master's degree
- Annual Earnings: $52,490
- Growth: 38.1%
- Annual Job Openings: 216,000
- Self-Employed: 0.3%
- Part-Time: 27.7%

The job openings listed here are shared with all other postsecondary teaching occupations.

Age Bracket	Percentage of Workers
45–54 Years Old	22.8%
55–64 Years Old	19.0%
65 or Older	5.5%

Teach courses in library science. Prepare course materials such as syllabi, homework assignments, and handouts. Prepare and deliver lectures to undergraduate and/or graduate students on topics such as collection development, archival methods, and indexing and abstracting. Evaluate and grade students' class work, assignments, and papers. Keep abreast of developments in their field by reading current literature, talking with colleagues, and participating in professional conferences. Initiate, facilitate, and moderate classroom discussions. Plan, evaluate, and revise curricula, course content, and course materials and methods of instruction. Conduct research in a particular field of knowledge and publish findings in professional journals, books, and/or electronic media. Maintain student attendance records, grades, and other required records. Collaborate with colleagues to address teaching and research issues. Advise students on academic and vocational curricula, and on career issues. Compile, administer, and grade examinations or assign this work to others. Supervise undergraduate and/or graduate teaching, internship, and research work. Maintain regularly scheduled office hours in order to advise and assist students. Write grant proposals to procure external research funding. Select and obtain materials and supplies such as textbooks. Serve on academic or administrative committees that deal with institutional policies, departmental matters, and academic issues. Participate in student recruitment, registration, and placement activities. Compile bibliographies of specialized materials for outside reading assignments. Perform administrative duties such as serving as

department head. **SKILLS**—Instructing; Learning Strategies; Writing; Active Learning; Service Orientation; Persuasion; Reading Comprehension; Social Perceptiveness.

GOE—Interest Area: 05. Education and Training. **Work Group:** 05.03. Postsecondary and Adult Teaching and Instructing. **Other Jobs in This Work Group:** Adult Literacy, Remedial Education, and GED Teachers and Instructors; Agricultural Sciences Teachers, Postsecondary; Anthropology and Archeology Teachers, Postsecondary; Architecture Teachers, Postsecondary; Area, Ethnic, and Cultural Studies Teachers, Postsecondary; Art, Drama, and Music Teachers, Postsecondary; Atmospheric, Earth, Marine, and Space Sciences Teachers, Postsecondary; Biological Science Teachers, Postsecondary; Business Teachers, Postsecondary; Chemistry Teachers, Postsecondary; Communications Teachers, Postsecondary; Computer Science Teachers, Postsecondary; Criminal Justice and Law Enforcement Teachers, Postsecondary; Economics Teachers, Postsecondary; Education Teachers, Postsecondary; Engineering Teachers, Postsecondary; English Language and Literature Teachers, Postsecondary; Environmental Science Teachers, Postsecondary; Farm and Home Management Advisors; Foreign Language and Literature Teachers, Postsecondary; Forestry and Conservation Science Teachers, Postsecondary; Geography Teachers, Postsecondary; Graduate Teaching Assistants; Health Specialties Teachers, Postsecondary; History Teachers, Postsecondary; Home Economics Teachers, Postsecondary; Law Teachers, Postsecondary; Mathematical Science Teachers, Postsecondary; Nursing Instructors and Teachers, Postsecondary; Philosophy and Religion Teachers, Postsecondary; Physics Teachers, Postsecondary; Political Science Teachers, Postsecondary; Psychology Teachers, Postsecondary; Recreation and Fitness Studies

Teachers, Postsecondary; Self-Enrichment Education Teachers; Social Work Teachers, Postsecondary; Sociology Teachers, Postsecondary; Vocational Education Teachers, Postsecondary. **PERSONALITY TYPE:** No data available.

EDUCATION/TRAINING PROGRAM(S)— Library Science/Librarianship; Teacher Education and Professional Development, Specific Subject Areas, Other.

WORK ENVIRONMENT—Sitting; indoors; physical proximity to others; sounds, noise levels are distracting or uncomfortable.

License Clerks

- Education/Training Required: Short-term on-the-job training
- Annual Earnings: $28,980
- Growth: 12.3%
- Annual Job Openings: 14,000
- Self-Employed: 2.6%
- Part-Time: 8.3%

The job openings listed here are shared with Court Clerks and Municipal Clerks.

Age Bracket	Percentage of Workers
45–54 Years Old	25.8%
55–64 Years Old	13.5%
65 or Older	2.2%

Issue licenses or permits to qualified applicants. Obtain necessary information; record data; advise applicants on requirements; collect fees; and issue licenses. May conduct oral, written, visual, or performance testing. Answer questions and provide advice to the public regarding licensing policies, procedures, and reg-ulations. Assemble photographs with printed license information in order to produce completed documents. Collect prescribed fees for licenses. Conduct and score oral, visual, written, or performance tests to determine applicant qualifications, and notify applicants of their scores. Evaluate information on applications to verify completeness and accuracy and to determine whether applicants are qualified to obtain desired licenses. Instruct customers in the completion of drivers' license application forms and other forms such as voter registration cards and organ donor forms. Maintain records of applications made and licensing fees collected. Operate specialized photographic equipment in order to obtain photographs for drivers' licenses and photo identification cards. Perform routine data entry and other office support activities including creating, sorting, photocopying, distributing, and filing documents. Question applicants to obtain required information, such as name, address, and age, and record data on prescribed forms. Stock counters with adequate supplies of forms, film, licenses, and other required materials. Update operational records and licensing information, using computer terminals. Code information on license applications for entry into computers. Inform customers by mail or telephone of additional steps they need to take to obtain licenses. Perform record checks on past and current licensees, as required by investigations. Prepare bank deposits, and take them to banks. Prepare lists of overdue accounts, license suspensions and issuances. Train other workers, and coordinate their work as necessary. Send by mail drivers' licenses to out-of-county or out-of-state applicants. Enforce canine licensing regulations, contacting non-compliant owners in person or by mail to inform them of the required regulations and potential enforcement actions. Perform driver education program enrollments for participating schools. Provide assistance in the preparation of insurance examinations covering a variety of types of insurance. SKILLS—Speaking.

GOE—Interest Area: 07. Government and Public Administration. Work Group: 07.04. Public Administration Clerical Support. Other Jobs in This Work Group: Court Clerks; Court Reporters; Municipal Clerks. PERSONALITY TYPE: Conventional. Conventional occupations frequently involve following set procedures and routines. These occupations can include working with data and details more than with ideas. Usually there is a clear line of authority to follow.

EDUCATION/TRAINING PROGRAM(S)—General Office Occupations and Clerical Services.

WORK ENVIRONMENT—Sitting; standing; indoors; disease or infections; spend time bending or twisting the body.

Licensed Practical and Licensed Vocational Nurses

- Education/Training Required: Postsecondary vocational training
- Annual Earnings: $34,650
- Growth: 20.2%
- Annual Job Openings: 105,000
- Self-Employed: 0.6%
- Part-Time: 19.1%

Age Bracket	Percentage of Workers
45–54 Years Old	30.5%
55–64 Years Old	13.2%
65 or Older	2.4%

Care for ill, injured, convalescent, or disabled persons in hospitals, nursing homes, clinics, private homes, group homes, and similar institutions. May work under the supervision of a registered nurse. Licensing required. Observe patients, charting and reporting changes in patients' conditions, such as adverse reactions to medication or treatment, and taking any necessary action. Administer prescribed medications or start intravenous fluids, and note times and amounts on patients' charts. Answer patients' calls and determine how to assist them. Measure and record patients' vital signs, such as height, weight, temperature, blood pressure, pulse and respiration. Provide basic patient care and treatments, such as taking temperatures and blood pressure, dressing wounds, treating bedsores, giving enemas, douches, alcohol rubs, and massages, or performing catheterizations. Help patients with bathing, dressing, personal hygiene, moving in bed, and standing and walking. Supervise nurses' aides and assistants. Work as part of a health care team to assess patient needs, plan and modify care and implement interventions. Record food and fluid intake and output. Evaluate nursing intervention outcomes, conferring with other health-care team members as necessary. Assemble and use equipment such as catheters, tracheotomy tubes, and oxygen suppliers. Collect samples such as blood, urine and sputum from patients, and perform routine laboratory tests on samples. Prepare patients for examinations, tests and treatments and explain procedures. Prepare food trays and examine them for conformance to prescribed diet. Apply compresses, ice bags, and hot water bottles. Clean rooms and make beds. Inventory and requisition supplies and instruments. Provide medical treatment and personal care to patients in private home settings, such as cooking, keeping rooms orderly, seeing that patients are comfortable and in good spirits, and instructing family members in simple nursing tasks. Sterilize equipment and supplies, using germicides, sterilizer, or autoclave. Assist in delivery, care, and feeding of infants. Wash and dress bodies of deceased persons. Make appointments, keep records and perform other clerical duties in doctors' offices and clinics. Set up equipment and prepare medical treatment rooms. **SKILLS**—Service Orientation; Science; Active Listening; Judgment and Decision Making; Time Management; Instructing; Operation Monitoring; Management of Personnel Resources.

GOE—Interest Area: 08. Health Science. **Work Group:** 08.08. Patient Care and Assistance. **Other Jobs in This Work Group:** Home Health Aides; Nursing Aides, Orderlies, and Attendants; Psychiatric Aides; Psychiatric Technicians. **PERSONALITY TYPE:** Social. Social occupations frequently involve working with, communicating with, and teaching people. These occupations often involve helping or providing service to others.

EDUCATION/TRAINING PROGRAM(S)— Licensed Practical Nurse Training (LPN, Cert, Dipl, AAS).

WORK ENVIRONMENT—Disease or infections; physical proximity to others; walking and running; sounds, noise levels are distracting or uncomfortable; sitting.

Licensing Examiners and Inspectors

- Education/Training Required: Long-term on-the-job training
- Annual Earnings: $48,530
- Growth: 9.8%
- Annual Job Openings: 20,000
- Self-Employed: 0.9%
- Part-Time: 5.3%

The job openings listed here are shared with Coroners, Environmental Compliance Inspectors, Equal Opportunity Representatives and Officers, Government Property Inspectors and Investigators, and Pressure Vessel Inspectors.

Age Bracket	Percentage of Workers
45–54 Years Old	40.5%
55–64 Years Old	15.1%
65 or Older	0.8%

Examine, evaluate, and investigate eligibility for, conformity with, or liability under licenses or permits. Administer oral, written, road, or flight tests to license applicants. Advise licensees and other individuals or groups concerning licensing, permit, or passport regulations. Evaluate applications, records, and documents in order to gather information about eligibility or liability issues. Issue licenses to individuals meeting standards. Prepare correspondence to inform concerned parties of licensing decisions and of appeals processes. Prepare reports of activities, evaluations, recommendations, and decisions. Report law or regulation violations to appropriate boards and agencies. Score tests and observe equipment operation and control in order to rate ability of applicants. Confer with and interview officials, technical or professional specialists, and applicants, in order to obtain information or to clarify facts relevant to licensing decisions. Visit establishments to verify that valid licenses and permits are displayed, and that licensing standards are being upheld. Warn violators of infractions or penalties. **SKILLS**—Speaking; Active Listening; Writing; Monitoring; Reading Comprehension; Judgment and Decision Making; Mathematics; Critical Thinking; Quality Control Analysis.

GOE—Interest Area: 07. Government and Public Administration. **Work Group:** 07.03. Regulations Enforcement. **Other Jobs in This Work Group:** Agricultural Inspectors; Aviation Inspectors; Child Support, Missing Persons, and Unemployment Insurance Fraud Investigators; Environmental Compliance Inspectors; Equal Opportunity Representatives and Officers; Financial Examiners; Fire Inspectors; Fish and Game Wardens; Forest Fire Inspectors and Prevention Specialists; Government Property Inspectors and Investigators; Immigration and Customs Inspectors; Marine Cargo Inspectors; Mechanical Inspectors; Motor Vehicle Inspectors; Nuclear Monitoring Technicians; Occupational Health and Safety Specialists; Pressure Vessel Inspectors; Railroad Inspectors; Tax Examiners, Collectors, and Revenue Agents. **PERSONALITY TYPE:** Conventional. Conventional occupations frequently involve following set procedures and routines. These occupations can include working with data and details more than with ideas. Usually there is a clear line of authority to follow.

EDUCATION/TRAINING PROGRAM(S)— No data available.

WORK ENVIRONMENT—Sitting; outdoors; walking and running; standing; very hot or cold.

Locksmiths and Safe Repairers

- Education/Training Required: Moderate-term on-the-job training
- Annual Earnings: $30,580
- Growth: 21.0%
- Annual Job Openings: 3,000
- Self-Employed: 16.8%
- Part-Time: 6.9%

Age Bracket	Percentage of Workers
45–54 Years Old	30.4%
55–64 Years Old	13.0%
65 or Older	4.3%

Repair and open locks; make keys; change locks and safe combinations; and install and repair safes. Cut new or duplicate keys, using keycutting machines. Keep records of company locks and keys. Insert new or repaired tumblers into locks in order to change combinations. Move picklocks in cylinders in order to open door locks without keys. Disassemble mechanical or electrical locking devices, and repair or replace worn tumblers, springs, and other parts, using hand tools. Repair and adjust safes, vault doors, and vault components, using hand tools, lathes, drill presses, and welding and acetylene cutting apparatus. Install safes, vault doors, and deposit boxes according to blueprints, using equipment such as powered drills, taps, dies, truck cranes, and dollies. Open safe locks by drilling. **SKILLS**—Installation; Repairing; Equipment Maintenance; Troubleshooting; Service Orientation; Equipment Selection; Technology Design; Management of Material Resources.

GOE—Interest Area: 13. Manufacturing. **Work Group:** 13.13. Machinery Repair. **Other Jobs in This Work Group:** Bicycle Repairers; Gas

Appliance Repairers; Hand and Portable Power Tool Repairers; Industrial Machinery Mechanics; Maintenance Workers, Machinery; Mechanical Door Repairers; Millwrights; Signal and Track Switch Repairers; Valve and Regulator Repairers. **PERSONALITY TYPE:** Realistic. Realistic occupations frequently involve work activities that include practical, hands-on problems and solutions. They often deal with plants, animals, and real-world materials like wood, tools, and machinery. Many of the occupations require working outside and do not involve a lot of paperwork or working closely with others.

EDUCATION/TRAINING PROGRAM(S)— Locksmithing and Safe Repair.

WORK ENVIRONMENT—Extremely bright or inadequate lighting; outdoors; outdoors, under cover; very hot or cold; in an enclosed vehicle or equipment; sounds, noise levels are distracting or uncomfortable.

Lodging Managers

- ◎ Education/Training Required: Work experience in a related occupation
- ◎ Annual Earnings: $39,100
- ◎ Growth: 6.6%
- ◎ Annual Job Openings: 10,000
- ◎ Self-Employed: 50.3%
- ◎ Part-Time: 7.2%

Age Bracket	Percentage of Workers
45–54 Years Old	22.5%
55–64 Years Old	17.5%
65 or Older	9.4%

Plan, direct, or coordinate activities of an organization or department that provides lodg- ing and other accommodations. Greet and register guests. Answer inquiries pertaining to hotel policies and services, and resolve occupants' complaints. Assign duties to workers, and schedule shifts. Coordinate front-office activities of hotels or motels, and resolve problems. Participate in financial activities such as the setting of room rates, the establishment of budgets, and the allocation of funds to departments. Confer and cooperate with other managers in order to ensure coordination of hotel activities. Collect payments, and record data pertaining to funds and expenditures. Manage and maintain temporary or permanent lodging facilities. Observe and monitor staff performance in order to ensure efficient operations and adherence to facility's policies and procedures. Train staff members in their duties. Show, rent, or assign accommodations. Develop and implement policies and procedures for the operation of a department or establishment. Inspect guest rooms, public areas, and grounds for cleanliness and appearance. Prepare required paperwork pertaining to departmental functions. Interview and hire applicants. Purchase supplies, and arrange for outside services, such as deliveries, laundry, maintenance and repair, and trash collection. Arrange telephone answering services, deliver mail and packages, and answer questions regarding locations for eating and entertainment. Perform marketing and public relations activities. Organize and coordinate the work of staff and convention personnel for meetings to be held at a particular facility. Receive and process advance registration payments, send out letters of confirmation, and return checks when registrations cannot be accepted. Meet with clients in order to schedule and plan details of conventions, banquets, receptions and other functions. Provide assistance to staff members by performing activities such as inspecting rooms, setting tables and doing laundry. **SKILLS—** Management of Financial Resources; Social Perceptiveness; Negotiation; Management of Material Resources; Management of Personnel Resources; Monitoring; Persuasion; Time Management.

GOE—Interest Area: 09. Hospitality, Tourism, and Recreation. **Work Group:** 09.01. Managerial Work in Hospitality and Tourism. **Other Jobs in This Work Group:** First-Line Supervisors/Managers of Food Preparation and Serving Workers; First-Line Supervisors/ Managers of Personal Service Workers; Food Service Managers; Gaming Managers; Gaming Supervisors. **PERSONALITY TYPE:** Enterprising. Enterprising occupations frequently involve starting up and carrying out projects. These occupations can involve leading people and making many decisions. They sometimes require risk taking and often deal with business.

EDUCATION/TRAINING PROGRAM(S)— Hospitality Administration/Management, General; Hospitality and Recreation Marketing Operations; Hotel/Motel Administration/ Management; Resort Management; Selling Skills and Sales Operations.

WORK ENVIRONMENT—Physical proximity to others; sitting; indoors; very hot or cold; sounds, noise levels are distracting or uncomfortable.

Logisticians

- Education/Training Required: Bachelor's degree
- Annual Earnings: $59,460
- Growth: 27.5%
- Annual Job Openings: 162,000
- Self-Employed: No data available
- Part-Time: 7.4%

Age Bracket	Percentage of Workers
45–54 Years Old	26.5%
55–64 Years Old	11.8%
65 or Older	5.9%

Analyze and coordinate the logistical functions of a firm or organization. Responsible for the entire life cycle of a product, including acquisition, distribution, internal allocation, delivery, and final disposal of resources. Develop and implement technical project management tools such as plans, schedules, and responsibility and compliance matrices. Develop proposals that include documentation for estimates. Direct and support the compilation and analysis of technical source data necessary for product development. Direct availability and allocation of materials, supplies, and finished products. Direct team activities, establishing task priorities, scheduling and tracking work assignments, providing guidance, and ensuring the availability of resources. Manage the logistical aspects of product life cycles, including coordination or provisioning of samples, and the minimization of obsolescence. Participate in the assessment and review of design alternatives and design change proposal impacts. Perform system life-cycle cost analysis, and develop component studies. Plan, organize, and execute logistics support activities such as maintenance planning, repair analysis, and test equipment recommendations. Provide project management services, including the provision and analysis of technical data. Redesign the movement of goods in order to maximize value and minimize costs. Report project plans, progress, and results. Stay informed of logistics technology advances, and apply appropriate technology in order to improve logistics processes. Collaborate with other departments as necessary to meet customer requirements, to take advantage of sales opportunities or, in the case of shortages, to minimize negative impacts on a business. Develop an understanding of customers' needs, and take actions to ensure that such needs are met. Explain proposed solutions to customers, management, or other interested parties through written proposals and oral presentations. Maintain and develop positive business relationships with a customer's key personnel involved in or directly relevant to a logistics activity. Manage subcontractor activities, reviewing proposals, developing performance specifications, and serving as liaisons between subcontractors and organizations. Protect and control proprietary materials. Review logistics performance with customers against targets, benchmarks and service agreements. **SKILLS**—No data available.

GOE—Interest Area: 04. Business and Administration. **Work Group:** 04.05. Accounting, Auditing, and Analytical Support. **Other Jobs in This Work Group:** Accountants; Auditors; Budget Analysts; Industrial Engineering Technicians; Management Analysts; Operations Research Analysts. **PERSONALITY TYPE:** No data available.

EDUCATION/TRAINING PROGRAM(S)— Logistics and Materials Management; Operations Management and Supervision; Transportation/Transportation Management.

WORK ENVIRONMENT—No data available.

Machinists

- Education/Training Required: Long-term on-the-job training
- Annual Earnings: $34,090
- Growth: 8.2%
- Annual Job Openings: 30,000
- Self-Employed: 2.7%
- Part-Time: 2.1%

Age Bracket	Percentage of Workers
45–54 Years Old	28.6%
55–64 Years Old	14.8%
65 or Older	1.5%

Set up and operate a variety of machine tools to produce precision parts and instruments. Includes precision instrument makers who fabricate, modify, or repair mechanical instruments. May also fabricate and modify parts to make or repair machine tools or maintain industrial machines, applying knowledge of mechanics, shop mathematics, metal properties, layout, and machining procedures. Calculate dimensions and tolerances using knowledge of mathematics and instruments such as micrometers and vernier calipers. Machine parts to specifications using machine tools such as lathes, milling machines, shapers, or grinders. Measure, examine, and test completed units in order to detect defects and ensure conformance to specifications, using precision instruments such as micrometers. Set up, adjust, and operate all of the basic machine tools and many specialized or advanced variation tools in order to perform precision machining operations. Align and secure holding fixtures, cutting tools, attachments, accessories, and materials onto machines. Monitor the feed and speed of machines during the machining process. Study sample parts, blueprints, drawings, and engineering information in order to determine methods and sequences of operations needed to fabricate products, and determine product dimensions and tolerances. Select the appropriate tools, machines, and materials to be used in preparation of machinery work. Lay out, measure, and mark metal stock in order to display placement of cuts. Observe and listen to operating machines or equipment in order to diagnose machine malfunctions and to determine need for adjustments or repairs. Check workpieces to ensure that they are properly lubricated and cooled. Maintain industrial machines, applying knowledge of mechanics, shop mathematics, metal properties, layout, and machining procedures. Position and fasten workpieces. Operate equipment to verify operational efficiency. Install repaired parts into equipment, or install new equipment. Clean and lubricate machines, tools, and equipment in order to remove grease, rust, stains, and foreign matter. Advise clients about the materials being used for finished products. Program computers and electronic instruments such as numerically controlled machine tools. Set controls to regulate machining, or enter commands to retrieve, input, or edit computerized machine control media. Confer with engineering, supervisory, and manufacturing personnel in order to exchange technical information. **SKILLS**—Operation Monitoring; Operation and Control; Equipment Maintenance; Quality Control Analysis; Installation; Troubleshooting; Equipment Selection; Repairing.

GOE—Interest Area: 13. Manufacturing. **Work Group:** 13.05. Production Machining

Technology. **Other Jobs in This Work Group:** Foundry Mold and Coremakers; Lay-Out Workers, Metal and Plastic; Model Makers, Metal and Plastic; Numerical Control Machine Tool Operators and Tenders, Metal and Plastic; Numerical Tool and Process Control Programmers; Patternmakers, Metal and Plastic; Tool and Die Makers; Tool Grinders, Filers, and Sharpeners. **PERSONALITY TYPE:** Realistic. Realistic occupations frequently involve work activities that include practical, hands-on problems and solutions. They often deal with plants, animals, and real-world materials like wood, tools, and machinery. Many of the occupations require working outside and do not involve a lot of paperwork or working closely with others.

EDUCATION/TRAINING PROGRAM(S)—Machine Shop Technology/Assistant; Machine Tool Technology/Machinist.

WORK ENVIRONMENT—Sounds, noise levels are distracting or uncomfortable; hazardous equipment; indoors, not environmentally controlled; contaminants; minor burns, cuts, bites, or stings.

Maids and Housekeeping Cleaners

- Education/Training Required: Short-term on-the-job training
- Annual Earnings: $17,000
- Growth: 9.2%
- Annual Job Openings: 352,000
- Self-Employed: 9.0%
- Part-Time: 31.9%

Age Bracket	Percentage of Workers
45–54 Years Old	23.9%
55–64 Years Old	14.1%
65 or Older	4.6%

Perform any combination of light cleaning duties to maintain private households or commercial establishments, such as hotels, restaurants, and hospitals, in a clean and orderly manner. Duties include making beds, replenishing linens, cleaning rooms and halls, and vacuuming. Move and arrange furniture, and turn mattresses. Observe precautions required to protect hotel and guest property, and report damage, theft, and found articles to supervisors. Plan menus, and cook and serve meals and refreshments following employer's instructions or own methods. Prepare rooms for meetings, and arrange decorations, media equipment, and furniture for social or business functions. Take care of pets by grooming, exercising, and/or feeding them. Wash dishes and clean kitchens, cooking utensils, and silverware. Answer telephones and doorbells. Care for children and/or elderly persons by overseeing their activities, providing companionship, and assisting them with dressing, bathing, eating, and other needs. Carry linens, towels, toilet items, and cleaning supplies, using wheeled carts. Purchase or order groceries and household supplies to keep kitchens stocked, and record expenditures. Run errands such as taking laundry to the cleaners and buying groceries. Clean rooms, hallways, lobbies, lounges, restrooms, corridors, elevators, stairways, locker rooms and other work areas so that health standards are met. Clean rugs, carpets, upholstered furniture, and/or draperies, using vacuum cleaners and/or shampooers. Empty wastebaskets, empty and clean ashtrays, and transport other trash and waste to disposal areas. Sweep, scrub, wax, and/or polish floors, using brooms, mops, and/or powered scrubbing and waxing machines. Dust and polish furniture and equipment. Keep storage areas and carts well-stocked, clean, and tidy. Polish silver accessories and metalwork such as fixtures and fittings. Remove debris from driveways, garages, and swimming pool areas. Replace light bulbs. Replenish supplies such as drinking glasses, linens, writing supplies, and bathroom items. Sort clothing and other articles, load washing machines, and iron and fold dried items. Sort, count, and mark clean linens, and store them in linen closets. Wash windows, walls, ceilings, and woodwork, waxing and polishing as necessary. Assign duties to other staff and give instructions regarding work methods and routines. **SKILLS**—None met the criteria.

GOE—Interest Area: 09. Hospitality, Tourism, and Recreation. **Work Group:** 09.03. Hospitality and Travel Services. **Other Jobs in This Work Group:** Baggage Porters and Bellhops; Concierges; Flight Attendants; Hotel, Motel, and Resort Desk Clerks; Janitors and Cleaners, Except Maids and Housekeeping Cleaners; Reservation and Transportation Ticket Agents; Tour Guides and Escorts; Transportation Attendants, Except Flight Attendants and Baggage Porters; Travel Agents; Travel Clerks; Travel Guides. **PERSONALITY TYPE:** Realistic. Realistic occupations frequently involve work activities that include practical, hands-on problems and solutions. They often deal with plants, animals, and real-world materials like wood, tools, and machinery. Many of the occupations require working outside and do not involve a lot of paperwork or working closely with others.

EDUCATION/TRAINING PROGRAM(S)— No data available.

M

WORK ENVIRONMENT—Standing; walking and running; spend time kneeling, crouching, stooping, or crawling; spend time making repetitive motions; spend time bending or twisting the body.

Maintenance and Repair Workers, General

- Education/Training Required: Moderate-term on-the-job training
- Annual Earnings: $30,930
- Growth: 16.3%
- Annual Job Openings: 155,000
- Self-Employed: 0.9%
- Part-Time: 4.5%

The job openings listed here are shared with Refractory Materials Repairers, Except Brickmasons.

Age Bracket	Percentage of Workers
45–54 Years Old	29.1%
55–64 Years Old	12.3%
65 or Older	5.5%

Perform work involving the skills of two or more maintenance or craft occupations to keep machines, mechanical equipment, or the structure of an establishment in repair. Duties may involve pipe fitting; boiler making; insulating; welding; machining; carpentry; repairing electrical or mechanical equipment; installing, aligning, and balancing new equipment; and repairing buildings, floors, or stairs. Repair or replace defective equipment parts using hand tools and power tools, and reassemble equipment. Perform routine preventive maintenance to ensure that machines continue to run smoothly, building systems operate efficiently, and the physical condition of buildings does not deteriorate. Inspect drives, motors, and belts, check fluid levels, replace filters, and perform other maintenance actions, following checklists. Use tools ranging from common hand and power tools, such as hammers, hoists, saws, drills, and wrenches, to precision measuring instruments and electrical and electronic testing devices. Assemble, install and/or repair wiring, electrical and electronic components, pipe systems and plumbing, machinery, and equipment. Diagnose mechanical problems and determine how to correct them, checking blueprints, repair manuals, and parts catalogs as necessary. Inspect, operate, and test machinery and equipment in order to diagnose machine malfunctions. Record maintenance and repair work performed and the costs of the work. Clean and lubricate shafts, bearings, gears, and other parts of machinery. Dismantle devices to gain access to and remove defective parts, using hoists, cranes, hand tools, and power tools. Plan and lay out repair work using diagrams, drawings, blueprints, maintenance manuals, and schematic diagrams. Order parts, supplies, and equipment from catalogs and suppliers, or obtain them from storerooms. Adjust functional parts of devices and control instruments, using hand tools, levels, plumb bobs, and straightedges. Paint and repair roofs, windows, doors, floors, woodwork, plaster, drywall, and other parts of building structures. Operate cutting torches or welding equipment to cut or join metal parts. Align and balance new equipment after installation. Inspect used parts to determine changes in dimensional requirements, using rules, calipers, micrometers, and other measuring instruments. Set up and operate machine tools to repair or fabricate machine parts, jigs and fixtures, and tools. Maintain and repair specialized equipment and machinery found in cafeterias, laundries, hospitals, stores, offices, and factories. **SKILLS**—Equipment

Maintenance; Installation; Repairing; Troubleshooting; Operation Monitoring; Equipment Selection; Operation and Control; Critical Thinking.

GOE—Interest Area: 02. Architecture and Construction. **Work Group:** 02.05. Systems and Equipment Installation, Maintenance, and Repair. **Other Jobs in This Work Group:** Central Office and PBX Installers and Repairers; Communication Equipment Mechanics, Installers, and Repairers; Electric Meter Installers and Repairers; Electrical and Electronics Repairers, Powerhouse, Substation, and Relay; Electrical Power-Line Installers and Repairers; Elevator Installers and Repairers; Frame Wirers, Central Office; Heating and Air Conditioning Mechanics; Home Appliance Installers; Meter Mechanics; Refrigeration Mechanics; Station Installers and Repairers, Telephone; Telecommunications Facility Examiners; Telecommunications Line Installers and Repairers. **PERSONALITY TYPE:** Realistic. Realistic occupations frequently involve work activities that include practical, hands-on problems and solutions. They often deal with plants, animals, and real-world materials like wood, tools, and machinery. Many of the occupations require working outside and do not involve a lot of paperwork or working closely with others.

EDUCATION/TRAINING PROGRAM(S)— Building/Construction Site Management/ Manager.

WORK ENVIRONMENT—Very hot or cold; minor burns, cuts, bites, or stings; contaminants; sounds, noise levels are distracting or uncomfortable; extremely bright or inadequate lighting.

Management Analysts

- Education/Training Required: Work experience plus degree
- Annual Earnings: $64,560
- Growth: 30.4%
- Annual Job Openings: 78,000
- Self-Employed: 29.8%
- Part-Time: 14.0%

Age Bracket	Percentage of Workers
45–54 Years Old	23.8%
55–64 Years Old	20.7%
65 or Older	6.8%

Conduct organizational studies and evaluations, design systems and procedures, conduct work simplifications and measurement studies, and prepare operations and procedures manuals to assist management in operating more efficiently and effectively. Includes program analysts and management consultants. Review forms and reports, and confer with management and users about format, distribution, and purpose, and to identify problems and improvements. Develop and implement records management program for filing, protection, and retrieval of records, and assure compliance with program. Interview personnel and conduct on-site observation to ascertain unit functions, work performed, and methods, equipment, and personnel used. Prepare manuals and train workers in use of new forms, reports, procedures or equipment, according to organizational policy. Design, evaluate, recommend, and approve changes of forms and reports. Recommend purchase of storage equipment, and design area layout to locate equipment in space available. Plan study of work problems and procedures, such as organizational change, communications, information flow, integrated production methods,

M

inventory control, or cost analysis. Gather and organize information on problems or procedures. Analyze data gathered and develop solutions or alternative methods of proceeding. Document findings of study and prepare recommendations for implementation of new systems, procedures, or organizational changes. Confer with personnel concerned to ensure successful functioning of newly implemented systems or procedures. **SKILLS**—Systems Evaluation; Systems Analysis; Management of Personnel Resources; Management of Material Resources; Operations Analysis; Judgment and Decision Making; Complex Problem Solving; Writing; Monitoring.

GOE—Interest Area: 04. Business and Administration. **Work Group:** 04.05. Accounting, Auditing, and Analytical Support. **Other Jobs in This Work Group:** Accountants; Auditors; Budget Analysts; Industrial Engineering Technicians; Logisticians; Operations Research Analysts. **PERSONALITY TYPE:** Enterprising. Enterprising occupations frequently involve starting up and carrying out projects. These occupations can involve leading people and making many decisions. They sometimes require risk taking and often deal with business.

EDUCATION/TRAINING PROGRAM(S)— Business Administration/Management; Business/Commerce, General.

WORK ENVIRONMENT—Sitting; indoors; walking and running.

Marine Cargo Inspectors

- Education/Training Required: Work experience in a related occupation
- Annual Earnings: $47,920
- Growth: 7.7%
- Annual Job Openings: 5,000
- Self-Employed: 0.4%
- Part-Time: 3.2%

The job openings listed here are shared with Aviation Inspectors, Freight Inspectors, Motor Vehicle Inspectors, Public Transportation Inspectors, and Railroad Inspectors.

Age Bracket	Percentage of Workers
45–54 Years Old	54.3%
55–64 Years Old	15.2%
65 or Older	2.2%

Inspect cargoes of seagoing vessels to certify compliance with health and safety regulations in cargo handling and stowage. Inspects loaded cargo in holds and cargo handling devices to determine compliance with regulations and need for maintenance. Reads vessel documents to ascertain cargo capabilities according to design and cargo regulations. Calculates gross and net tonnage, hold capacities, volume of stored fuel and water, cargo weight, and ship stability factors, using mathematical formulas. Determines type of license and safety equipment required, and computes applicable tolls and wharfage fees. Examines blueprints of ship and takes physical measurements to determine capacity and depth of vessel in water, using measuring instruments. Writes certificates of admeasurement, listing details, such as design, length, depth, and breadth of vessel, and method of propulsion. Issues certificate of compliance when violations are not detected or recommends remedial procedures to correct deficiencies. Times roll of ship, using stopwatch. Analyzes data, formulates recommendations, and writes reports of findings. Advises crew in techniques of stowing dangerous and heavy cargo, according to knowledge of hazardous cargo. **SKILLS**—Mathematics; Writing; Systems Evaluation; Systems Analysis; Reading Comprehension; Active Listening; Speaking; Judgment and Decision Making.

GOE—Interest Area: 07. Government and Public Administration. **Work Group:** 07.03. Regulations Enforcement. **Other Jobs in This Work Group:** Agricultural Inspectors; Aviation Inspectors; Child Support, Missing Persons, and Unemployment Insurance Fraud Investigators; Environmental Compliance Inspectors; Equal Opportunity Representatives and Officers; Financial Examiners; Fire Inspectors; Fish and Game Wardens; Forest Fire Inspectors and Prevention Specialists; Government Property Inspectors and Investigators; Immigration and Customs Inspectors; Licensing Examiners and Inspectors; Mechanical Inspectors; Motor Vehicle Inspectors; Nuclear Monitoring Technicians; Occupational Health and Safety Specialists; Pressure Vessel Inspectors; Railroad Inspectors; Tax Examiners, Collectors, and Revenue Agents. **PERSONALITY TYPE:** Conventional. Conventional occupations frequently involve following set procedures and routines. These occupations can include working with data and details more than with ideas. Usually there is a clear line of authority to follow.

EDUCATION/TRAINING PROGRAM(S)— No data available.

WORK ENVIRONMENT—Outdoors; walking and running; extremely bright or inadequate lighting; standing; very hot or cold.

Marriage and Family Therapists

- Education/Training Required: Master's degree
- Annual Earnings: $40,440
- Growth: 22.4%
- Annual Job Openings: 3,000
- Self-Employed: 4.2%
- Part-Time: 14.6%

Age Bracket	Percentage of Workers
45–54 Years Old	28.0%
55–64 Years Old	13.4%
65 or Older	2.3%

Diagnose and treat mental and emotional disorders, whether cognitive, affective, or behavioral, within the context of marriage and family systems. Apply psychotherapeutic and family systems theories and techniques in the delivery of professional services to individuals, couples, and families for the purpose of treating such diagnosed nervous and mental disorders. Ask questions that will help clients identify their feelings and behaviors. Collect information about clients, using techniques such as testing, interviewing, discussion, and observation. Confer with clients in order to develop plans for post-treatment activities. Counsel clients on concerns such as unsatisfactory relationships, divorce and separation, child rearing, home management, and financial difficulties. Determine whether clients should be counseled or referred to other specialists in such fields as medicine, psychiatry and legal aid. Develop and implement individualized treatment plans addressing family relationship problems. Encourage individuals and family members to develop and use skills and strategies for confronting their problems in a constructive manner. Maintain case files that include activities, progress notes, evaluations, and recommendations. Confer with other counselors in order to analyze individual cases and to coordinate counseling services. Contact doctors, schools, social workers, juvenile counselors, law enforcement personnel and others to gather information in order to make recommendations to courts for the resolution of child custody or visitation disputes. Follow up on results of counseling programs and clients' adjustments in order to determine effectiveness of programs. Provide family counseling and treatment services to inmates participating in substance abuse programs. Provide instructions to clients on how to obtain help with legal, financial, and other personal issues. Supervise other counselors, social service staff and assistants. Write evaluations of parents and children for use by courts deciding divorce and custody cases, testifying in court if necessary. Provide public education and consultation to other professionals or groups regarding counseling services, issues and methods. **SKILLS**—No data available.

GOE—**Interest Area:** 10. Human Service. **Work Group:** 10.01. Counseling and Social Work. **Other Jobs in This Work Group:** Child, Family, and School Social Workers; Clinical Psychologists; Counseling Psychologists; Medical and Public Health Social Workers; Mental Health and Substance Abuse Social Workers; Mental Health Counselors; Probation Officers and Correctional Treatment Specialists; Rehabilitation Counselors; Residential Advisors; Social and Human Service Assistants; Substance Abuse and Behavioral Disorder Counselors. **PERSONALITY TYPE:** No data available.

EDUCATION/TRAINING PROGRAM(S)— Clinical Pastoral Counseling/Patient Counseling; Marriage and Family Therapy/Counseling; Social Work.

WORK ENVIRONMENT—No data available.

Materials Inspectors

- Education/Training Required: Moderate-term on-the-job training
- Annual Earnings: $28,630
- Growth: 4.7%
- Annual Job Openings: 87,000
- Self-Employed: 1.2%
- Part-Time: 5.0%

The job openings listed here are shared with Electrical and Electronic Inspectors and Testers; Mechanical Inspectors; Precision Devices Inspectors and Testers; and Production Inspectors, Testers, Graders, Sorters, Samplers, Weighers.

Age Bracket	Percentage of Workers
45–54 Years Old	27.3%
55–64 Years Old	15.0%
65 or Older	2.2%

Examine and inspect materials and finished parts and products for defects and wear and to ensure conformance with work orders, diagrams, blueprints, and template specifications. Usually specialize in a single phase of inspection. Inspects materials, products, and work in progress for conformance to specifications, and adjusts process or assembly equipment to meet standards. Collects samples for testing, and computes findings. Reads dials and meters to verify functioning of equipment according to specifications. Analyzes and interprets blueprints, sample data, and other materials to determine, change, or measure specifications or inspection and testing procedures. Tests and measures finished products, components, or assemblies for functioning, operation, accuracy, or assembly to verify adherence to functional specifications. Observes and monitors production operations and equipment to ensure proper assembly of parts, or assists in testing and monitoring activities. Marks items for acceptance or rejection, records test results and inspection data, and compares findings with specifications to ensure conformance to standards. Confers with vendors and others regarding inspection results, recommends corrective procedures, and compiles reports of results, recommendations, and needed repairs. Supervises testing or drilling activities, and adjusts equipment to obtain sample fluids or to direct drilling. Operates or tends machinery and equipment, and uses hand tools. Fabricates, installs, positions, or connects components, parts, finished products, or instruments for testing or operational purposes. **SKILLS**—Quality Control Analysis; Operation Monitoring; Troubleshooting; Operation and Control; Technology Design; Installation; Science; Mathematics.

GOE—Interest Area: 13. Manufacturing. **Work Group:** 13.07. Production Quality Control. **Other Jobs in This Work Group:** Electrical and Electronic Inspectors and Testers; Graders and Sorters, Agricultural Products; Precision Devices Inspectors and Testers; Production Inspectors, Testers, Graders, Sorters, Samplers, Weighers. **PERSONALITY TYPE:** Realistic. Realistic occupations frequently involve work activities that include practical, hands-on problems and solutions. They often deal with plants, animals, and real-world materials like wood, tools, and machinery. Many of the occupations require working outside and do not involve a lot of paperwork or working closely with others.

EDUCATION/TRAINING PROGRAM(S)— Quality Control Technology/Technician.

WORK ENVIRONMENT—Standing; hazardous equipment; walking and running; common protective or safety equipment; very hot or cold; minor burns, cuts, bites, or stings.

Mathematical Science Teachers, Postsecondary

- Education/Training Required: Master's degree
- Annual Earnings: $53,250
- Growth: 38.1%
- Annual Job Openings: 216,000
- Self-Employed: 0.3%
- Part-Time: 27.7%

The job openings listed here are shared with all other postsecondary teaching occupations.

Age Bracket	Percentage of Workers
45–54 Years Old	22.8%
55–64 Years Old	19.0%
65 or Older	5.5%

Teach courses pertaining to mathematical concepts, statistics, and actuarial science and to the application of original and standardized mathematical techniques in solving specific problems and situations. Evaluate and grade students' class work, assignments, and papers. Compile, administer, and grade examinations or assign this work to others. Prepare and deliver lectures to undergraduate and/or graduate students on topics such as linear algebra, differential equations, and discrete mathematics. Prepare course materials such as syllabi, homework assignments, and handouts. Maintain student attendance records, grades, and other required records. Maintain regularly scheduled office hours in order to advise and assist students. Plan, evaluate, and revise curricula, course content, and course materials and methods of instruction. Initiate, facilitate, and moderate classroom discussions. Select and obtain materials and supplies such as textbooks. Keep abreast of developments in their field by reading current literature, talking with colleagues, and participating in professional conferences. Advise students on academic and vocational curricula, and on career issues. Collaborate with colleagues to address teaching and research issues. Serve on academic or administrative committees that deal with institutional policies, departmental matters, and academic issues. Participate in student recruitment, registration, and placement activities. Perform administrative duties such as serving as department head. Conduct research in a particular field of knowledge and publish findings in books, professional journals, and/or electronic media. Supervise undergraduate and/or graduate teaching, internship, and research work. Act as advisers to student organizations. **SKILLS**—Instructing; Mathematics; Learning Strategies; Critical Thinking; Active Learning; Speaking; Social Perceptiveness; Complex Problem Solving.

GOE—**Interest Area:** 05. Education and Training. **Work Group:** 05.03. Postsecondary and Adult Teaching and Instructing. **Other Jobs in This Work Group:** Adult Literacy, Remedial Education, and GED Teachers and Instructors; Agricultural Sciences Teachers, Postsecondary; Anthropology and Archeology Teachers, Postsecondary; Architecture Teachers, Postsecondary; Area, Ethnic, and Cultural Studies Teachers, Postsecondary; Art, Drama, and Music Teachers,

Postsecondary; Atmospheric, Earth, Marine, and Space Sciences Teachers, Postsecondary; Biological Science Teachers, Postsecondary; Business Teachers, Postsecondary; Chemistry Teachers, Postsecondary; Communications Teachers, Postsecondary; Computer Science Teachers, Postsecondary; Criminal Justice and Law Enforcement Teachers, Postsecondary; Economics Teachers, Postsecondary; Education Teachers, Postsecondary; Engineering Teachers, Postsecondary; English Language and Literature Teachers, Postsecondary; Environmental Science Teachers, Postsecondary; Farm and Home Management Advisors; Foreign Language and Literature Teachers, Postsecondary; Forestry and Conservation Science Teachers, Postsecondary; Geography Teachers, Postsecondary; Graduate Teaching Assistants; Health Specialties Teachers, Postsecondary; History Teachers, Postsecondary; Home Economics Teachers, Postsecondary; Law Teachers, Postsecondary; Library Science Teachers, Postsecondary; Nursing Instructors and Teachers, Postsecondary; Philosophy and Religion Teachers, Postsecondary; Physics Teachers, Postsecondary; Political Science Teachers, Postsecondary; Psychology Teachers, Postsecondary; Recreation and Fitness Studies Teachers, Postsecondary; Self-Enrichment Education Teachers; Social Work Teachers, Postsecondary; Sociology Teachers, Postsecondary; Vocational Education Teachers, Postsecondary. **PERSONALITY TYPE:** Investigative. Investigative occupations frequently involve working with ideas and require an extensive amount of thinking. These occupations can involve searching for facts and figuring out problems mentally.

EDUCATION/TRAINING PROGRAM(S)— Algebra and Number Theory; Analysis and Functional Analysis; Applied Mathematics; Business Statistics; Geometry/Geometric

Analysis; Logic; Mathematical Statistics and Probability; Mathematics and Statistics, Other; Mathematics, General; Mathematics, Other; Statistics, General; Topology and Foundations.

WORK ENVIRONMENT—Physical proximity to others; sitting; indoors; sounds, noise levels are distracting or uncomfortable.

Mechanical Inspectors

- Education/Training Required: Moderate-term on-the-job training
- Annual Earnings: $28,630
- Growth: 4.7%
- Annual Job Openings: 87,000
- Self-Employed: 1.2%
- Part-Time: 5.0%

The job openings listed here are shared with Electrical and Electronic Inspectors and Testers; Materials Inspectors; Precision Devices Inspectors and Testers; and Production Inspectors, Testers, Graders, Sorters, Samplers, Weighers.

Age Bracket	Percentage of Workers
45–54 Years Old	27.3%
55–64 Years Old	15.0%
65 or Older	2.2%

Inspect and test mechanical assemblies and systems, such as motors, vehicles, and transportation equipment for defects and wear to ensure compliance with specifications. Tests and measures finished products, components, or assemblies for functioning, operation, accuracy, or assembly to verify adherence to functional specifications. Inspects materials, products, and work in progress for conformance to specifications, and adjusts process or assembly equip-

ment to meet standards. Starts and operates finished products for testing or inspection. Reads dials and meters to ensure that equipment is operating according to specifications. Collects samples for testing, and computes findings. Marks items for acceptance or rejection, records test results and inspection data, and compares findings with specifications to ensure conformance to standards. Discards or rejects products, materials, and equipment not meeting specifications. Reads and interprets materials, such as work orders, inspection manuals, and blueprints, to determine inspection and test procedures. Analyzes and interprets sample data. Installs and positions new or replacement parts, components, and instruments. Estimates and records operational data. Completes necessary procedures to satisfy licensing requirements, and indicates concurrence with acceptance or rejection decisions. Confers with vendors and others regarding inspection results, recommends corrective procedures, and compiles reports of results, recommendations, and needed repairs. Cleans and maintains test equipment and instruments to ensure proper functioning. **SKILLS**—Quality Control Analysis; Science; Installation; Operation Monitoring; Troubleshooting; Operation and Control; Equipment Maintenance; Repairing.

GOE—Interest Area: 07. Government and Public Administration. **Work Group:** 07.03. Regulations Enforcement. **Other Jobs in This Work Group:** Agricultural Inspectors; Aviation Inspectors; Child Support, Missing Persons, and Unemployment Insurance Fraud Investigators; Environmental Compliance Inspectors; Equal Opportunity Representatives and Officers; Financial Examiners; Fire Inspectors; Fish and Game Wardens; Forest Fire Inspectors and Prevention Specialists; Government Property Inspectors and Investigators; Immigration and

Customs Inspectors; Licensing Examiners and Inspectors; Marine Cargo Inspectors; Motor Vehicle Inspectors; Nuclear Monitoring Technicians; Occupational Health and Safety Specialists; Pressure Vessel Inspectors; Railroad Inspectors; Tax Examiners, Collectors, and Revenue Agents. **PERSONALITY TYPE:** Realistic. Realistic occupations frequently involve work activities that include practical, hands-on problems and solutions. They often deal with plants, animals, and real-world materials like wood, tools, and machinery. Many of the occupations require working outside and do not involve a lot of paperwork or working closely with others.

EDUCATION/TRAINING PROGRAM(S)— Quality Control Technology/Technician.

WORK ENVIRONMENT—Standing; walking and running; hazardous equipment; sounds, noise levels are distracting or uncomfortable; common protective or safety equipment.

Medical and Clinical Laboratory Technicians

- Education/Training Required: Associate degree
- Annual Earnings: $31,440
- Growth: 19.4%
- Annual Job Openings: 21,000
- Self-Employed: 1.6%
- Part-Time: 16.0%

Age Bracket	Percentage of Workers
45–54 Years Old	29.6%
55–64 Years Old	11.6%
65 or Older	1.0%

Perform routine medical laboratory tests for the diagnosis, treatment, and prevention of disease. May work under the supervision of a medical technologist. Conduct chemical analyses of body fluids, such as blood and urine, using microscope or automatic analyzer to detect abnormalities or diseases, and enter findings into computer. Set up, adjust, maintain and clean medical laboratory equipment. Analyze the results of tests and experiments to ensure conformity to specifications, using special mechanical and electrical devices. Analyze and record test data to issue reports that use charts, graphs and narratives. Perform medical research to further control and cure disease. Conduct blood tests for transfusion purposes and perform blood counts. Obtain specimens, cultivating, isolating and identifying microorganisms for analysis. Examine cells stained with dye to locate abnormalities. Collect blood or tissue samples from patients, observing principles of asepsis to obtain blood sample. Consult with a pathologist to determine a final diagnosis when abnormal cells are found. Inoculate fertilized eggs, broths, or other bacteriological media with organisms. Cut, stain and mount tissue samples for examination by pathologists. Supervise and instruct other technicians and laboratory assistants. Prepare standard volumetric solutions and reagents to be combined with samples, following standardized formulas or experimental procedures. Prepare vaccines and serums by standard laboratory methods, testing for virus inactivity and sterility. Test raw materials, processes and finished products to determine quality and quantity of materials or characteristics of a substance. **SKILLS**—Equipment Maintenance; Science; Troubleshooting; Instructing; Monitoring; Service Orientation; Operation Monitoring; Quality Control Analysis; Time Management.

GOE—**Interest Area:** 08. Health Science. **Work Group:** 08.06. Medical Technology. **Other Jobs in This Work Group:** Biological Technicians; Cardiovascular Technologists and Technicians; Diagnostic Medical Sonographers; Medical and Clinical Laboratory Technologists; Medical Equipment Preparers; Medical Records and Health Information Technicians; Nuclear Medicine Technologists; Opticians, Dispensing; Orthotists and Prosthetists; Radiologic Technicians; Radiologic Technologists. **PERSONALITY TYPE:** Realistic. Realistic occupations frequently involve work activities that include practical, hands-on problems and solutions. They often deal with plants, animals, and real-world materials like wood, tools, and machinery. Many of the occupations require working outside and do not involve a lot of paperwork or working closely with others.

EDUCATION/TRAINING PROGRAM(S)—
Blood Bank Technology Specialist; Clinical/Medical Laboratory Technician; Clinical/Medical Laboratory Technician/Assistant (Certificate); Hematology Technology/Technician; Histologic Technician.

WORK ENVIRONMENT—Disease or infections; hazardous conditions; physical proximity to others; indoors; contaminants.

Medical and Clinical Laboratory Technologists

- Education/Training Required: Bachelor's degree
- Annual Earnings: $46,710
- Growth: 19.3%
- Annual Job Openings: 21,000
- Self-Employed: 1.6%
- Part-Time: 16.0%

Age Bracket	Percentage of Workers
45–54 Years Old	29.6%
55–64 Years Old	11.6%
65 or Older	1.0%

Perform complex medical laboratory tests for diagnosis, treatment, and prevention of disease. May train or supervise staff. Analyze laboratory findings to check the accuracy of the results. Conduct chemical analysis of body fluids, including blood, urine, and spinal fluid, to determine presence of normal and abnormal components. Operate, calibrate and maintain equipment used in quantitative and qualitative analysis, such as spectrophotometers, calorimeters, flame photometers, and computer-controlled analyzers. Enter data from analysis of medical tests and clinical results into computer for storage. Analyze samples of biological material for chemical content or reaction. Establish and monitor programs to ensure the accuracy of laboratory results. Set up, clean, and maintain laboratory equipment. Provide technical information about test results to physicians, family members and researchers. Supervise, train, and direct lab assistants, medical and clinical laboratory technicians and technologists, and other

M

medical laboratory workers engaged in laboratory testing. Develop, standardize, evaluate, and modify procedures, techniques and tests used in the analysis of specimens and in medical laboratory experiments. Cultivate, isolate, and assist in identifying microbial organisms, and perform various tests on these microorganisms. Study blood samples to determine the number of cells and their morphology, as well as the blood group, type and compatibility for transfusion purposes, using microscopic technique. Obtain, cut, stain, and mount biological material on slides for microscopic study and diagnosis, following standard laboratory procedures. Select and prepare specimen and media for cell culture, using aseptic technique and knowledge of medium components and cell requirements. Conduct medical research under direction of microbiologist or biochemist. Harvest cell cultures at optimum time based on knowledge of cell cycle differences and culture conditions. **SKILLS—** Equipment Maintenance; Operation Monitoring; Quality Control Analysis; Science; Troubleshooting; Repairing; Operation and Control; Instructing.

GOE—Interest Area: 08. Health Science. **Work Group:** 08.06. Medical Technology. **Other Jobs in This Work Group:** Biological Technicians; Cardiovascular Technologists and Technicians; Diagnostic Medical Sonographers; Medical and Clinical Laboratory Technicians; Medical Equipment Preparers; Medical Records and Health Information Technicians; Nuclear Medicine Technologists; Opticians, Dispensing; Orthotists and Prosthetists; Radiologic Technicians; Radiologic Technologists. **PERSONALITY TYPE:** Investigative. Investigative occupations frequently involve working with ideas and require an extensive amount of thinking. These occupations can involve searching for facts and figuring out problems mentally.

EDUCATION/TRAINING PROGRAM(S)— Clinical Laboratory Science/Medical Technology/Technologist; Clinical/Medical Laboratory Science and Allied Professions, Other; Clinical/Medical Laboratory Science and Allied Professions, Other; Cytogenetics/Genetics/Clinical Genetics Technology/Technologists; Gytotechnology/Cytotechnologist; Histologic Technology/Histotechnologist; Renal/Dialysis Technologist/Technician.

WORK ENVIRONMENT—Disease or infections; contaminants; hazardous conditions; sounds, noise levels are distracting or uncomfortable; physical proximity to others.

Medical and Health Services Managers

- Education/Training Required: Work experience plus degree
- Annual Earnings: $68,320
- Growth: 29.3%
- Annual Job Openings: 33,000
- Self-Employed: 5.3%
- Part-Time: 5.4%

Age Bracket	Percentage of Workers
45–54 Years Old	39.6%
55–64 Years Old	14.8%
65 or Older	2.5%

Plan, direct, or coordinate medicine and health services in hospitals, clinics, managed care organizations, public health agencies, or similar organizations. Direct, supervise and evaluate work activities of medical, nursing, technical, clerical, service, maintenance, and other personnel. Establish objectives and evaluative or operational criteria for units they manage. Direct or conduct recruitment, hiring and training of personnel. Develop and maintain computerized record management systems to store and process data, such as personnel activities and information, and to produce reports. Develop and implement organizational policies and procedures for the facility or medical unit. Conduct and administer fiscal operations, including accounting, planning budgets, authorizing expenditures, establishing rates for services, and coordinating financial reporting. Establish work schedules and assignments for staff, according to workload, space and equipment availability. Maintain communication between governing boards, medical staff, and department heads by attending board meetings and coordinating interdepartmental functioning. Monitor the use of diagnostic services, inpatient beds, facilities, and staff to ensure effective use of resources and assess the need for additional staff, equipment, and services. Maintain awareness of advances in medicine, computerized diagnostic and treatment equipment, data processing technology, government regulations, health insurance changes, and financing options. Manage change in integrated health care delivery systems, such as work restructuring, technological innovations, and shifts in the focus of care. Prepare activity reports to inform management of the status and implementation plans of programs, services, and quality initiatives. Plan, implement and administer programs and services in a health care or medical facility, including personnel administration, training, and coordination of medical, nursing and physical plant staff. Consult with medical, business, and community groups to discuss service problems, respond to community needs, enhance public relations, coordinate activities and plans, and promote health programs. Inspect facilities and recommend building or equipment modifications to ensure emergency readiness and compliance to access, safety, and sanitation regulations. **SKILLS**—Management of Personnel Resources; Persuasion; Service Orientation; Management of Material Resources; Learning Strategies; Social Perceptiveness; Critical Thinking; Monitoring; Management of Financial Resources.

GOE—**Interest Area:** 08. Health Science. **Work Group:** 08.01. Managerial Work in Medical and Health Services. **Other Jobs in This Work Group:** Coroners; First-Line Supervisors and Manager/Supervisors—Animal Care Workers, Except Livestock. **PERSONALITY TYPE:** Enterprising. Enterprising occupations frequently involve starting up and carrying out projects. These occupations can involve leading people and making many decisions. They sometimes require risk taking and often deal with business.

EDUCATION/TRAINING PROGRAM(S)—Community Health and Preventive Medicine ; Health and Medical Administrative Services, Other; Health Information/Medical Records Administration/Administrator; Health Services Administration; Health Unit Manager/Ward Supervisor; Health/Health Care Administration/Management; Hospital and Health Care Facilities Administration/Management; Nursing Administration (MSN, MS, PhD); Public Health, General (MPH, DPH).

WORK ENVIRONMENT—Disease or infections; exposed to radiation; physical proximity to others; sounds, noise levels are distracting or uncomfortable; sitting.

M

Medical and Public Health Social Workers

◎ Education/Training Required: Bachelor's degree
◎ Annual Earnings: $40,780
◎ Growth: 28.6%
◎ Annual Job Openings: 18,000
◎ Self-Employed: 1.7%
◎ Part-Time: 8.7%

Age Bracket	Percentage of Workers
45–54 Years Old	26.4%
55–64 Years Old	12.9%
65 or Older	1.9%

Provide persons, families, or vulnerable populations with the psychosocial support needed to cope with chronic, acute, or terminal illnesses, such as Alzheimer's, cancer, or AIDS. Services include advising family care givers, providing patient education and counseling, and making necessary referrals for other social services. Collaborate with other professionals to evaluate patients' medical or physical condition and to assess client needs. Investigate child abuse or neglect cases and take authorized protective action when necessary. Refer patient, client, or family to community resources to assist in recovery from mental or physical illness and to provide access to services such as financial assistance, legal aid, housing, job placement or education. Counsel clients and patients in individual and group sessions to help them overcome dependencies, recover from illness, and adjust to life. Organize support groups or counsel family members to assist them in understanding, dealing with, and supporting the client or patient. Advocate for clients or patients to resolve crises. Identify environmental impedi-

ments to client or patient progress through interviews and review of patient records. Utilize consultation data and social work experience to plan and coordinate client or patient care and rehabilitation, following through to ensure service efficacy. Modify treatment plans to comply with changes in clients' status. Monitor, evaluate, and record client progress according to measurable goals described in treatment and care plan. Supervise and direct other workers providing services to clients or patients. Develop or advise on social policy and assist in community development. Oversee Medicaid- and Medicare-related paperwork and record-keeping in hospitals. Conduct social research to advance knowledge in the social work field. Plan and conduct programs to combat social problems, prevent substance abuse, or improve community health and counseling services. **SKILLS—** Social Perceptiveness; Service Orientation; Negotiation; Coordination; Active Listening; Learning Strategies; Critical Thinking; Speaking; Instructing.

GOE—Interest Area: 10. Human Service. **Work Group:** 10.01. Counseling and Social Work. **Other Jobs in This Work Group:** Child, Family, and School Social Workers; Clinical Psychologists; Counseling Psychologists; Marriage and Family Therapists; Mental Health and Substance Abuse Social Workers; Mental Health Counselors; Probation Officers and Correctional Treatment Specialists; Rehabilitation Counselors; Residential Advisors; Social and Human Service Assistants; Substance Abuse and Behavioral Disorder Counselors. **PERSONALITY TYPE:** Social. Social occupations frequently involve working with, communicating with, and teaching people. These occupations often involve helping or providing service to others.

EDUCATION/TRAINING PROGRAM(S)—
Clinical/Medical Social Work.

WORK ENVIRONMENT—Physical proximity to others; disease or infections; sounds, noise levels are distracting or uncomfortable; sitting; contaminants.

Medical Equipment Repairers

- Education/Training Required: Associate degree
- Annual Earnings: $38,590
- Growth: 14.8%
- Annual Job Openings: 4,000
- Self-Employed: 23.2%
- Part-Time: 10.1%

Age Bracket	Percentage of Workers
45–54 Years Old	29.0%
55–64 Years Old	11.3%
65 or Older	8.1%

Test, adjust, or repair biomedical or electromedical equipment. Inspect and test malfunctioning medical and related equipment following manufacturers' specifications, using test and analysis instruments. Examine medical equipment and facility's structural environment and check for proper use of equipment, to protect patients and staff from electrical or mechanical hazards and to ensure compliance with safety regulations. Disassemble malfunctioning equipment and remove, repair and replace defective parts such as motors, clutches or transformers. Keep records of maintenance, repair, and required updates of equipment. Perform preventive maintenance or service such as cleaning, lubricating and adjusting equipment. Test and calibrate components and equipment following manufacturers' manuals and troubleshooting techniques, using hand tools, power tools and measuring devices. Explain and demonstrate correct operation and preventive maintenance of medical equipment to personnel. Study technical manuals and attend training sessions provided by equipment manufacturers to maintain current knowledge. Plan and carry out work assignments, using blueprints, schematic drawings, technical manuals, wiring diagrams, and liquid and air flow sheets, while following prescribed regulations, directives, and other instructions as required. Solder loose connections, using soldering iron. Test, evaluate, and classify excess or in-use medial equipment and determine serviceability, condition, and disposition in accordance with regulations. Research catalogs and repair part lists to locate sources for repair parts, requisitioning parts and recording their receipt. Evaluate technical specifications to identify equipment and systems best suited for intended use and possible purchase based on specifications, user needs and technical requirements. Contribute expertise to develop medical maintenance standard operating procedures. Compute power and space requirements for installing medical, dental or related equipment and install units to manufacturers' specifications. Supervise and advise subordinate personnel. **SKILLS**—Repairing; Installation; Equipment Maintenance; Troubleshooting; Systems Analysis; Instructing; Service Orientation; Operation Monitoring.

GOE—Interest Area: 13. Manufacturing. **Work Group:** 13.15. Medical and Technical Equipment Repair. **Other Jobs in This Work Group:** Camera and Photographic Equipment

Repairers; Watch Repairers. **PERSONALITY TYPE:** Realistic. Realistic occupations frequently involve work activities that include practical, hands-on problems and solutions. They often deal with plants, animals, and real-world materials like wood, tools, and machinery. Many of the occupations require working outside and do not involve a lot of paperwork or working closely with others.

EDUCATION/TRAINING PROGRAM(S)— Biomedical Technology/Technician.

WORK ENVIRONMENT—Contaminants; physical proximity to others; cramped work space, awkward positions; extremely bright or inadequate lighting; hazardous conditions.

Medical Secretaries

- ◎ Education/Training Required: Postsecondary vocational training
- ◎ Annual Earnings: $27,030
- ◎ Growth: 17.2%
- ◎ Annual Job Openings: 50,000
- ◎ Self-Employed: 1.6%
- ◎ Part-Time: 17.5%

Age Bracket	Percentage of Workers
45–54 Years Old	28.6%
55–64 Years Old	16.3%
65 or Older	3.2%

Perform secretarial duties utilizing specific knowledge of medical terminology and hospital, clinic, or laboratory procedures. Duties include scheduling appointments, billing patients, and compiling and recording medical charts, reports, and correspondence. Schedule and confirm patient diagnostic appointments, surgeries and medical consultations. Compile and record medical charts, reports, and correspondence, using typewriter or personal computer. Answer telephones, and direct calls to appropriate staff. Receive and route messages and documents such as laboratory results to appropriate staff. Greet visitors, ascertain purpose of visit, and direct them to appropriate staff. Interview patients in order to complete documents, case histories, and forms such as intake and insurance forms. Maintain medical records, technical library and correspondence files. Operate office equipment such as voice mail messaging systems, and use word processing, spreadsheet, and other software applications to prepare reports, invoices, financial statements, letters, case histories and medical records. Transmit correspondence and medical records by mail, e-mail, or fax. Perform various clerical and administrative functions, such as ordering and maintaining an inventory of supplies. Arrange hospital admissions for patients. Transcribe recorded messages and practitioners' diagnoses and recommendations into patients' medical records. Perform bookkeeping duties, such as credits and collections, preparing and sending financial statements and bills, and keeping financial records. Complete insurance and other claim forms. Prepare correspondence and assist physicians or medical scientists with preparation of reports, speeches, articles and conference proceedings. **SKILLS—**Social Perceptiveness; Instructing; Active Listening; Writing; Time Management; Management of Personnel Resources; Speaking; Management of Material Resources.

GOE—Interest Area: 04. Business and Administration. **Work Group:** 04.04. Secretarial Support. **Other Jobs in This Work Group:** Executive Secretaries and Administrative Assistants; Legal Secretaries; Secretaries, Except

Legal, Medical, and Executive. **PERSONALITY TYPE:** Conventional. Conventional occupations frequently involve following set procedures and routines. These occupations can include working with data and details more than with ideas. Usually there is a clear line of authority to follow.

EDUCATION/TRAINING PROGRAM(S)— Medical Administrative/Executive Assistant and Medical Secretary; Medical Insurance Specialist/Medical Biller ; Medical Office Assistant/Specialist .

WORK ENVIRONMENT—Sounds, noise levels are distracting or uncomfortable; physical proximity to others; disease or infections; sitting; exposed to radiation.

Mental Health and Substance Abuse Social Workers

- ◎ Education/Training Required: Master's degree
- ◎ Annual Earnings: $34,310
- ◎ Growth: 34.5%
- ◎ Annual Job Openings: 17,000
- ◎ Self-Employed: 1.6%
- ◎ Part-Time: 8.7%

Age Bracket	Percentage of Workers
45–54 Years Old	26.4%
55–64 Years Old	12.9%
65 or Older	1.9%

Assess and treat individuals with mental, emotional, or substance abuse problems, including abuse of alcohol, tobacco, and/or other drugs.

Activities may include individual and group therapy, crisis intervention, case management, client advocacy, prevention, and education. Counsel clients in individual and group sessions to assist them in dealing with substance abuse, mental and physical illness, poverty, unemployment, or physical abuse. Interview clients, review records, and confer with other professionals to evaluate mental or physical condition of client or patient. Collaborate with counselors, physicians, and nurses to plan and coordinate treatment, drawing on social work experience and patient needs. Monitor, evaluate, and record client progress with respect to treatment goals. Refer patient, client, or family to community resources for housing or treatment to assist in recovery from mental or physical illness, following through to ensure service efficacy. Counsel and aid family members to assist them in understanding, dealing with, and supporting the client or patient. Modify treatment plans according to changes in client status. Plan and conduct programs to prevent substance abuse, to combat social problems, or to improve health and counseling services in community. Supervise and direct other workers who provide services to clients or patients. Develop or advise on social policy and assist in community development. **SKILLS**—Social Perceptiveness; Service Orientation; Negotiation; Persuasion; Active Listening; Judgment and Decision Making; Active Learning; Instructing.

GOE—Interest Area: 10. Human Service. **Work Group:** 10.01. Counseling and Social Work. **Other Jobs in This Work Group:** Child, Family, and School Social Workers; Clinical Psychologists; Counseling Psychologists; Marriage and Family Therapists; Medical and Public Health Social Workers; Mental Health Counselors; Probation Officers and Correctional Treatment Specialists;

Rehabilitation Counselors; Residential Advisors; Social and Human Service Assistants; Substance Abuse and Behavioral Disorder Counselors. **PERSONALITY TYPE:** Social. Social occupations frequently involve working with, communicating with, and teaching people. These occupations often involve helping or providing service to others.

EDUCATION/TRAINING PROGRAM(S)— Clinical/Medical Social Work.

WORK ENVIRONMENT—Sounds, noise levels are distracting or uncomfortable; sitting; physical proximity to others; in an enclosed vehicle or equipment; disease or infections.

Mental Health Counselors

- Education/Training Required: Master's degree
- Annual Earnings: $33,400
- Growth: 26.7%
- Annual Job Openings: 13,000
- Self-Employed: 4.1%
- Part-Time: 14.6%

Age Bracket	Percentage of Workers
45–54 Years Old	28.0%
55–64 Years Old	13.4%
65 or Older	2.3%

Counsel with emphasis on prevention. Work with individuals and groups to promote optimum mental health. May help individuals deal with addictions and substance abuse; family, parenting, and marital problems; suicide; stress management; problems with self-esteem; and issues associated with aging and mental and emotional health. Maintain confidentiality of records relating to clients' treatment. Encourage clients to express their feelings and discuss what is happening in their lives, and help them to develop insight into themselves and their relationships. Guide clients in the development of skills and strategies for dealing with their problems. Prepare and maintain all required treatment records and reports. Counsel clients and patients, individually and in group sessions, to assist in overcoming dependencies, adjusting to life, and making changes. Collect information about clients through interviews, observation, and tests. Act as client advocates in order to coordinate required services or to resolve emergency problems in crisis situations. Develop and implement treatment plans based on clinical experience and knowledge. Collaborate with other staff members to perform clinical assessments and develop treatment plans. Evaluate clients' physical or mental condition based on review of client information. Meet with families, probation officers, police, and other interested parties in order to exchange necessary information during the treatment process. Refer patients, clients, or family members to community resources or to specialists as necessary. Counsel family members to assist them in understanding, dealing with, and supporting clients or patients. Evaluate the effectiveness of counseling programs and clients' progress in resolving identified problems and moving towards defined objectives. Plan, organize and lead structured programs of counseling, work, study, recreation and social activities for clients. Modify treatment activities and approaches as needed in order to comply with changes in clients' status. Learn about new developments in their field by reading professional literature, attending courses and seminars, and establishing and maintaining contact with other social service agencies. Discuss with individual patients their plans for life after leaving therapy. Gather information about community mental health needs and resources that could be used in conjunction with therapy. Monitor clients' use of medications. **SKILLS**—Social Perceptiveness; Service Orientation; Learning Strategies; Negotiation; Persuasion; Active Listening; Critical Thinking; Speaking; Active Learning; Instructing.

GOE—Interest Area: 10. Human Service. **Work Group:** 10.01. Counseling and Social Work. **Other Jobs in This Work Group:** Child, Family, and School Social Workers; Clinical Psychologists; Counseling Psychologists; Marriage and Family Therapists; Medical and Public Health Social Workers; Mental Health and Substance Abuse Social Workers; Probation Officers and Correctional Treatment Specialists; Rehabilitation Counselors; Residential Advisors; Social and Human Service Assistants; Substance Abuse and Behavioral Disorder Counselors. **PERSONALITY TYPE:** Social. Social occupations frequently involve working with, communicating with, and teaching people. These occupations often involve helping or providing service to others.

EDUCATION/TRAINING PROGRAM(S)— Clinical/Medical Social Work; Mental and Social Health Services and Allied Professions, Other; Mental Health Counseling/Counselor; Substance Abuse/Addiction Counseling.

WORK ENVIRONMENT—Sitting; physical proximity to others; sounds, noise levels are distracting or uncomfortable; disease or infections; indoors, not environmentally controlled.

Middle School Teachers, Except Special and Vocational Education

- Education/Training Required: Bachelor's degree
- Annual Earnings: $44,180
- Growth: 9.0%
- Annual Job Openings: 69,000
- Self-Employed: 0.1%
- Part-Time: 9.2%

Age Bracket	Percentage of Workers
45–54 Years Old	28.0%
55–64 Years Old	14.5%
65 or Older	2.0%

Teach students in public or private schools in one or more subjects at the middle, intermediate, or junior high level, which falls between elementary and senior high school as defined by applicable state laws and regulations. Establish and enforce rules for behavior and procedures for maintaining order among the students for whom they are responsible. Adapt teaching methods and instructional materials to meet students' varying needs and interests. Instruct through lectures, discussions, and demonstrations in one or more subjects such as English, mathematics, or social studies. Prepare, administer, and grade tests and assignments in order to evaluate students' progress. Establish clear objectives for all lessons, units, and projects, and communicate these objectives to students. Plan and conduct activities for a balanced program of instruction, demonstration, and work time that provides students with opportunities to observe, question, and investigate. Maintain accurate, complete, and correct student records as required by laws, district policies, and administrative regulations. Observe and evaluate students' performance, behavior, social development, and physical health. Prepare materials and classrooms for class activities. Assign lessons and correct homework. Enforce all administration policies and rules governing students. Confer with parents or guardians, other teachers, counselors, and administrators in order to resolve students' behavioral and academic problems. Prepare students for later grades by encouraging them to explore learning opportunities and to persevere with challenging tasks. Prepare objectives and outlines for courses of study, following curriculum guidelines or requirements of states and schools. Meet with parents and guardians to discuss their children's progress, and to determine their priorities for their children and their resource needs. Guide and counsel students with adjustment and/or academic problems, or special academic interests. Meet with other professionals to discuss individual students' needs and progress. Prepare and implement remedial programs for students requiring extra help. Prepare for assigned classes, and show written evidence of preparation upon request of immediate supervisors. Use computers, audiovisual aids, and other equipment and materials to supplement presentations. **SKILLS**—Instructing; Learning Strategies; Social Perceptiveness; Time Management; Monitoring; Negotiation; Persuasion; Service Orientation.

GOE—**Interest Area:** 05. Education and Training. **Work Group:** 05.02. Preschool, Elementary, and Secondary Teaching and Instructing. **Other Jobs in This Work Group:** Elementary School Teachers, Except Special Education; Kindergarten Teachers, Except Special Education; Preschool Teachers, Except Special Education; Secondary School Teachers, Except Special and Vocational Education; Special Education Teachers, Middle School; Special Education Teachers, Preschool, Kindergarten, and Elementary School; Special Education Teachers, Secondary School; Teacher Assistants; Vocational Education Teachers, Middle School; Vocational Education Teachers, Secondary School. **PERSONALITY TYPE:** Social. Social occupations frequently involve working with, communicating with, and teaching people. These occupations often involve helping or providing service to others.

EDUCATION/TRAINING PROGRAM(S)— Art Teacher Education; Computer Teacher Education; English/Language Arts Teacher Education; Family and Consumer Sciences/Home Economics Teacher Education; Foreign Language Teacher Education; Health Occupations Teacher Education; Health Teacher Education; History Teacher Education; Junior High/Intermediate/Middle School Education and Teaching; Mathematics Teacher Education; Music Teacher Education; Physical Education Teaching and Coaching; Reading Teacher Education; others.

WORK ENVIRONMENT—Physical proximity to others; sounds, noise levels are distracting or uncomfortable; standing; contaminants; walking and running.

Mobile Heavy Equipment Mechanics, Except Engines

- Education/Training Required: Postsecondary vocational training
- Annual Earnings: $38,630
- Growth: 9.6%
- Annual Job Openings: 12,000
- Self-Employed: 4.4%
- Part-Time: 2.8%

Age Bracket	Percentage of Workers
45–54 Years Old	35.0%
55–64 Years Old	12.5%
65 or Older	2.5%

Diagnose, adjust, repair, or overhaul mobile mechanical, hydraulic, and pneumatic equipment, such as cranes, bulldozers, graders, and conveyors, used in construction, logging, and surface mining. Test mechanical products and equipment after repair or assembly to ensure proper performance and compliance with manufacturers' specifications. Repair and replace damaged or worn parts. Operate and inspect machines or heavy equipment in order to diagnose defects. Diagnose faults or malfunctions to determine required repairs, using engine diagnostic equipment such as computerized test equipment and calibration devices. Dismantle and reassemble heavy equipment using hoists and hand tools. Clean, lubricate, and perform other routine maintenance work on equipment and vehicles. Examine parts for damage or excessive wear, using micrometers and gauges. Schedule maintenance for industrial machines and equipment, and keep equipment service records. Read and understand operating manuals, blueprints, and technical drawings. Overhaul and test machines or equipment to ensure operating efficiency. Assemble gear systems, and align frames and gears. Fit bearings to adjust, repair, or overhaul mobile mechanical, hydraulic, and pneumatic equipment. Weld or solder broken parts and structural members, using electric or gas welders and soldering tools. Clean parts by spraying them with grease solvent or immersing them in tanks of solvent. Adjust, maintain, and repair or replace subassemblies, such as transmissions and crawler heads, using hand tools, jacks, and cranes. Adjust and maintain industrial machinery, using control and regulating devices. Fabricate needed parts or items from sheet metal. Direct workers who are assembling or disassembling equipment or cleaning parts. **SKILLS**—Installation; Equipment Maintenance; Repairing; Troubleshooting; Operation Monitoring; Equipment Selection; Operation and Control; Persuasion; Technology Design.

GOE—Interest Area: 13. Manufacturing. **Work Group:** 13.14. Vehicle and Facility Mechanical Work. **Other Jobs in This Work Group:** Aircraft Body and Bonded Structure Repairers; Aircraft Engine Specialists; Aircraft Rigging Assemblers; Aircraft Structure Assemblers, Precision; Aircraft Systems Assemblers, Precision; Airframe-and-Power-Plant Mechanics; Automotive Body and Related Repairers; Automotive Glass Installers and Repairers; Automotive Master Mechanics; Automotive Specialty Technicians; Bus and Truck Mechanics and Diesel Engine Specialists; Farm Equipment Mechanics; Fiberglass Laminators and Fabricators; Motorboat Mechanics; Motorcycle Mechanics; Outdoor Power Equipment and Other Small Engine Mechanics; Rail Car Repairers; Recreational Vehicle Service Technicians; Tire Repairers and Changers. **PERSONALITY TYPE:** Realistic.

Realistic occupations frequently involve work activities that include practical, hands-on problems and solutions. They often deal with plants, animals, and real-world materials like wood, tools, and machinery. Many of the occupations require working outside and do not involve a lot of paperwork or working closely with others.

EDUCATION/TRAINING PROGRAM(S)— Agricultural Mechanics and Equipment/ Machine Technology; Heavy Equipment Maintenance/Technology/Technician.

WORK ENVIRONMENT—Contaminants; sounds, noise levels are distracting or uncomfortable; hazardous equipment; indoors, not environmentally controlled; in an open vehicle or equipment; very hot or cold.

Motor Vehicle Inspectors

- Education/Training Required: Work experience in a related occupation
- Annual Earnings: $47,920
- Growth: 7.7%
- Annual Job Openings: 5,000
- Self-Employed: 0.4%
- Part-Time: 3.2%

The job openings listed here are shared with Aviation Inspectors, Freight Inspectors, Marine Cargo Inspectors, Public Transportation Inspectors, and Railroad Inspectors.

Age Bracket	Percentage of Workers
45–54 Years Old	54.3%
55–64 Years Old	15.2%
65 or Older	2.2%

Inspect automotive vehicles to ensure compliance with governmental regulations and safety standards. Inspects truck accessories, air lines and electric circuits, and reports needed repairs. Examines vehicles for damage, and drives vehicle to detect malfunctions. Tests vehicle components for wear, damage, or improper adjustment, using mechanical or electrical devices. Applies inspection sticker to vehicles that pass inspection, and rejection sticker to vehicles that fail. Prepares report on each vehicle for follow-up action by owner or police. Prepares and keeps record of vehicles delivered. Positions trailer and drives car onto truck trailer. Notifies authorities of owners having illegal equipment installed on vehicle. Services vehicles with fuel and water. **SKILLS—**Science; Troubleshooting; Quality Control Analysis; Operation Monitoring; Technology Design; Systems Evaluation; Equipment Maintenance.

GOE—Interest Area: 07. Government and Public Administration. **Work Group:** 07.03. Regulations Enforcement. **Other Jobs in This Work Group:** Agricultural Inspectors; Aviation Inspectors; Child Support, Missing Persons, and Unemployment Insurance Fraud Investigators; Environmental Compliance Inspectors; Equal Opportunity Representatives and Officers; Financial Examiners; Fire Inspectors; Fish and Game Wardens; Forest Fire Inspectors and Prevention Specialists; Government Property Inspectors and Investigators; Immigration and Customs Inspectors; Licensing Examiners and Inspectors; Marine Cargo Inspectors; Mechanical Inspectors; Nuclear Monitoring Technicians; Occupational Health and Safety Specialists; Pressure Vessel Inspectors; Railroad Inspectors; Tax Examiners, Collectors, and Revenue Agents. **PERSONALITY TYPE:** Realistic. Realistic occupations frequently involve work activities that include practical, hands-on problems and solutions. They often deal with plants, animals, and real-world materials like wood, tools, and machinery. Many of the occupations require working outside and do not involve a lot of paperwork or working closely with others.

EDUCATION/TRAINING PROGRAM(S)— No data available.

WORK ENVIRONMENT—Outdoors; standing; spend time bending or twisting the body; minor burns, cuts, bites, or stings; spend time kneeling, crouching, stooping, or crawling.

Multi-Media Artists and Animators

- Education/Training Required: Bachelor's degree
- Annual Earnings: $49,900
- Growth: 15.8%
- Annual Job Openings: 12,000
- Self-Employed: 53.5%
- Part-Time: 20.0%

Age Bracket	Percentage of Workers
45–54 Years Old	25.5%
55–64 Years Old	17.0%
65 or Older	5.7%

Create special effects, animation, or other visual images using film, video, computers, or other electronic tools and media for use in products or creations, such as computer games, movies, music videos, and commercials. Design complex graphics and animation, using independent judgment, creativity, and computer equipment. Create two-dimensional and three-dimensional images depicting objects in motion or illustrating a process, using computer animation or modeling programs. Make objects or characters appear lifelike by manipulating light, color, texture, shadow, and transparency, and/or manipulating static images to give the illusion of motion. Assemble, typeset, scan and produce digital camera-ready art or film negatives and printer's proofs. Apply story development, directing, cinematography, and editing to animation to create storyboards that show the flow of the animation and map out key scenes and characters. Script, plan, and create animated narrative sequences under tight deadlines, using computer software and hand drawing techniques. Create basic designs, drawings, and illustrations for product labels, cartons, direct mail, or television. Create pen-and-paper images to be scanned, edited, colored, textured or animated by computer. Develop briefings, brochures, multimedia presentations, web pages, promotional products, technical illustrations, and computer artwork for use in products, technical manuals, literature, newsletters and slide shows. **SKILLS—**Operations Analysis; Technology Design; Time Management; Active Listening; Persuasion; Reading Comprehension; Judgment and Decision Making; Active Learning.

GOE—Interest Area: 03. Arts and Communication. **Work Group:** 03.09. Media Technology. **Other Jobs in This Work Group:** Audio and Video Equipment Technicians; Broadcast Technicians; Camera Operators, Television, Video, and Motion Picture; Film and Video Editors; Photographic Hand Developers; Photographic Reproduction Technicians; Photographic Retouchers and Restorers; Professional Photographers; Radio Operators; Sound Engineering Technicians. **PERSONALITY TYPE:** No data available.

EDUCATION/TRAINING PROGRAM(S)— Animation, Interactive Technology, Video Graphics and Special Effects; Drawing; Graphic Design; Intermedia/Multimedia; Painting; Printmaking; Web Page, Digital/Multimedia and Information Resources Design.

WORK ENVIRONMENT—Sitting; indoors; sounds, noise levels are distracting or uncomfortable; physical proximity to others.

Municipal Clerks

- Education/Training Required: Short-term on-the-job training
- Annual Earnings: $28,980
- Growth: 12.3%
- Annual Job Openings: 14,000
- Self-Employed: 2.6%
- Part-Time: 8.3%

The job openings listed here are shared with Court Clerks and License Clerks.

Age Bracket	Percentage of Workers
45–54 Years Old	25.8%
55–64 Years Old	13.5%
65 or Older	2.2%

Draft agendas and bylaws for town or city council; record minutes of council meetings; answer official correspondence; keep fiscal records and accounts; and prepare reports on civic needs. Participate in the administration of municipal elections, including preparation and distribution of ballots, appointment and training of election officers, and tabulation and certification of results. Record and edit the minutes of meetings, then distribute them to appropriate officials and staff members. Plan and direct the maintenance, filing, safekeeping, and computerization of all municipal documents. Issue public notification of all official activities and meetings. Maintain and update documents such as municipal codes and city charters. Prepare meeting agendas and packets of related information. Prepare ordinances, resolutions, and proclamations so that they can be executed, recorded, archived, and distributed. Respond to requests for information from the public, other municipalities, state officials, and state and federal legislative offices. Maintain fiscal records and accounts. Perform budgeting duties, including assisting in budget preparation, expenditure review, and budget administration. Perform general office duties such as taking and transcribing dictation, typing and proofreading correspondence, distributing and filing official forms, and scheduling appointments. Coordinate and maintain office-tracking systems for correspondence and follow-up actions. Research information in the municipal archives upon request of public officials and private citizens. Perform contract administration duties, assisting with bid openings and the awarding of contracts. Collaborate with other staff to assist in the development and implementation of goals, objectives, policies, and priorities. Represent municipalities at community events, and serve as liaisons on community committees. Serve as a notary of the public. Issue various permits and licenses, including marriage, fishing, hunting, and dog licenses, and collect appropriate fees. Provide assistance to persons with disabilities in reaching less accessible areas of municipal facilities. Process claims against the municipality, maintaining files and log of claims, and coordinate claim response and handling with municipal claims administrators. **SKILLS—** Service Orientation; Social Perceptiveness; Management of Financial Resources; Active Listening; Writing; Persuasion; Instructing; Management of Personnel Resources.

GOE—**Interest Area:** 07. Government and Public Administration. **Work Group:** 07.04. Public Administration Clerical Support. **Other Jobs in This Work Group:** Court Clerks; Court Reporters; License Clerks. **PERSONALITY TYPE:** Conventional. Conventional occupations frequently involve following set procedures and routines. These occupations can include working with data and details more than with ideas. Usually there is a clear line of authority to follow.

EDUCATION/TRAINING PROGRAM(S)— General Office Occupations and Clerical Services.

WORK ENVIRONMENT—Sitting; physical proximity to others; indoors; sounds, noise levels are distracting or uncomfortable.

Municipal Fire Fighting and Prevention Supervisors

- Education/Training Required: Work experience in a related occupation
- Annual Earnings: $59,760
- Growth: 18.7%
- Annual Job Openings: 8,000
- Self-Employed: 0%
- Part-Time: 0.1%

The job openings listed here are shared with Forest Fire Fighting and Prevention Supervisors.

Age Bracket	Percentage of Workers
45–54 Years Old	57.1%
55–64 Years Old	4.8%
65 or Older	2.4%

Supervise fire fighters who control and extinguish municipal fires, protect life and property, and conduct rescue efforts. Assign firefighters to jobs at strategic locations in order to facilitate rescue of persons and maximize application of extinguishing agents. Provide emergency medical services as required, and perform light to heavy rescue functions at emergencies. Assess nature and extent of fire, condition of building, danger to adjacent buildings, and water supply status in order to determine crew or company requirements. Instruct and drill fire department personnel in assigned duties, including firefighting, medical care, hazardous materials response, fire prevention, and related subjects. Evaluate the performance of assigned firefighting personnel. Direct the training of firefighters, assigning of instructors to training classes, and providing of supervisors with reports on training progress and status. Prepare activity reports listing fire call locations, actions taken, fire types and probable causes, damage estimates, and situation dispositions. Maintain required maps and records. Attend in-service training classes to remain current in knowledge of codes, laws, ordinances, and regulations. Evaluate fire station procedures in order to ensure efficiency and enforcement of departmental regulations. Direct firefighters in station maintenance duties, and participate in these duties. Compile and maintain equipment and personnel records, including accident reports. Direct investigation of cases of suspected arson, hazards, and false alarms and submit reports outlining findings. Recommend personnel actions related to disciplinary procedures, performance, leaves of absence, and grievances. Supervise and participate in the inspection of properties in order to ensure that they are in compliance with applicable fire codes, ordinances, laws, regulations, and standards. Write and submit proposals for repair, modification, or replacement of firefighting equipment.

M

Coordinate the distribution of fire prevention promotional materials. Identify corrective actions needed to bring properties into compliance with applicable fire codes and ordinances and conduct follow-up inspections to see if corrective actions have been taken. **SKILLS**—Service Orientation; Management of Personnel Resources; Equipment Maintenance; Coordination; Instructing; Operation Monitoring; Judgment and Decision Making; Management of Material Resources.

GOE—Interest Area: 12. Law and Public Safety. **Work Group:** 12.01. Managerial Work in Law and Public Safety. **Other Jobs in This Work Group:** Emergency Management Specialists; First-Line Supervisors/Managers of Correctional Officers; First-Line Supervisors/Managers of Police and Detectives; Forest Fire Fighting and Prevention Supervisors. **PERSONALITY TYPE:** Realistic. Realistic occupations frequently involve work activities that include practical, hands-on problems and solutions. They often deal with plants, animals, and real-world materials like wood, tools, and machinery. Many of the occupations require working outside and do not involve a lot of paperwork or working closely with others.

EDUCATION/TRAINING PROGRAM(S)— Fire Protection and Safety Technology/ Technician; Fire Services Administration.

WORK ENVIRONMENT—Sounds, noise levels are distracting or uncomfortable; very hot or cold; physical proximity to others; contaminants; hazardous conditions.

Music Arrangers and Orchestrators

- Education/Training Required: Work experience plus degree
- Annual Earnings: $34,800
- Growth: 13.5%
- Annual Job Openings: 8,000
- Self-Employed: 39.3%
- Part-Time: 39.5%

The job openings listed here are shared with Composers and Music Directors.

Age Bracket	Percentage of Workers
45–54 Years Old	23.5%
55–64 Years Old	11.2%
65 or Older	10.6%

Write and transcribe musical scores. Composes musical scores for orchestra, band, choral group, or individual instrumentalist or vocalist, using knowledge of music theory and instrumental and vocal capabilities. Transposes music from one voice or instrument to another to accommodate particular musician in musical group. Adapts musical composition for orchestra, band, choral group, or individual to style for which it was not originally written. Copies parts from score for individual performers. Determines voice, instrument, harmonic structure, rhythm, tempo, and tone balance to achieve desired effect. Transcribes musical parts from score written by arranger or orchestrator for each instrument or voice, using knowledge of music composition. **SKILLS**—Coordination; Writing; Operations Analysis.

GOE—Interest Area: 03. Arts and Communication. **Work Group:** 03.07. Music. **Other Jobs in This Work Group:** Composers; Music Directors; Musicians, Instrumental;

Singers; Talent Directors. **PERSONALITY TYPE:** Artistic. Artistic occupations frequently involve working with forms, designs, and patterns. They often require self-expression, and the work can be done without following a clear set of rules.

EDUCATION/TRAINING PROGRAM(S)— Conducting; Music Management and Merchandising; Music Performance, General; Music Theory and Composition; Music, Other; Musicology and Ethnomusicology; Religious/ Sacred Music; Voice and Opera.

WORK ENVIRONMENT—Sitting; indoors; standing.

Music Directors

- Education/Training Required: Master's degree
- Annual Earnings: $34,800
- Growth: 13.5%
- Annual Job Openings: 8,000
- Self-Employed: 39.3%
- Part-Time: 39.5%

The job openings listed here are shared with Composers and Music Arrangers and Orchestrators.

Age Bracket	Percentage of Workers
45–54 Years Old	23.5%
55–64 Years Old	11.2%
65 or Older	10.6%

Direct and conduct instrumental or vocal performances by musical groups, such as orchestras or choirs. Assign and review staff work in such areas as scoring, arranging, and copying music, and vocal coaching. Collaborate with music librarians to ensure availability of scores.

Engage services of composers to write scores. Meet with composers to discuss interpretations of their work. Perform administrative tasks such as applying for grants, developing budgets, negotiating contracts, and designing and printing programs and other promotional materials. Transcribe musical compositions and melodic lines to adapt them to a particular group, or to create a particular musical style. Confer with clergy to select music for church services. Coordinate and organize tours, or hire touring companies to arrange concert dates, venues, accommodations, and transportation for longer tours. Plan and implement fund-raising and promotional activities. Audition and select performers for musical presentations. Conduct guest soloists in addition to ensemble members. Consider such factors as ensemble size and abilities, availability of scores, and the need for musical variety, in order to select music to be performed. Direct groups at rehearsals and live or recorded performances in order to achieve desired effects such as tonal and harmonic balance dynamics, rhythm, and tempo. Meet with soloists and concertmasters to discuss and prepare for performances. Plan and schedule rehearsals and performances, and arrange details such as locations, accompanists, and instrumentalists. Position members within groups to obtain balance among instrumental or vocal sections. Study scores to learn the music in detail, and to develop interpretations. Use gestures to shape the music being played, communicating desired tempo, phrasing, tone, color, pitch, volume, and other performance aspects. **SKILLS—** Management of Personnel Resources; Coordination; Instructing; Time Management; Monitoring; Learning Strategies; Social Perceptiveness; Operations Analysis.

GOE—Interest Area: 03. Arts and Communication. **Work Group:** 03.07. Music.

Other Jobs in This Work Group: Composers; Music Arrangers and Orchestrators; Musicians, Instrumental; Singers; Talent Directors. **PERSONALITY TYPE:** Artistic. Artistic occupations frequently involve working with forms, designs, and patterns. They often require self-expression, and the work can be done without following a clear set of rules.

EDUCATION/TRAINING PROGRAM(S)— Conducting; Music Management and Merchandising; Music Performance, General; Music Theory and Composition; Music, Other; Musicology and Ethnomusicology; Religious/Sacred Music; Voice and Opera.

WORK ENVIRONMENT—Standing; sitting; spend time making repetitive motions; indoors; outdoors.

Nursery and Greenhouse Managers

- ☉ Education/Training Required: Work experience plus degree
- ☉ Annual Earnings: $50,720
- ☉ Growth: 5.1%
- ☉ Annual Job Openings: 25,000
- ☉ Self-Employed: 0.9%
- ☉ Part-Time: 9.2%

The job openings listed here are shared with Agricultural Crop Farm Managers and Fish Hatchery Managers.

Age Bracket	Percentage of Workers
45–54 Years Old	29.6%
55–64 Years Old	17.5%
65 or Older	12.6%

Plan, organize, direct, control, and coordinate activities of workers engaged in propagating, cultivating, and harvesting horticultural specialties, such as trees, shrubs, flowers, mushrooms, and other plants. Confer with horticultural personnel in order to plan facility renovations or additions. Construct structures and accessories such as greenhouses and benches. Coordinate clerical, recordkeeping, inventory, requisitioning, and marketing activities. Cut and prune trees, shrubs, flowers, and plants. Graft plants. Inspect facilities and equipment for signs of disrepair, and perform necessary maintenance work. Negotiate contracts such as those for land leases or tree purchases. Assign work schedules and duties to nursery or greenhouse staff, and supervise their work. Determine plant growing conditions, such as greenhouses, hydroponics, or natural settings, and set planting and care schedules. Determine types and quantities of horticultural plants to be grown, based on budgets, projected sales volumes, and/or executive directives. Explain and enforce safety regulations and policies. Hire employees, and train them in gardening techniques. Identify plants as well as problems such as diseases, weeds, and insect pests. Manage nurseries that grow horticultural plants for sale to trade or retail customers, for display or exhibition, or for research. Select and purchase seeds, plant nutrients, disease control chemicals, and garden and lawn care equipment. Tour work areas to observe work being done, to inspect crops, and to evaluate plant and soil conditions. Apply pesticides and fertilizers to plants. Position and regulate plant irrigation systems, and program environmental and irrigation control computers. Prepare soil for planting, and plant or transplant seeds, bulbs, and cuttings. Provide information to customers on the care of trees, shrubs, flowers, plants, and lawns. **SKILLS—**Management of Personnel Resources; Management of

Financial Resources; Management of Material Resources; Negotiation; Systems Analysis; Systems Evaluation; Coordination; Operations Analysis; Time Management.

GOE—Interest Area: 01. Agriculture and Natural Resources. **Work Group:** 01.01. Managerial Work in Agriculture and Natural Resources. **Other Jobs in This Work Group:** Agricultural Crop Farm Managers; Farmers and Ranchers; First-Line Supervisors and Manager/Supervisors—Agricultural Crop Workers; First-Line Supervisors and Manager/Supervisors—Animal Husbandry Workers; First-Line Supervisors and Manager/Supervisors—Extractive Workers; First-Line Supervisors and Manager/Supervisors—Fishery Workers; First-Line Supervisors and Manager/Supervisors—Horticultural Workers; First-Line Supervisors and Manager/Supervisors—Landscaping Workers; First-Line Supervisors and Manager/Supervisors—Logging Workers; Fish Hatchery Managers; Lawn Service Managers; Park Naturalists; Purchasing Agents and Buyers, Farm Products. **PERSONALITY TYPE:** Enterprising. Enterprising occupations frequently involve starting up and carrying out projects. These occupations can involve leading people and making many decisions. They sometimes require risk taking and often deal with business.

EDUCATION/TRAINING PROGRAM(S) —Agribusiness/Agricultural Business Operations; Agricultural Business and Management, General; Greenhouse Operations and Management; Horticultural Science; Ornamental Horticulture; Plant Nursery Operations and Management; Plant Protection and Integrated Pest Management.

WORK ENVIRONMENT—Outdoors; spend time kneeling, crouching, stooping, or crawling; very hot or cold; standing; minor burns, cuts, bites, or stings.

Nursing Instructors and Teachers, Postsecondary

- Education/Training Required: Master's degree
- Annual Earnings: $52,720
- Growth: 38.1%
- Annual Job Openings: 216,000
- Self-Employed: 0.3%
- Part-Time: 27.7%

The job openings listed here are shared with all other postsecondary teaching occupations.

Age Bracket	Percentage of Workers
45–54 Years Old	22.8%
55–64 Years Old	19.0%
65 or Older	5.5%

Demonstrate and teach patient care in classroom and clinical units to nursing students. Includes both teachers primarily engaged in teaching and those who do a combination of both teaching and research. Initiate, facilitate, and moderate classroom discussions. Prepare and deliver lectures to undergraduate and/or graduate students on topics such as pharmacology, mental health nursing, and community health care practices. Keep abreast of developments in their field by reading current literature, talking with colleagues, and participating in professional conferences. Prepare course materials such as syllabi, homework assignments, and handouts. Supervise students' laboratory and clinical work.

Evaluate and grade students' class work, laboratory and clinic work, assignments, and papers. Collaborate with colleagues to address teaching and research issues. Plan, evaluate, and revise curricula, course content, and course materials and methods of instruction. Assess clinical education needs, and patient and client teaching needs, utilizing a variety of methods. Compile, administer, and grade examinations or assign this work to others. Advise students on academic and vocational curricula, and on career issues. Maintain student attendance records, grades, and other required records. Maintain regularly scheduled office hours in order to advise and assist students. Supervise undergraduate and/or graduate teaching, internship, and research work. Conduct research in a particular field of knowledge and publish findings in professional journals, books, and/or electronic media. Participate in student recruitment, registration, and placement activities. Serve on academic or administrative committees that deal with institutional policies, departmental matters, and academic issues. Coordinate training programs with area universities, clinics, hospitals, health agencies, and/or vocational schools. Compile bibliographies of specialized materials for outside reading assignments. Select and obtain materials and supplies such as textbooks and laboratory equipment. Participate in campus and community events. Write grant proposals to procure external research funding. Act as advisers to student organizations. Demonstrate patient care in clinical units of hospitals. Perform administrative duties such as serving as department head. **SKILLS**—Instructing; Social Perceptiveness; Science; Learning Strategies; Writing; Service Orientation; Reading Comprehension; Persuasion.

GOE—Interest Area: 05. Education and Training. **Work Group:** 05.03. Postsecondary and Adult Teaching and Instructing. **Other Jobs in This Work Group:** Adult Literacy, Remedial Education, and GED Teachers and Instructors; Agricultural Sciences Teachers, Postsecondary; Anthropology and Archeology Teachers, Postsecondary; Architecture Teachers, Postsecondary; Area, Ethnic, and Cultural Studies Teachers, Postsecondary; Art, Drama, and Music Teachers, Postsecondary; Atmospheric, Earth, Marine, and Space Sciences Teachers, Postsecondary; Biological Science Teachers, Postsecondary; Business Teachers, Postsecondary; Chemistry Teachers, Postsecondary; Communications Teachers, Postsecondary; Computer Science Teachers, Postsecondary; Criminal Justice and Law Enforcement Teachers, Postsecondary; Economics Teachers, Postsecondary; Education Teachers, Postsecondary; Engineering Teachers, Postsecondary; English Language and Literature Teachers, Postsecondary; Environmental Science Teachers, Postsecondary; Farm and Home Management Advisors; Foreign Language and Literature Teachers, Postsecondary; Forestry and Conservation Science Teachers, Postsecondary; Geography Teachers, Postsecondary; Graduate Teaching Assistants; Health Specialties Teachers, Postsecondary; History Teachers, Postsecondary; Home Economics Teachers, Postsecondary; Law Teachers, Postsecondary; Library Science Teachers, Postsecondary; Mathematical Science Teachers, Postsecondary; Philosophy and Religion Teachers, Postsecondary; Physics Teachers, Postsecondary; Political Science Teachers, Postsecondary; Psychology Teachers, Postsecondary; Recreation and Fitness Studies Teachers, Postsecondary; Self-Enrichment Education Teachers; Social Work Teachers, Postsecondary; Sociology Teachers, Postsecondary; Vocational Education Teachers, Postsecondary. **PERSONALITY TYPE:** Social. Social occupations frequently involve working with, communicating with, and teaching people. These occupations often involve helping or providing service to others.

EDUCATION/TRAINING PROGRAM(S)— Adult Health Nurse/Nursing; Family Practice Nurse/Nurse Practitioner; Maternal/Child Health Nurse/Nursing; Nurse Anesthetist; Nurse Midwife/Nursing Midwifery; Nursing— Registered Nurse Training (RN, ASN, BSN, MSN); Nursing Clinical Specialist; Nursing Science (MS, PhD); Nursing, Other; Pediatric Nurse/Nursing; Perioperative/Operating and Surgical Nurse/Nur; Pre-Nursing Studies; Psychiatric/Mental Health Nurse/Nursing; Public Health/Community Nurse/Nursing.

WORK ENVIRONMENT—Physical proximity to others; disease or infections; sitting; contaminants; indoors.

Obstetricians and Gynecologists

- ◎ Education/Training Required: First professional degree
- ◎ Annual Earnings: more than $145,600
- ◎ Growth: 19.5%
- ◎ Annual Job Openings: 38,000
- ◎ Self-Employed: 16.9%
- ◎ Part-Time: 8.1%

The job openings listed here are shared with Anesthesiologists; Family and General Practitioners; Internists, General; Pediatricians, General; Psychiatrists; and Surgeons.

Age Bracket	Percentage of Workers
45–54 Years Old	29.3%
55–64 Years Old	13.4%
65 or Older	5.4%

Diagnose, treat, and help prevent diseases of women, especially those affecting the reproductive system and the process of childbirth. Advise patients and community members concerning diet, activity, hygiene, and disease prevention. Analyze records, reports, test results, or examination information to diagnose medical condition of patient. Care for and treat women during prenatal, natal and post-natal periods. Collect, record, and maintain patient information, such as medical histories, reports, and examination results. Explain procedures and discuss test results or prescribed treatments with patients. Monitor patients' condition and progress and re-evaluate treatments as necessary. Perform cesarean sections or other surgical procedures as needed to preserve patients' health and deliver babies safely. Prescribe or administer therapy, medication, and other specialized medical care to treat or prevent illness, disease, or injury. Refer patient to medical specialist or other practitioner when necessary. Treat diseases of female organs. Conduct research to develop or test medications, treatments, or procedures to prevent or control disease or injury. Consult with, or provide consulting services to, other physicians. Direct and coordinate activities of nurses, students, assistants, specialists, therapists, and other medical staff. Plan, implement, or administer health programs in hospitals, businesses, or communities for prevention and treatment of injuries or illnesses. Prepare government and organizational reports on birth, death, and disease statistics, workforce evaluations, or the medical status of individuals. **SKILLS—**Science; Systems Evaluation; Reading Comprehension; Active Learning; Judgment and Decision Making; Management of Personnel Resources; Systems Analysis; Social Perceptiveness.

GOE—Interest Area: 08. Health Science. **Work Group:** 08.02. Medicine and Surgery. **Other Jobs**

in This Work Group: Anesthesiologists; Family and General Practitioners; Internists, General; Medical Assistants; Medical Transcriptionists; Pediatricians, General; Pharmacists; Pharmacy Aides; Pharmacy Technicians; Physician Assistants; Psychiatrists; Registered Nurses; Surgeons; Surgical Technologists. **PERSONALITY TYPE:** Investigative. Investigative occupations frequently involve working with ideas and require an extensive amount of thinking. These occupations can involve searching for facts and figuring out problems mentally.

EDUCATION/TRAINING PROGRAM(S)— Neonatal-Perinatal Medicine; Obstetrics and Gynecology.

WORK ENVIRONMENT—Disease or infections; common protective or safety equipment; walking and running; spend time bending or twisting the body; indoors; standing.

Operations Research Analysts

- Education/Training Required: Master's degree
- Annual Earnings: $60,230
- Growth: 6.2%
- Annual Job Openings: 6,000
- Self-Employed: 5.8%
- Part-Time: 2.7%

Age Bracket	Percentage of Workers
45–54 Years Old	34.7%
55–64 Years Old	13.7%
65 or Older	close to 0%

Formulate and apply mathematical modeling and other optimizing methods using a computer to develop and interpret information that assists management with decision making, policy formulation, or other managerial functions. May develop related software, service, or products. Frequently concentrates on collecting and analyzing data and developing decision support software. May develop and supply optimal time, cost, or logistics networks for program evaluation, review, or implementation. Analyze information obtained from management in order to conceptualize and define operational problems. Break systems into their component parts, assign numerical values to each component, and examine the mathematical relationships between them. Collaborate with senior managers and decision-makers to identify and solve a variety of problems, and to clarify management objectives. Define data requirements; then gather and validate information, applying judgment and statistical tests. Design, conduct, and evaluate experimental operational models in cases where models cannot be developed from existing data. Formulate mathematical or simulation models of problems, relating constants and variables, restrictions, alternatives, conflicting objectives, and their numerical parameters. Observe the current system in operation, and gather and analyze information about each of the parts of component problems, using a variety of sources. Perform validation and testing of models to ensure adequacy; reformulate models as necessary. Prepare management reports defining and evaluating problems and recommending solutions. Specify manipulative or computational methods to be applied to models. Study and analyze information about alternative courses of action in order to determine which plan will offer the best outcomes. Collaborate with others in the organization to ensure successful implementation of chosen problem solutions. Develop and apply time and cost networks in order to plan, control, and review large projects. Develop business methods and procedures, including accounting systems, file systems, office systems, logistics systems, and production schedules. **SKILLS**—Systems Evaluation; Systems Analysis; Mathematics; Judgment and Decision Making; Science; Monitoring; Complex Problem Solving; Operations Analysis.

GOE—Interest Area: 04. Business and Administration. **Work Group:** 04.05. Accounting, Auditing, and Analytical Support. **Other Jobs in This Work Group:** Accountants; Auditors; Budget Analysts; Industrial Engineering Technicians; Logisticians; Management Analysts. **PERSONALITY TYPE:** Investigative. Investigative occupations frequently involve working with ideas and require an extensive amount of thinking. These occupations can involve searching for facts and figuring out problems mentally.

EDUCATION/TRAINING PROGRAM(S)— Management Science, General; Management Sciences and Quantitative Methods, Other; Operations Research.

WORK ENVIRONMENT—Sitting; indoors.

Optometrists

◎ Education/Training Required: First professional degree

◎ Annual Earnings: $88,290

◎ Growth: 17.1%

◎ Annual Job Openings: 2,000

◎ Self-Employed: 29.2%

◎ Part-Time: 25.1%

Age Bracket	Percentage of Workers
45–54 Years Old	27.0%
55–64 Years Old	8.1%
65 or Older	8.1%

Diagnose, manage, and treat conditions and diseases of the human eye and visual system. Examine eyes and visual system, diagnose problems or impairments, prescribe corrective lenses, and provide treatment. May prescribe therapeutic drugs to treat specific eye conditions. Examine eyes, using observation, instruments and pharmaceutical agents, to determine visual acuity and perception, focus and coordination and to diagnose diseases and other abnormalities such as glaucoma or color blindness. Analyze test results and develop a treatment plan. Prescribe, supply, fit and adjust eyeglasses, contact lenses and other vision aids. Prescribe medications to treat eye diseases if state laws permit. Educate and counsel patients on contact lens care, visual hygiene, lighting arrangements and safety factors. Consult with and refer patients to ophthalmologist or other health care practitioner if additional medical treatment is determined necessary. Remove foreign bodies from the eye. Provide patients undergoing eye surgeries, such as cataract and laser vision correction, with pre- and post-operative care. Prescribe therapeutic procedures to correct or conserve vision. Provide vision therapy and low vision rehabilitation. **SKILLS**—Science; Management of Personnel Resources; Judgment and Decision Making; Active Listening; Persuasion; Service Orientation; Reading Comprehension; Active Learning; Instructing.

GOE—Interest Area: 08. Health Science. **Work Group:** 08.04. Health Specialties. **Other Jobs in This Work Group:** Chiropractors; Podiatrists. **PERSONALITY TYPE:** Investigative. Investigative occupations frequently involve working with ideas and require an extensive amount of thinking. These occupations can involve searching for facts and figuring out problems mentally.

EDUCATION/TRAINING PROGRAM(S)—Optometry (OD).

WORK ENVIRONMENT—Physical proximity to others; disease or infections; sitting; indoors.

Oral and Maxillofacial Surgeons

- Education/Training Required: First professional degree
- Annual Earnings: more than $145,600
- Growth: 4.1%
- Annual Job Openings: 7,000
- Self-Employed: 39.9%
- Part-Time: 22.3%

The job openings listed here are shared with Dentists, General; Orthodontists; and Prosthodontists.

Age Bracket	Percentage of Workers
45–54 Years Old	28.2%
55–64 Years Old	19.7%
65 or Older	6.4%

Perform surgery on mouth, jaws, and related head and neck structure to execute difficult and multiple extractions of teeth, to remove tumors and other abnormal growths, to correct abnormal jaw relations by mandibular or maxillary revision, to prepare mouth for insertion of dental prosthesis, or to treat fractured jaws. Administer general and local anesthetics. Collaborate with other professionals such as restorative dentists and orthodontists in order to plan treatment. Perform surgery on the mouth and jaws in order to treat conditions such as cleft lip and palate and jaw growth problems. Perform surgery to prepare the mouth for dental implants, and to aid in the regeneration of defi-cient bone and gum tissues. Provide emergency treatment of facial injuries including facial lacerations, intra-oral lacerations, and fractured facial bones. Remove impacted, damaged, and non-restorable teeth. Remove tumors and other abnormal growths of the oral and facial regions, using surgical instruments. Restore form and function by moving skin, bone, nerves, and other tissues from other parts of the body in order to reconstruct the jaws and face. Evaluate the position of the wisdom teeth in order to determine whether problems exist currently or might occur in the future. Perform minor cosmetic procedures such as chin and cheek-bone enhancements, and minor facial rejuvenation procedures including the use of Botox and laser technology. Treat infections of the oral cavity, salivary glands, jaws, and neck. Treat problems affecting the oral mucosa such as mouth ulcers and infections. Treat snoring problems, using laser surgery. **SKILLS**—Science; Reading Comprehension; Judgment and Decision Making; Critical Thinking; Active Learning; Learning Strategies; Speaking; Service Orientation.

GOE—Interest Area: 08. Health Science. **Work Group:** 08.03. Dentistry. **Other Jobs in This Work Group:** Dental Assistants; Dental Hygienists; Dentists, General; Orthodontists; Prosthodontists. **PERSONALITY TYPE:** Investigative. Investigative occupations frequently involve working with ideas and require an extensive amount of thinking. These occupations can involve searching for facts and figuring out problems mentally.

EDUCATION/TRAINING PROGRAM(S)— Dental/Oral Surgery Specialty; Oral/Maxillofacial Surgery (Cert, MS, PhD).

WORK ENVIRONMENT—Common protective or safety equipment; disease or infections; indoors; standing; using hands on objects, tools, or controls.

Orthodontists

- Education/Training Required: First professional degree
- Annual Earnings: more than $145,600
- Growth: 4.1%
- Annual Job Openings: 7,000
- Self-Employed: 39.9%
- Part-Time: 22.3%

The job openings listed here are shared with Dentists, General; Oral and Maxillofacial Surgeons; and Prosthodontists.

Age Bracket	Percentage of Workers
45–54 Years Old	28.2%
55–64 Years Old	19.7%
65 or Older	6.4%

Examine, diagnose, and treat dental malocclusions and oral cavity anomalies. Design and fabricate appliances to realign teeth and jaws to produce and maintain normal function and to improve appearance. Adjust dental appliances periodically in order to produce and maintain normal function. Coordinate orthodontic services with other dental and medical services. Design and fabricate appliances, such as space maintainers, retainers, and labial and lingual arch wires. Diagnose teeth and jaw or other dental-facial abnormalities. Examine patients in order to assess abnormalities of jaw development, tooth position, and other dental-facial structures. Fit dental appliances in patients' mouths in order to alter the position and relationship of teeth and jaws, and to realign teeth. Prepare diagnostic and treatment records. Provide patients with proposed treatment plans and cost estimates. Study diagnostic records such as medical/dental histories, plaster models of the teeth, photos of a patient's face and teeth, and X rays in order to develop patient treatment plans. Instruct dental officers and technical assistants in orthodontic procedures and techniques. **SKILLS**—Science; Technology Design; Reading Comprehension; Active Learning; Operations Analysis; Service Orientation; Critical Thinking; Complex Problem Solving; Equipment Selection.

GOE—Interest Area: 08. Health Science. **Work Group:** 08.03. Dentistry. **Other Jobs in This Work Group:** Dental Assistants; Dental Hygienists; Dentists, General; Oral and Maxillofacial Surgeons; Prosthodontists. **PERSONALITY TYPE:** Investigative. Investigative occupations frequently involve working with ideas and require an extensive amount of thinking. These occupations can involve searching for facts and figuring out problems mentally.

EDUCATION/TRAINING PROGRAM(S)—Orthodontics Specialty; Orthodontics/Orthodontology (Cert, MS, PhD).

WORK ENVIRONMENT—Common protective or safety equipment; standing; indoors; disease or infections; sitting.

Painters and Illustrators

- Education/Training Required: Long-term on-the-job training
- Annual Earnings: $41,240
- Growth: 16.5%
- Annual Job Openings: 4,000
- Self-Employed: 55.5%
- Part-Time: 23.1%

The job openings listed here are shared with Cartoonists, Sculptors, and Sketch Artists.

Age Bracket	Percentage of Workers
45–54 Years Old	25.5%
55–64 Years Old	17.0%
65 or Older	5.7%

Paint or draw subject material to produce original artwork or illustrations, using watercolors, oils, acrylics, tempera, or other paint mediums. Renders drawings, illustrations, and sketches of buildings, manufactured products, or models, working from sketches, blueprints, memory, or reference materials. Paints scenic backgrounds, murals, and portraiture for motion picture and television production sets, glass artworks, and exhibits. Etches, carves, paints, or draws artwork on material, such as stone, glass, canvas, wood, and linoleum. Develops drawings, paintings, diagrams, and models of medical or biological subjects for use in publications, exhibits, consultations, research, and teaching. Studies style, techniques, colors, textures, and materials used by artist to maintain consistency in reconstruction or retouching procedures. Removes painting from frame or paint layer from canvas to restore artwork, following specified technique and equipment. Examines surfaces of paintings and proofs of artwork, using magnifying device, to determine method of restoration or needed corrections. Installs finished stained glass in window or door frame. Assembles, leads, and solders finished glass to fabricate stained glass article. Applies select solvents and cleaning agents to clean surface of painting and remove accretions, discolorations, and deteriorated varnish. Performs tests to determine factors, such as age, structure, pigment stability, and probable reaction to various cleaning agents and solvents. Confers with professional personnel or client to discuss objectives of artwork, develop illustration ideas, and theme to be portrayed. Brushes or sprays protective or decorative finish on completed background panels, informational legends, exhibit accessories, or finished painting. Integrates and develops visual elements, such as line, space, mass, color, and perspective to produce desired effect. **SKILLS**—Operations Analysis; Management of Material Resources; Installation; Quality Control Analysis; Repairing.

GOE—Interest Area: 03. Arts and Communication. **Work Group:** 03.04. Studio Art. **Other Jobs in This Work Group:** Cartoonists; Craft Artists; Potters; Sculptors; Sketch Artists. **PERSONALITY TYPE:** Artistic. Artistic occupations frequently involve working with forms, designs, and patterns. They often require self-expression, and the work can be done without following a clear set of rules.

EDUCATION/TRAINING PROGRAM(S)—Art/Art Studies, General; Art/Art Studies, General; Drawing; Fine Arts and Art Studies, Other; Fine/Studio Arts, General; Medical Illustration/Medical Illustrator.

WORK ENVIRONMENT—Sitting; spend time making repetitive motions; standing; indoors; minor burns, cuts, bites, or stings.

Pediatricians, General

- Education/Training Required: First professional degree
- Annual Earnings: $135,450
- Growth: 19.5%
- Annual Job Openings: 38,000
- Self-Employed: 16.9%
- Part-Time: 8.1%

The job openings listed here are shared with Anesthesiologists; Family and General Practitioners; Internists, General; Obstetricians and Gynecologists, General; Psychiatrists; and Surgeons.

Age Bracket	Percentage of Workers
45–54 Years Old	29.3%
55–64 Years Old	13.4%
65 or Older	5.4%

Diagnose, treat, and help prevent children's diseases and injuries. Advise patients, parents or guardians and community members concerning diet, activity, hygiene, and disease prevention. Collect, record, and maintain patient information, such as medical history, reports, and examination results. Examine children regularly to assess their growth and development. Examine patients or order, perform and interpret diagnostic tests to obtain information on medical condition and determine diagnosis. Explain procedures and discuss test results or prescribed treatments with patients and parents or guardians. Monitor patients' condition and progress and re-evaluate treatments as necessary. Plan and execute medical care programs to aid in the mental and physical growth and development of children and adolescents. Prescribe or administer treatment, therapy, medication, vaccination, and other specialized medical care to treat or prevent illness, disease, or injury in infants and children. Refer patient to medical specialist or other practitioner when necessary. Treat children who have minor illnesses, acute and chronic health problems, and growth and development concerns. Conduct research to study anatomy and develop or test medications, treatments, or procedures to prevent, or control disease or injury. Direct and coordinate activities of nurses, students, assistants, specialists, therapists, and other medical staff. Operate on patients to remove, repair, or improve functioning of diseased or injured body parts and systems. Plan, implement, or administer health programs or standards in hospital, business, or community for information, prevention, or treatment of injury or illness. Provide consulting services to other physicians. Prepare reports for government or management of birth, death, and disease statistics, workforce evaluations, or medical status of individuals. **SKILLS**—Science; Systems Evaluation; Reading Comprehension; Active Learning; Judgment and Decision Making; Management of Personnel Resources; Systems Analysis; Social Perceptiveness.

GOE—Interest Area: 08. Health Science. **Work Group:** 08.02. Medicine and Surgery. **Other Jobs in This Work Group:** Anesthesiologists; Family and General Practitioners; Internists, General; Medical Assistants; Medical Transcriptionists; Obstetricians and Gynecologists; Pharmacists; Pharmacy Aides; Pharmacy Technicians; Physician Assistants; Psychiatrists; Registered Nurses; Surgeons; Surgical Technologists. **PERSONALITY TYPE:** Investigative. Investigative occupations frequently involve working with ideas and require an extensive amount of thinking. These occupations can involve searching for facts and figuring out problems mentally.

EDUCATION/TRAINING PROGRAM(S)— Child/Pediatric Neurology; Family Medicine; Neonatal-Perinatal Medicine; Pediatric Cardiology; Pediatric Endocrinology; Pediatric Hemato-Oncology; Pediatric Nephrology; Pediatric Orthopedics; Pediatric Surgery; Pediatrics.

WORK ENVIRONMENT—Disease or infections; common protective or safety equipment; walking and running; spend time bending or twisting the body; indoors; standing.

Personal and Home Care Aides

- Education/Training Required: Short-term on-the-job training
- Annual Earnings: $17,020
- Growth: 40.5%
- Annual Job Openings: 154,000
- Self-Employed: 7.1%
- Part-Time: 34.0%

Age Bracket	Percentage of Workers
45–54 Years Old	23.4%
55–64 Years Old	17.0%
65 or Older	8.4%

Assist elderly or disabled adults with daily living activities at the person's home or in a daytime non-residential facility. Duties performed at a place of residence may include keeping house (making beds, doing laundry, washing dishes) and preparing meals. May provide meals and supervised activities at non-residential care facilities. May advise families, the elderly, and disabled on such things as nutrition, cleanliness, and household utilities. Perform health-care related tasks, such as monitoring vital signs and medication, under the direction of registered nurses and physiotherapists. Administer bedside and personal care, such as ambulation and personal hygiene assistance. Prepare and maintain records of client progress and services performed, reporting changes in client condition to manager or supervisor. Perform housekeeping duties, such as cooking, cleaning, washing clothes and dishes, and running errands. Care for individuals and families during periods of incapacitation, family disruption or convalescence, providing companionship, personal care and help in adjusting to new lifestyles. Instruct and advise clients on issues such as household cleanliness, utilities, hygiene, nutrition and infant care. Plan, shop for, and prepare meals, including special diets, and assist families in planning, shopping for, and preparing nutritious meals. Participate in case reviews, consulting with the team caring for the client, to evaluate the client's needs and plan for continuing services. Transport clients to locations outside the home, such as to physicians' offices or on outings, using a motor vehicle. Train family members to provide bedside care. Provide clients with communication assistance, typing their correspondence and obtaining information for them. **SKILLS**—Social Perceptiveness; Persuasion; Service Orientation; Learning Strategies; Coordination; Instructing; Active Listening; Critical Thinking.

GOE—Interest Area: 10. Human Service. **Work Group:** 10.03. Child/Personal Care and Services. **Other Jobs in This Work Group:** Child Care Workers; Funeral Attendants; Nannies. **PERSONALITY TYPE:** Social. Social occupations frequently involve working with, communicating with, and teaching people. These occupations often involve helping or providing service to others.

EDUCATION/TRAINING PROGRAM(S)— No data available.

WORK ENVIRONMENT—Physical proximity to others; in an enclosed vehicle or equipment; disease or infections; minor burns, cuts, bites, or stings; standing.

Personal Financial Advisors

- Education/Training Required: Bachelor's degree
- Annual Earnings: $62,450
- Growth: 34.6%
- Annual Job Openings: 18,000
- Self-Employed: 37.7%
- Part-Time: 7.0%

Age Bracket	Percentage of Workers
45–54 Years Old	24.8%
55–64 Years Old	16.2%
65 or Older	3.2%

Advise clients on financial plans utilizing knowledge of tax and investment strategies, securities, insurance, pension plans, and real estate. Duties include assessing clients' assets, liabilities, cash flow, insurance coverage, tax status, and financial objectives to establish investment strategies. Analyze financial information obtained from clients to determine strategies for meeting clients' financial objectives. Answer clients' questions about the purposes and details of financial plans and strategies. Build and maintain client bases, keeping current client plans up-to-date and recruiting new clients on an ongoing basis. Contact clients periodically to determine if there have been changes in their financial status. Devise debt liquidation plans that include payoff priorities and timelines. Explain and document for clients the types of services that are to be provided, and the responsibilities to be taken by the personal financial advisor. Explain to individuals and groups the details of financial assistance available to college and university students, such as loans, grants, and scholarships. Guide clients in the gathering of information such as bank account records, income tax returns, life and disability insurance records, pension plan information, and wills. Implement financial planning recommendations, or refer clients to someone who can assist them with plan implementation. Interview clients to determine their current income, expenses, insurance coverage, tax status, financial objectives, risk tolerance, and other information needed to develop a financial plan. Monitor financial market trends to ensure that plans are effective, and to identify any necessary updates. Prepare and interpret for clients information such as investment performance reports, financial document summaries, and income projections. Recommend strategies clients can use to achieve their financial goals and objectives, including specific recommendations in such areas as cash management, insurance coverage, and investment planning. Research and investigate available investment opportunities to determine whether they fit into financial plans. Review clients' accounts and plans regularly to determine whether life changes, economic changes, or financial performance indicate a need for plan reassessment. Sell financial products such as stocks, bonds, mutual funds, and insurance if licensed to do so. **SKILLS**—Service Orientation; Speaking; Management of Financial Resources; Active Listening; Judgment and Decision Making; Mathematics; Critical Thinking; Reading Comprehension; Writing.

GOE—Interest Area: 06. Finance and Insurance. **Work Group:** 06.05. Finance/Insurance Sales and Support. **Other Jobs in This Work Group:** Advertising Sales Agents; Insurance Sales Agents; Sales Agents, Financial Services; Sales Agents, Securities and Commodities. **PERSONALITY TYPE:** Social. Social occupations frequently involve working with, communicating with, and teaching peo-

P

ple. These occupations often involve helping or providing service to others.

EDUCATION/TRAINING PROGRAM(S)— Finance, General; Financial Planning and Services.

WORK ENVIRONMENT—Sitting; indoors; walking and running.

Personnel Recruiters

- ◎ Education/Training Required: Bachelor's degree
- ◎ Annual Earnings: $41,190
- ◎ Growth: 27.3%
- ◎ Annual Job Openings: 29,000
- ◎ Self-Employed: 0.8%
- ◎ Part-Time: 7.7%

The job openings listed here are shared with Employment Interviewers, Private or Public Employment Service.

Age Bracket	Percentage of Workers
45–54 Years Old	26.6%
55–64 Years Old	13.4%
65 or Older	1.6%

Seek out, interview, and screen applicants to fill existing and future job openings and promote career opportunities within an organization. Establish and maintain relationships with hiring managers to stay abreast of current and future hiring and business needs. Interview applicants to obtain information on work history, training, education, and job skills. Maintain current knowledge of Equal Employment Opportunity (EEO) and affirmative action guidelines and laws, such as the Americans with Disabilities Act. Perform searches for qualified candidates according to relevant job criteria, using computer databases, networking, Internet recruiting resources, cold calls, media, recruiting firms, and employee referrals. Prepare and maintain employment records. Contact applicants to inform them of employment possibilities, consideration, and selection. Inform potential applicants about facilities, operations, benefits, and job or career opportunities in organizations. Screen and refer applicants to hiring personnel in the organization, making hiring recommendations when appropriate. Arrange for interviews and provide travel arrangements as necessary. Advise managers and employees on staffing policies and procedures. Review and evaluate applicant qualifications or eligibility for specified licensing, according to established guidelines and designated licensing codes. Hire applicants and authorize paperwork assigning them to positions. Conduct reference and background checks on applicants. Evaluate recruitment and selection criteria to ensure conformance to professional, statistical, and testing standards, recommending revision as needed. Recruit applicants for open positions, arranging job fairs with college campus representatives. Advise management on organizing, preparing, and implementing recruiting and retention programs. Supervise personnel clerks performing filing, typing and record-keeping duties. Project yearly recruitment expenditures for budgetary consideration and control. **SKILLS—**Management of Personnel Resources; Negotiation; Persuasion; Service Orientation; Time Management; Social Perceptiveness; Management of Financial Resources; Active Listening.

GOE—Interest Area: 04. Business and Administration. **Work Group:** 04.03. Human Resources Support. **Other Jobs in This Work Group:** Compensation, Benefits, and Job Analysis Specialists; Employment Interviewers,

Private or Public Employment Service; Training and Development Specialists. **PERSONALITY TYPE:** Enterprising. Enterprising occupations frequently involve starting up and carrying out projects. These occupations can involve leading people and making many decisions. They sometimes require risk taking and often deal with business.

EDUCATION/TRAINING PROGRAM(S)—Human Resources Management/Personnel Administration, General; Labor and Industrial Relations.

WORK ENVIRONMENT—Sitting; sounds, noise levels are distracting or uncomfortable; contaminants; indoors; physical proximity to others.

Pharmacists

- Education/Training Required: First professional degree
- Annual Earnings: $87,160
- Growth: 30.1%
- Annual Job Openings: 23,000
- Self-Employed: 3.4%
- Part-Time: 17.3%

Age Bracket	Percentage of Workers
45–54 Years Old	19.0%
55–64 Years Old	15.9%
65 or Older	6.5%

Compound and dispense medications following prescriptions issued by physicians, dentists, or other authorized medical practitioners. Review prescriptions to assure accuracy, to ascertain the needed ingredients, and to evaluate their suitability. Provide information and advice regarding drug interactions, side effects, dosage and proper medication storage. Analyze prescribing trends to monitor patient compliance and to prevent excessive usage or harmful interactions. Order and purchase pharmaceutical supplies, medical supplies, and drugs, maintaining stock and storing and handling it properly. Maintain records, such as pharmacy files, patient profiles, charge system files, inventories, control records for radioactive nuclei, and registries of poisons, narcotics, and controlled drugs. Provide specialized services to help patients manage conditions such as diabetes, asthma, smoking cessation, or high blood pressure. Advise customers on the selection of medication brands, medical equipment and health-care supplies. Collaborate with other health care professionals to plan, monitor, review, and evaluate the quality and effectiveness of drugs and drug regimens, providing advice on drug applications and characteristics. Compound and dispense medications as prescribed by doctors and dentists, by calculating, weighing, measuring, and mixing ingredients, or oversee these activities. Offer health promotion and prevention activities, for example, training people to use devices such as blood pressure or diabetes monitors. Refer patients to other health professionals and agencies when appropriate. Prepare sterile solutions and infusions for use in surgical procedures, emergency rooms, or patients' homes. Plan, implement, and maintain procedures for mixing, packaging, and labeling pharmaceuticals, according to policy and legal requirements, to ensure quality, security, and proper disposal. Assay radiopharmaceuticals, verify rates of disintegration, and calculate the volume required to produce the desired results, to ensure proper dosages. Manage pharmacy operations, hiring and supervising staff, performing administrative duties, and buying and selling non-pharmaceutical merchandise. Work in hospitals, clinics, or for

HMOs, dispensing prescriptions, serving as a medical team consultants, or specializing in specific drug therapy areas such as oncology or nuclear pharmacotherapy. **SKILLS**—Social Perceptiveness; Instructing; Reading Comprehension; Active Listening; Science; Critical Thinking; Speaking; Active Learning.

GOE—Interest Area: 08. Health Science. **Work Group:** 08.02. Medicine and Surgery. **Other Jobs in This Work Group:** Anesthesiologists; Family and General Practitioners; Internists, General; Medical Assistants; Medical Transcriptionists; Obstetricians and Gynecologists; Pediatricians, General; Pharmacy Aides; Pharmacy Technicians; Physician Assistants; Psychiatrists; Registered Nurses; Surgeons; Surgical Technologists. **PERSONALITY TYPE:** Investigative. Investigative occupations frequently involve working with ideas and require an extensive amount of thinking. These occupations can involve searching for facts and figuring out problems mentally.

EDUCATION/TRAINING PROGRAM(S)—Clinical and Industrial Drug Development (MS, PhD); Clinical, Hospital, and Managed Care Pharmacy (MS, PhD); Industrial and Physical Pharmacy and Cosmetic Sciences (MS, PhD); Medicinal and Pharmaceutical Chemistry (MS, PhD); Natural Products Chemistry and Pharmacognosy (MS, PhD); Pharmaceutics and Drug Design (MS, PhD); Pharmacoeconomics/Pharmaceutical Economics (MS, PhD); Pharmacy (PharmD, BS/BPharm); Pharmacy Administration and Pharmacy Policy and Regulatory Affairs (MS, PhD); others.

WORK ENVIRONMENT—Physical proximity to others; disease or infections; standing; indoors; sounds, noise levels are distracting or uncomfortable.

Philosophy and Religion Teachers, Postsecondary

- Education/Training Required: Master's degree
- Annual Earnings: $52,580
- Growth: 38.1%
- Annual Job Openings: 216,000
- Self-Employed: 0.3%
- Part-Time: 27.7%

The job openings listed here are shared with all other postsecondary teaching occupations.

Age Bracket	Percentage of Workers
45–54 Years Old	22.8%
55–64 Years Old	19.0%
65 or Older	5.5%

Teach courses in philosophy, religion, and theology. Evaluate and grade students' class work, assignments, and papers. Initiate, facilitate, and moderate classroom discussions. Prepare and deliver lectures to undergraduate and/or graduate students on topics such as ethics, logic, and contemporary religious thought. Prepare course materials such as syllabi, homework assignments, and handouts. Compile, administer, and grade examinations or assign this work to others. Keep abreast of developments in their field by reading current literature, talking with colleagues, and participating in professional conferences. Maintain student attendance records, grades, and other required records. Plan, evaluate, and revise curricula, course content, and course materials and methods of instruction. Maintain regularly scheduled office hours in order to advise and assist students. Select and obtain materials and supplies such as textbooks.

Advise students on academic and vocational curricula, and on career issues. Conduct research in a particular field of knowledge and publish findings in professional journals, books, and/or electronic media. Perform administrative duties such as serving as department head. Serve on academic or administrative committees that deal with institutional policies, departmental matters, and academic issues. Collaborate with colleagues to address teaching and research issues. Participate in campus and community events. Compile bibliographies of specialized materials for outside reading assignments. Participate in student recruitment, registration, and placement activities. Supervise undergraduate and/or graduate teaching, internship, and research work. **SKILLS**—Instructing; Learning Strategies; Writing; Critical Thinking; Reading Comprehension; Social Perceptiveness; Persuasion; Speaking.

GOE—Interest Area: 05. Education and Training. **Work Group:** 05.03. Postsecondary and Adult Teaching and Instructing. **Other Jobs in This Work Group:** Adult Literacy, Remedial Education, and GED Teachers and Instructors; Agricultural Sciences Teachers, Postsecondary; Anthropology and Archeology Teachers, Postsecondary; Architecture Teachers, Postsecondary; Area, Ethnic, and Cultural Studies Teachers, Postsecondary; Art, Drama, and Music Teachers, Postsecondary; Atmospheric, Earth, Marine, and Space Sciences Teachers, Postsecondary; Biological Science Teachers, Postsecondary; Business Teachers, Postsecondary; Chemistry Teachers, Postsecondary; Communications Teachers, Postsecondary; Computer Science Teachers, Postsecondary; Criminal Justice and Law Enforcement Teachers, Postsecondary; Economics Teachers, Postsecondary; Education Teachers, Postsecondary; Engineering Teachers, Postsecondary; English Language and Literature Teachers, Postsecondary; Environmental Science Teachers, Postsecondary; Farm and Home Management Advisors; Foreign Language and Literature Teachers, Postsecondary; Forestry and Conservation Science Teachers, Postsecondary; Geography Teachers, Postsecondary; Graduate Teaching Assistants; Health Specialties Teachers, Postsecondary; History Teachers, Postsecondary; Home Economics Teachers, Postsecondary; Law Teachers, Postsecondary; Library Science Teachers, Postsecondary; Mathematical Science Teachers, Postsecondary; Nursing Instructors and Teachers, Postsecondary; Physics Teachers, Postsecondary; Political Science Teachers, Postsecondary; Psychology Teachers, Postsecondary; Recreation and Fitness Studies Teachers, Postsecondary; Self-Enrichment Education Teachers; Social Work Teachers, Postsecondary; Sociology Teachers, Postsecondary; Vocational Education Teachers, Postsecondary. **PERSONALITY TYPE:** No data available.

EDUCATION/TRAINING PROGRAM(S)—Bible/Biblical Studies; Buddhist Studies; Christian Studies; Divinity/Ministry (BD, MDiv.); Ethics; Hindu Studies; Missions/Missionary Studies and Missiology; Pastoral Counseling and Specialized Ministries, Other; Pastoral Studies/Counseling; Philosophy; Philosophy and Religion, Other; Philosophy, Other; Pre-Theology/Pre-Ministerial Studies; Rabbinical Studies (M.H.L./Rav); Religion/Religious Studies; Religious Education; Religious/Sacred Music; Talmudic Studies; others.

WORK ENVIRONMENT—Sitting; physical proximity to others; indoors.

Physicists

- Education/Training Required: Doctoral degree
- Annual Earnings: $87,480
- Growth: 6.9%
- Annual Job Openings: 1,000
- Self-Employed: 9.9%
- Part-Time: 2.4%

Age Bracket	Percentage of Workers
45–54 Years Old	22.2%
55–64 Years Old	33.3%
65 or Older	11.1%

Conduct research into the phases of physical phenomena, develop theories and laws on the basis of observation and experiments, and devise methods to apply laws and theories to industry and other fields. Analyze data from research conducted to detect and measure physical phenomena. Describe and express observations and conclusions in mathematical terms. Design computer simulations to model physical data so that it can be better understood. Develop theories and laws on the basis of observation and experiments, and apply these theories and laws to problems in areas such as nuclear energy, optics, and aerospace technology. Observe the structure and properties of matter, and the transformation and propagation of energy, using equipment such as masers, lasers, and telescopes, in order to explore and identify the basic principles governing these phenomena. Perform complex calculations as part of the analysis and evaluation of data, using computers. Report experimental results by writing papers for scientific journals or by presenting information at scientific conferences. Collaborate with other scientists in the design, development, and testing of experimental, industrial, or medical equipment, instrumentation, and procedures. Conduct application evaluations and analyze results in order to determine commercial, industrial, scientific, medical, military, or other uses for electro-optical devices. Develop manufacturing, assembly, and fabrication processes of lasers, masers, infrared, and other light-emitting and light-sensitive devices. Provide support services for activities such as radiation therapy, diagnostic imaging, or seismology. Teach physics to students. Advise authorities of procedures to be followed in radiation incidents or hazards, and assist in civil defense planning. Conduct research pertaining to potential environmental impacts of atomic energy-related industrial development in order to determine licensing qualifications. Develop standards of permissible concentrations of radioisotopes in liquids and gases. Direct testing and monitoring of contamination of radioactive equipment, and recording of personnel and plant area radiation exposure data. **SKILLS**—Science; Mathematics; Writing; Technology Design; Active Learning; Reading Comprehension; Critical Thinking; Operations Analysis; Management of Personnel Resources.

GOE—Interest Area: 15. Scientific Research, Engineering, and Mathematics. **Work Group:** 15.02. Physical Sciences. **Other Jobs in This Work Group:** Astronomers; Atmospheric and Space Scientists; Chemists; Geographers; Geologists; Hydrologists; Materials Scientists. **PERSONALITY TYPE:** Investigative. Investigative occupations frequently involve working with ideas and require an extensive amount of thinking. These occupations can involve searching for facts and figuring out problems mentally.

EDUCATION/TRAINING PROGRAM(S)— Acoustics; Astrophysics; Atomic/Molecular Physics; Elementary Particle Physics;

Health/Medical Physics; Nuclear Physics; Optics/Optical Sciences; Physics, General; Physics, Other; Plasma and High-Temperature Physics; Solid State and Low-Temperature Physics; Theoretical and Mathematical Physics.

WORK ENVIRONMENT—Sitting; specialized protective or safety equipment; indoors; exposed to radiation; hazardous conditions.

Physics Teachers, Postsecondary

- Education/Training Required: Master's degree
- Annual Earnings: $65,280
- Growth: 38.1%
- Annual Job Openings: 216,000
- Self-Employed: 0.3%
- Part-Time: 27.7%

The job openings listed here are shared with all other postsecondary teaching occupations.

Age Bracket	Percentage of Workers
45–54 Years Old	22.8%
55–64 Years Old	19.0%
65 or Older	5.5%

Teach courses pertaining to the laws of matter and energy. Includes both teachers primarily engaged in teaching and those who do a combination of both teaching and research. Evaluate and grade students' class work, laboratory work, assignments, and papers. Prepare and deliver lectures to undergraduate and/or graduate students on topics such as quantum mechanics, particle physics, and optics. Compile, administer, and grade examinations or assign this work to others. Maintain student attendance records, grades, and other required records. Supervise students' laboratory work. Prepare course materials such as syllabi, homework assignments, and handouts. Maintain regularly scheduled office hours in order to advise and assist students. Supervise undergraduate and/or graduate teaching, internship, and research work. Keep abreast of developments in their field by reading current literature, talking with colleagues, and participating in professional conferences. Plan, evaluate, and revise curricula, course content, and course materials and methods of instruction. Initiate, facilitate, and moderate classroom discussions. Conduct research in a particular field of knowledge and publish findings in professional journals, books, and/or electronic media. Advise students on academic and vocational curricula, and on career issues. Select and obtain materials and supplies such as textbooks and laboratory equipment. Collaborate with colleagues to address teaching and research issues. Participate in student recruitment, registration, and placement activities. Serve on academic or administrative committees that deal with institutional policies, departmental matters, and academic issues. Write grant proposals to procure external research funding. Perform administrative duties such as serving as department head. **SKILLS**—Science; Instructing; Learning Strategies; Mathematics; Programming; Critical Thinking; Active Learning; Reading Comprehension.

GOE—Interest Area: 05. Education and Training. **Work Group:** 05.03. Postsecondary and Adult Teaching and Instructing. **Other Jobs in This Work Group:** Adult Literacy, Remedial Education, and GED Teachers and Instructors; Agricultural Sciences Teachers, Postsecondary; Anthropology and Archeology Teachers, Postsecondary; Architecture Teachers, Postsecondary; Area, Ethnic, and Cultural Studies Teachers, Postsecondary; Art, Drama, and Music Teachers, Postsecondary; Atmospheric, Earth, Marine, and Space Sciences Teachers, Postsecondary; Biological Science Teachers, Postsecondary; Business Teachers, Postsecondary; Chemistry Teachers, Postsecondary; Communications Teachers, Postsecondary; Computer Science Teachers, Postsecondary; Criminal Justice and Law Enforcement Teachers, Postsecondary; Economics Teachers, Postsecondary; Education Teachers, Postsecondary; Engineering Teachers, Postsecondary; English Language and Literature Teachers, Postsecondary; Environmental Science Teachers, Postsecondary; Farm and Home Management Advisors; Foreign Language and Literature Teachers, Postsecondary; Forestry and Conservation Science Teachers, Postsecondary; Geography Teachers, Postsecondary; Graduate Teaching Assistants; Health Specialties Teachers, Postsecondary; History Teachers, Postsecondary; Home Economics Teachers, Postsecondary; Law Teachers, Postsecondary; Library Science Teachers, Postsecondary; Mathematical Science Teachers, Postsecondary; Nursing Instructors and Teachers, Postsecondary; Philosophy and Religion Teachers, Postsecondary; Political Science Teachers, Postsecondary; Psychology Teachers, Postsecondary; Recreation and Fitness Studies Teachers, Postsecondary; Self-Enrichment Education Teachers; Social Work Teachers, Postsecondary; Sociology Teachers, Postsecondary; Vocational Education Teachers, Postsecondary. **PERSONALITY TYPE:** Investigative. Investigative occupations frequently involve working with ideas and require an extensive amount of thinking. These occupations can involve searching for facts and figuring out problems mentally.

EDUCATION/TRAINING PROGRAM(S)— Acoustics; Atomic/Molecular Physics; Elemen-

tary Particle Physics; Nuclear Physics; Optics/Optical Sciences; Physics, General; Physics, Other; Plasma and High-Temperature Physics; Solid State and Low-Temperature Physics; Theoretical and Mathematical Physics.

WORK ENVIRONMENT—Sitting; indoors; physical proximity to others; sounds, noise levels are distracting or uncomfortable; contaminants; hazardous conditions.

Podiatrists

- Education/Training Required: First professional degree
- Annual Earnings: $97,290
- Growth: 15.0%
- Annual Job Openings: 1,000
- Self-Employed: 44.4%
- Part-Time: 15.6%

Age Bracket	Percentage of Workers
45–54 Years Old	27.3%
55–64 Years Old	9.1%
65 or Older	9.1%

Diagnose and treat diseases and deformities of the human foot. Advise patients about treatments and foot care techniques necessary for prevention of future problems. Correct deformities by means of plaster casts and strapping. Diagnose diseases and deformities of the foot using medical histories, physical examinations, X rays, and laboratory test results. Make and fit prosthetic appliances. Prescribe medications, corrective devices, physical therapy, or surgery. Refer patients to physicians when symptoms indicative of systemic disorders, such as arthritis or diabetes, are observed in feet and legs. Treat bone, muscle, and joint disorders affecting the feet. Treat conditions such as corns, calluses, ingrown nails, tumors, shortened tendons, bunions, cysts, and abscesses by surgical methods. Treat deformities using mechanical methods, such as whirlpool or paraffin baths, and electrical methods, such as short wave and low voltage currents. Educate the public about the benefits of foot care through techniques such as speaking engagements, advertising, and other forums. Perform administrative duties such as hiring employees, ordering supplies, and keeping records. **SKILLS**—Active Learning; Reading Comprehension; Technology Design; Judgment and Decision Making; Systems Evaluation; Equipment Selection; Active Listening; Service Orientation; Complex Problem Solving.

GOE—**Interest Area:** 08. Health Science. **Work Group:** 08.04. Health Specialties. **Other Jobs in This Work Group:** Chiropractors; Optometrists. **PERSONALITY TYPE:** Social. Social occupations frequently involve working with, communicating with, and teaching people. These occupations often involve helping or providing service to others.

EDUCATION/TRAINING PROGRAM(S)— Podiatric Medicine/Podiatry (DPM).

WORK ENVIRONMENT—Disease or infections; common protective or safety equipment; minor burns, cuts, bites, or stings; indoors; exposed to radiation.

Poets and Lyricists

- Education/Training Required: Bachelor's degree
- Annual Earnings: $45,460
- Growth: 16.1%
- Annual Job Openings: 23,000
- Self-Employed: 67.9%
- Part-Time: 24.2%

The job openings listed here are shared with Caption Writers, Copy Writers, and Creative Writers.

Age Bracket	Percentage of Workers
45–54 Years Old	24.7%
55–64 Years Old	16.3%
65 or Older	7.4%

Write poetry or song lyrics for publication or performance. Writes words to fit musical compositions, including lyrics for operas, musical plays, and choral works. Chooses subject matter and suitable form to express personal feeling and experience or ideas or to narrate story or event. Adapts text to accommodate musical requirements of composer and singer. Writes narrative, dramatic, lyric, or other types of poetry for publication. **SKILLS**—Writing; Reading Comprehension.

GOE—**Interest Area:** 03. Arts and Communication. **Work Group:** 03.02. Writing and Editing. **Other Jobs in This Work Group:** Copy Writers; Creative Writers; Editors; Technical Writers. **PERSONALITY TYPE:** Artistic. Artistic occupations frequently involve working with forms, designs, and patterns. They often require self-expression, and the work can be done without following a clear set of rules.

EDUCATION/TRAINING PROGRAM(S)— Communications Studies/Speech Communication and Rhetoric; Creative Writing; English Composition.

WORK ENVIRONMENT—Sitting; indoors.

Political Science Teachers, Postsecondary

- Education/Training Required: Master's degree
- Annual Earnings: $59,530
- Growth: 38.1%
- Annual Job Openings: 216,000
- Self-Employed: 0.3%
- Part-Time: 27.7%

The job openings listed here are shared with all other postsecondary teaching occupations.

Age Bracket	Percentage of Workers
45–54 Years Old	22.8%
55–64 Years Old	19.0%
65 or Older	5.5%

Teach courses in political science, international affairs, and international relations. Initiate, facilitate, and moderate classroom discussions. Prepare and deliver lectures to undergraduate and/or graduate students on topics such as classical political thought, international relations, and democracy and citizenship. Evaluate and grade students' class work, assignments, and papers. Compile, administer, and grade examinations or assign this work to others. Prepare course materials such as syllabi, homework assignments, and handouts. Keep abreast of developments in their field by reading current literature, talking with colleagues, and partici-

pating in professional conferences. Plan, evaluate, and revise curricula, course content, and course materials and methods of instruction. Maintain student attendance records, grades, and other required records. Maintain regularly scheduled office hours in order to advise and assist students. Advise students on academic and vocational curricula, and on career issues. Select and obtain materials and supplies such as textbooks. Conduct research in a particular field of knowledge and publish findings in professional journals, books, and/or electronic media. Supervise undergraduate and/or graduate teaching, internship, and research work. Collaborate with colleagues to address teaching and research issues. Serve on academic or administrative committees that deal with institutional policies, departmental matters, and academic issues. Participate in campus and community events. Participate in student recruitment, registration, and placement activities. Compile bibliographies of specialized materials for outside reading assignments. Act as advisers to student organizations. Perform administrative duties such as serving as department head. **SKILLS—** Instructing; Learning Strategies; Persuasion; Writing; Critical Thinking; Reading Comprehension; Speaking; Active Learning.

GOE—Interest Area: 05. Education and Training. **Work Group:** 05.03. Postsecondary and Adult Teaching and Instructing. **Other Jobs in This Work Group:** Adult Literacy, Remedial Education, and GED Teachers and Instructors; Agricultural Sciences Teachers, Postsecondary; Anthropology and Archeology Teachers, Postsecondary; Architecture Teachers, Postsecondary; Area, Ethnic, and Cultural Studies Teachers, Postsecondary; Art, Drama, and Music Teachers, Postsecondary; Atmospheric, Earth, Marine, and Space Sciences Teachers, Postsecondary; Biological Science Teachers, Postsecondary;

Business Teachers, Postsecondary; Chemistry Teachers, Postsecondary; Communications Teachers, Postsecondary; Computer Science Teachers, Postsecondary; Criminal Justice and Law Enforcement Teachers, Postsecondary; Economics Teachers, Postsecondary; Education Teachers, Postsecondary; Engineering Teachers, Postsecondary; English Language and Literature Teachers, Postsecondary; Environmental Science Teachers, Postsecondary; Farm and Home Management Advisors; Foreign Language and Literature Teachers, Postsecondary; Forestry and Conservation Science Teachers, Postsecondary; Geography Teachers, Postsecondary; Graduate Teaching Assistants; Health Specialties Teachers, Postsecondary; History Teachers, Postsecondary; Home Economics Teachers, Postsecondary; Law Teachers, Postsecondary; Library Science Teachers, Postsecondary; Mathematical Science Teachers, Postsecondary; Nursing Instructors and Teachers, Postsecondary; Philosophy and Religion Teachers, Postsecondary; Physics Teachers, Postsecondary; Psychology Teachers, Postsecondary; Recreation and Fitness Studies Teachers, Postsecondary; Self-Enrichment Education Teachers; Social Work Teachers, Postsecondary; Sociology Teachers, Postsecondary; Vocational Education Teachers, Postsecondary. **PERSONALITY TYPE:** Social. Social occupations frequently involve working with, communicating with, and teaching people. These occupations often involve helping or providing service to others.

EDUCATION/TRAINING PROGRAM(S)— American Government and Politics (United States); Political Science and Government, General; Political Science and Government, Other; Social Science Teacher Education.

WORK ENVIRONMENT—Sitting; indoors; physical proximity to others.

Postal Service Mail Carriers

- Education/Training Required: Short-term on-the-job training
- Annual Earnings: $45,880
- Growth: –0.5%
- Annual Job Openings: 20,000
- Self-Employed: 0%
- Part-Time: 6.5%

Age Bracket	Percentage of Workers
45–54 Years Old	37.5%
55–64 Years Old	16.1%
65 or Older	2.2%

Sort mail for delivery. Deliver mail on established route by vehicle or on foot. Bundle mail in preparation for delivery or transportation to relay boxes. Deliver mail to residences and business establishments along specified routes by walking and/or driving, using a combination of satchels, carts, cars, and small trucks. Enter change of address orders into computers that process forwarding address stickers. Hold mail for customers who are away from delivery locations. Leave notices telling patrons where to collect mail that could not be delivered. Maintain accurate records of deliveries. Meet schedules for the collection and return of mail. Record address changes and redirect mail for those addresses. Return incorrectly addressed mail to senders. Return to the post office with mail collected from homes, businesses, and public mailboxes. Sign for cash-on-delivery and registered mail before leaving the post office. Sort mail for delivery, arranging it in delivery sequence. Travel to post offices to pick up the mail for routes and/or pick up mail from postal relay boxes. Turn in money and receipts collected along mail routes.

P

Answer customers' questions about postal services and regulations. Complete forms that notify publishers of address changes. Obtain signed receipts for registered, certified, and insured mail; collect associated charges; and complete any necessary paperwork. Provide customers with change of address cards and other forms. Register, certify, and insure parcels and letters. Report any unusual circumstances concerning mail delivery, including the condition of street letter boxes. Sell stamps and money orders. **SKILLS**—None met the criteria.

GOE—Interest Area: 16. Transportation, Distribution, and Logistics. **Work Group:** 16.06. Other Services Requiring Driving. **Other Jobs in This Work Group:** Ambulance Drivers and Attendants, Except Emergency Medical Technicians; Bus Drivers, School; Bus Drivers, Transit and Intercity; Couriers and Messengers; Driver/Sales Workers; Parking Lot Attendants; Taxi Drivers and Chauffeurs. **PERSONALITY TYPE:** Conventional. Conventional occupations frequently involve following set procedures and routines. These occupations can include working with data and details more than with ideas. Usually there is a clear line of authority to follow.

EDUCATION/TRAINING PROGRAM(S)—General Office Occupations and Clerical Services.

WORK ENVIRONMENT—Outdoors; walking and running; very hot or cold; minor burns, cuts, bites, or stings; standing.

Precision Devices Inspectors and Testers

- Education/Training Required: Moderate-term on-the-job training
- Annual Earnings: $28,630
- Growth: 4.7%
- Annual Job Openings: 87,000
- Self-Employed: 1.2%
- Part-Time: 5.0%

The job openings listed here are shared with Electrical and Electronic Inspectors and Testers; Materials Inspectors; Mechanical Inspectors; and Production Inspectors, Testers, Graders, Sorters, Samplers, Weighers.

Age Bracket	Percentage of Workers
45–54 Years Old	27.3%
55–64 Years Old	15.0%
65 or Older	2.2%

Verify accuracy of and adjust precision devices, such as meters and gauges, testing instruments, clock and watch mechanisms, to ensure operation of device is in accordance with design specifications. Inspects materials, products, and work in progress for conformance to specifications, and adjusts process or assembly equipment to meet standards. Reads dials and meters to verify functioning of equipment according to specifications. Tests and measures finished products, components, or assemblies for functioning, operation, accuracy, or assembly to verify adherence to functional specifications. Marks items for acceptance or rejection, records test results and inspection data, and compares findings with specifications to ensure conformance to standards. Completes necessary procedures to satisfy licensing requirements. Computes and/or calculates data and other information. Confers with vendors and others regarding inspection results and recommends corrective procedures. Disassembles defective parts and components. Estimates operational data to meet acceptable standards. Operates or tends machinery and equipment, and uses hand tools. Discards or rejects products, materials, and equipment not meeting specifications. Analyzes and interprets blueprints, sample data, and other materials to determine, change, or measure specifications or inspection and testing procedures. Fabricates, installs, positions, or connects components, parts, finished products, or instruments for testing or operational purposes. Cleans and maintains test equipment and instruments and certifies that precision instruments meet standards. **SKILLS**—Quality Control Analysis; Operation Monitoring; Technology Design; Installation; Science; Troubleshooting; Equipment Maintenance; Operation and Control.

GOE—**Interest Area:** 13. Manufacturing. **Work Group:** 13.07. Production Quality Control. **Other Jobs in This Work Group:** Electrical and Electronic Inspectors and Testers; Graders and Sorters, Agricultural Products; Materials Inspectors; Production Inspectors, Testers, Graders, Sorters, Samplers, Weighers. **PERSONALITY TYPE:** Realistic. Realistic occupations frequently involve work activities that include practical, hands-on problems and solutions. They often deal with plants, animals, and real-world materials like wood, tools, and machinery. Many of the occupations require working outside and do not involve a lot of paperwork or working closely with others.

EDUCATION/TRAINING PROGRAM(S)— Quality Control Technology/Technician.

WORK ENVIRONMENT—Sitting; common protective or safety equipment; walking and running; spend time making repetitive motions; indoors; standing.

Precision Dyers

- Education/Training Required: Moderate-term on-the-job training
- Annual Earnings: $17,350
- Growth: 12.3%
- Annual Job Openings: 47,000
- Self-Employed: 6.8%
- Part-Time: 16.9%

The job openings listed here are shared with Laundry and Drycleaning Machine Operators and Tenders, Except Pressing; and Spotters, Dry Cleaning.

Age Bracket	Percentage of Workers
45–54 Years Old	25.9%
55–64 Years Old	17.1%
65 or Older	5.2%

Change or restore the color of articles, such as garments, drapes, and slipcovers, by means of dyes. Work requires knowledge of the composition of the textiles being dyed or restored; the chemical properties of bleaches and dyes; and their effects upon such textiles. Matches sample color, applying knowledge of bleaching agent and dye properties, and type, construction, condition, and color of article. Immerses article in bleaching bath to strip colors. Immerses article in dye solution and stirs with stick, or dyes article in rotary-drum or paddle dyeing machine. Rinses article in water and acetic acid solution to remove excess dye and to fix colors. Dissolves dye or bleaching chemicals in water. Operates or directs operation of extractor and drier. Sprays or brushes article with prepared solution to remove stains. Measures and mixes amounts of bleaches, dyes, oils, and acids, following formulas. Applies dye to article, using spray gun, electrically rotated brush, or handbrush. Examines article to identify fabric and original dye by sight, touch, or by testing sample with fire or chemical reagent. Tests dye on swatch of fabric, to ensure color match. **SKILLS**—Science.

GOE—Interest Area: 13. Manufacturing. **Work Group:** 13.11. Apparel, Shoes, Leather, and Fabric Care. **Other Jobs in This Work Group:** Custom Tailors; Fabric Menders, Except Garment; Laundry and Drycleaning Machine Operators and Tenders, Except Pressing; Pressers, Delicate Fabrics; Pressers, Hand; Shoe and Leather Workers and Repairers; Shop and Alteration Tailors; Spotters, Dry Cleaning; Upholsterers. **PERSONALITY TYPE:** Realistic. Realistic occupations frequently involve work activities that include practical, hands-on problems and solutions. They often deal with plants, animals, and real-world materials like wood, tools, and machinery. Many of the occupations require working outside and do not involve a lot of paperwork or working closely with others.

EDUCATION/TRAINING PROGRAM(S)— No data available.

WORK ENVIRONMENT—Standing; spend time bending or twisting the body; indoors; walking and running; hazardous conditions.

Pressure Vessel Inspectors

- ◎ Education/Training Required: Long-term on-the-job training
- ◎ Annual Earnings: $48,530
- ◎ Growth: 9.8%
- ◎ Annual Job Openings: 20,000
- ◎ Self-Employed: 0.9%
- ◎ Part-Time: 5.3%

The job openings listed here are shared with Coroners, Environmental Compliance Inspectors, Equal Opportunity Representatives and Officers, Government Property Inspectors and Investigators, and Licensing Examiners and Inspectors.

Age Bracket	Percentage of Workers
45–54 Years Old	40.5%
55–64 Years Old	15.1%
65 or Older	0.8%

Inspect pressure vessel equipment for conformance with safety laws and standards regulating their design, fabrication, installation, repair, and operation. Inspects drawings, designs, and specifications for piping, boilers and other vessels. Performs standard tests to verify condition of equipment and calibration of meters and gauges, using test equipment and hand tools. Inspects gas mains to determine that rate of flow, pressure, location, construction, or installation conform to standards. Evaluates factors, such as materials used, safety devices, regulators, construction quality, riveting, welding, pitting, corrosion, cracking, and safety valve operation. Calculates allowable limits of pressure, strength, and stresses. Examines permits and inspection records to determine that inspection schedule and remedial actions conform to procedures and regulations. Keeps records and prepares reports of inspections and investigations for administrative or legal authorities. Investigates accidents to determine causes and to develop methods of preventing recurrences. Confers with engineers, manufacturers, contractors, owners, and operators concerning problems in construction, operation, and repair. Witnesses acceptance and installation tests. Recommends or orders actions to correct violations of legal requirements or to eliminate unsafe conditions. **SKILLS**—Quality Control Analysis; Operation Monitoring; Mathematics; Science; Operations Analysis; Systems Evaluation; Writing; Systems Analysis.

GOE—Interest Area: 07. Government and Public Administration. **Work Group:** 07.03. Regulations Enforcement. **Other Jobs in This Work Group:** Agricultural Inspectors; Aviation Inspectors; Child Support, Missing Persons, and Unemployment Insurance Fraud Investigators; Environmental Compliance Inspectors; Equal Opportunity Representatives and Officers; Financial Examiners; Fire Inspectors; Fish and Game Wardens; Forest Fire Inspectors and Prevention Specialists; Government Property Inspectors and Investigators; Immigration and Customs Inspectors; Licensing Examiners and Inspectors; Marine Cargo Inspectors; Mechanical Inspectors; Motor Vehicle Inspectors; Nuclear Monitoring Technicians; Occupational Health and Safety Specialists; Railroad Inspectors; Tax Examiners, Collectors, and Revenue Agents. **PERSONALITY TYPE:** Realistic. Realistic occupations frequently involve work activities that include practical, hands-on problems and solutions. They often deal with plants, animals, and real-world materials like wood, tools, and machinery. Many of the occupations require working outside and do not involve a lot of paperwork or working closely with others.

EDUCATION/TRAINING PROGRAM(S)— No data available.

WORK ENVIRONMENT—Standing; very hot or cold; common protective or safety equipment; extremely bright or inadequate lighting; indoors.

Private Detectives and Investigators

- ◎ Education/Training Required: Work experience in a related occupation
- ◎ Annual Earnings: $32,510
- ◎ Growth: 25.3%
- ◎ Annual Job Openings: 9,000
- ◎ Self-Employed: 34.7%
- ◎ Part-Time: 7.8%

Age Bracket	Percentage of Workers
45–54 Years Old	25.0%
55–64 Years Old	20.3%
65 or Older	3.1%

Detect occurrences of unlawful acts or infractions of rules in private establishment, or seek, examine, and compile information for client. Apprehend suspects and release them to law enforcement authorities or security personnel. Conduct background investigations of individuals, such as pre-employment checks, to obtain information about an individual's character, financial status or personal history. Conduct private investigations on a paid basis. Confer with establishment officials, security departments, police, or postal officials to identify problems, provide information, and receive instructions. Monitor industrial or commercial properties to enforce conformance to establishment rules, and

P

to protect people or property. Observe and document activities of individuals in order to detect unlawful acts or to obtain evidence for cases, using binoculars and still or video cameras. Obtain and analyze information on suspects, crimes, and disturbances in order to solve cases, to identify criminal activity, and to gather information for court cases. Perform undercover operations such as evaluating the performance and honesty of employees by posing as customers or employees. Question persons to obtain evidence for cases of divorce, child custody, or missing persons, or information about individuals' character or financial status. Search computer databases, credit reports, public records, tax and legal filings, and other resources in order to locate persons or to compile information for investigations. Write reports and case summaries to document investigations. Alert appropriate personnel to suspects' locations. Count cash, and review transactions, sales checks, and register tapes in order to verify amounts and to identify shortages. Expose fraudulent insurance claims or stolen funds. Investigate companies' financial standings or locate funds stolen by embezzlers, using accounting skills. Testify at hearings and court trials to present evidence. Warn troublemakers causing problems on establishment premises, and eject them from premises when necessary. **SKILLS**—Systems Evaluation; Persuasion; Systems Analysis; Active Listening; Critical Thinking; Social Perceptiveness; Writing; Speaking.

GOE—Interest Area: 12. Law and Public Safety. **Work Group:** 12.05. Safety and Security. **Other Jobs in This Work Group:** Animal Control Workers; Crossing Guards; Gaming Surveillance Officers and Gaming Investigators; Lifeguards, Ski Patrol, and Other Recreational Protective Service Workers; Security Guards. **PERSONALITY TYPE:** Enterprising.

Enterprising occupations frequently involve starting up and carrying out projects. These occupations can involve leading people and making many decisions. They sometimes require risk taking and often deal with business.

EDUCATION/TRAINING PROGRAM(S)— Criminal Justice/Police Science.

WORK ENVIRONMENT—Standing; outdoors; walking and running; climbing ladders, scaffolds, or poles; spend time bending or twisting the body.

Private Sector Executives

- Education/Training Required: Work experience plus degree
- Annual Earnings: $141,820
- Growth: 16.7%
- Annual Job Openings: 63,000
- Self-Employed: 14.6%
- Part-Time: 5.3%

The job openings listed here are shared with Chief Executives and Government Service Executives.

Age Bracket	Percentage of Workers
45–54 Years Old	36.2%
55–64 Years Old	20.3%
65 or Older	5.3%

Determine and formulate policies and business strategies and provide overall direction of private sector organizations. Plan, direct, and coordinate operational activities at the highest level of management with the help of subordinate managers. Directs, plans, and implements policies and objectives of organization or business in accordance with charter and board of directors. Directs activities of organization to plan procedures, establish responsibilities, and coordinate functions among departments and sites. Analyzes operations to evaluate performance of company and staff and to determine areas of cost reduction and program improvement. Confers with board members, organization officials, and staff members to establish policies and formulate plans. Reviews financial statements and sales and activity reports to ensure that organization's objectives are achieved. Assigns or delegates responsibilities to subordinates. Directs and coordinates activities of business involved with buying and selling investment products and financial services. Establishes internal control procedures. Presides over or serves on board of directors, management committees, or other governing boards. Directs inservice training of staff. Administers program for selection of sites, construction of buildings, and provision of equipment and supplies. Screens, selects, hires, transfers, and discharges employees. Promotes objectives of institution or business before associations, public, government agencies, or community groups. Negotiates or approves contracts with suppliers and distributors, and with maintenance, janitorial, and security providers. Prepares reports and budgets. Directs non-merchandising departments of business, such as advertising, purchasing, credit, and accounting. Directs and coordinates activities of business or department concerned with production, pricing, sales, and/or distribution of products. Directs and coordinates organization's financial and budget activities to fund operations, maximize investments, and increase efficiency. **SKILLS**—Management of Financial Resources; Systems Evaluation; Systems Analysis; Management of Personnel Resources; Judgment and Decision Making; Management of Material Resources; Coordination; Negotiation.

GOE—Interest Area: 04. Business and Administration. **Work Group:** 04.01. Managerial Work in General Business. **Other Jobs in This Work Group:** Chief Executives; Compensation and Benefits Managers; General and Operations Managers; Human Resources Managers; Training and Development Managers. **PERSONALITY TYPE:** Enterprising. Enterprising occupations frequently involve starting up and carrying out projects. These occupations can involve leading people and making many decisions. They sometimes require risk taking and often deal with business.

EDUCATION/TRAINING PROGRAM(S)— Business Administration/Management; Entrepreneurship/Entrepreneurial Studies; International Business/Trade/Commerce; Transportation/Transportation Management.

WORK ENVIRONMENT—Sitting; indoors; walking and running.

Probation Officers and Correctional Treatment Specialists

- Education/Training Required: Bachelor's degree
- Annual Earnings: $39,760
- Growth: 14.7%
- Annual Job Openings: 15,000
- Self-Employed: 0.2%
- Part-Time: 10.6%

Age Bracket	Percentage of Workers
45–54 Years Old	27.7%
55–64 Years Old	11.4%
65 or Older	2.9%

Provide social services to assist in rehabilitation of law offenders in custody or on probation or parole. Make recommendations for actions involving formulation of rehabilitation plan and treatment of offender, including conditional release and education and employment stipulations. Prepare and maintain case folder for each assigned inmate or offender. Write reports describing offenders' progress. Inform offenders or inmates of requirements of conditional release, such as office visits, restitution payments, or educational and employment stipulations. Discuss with offenders how such issues as drug and alcohol abuse, and anger management problems might have played roles in their criminal behavior. Gather information about offenders' backgrounds by talking to offenders, their families and friends, and other people who have relevant information. Develop rehabilitation programs for assigned offenders or inmates, establishing rules of conduct, goals, and objectives. Develop liaisons and networks with other parole officers, community agencies, staff in correctional institutions, psychiatric facilities and after-care agencies in order to make plans for helping offenders with life adjustments. Arrange for medical, mental health, or substance abuse treatment services according to individual needs and/or court orders. Provide offenders or inmates with assistance in matters concerning detainers, sentences in other jurisdictions, writs, and applications for social assistance. Arrange for post-release services such as employment, housing, counseling, education, and social activities. Recommend remedial action or initiate court action when terms of probation or parole are not complied with. Interview probationers and parolees regularly to evaluate their progress in accomplishing goals and maintaining the terms specified in their probation contracts and rehabilitation plans. Supervise people on community-based sentences, including people on electronically monitored home detention. Assess the suitability of penitentiary inmates for release under parole and statutory release programs, and submit recommendations to parole boards. Investigate alleged parole violations, using interviews, surveillance, and search and seizure. Conduct prehearing and presentencing investigations, and testify in court regarding offenders' backgrounds and recommended sentences and sentencing conditions. **SKILLS**—Social Perceptiveness; Persuasion; Time Management; Negotiation; Learning Strategies; Management of Personnel Resources; Coordination; Instructing.

GOE—Interest Area: 10. Human Service. **Work Group:** 10.01. Counseling and Social Work. **Other Jobs in This Work Group:** Child, Family, and School Social Workers; Clinical Psychologists; Counseling Psychologists; Marriage and Family Therapists; Medical and Public Health Social Workers; Mental Health and Substance Abuse Social Workers; Mental Health Counselors; Rehabilitation Counselors; Residential Advisors; Social and Human Service Assistants; Substance Abuse and Behavioral Disorder Counselors. **PERSONALITY TYPE:** Social. Social occupations frequently involve working with, communicating with, and teaching people. These occupations often involve helping or providing service to others.

EDUCATION/TRAINING PROGRAM(S)—Social Work.

WORK ENVIRONMENT—Disease or infections; very hot or cold; physical proximity to others; indoors, not environmentally controlled; outdoors.

Product Safety Engineers

- Education/Training Required: Bachelor's degree
- Annual Earnings: $64,320
- Growth: 7.9%
- Annual Job Openings: 4,000
- Self-Employed: 1.6%
- Part-Time: 1.5%

The job openings listed here are shared with Fire-Prevention and Protection Engineers and Product Safety Engineers.

Age Bracket	Percentage of Workers
45–54 Years Old	23.3%
55–64 Years Old	14.4%
65 or Older	2.8%

Develop and conduct tests to evaluate product safety levels and recommend measures to reduce or eliminate hazards. Conduct research to evaluate safety levels for products. Evaluate potential health hazards or damage that could occur from product misuse. Investigate causes of accidents, injuries, or illnesses related to product usage in order to develop solutions to minimize or prevent recurrence. Participate in preparation of product usage and precautionary label instructions. Recommend procedures for detection, prevention, and elimination of physical, chemical, or other product hazards. Report accident investigation findings. **SKILLS**—Quality Control Analysis; Operations Analysis; Science; Mathematics; Technology Design; Writing; Active Learning; Troubleshooting.

GOE—Interest Area: 15. Scientific Research, Engineering, and Mathematics. **Work Group:** 15.08. Industrial and Safety Engineering. **Other**

Jobs in This Work Group: Fire-Prevention and Protection Engineers; Industrial Engineers; Industrial Safety and Health Engineers. **PERSONALITY TYPE:** Investigative. Investigative occupations frequently involve working with ideas and require an extensive amount of thinking. These occupations can involve searching for facts and figuring out problems mentally.

EDUCATION/TRAINING PROGRAM(S)— Environmental/Environmental Health Engineering.

WORK ENVIRONMENT—Specialized protective or safety equipment; sitting; indoors; standing; walking and running.

Production Inspectors, Testers, Graders, Sorters, Samplers, Weighers

- Education/Training Required: Moderate-term on-the-job training
- Annual Earnings: $28,630
- Growth: 4.7%
- Annual Job Openings: 87,000
- Self-Employed: 1.2%
- Part-Time: 5.0%

The job openings listed here are shared with Electrical and Electronic Inspectors and Testers; Materials Inspectors; Mechanical Inspectors; and Precision Devices Inspectors and Testers.

Age Bracket	Percentage of Workers
45–54 Years Old	27.3%
55–64 Years Old	15.0%
65 or Older	2.2%

Inspect, test, grade, sort, sample, or weigh nonagricultural raw materials or processed, machined, fabricated, or assembled parts or products. Work may be performed before, during, or after processing. Grades, classifies, and sorts products according to size, weight, color, or other specifications. Marks, affixes, or stamps product or container to identify defects, or denote grade or size information. Records inspection or test data, such as weight, temperature, grade, or moisture content, and number inspected or graded. Collects or selects samples for testing or for use as model. Discards or routes defective products or contaminants for rework or reuse. Notifies supervisor or specified personnel of deviations from specifications, machine malfunctions, or need for equipment maintenance. Reads work order to determine inspection criteria and to verify identification numbers and product type. Uses or operates product to test functional performance. Computes percentages or averages, using formulas and calculator, and prepares reports of inspection or test findings. Sets controls, starts machine, and observes machine which automatically sorts or inspects products. Counts number of product tested or inspected, and stacks or arranges for further processing, shipping, or packing. Cleans, trims, makes adjustments, or repairs product or processing equipment to correct defects found during inspection. Transports inspected or tested products to other work stations, using handtruck or lift truck. Wraps and packages product for shipment or delivery. Weighs materials, products, containers, or samples to verify packaging weight, to determine percentage of each ingredient, or to determine sorting. Compares color, shape, texture, or grade of product or material with color chart, template, or sample, to verify conformance to standards. Tests samples, materials, or products, using test equipment, such as thermometer, voltmeter, moisture meter, or tensiometer, for conformance to specifications. Measures dimensions of product, using measuring instruments, such as rulers, calipers, gauges, or micrometers, to verify conformance to specifications. Examines product or monitors processing of product, using any or all of five senses, to determine defects or grade. **SKILLS**—Quality Control Analysis; Operation Monitoring; Operation and Control; Troubleshooting; Repairing; Management of Material Resources; Equipment Maintenance.

GOE—**Interest Area:** 13. Manufacturing. **Work Group:** 13.07. Production Quality Control. **Other Jobs in This Work Group:** Electrical and Electronic Inspectors and Testers; Graders and Sorters, Agricultural Products; Materials Inspectors; Precision Devices Inspectors and Testers. **PERSONALITY TYPE:** Realistic. Realistic occupations frequently involve work activities that include practical, hands-on problems and solutions. They often deal with plants, animals, and real-world materials like wood, tools, and machinery. Many of the occupations require working outside and do not involve a lot of paperwork or working closely with others.

EDUCATION/TRAINING PROGRAM(S)— Quality Control Technology/Technician.

WORK ENVIRONMENT—Walking and running; spend time bending or twisting the body; indoors; using hands on objects, tools, or controls; sitting.

Property, Real Estate, and Community Association Managers

- Education/Training Required: Bachelor's degree
- Annual Earnings: $41,540
- Growth: 12.8%
- Annual Job Openings: 35,000
- Self-Employed: 46.0%
- Part-Time: 15.3%

Age Bracket	Percentage of Workers
45–54 Years Old	24.3%
55–64 Years Old	20.6%
65 or Older	11.5%

Plan, direct, or coordinate selling, buying, leasing, or governance activities of commercial, industrial, or residential real estate properties. Act as liaisons between on-site managers or tenants and owners. Confer regularly with community association members to ensure their needs are being met. Determine and certify the eligibility of prospective tenants, following government regulations. Direct and coordinate the activities of staff and contract personnel, and evaluate their performance. Direct collection of monthly assessments, rental fees, and deposits and payment of insurance premiums, mortgage, taxes, and incurred operating expenses. Inspect grounds, facilities, and equipment routinely to determine necessity of repairs or maintenance. Investigate complaints, disturbances and violations, and resolve problems, following management rules and regulations. Maintain records of sales, rental or usage activity, special permits issued, maintenance and operating costs, or property availability. Manage and oversee operations, maintenance, administration, and improvement of commercial, industrial, or residential properties. Market vacant space to prospective tenants through leasing agents, advertising, or other methods. Meet with prospective tenants to show properties, explain terms of occupancy, and provide information about local areas. Negotiate the sale, lease, or development of property, and complete or review appropriate documents and forms. Plan, schedule, and coordinate general maintenance, major repairs, and remodeling or construction projects for commercial or residential properties. Prepare and administer contracts for provision of property services such as cleaning, maintenance, and security services. Prepare detailed budgets and financial reports for properties. Purchase building and maintenance supplies, equipment, or furniture. Analyze information on property values, taxes, zoning, population growth, and traffic volume and patterns in order to determine if properties should be acquired. Clean common areas, change light bulbs, and make minor property repairs. Confer with legal authorities to ensure that renting and advertising practices are not discriminatory and that properties comply with state and federal regulations. **SKILLS**—Management of Financial Resources; Management of Personnel Resources; Management of Material Resources; Negotiation; Systems Evaluation; Coordination; Systems Analysis; Judgment and Decision Making.

GOE—Interest Area: 14. Retail and Wholesale Sales and Service. **Work Group:** 14.01. Managerial Work in Retail/Wholesale Sales and Service. **Other Jobs in This Work Group:** Advertising and Promotions Managers; First-Line Supervisors/Managers of Non-Retail Sales Workers; First-Line Supervisors/Managers of Retail Sales Workers; Funeral Directors;

Marketing Managers; Purchasing Managers; Sales Managers. **PERSONALITY TYPE:** Enterprising. Enterprising occupations frequently involve starting up and carrying out projects. These occupations can involve leading people and making many decisions. They sometimes require risk taking and often deal with business.

EDUCATION/TRAINING PROGRAM(S)— Real Estate.

WORK ENVIRONMENT—Sitting; walking and running; outdoors; spend time bending or twisting the body; indoors.

Prosthodontists

- ◎ Education/Training Required: First professional degree
- ◎ Annual Earnings: more than $145,600
- ◎ Growth: 4.1%
- ◎ Annual Job Openings: 7,000
- ◎ Self-Employed: 39.9%
- ◎ Part-Time: 22.3%

The job openings listed here are shared with Dentists, General; Oral and Maxillofacial Surgeons; and Orthodontists.

Age Bracket	Percentage of Workers
45–54 Years Old	28.2%
55–64 Years Old	19.7%
65 or Older	6.4%

Construct oral prostheses to replace missing teeth and other oral structures to correct natural and acquired deformation of mouth and jaws, to restore and maintain oral function, such as chewing and speaking, and to improve appearance. Collaborate with general dentists, specialists, and other health professionals in order to develop solutions to dental and oral health concerns. Design and fabricate dental prostheses, or supervise dental technicians and laboratory bench workers who construct the devices. Fit prostheses to patients, making any necessary adjustments and modifications. Measure and take impressions of patients' jaws and teeth in order to determine the shape and size of dental prostheses, using face bows, dental articulators, recording devices, and other materials. Replace missing teeth and associated oral structures with permanent fixtures, such as crowns and bridges, or removable fixtures, such as dentures. Restore function and aesthetics to traumatic injury victims, or to individuals with diseases or birth defects. Bleach discolored teeth in order to brighten and whiten them. Place veneers onto teeth in order to conceal defects. Repair, reline, and/or rebase dentures. Treat facial pain and jaw joint problems. Use bonding technology on the surface of the teeth in order to change tooth shape or to close gaps. **SKILLS—** Science; Technology Design; Reading Comprehension; Judgment and Decision Making; Critical Thinking; Service Orientation; Equipment Selection; Mathematics; Operations Analysis.

GOE—Interest Area: 08. Health Science. **Work Group:** 08.03. Dentistry. **Other Jobs in This Work Group:** Dental Assistants; Dental Hygienists; Dentists, General; Oral and Maxillofacial Surgeons; Orthodontists. **PERSONALITY TYPE:** Investigative. Investigative occupations frequently involve working with ideas and require an extensive amount of thinking. These occupations can involve searching for facts and figuring out problems mentally.

EDUCATION/TRAINING PROGRAM(S)— Prosthodontics Specialty; Prosthodontics/ Prosthodontology (Cert, MS, PhD).

WORK ENVIRONMENT—Common protective or safety equipment; indoors; sitting; standing; spend time bending or twisting the body.

Psychiatrists

- Education/Training Required: First professional degree
- Annual Earnings: more than $145,600
- Growth: 19.5%
- Annual Job Openings: 38,000
- Self-Employed: 16.9%
- Part-Time: 8.1%

The job openings listed here are shared with Anesthesiologists; Family and General Practitioners; Internists, General; Obstetricians and Gynecologists, General; Pediatricians, General; and Surgeons.

Age Bracket	Percentage of Workers
45–54 Years Old	29.3%
55–64 Years Old	13.4%
65 or Older	5.4%

Diagnose, treat, and help prevent disorders of the mind. Analyze and evaluate patient data and test or examination findings to diagnose nature and extent of mental disorder. Prescribe, direct, and administer psychotherapeutic treatments or medications to treat mental, emotional, or behavioral disorders. Collaborate with physicians, psychologists, social workers, psychiatric nurses, or other professionals to discuss treatment plans and progress. Gather and maintain patient information and records, including social and medical history obtained from patients, relatives, and other professionals. Counsel outpatients and other patients during office visits. Design individualized care plans, using a variety of treatments. Examine or conduct laboratory or diagnostic tests on patient to provide information on general physical condition and mental disorder. Advise and inform guardians, relatives, and significant others of patients' conditions and treatment. Review and evaluate treatment procedures and outcomes of other psychiatrists and medical professionals. Teach, conduct research, and publish findings to increase understanding of mental, emotional, and behavioral states and disorders. Prepare and submit case reports and summaries to government and mental health agencies. Serve on committees to promote and maintain community mental health services and delivery systems. **SKILLS**—Social Perceptiveness; Persuasion; Active Learning; Science; Active Listening; Negotiation; Systems Analysis; Learning Strategies; Complex Problem Solving.

GOE—Interest Area: 08. Health Science. **Work Group:** 08.02. Medicine and Surgery. **Other Jobs in This Work Group:** Anesthesiologists; Family and General Practitioners; Internists, General; Medical Assistants; Medical Transcriptionists; Obstetricians and Gynecologists; Pediatricians, General; Pharmacists; Pharmacy Aides; Pharmacy Technicians; Physician Assistants; Registered Nurses; Surgeons; Surgical Technologists. **PERSONALITY TYPE:** Investigative. Investigative occupations frequently involve working with ideas and require an extensive amount of thinking. These occupations can involve searching for facts and figuring out problems mentally.

EDUCATION/TRAINING PROGRAM(S)— Child Psychiatry; Psychiatry; Psysical Medical and Rehabilitation/Psychiatry.

WORK ENVIRONMENT—Sitting; physical proximity to others; disease or infections; indoors; sounds, noise levels are distracting or uncomfortable.

Psychology Teachers, Postsecondary

- ◉ Education/Training Required: Master's degree
- ◉ Annual Earnings: $55,750
- ◉ Growth: 38.1%
- ◉ Annual Job Openings: 216,000
- ◉ Self-Employed: 0.3%
- ◉ Part-Time: 27.7%

The job openings listed here are shared with all other postsecondary teaching occupations.

Age Bracket	Percentage of Workers
45–54 Years Old	22.8%
55–64 Years Old	19.0%
65 or Older	5.5%

Teach courses in psychology, such as child, clinical, and developmental psychology, and psychological counseling. Prepare and deliver lectures to undergraduate and/or graduate students on topics such as abnormal psychology, cognitive processes, and work motivation. Evaluate and grade students' class work, laboratory work, assignments, and papers. Initiate, facilitate, and moderate classroom discussions. Compile, administer, and grade examinations or assign this work to others. Keep abreast of developments in their field by reading current literature, talking with colleagues, and participating in professional conferences. Prepare course materials such as syllabi, homework assignments, and handouts. Plan, evaluate, and revise curricula, course content, and course materials and methods of instruction. Maintain student attendance records, grades, and other required records. Supervise undergraduate and/or graduate teaching, internship, and research work. Maintain regularly scheduled office hours in order to advise and assist students. Conduct research in a particular field of knowledge and publish findings in professional journals, books, and/or electronic media. Advise students on academic and vocational curricula, and on career issues. Select and obtain materials and supplies such as textbooks. Collaborate with colleagues to address teaching and research issues. Serve on academic or administrative committees that deal with institutional policies, departmental matters, and academic issues. Compile bibliographies of specialized materials for outside reading assignments. Participate in student recruitment, registration, and placement activities. Supervise students' laboratory work. Perform administrative duties such as serving as department head. Act as advisers to student organizations. Write grant proposals to procure external research funding. **SKILLS**—Instructing; Learning Strategies; Social Perceptiveness; Active Learning; Critical Thinking; Persuasion; Science; Reading Comprehension; Writing.

GOE—Interest Area: 05. Education and Training. **Work Group:** 05.03. Postsecondary and Adult Teaching and Instructing. **Other Jobs in This Work Group:** Adult Literacy, Remedial Education, and GED Teachers and Instructors; Agricultural Sciences Teachers, Postsecondary; Anthropology and Archeology Teachers, Postsecondary; Architecture Teachers, Postsecondary; Area, Ethnic, and Cultural Studies Teachers, Postsecondary; Art, Drama, and Music Teachers, Postsecondary; Atmospheric, Earth, Marine, and Space Sciences Teachers, Postsecondary; Biological Science Teachers, Postsecondary; Business Teachers, Postsecondary; Chemistry Teachers, Postsecondary; Communications Teachers, Postsecondary; Computer Science Teachers, Postsecondary; Criminal Justice and Law Enforcement Teachers, Postsecondary;

Economics Teachers, Postsecondary; Education Teachers, Postsecondary; Engineering Teachers, Postsecondary; English Language and Literature Teachers, Postsecondary; Environmental Science Teachers, Postsecondary; Farm and Home Management Advisors; Foreign Language and Literature Teachers, Postsecondary; Forestry and Conservation Science Teachers, Postsecondary; Geography Teachers, Postsecondary; Graduate Teaching Assistants; Health Specialties Teachers, Postsecondary; History Teachers, Postsecondary; Home Economics Teachers, Postsecondary; Law Teachers, Postsecondary; Library Science Teachers, Postsecondary; Mathematical Science Teachers, Postsecondary; Nursing Instructors and Teachers, Postsecondary; Philosophy and Religion Teachers, Postsecondary; Physics Teachers, Postsecondary; Political Science Teachers, Postsecondary; Recreation and Fitness Studies Teachers, Postsecondary; Self-Enrichment Education Teachers; Social Work Teachers, Postsecondary; Sociology Teachers, Postsecondary; Vocational Education Teachers, Postsecondary. **PERSONALITY TYPE:** Social. Social occupations frequently involve working with, communicating with, and teaching people. These occupations often involve helping or providing service to others.

EDUCATION/TRAINING PROGRAM(S)— Clinical Psychology; Cognitive Psychology and Psycholinguistics; Community Psychology; Comparative Psychology; Counseling Psychology; Developmental and Child Psychology; Educational Psychology; Experimental Psychology; Industrial and Organizational Psychology; Marriage and Family Therapy/Counseling; Personality Psychology; Physiological Psychology/Psychobiology; Psychology Teacher Education; Psychology, General; Psychology, Other; Psychometrics and Quantitative Psychology; others.

WORK ENVIRONMENT—Sitting; indoors; physical proximity to others; sounds, noise levels are distracting or uncomfortable.

Public Relations Managers

- Education/Training Required: Work experience plus degree
- Annual Earnings: $73,960
- Growth: 23.4%
- Annual Job Openings: 10,000
- Self-Employed: 0.9%
- Part-Time: 4.8%

Age Bracket	Percentage of Workers
45–54 Years Old	43.5%
55–64 Years Old	6.5%
65 or Older	close to 0%

Plan and direct public relations programs designed to create and maintain a favorable public image for employer or client; or if engaged in fundraising, plan and direct activities to solicit and maintain funds for special projects and nonprofit organizations. Identify main client groups and audiences and determine the best way to communicate publicity information to them. Write interesting and effective press releases, prepare information for media kits and develop and maintain company internet or intranet web pages. Develop and maintain the company's corporate image and identity, which includes the use of logos and signage. Manage communications budgets. Manage special events such as sponsorship of races, parties introducing new products, or other activities the firm supports in order to gain public attention through the media without advertising directly. Draft speeches for company executives, and arrange interviews and other forms of contact for them. Assign, supervise and review the activities of public relations staff. Evaluate advertising and promotion programs for compatibility with public relations efforts. Establish and maintain effective working relationships with local and municipal government officials and media representatives. Confer with labor relations managers to develop internal communications that keep employees informed of company activities. Direct activities of external agencies, establishments and departments that develop and implement communication strategies and information programs. Formulate policies and procedures related to public information programs, working with public relations executives. Respond to requests for information about employers' activities or status. Establish goals for soliciting funds, develop policies for collection and safeguarding of contributions, and coordinate disbursement of funds. Facilitate consumer relations, or the relationship between parts of the company such as the managers and employees, or different branch offices. Maintain company archives. Manage in-house communication courses. Produce films and other video products, regulate their distribution, and operate film library. **SKILLS**—Social Perceptiveness; Management of Financial Resources; Service Orientation; Monitoring; Persuasion; Writing; Coordination; Negotiation.

GOE—Interest Area: 03. Arts and Communication. **Work Group:** 03.01. Managerial Work in Arts and Communication. **Other Jobs in This Work Group:** Agents and Business Managers of Artists, Performers, and Athletes; Art Directors; Producers; Program Directors; Technical Directors/Managers. **PERSONALITY TYPE:** No data available.

EDUCATION/TRAINING PROGRAM(S)— Public Relations/Image Management.

WORK ENVIRONMENT—Sitting; physical proximity to others; in an enclosed vehicle or equipment; indoors; extremely bright or inadequate lighting.

Public Transportation Inspectors

- Education/Training Required: Work experience in a related occupation
- Annual Earnings: $47,920
- Growth: 7.7%
- Annual Job Openings: 5,000
- Self-Employed: 0.4%
- Part-Time: 3.2%

The job openings listed here are shared with Aviation Inspectors, Freight Inspectors, Marine Cargo Inspectors, Motor Vehicle Inspectors, and Railroad Inspectors.

Age Bracket	Percentage of Workers
45–54 Years Old	54.3%
55–64 Years Old	15.2%
65 or Older	2.2%

Monitor operation of public transportation systems to ensure good service and compliance with regulations. Investigate accidents, equipment failures, and complaints. Observes employees performing assigned duties to note their deportment, treatment of passengers, and adherence to company regulations and schedules. Observes and records time required to load and unload passengers or freight volume of traffic on vehicle and at stops. Investigates schedule delays, accidents, and complaints. Inspects company vehicles and other property for evidence of abuse, damage, and mechanical malfunction and directs repair. Determines need for changes in service, such as additional vehicles, route changes, and revised schedules to improve service and efficiency. Drives automobile along route to detect conditions hazardous to equipment and passengers and negotiates with local governments to eliminate hazards. Submits written reports to management with recommendations for improving service. Reports disruptions to service. Assists in dispatching equipment when necessary. Recommends promotions and disciplinary actions involving transportation personnel. **SKILLS**—Operations Analysis; Writing; Systems Evaluation; Management of Personnel Resources; Monitoring; Speaking; Systems Analysis; Negotiation.

GOE—Interest Area: 16. Transportation, Distribution, and Logistics. **Work Group:** 16.07. Transportation Support Work. **Other Jobs in This Work Group:** Bridge and Lock Tenders; Cargo and Freight Agents; Cleaners of Vehicles and Equipment; Freight Inspectors; Railroad Yard Workers; Stevedores, Except Equipment Operators; Traffic Technicians; Train Crew Members. **PERSONALITY TYPE:** Enterprising. Enterprising occupations frequently involve starting up and carrying out projects. These occupations can involve leading people and making many decisions. They sometimes require risk taking and often deal with business.

EDUCATION/TRAINING PROGRAM(S)— No data available.

WORK ENVIRONMENT—Outdoors; sitting; walking and running; very hot or cold; extremely bright or inadequate lighting.

Purchasing Agents, Except Wholesale, Retail, and Farm Products

- Education/Training Required: Work experience in a related occupation
- Annual Earnings: $48,360
- Growth: 11.2%
- Annual Job Openings: 29,000
- Self-Employed: 1.3%
- Part-Time: 5.5%

Age Bracket	Percentage of Workers
45–54 Years Old	29.8%
55–64 Years Old	12.3%
65 or Older	2.1%

Purchase machinery, equipment, tools, parts, supplies, or services necessary for the operation of an establishment. Purchase raw or semi-finished materials for manufacturing. Purchase the highest quality merchandise at the lowest possible price and in correct amounts. Prepare purchase orders, solicit bid proposals and review requisitions for goods and services. Research and evaluate suppliers based on price, quality, selection, service, support, availability, reliability, production and distribution capabilities, and the supplier's reputation and history. Analyze price proposals, financial reports, and other data and information to determine reasonable prices. Monitor and follow applicable laws and regulations. Negotiate, or renegotiate, and administer contracts with suppliers, vendors, and other representatives. Monitor shipments to ensure that goods come in on time, and in the event of problems trace shipments and follow up unde-

P

livered goods. Confer with staff, users, and vendors to discuss defective or unacceptable goods or services and determine corrective action. Evaluate and monitor contract performance to ensure compliance with contractual obligations and to determine need for changes. Maintain and review computerized or manual records of items purchased, costs, delivery, product performance, and inventories. Review catalogs, industry periodicals, directories, trade journals, and Internet sites, and consult with other department personnel to locate necessary goods and services. Study sales records and inventory levels of current stock to develop strategic purchasing programs that facilitate employee access to supplies. Interview vendors and visit suppliers' plants and distribution centers to examine and learn about products, services and prices. Arrange the payment of duty and freight charges. Hire, train and/or supervise purchasing clerks, buyers, and expediters. Write and review product specifications, maintaining a working technical knowledge of the goods or services to be purchased. Monitor changes affecting supply and demand, tracking market conditions, price trends, or futures markets. Formulate policies and procedures for bid proposals and procurement of goods and services. **SKILLS**—Time Management; Management of Personnel Resources; Negotiation; Persuasion; Speaking; Coordination; Writing; Monitoring; Judgment and Decision Making.

GOE—Interest Area: 14. Retail and Wholesale Sales and Service. **Work Group:** 14.05. Purchasing. **Other Jobs in This Work Group:** Wholesale and Retail Buyers, Except Farm Products. **PERSONALITY TYPE:** Enterprising. Enterprising occupations frequently involve starting up and carrying out projects. These occupations can involve leading people and making many decisions. They some-

times require risk taking and often deal with business.

EDUCATION/TRAINING PROGRAM(S)—Merchandising and Buying Operations; Sales, Distribution, and Marketing Operations, General; Sales, Distribution, and Marketing Operations, General.

WORK ENVIRONMENT—Sitting; physical proximity to others; sounds, noise levels are distracting or uncomfortable; indoors, not environmentally controlled; very hot or cold; cramped work space, awkward positions.

Purchasing Managers

- Education/Training Required: Work experience plus degree
- Annual Earnings: $74,300
- Growth: 4.8%
- Annual Job Openings: 9,000
- Self-Employed: 0.2%
- Part-Time: 2.6%

Age Bracket	Percentage of Workers
45–54 Years Old	35.5%
55–64 Years Old	15.4%
65 or Older	1.8%

Plan, direct, or coordinate the activities of buyers, purchasing officers, and related workers involved in purchasing materials, products, and services. Maintain records of goods ordered and received. Locate vendors of materials, equipment or supplies, and interview them in order to determine product availability and terms of sales. Prepare and process requisitions and purchase orders for supplies and equipment. Control purchasing department budgets. Interview and hire staff, and oversee staff training. Review purchase order claims and contracts for conformance to company policy. Analyze market and delivery systems in order to assess present and future material availability. Develop and implement purchasing and contract management instructions, policies, and procedures. Participate in the development of specifications for equipment, products or substitute materials. Resolve vendor or contractor grievances, and claims against suppliers. Represent companies in negotiating contracts and formulating policies with suppliers. Review, evaluate, and approve specifications for issuing and awarding bids. Direct and coordinate activities of personnel engaged in buying, selling, and distributing materials, equipment, machinery, and supplies. Prepare bid awards requiring board approval. Prepare reports regarding market conditions and merchandise costs. Administer on-line purchasing systems. **SKILLS**—Negotiation; Management of Material Resources; Management of Financial Resources; Operations Analysis; Persuasion; Time Management; Active Learning; Coordination.

GOE—Interest Area: 14. Retail and Wholesale Sales and Service. **Work Group:** 14.01. Managerial Work in Retail/Wholesale Sales and Service. **Other Jobs in This Work Group:** Advertising and Promotions Managers; First-Line Supervisors/Managers of Non-Retail Sales Workers; First-Line Supervisors/Managers of Retail Sales Workers; Funeral Directors; Marketing Managers; Property, Real Estate, and Community Association Managers; Sales Managers. **PERSONALITY TYPE:** Enterprising. Enterprising occupations frequently involve starting up and carrying out projects. These occupations can involve leading people and making many decisions. They sometimes require risk taking and often deal with business.

EDUCATION/TRAINING PROGRAM(S)—Purchasing, Procurement/Acquisitions and Contracts Management.

WORK ENVIRONMENT—Sounds, noise levels are distracting or uncomfortable; sitting; very hot or cold; contaminants; indoors; indoors, not environmentally controlled.

Railroad Inspectors

- Education/Training Required: Work experience in a related occupation
- Annual Earnings: $47,920
- Growth: 7.7%
- Annual Job Openings: 5,000
- Self-Employed: 0.4%
- Part-Time: 3.2%

The job openings listed here are shared with Aviation Inspectors, Freight Inspectors, Marine Cargo Inspectors, Motor Vehicle Inspectors, and Public Transportation Inspectors.

Age Bracket	Percentage of Workers
45–54 Years Old	54.3%
55–64 Years Old	15.2%
65 or Older	2.2%

Inspect railroad equipment, roadbed, and track to ensure safe transport of people or cargo. Fills paint container on rail-detector car used to mark section of defective rail with paint. Directs crews to repair or replace defective equipment or to re-ballast roadbed. Places lanterns or flags in front and rear of train to signal that inspection is being performed. Seals leaks found during inspection that can be sealed with caulking compound. Replaces defective brake rod pins and tightens safety appliances. Notifies train dispatcher of rail-car to be moved to shop for repair. Makes minor repairs. Packs brake bearings with grease. Inspects signals and track wiring to determine continuity of electrical connections. Examines roadbed, switches, fishplates, rails, and ties to detect damage or wear. Examines locomotives and cars to detect damage or structural defects. Inspects and tests completed work. Operates switches to determine working conditions. Tests and synchronizes rail-flaw-detection machine, using circuit tester and hand tools, and reloads machine with paper and ink. Starts machine and signals worker to operate rail-detector car. Prepares reports on repairs made and equipment, railcars, or roadbed needing repairs. Tags rail cars needing immediate repair. **SKILLS**—Repairing; Troubleshooting; Operation Monitoring; Equipment Maintenance; Quality Control Analysis; Management of Personnel Resources; Systems Analysis; Science; Time Management.

GOE—Interest Area: 07. Government and Public Administration. **Work Group:** 07.03. Regulations Enforcement. **Other Jobs in This Work Group:** Agricultural Inspectors; Aviation Inspectors; Child Support, Missing Persons, and Unemployment Insurance Fraud Investigators; Environmental Compliance Inspectors; Equal Opportunity Representatives and Officers; Financial Examiners; Fire Inspectors; Fish and Game Wardens; Forest Fire Inspectors and Prevention Specialists; Government Property Inspectors and Investigators; Immigration and Customs Inspectors; Licensing Examiners and Inspectors; Marine Cargo Inspectors; Mechanical Inspectors; Motor Vehicle Inspectors; Nuclear Monitoring Technicians; Occupational Health and Safety Specialists; Pressure Vessel Inspectors; Tax Examiners, Collectors, and Revenue Agents. **PERSONALITY TYPE:** Realistic. Realistic occupations frequently involve work activities that include practical, hands-on problems and solutions. They often deal with plants, animals, and real-world materials like wood, tools, and machinery. Many of the occupations require working outside and do not involve a lot of paperwork or working closely with others.

EDUCATION/TRAINING PROGRAM(S)— No data available.

WORK ENVIRONMENT—Outdoors; standing; hazardous equipment; walking and running; spend time bending or twisting the body.

Real Estate Brokers

- Education/Training Required: Work experience in a related occupation
- Annual Earnings: $56,970
- Growth: 2.4%
- Annual Job Openings: 11,000
- Self-Employed: 59.1%
- Part-Time: 14.8%

Age Bracket	Percentage of Workers
45–54 Years Old	25.3%
55–64 Years Old	23.5%
65 or Older	9.9%

Operate real estate office or work for commercial real estate firm, overseeing real estate transactions. Other duties usually include selling real estate or renting properties and arranging loans. Sell, for a fee, real estate owned by others. Obtain agreements from property owners to place properties for sale with real estate firms. Monitor fulfillment of purchase contract terms to ensure that they are handled in a timely manner. Compare a property with similar properties that have recently sold, in order to determine its competitive market price. Act as an intermediary in negotiations between buyers and sellers over property prices and settlement details, and during the closing of sales. Generate lists of properties for sale, their locations and descriptions, and available financing options, using computers. Maintain knowledge of real estate law, local economies, fair housing laws, and types of available mortgages, financing options and government programs. Check work completed by loan officers, attorneys, and other professionals to ensure that it is performed properly. Arrange for financing of property purchases. Appraise property values, assessing income potential when relevant. Maintain awareness of current income tax regulations, local zoning, building and tax laws, and growth possibilities of the area where a property is located. Manage and operate real estate offices, handling associated business details. Supervise agents who handle real estate transactions. Rent properties or manage rental properties. Arrange for title searches of properties being sold. Give buyers virtual tours of properties in which they are interested, using computers. Review property details to ensure that environmental regulations are met. Develop, sell, or lease property used for industry or manufacturing. **SKILLS**—Management of Financial Resources; Negotiation; Persuasion; Service Orientation; Active Listening; Judgment and Decision Making; Mathematics; Complex Problem Solving; Time Management.

GOE—Interest Area: 14. Retail and Wholesale Sales and Service. **Work Group:** 14.03. General Sales. **Other Jobs in This Work Group:** Parts Salespersons; Real Estate Sales Agents; Retail Salespersons; Sales Representatives, Wholesale and Manufacturing, Except Technical and Scientific Products; Service Station Attendants. **PERSONALITY TYPE:** No data available.

EDUCATION/TRAINING PROGRAM(S)— Real Estate.

WORK ENVIRONMENT—In an enclosed vehicle or equipment; outdoors; physical proximity to others; sitting; indoors, not environmentally controlled; very hot or cold.

Real Estate Sales Agents

- Education/Training Required: Postsecondary vocational training
- Annual Earnings: $36,950
- Growth: 5.7%
- Annual Job Openings: 34,000
- Self-Employed: 59.0%
- Part-Time: 14.8%

Age Bracket	Percentage of Workers
45–54 Years Old	25.3%
55–64 Years Old	23.5%
65 or Older	9.9%

Rent, buy, or sell property for clients. Perform duties such as study property listings, interview prospective clients, accompany clients to property site, discuss conditions of sale, and draw up real estate contracts. Includes agents who represent buyer. Present purchase offers to sellers for consideration. Confer with escrow companies, lenders, home inspectors, and pest control operators to ensure that terms and conditions of purchase agreements are met before closing dates. Interview clients to determine what kinds of properties they are seeking. Prepare documents such as representation contracts, purchase agreements, closing statements, deeds and leases. Coordinate property closings, overseeing signing of documents and disbursement of funds. Act as an intermediary in negotiations between buyers and sellers, generally representing one or the other. Promote sales of properties through advertisements, open houses, and participation in multiple listing services. Compare a property with similar properties that have recently sold in order to determine its competitive market price. Coordinate appointments to show homes to prospective buyers. Generate lists of properties that are compatible with buyers' needs and financial resources. Display commercial, industrial, agricultural, and residential properties to clients and explain their features. Arrange for title searches to determine whether clients have clear property titles. Review plans for new construction with clients, enumerating and recommending available options and features. Answer clients' questions regarding construction work, financing, maintenance, repairs, and appraisals. Inspect condition of premises, and arrange for necessary maintenance or notify owners of maintenance needs. Accompany buyers during visits to and inspections of property, advising them on the suitability and value of the homes they are visiting. Advise sellers on how to make homes more appealing to potential buyers. Arrange meetings between buyers and sellers when details of transactions need to be negotiated. Advise clients on market conditions, prices, mortgages, legal requirements and related matters. Evaluate mortgage options to help clients obtain financing at the best prevailing rates and terms. Review property listings, trade journals, and relevant literature, and attend conventions, seminars, and staff and association meetings in order to remain knowledgeable about real estate markets. **SKILLS**—Negotiation; Service Orientation; Time Management; Coordination; Social Perceptiveness; Speaking; Active Listening; Writing.

GOE—Interest Area: 14. Retail and Wholesale Sales and Service. **Work Group:** 14.03. General

Sales. **Other Jobs in This Work Group:** Parts Salespersons; Real Estate Brokers; Retail Salespersons; Sales Representatives, Wholesale and Manufacturing, Except Technical and Scientific Products; Service Station Attendants. **PERSONALITY TYPE:** Enterprising. Enterprising occupations frequently involve starting up and carrying out projects. These occupations can involve leading people and making many decisions. They sometimes require risk taking and often deal with business.

EDUCATION/TRAINING PROGRAM(S)— Real Estate.

WORK ENVIRONMENT—In an enclosed vehicle or equipment; outdoors; very hot or cold; sitting; physical proximity to others.

Recreation and Fitness Studies Teachers, Postsecondary

- Education/Training Required: Master's degree
- Annual Earnings: $45,400
- Growth: 38.1%
- Annual Job Openings: 216,000
- Self-Employed: 0.3%
- Part-Time: 27.7%

The job openings listed here are shared with all other postsecondary teaching occupations.

Age Bracket	Percentage of Workers
45–54 Years Old	22.8%
55–64 Years Old	19.0%
65 or Older	5.5%

Teach courses pertaining to recreation, leisure, and fitness studies, including exercise physiology and facilities management. Evaluate and grade students' class work, assignments, and papers. Maintain student attendance records, grades, and other required records. Prepare and deliver lectures to undergraduate and/or graduate students on topics such as anatomy, therapeutic recreation, and conditioning theory. Prepare course materials such as syllabi, homework assignments, and handouts. Compile, administer, and grade examinations or assign this work to others. Maintain regularly scheduled office hours in order to advise and assist students. Plan, evaluate, and revise curricula, course content, and course materials and methods of instruction. Initiate, facilitate, and moderate classroom discussions. Keep abreast of developments in their field by reading current literature, talking with colleagues, and participating in professional conferences. Advise students on academic and vocational curricula, and on career issues. Participate in student recruitment, registration, and placement activities. Collaborate with colleagues to address teaching and research issues. Select and obtain materials and supplies such as textbooks. Participate in campus and community events. Serve on academic or administrative committees that deal with institutional policies, departmental matters, and academic issues. Compile bibliographies of specialized materials for outside reading assignments. Supervise undergraduate and/or graduate teaching, internship, and research work. Perform administrative duties such as serving as department heads. Prepare students to act as sports coaches. Conduct research in a particular field of knowledge and publish findings in professional journals, books, and/or electronic media. Act as advisers to student organizations. **SKILLS**—Instructing; Learning Strategies; Social Perceptiveness; Persuasion; Time Management; Service Orientation; Active Learning; Monitoring; Negotiation.

GOE—Interest Area: 05. Education and Training. **Work Group:** 05.03. Postsecondary and Adult Teaching and Instructing. **Other Jobs in This Work Group:** Adult Literacy, Remedial Education, and GED Teachers and Instructors; Agricultural Sciences Teachers, Postsecondary; Anthropology and Archeology Teachers, Postsecondary; Architecture Teachers, Postsecondary; Area, Ethnic, and Cultural Studies Teachers, Postsecondary; Art, Drama, and Music Teachers, Postsecondary; Atmospheric, Earth, Marine, and Space Sciences Teachers, Postsecondary; Biological Science Teachers, Postsecondary; Business Teachers, Postsecondary; Chemistry Teachers, Postsecondary; Communications Teachers, Postsecondary; Computer Science Teachers, Postsecondary; Criminal Justice and Law Enforcement Teachers, Postsecondary; Economics Teachers, Postsecondary; Education Teachers, Postsecondary; Engineering Teachers, Postsecondary; English Language and Literature Teachers, Postsecondary; Environmental Science Teachers, Postsecondary; Farm and Home Management Advisors; Foreign Language and Literature Teachers, Postsecondary; Forestry and Conservation Science Teachers, Postsecondary; Geography Teachers, Postsecondary; Graduate Teaching Assistants; Health Specialties Teachers, Postsecondary; History Teachers, Postsecondary; Home Economics Teachers, Postsecondary; Law Teachers, Postsecondary; Library Science Teachers, Postsecondary; Mathematical Science Teachers, Postsecondary; Nursing Instructors and Teachers, Postsecondary; Philosophy and Religion Teachers, Postsecondary; Physics Teachers, Postsecondary; Political Science Teachers, Postsecondary; Psychology Teachers, Postsecondary; Self-Enrichment Education Teachers; Social Work Teachers, Postsecondary;

Sociology Teachers, Postsecondary; Vocational Education Teachers, Postsecondary. **PERSONALITY TYPE:** No data available.

EDUCATION/TRAINING PROGRAM(S)— Health and Physical Education, General; Parks, Recreation and Leisure Studies; Sport and Fitness Administration/Management.

WORK ENVIRONMENT—Physical proximity to others; outdoors; sounds, noise levels are distracting or uncomfortable; sitting; very hot or cold; extremely bright or inadequate lighting.

Refractory Materials Repairers, Except Brickmasons

- Education/Training Required: Moderate-term on-the-job training
- Annual Earnings: $39,610
- Growth: 16.3%
- Annual Job Openings: 155,000
- Self-Employed: 6.1%
- Part-Time: 2.1%

The job openings listed here are shared with Maintenance and Repair Workers, General.

Age Bracket	Percentage of Workers
45–54 Years Old	32.0%
55–64 Years Old	13.5%
65 or Older	1.3%

Build or repair furnaces, kilns, cupolas, boilers, converters, ladles, soaking pits, ovens, etc., using refractory materials. Bolt sections of wooden molds together, using wrenches, and line molds with paper to prevent clay from sticking to molds. Chip slag from linings of ladles or remove linings when beyond repair, using hammers and chisels. Disassemble molds, and cut, chip, and smooth clay structures such as floaters, drawbars, and L-blocks. Drill holes in furnace walls, bolt overlapping layers of plastic to walls, and hammer surfaces to compress layers into solid sheets. Dry and bake new linings by placing inverted linings over burners, building fires in ladles, or by using blowtorches. Dump and tamp clay in molds, using tamping tools. Fasten stopper heads to rods with metal pins to assemble refractory stoppers used to plug pouring nozzles of steel ladles. Install clay structures in melting tanks and drawing kilns to control the flow and temperature of molten glass, using hoists and hand tools. Measure furnace walls to determine dimensions, then cut required number of sheets from plastic block, using saws. Mix specified amounts of sand, clay, mortar powder, and water to form refractory clay or mortar, using shovels or mixing machines. Reline or repair ladles and pouring spouts with refractory clay, using trowels. Remove worn or damaged plastic block refractory linings of furnaces, using hand tools. Spread mortar on stopper heads and rods, using trowels, and slide brick sleeves over rods to form refractory jackets. Tighten locknuts holding refractory stopper assemblies together, spread mortar on jackets to seal sleeve joints, and dry mortar in ovens. Climb scaffolding, carrying hoses, and spray surfaces of cupolas with refractory mixtures, using spray equipment. Install preformed metal scaffolding in interiors of cupolas, using hand tools. Transfer clay structures to curing ovens, melting tanks, and drawing kilns, using forklifts. **SKILLS—**Repairing; Installation; Operation and Control; Equipment Maintenance; Troubleshooting; Science; Equipment Selection; Operation Monitoring.

GOE—Interest Area: 02. Architecture and Construction. **Work Group:** 02.04. Construction Crafts. **Other Jobs in This Work**

R

Group: Boat Builders and Shipwrights; Boilermakers; Brattice Builders; Brickmasons and Blockmasons; Carpet Installers; Ceiling Tile Installers; Cement Masons and Concrete Finishers; Commercial Divers; Construction Carpenters; Crane and Tower Operators; Dragline Operators; Drywall Installers; Electricians; Fence Erectors; Floor Layers, Except Carpet, Wood, and Hard Tiles; Floor Sanders and Finishers; Glaziers; Grader, Bulldozer, and Scraper Operators; Hazardous Materials Removal Workers; Insulation Workers, Floor, Ceiling, and Wall; Insulation Workers, Mechanical; Manufactured Building and Mobile Home Installers; Operating Engineers; Painters, Construction and Maintenance; Paperhangers; Paving, Surfacing, and Tamping Equipment Operators; Pile-Driver Operators; Pipe Fitters; Pipelayers; Pipelaying Fitters; Plasterers and Stucco Masons; Plumbers; Rail-Track Laying and Maintenance Equipment Operators; Reinforcing Iron and Rebar Workers; Riggers; Roofers; Rough Carpenters; Security and Fire Alarm Systems Installers; Segmental Pavers; Sheet Metal Workers; Ship Carpenters and Joiners; Stone Cutters and Carvers; Stonemasons; Structural Iron and Steel Workers; Tapers; Terrazzo Workers and Finishers; Tile and Marble Setters. **PERSONALITY TYPE:** Realistic. Realistic occupations frequently involve work activities that include practical, hands-on problems and solutions. They often deal with plants, animals, and real-world materials like wood, tools, and machinery. Many of the occupations require working outside and do not involve a lot of paperwork or working closely with others.

EDUCATION/TRAINING PROGRAM(S)— Industrial Mechanics and Maintenance Technology.

WORK ENVIRONMENT—Hazardous equipment; very hot or cold; common protective or safety equipment; climbing ladders, scaffolds, or poles; extremely bright or inadequate lighting.

Registered Nurses

- ◎ Education/Training Required: Associate degree
- ◎ Annual Earnings: $53,640
- ◎ Growth: 27.3%
- ◎ Annual Job Openings: 215,000
- ◎ Self-Employed: 1.2%
- ◎ Part-Time: 22.0%

Age Bracket	Percentage of Workers
45–54 Years Old	31.3%
55–64 Years Old	12.5%
65 or Older	2.1%

Assess patient health problems and needs, develop and implement nursing care plans, and maintain medical records. Administer nursing care to ill, injured, convalescent, or disabled patients. May advise patients on health maintenance and disease prevention or provide case management. Licensing or registration required. Includes advance practice nurses such as: nurse practitioners, clinical nurse specialists, certified nurse midwives, and certified registered nurse anesthetists. Advanced practice nursing is practiced by RNs who have specialized formal, post-basic education and who function in highly autonomous and specialized roles. Maintain accurate, detailed reports and records. Monitor, record and report symptoms and changes in patients' conditions. Record patients' medical information and vital signs.

Modify patient treatment plans as indicated by patients' responses and conditions. Consult and coordinate with health care team members to assess, plan, implement and evaluate patient care plans. Order, interpret, and evaluate diagnostic tests to identify and assess patient's condition. Monitor all aspects of patient care, including diet and physical activity. Direct and supervise less skilled nursing/health care personnel, or supervise a particular unit on one shift. Prepare patients for, and assist with, examinations and treatments. Observe nurses and visit patients to ensure that proper nursing care is provided. Assess the needs of individuals, families and/or communities, including assessment of individuals' home and/or work environments to identify potential health or safety problems. Instruct individuals, families and other groups on topics such as health education, disease prevention and childbirth, and develop health improvement programs. Prepare rooms, sterile instruments, equipment and supplies, and ensure that stock of supplies is maintained. Inform physician of patient's condition during anesthesia. Deliver infants and provide prenatal and postpartum care and treatment under obstetrician's supervision. Administer local, inhalation, intravenous, and other anesthetics. Provide health care, first aid, immunizations and assistance in convalescence and rehabilitation in locations such as schools, hospitals, and industry. Perform physical examinations, make tentative diagnoses, and treat patients en route to hospitals or at disaster site triage centers. Conduct specified laboratory tests. Hand items to surgeons during operations. Prescribe or recommend drugs, medical devices or other forms of treatment, such as physical therapy, inhalation therapy, or related therapeutic procedures. Direct and coordinate infection control programs, advising and consulting with specified personnel about necessary precautions.

SKILLS—Social Perceptiveness; Service Orientation; Instructing; Time Management; Learning Strategies; Coordination; Critical Thinking; Active Learning; Monitoring.

GOE—**Interest Area:** 08. Health Science. **Work Group:** 08.02. Medicine and Surgery. **Other Jobs in This Work Group:** Anesthesiologists; Family and General Practitioners; Internists, General; Medical Assistants; Medical Transcriptionists; Obstetricians and Gynecologists; Pediatricians, General; Pharmacists; Pharmacy Aides; Pharmacy Technicians; Physician Assistants; Psychiatrists; Surgeons; Surgical Technologists. **PERSONALITY TYPE:** Social. Social occupations frequently involve working with, communicating with, and teaching people. These occupations often involve helping or providing service to others.

EDUCATION/TRAINING PROGRAM(S)—Adult Health Nurse/Nursing; Critical Care Nursing; Family Practice Nurse/Nurse Practitioner; Maternal/Child Health Nurse/Nursing; Nurse Anesthetist; Nurse Midwife/Nursing Midwifery; Nursing—Registered Nurse Training (RN, ASN, BSN, MSN); Nursing Clinical Specialist; Nursing Science (MS, PhD); Nursing, Other; Occupational and Environmental Health Nursing; Pediatric Nurse/Nursing; Perioperative/Operating Room and Surgical Nurse/Nursing; Psychiatric/Mental Health Nurse/Nursing; others.

WORK ENVIRONMENT—Physical proximity to others; disease or infections; contaminants; sounds, noise levels are distracting or uncomfortable; cramped work space, awkward positions.

Rehabilitation Counselors

- ◎ Education/Training Required: Master's degree
- ◎ Annual Earnings: $27,900
- ◎ Growth: 33.8%
- ◎ Annual Job Openings: 19,000
- ◎ Self-Employed: 4.4%
- ◎ Part-Time: 14.6%

Age Bracket	Percentage of Workers
45–54 Years Old	28.0%
55–64 Years Old	13.4%
65 or Older	2.3%

Counsel individuals to maximize the independence and employability of persons coping with personal, social, and vocational difficulties that result from birth defects, illness, disease, accidents, or the stress of daily life. Coordinate activities for residents of care and treatment facilities. Assess client needs and design and implement rehabilitation programs that may include personal and vocational counseling, training, and job placement. Analyze information from interviews, educational and medical records, consultation with other professionals, and diagnostic evaluations, in order to assess clients' abilities, needs, and eligibility for services. Arrange for physical, mental, academic, vocational, and other evaluations to obtain information for assessing clients' needs and developing rehabilitation plans. Collaborate with clients' families to implement rehabilitation plans that include behavioral, residential, social, and/or employment goals. Confer with clients to discuss their options and goals so that rehabilitation programs and plans for accessing needed services can be developed. Confer with physicians, psychologists, occupational therapists, and other professionals, in order to develop and implement client rehabilitation programs. Develop and maintain relationships with community referral sources such as schools and community groups. Develop rehabilitation plans that fit clients' aptitudes, education levels, physical abilities, and career goals. Direct case service allocations, authorizing expenditures and payments. Maintain close contact with clients during job training and placements, in order to resolve problems and evaluate placement adequacy. Monitor and record clients' progress in order to ensure that goals and objectives are met. Prepare and maintain records and case files, including documentation such as clients' personal and eligibility information, services provided, narratives of client contacts, and relevant correspondence. Arrange for on-site job coaching or assistive devices such as specially equipped wheelchairs in order to help clients adapt to work or school environments. Collaborate with community agencies to establish facilities and programs to assist persons with disabilities. Develop diagnostic procedures for determining clients' needs. Locate barriers to client employment, such as inaccessible work sites, inflexible schedules, and transportation problems, and work with clients to develop strategies for overcoming these barriers. Participate in job development and placement programs, contacting prospective employers, placing clients in jobs, and evaluating the success of placements. **SKILLS**—No data available.

GOE—Interest Area: 10. Human Service. **Work Group:** 10.01. Counseling and Social Work. **Other Jobs in This Work Group:** Child, Family, and School Social Workers; Clinical Psychologists; Counseling Psychologists; Marriage and Family Therapists; Medical and Public Health Social Workers; Mental Health and Substance Abuse Social Workers; Mental Health Counselors; Probation Officers and Correctional Treatment Specialists; Residential Advisors; Social and Human Service Assistants; Substance Abuse and Behavioral Disorder Counselors. **PERSONALITY TYPE:** No data available.

EDUCATION/TRAINING PROGRAM(S)— Assistive/Augmentative Technology and Rehabiliation Engineering; Rehabilitation Counseling/Counselor.

WORK ENVIRONMENT—No data available.

Sales Representatives, Agricultural

- ◎ Education/Training Required: Moderate-term on-the-job training
- ◎ Annual Earnings: $59,390
- ◎ Growth: 19.3%
- ◎ Annual Job Openings: 44,000
- ◎ Self-Employed: 4.6%
- ◎ Part-Time: 8.1%

The job openings listed here are shared with Sales Representatives, Chemical and Pharmaceutical; Sales Representatives, Electrical/Electronic; Sales Representatives, Instruments; Sales Representatives, Mechanical Equipment and Supplies; and Sales Representatives, Medical.

Age Bracket	Percentage of Workers
45–54 Years Old	24.0%
55–64 Years Old	13.3%
65 or Older	2.9%

Sell agricultural products and services, such as animal feeds, farm and garden equipment, and

dairy, poultry, and veterinarian supplies. Solicits orders from customers in person or by phone. Demonstrates use of agricultural equipment or machines. Recommends changes in customer use of agricultural products to improve production. Prepares reports of business transactions. Informs customer of estimated delivery schedule, service contracts, warranty, or other information pertaining to purchased products. Displays or shows customer agricultural related products. Compiles lists of prospective customers for use as sales leads. Prepares sales contracts for orders obtained. Consults with customer regarding installation, set-up, or layout of agricultural equipment and machines. Quotes prices and credit terms. **SKILLS**—Persuasion; Negotiation; Speaking; Active Listening; Writing; Mathematics; Instructing.

GOE—Interest Area: 14. Retail and Wholesale Sales and Service. **Work Group:** 14.02. Technical Sales. **Other Jobs in This Work Group:** Sales Engineers; Sales Representatives, Chemical and Pharmaceutical; Sales Representatives, Electrical/Electronic; Sales Representatives, Instruments; Sales Representatives, Mechanical Equipment and Supplies; Sales Representatives, Medical. **PERSONALITY TYPE:** Enterprising. Enterprising occupations frequently involve starting up and carrying out projects. These occupations can involve leading people and making many decisions. They sometimes require risk taking and often deal with business.

EDUCATION/TRAINING PROGRAM(S)— Business, Management, Marketing, and Related Support Services; Selling Skills and Sales Operations.

WORK ENVIRONMENT—Standing; outdoors; sitting; hazardous equipment; walking and running.

Sales Representatives, Chemical and Pharmaceutical

- Education/Training Required: Moderate-term on-the-job training
- Annual Earnings: $59,390
- Growth: 19.3%
- Annual Job Openings: 44,000
- Self-Employed: 4.6%
- Part-Time: 8.1%

The job openings listed here are shared with Sales Representatives, Agricultural; Sales Representatives, Electrical/Electronic; Sales Representatives, Instruments; Sales Representatives, Mechanical Equipment and Supplies; and Sales Representatives, Medical.

Age Bracket	Percentage of Workers
45–54 Years Old	24.0%
55–64 Years Old	13.3%
65 or Older	2.9%

Sell chemical or pharmaceutical products or services, such as acids, industrial chemicals, agricultural chemicals, medicines, drugs, and water treatment supplies. Promotes and sells pharmaceutical and chemical products to potential customers. Explains water treatment package benefits to customer and sells chemicals to treat and resolve water process problems. Estimates and advises customer of service costs to correct water-treatment process problems. Discusses characteristics and clinical studies pertaining to pharmaceutical products with physicians, dentists, hospitals, and retail/wholesale establishments. Distributes drug samples to customer and takes orders for pharmaceutical supply items from customer. Inspects, tests, and observes chemical changes in water system equipment, utilizing test kit, reference manual, and knowledge of chemical treatment. **SKILLS**—Science; Persuasion; Speaking; Social Perceptiveness; Active Listening; Negotiation.

GOE—Interest Area: 14. Retail and Wholesale Sales and Service. **Work Group:** 14.02. Technical Sales. **Other Jobs in This Work Group:** Sales Engineers; Sales Representatives, Agricultural; Sales Representatives, Electrical/Electronic; Sales Representatives, Instruments; Sales Representatives, Mechanical Equipment and Supplies; Sales Representatives, Medical. **PERSONALITY TYPE:** Enterprising. Enterprising occupations frequently involve starting up and carrying out projects. These occupations can involve leading people and making many decisions. They sometimes require risk taking and often deal with business.

EDUCATION/TRAINING PROGRAM(S)— Business, Management, Marketing, and Related Support Services; Selling Skills and Sales Operations.

WORK ENVIRONMENT—Sitting; standing; walking and running; outdoors; spend time bending or twisting the body.

Sales Representatives, Electrical/Electronic

- ◎ Education/Training Required: Moderate-term on-the-job training
- ◎ Annual Earnings: $59,390
- ◎ Growth: 19.3%
- ◎ Annual Job Openings: 44,000
- ◎ Self-Employed: 4.6%
- ◎ Part-Time: 8.1%

The job openings listed here are shared with Sales Representatives, Agricultural; Sales Representatives, Chemical and Pharmaceutical; Sales Representatives, Instruments; Sales Representatives, Mechanical Equipment and Supplies; and Sales Representatives, Medical.

Age Bracket	Percentage of Workers
45–54 Years Old	24.0%
55–64 Years Old	13.3%
65 or Older	2.9%

Sell electrical, electronic, or related products or services, such as communication equipment, radiographic-inspection equipment and services, ultrasonic equipment, electronics parts, computers, and EDP systems. Analyzes communication needs of customer and consults with staff engineers regarding technical problems. Trains establishment personnel in equipment use, utilizing knowledge of electronics and product sold. Recommends equipment to meet customer requirements, considering salable features, such as flexibility, cost, capacity, and economy of operation. Negotiates terms of sale and services with customer. Sells electrical or electronic equipment, such as computers, data processing and radiographic equipment to businesses and industrial establishments. **SKILLS**—Persuasion; Negotiation; Instructing; Operations Analysis; Active Listening; Equipment Selection; Speaking; Technology Design.

GOE—Interest Area: 14. Retail and Wholesale Sales and Service. **Work Group:** 14.02. Technical Sales. **Other Jobs in This Work Group:** Sales Engineers; Sales Representatives, Agricultural; Sales Representatives, Chemical and Pharmaceutical; Sales Representatives, Instruments; Sales Representatives, Mechanical Equipment and Supplies; Sales Representatives, Medical. **PERSONALITY TYPE:** Enterprising. Enterprising occupations frequently involve starting up and carrying out projects. These occupations can involve leading people and making many decisions. They sometimes require risk taking and often deal with business.

EDUCATION/TRAINING PROGRAM(S)—Business, Management, Marketing, and Related Support Services; Selling Skills and Sales Operations.

WORK ENVIRONMENT—Standing; sitting; indoors; walking and running.

Sales Representatives, Instruments

- ◎ Education/Training Required: Moderate-term on-the-job training
- ◎ Annual Earnings: $59,390
- ◎ Growth: 19.3%
- ◎ Annual Job Openings: 44,000
- ◎ Self-Employed: 4.6%
- ◎ Part-Time: 8.1%

The job openings listed here are shared with Sales Representatives, Agricultural; Sales Representatives, Chemical and Pharmaceutical; Sales Representatives, Electrical/Electronic; Sales Representatives, Mechanical Equipment and Supplies; and Sales Representatives, Medical.

Age Bracket	Percentage of Workers
45–54 Years Old	24.0%
55–64 Years Old	13.3%
65 or Older	2.9%

Sell precision instruments, such as dynamometers and spring scales, and laboratory, navigation, and surveying instruments. Assists customer with product selection, utilizing knowledge of engineering specifications and catalog resources. Evaluates customer needs and emphasizes product features based on technical knowledge of product capabilities and limitations. Sells weighing and other precision instruments, such as spring scales, dynamometers, and laboratory, navigational, and surveying instruments to customer. SKILLS—Persuasion; Active Listening; Speaking; Service Orientation.

GOE—Interest Area: 14. Retail and Wholesale Sales and Service. Work Group: 14.02. Technical Sales. Other Jobs in This Work Group: Sales Engineers; Sales Representatives, Agricultural; Sales Representatives, Chemical and Pharmaceutical; Sales Representatives, Electrical/Electronic; Sales Representatives, Mechanical Equipment and Supplies; Sales Representatives, Medical. PERSONALITY TYPE: Enterprising. Enterprising occupations frequently involve starting up and carrying out projects. These occupations can involve leading people and making many decisions. They sometimes require risk taking and often deal with business.

EDUCATION/TRAINING PROGRAM(S)—Business, Management, Marketing, and Related Support Services; Selling Skills and Sales Operations.

WORK ENVIRONMENT—Standing; sitting; indoors.

Sales Representatives, Mechanical Equipment and Supplies

◎ Education/Training Required: Moderate-term on-the-job training
◎ Annual Earnings: $59,390
◎ Growth: 19.3%
◎ Annual Job Openings: 44,000
◎ Self-Employed: 4.6%
◎ Part-Time: 8.1%

The job openings listed here are shared with Sales Representatives, Agricultural; Sales Representatives, Chemical and Pharmaceutical; Sales Representatives, Electrical/Electronic; Sales Representatives, Instruments; and Sales Representatives, Medical.

Age Bracket	Percentage of Workers
45–54 Years Old	24.0%
55–64 Years Old	13.3%
65 or Older	2.9%

Sell mechanical equipment, machinery, materials, and supplies, such as aircraft and railroad equipment and parts, construction machinery, material-handling equipment, industrial machinery, and welding equipment. Recommends and sells textile, industrial, construction, railroad, and oil field machinery, equipment, materials, and supplies, and services utilizing knowledge of machine operations. Computes installation or production costs, estimates savings, and prepares and submits bid specifications to customer for review and approval. Submits orders for product and follows-up on order to verify material list accuracy and delivery schedule meets project deadline. Appraises equipment and verifies customer credit rating to establish trade-in value and contract terms. Reviews existing machinery/equipment placement and diagrams proposal to illustrate efficient space utilization, using standard measuring devices and templates. Attends sales and trade meetings and reads related publications to obtain current market condition information, business trends, and industry developments. Inspects establishment premises to verify installation feasibility, and obtains building blueprints and elevator specifications to submit to engineering department for bid. Demonstrates and explains use of installed equipment and production processes. Arranges for installation and test-operation of machinery and recommends solutions to product-related problems. Contacts current and potential customers, visits establishments to evaluate needs, and promotes sale of products and services. **SKILLS**—Operations Analysis; Negotiation; Persuasion; Equipment Selection; Active Listening; Speaking; Instructing; Reading Comprehension.

GOE—**Interest Area:** 14. Retail and Wholesale Sales and Service. **Work Group:** 14.02. Technical Sales. **Other Jobs in This Work Group:** Sales Engineers; Sales Representatives, Agricultural; Sales Representatives, Chemical and Pharmaceutical; Sales Representatives, Electrical/Electronic; Sales Representatives, Instruments; Sales Representatives, Medical. **PERSONALITY TYPE:** Enterprising. Enterprising occupations frequently involve starting up and carrying out projects. These occupations can involve leading people and making many decisions. They sometimes require risk taking and often deal with business.

EDUCATION/TRAINING PROGRAM(S)—Business, Management, Marketing, and Related Support Services; Selling Skills and Sales Operations.

WORK ENVIRONMENT—Walking and running; standing; sitting; indoors; outdoors.

Sales Representatives, Medical

- Education/Training Required: Moderate-term on-the-job training
- Annual Earnings: $59,390
- Growth: 19.3%
- Annual Job Openings: 44,000
- Self-Employed: 4.6%
- Part-Time: 8.1%

The job openings listed here are shared with Sales Representatives, Agricultural; Sales Representatives, Chemical and Pharmaceutical; Sales Representatives, Electrical/Electronic; Sales Representatives, Instruments; and Sales Representatives, Mechanical Equipment and Supplies.

Age Bracket	Percentage of Workers
45–54 Years Old	24.0%
55–64 Years Old	13.3%
65 or Older	2.9%

Sell medical equipment, products, and services. Does not include pharmaceutical sales representatives. Promotes sale of medical and dental equipment, supplies, and services to doctors, dentists, hospitals, medical schools, and retail establishments. Writes specifications to order custom-made surgical appliances, using customer measurements and physician prescriptions. Advises customer regarding office layout, legal and insurance regulations, cost analysis, and collection methods. Designs and fabricates custom-made medical appliances. Selects surgical appliances from stock and fits and sells appliance to customer. Studies data describing new products to accurately recommend purchase of equipment and supplies. **SKILLS**—Technology Design; Negotiation; Persuasion; Operations Analysis; Active Listening; Writing; Speaking; Reading Comprehension; Service Orientation; Equipment Selection.

GOE—**Interest Area:** 14. Retail and Wholesale Sales and Service. **Work Group:** 14.02. Technical Sales. **Other Jobs in This Work Group:** Sales Engineers; Sales Representatives, Agricultural; Sales Representatives, Chemical and Pharmaceutical; Sales Representatives, Electrical/Electronic; Sales Representatives, Instruments; Sales Representatives, Mechanical Equipment and Supplies. **PERSONALITY TYPE:** Enterprising. Enterprising occupations frequently involve starting up and carrying out projects. These occupations can involve leading people and making many decisions. They sometimes require risk taking and often deal with business.

EDUCATION/TRAINING PROGRAM(S)— Business, Management, Marketing, and Related Support Services; Selling Skills and Sales Operations.

WORK ENVIRONMENT—Standing; walking and running; indoors; sitting.

Sales Representatives, Wholesale and Manufacturing, Except Technical and Scientific Products

- ◎ Education/Training Required: Moderate-term on-the-job training
- ◎ Annual Earnings: $46,090
- ◎ Growth: 19.1%
- ◎ Annual Job Openings: 160,000
- ◎ Self-Employed: 4.6%
- ◎ Part-Time: 8.1%

Age Bracket	Percentage of Workers
45–54 Years Old	24.0%
55–64 Years Old	13.3%
65 or Older	2.9%

Sell goods for wholesalers or manufacturers to businesses or groups of individuals. Work requires substantial knowledge of items sold. Answer customers' questions about products, prices, availability, product uses, and credit terms. Arrange and direct delivery and installation of products and equipment. Contact regular and prospective customers to demonstrate products, explain product features, and solicit orders. Estimate or quote prices, credit or contract terms, warranties, and delivery dates. Forward orders to manufacturers. Identify prospective customers by using business directories, following leads from existing clients, participating in organizations and clubs, and attending trade shows and conferences. Monitor market conditions, product innovations, and competitors' products, prices, and sales. Negotiate details of contracts and payments, and

S

prepare sales contracts and order forms. Prepare drawings, estimates, and bids that meet specific customer needs. Provide customers with product samples and catalogs. Recommend products to customers, based on customers' needs and interests. Buy products from manufacturers or brokerage firms, and distribute them to wholesale and retail clients. Check stock levels and reorder merchandise as necessary. Consult with clients after sales or contract signings in order to resolve problems and to provide ongoing support. Negotiate with retail merchants to improve product exposure such as shelf positioning and advertising. Obtain credit information about prospective customers. Perform administrative duties, such as preparing sales budgets and reports, keeping sales records, and filing expense account reports. Plan, assemble, and stock product displays in retail stores, or make recommendations to retailers regarding product displays, promotional programs, and advertising. Train customers' employees to operate and maintain new equipment. **SKILLS**—Negotiation; Management of Material Resources; Persuasion; Service Orientation; Speaking; Social Perceptiveness; Writing; Instructing; Systems Evaluation.

GOE—Interest Area: 14. Retail and Wholesale Sales and Service. **Work Group:** 14.03. General Sales. **Other Jobs in This Work Group:** Parts Salespersons; Real Estate Brokers; Real Estate Sales Agents; Retail Salespersons; Service Station Attendants. **PERSONALITY TYPE:** Enterprising. Enterprising occupations frequently involve starting up and carrying out projects. These occupations can involve leading people and making many decisions. They sometimes require risk taking and often deal with business.

EDUCATION/TRAINING PROGRAM(S)—Apparel and Accessories Marketing Operations; Business, Management, Marketing, and Related Support Services; Fashion Merchandising; General Merchandising, Sales, and Related Marketing Operations, Other; Sales, Distribution, and Marketing Operations, General; Sales, Distribution, and Marketing Operations, General; Sepecialized Merchandising, Sales, and Related Marketing Operations, Other; Special Products Marketing Operations.

WORK ENVIRONMENT—Sitting; standing; walking and running; outdoors; indoors.

School Psychologists

- ◎ Education/Training Required: Doctoral degree
- ◎ Annual Earnings: $56,360
- ◎ Growth: 24.4%
- ◎ Annual Job Openings: 17,000
- ◎ Self-Employed: 25.4%
- ◎ Part-Time: 27.2%

The job openings listed here are shared with Clinical Psychologists and Counseling Psychologists.

Age Bracket	Percentage of Workers
45–54 Years Old	33.0%
55–64 Years Old	23.8%
65 or Older	7.6%

Investigate processes of learning and teaching and develop psychological principles and techniques applicable to educational problems. Compile and interpret students' test results, along with information from teachers and parents, in order to diagnose conditions, and to help assess eligibility for special services. Report any pertinent information to the proper authorities in cases of child endangerment, neglect, or abuse. Assess an individual child's needs, limitations, and potential, using observation, review of school records, and consultation with parents and school personnel. Select, administer, and score psychological tests. Provide consultation to parents, teachers, administrators, and others on topics such as learning styles and behavior modification techniques. Promote an understanding of child development and its relationship to learning and behavior. Collaborate with other educational professionals to develop teaching strategies and school programs. Counsel children and families to help solve conflicts and problems in learning and adjustment. Develop individualized educational plans in collaboration with teachers and other staff members. Maintain student records, including special education reports, confidential records, records of services provided, and behavioral data. Serve as a resource to help families and schools deal with crises, such as separation and loss. Attend workshops, seminars, and/or professional meetings in order to remain informed of new developments in school psychology. Design classes and programs to meet the needs of special students. Refer students and their families to appropriate community agencies for medical, vocational, or social services. Initiate and direct efforts to foster tolerance, understanding, and appreciation of diversity in school communities. Collect and analyze data to evaluate the effectiveness of academic programs and other services, such as behavioral management systems. Provide educational programs on topics such as classroom management, teaching strategies, or parenting skills. Conduct research to generate new knowledge that can be used to address learning and behavior issues. **SKILLS**—Social Perceptiveness; Learning Strategies; Negotiation; Persuasion; Service Orientation; Writing; Active Learning; Coordination.

GOE—Interest Area: 15. Scientific Research, Engineering, and Mathematics. **Work Group:** 15.04. Social Sciences. **Other Jobs in This Work Group:** Anthropologists; Archeologists; Economists; Historians; Industrial-Organizational Psychologists; Political Scientists; Sociologists. **PERSONALITY TYPE:** Investigative. Investigative occupations frequently involve working with ideas and require an extensive amount of thinking. These occupations can involve searching for facts and figuring out problems mentally.

EDUCATION/TRAINING PROGRAM(S)— Clinical Psychology; Counseling Psychology; Developmental and Child Psychology; Psychoanalysis and Psychotherapy; Psychology, General; School Psychology.

WORK ENVIRONMENT—Sitting; physical proximity to others; sounds, noise levels are distracting or uncomfortable; indoors; disease or infections.

Sculptors

- Education/Training Required: Long-term on-the-job training
- Annual Earnings: $41,240
- Growth: 16.5%
- Annual Job Openings: 4,000
- Self-Employed: 55.5%
- Part-Time: 23.1%

The job openings listed here are shared with Cartoonists, Painters and Illustrators, and Sketch Artists.

Age Bracket	Percentage of Workers
45–54 Years Old	25.5%
55–64 Years Old	17.0%
65 or Older	5.7%

Design and construct three-dimensional art works, using materials such as stone, wood, plaster, and metal and employing various manual and tool techniques. Carves objects from stone, concrete, plaster, wood, or other material, using abrasives and tools, such as chisels, gouges, and mall. Models substances, such as clay or wax, using fingers and small hand tools to form objects. Cuts, bends, laminates, arranges, and fastens individual or mixed raw and manufactured materials and products to form works of art. Constructs artistic forms from metal or stone, using metalworking, welding, or masonry tools and equipment. **SKILLS**—None met the criteria.

GOE—Interest Area: 03. Arts and Communication. **Work Group:** 03.04. Studio Art. **Other Jobs in This Work Group:** Cartoonists; Craft Artists; Painters and Illustrators; Potters; Sketch Artists. **PERSONALITY TYPE:** Artistic. Artistic occupations frequently involve working with forms, designs, and patterns. They often require self-expression, and the work can be done without following a clear set of rules.

EDUCATION/TRAINING PROGRAM(S)— Art/Art Studies, General; Art/Art Studies, General; Fine Arts and Art Studies, Other; Fine/Studio Arts, General; Sculpture.

WORK ENVIRONMENT—Using hands on objects, tools, or controls; standing; spend time bending or twisting the body; sitting; minor burns, cuts, bites, or stings.

Secondary School Teachers, Except Special and Vocational Education

- Education/Training Required: Bachelor's degree
- Annual Earnings: $46,120
- Growth: 18.2%
- Annual Job Openings: 118,000
- Self-Employed: 0%
- Part-Time: 8.8%

Age Bracket	Percentage of Workers
45–54 Years Old	31.0%
55–64 Years Old	15.7%
65 or Older	2.0%

Instruct students in secondary public or private schools in one or more subjects at the secondary level, such as English, mathematics, or social studies. May be designated according to subject matter specialty, such as typing instructors, commercial teachers, or English teachers. Establish and enforce rules for behavior and procedures for maintaining order among the students for whom they are responsible. Instruct through lectures, discussions, and demonstrations in one or more subjects such as English, mathematics, or social studies. Establish clear objectives for all lessons, units, and projects, and communicate those objectives to students. Prepare, administer, and grade tests and assignments to evaluate students' progress. Prepare materials and classrooms for class activities. Adapt teaching methods and instructional materials to meet students' varying needs and interests. Maintain accurate and complete student records as required by laws, district policies, and administrative regulations. Assign and grade class work and homework. Observe and evaluate students' performance, behavior, social development, and physical health. Enforce all administration policies and rules governing students. Plan and conduct activities for a balanced program of instruction, demonstration, and work time that provides students with opportunities to observe, question, and investigate. Prepare students for later grades by encouraging them to explore learning opportunities and to persevere with challenging tasks. Guide and counsel students with adjustment and/or academic problems, or special academic interests. Instruct and monitor students in the use and care of equipment and materials, in order to prevent injuries and damage. Prepare for assigned classes, and show written evidence of preparation upon request of immediate supervisors. Use computers, audiovisual aids, and other equipment and materials to supplement presentations. Meet with parents and guardians to discuss their children's progress, and to determine their priorities for their children and their resource needs. Confer with parents or guardians, other teachers, counselors, and administrators in order to resolve students' behavioral and academic problems. Prepare objectives and outlines for courses of study, following curriculum guidelines or requirements of states and schools. Meet with other professionals to discuss individual students' needs and progress. **SKILLS**—Learning Strategies; Instructing; Social Perceptiveness; Persuasion; Monitoring; Time Management; Service Orientation; Negotiation.

GOE—Interest Area: 05. Education and Training. **Work Group:** 05.02. Preschool, Elementary, and Secondary Teaching and Instructing. **Other Jobs in This Work Group:** Elementary School Teachers, Except Special Education; Kindergarten Teachers, Except Special Education; Middle School Teachers, Except Special and Vocational Education; Preschool Teachers, Except Special Education; Special Education Teachers, Middle School; Special Education Teachers, Preschool, Kindergarten, and Elementary School; Special Education Teachers, Secondary School; Teacher Assistants; Vocational Education Teachers, Middle School; Vocational Education Teachers, Secondary School. **PERSONALITY TYPE:** Social. Social occupations frequently involve working with, communicating with, and teaching people. These occupations often involve helping or providing service to others.

EDUCATION/TRAINING PROGRAM(S)—Agricultural Teacher Education; Art Teacher Education; Biology Teacher Education; Business Teacher Education; Chemistry Teacher Education; Computer Teacher Education; Drama and Dance Teacher Education; Driver and Safety Teacher Education; English/Language Arts Teacher Education; Family and Consumer Sciences/Home Economics Teacher Education; Foreign Language Teacher Education; French Language Teacher Education; Geography Teacher Education; German Language Teacher Education; others.

WORK ENVIRONMENT—Physical proximity to others; sounds, noise levels are distracting or uncomfortable; contaminants; standing; indoors.

Security Guards

- Education/Training Required: Short-term on-the-job training
- Annual Earnings: $20,520
- Growth: 31.9%
- Annual Job Openings: 228,000
- Self-Employed: 0.9%
- Part-Time: 15.1%

Age Bracket	Percentage of Workers
45–54 Years Old	18.1%
55–64 Years Old	15.9%
65 or Older	8.5%

Guard, patrol, or monitor premises to prevent theft, violence, or infractions of rules. Patrol industrial and commercial premises to prevent and detect signs of intrusion and ensure security of doors, windows, and gates. Answer alarms and investigate disturbances. Monitor and authorize entrance and departure of employees, visitors, and other persons to guard against theft and maintain security of premises. Write reports of daily activities and irregularities, such as equipment or property damage, theft, presence of unauthorized persons, or unusual occurrences. Call police or fire departments in cases of emergency, such as fire or presence of unauthorized persons. Circulate among visitors, patrons, and employees to preserve order and protect property. Answer telephone calls to take messages, answer questions, and provide information during nonbusiness hours or when switchboard is closed. Warn persons of rule infractions or violations, and apprehend or evict violators from premises, using force when necessary. Operate detecting devices to screen individuals and prevent passage of prohibited articles into restricted areas. Escort or drive motor vehicle to transport individuals to specified locations and to provide personal protection. Inspect and adjust security systems, equipment, and machinery to ensure operational use and to detect evidence of tampering. Drive and guard armored vehicle to transport money and valuables to prevent theft and ensure safe delivery. **SKILLS**—Social Perceptiveness; Negotiation; Learning Strategies; Speaking; Active Listening; Time Management; Writing; Monitoring.

GOE—Interest Area: 12. Law and Public Safety. **Work Group:** 12.05. Safety and Security. **Other Jobs in This Work Group:** Animal Control Workers; Crossing Guards; Gaming Surveillance Officers and Gaming Investigators; Lifeguards, Ski Patrol, and Other Recreational Protective Service Workers; Private Detectives and Investigators. **PERSONALITY TYPE:** Social. Social occupations frequently involve working with, communicating with, and teaching people. These occupations often involve helping or providing service to others.

EDUCATION/TRAINING PROGRAM(S)—Securities Services Administration/Management; Security and Loss Prevention Services.

WORK ENVIRONMENT—Very hot or cold; sounds, noise levels are distracting or uncomfortable; extremely bright or inadequate lighting; physical proximity to others; outdoors.

Self-Enrichment Education Teachers

- Education/Training Required: Work experience in a related occupation
- Annual Earnings: $31,530
- Growth: 40.1%
- Annual Job Openings: 39,000
- Self-Employed: 19.9%
- Part-Time: 41.0%

Age Bracket	Percentage of Workers
45–54 Years Old	22.4%
55–64 Years Old	14.8%
65 or Older	5.1%

Teach or instruct courses other than those that normally lead to an occupational objective or degree. Courses may include self-improvement, nonvocational, and nonacademic subjects. Teaching may or may not take place in a traditional educational institution. Conduct classes, workshops, and demonstrations, and provide individual instruction to teach topics and skills such as cooking, dancing, writing, physical fitness, photography, personal finance, and flying. Instruct students individually and in groups, using various teaching methods such as lectures, discussions, and demonstrations. Adapt teaching methods and instructional materials to meet students' varying needs and interests. Assign and grade class work and homework. Confer with other teachers and professionals to plan and schedule lessons promoting learning and development. Enforce policies and rules governing students. Establish clear objectives for all lessons, units, and projects, and communicate those objectives to students. Instruct and monitor students in use and care of equipment and materials, in order to prevent injury and damage. Maintain accurate and complete student records as required by administrative policy. Meet with other instructors to discuss individual students and their progress. Monitor students' performance in order to make suggestions for improvement, and to ensure that they satisfy course standards, training requirements, and objectives. Observe students to determine qualifications, limitations, abilities, interests, and other individual characteristics. Plan and conduct activities for a balanced program of instruction, demonstration, and work time that provides students with opportunities to observe, question, and investigate. Plan and supervise class projects, field trips, visits by guest speakers, contests, or other experiential activities, and guide students in learning from those activities. Prepare and administer written, oral, and performance tests, and issue grades in accordance with performance. Prepare and implement remedial programs for students requiring extra help. Prepare instructional program objectives, outlines, and lesson plans. Prepare materials and classrooms for class activities. Prepare students for further development by encouraging them to explore learning opportunities and to persevere with challenging tasks. Review instructional content, methods, and student evaluations in order to assess strengths and weaknesses, and to develop recommendations for course revision, development, or elimination. **SKILLS**—Instructing; Writing; Speaking; Learning Strategies; Service Orientation; Systems Evaluation; Reading Comprehension; Active Listening; Judgment and Decision Making; Management of Material Resources.

GOE—Interest Area: 05. Education and Training. **Work Group:** 05.03. Postsecondary and Adult Teaching and Instructing. **Other Jobs in This Work Group:** Adult Literacy, Remedial Education, and GED Teachers and Instructors; Agricultural Sciences Teachers, Postsecondary; Anthropology and Archeology Teachers, Postsecondary; Architecture Teachers, Postsecondary; Area, Ethnic, and Cultural Studies Teachers, Postsecondary; Art, Drama, and Music Teachers, Postsecondary; Atmospheric, Earth, Marine, and Space Sciences Teachers, Postsecondary; Biological Science Teachers, Postsecondary; Business Teachers, Postsecondary; Chemistry Teachers, Postsecondary; Communications Teachers, Postsecondary; Computer Science Teachers, Postsecondary; Criminal Justice and

Law Enforcement Teachers, Postsecondary; Economics Teachers, Postsecondary; Education Teachers, Postsecondary; Engineering Teachers, Postsecondary; English Language and Literature Teachers, Postsecondary; Environmental Science Teachers, Postsecondary; Farm and Home Management Advisors; Foreign Language and Literature Teachers, Postsecondary; Forestry and Conservation Science Teachers, Postsecondary; Geography Teachers, Postsecondary; Graduate Teaching Assistants; Health Specialties Teachers, Postsecondary; History Teachers, Postsecondary; Home Economics Teachers, Postsecondary; Law Teachers, Postsecondary; Library Science Teachers, Postsecondary; Mathematical Science Teachers, Postsecondary; Nursing Instructors and Teachers, Postsecondary; Philosophy and Religion Teachers, Postsecondary; Physics Teachers, Postsecondary; Political Science Teachers, Postsecondary; Psychology Teachers, Postsecondary; Recreation and Fitness Studies Teachers, Postsecondary; Social Work Teachers, Postsecondary; Sociology Teachers, Postsecondary; Vocational Education Teachers, Postsecondary. **PERSONALITY TYPE:** Social. Social occupations frequently involve working with, communicating with, and teaching people. These occupations often involve helping or providing service to others.

EDUCATION/TRAINING PROGRAM(S)— Adult and Continuing Education and Teaching.

WORK ENVIRONMENT—Sitting; standing; walking and running; indoors.

Sketch Artists

- Education/Training Required: Long-term on-the-job training
- Annual Earnings: $41,240
- Growth: 16.5%
- Annual Job Openings: 4,000
- Self-Employed: 55.5%
- Part-Time: 23.1%

The job openings listed here are shared with Cartoonists, Painters and Illustrators, and Sculptors.

Age Bracket	Percentage of Workers
45–54 Years Old	25.5%
55–64 Years Old	17.0%
65 or Older	5.7%

Sketch likenesses of subjects according to observation or descriptions either to assist law enforcement agencies in identifying suspects, to depict court room scenes, or for entertainment purposes of patrons, using mediums such as pencil, charcoal, and pastels. Draws sketch, profile, or likeness of posed subject or photograph, using pencil, charcoal, pastels, or other medium. Assembles and arranges outlines of features to form composite image, according to information provided by witness or victim. Alters copy of composite image until witness or victim is satisfied that composite is best possible representation of suspect. Poses subject to accentuate most pleasing features or profile. Classifies and codes components of image, using established system, to help identify suspect. Prepares series of simple line drawings conforming to description of suspect and presents drawings to informant for selection of sketch. Interviews crime victims and witnesses to obtain descriptive information concerning physical build, sex, nationality, and facial features of unidentified suspect. Measures distances and develops sketches of crime scene from photograph and measurements. Searches police photograph records, using classification and coding system to determine if existing photograph of suspects is available. Operates photocopy or similar machine to reproduce composite image. **SKILLS**—Active Listening; Social Perceptiveness; Speaking.

GOE—Interest Area: 03. Arts and Communication. **Work Group:** 03.04. Studio Art. **Other Jobs in This Work Group:** Cartoonists; Craft Artists; Painters and Illustrators; Potters; Sculptors. **PERSONALITY TYPE:** Artistic. Artistic occupations frequently involve working with forms, designs, and patterns. They often require self-expression, and the work can be done without following a clear set of rules.

EDUCATION/TRAINING PROGRAM(S)—Art/Art Studies, General; Art/Art Studies, General; Drawing; Fine/Studio Arts, General.

WORK ENVIRONMENT—Sitting; spend time making repetitive motions; indoors; extremely bright or inadequate lighting; using hands on objects, tools, or controls.

Social and Community Service Managers

- Education/Training Required: Bachelor's degree
- Annual Earnings: $48,330
- Growth: 27.7%
- Annual Job Openings: 19,000
- Self-Employed: 6.6%
- Part-Time: 10.7%

Age Bracket	Percentage of Workers
45–54 Years Old	27.7%
55–64 Years Old	19.9%
65 or Older	3.9%

Plan, organize, or coordinate the activities of a social service program or community outreach organization. Oversee the program or organization's budget and policies regarding participant involvement, program requirements, and benefits. Work may involve directing social workers, counselors, or probation officers. Establish and maintain relationships with other agencies and organizations in community in order to meet community needs and to ensure that services are not duplicated. Prepare and maintain records and reports, such as budgets, personnel records, or training manuals. Direct activities of professional and technical staff members and volunteers. Evaluate the work of staff and volunteers in order to ensure that programs are of appropriate quality and that resources are used effectively. Establish and oversee administrative procedures to meet objectives set by boards of directors or senior management. Participate in the determination of organizational policies regarding such issues as participant eligibility, program requirements, and program benefits. Research and analyze member or community needs in order to determine program directions and goals. Speak to community groups to explain and interpret agency purposes, programs, and policies. Recruit, interview, and hire or sign up volunteers and staff. Represent organizations in relations with governmental and media institutions. Plan and administer budgets for programs, equipment and support services. Analyze proposed legislation, regulations, or rule changes in order to determine how agency services could be impacted. Act as consultants to agency staff and other community programs

S

regarding the interpretation of program-related federal, state, and county regulations and policies. Implement and evaluate staff training programs. Direct fund-raising activities and the preparation of public relations materials. **SKILLS**—Social Perceptiveness; Management of Personnel Resources; Service Orientation; Negotiation; Persuasion; Instructing; Monitoring; Learning Strategies.

GOE—Interest Area: 07. Government and Public Administration. **Work Group:** 07.01. Managerial Work in Government and Public Administration. **Other Jobs in This Work Group:** Government Service Executives. **PERSONALITY TYPE:** Social. Social occupations frequently involve working with, communicating with, and teaching people. These occupations often involve helping or providing service to others.

EDUCATION/TRAINING PROGRAM(S)—Business Administration/Management; Business, Management, Marketing, and Related Support Services; Business/Commerce, General; Community Organization and Advocacy; Entrepreneurship/Entrepreneurial Studies; Human Services, General; Non-Profit/Public/Organizational Management; Public Administration.

WORK ENVIRONMENT—Sitting; sounds, noise levels are distracting or uncomfortable; in an enclosed vehicle or equipment; physical proximity to others; indoors.

Social and Human Service Assistants

- Education/Training Required: Moderate-term on-the-job training
- Annual Earnings: $24,730
- Growth: 48.7%
- Annual Job Openings: 63,000
- Self-Employed: 0.2%
- Part-Time: 10.6%

Age Bracket	Percentage of Workers
45–54 Years Old	27.7%
55–64 Years Old	11.4%
65 or Older	2.9%

Assist professionals from a wide variety of fields, such as psychology, rehabilitation, or social work, to provide client services, as well as support for families. May assist clients in identifying available benefits and social and community services and help clients obtain them. May assist social workers with developing, organizing, and conducting programs to prevent and resolve problems relevant to substance abuse, human relationships, rehabilitation, or adult daycare. Provide information on and refer individuals to public or private agencies and community services for assistance. Keep records and prepare reports for owner or management concerning visits with clients. Visit individuals in homes or attend group meetings to provide information on agency services, requirements and procedures. Advise clients regarding food stamps, child care, food, money management, sanitation, and housekeeping. Submit to and review reports and problems with superior. Oversee day-to-day group activities of residents in institution. Interview individuals and family members to compile information on social, educational, criminal, institutional, or drug history. Meet with youth groups to acquaint them with consequences of delinquent acts. Transport and accompany clients to shopping area and to appointments, using automobile. Explain rules established by owner or management, such as sanitation and maintenance requirements, and parking regulations. Observe and discuss meal preparation and suggest alternate methods of food preparation. Demonstrate use and care of equipment for tenant use. Consult with supervisor concerning programs for individual families. Monitor free, supplementary meal program to ensure cleanliness of facility and that eligibility guidelines are met for persons receiving meals. Observe clients' food selections and recommend alternate economical and nutritional food choices. Inform tenants of facilities, such as laundries and playgrounds. Care for children in client's home during client's appointments. Assist in locating housing for displaced individuals. Assist clients with preparation of forms, such as tax or rent forms. Assist in planning of food budget, utilizing charts and sample budgets. **SKILLS—**Social Perceptiveness; Service Orientation; Management of Financial Resources; Learning Strategies; Instructing; Time Management; Speaking; Active Listening.

GOE—Interest Area: 10. Human Service. **Work Group:** 10.01. Counseling and Social Work. **Other Jobs in This Work Group:** Child, Family, and School Social Workers; Clinical Psychologists; Counseling Psychologists; Marriage and Family Therapists; Medical and Public Health Social Workers; Mental Health and Substance Abuse Social Workers; Mental Health Counselors; Probation Officers and Correctional Treatment Specialists; Rehabilitation Counselors; Residential Advisors; Substance Abuse and Behavioral Disorder Counselors. **PERSONALITY TYPE:** Social.

Social occupations frequently involve working with, communicating with, and teaching people. These occupations often involve helping or providing service to others.

EDUCATION/TRAINING PROGRAM(S)— Mental and Social Health Services and Allied Professions, Other.

WORK ENVIRONMENT—Sitting; in an enclosed vehicle or equipment; sounds, noise levels are distracting or uncomfortable; physical proximity to others; extremely bright or inadequate lighting.

Social Work Teachers, Postsecondary

- ◉ Education/Training Required: Master's degree
- ◉ Annual Earnings: $52,160
- ◉ Growth: 38.1%
- ◉ Annual Job Openings: 216,000
- ◉ Self-Employed: 0.3%
- ◉ Part-Time: 27.7%

The job openings listed here are shared with all other postsecondary teaching occupations.

Age Bracket	Percentage of Workers
45–54 Years Old	22.8%
55–64 Years Old	19.0%
65 or Older	5.5%

Teach courses in social work. Initiate, facilitate, and moderate classroom discussions. Evaluate and grade students' class work, assignments, and papers. Prepare and deliver lectures to undergraduate and/or graduate students on topics such as family behavior, child and adolescent mental health, and social intervention evaluation. Keep abreast of developments in their field by reading current literature, talking with colleagues, and participating in professional conferences. Conduct research in a particular field of knowledge and publish findings in professional journals, books, and/or electronic media. Supervise students' laboratory work and fieldwork. Prepare course materials such as syllabi, homework assignments, and handouts. Supervise undergraduate and/or graduate teaching, internship, and research work. Maintain regularly scheduled office hours in order to advise and assist students. Plan, evaluate, and revise curricula, course content, and course materials and methods of instruction. Collaborate with colleagues, and with community agencies, in order to address teaching and research issues. Compile, administer, and grade examinations or assign this work to others. Advise students on academic and vocational curricula, and on career issues. Maintain student attendance records, grades, and other required records. Write grant proposals to procure external research funding. Serve on academic or administrative committees that deal with institutional policies, departmental matters, and academic issues. Perform administrative duties such as serving as department head. Compile bibliographies of specialized materials for outside reading assignments. Select and obtain materials and supplies such as textbooks and laboratory equipment. Participate in student recruitment, registration, and placement activities. Participate in campus and community events. Provide professional consulting services to government and/or industry. Act as advisers to student organizations. **SKILLS**—Social Perceptiveness; Instructing; Service Orientation; Learning Strategies; Negotiation; Critical Thinking; Writing; Active Learning; Coordination.

GOE—Interest Area: 05. Education and Training. **Work Group:** 05.03. Postsecondary and Adult Teaching and Instructing. **Other Jobs in This Work Group:** Adult Literacy, Remedial Education, and GED Teachers and Instructors; Agricultural Sciences Teachers, Postsecondary; Anthropology and Archeology Teachers, Postsecondary; Architecture Teachers, Postsecondary; Area, Ethnic, and Cultural Studies Teachers, Postsecondary; Art, Drama, and Music Teachers, Postsecondary; Atmospheric, Earth, Marine, and Space Sciences Teachers, Postsecondary; Biological Science Teachers, Postsecondary; Business Teachers, Postsecondary; Chemistry Teachers, Postsecondary; Communications Teachers, Postsecondary; Computer Science Teachers, Postsecondary; Criminal Justice and Law Enforcement Teachers, Postsecondary; Economics Teachers, Postsecondary; Education Teachers, Postsecondary; Engineering Teachers, Postsecondary; English Language and Literature Teachers, Postsecondary; Environmental Science Teachers, Postsecondary; Farm and Home Management Advisors; Foreign Language and Literature Teachers, Postsecondary; Forestry and Conservation Science Teachers, Postsecondary; Geography Teachers, Postsecondary; Graduate Teaching Assistants; Health Specialties Teachers, Postsecondary; History Teachers, Postsecondary; Home Economics Teachers, Postsecondary; Law Teachers, Postsecondary; Library Science Teachers, Postsecondary; Mathematical Science Teachers, Postsecondary; Nursing Instructors and Teachers, Postsecondary; Philosophy and Religion Teachers, Postsecondary; Physics Teachers, Postsecondary; Political Science Teachers, Postsecondary; Psychology Teachers, Postsecondary; Recreation and Fitness Studies Teachers, Postsecondary; Self-Enrichment Education Teachers; Sociology Teachers, Postsecondary; Vocational Education Teachers,

Postsecondary. **PERSONALITY TYPE:** No data available.

EDUCATION/TRAINING PROGRAM(S)—Clinical/Medical Social Work; Social Work; Teacher Education and Professional Development, Specific Subject Areas, Other.

WORK ENVIRONMENT—Sitting; indoors; sounds, noise levels are distracting or uncomfortable.

Sociologists

- Education/Training Required: Master's degree
- Annual Earnings: $56,790
- Growth: 13.4%
- Annual Job Openings: fewer than 500
- Self-Employed: 0%
- Part-Time: 8.6%

Age Bracket	Percentage of Workers
45–54 Years Old	50.0%
55–64 Years Old	less than 25.0%
65 or Older	close to 0%

Study human society and social behavior by examining the groups and social institutions that people form, as well as various social, religious, political, and business organizations. May study the behavior and interaction of groups, trace their origin and growth, and analyze the influence of group activities on individual members. Prepare publications and reports containing research findings. Analyze and interpret data in order to increase the understanding of human social behavior. Plan and conduct research to develop and test theories about societal issues such as crime, group relations, poverty, and aging. Collect data about the attitudes, values, and behaviors of people in groups, using observation, interviews, and review of documents. Develop, implement, and evaluate methods of data collection, such as questionnaires or interviews. Teach sociology. Direct work of statistical clerks, statisticians, and others who compile and evaluate research data. Consult with and advise individuals such as administrators, social workers, and legislators regarding social issues and policies, as well as the implications of research findings. Collaborate with research workers in other disciplines. Develop approaches to the solution of groups' problems, based on research findings in sociology and related disciplines. Observe group interactions and role affiliations to collect data, identify problems, evaluate progress, and determine the need for additional change. Develop problem intervention procedures, utilizing techniques such as interviews, consultations, role playing, and participant observation of group interactions. **SKILLS**—Science; Writing; Management of Financial Resources; Critical Thinking; Reading Comprehension; Active Learning; Complex Problem Solving; Time Management; Management of Personnel Resources.

GOE—**Interest Area:** 15. Scientific Research, Engineering, and Mathematics. **Work Group:** 15.04. Social Sciences. **Other Jobs in This Work Group:** Anthropologists; Archeologists; Economists; Educational Psychologists; Historians; Industrial-Organizational Psychologists; Political Scientists. **PERSONALITY TYPE:** Investigative. Investigative occupations frequently involve working with ideas and require an extensive amount of thinking. These occupations can involve searching for facts and figuring out problems mentally.

EDUCATION/TRAINING PROGRAM(S)—Criminology; Demography and Population Studies; Sociology; Urban Studies/Affairs.

WORK ENVIRONMENT—Sitting; indoors.

Sociology Teachers, Postsecondary

- ◉ Education/Training Required: Master's degree
- ◉ Annual Earnings: $54,600
- ◉ Growth: 38.1%
- ◉ Annual Job Openings: 216,000
- ◉ Self-Employed: 0.3%
- ◉ Part-Time: 27.7%

The job openings listed here are shared with all other postsecondary teaching occupations.

Age Bracket	Percentage of Workers
45–54 Years Old	22.8%
55–64 Years Old	19.0%
65 or Older	5.5%

Teach courses in sociology. Evaluate and grade students' class work, assignments, and papers. Prepare and deliver lectures to undergraduate and/or graduate students on topics such as race and ethnic relations, measurement and data collection, and workplace social relations. Initiate, facilitate, and moderate classroom discussions. Compile, administer, and grade examinations or assign this work to others. Prepare course materials such as syllabi, homework assignments, and handouts. Keep abreast of developments in their field by reading current literature, talking with colleagues, and participating in professional conferences. Maintain student attendance records, grades, and other required records. Maintain regularly scheduled office hours in order to advise and assist students. Plan, evaluate, and revise curricula, course content, and course materials and methods of instruction. Advise students on academic and vocational curricula, and on career issues. Collaborate with colleagues to address teaching and research issues. Conduct research in a particular field of knowledge and publish findings in professional journals, books, and/or electronic media. Select and obtain materials and supplies such as textbooks and laboratory equipment. Supervise undergraduate and/or graduate teaching, internship, and research work. Serve on academic or administrative committees that deal with institutional policies, departmental matters, and academic issues. Participate in student recruitment, registration, and placement activities. Perform administrative duties such as serving as department head. Supervise students' laboratory work and fieldwork. Write grant proposals to procure external research funding. Act as advisers to student organizations. **SKILLS**—Instructing; Learning Strategies; Social Perceptiveness; Writing; Active Learning; Critical Thinking; Persuasion; Speaking.

GOE—Interest Area: 05. Education and Training. **Work Group:** 05.03. Postsecondary and Adult Teaching and Instructing. **Other Jobs in This Work Group:** Adult Literacy, Remedial Education, and GED Teachers and Instructors; Agricultural Sciences Teachers, Postsecondary; Anthropology and Archeology Teachers, Postsecondary; Architecture Teachers, Postsecondary; Area, Ethnic, and Cultural Studies Teachers, Postsecondary; Art, Drama, and Music Teachers, Postsecondary; Atmospheric, Earth, Marine, and Space Sciences Teachers, Postsecondary; Biological Science Teachers, Postsecondary; Business Teachers, Postsecondary; Chemistry

Teachers, Postsecondary; Communications Teachers, Postsecondary; Computer Science Teachers, Postsecondary; Criminal Justice and Law Enforcement Teachers, Postsecondary; Economics Teachers, Postsecondary; Education Teachers, Postsecondary; Engineering Teachers, Postsecondary; English Language and Literature Teachers, Postsecondary; Environmental Science Teachers, Postsecondary; Farm and Home Management Advisors; Foreign Language and Literature Teachers, Postsecondary; Forestry and Conservation Science Teachers, Postsecondary; Geography Teachers, Postsecondary; Graduate Teaching Assistants; Health Specialties Teachers, Postsecondary; History Teachers, Postsecondary; Home Economics Teachers, Postsecondary; Law Teachers, Postsecondary; Library Science Teachers, Postsecondary; Mathematical Science Teachers, Postsecondary; Nursing Instructors and Teachers, Postsecondary; Philosophy and Religion Teachers, Postsecondary; Physics Teachers, Postsecondary; Political Science Teachers, Postsecondary; Psychology Teachers, Postsecondary; Recreation and Fitness Studies Teachers, Postsecondary; Self-Enrichment Education Teachers; Social Work Teachers, Postsecondary; Vocational Education Teachers, Postsecondary. **PERSONALITY TYPE:** Social. Social occupations frequently involve working with, communicating with, and teaching people. These occupations often involve helping or providing service to others.

EDUCATION/TRAINING PROGRAM(S)— Social Science Teacher Education; Sociology.

WORK ENVIRONMENT—Sitting; physical proximity to others; indoors; sounds, noise levels are distracting or uncomfortable.

Special Education Teachers, Middle School

- Education/Training Required: Bachelor's degree
- Annual Earnings: $45,000
- Growth: 30.0%
- Annual Job Openings: 59,000
- Self-Employed: 0.3%
- Part-Time: 9.3%

The job openings listed here are shared with Special Education Teachers, Preschool, Kindergarten, and Elementary School, and Special Education Teachers, Secondary School.

Age Bracket	Percentage of Workers
45–54 Years Old	30.8%
55–64 Years Old	15.9%
65 or Older	1.6%

Teach middle school subjects to educationally and physically handicapped students. Includes teachers who specialize and work with audibly and visually handicapped students and those who teach basic academic and life processes skills to the mentally impaired. Establish and enforce rules for behavior and policies and procedures to maintain order among students. Maintain accurate and complete student records, and prepare reports on children and activities, as required by laws, district policies, and administrative regulations. Prepare materials and classrooms for class activities. Confer with parents, administrators, testing specialists, social workers, and professionals to develop individual educational plans designed to promote students' educational, physical, and social development. Develop and implement strategies to meet the needs of students with a variety of handicapping conditions. Teach socially acceptable behavior, employing techniques such as behavior modification and positive reinforcement. Modify the general education curriculum for special-needs students based upon a variety of instructional techniques and instructional technology. Employ special educational strategies and techniques during instruction to improve the development of sensory- and perceptual-motor skills, language, cognition, and memory. Confer with parents or guardians, other teachers, counselors, and administrators in order to resolve students' behavioral and academic problems. Instruct through lectures, discussions, and demonstrations in one or more subjects such as English, mathematics, or social studies. Coordinate placement of students with special needs into mainstream classes. Meet with parents and guardians to discuss their children's progress, and to determine their priorities for their children and their resource needs. Prepare, administer, and grade tests and assignments to evaluate students' progress. Guide and counsel students with adjustment and/or academic problems, or special academic interests. Observe and evaluate students' performance, behavior, social development, and physical health. Establish clear objectives for all lessons, units, and projects, and communicate those objectives to students. Teach students personal development skills such as goal setting, independence, and self-advocacy. Plan and conduct activities for a balanced program of instruction, demonstration, and work time that provides students with opportunities to observe, question, and investigate. **SKILLS**—Learning Strategies; Instructing; Social Perceptiveness; Persuasion; Monitoring; Negotiation; Time Management; Service Orientation.

GOE—Interest Area: 05. Education and Training. **Work Group:** 05.02. Preschool, Elementary, and Secondary Teaching and Instructing. **Other Jobs in This Work Group:** Elementary School Teachers, Except Special Education; Kindergarten Teachers, Except Special Education; Middle School Teachers, Except Special and Vocational Education; Preschool Teachers, Except Special Education; Secondary School Teachers, Except Special and Vocational Education; Special Education Teachers, Preschool, Kindergarten, and Elementary School; Special Education Teachers, Secondary School; Teacher Assistants; Vocational Education Teachers, Middle School; Vocational Education Teachers, Secondary School. **PERSONALITY TYPE:** Social. Social occupations frequently involve working with, communicating with, and teaching people. These occupations often involve helping or providing service to others.

EDUCATION/TRAINING PROGRAM(S)—Special Education, General.

WORK ENVIRONMENT—Physical proximity to others; sounds, noise levels are distracting or uncomfortable; contaminants; disease or infections; sitting.

Special Education Teachers, Preschool, Kindergarten, and Elementary School

- Education/Training Required: Bachelor's degree
- Annual Earnings: $44,330
- Growth: 30.0%
- Annual Job Openings: 59,000
- Self-Employed: 0.3%
- Part-Time: 9.3%

The job openings listed here are shared with Special Education Teachers, Middle School, and Special Education Teachers, Secondary School.

Age Bracket	Percentage of Workers
45–54 Years Old	30.8%
55–64 Years Old	15.9%
65 or Older	1.6%

Teach elementary and preschool school subjects to educationally and physically handicapped students. Includes teachers who specialize and work with audibly and visually handicapped students and those who teach basic academic and life processes skills to the mentally impaired. Instruct students in academic subjects, using a variety of techniques such as phonetics, multisensory learning, and repetition, in order to reinforce learning and to meet students' varying needs and interests. Employ special educational strategies and techniques during instruction to improve the development of sensory- and perceptual-motor skills, language, cognition, and memory. Teach socially acceptable behavior, employing techniques such as behavior modification and positive reinforcement. Modify the general education curriculum for special-needs students based upon a variety of instructional techniques and technologies. Meet with parents and guardians to discuss their children's progress, and to determine their priorities for their children and their resource needs. Plan and conduct activities for a balanced program of instruction, demonstration, and work time that provides students with opportunities to observe, question, and investigate. Establish and enforce rules for behavior and policies and procedures to maintain order among the students for whom they are responsible. Confer with parents, administrators, testing specialists, social workers, and professionals to develop individual educational plans designed to promote students' educational, physical, and social development. Maintain accurate and complete student records, and prepare reports on children and activities, as required by laws, district policies, and administrative regulations. Establish clear objectives for all lessons, units, and projects, and communicate those objectives to students. Develop and implement strategies to meet the needs of students with a variety of handicapping conditions. Prepare classrooms for class activities and provide a variety of materials and resources for children to explore, manipulate, and use, both in learning activities and imaginative play. Confer with parents or guardians, teachers, counselors, and administrators in order to resolve students' behavioral and academic problems. Observe and evaluate students' performance, behavior, social development, and physical health. Teach students personal development skills such as goal setting, independence, and self-advocacy. **SKILLS—** Instructing; Learning Strategies; Social Perceptiveness; Time Management; Monitoring; Negotiation; Coordination; Service Orientation.

GOE—Interest Area: 05. Education and Training. **Work Group:** 05.02. Preschool, Elementary, and Secondary Teaching and Instructing. **Other Jobs in This Work Group:** Elementary School Teachers, Except Special Education; Kindergarten Teachers, Except Special Education; Middle School Teachers, Except Special and Vocational Education; Preschool Teachers, Except Special Education; Secondary School Teachers, Except Special and Vocational Education; Special Education Teachers, Middle School; Special Education Teachers, Secondary School; Teacher Assistants; Vocational Education Teachers, Middle School; Vocational Education Teachers, Secondary School. **PERSONALITY TYPE:** Social. Social occupations frequently involve working with, communicating with, and teaching people. These occupations often involve helping or providing service to others.

EDUCATION/TRAINING PROGRAM(S)— Education/Teaching of Individuals with Autism; Education/Teaching of Individuals with Emotional Disturbances; Education/Teaching of Individuals with Hearing Impairments, Including Deafness; Education/Teaching of Individuals with Mental Retardation; Education/Teaching of Individuals with Multiple Disabilities; others.

WORK ENVIRONMENT—Physical proximity to others; sounds, noise levels are distracting or uncomfortable; standing; very hot or cold; contaminants.

Special Education Teachers, Secondary School

- Education/Training Required: Bachelor's degree
- Annual Earnings: $46,300
- Growth: 30.0%
- Annual Job Openings: 59,000
- Self-Employed: 0.3%
- Part-Time: 9.3%

The job openings listed here are shared with Special Education Teachers, Middle School, and Special Education Teachers, Preschool, Kindergarten, and Elementary School.

Age Bracket	Percentage of Workers
45–54 Years Old	30.8%
55–64 Years Old	15.9%
65 or Older	1.6%

Teach secondary school subjects to educationally and physically handicapped students. Includes teachers who specialize and work with audibly and visually handicapped students and those who teach basic academic and life processes skills to the mentally impaired. Maintain accurate and complete student records, and prepare reports on children and activities, as required by laws, district policies, and administrative regulations. Teach socially acceptable behavior, employing techniques such as behavior modification and positive reinforcement. Prepare materials and classrooms for class activities. Establish and enforce rules for behavior and policies and procedures to maintain order among students. Confer with parents, administrators, testing specialists, social workers, and professionals to develop individual educational plans designed to promote students' educational, physical, and social development. Instruct through lectures, discussions, and demonstrations in one or more subjects such as English, mathematics, or social studies. Employ special educational strategies and techniques during instruction to improve the development of sensory- and perceptual-motor skills, language, cognition, and memory. Plan and conduct activities for a balanced program of instruction, demonstration, and work time that provides students with opportunities to observe, question, and investigate. Teach personal development skills such as goal setting, independence, and self-advocacy. Prepare students for later grades by encouraging them to explore learning opportunities and to persevere with challenging tasks. Establish clear objectives for all lessons, units, and projects, and communicate those objectives to students. Develop and implement strategies to meet the needs of students with a variety of handicapping conditions. Modify the general education curriculum for special-needs students, based upon a variety of instructional techniques and technologies. Meet with other professionals to discuss individual students' needs and progress. Confer with parents or guardians, other teachers, counselors, and administrators in order to resolve students' behavioral and academic problems. Meet with parents and guardians to discuss their children's progress, and to determine their priorities for their children and their resource needs. Guide and counsel students with adjustment and/or academic problems, or special academic interests. **SKILLS**—Learning Strategies; Social Perceptiveness; Instructing; Negotiation; Persuasion; Service Orientation; Time Management; Coordination.

GOE—Interest Area: 05. Education and Training. **Work Group:** 05.02. Preschool, Elementary, and Secondary Teaching and Instructing. **Other Jobs in This Work Group:** Elementary School Teachers, Except Special Education; Kindergarten Teachers, Except Special Education; Middle School Teachers, Except Special and Vocational Education; Preschool Teachers, Except Special Education; Secondary School Teachers, Except Special and Vocational Education; Special Education Teachers, Middle School; Special Education Teachers, Preschool, Kindergarten, and Elementary School; Teacher Assistants; Vocational Education Teachers, Middle School; Vocational Education Teachers, Secondary School. **PERSONALITY TYPE:** Social. Social occupations frequently involve working with, communicating with, and teaching people. These occupations often involve helping or providing service to others.

EDUCATION/TRAINING PROGRAM(S)— Special Education, General.

WORK ENVIRONMENT—Physical proximity to others; sounds, noise levels are distracting or uncomfortable; extremely bright or inadequate lighting; contaminants; sitting.

Speech-Language Pathologists

- Education/Training Required: Master's degree
- Annual Earnings: $53,790
- Growth: 27.2%
- Annual Job Openings: 10,000
- Self-Employed: 8.2%
- Part-Time: 28.1%

Age Bracket	Percentage of Workers
45–54 Years Old	34.4%
55–64 Years Old	5.4%
65 or Older	1.1%

Assess and treat persons with speech, language, voice, and fluency disorders. May select alternative communication systems and teach their use. May perform research related to speech and language problems. Monitor patients' progress and adjust treatments accordingly. Evaluate hearing and speech/language test results and medical or background information to diagnose and plan treatment for speech, language, fluency, voice, and swallowing disorders. Administer hearing or speech/language evaluations, tests, or examinations to patients to collect information on type and degree of impairments, using written and oral tests and special instruments. Record information on the initial evaluation, treatment, progress, and discharge of clients. Develop and implement treatment plans for problems such as stuttering, delayed language, swallowing disorders, and inappropriate pitch or harsh voice problems, based on own assessments and recommendations of physicians, psychologists, and social workers. Develop individual or group programs in schools to deal with speech or language problems. Instruct clients in techniques for more effective communication, including sign language, lip reading, and voice improvement. Teach clients to control or strengthen tongue, jaw, face muscles, and breathing mechanisms. Develop speech exercise programs to reduce disabilities. Consult with and advise educators or medical staff on speech or hearing topics such as communication strategies and speech and language stimulation. Instruct patients and family members in strategies to cope with or avoid communication-related misunderstandings. Design, develop, and employ alternative diagnostic or communication devices and strategies. Conduct lessons and direct educational or therapeutic games to assist teachers dealing with speech problems. Refer clients to additional medical or educational services if needed. Participate in conferences or training, or publish research results, to share knowledge of new hearing or speech disorder treatment methods or technologies. Communicate with non-speaking students, using sign language or computer technology. Provide communication instruction to dialect speakers or students with limited English proficiency. Use computer applications to identify and assist with communication disabilities. **SKILLS**—Instructing; Social Perceptiveness; Learning Strategies; Service Orientation; Time Management; Speaking; Active Learning; Coordination.

GOE—Interest Area: 08. Health Science. **Work Group:** 08.07. Medical Therapy. **Other Jobs in This Work Group:** Audiologists; Massage Therapists; Occupational Therapist Aides; Occupational Therapist Assistants; Occupational Therapists; Physical Therapist Aides; Physical Therapist Assistants; Physical Therapists; Radiation Therapists; Recreational Therapists; Respiratory Therapists; Respiratory Therapy Technicians. **PERSONALITY TYPE:** Social. Social occupations frequently involve working with, communicating with, and teaching people. These occupations often involve helping or providing service to others.

EDUCATION/TRAINING PROGRAM(S)— Audiology/Audiologist and Speech-Language Pathology/Pathologist; Communication Disorders Sciences and Services, Other; Communication Disorders, General; Speech-Language Pathology/Pathologist.

WORK ENVIRONMENT—Physical proximity to others; sitting; sounds, noise levels are distracting or uncomfortable; disease or infections; contaminants.

Spotters, Dry Cleaning

- Education/Training Required: Moderate-term on-the-job training
- Annual Earnings: $17,350
- Growth: 12.3%
- Annual Job Openings: 47,000
- Self-Employed: 6.8%
- Part-Time: 16.9%

The job openings listed here are shared with Laundry and Drycleaning Machine Operators and Tenders, Except Pressing; and Precision Dyers.

Age Bracket	Percentage of Workers
45–54 Years Old	25.9%
55–64 Years Old	17.1%
65 or Older	5.2%

Identify stains in wool, synthetic, and silk garments and household fabrics and apply chemical solutions to remove stain. Determine spotting procedures on basis of type of fabric and nature of stain. Sprays steam, water, or air over spot to flush out chemicals, dry material, raise nap, or brighten color. Cleans fabric using vacuum or airhose. Spreads article on worktable and positions stain over vacuum head or on marble slab. Mixes bleaching agent with hot water in vats and soaks material until it is bleached. Applies bleaching powder to spot, and sprays with steam to remove stains from certain fabrics which do not respond to other cleaning solvents. Sprinkles chemical solvents over stain and pats area with brush or sponge until stain is removed. Inspects spots to ascertain composition and select solvent. Operates drycleaning machine. Applies chemicals to neutralize effect of solvents. **SKILLS**—Operation Monitoring.

GOE—Interest Area: 13. Manufacturing. **Work Group:** 13.11. Apparel, Shoes, Leather, and Fabric Care. **Other Jobs in This Work Group:** Custom Tailors; Fabric Menders, Except Garment; Laundry and Drycleaning Machine Operators and Tenders, Except Pressing; Precision Dyers; Pressers, Delicate Fabrics; Pressers, Hand; Shoe and Leather Workers and Repairers; Shop and Alteration Tailors; Upholsterers. **PERSONALITY TYPE:** Realistic. Realistic occupations frequently involve work activities that include practical, hands-on problems and solutions. They often deal with plants, animals, and real-world materials like wood, tools, and machinery. Many of the occupations require working outside and do not involve a lot of paperwork or working closely with others.

EDUCATION/TRAINING PROGRAM(S)— No data available.

WORK ENVIRONMENT—Hazardous conditions; contaminants; minor burns, cuts, bites, or stings; standing; using hands on objects, tools, or controls.

Station Installers and Repairers, Telephone

- Education/Training Required: Long-term on-the-job training
- Annual Earnings: $50,270
- Growth: –0.6%
- Annual Job Openings: 23,000
- Self-Employed: 4.6%
- Part-Time: 1.7%

The job openings listed here are shared with Central Office and PBX Installers and Repairers; Communication Equipment Mechanics, Installers, and Repairers; Frame Wirers, Central Office; and Telecommunications Facility Examiners.

Age Bracket	Percentage of Workers
45–54 Years Old	29.5%
55–64 Years Old	9.6%
65 or Older	1.2%

Install and repair telephone station equipment, such as telephones, coin collectors, telephone booths, and switching-key equipment. Installs communication equipment, such as intercommunication systems and related apparatus, using schematic diagrams, testing devices, and hand tools. Assembles telephone equipment, mounts brackets, and connects wire leads, using hand tools and following installation diagrams or work order. Analyzes equipment operation, using testing devices to locate and diagnose nature of malfunction and ascertain needed repairs. Operates and tests equipment to ensure elimination of malfunction. Climbs poles to install or repair outside service lines. Disassembles components and replaces, cleans, adjusts and repairs parts, wires, switches, relays, circuits, or signaling units, using hand tools. Repairs cables, lays out plans for new equipment, and estimates material required. **SKILLS**—Troubleshooting; Installation; Repairing; Equipment Maintenance; Quality Control Analysis; Operations Analysis; Technology Design; Operation Monitoring; Operation and Control.

GOE—Interest Area: 02. Architecture and Construction. **Work Group:** 02.05. Systems and Equipment Installation, Maintenance, and Repair. **Other Jobs in This Work Group:** Central Office and PBX Installers and Repairers; Communication Equipment Mechanics, Installers, and Repairers; Electric Meter Installers and Repairers; Electrical and Electronics Repairers, Powerhouse, Substation, and Relay; Electrical Power-Line Installers and Repairers; Elevator Installers and Repairers; Frame Wirers; Central Office; Heating and Air Conditioning Mechanics; Home Appliance Installers; Maintenance and Repair Workers, General; Meter Mechanics; Refrigeration Mechanics; Telecommunications Facility Examiners; Telecommunications Line Installers and Repairers. **PERSONALITY TYPE:** Realistic. Realistic occupations frequently involve work activities that include practical, hands-on problems and solutions. They often deal with plants, animals, and real-world materials like wood, tools, and machinery. Many of the occupations require working outside and do not involve a lot of paperwork or working closely with others.

EDUCATION/TRAINING PROGRAM(S)—Communications Systems Installation and Repair Technology.

WORK ENVIRONMENT—Climbing ladders, scaffolds, or poles; common protective or safety equipment; high places; standing; very hot or cold.

Storage and Distribution Managers

- ◉ Education/Training Required: Work experience in a related occupation
- ◉ Annual Earnings: $67,300
- ◉ Growth: 19.7%
- ◉ Annual Job Openings: 13,000
- ◉ Self-Employed: 1.1%
- ◉ Part-Time: 2.4%

The job openings listed here are shared with Transportation Managers.

Age Bracket	Percentage of Workers
45–54 Years Old	28.0%
55–64 Years Old	11.6%
65 or Older	1.3%

Plan, direct, and coordinate the storage and distribution operations within an organization or the activities of organizations that are engaged in storing and distributing materials and products. Supervise the activities of workers engaged in receiving, storing, testing, and shipping products or materials. Plan, develop, and implement warehouse safety and security programs and activities. Review invoices, work orders, consumption reports, and demand forecasts in order to estimate peak delivery periods and to issue work assignments. Schedule and monitor air or surface pickup, delivery, or distribution of products or materials. Interview, select, and train warehouse and supervisory personnel. Confer with department heads to coordinate warehouse activities, such as production, sales, records control, and purchasing. Respond to customers' or shippers' questions and complaints regarding storage and distribution services. Inspect physical conditions of warehouses, vehicle fleets and equipment, and order testing, maintenance, repair, or replacement as necessary. Develop and document standard and emergency operating procedures for receiving, handling, storing, shipping, or salvaging products or materials. Examine products or materials in order to estimate quantities or weight and type of container required for storage or transport. Negotiate with carriers, warehouse operators and insurance company representatives for services and preferential rates. Issue shipping instructions and provide routing information to ensure that delivery times and locations are coordinated. Examine invoices and shipping manifests for conformity to tariff and customs regulations. Prepare and manage departmental budgets. Prepare or direct preparation of correspondence, reports, and operations, maintenance, and safety manuals. Arrange for necessary shipping documentation, and contact customs officials in order to effect release of shipments. Advise sales and billing departments of transportation charges for customers' accounts. Evaluate freight costs and the inventory costs associated with transit times in order to ensure that costs are appropriate. Participate in setting transportation and service rates. Track and trace goods while they are en route to their destinations, expediting orders when necessary. **SKILLS**—Management of Personnel Resources; Operations Analysis; Monitoring; Persuasion; Service Orientation; Management of Material Resources; Social Perceptiveness; Systems Analysis.

GOE—Interest Area: 16. Transportation, Distribution, and Logistics. **Work Group:** 16.01. Managerial Work in Transportation. **Other Jobs in This Work Group:** Aircraft Cargo Handling Supervisors; First-Line Supervisors/ Managers of Transportation and Material-Moving Machine and Vehicle Operators; Postmasters and Mail Superintendents; Railroad Conductors and Yardmasters; Transportation Managers. **PERSONALITY TYPE:** Enterprising. Enterprising occupations frequently involve starting up and carrying out projects. These occupations can involve leading people and making many decisions. They sometimes require risk taking and often deal with business.

EDUCATION/TRAINING PROGRAM(S)— Aeronautics/Aviation/Aerospace Science and Technology, General; Aviation/Airway Management and Operations; Business Administration/Management; Logistics and Materials Management; Public Administration; Transportation/Transportation Management.

S

WORK ENVIRONMENT—Very hot or cold; indoors, not environmentally controlled; contaminants; sounds, noise levels are distracting or uncomfortable; sitting.

Substance Abuse and Behavioral Disorder Counselors

- ◎ Education/Training Required: Master's degree
- ◎ Annual Earnings: $32,630
- ◎ Growth: 23.3%
- ◎ Annual Job Openings: 10,000
- ◎ Self-Employed: 4.5%
- ◎ Part-Time: 14.6%

Age Bracket	Percentage of Workers
45–54 Years Old	28.0%
55–64 Years Old	13.4%
65 or Older	2.3%

Counsel and advise individuals with alcohol, tobacco, drug, or other problems, such as gambling and eating disorders. May counsel individuals, families, or groups or engage in prevention programs. Counsel clients and patients, individually and in group sessions, to assist in overcoming dependencies, adjusting to life, and making changes. Complete and maintain accurate records and reports regarding the patients' histories and progress, services provided, and other required information. Develop client treatment plans based on research, clinical experience, and client histories. Review and evaluate clients' progress in relation to measurable goals described in treatment and care plans. Interview clients, review records, and confer with other professionals in order to evaluate individuals' mental and physical condition, and to determine their suitability for participation in a specific program. Intervene as advocate for clients or patients in order to resolve emergency problems in crisis situations. Provide clients or family members with information about addiction issues and about available services and programs, making appropriate referrals when necessary. Modify treatment plans to comply with changes in client status. Coordinate counseling efforts with mental health professionals and other health professionals such as doctors, nurses, and social workers. Attend training sessions in order to increase knowledge and skills. Plan and implement follow-up and aftercare programs for clients to be discharged from treatment programs. Conduct chemical dependency program orientation sessions. Counsel family members to assist them in understanding, dealing with, and supporting clients or patients. Participate in case conferences and staff meetings. Act as liaisons between clients and medical staff. Coordinate activities with courts, probation officers, community services and other post-treatment agencies. Confer with family members or others close to clients in order to keep them informed of treatment planning and progress. Instruct others in program methods, procedures, and functions. Follow progress of discharged patients in order to determine effectiveness of treatments. Develop, implement, and evaluate public education, prevention, and health promotion programs, working in collaboration with organizations, institutions and communities. **SKILLS**—Social Perceptiveness; Persuasion; Service Orientation; Negotiation; Instructing; Learning Strategies; Active Listening; Time Management.

GOE—Interest Area: 10. Human Service. **Work Group:** 10.01. Counseling and Social Work. **Other Jobs in This Work Group:** Child,

Family, and School Social Workers; Clinical Psychologists; Counseling Psychologists; Marriage and Family Therapists; Medical and Public Health Social Workers; Mental Health and Substance Abuse Social Workers; Mental Health Counselors; Probation Officers and Correctional Treatment Specialists; Rehabilitation Counselors; Residential Advisors; Social and Human Service Assistants. **PERSONALITY TYPE:** Social. Social occupations frequently involve working with, communicating with, and teaching people. These occupations often involve helping or providing service to others.

EDUCATION/TRAINING PROGRAM(S)— Clinical/Medical Social Work; Mental and Social Health Services and Allied Professions, Other; Substance Abuse/Addiction Counseling.

WORK ENVIRONMENT—Sitting; physical proximity to others; disease or infections; indoors; sounds, noise levels are distracting or uncomfortable.

Subway and Streetcar Operators

- ◎ Education/Training Required: Moderate-term on-the-job training
- ◎ Annual Earnings: $47,560
- ◎ Growth: 13.2%
- ◎ Annual Job Openings: 2,000
- ◎ Self-Employed: 0%
- ◎ Part-Time: 8.8%

Age Bracket	Percentage of Workers
45–54 Years Old	27.3%
55–64 Years Old	18.2%
65 or Older	less than 4.5%

Operate subway or elevated suburban train with no separate locomotive, or electric-powered streetcar to transport passengers. May handle fares. Drive and control rail-guided public transportation, such as subways, elevated trains, and electric-powered streetcars, trams, or trolleys, in order to transport passengers. Make announcements to passengers, such as notifications of upcoming stops or schedule delays. Operate controls to open and close transit vehicle doors. Regulate vehicle speed and the time spent at each stop, in order to maintain schedules. Report delays, mechanical problems, and emergencies to supervisors or dispatchers, using radios. Monitor lights indicating obstructions or other trains ahead and watch for car and truck traffic at crossings to stay alert to potential hazards. Attend meetings on driver and passenger safety in order to learn ways in which job performance might be affected. Collect fares from passengers, and issue change and transfers. Complete reports, including shift summaries and incident or accident reports. Direct emergency evacuation procedures. Greet passengers, provide information, and answer questions concerning fares, schedules, transfers, and routings. Record transactions and coin receptor readings in order to verify the amount of money collected. **SKILLS**—Operation and Control; Operation Monitoring.

GOE—**Interest Area:** 16. Transportation, Distribution, and Logistics. **Work Group:** 16.04. Rail Vehicle Operation. **Other Jobs in This Work Group:** Locomotive Engineers; Locomotive Firers; Rail Yard Engineers, Dinkey Operators, and Hostlers. **PERSONALITY TYPE:** Realistic. Realistic occupations frequently involve work activities that include practical, hands-on problems and solutions. They often deal with plants, animals, and real-world materials like wood, tools, and machinery. Many of the occupations require working outside and do not involve a lot of paperwork or working closely with others.

EDUCATION/TRAINING PROGRAM(S)— Truck and Bus Driver/Commercial Vehicle Operation.

WORK ENVIRONMENT—Sitting; using hands on objects, tools, or controls; outdoors; spend time making repetitive motions; very hot or cold; standing.

Surgeons

- ◎ Education/Training Required: First professional degree
- ◎ Annual Earnings: more than $145,600
- ◎ Growth: 19.5%
- ◎ Annual Job Openings: 38,000
- ◎ Self-Employed: 16.9%
- ◎ Part-Time: 8.1%

The job openings listed here are shared with Anesthesiologists; Family and General Practitioners; Internists, General; Obstetricians and Gynecologists, General; Pediatricians, General; and Psychiatrists.

Age Bracket	Percentage of Workers
45–54 Years Old	29.3%
55–64 Years Old	13.4%
65 or Older	5.4%

Treat diseases, injuries, and deformities by invasive methods, such as manual manipulation or by using instruments and appliances. Analyze patient's medical history, medication allergies, physical condition, and examination results to verify operation's necessity and to determine best procedure. Prescribe preoperative and postoperative treatments and procedures,

such as sedatives, diets, antibiotics, and preparation and treatment of the patient's operative area. Direct and coordinate activities of nurses, assistants, specialists, residents and other medical staff. Examine patient to provide information on medical condition and surgical risk. Follow established surgical techniques during the operation. Operate on patients to correct deformities, repair injuries, prevent and treat diseases, or improve or restore patients' functions. Refer patient to medical specialist or other practitioners when necessary. Conduct research to develop and test surgical techniques that can improve operating procedures and outcomes. Examine instruments, equipment, and operating room to ensure sterility. Manage surgery services, including planning, scheduling and coordination, determination of procedures, and procurement of supplies and equipment. Prepare case histories. Provide consultation and surgical assistance to other physicians and surgeons. Diagnose bodily disorders and orthopedic conditions and provide treatments, such as medicines and surgeries, in clinics, hospital wards, and operating rooms. **SKILLS—**Science; Systems Evaluation; Management of Personnel Resources; Judgment and Decision Making; Systems Analysis; Operation and Control; Reading Comprehension; Coordination.

GOE—Interest Area: 08. Health Science. **Work Group:** 08.02. Medicine and Surgery. **Other Jobs in This Work Group:** Anesthesiologists; Family and General Practitioners; Internists, General; Medical Assistants; Medical Transcriptionists; Obstetricians and Gynecologists; Pediatricians, General; Pharmacists; Pharmacy Aides; Pharmacy Technicians; Physician Assistants; Psychiatrists; Registered Nurses; Surgical Technologists. **PERSONALITY TYPE:** Investigative. Investigative occupations frequently involve working with ideas and require an extensive amount of thinking. These occupations can involve searching for facts and figuring out problems mentally.

EDUCATION/TRAINING PROGRAM(S)— Adult Reconstructive Orthopedics (Orthopedic Surgery); Colon and Rectal Surgery; Critical Care Surgery; General Surgery; Hand Surgery; Neurological Surgery/Neurosurgery; Orthopedic Surgery of the Spine; Orthopedics/Orthopedic Surgery; Otolaryngology; Pediatric Orthopedics; Pediatric Surgery; Plastic Surgery; Sports Medicine; Thoracic Surgery; Urology; Vascular Surgery.

WORK ENVIRONMENT—Disease or infections; common protective or safety equipment; standing; specialized protective or safety equipment; indoors; using hands on objects, tools, or controls.

Tax Preparers

- ◎ Education/Training Required:
  Moderate-term on-the-job training
- ◎ Annual Earnings: $26,130
- ◎ Growth: 23.2%
- ◎ Annual Job Openings: 11,000
- ◎ Self-Employed: 26.2%
- ◎ Part-Time: 20.3%

Age Bracket	Percentage of Workers
45–54 Years Old	19.8%
55–64 Years Old	22.0%
65 or Older	13.2%

Prepare tax returns for individuals or small businesses but do not have the background or responsibilities of an accredited or certified public accountant. Check data input or verify totals on forms prepared by others to detect errors in arithmetic, data entry, or procedures. Compute taxes owed or overpaid, using adding machines or personal computers, and complete entries on forms, following tax form instructions and tax tables. Interview clients to obtain additional information on taxable income and deductible expenses and allowances. Prepare or assist in preparing simple to complex tax returns for individuals or small businesses. Review financial records such as income statements and documentation of expenditures in order to determine forms needed to prepare tax returns. Use all appropriate adjustments, deductions, and credits to keep clients' taxes to a minimum. Calculate form preparation fees according to return complexity and processing time required. Consult tax law handbooks or bulletins in order to determine procedures for preparation of atypical returns. Furnish taxpayers with sufficient information and advice in order to ensure correct tax form completion. **SKILLS—** Mathematics; Reading Comprehension; Active Listening; Speaking; Active Learning; Judgment and Decision Making; Monitoring.

GOE—Interest Area: 04. Business and Administration. **Work Group:** 04.06. Mathematical Clerical Support. **Other Jobs in This Work Group:** Billing, Cost, and Rate Clerks; Bookkeeping, Accounting, and Auditing Clerks; Brokerage Clerks; Payroll and Timekeeping Clerks; Statement Clerks. **PERSONALITY TYPE:** Conventional. Conventional occupations frequently involve following set procedures and routines. These occupations can include working with data and details more than with ideas. Usually there is a clear line of authority to follow.

EDUCATION/TRAINING PROGRAM(S)— Accounting Technology/Technician and Bookkeeping; Taxation.

T

WORK ENVIRONMENT—Sitting; spend time making repetitive motions; indoors.

Taxi Drivers and Chauffeurs

- Education/Training Required: Short-term on-the-job training
- Annual Earnings: $19,790
- Growth: 21.7%
- Annual Job Openings: 28,000
- Self-Employed: 4.8%
- Part-Time: 17.3%

Age Bracket	Percentage of Workers
45–54 Years Old	23.1%
55–64 Years Old	20.6%
65 or Older	10.5%

Drive automobiles, vans, or limousines to transport passengers. May occasionally carry cargo. Test vehicle equipment such as lights, brakes, horns, and windshield wipers, in order to ensure proper operation. Notify dispatchers or company mechanics of vehicle problems. Drive taxicabs, limousines, company cars, or privately owned vehicles in order to transport passengers. Follow regulations governing taxi operation and ensure that passengers follow safety regulations. Pick up passengers at prearranged locations, at taxi stands, or by cruising streets in high traffic areas. Perform routine vehicle maintenance, such as regulating tire pressure and adding gasoline, oil, and water. Communicate with dispatchers by radio, telephone, or computer in order to exchange information and receive requests for passenger service. Record name, date, and taxi identification information on trip sheets, along with trip information such as time and place of pickup and drop-off, and total fee. Complete accident reports when necessary. Provide passengers with assistance entering and exiting vehicles, and help them with any luggage. Arrange to pick up particular customers or groups on a regular schedule. Vacuum and clean interiors, and wash and polish exteriors of automobiles. Pick up or meet employers according to requests, appointments, or schedules. Operate vans with special equipment, such as wheelchair lifts to transport people with special needs. Collect fares or vouchers from passengers; and make change and/or issue receipts, as necessary. Determine fares based on trip distances and times, using taximeters and fee schedules, and announce fares to passengers. Perform minor vehicle repairs such as cleaning spark plugs, or take vehicles to mechanics for servicing. Turn the taximeter on when passengers enter the cab, and turn it off when they reach the final destination. Report to taxicab services or garages in order to receive vehicle assignments. Perform errands for customers or employers, such as delivering or picking up mail and packages. Provide passengers with information about the local area and points of interest, and/or give advice on hotels and restaurants. **SKILLS**—Service Orientation; Installation; Operation and Control; Equipment Maintenance; Social Perceptiveness; Learning Strategies; Negotiation; Instructing.

GOE—Interest Area: 16. Transportation, Distribution, and Logistics. **Work Group:** 16.06. Other Services Requiring Driving. **Other Jobs in This Work Group:** Ambulance Drivers and Attendants, Except Emergency Medical Technicians; Bus Drivers, School; Bus Drivers, Transit and Intercity; Couriers and Messengers; Driver/Sales Workers; Parking Lot Attendants; Postal Service Mail Carriers. **PERSONALITY**

TYPE: Realistic. Realistic occupations frequently involve work activities that include practical, hands-on problems and solutions. They often deal with plants, animals, and real-world materials like wood, tools, and machinery. Many of the occupations require working outside and do not involve a lot of paperwork or working closely with others.

EDUCATION/TRAINING PROGRAM(S)— Truck and Bus Driver/Commercial Vehicle Operation.

WORK ENVIRONMENT—In an enclosed vehicle or equipment; sitting; contaminants; extremely bright or inadequate lighting; physical proximity to others.

Teacher Assistants

- Education/Training Required: Short-term on-the-job training
- Annual Earnings: $19,760
- Growth: 23.0%
- Annual Job Openings: 259,000
- Self-Employed: 0.3%
- Part-Time: 41.1%

Age Bracket	Percentage of Workers
45–54 Years Old	28.5%
55–64 Years Old	12.4%
65 or Older	1.9%

Perform duties that are instructional in nature or deliver direct services to students or parents. Serve in a position for which a teacher or another professional has ultimate responsibility for the design and implementation of educational programs and services. Discuss assigned duties with classroom teachers in order to coordinate instructional efforts. Prepare lesson materials, bulletin board displays, exhibits, equipment, and demonstrations. Present subject matter to students under the direction and guidance of teachers, using lectures, discussions, or supervised role-playing methods. Tutor and assist children individually or in small groups in order to help them master assignments and to reinforce learning concepts presented by teachers. Supervise students in classrooms, halls, cafeterias, school yards, and gymnasiums, or on field trips. Conduct demonstrations to teach such skills as sports, dancing, and handicrafts. Distribute teaching materials such as textbooks, workbooks, papers, and pencils to students. Distribute tests and homework assignments, and collect them when they are completed. Enforce administration policies and rules governing students. Grade homework and tests, and compute and record results, using answer sheets or electronic marking devices. Instruct and monitor students in the use and care of equipment and materials, in order to prevent injuries and damage. Observe students' performance, and record relevant data to assess progress. Organize and label materials, and display students' work in a manner appropriate for their eye levels and perceptual skills. Organize and supervise games and other recreational activities to promote physical, mental, and social development. Participate in teacher-parent conferences regarding students' progress or problems. Plan, prepare, and develop various teaching aids such as bibliographies, charts, and graphs. Prepare lesson outlines and plans in assigned subject areas, and submit outlines to teachers for review. Provide extra assistance to students with special needs, such as non-English-speaking students or those with physical and mental disabilities. Take class attendance, and maintain attendance records. Assist in bus loading and unloading. Assist librarians in school libraries. Attend staff meetings, and serve on committees as required. Carry out therapeutic regimens such as behavior modification and personal development programs under the supervision of special education instructors, psychologists, or speech-language pathologists. **SKILLS**—Instructing; Learning Strategies; Service Orientation; Speaking; Social Perceptiveness; Active Listening; Reading Comprehension; Writing.

GOE—Interest Area: 05. Education and Training. **Work Group:** 05.02. Preschool, Elementary, and Secondary Teaching and Instructing. **Other Jobs in This Work Group:** Elementary School Teachers, Except Special Education; Kindergarten Teachers, Except Special Education; Middle School Teachers, Except Special and Vocational Education; Preschool Teachers, Except Special Education; Secondary School Teachers, Except Special and Vocational Education; Special Education Teachers, Middle School; Special Education Teachers, Preschool, Kindergarten, and Elementary School; Special Education Teachers, Secondary School; Vocational Education Teachers, Middle School; Vocational Education Teachers, Secondary School. **PERSONALITY TYPE:** Social. Social occupations frequently involve working with, communicating with, and teaching people. These occupations often involve helping or providing service to others.

EDUCATION/TRAINING PROGRAM(S)— Teacher Assistant/Aide; Teaching Assistant/Aides, Other.

WORK ENVIRONMENT—Sitting; standing; walking and running; indoors; disease or infections.

Technical Writers

- Education/Training Required: Bachelor's degree
- Annual Earnings: $54,390
- Growth: 27.1%
- Annual Job Openings: 6,000
- Self-Employed: 7.3%
- Part-Time: 5.5%

Age Bracket	Percentage of Workers
45–54 Years Old	34.5%
55–64 Years Old	13.8%
65 or Older	less than 0.9%

Write technical materials, such as equipment manuals, appendices, or operating and maintenance instructions. May assist in layout work. Organize material and complete writing assignment according to set standards regarding order, clarity, conciseness, style, and terminology. Maintain records and files of work and revisions. Edit, standardize, or make changes to material prepared by other writers or establishment personnel. Confer with customer representatives, vendors, plant executives, or publisher to establish technical specifications and to determine subject material to be developed for publication. Review published materials and recommend revisions or changes in scope, format, content, and methods of reproduction and binding. Select photographs, drawings, sketches, diagrams, and charts to illustrate material. Study drawings, specifications, mockups, and product samples to integrate and delineate technology, operating procedure, and production sequence and detail. Interview production and engineering personnel and read journals and other material to become familiar with product technologies and production methods. Observe production, developmental, and experimental activities to determine operating procedure and detail. Arrange for typing, duplication, and distribution of material. Assist in laying out material for publication. Analyze developments in specific field to determine need for revisions in previously published materials and development of new material. Review manufacturer's and trade catalogs, drawings and other data relative to operation, maintenance, and service of equipment. Draw sketches to illustrate specified materials or assembly sequence. **SKILLS**—Writing; Coordination; Active Listening; Active Learning; Reading Comprehension; Technology Design; Speaking; Learning Strategies; Service Orientation.

GOE—Interest Area: 03. Arts and Communication. **Work Group:** 03.02. Writing and Editing. **Other Jobs in This Work Group:** Copy Writers; Creative Writers; Editors; Poets and Lyricists. **PERSONALITY TYPE:** Artistic. Artistic occupations frequently involve working with forms, designs, and patterns. They often require self-expression, and the work can be done without following a clear set of rules.

EDUCATION/TRAINING PROGRAM(S)— Business/Corporate Communications; Communications Studies/Speech Communication and Rhetoric; Technical and Business Writing.

WORK ENVIRONMENT—Sitting; sounds, noise levels are distracting or uncomfortable; extremely bright or inadequate lighting; indoors; physical proximity to others.

Telecommunications Facility Examiners

- Education/Training Required: Long-term on-the-job training
- Annual Earnings: $50,270
- Growth: –0.6%
- Annual Job Openings: 23,000
- Self-Employed: 4.6%
- Part-Time: 1.7%

The job openings listed here are shared with Central Office and PBX Installers and Repairers; Communication Equipment Mechanics, Installers, and Repairers; Frame Wirers, Central Office; and Station Installers and Repairers, Telephone.

Age Bracket	Percentage of Workers
45–54 Years Old	29.5%
55–64 Years Old	9.6%
65 or Older	1.2%

Examine telephone transmission facilities to determine equipment requirements for providing subscribers with new or additional telephone services. Examines telephone transmission facilities to determine requirements for new or additional telephone services. Visits subscribers' premises to arrange for new installations, such as telephone booths and telephone poles. Designates cables available for use. Climbs telephone poles or stands on truck-mounted boom to examine terminal boxes for available connections. **SKILLS**— Technology Design; Installation.

GOE—Interest Area: 02. Architecture and Construction. **Work Group:** 02.05. Systems and Equipment Installation, Maintenance, and Repair. **Other Jobs in This Work Group:** Central Office and PBX Installers and Repairers; Communication Equipment Mechanics, Installers, and Repairers; Electric Meter Installers and Repairers; Electrical and Electronics Repairers, Powerhouse, Substation, and Relay; Electrical Power-Line Installers and Repairers; Elevator Installers and Repairers; Frame Wirers, Central Office; Heating and Air Conditioning Mechanics; Home Appliance Installers; Maintenance and Repair Workers, General; Meter Mechanics; Refrigeration Mechanics; Station Installers and Repairers, Telephone; Telecommunications Line Installers and Repairers. **PERSONALITY TYPE:** Realistic. Realistic occupations frequently involve work activities that include practical, hands-on problems and solutions. They often deal with plants, animals, and real-world materials like wood, tools, and machinery. Many of the occupations require working outside and do not involve a lot of paperwork or working closely with others.

EDUCATION/TRAINING PROGRAM(S)— Communications Systems Installation and Repair Technology.

WORK ENVIRONMENT—Climbing ladders, scaffolds, or poles; high places; outdoors; hazardous conditions; common protective or safety equipment.

Tractor-Trailer Truck Drivers

- ◎ Education/Training Required: Moderate-term on-the-job training
- ◎ Annual Earnings: $33,870
- ◎ Growth: 19.0%
- ◎ Annual Job Openings: 299,000
- ◎ Self-Employed: 13.1%
- ◎ Part-Time: 7.7%

The job openings listed here are shared with Truck Drivers, Heavy.

Age Bracket	Percentage of Workers
45–54 Years Old	24.1%
55–64 Years Old	13.6%
65 or Older	3.8%

Drive tractor-trailer truck to transport products, livestock, or materials to specified destinations. Drives tractor-trailer combination, applying knowledge of commercial driving regulations, to transport and deliver products, livestock, or materials, usually over long distance. Maneuvers truck into loading or unloading position, following signals from loading crew as needed. Drives truck to weigh station before and after loading, and along route to document weight and conform to state regulations. Maintains driver log according to I.C.C. regulations. Inspects truck before and after trips and submits report indicating truck condition. Reads bill of lading to determine assignment. Fastens chain or binders to secure load on trailer during transit. Loads or unloads, or assists in loading and unloading truck. Works as member of two-person team driving tractor with sleeper bunk behind cab. Services truck with oil, fuel, and radiator fluid to maintain tractor-trailer. Obtains customer's signature or collects payment for services. Inventories and inspects goods to be moved. Wraps goods using pads, packing paper, and containers, and secures load to trailer wall using straps. Gives directions to helper in packing and moving goods to trailer. **SKILLS—**Operation and Control; Equipment Maintenance; Repairing; Troubleshooting; Management of Material Resources; Operation Monitoring.

GOE—Interest Area: 16. Transportation, Distribution, and Logistics. **Work Group:** 16.03. Truck Driving. **Other Jobs in This Work Group:** Truck Drivers, Heavy; Truck Drivers, Light or Delivery Services. **PERSONALITY**

TYPE: Realistic. Realistic occupations frequently involve work activities that include practical, hands-on problems and solutions. They often deal with plants, animals, and real-world materials like wood, tools, and machinery. Many of the occupations require working outside and do not involve a lot of paperwork or working closely with others.

EDUCATION/TRAINING PROGRAM(S)— Truck and Bus Driver/Commercial Vehicle Operation.

WORK ENVIRONMENT—Sitting; extremely bright or inadequate lighting; outdoors; very hot or cold; spend time bending or twisting the body.

Training and Development Managers

- ⦿ Education/Training Required: Work experience plus degree
- ⦿ Annual Earnings: $70,430
- ⦿ Growth: 19.4%
- ⦿ Annual Job Openings: 21,000
- ⦿ Self-Employed: 0%
- ⦿ Part-Time: 3.7%

The job openings listed here are shared with Compensation and Benefits Managers.

Age Bracket	Percentage of Workers
45–54 Years Old	31.9%
55–64 Years Old	17.5%
65 or Older	0.8%

Plan, direct, or coordinate the training and development activities and staff of an organization. Conduct orientation sessions and arrange on-the-job training for new hires. Evaluate instructor performance and the effectiveness of training programs, providing recommendations for improvement. Develop testing and evaluation procedures. Conduct or arrange for ongoing technical training and personal development classes for staff members. Confer with management and conduct surveys to identify training needs based on projected production processes, changes, and other factors. Develop and organize training manuals, multimedia visual aids, and other educational materials. Plan, develop, and provide training and staff development programs, using knowledge of the effectiveness of methods such as classroom training, demonstrations, on-the-job training, meetings, conferences, and workshops. Analyze training needs to develop new training programs or modify and improve existing programs. Review and evaluate training and apprenticeship programs for compliance with government standards. Train instructors and supervisors in techniques and skills for training and dealing with employees. Coordinate established courses with technical and professional courses provided by community schools and designate training procedures. Prepare training budget for department or organization. **SKILLS—**Management of Personnel Resources; Learning Strategies; Management of Financial Resources; Service Orientation; Negotiation; Instructing; Social Perceptiveness; Persuasion.

GOE—Interest Area: 04. Business and Administration. **Work Group:** 04.01. Managerial Work in General Business. **Other Jobs in This Work Group:** Chief Executives; Compensation and Benefits Managers; General and Operations Managers; Human Resources Managers; Private Sector Executives. **PERSONALITY TYPE:** Enterprising. Enterprising occupations frequently involve starting up and carrying out projects. These occupations can involve leading people and making many decisions. They sometimes require risk taking and often deal with business.

EDUCATION/TRAINING PROGRAM(S)— Human Resources Development; Human Resources Management/Personnel Administration, General.

WORK ENVIRONMENT—Physical proximity to others; sitting; sounds, noise levels are distracting or uncomfortable; very hot or cold; extremely bright or inadequate lighting; contaminants.

Training and Development Specialists

- Education/Training Required: Bachelor's degree
- Annual Earnings: $45,370
- Growth: 27.9%
- Annual Job Openings: 35,000
- Self-Employed: 0.8%
- Part-Time: 7.7%

Age Bracket	Percentage of Workers
45–54 Years Old	26.6%
55–64 Years Old	13.4%
65 or Older	1.6%

Conduct training and development programs for employees. Coordinate recruitment and placement of training program participants. Evaluate training materials prepared by instructors, such as outlines, text, and handouts. Develop alternative training methods if expected improvements are not seen. Assess training needs through surveys, interviews with employees, focus groups, and/or consultation with managers, instructors or customer representatives. Screen, hire, and assign workers to positions based on qualifications. Select and assign instructors to conduct training. Devise programs to develop executive potential among employees in lower-level positions. Design, plan, organize and direct orientation and training for employees or customers of industrial or commercial establishment. Negotiate contracts with clients, including desired training outcomes, fees and expenses. Supervise instructors, evaluate instructor performance, and refer instructors to classes for skill development. Monitor training costs to ensure budget is not exceeded, and prepare budget reports to justify expenditures. Refer trainees to employer relations representatives, to locations offering job placement assistance, or to appropriate social services agencies if warranted. Keep up with developments in area of expertise by reading current journals, books and magazine articles. Present information, using a variety of instructional techniques and formats such as role playing, simulations, team exercises, group discussions, videos and lectures. Schedule classes based on availability of classrooms, equipment, and instructors. Organize and develop, or obtain, training procedure manuals and guides and course materials such as handouts and visual materials. Offer specific training programs to help workers maintain or improve job skills. Monitor, evaluate and record training activities and program effectiveness. Attend meetings and seminars to obtain information for use in training programs, or to inform management of training program status. **SKILLS—**Service Orientation; Social Perceptiveness; Instructing; Writing; Speaking; Persuasion; Active Learning; Learning Strategies; Time Management.

GOE—Interest Area: 04. Business and Administration. **Work Group:** 04.03. Human Resources Support. **Other Jobs in This Work Group:** Compensation, Benefits, and Job Analysis Specialists; Employment Interviewers, Private or Public Employment Service; Personnel Recruiters. **PERSONALITY TYPE:** Social. Social occupations frequently involve working with, communicating with, and teaching people. These occupations often involve helping or providing service to others.

EDUCATION/TRAINING PROGRAM(S)— Human Resources Management/Personnel Administration, General; Organizational Behavior Studies.

WORK ENVIRONMENT—Physical proximity to others; sounds, noise levels are distracting or uncomfortable; in an enclosed vehicle or equipment; sitting; cramped work space, awkward positions.

Transportation Managers

- Education/Training Required: Work experience in a related occupation
- Annual Earnings: $67,300
- Growth: 19.7%
- Annual Job Openings: 13,000
- Self-Employed: 1.1%
- Part-Time: 2.4%

The job openings listed here are shared with Storage and Distribution Managers.

Age Bracket	Percentage of Workers
45–54 Years Old	28.0%
55–64 Years Old	11.6%
65 or Older	1.3%

Plan, direct, and coordinate the transportation operations within an organization or the activities of organizations that provide transportation services. Direct activities related to dispatching, routing, and tracking transportation vehicles, such as aircraft and railroad cars. Plan, organize and manage the work of subordinate staff to ensure that the work is accomplished in a manner consistent with organizational requirements. Direct investigations to verify and resolve customer or shipper complaints. Serve as contact persons for all workers within assigned territories. Implement schedule and policy changes. Collaborate with other managers and staff members in order to formulate and implement policies, procedures, goals, and objectives. Monitor operations to ensure that staff members comply with administrative policies and procedures, safety rules, union contracts, and government regulations. Promote safe work activities by conducting safety audits, attending company safety meetings, and meeting with individual staff members. Develop criteria, application instructions, procedural manuals, and contracts for federal and state public transportation programs. Monitor spending to ensure that expenses are consistent with approved budgets. Direct and coordinate, through subordinates, activities of operations department in order to obtain use of equipment, facilities, and human resources. Direct activities of staff performing repairs and maintenance to equipment, vehicles, and facilities. Conduct investigations in cooperation with government agencies to determine causes of transportation accidents and to improve safety procedures. Analyze expenditures and other financial information in order to develop plans, policies, and budgets for increasing profits and improving services. Negotiate and authorize contracts with equipment and materials suppliers, and monitor contract fulfillment. Supervise workers assigning tariff classifications and preparing billing. Set operations policies and standards, including determination of safety procedures for the handling of dangerous goods. Recommend or authorize capital expenditures for acquisition of new equipment or property in order to increase efficiency and services of operations department. Prepare management recommendations, such as proposed fee and tariff increases or schedule changes. **SKILLS**— Negotiation; Time Management; Coordination; Instructing; Monitoring; Critical Thinking; Management of Financial Resources; Management of Personnel Resources.

GOE—Interest Area: 16. Transportation, Distribution, and Logistics. **Work Group:** 16.01. Managerial Work in Transportation. **Other Jobs in This Work Group:** Aircraft Cargo Handling Supervisors; First-Line Supervisors/Managers of Transportation and Material-Moving Machine and Vehicle Operators; Postmasters and Mail Superintendents; Railroad Conductors and Yardmasters; Storage and Distribution Managers. **PERSONALITY TYPE:** Enterprising. Enterprising occupations frequently involve starting up and carrying out projects. These occupations can involve leading people and making many decisions. They sometimes require risk taking and often deal with business.

EDUCATION/TRAINING PROGRAM(S)— Aeronautics/Aviation/Aerospace Science and Technology, General; Aviation/Airway Management and Operations; Business Administration/Management; Logistics and Materials Management; Public Administration; Transportation/Transportation Management.

WORK ENVIRONMENT—Sitting; sounds, noise levels are distracting or uncomfortable; physical proximity to others; very hot or cold; indoors.

Treasurers, Controllers, and Chief Financial Officers

- Education/Training Required: Work experience plus degree
- Annual Earnings: $83,780
- Growth: 18.3%
- Annual Job Openings: 71,000
- Self-Employed: 3.1%
- Part-Time: 4.8%

The job openings listed here are shared with Financial Managers, Branch or Department.

Age Bracket	Percentage of Workers
45–54 Years Old	26.6%
55–64 Years Old	13.4%
65 or Older	1.8%

Plan, direct, and coordinate the financial activities of an organization at the highest level of management. Includes financial reserve officers. Coordinate and direct the financial planning, budgeting, procurement, or investment activities of all or part of an organization. Develop internal control policies, guidelines, and procedures for activities such as budget administration, cash and credit management, and accounting. Prepare or direct preparation of financial statements, business activity reports, financial position forecasts, annual budgets, and/or reports required by regulatory agencies. Advise management on short-term and long-term financial objectives, policies, and actions. Analyze the financial details of past, present, and expected operations in order to identify development opportunities and areas where improvement is needed. Delegate authority for the receipt, disbursement, banking, protection, and custody of funds, securities, and financial instruments. Evaluate needs for procurement of funds and investment of surpluses, and make appropriate recommendations. Lead staff training and development in budgeting and financial management areas. Maintain current knowledge of organizational policies and procedures, federal and state policies and directives, and current accounting standards. Supervise employees performing financial reporting, accounting, billing, collections, payroll, and budgeting duties. Conduct or coordinate audits of company accounts and financial transactions to ensure compliance with state and federal requirements and statutes. Develop and maintain relationships with banking, insurance, and non-organizational accounting personnel in order to facilitate financial activities. Monitor and evaluate the performance of accounting and other financial staff; recommend and implement personnel actions such as promotions and dismissals. Monitor financial activities and details such as reserve levels to ensure that all legal and regulatory requirements are met. Perform tax planning work. Provide direction and assistance to other organizational units regarding accounting and budgeting policies and procedures, and efficient control and utilization of financial resources. Receive and record requests for disbursements; authorize disbursements in accordance with policies and procedures. **SKILLS**—Management of Financial Resources; Systems Analysis; Systems Evaluation; Judgment and Decision Making; Complex Problem Solving; Mathematics; Management of Personnel Resources; Critical Thinking; Operations Analysis.

GOE—Interest Area: 06. Finance and Insurance. **Work Group:** 06.01. Managerial Work in Finance and Insurance. **Other Jobs in This Work Group:** Financial Managers, Branch

or Department. **PERSONALITY TYPE:** Enterprising. Enterprising occupations frequently involve starting up and carrying out projects. These occupations can involve leading people and making many decisions. They sometimes require risk taking and often deal with business.

EDUCATION/TRAINING PROGRAM(S)— Accounting and Business/Management; Accounting and Finance; Credit Management; Finance and Financial Management Services, Other; Finance, General; International Finance; Public Finance.

WORK ENVIRONMENT—Sitting; indoors; standing; walking and running.

Truck Drivers, Heavy

- Education/Training Required: Moderate-term on-the-job training
- Annual Earnings: $33,870
- Growth: 19.0%
- Annual Job Openings: 299,000
- Self-Employed: 13.1%
- Part-Time: 7.7%

The job openings listed here are shared with Tractor-Trailer Truck Drivers.

Age Bracket	Percentage of Workers
45–54 Years Old	24.1%
55–64 Years Old	13.6%
65 or Older	3.8%

Drive truck with capacity of more than three tons to transport materials to specified destinations. Drives truck with capacity of more than 3 tons to transport and deliver cargo, materials, or damaged vehicle. Maintains radio or telephone contact with base or supervisor to receive instructions or be dispatched to new location. Maintains truck log according to state and federal regulations. Keeps record of materials and products transported. Position blocks and ties rope around items to secure cargo for transport. Cleans, inspects, and services vehicle. Operates equipment on vehicle to load, unload, or disperse cargo or materials. Obtains customer signature or collects payment for goods delivered and delivery charges. Assists in loading and unloading truck manually. **SKILLS—** Equipment Maintenance; Repairing; Operation Monitoring; Operation and Control.

GOE—Interest Area: 16. Transportation, Distribution, and Logistics. **Work Group:** 16.03. Truck Driving. **Other Jobs in This Work Group:** Tractor-Trailer Truck Drivers; Truck Drivers, Light or Delivery Services. **PERSONALITY TYPE:** Realistic. Realistic occupations frequently involve work activities that include practical, hands-on problems and solutions. They often deal with plants, animals, and real-world materials like wood, tools, and machinery. Many of the occupations require working outside and do not involve a lot of paperwork or working closely with others.

EDUCATION/TRAINING PROGRAM(S)— Truck and Bus Driver/Commercial Vehicle Operation.

WORK ENVIRONMENT—Sitting; outdoors; extremely bright or inadequate lighting; very hot or cold; hazardous equipment; spend time bending or twisting the body.

Truck Drivers, Light or Delivery Services

◉ Education/Training Required: Short-term on-the-job training

◉ Annual Earnings: $24,420

◉ Growth: 23.2%

◉ Annual Job Openings: 219,000

◉ Self-Employed: 4.7%

◉ Part-Time: 17.3%

Age Bracket	Percentage of Workers
45–54 Years Old	24.1%
55–64 Years Old	13.6%
65 or Older	3.8%

Drive a truck or van with a capacity of under 26,000 GVW, primarily to deliver or pick up merchandise or to deliver packages within a specified area. May require use of automatic routing or location software. May load and unload truck. Drive vehicles with capacities under three tons in order to transport materials to and from specified destinations such as railroad stations, plants, residences and offices, or within industrial yards. Inspect and maintain vehicle supplies and equipment, such as gas, oil, water, tires, lights, and brakes in order to ensure that vehicles are in proper working condition. Load and unload trucks, vans, or automobiles. Obey traffic laws, and follow established traffic and transportation procedures. Read maps, and follow written and verbal geographic directions. Verify the contents of inventory loads against shipping papers. Maintain records such as vehicle logs, records of cargo, or billing statements in accordance with regulations. Perform emergency repairs such as changing tires or installing light bulbs, fuses, tire chains, and spark plugs. Present bills and receipts, and collect payments for goods delivered or loaded. Report any mechanical problems encountered with vehicles. Report delays, accidents, or other traffic and transportation situations to bases or other vehicles, using telephones or mobile two-way radios. Turn in receipts and money received from deliveries. Drive trucks equipped with public address systems through city streets in order to broadcast announcements for advertising or publicity purposes. Sell and keep records of sales for products from truck inventory. Use and maintain the tools and equipment found on commercial vehicles, such as weighing and measuring devices. **SKILLS**—Repairing; Equipment Maintenance; Operation Monitoring; Operation and Control; Troubleshooting.

GOE—Interest Area: 16. Transportation, Distribution, and Logistics. **Work Group:** 16.03. Truck Driving. **Other Jobs in This Work Group:** Tractor-Trailer Truck Drivers; Truck Drivers, Heavy. **PERSONALITY TYPE:** Realistic. Realistic occupations frequently involve work activities that include practical, hands-on problems and solutions. They often deal with plants, animals, and real-world materials like wood, tools, and machinery. Many of the occupations require working outside and do not involve a lot of paperwork or working closely with others.

EDUCATION/TRAINING PROGRAM(S)— Truck and Bus Driver/Commercial Vehicle Operation.

WORK ENVIRONMENT—Sitting; outdoors; very hot or cold; extremely bright or inadequate lighting; spend time bending or twisting the body.

Veterinarians

- Education/Training Required: First professional degree
- Annual Earnings: $68,280
- Growth: 25.1%
- Annual Job Openings: 4,000
- Self-Employed: 27.7%
- Part-Time: 10.6%

Age Bracket	Percentage of Workers
45–54 Years Old	28.8%
55–64 Years Old	15.3%
65 or Older	6.8%

Diagnose and treat diseases and dysfunctions of animals. May engage in a particular function, such as research and development, consultation, administration, technical writing, sale or production of commercial products, or rendering of technical services to commercial firms or other organizations. Includes veterinarians who inspect livestock. Examine animals to detect and determine the nature of diseases or injuries. Treat sick or injured animals by prescribing medication, setting bones, dressing wounds, or performing surgery. Inoculate animals against various diseases such as rabies and distemper. Collect body tissue, feces, blood, urine, or other body fluids for examination and analysis. Operate diagnostic equipment such as radiographic and ultrasound equipment, and interpret the resulting images. Advise animal owners regarding sanitary measures, feeding, and general care necessary to promote health of animals. Educate the public about diseases that can be spread from animals to humans. Train and supervise workers who handle and care for animals. Provide care to a wide range of animals or specialize in a particular species, such as horses or exotic birds. Euthanize animals. Establish and conduct quarantine and testing procedures that prevent the spread of diseases to other animals or to humans, and that comply with applicable government regulations. Conduct postmortem studies and analyses to determine the causes of animals' deaths. Perform administrative duties such as scheduling appointments, accepting payments from clients, and maintaining business records. Direct the overall operations of animal hospitals, clinics, or mobile services to farms. Drive mobile clinic vans to farms so that health problems can be treated and/or prevented. Specialize in a particular type of treatment such as dentistry, pathology, nutrition, surgery, microbiology, or internal medicine. Inspect and test horses, sheep, poultry, and other animals to detect the presence of communicable diseases. Plan and execute animal nutrition and reproduction programs. Research diseases to which animals could be susceptible. Inspect animal housing facilities to determine their cleanliness and adequacy. Determine the effects of drug therapies, antibiotics, or new surgical techniques by testing them on animals. **SKILLS**—Science; Instructing; Management of Financial Resources; Reading Comprehension; Service Orientation; Complex Problem Solving; Management of Personnel Resources; Active Learning; Judgment and Decision Making.

GOE—Interest Area: 08. Health Science. **Work Group:** 08.05. Animal Care. **Other Jobs in This Work Group:** Animal Breeders; Animal Trainers; Nonfarm Animal Caretakers; Veterinary Assistants and Laboratory Animal Caretakers; Veterinary Technologists and Technicians. **PERSONALITY TYPE:** Investigative. Investigative occupations frequently involve working with ideas and require an extensive amount of thinking. These occupations can involve searching for facts and figuring out problems mentally.

EDUCATION/TRAINING PROGRAM(S)—Comparative and Laboratory Animal Medicine (Cert, MS, PhD); Laboratory Animal Medicine; Large Animal/Food Animal and Equine Surgery and Medicine (Cert, MS, PhD); Small/Companion Animal Surgery and Medicine (Cert, MS, PhD); Theriogenology; Veterinary Anatomy (Cert, MS, PhD); Veterinary Anesthesiology; Veterinary Biomedical and Clinical Sciences, Other (Cert, MS. PhD); Veterinary Dentistry; Veterinary Dermatology; Veterinary Emergency and Critical Care Medicine; others.

WORK ENVIRONMENT—Contaminants; physical proximity to others; disease or infections; sounds, noise levels are distracting or uncomfortable; exposed to radiation.

Vocational Education Teachers, Postsecondary

- Education/Training Required: Work experience in a related occupation
- Annual Earnings: $41,170
- Growth: 38.1%
- Annual Job Openings: 216,000
- Self-Employed: 0.3%
- Part-Time: 27.7%

The job openings listed here are shared with all other postsecondary teaching occupations.

Age Bracket	Percentage of Workers
45–54 Years Old	22.8%
55–64 Years Old	19.0%
65 or Older	5.5%

Teach or instruct vocational or occupational subjects at the postsecondary level (but at less than the baccalaureate) to students who have graduated or left high school. Includes correspondence school instructors; industrial, commercial and government training instructors; and adult education teachers and instructors who prepare persons to operate industrial machinery and equipment and transportation and communications equipment. Teaching may take place in public or private schools whose primary business is education or in a school associated with an organization whose primary business is other than education. Supervise and monitor students' use of tools and equipment. Observe and evaluate students' work to determine progress, provide feedback, and make suggestions for improvement. Present lectures and conduct discussions to increase students' knowledge and competence, using visual aids such as graphs, charts, videotapes, and slides. Administer oral, written, or performance tests in order to measure progress, and to evaluate training effectiveness. Prepare reports and maintain records such as student grades, attendance rolls, and training activity details. Supervise independent or group projects, field placements, laboratory work, or other training. Determine training needs of students or workers. Provide individualized instruction and tutorial and/or remedial instruction. Conduct on-the-job training, classes, or training sessions to teach and demonstrate principles, techniques, procedures, and/or methods of designated subjects. Develop curricula, and plan course content and methods of instruction. Prepare outlines of instructional programs and training schedules, and establish course goals. Integrate academic and vocational curricula so that students can obtain a variety of skills. Develop teaching aids such as instructional software, multimedia visual aids, or study materials. Select and assemble books, materials, supplies, and equipment for training, courses, or projects. Advise students on course selection, career decisions, and other academic and vocational concerns. Participate in conferences, seminars, and training sessions to keep abreast of developments in the field; integrate relevant information into training programs. Serve on faculty and school committees concerned with budgeting, curriculum revision, and course and diploma requirements. Review enrollment applications, and correspond with applicants to obtain additional information. Arrange for lectures by experts in designated fields. **SKILLS—** Instructing; Learning Strategies; Social Perceptiveness; Service Orientation; Time Management; Speaking; Persuasion; Active Learning; Negotiation.

GOE—Interest Area: 05. Education and Training. **Work Group:** 05.03. Postsecondary and Adult Teaching and Instructing. **Other Jobs in This Work Group:** Adult Literacy, Remedial Education, and GED Teachers and Instructors; Agricultural Sciences Teachers, Postsecondary; Anthropology and Archeology Teachers, Postsecondary; Architecture Teachers, Postsecondary; Area, Ethnic, and Cultural Studies Teachers, Postsecondary; Art, Drama, and Music Teachers, Postsecondary; Atmospheric, Earth, Marine, and Space Sciences Teachers, Postsecondary; Biological Science Teachers, Postsecondary; Business Teachers, Postsecondary; Chemistry Teachers, Postsecondary; Communications Teachers, Postsecondary; Computer Science Teachers, Postsecondary; Criminal Justice and Law Enforcement Teachers, Postsecondary; Economics Teachers, Postsecondary; Education Teachers, Postsecondary; Engineering Teachers, Postsecondary; English Language and Literature Teachers, Postsecondary; Environmental Science Teachers,

Postsecondary; Farm and Home Management Advisors; Foreign Language and Literature Teachers, Postsecondary; Forestry and Conservation Science Teachers, Postsecondary; Geography Teachers, Postsecondary; Graduate Teaching Assistants; Health Specialties Teachers, Postsecondary; History Teachers, Postsecondary; Home Economics Teachers, Postsecondary; Law Teachers, Postsecondary; Library Science Teachers, Postsecondary; Mathematical Science Teachers, Postsecondary; Nursing Instructors and Teachers, Postsecondary; Philosophy and Religion Teachers, Postsecondary; Physics Teachers, Postsecondary; Political Science Teachers, Postsecondary; Psychology Teachers, Postsecondary; Recreation and Fitness Studies Teachers, Postsecondary; Self-Enrichment Education Teachers; Social Work Teachers, Postsecondary; Sociology Teachers, Post-secondary. **PERSONALITY TYPE:** Social. Social occupations frequently involve working with, communicating with, and teaching people. These occupations often involve helping or providing service to others.

EDUCATION/TRAINING PROGRAM(S)— Agricultural Teacher Education; Business Teacher Education; Health Occupations Teacher Education; Sales and Marketing Operations/Marketing and Distribution Teacher Education; Teacher Education and Professional Development, Specific Subject Areas, Other; Technical Teacher Education; Technology Teacher Education/Industrial Arts Teacher Education; Trade and Industrial Teacher Education.

WORK ENVIRONMENT—Physical proximity to others; contaminants; sounds, noise levels are distracting or uncomfortable; sitting; hazardous conditions.

Vocational Education Teachers, Secondary School

- Education/Training Required: Work experience plus degree
- Annual Earnings: $46,650
- Growth: 9.0%
- Annual Job Openings: 12,000
- Self-Employed: 0%
- Part-Time: 8.8%

Age Bracket	Percentage of Workers
45–54 Years Old	31.0%
55–64 Years Old	15.7%
65 or Older	2.0%

Teach or instruct vocational or occupational subjects at the secondary school level. Prepare materials and classroom for class activities. Maintain accurate and complete student records as required by law, district policy, and administrative regulations. Instruct students individually and in groups, using various teaching methods such as lectures, discussions, and demonstrations. Establish and enforce rules for behavior and procedures for maintaining order among the students for whom they are responsible. Observe and evaluate students' performance, behavior, social development, and physical health. Instruct and monitor students the in use and care of equipment and materials, in order to prevent injury and damage. Plan and conduct activities for a balanced program of instruction, demonstration, and work time that provides students with opportunities to observe, question, and investigate. Prepare, administer, and grade tests and assignments in order to evaluate students' progress. Enforce all administration policies and rules governing students. Assign and grade class work and homework. Instruct students in the knowledge and skills required in a specific occupation or occupational field, using a systematic plan of lectures; discussions; audiovisual presentations; and laboratory, shop, and field studies. Establish clear objectives for all lessons, units, and projects, and communicate those objectives to students. Use computers, audiovisual aids, and other equipment and materials to supplement presentations. Plan and supervise work-experience programs in businesses, industrial shops, and school laboratories. Prepare students for later grades by encouraging them to explore learning opportunities and to persevere with challenging tasks. Confer with parents or guardians, other teachers, counselors, and administrators in order to resolve students' behavioral and academic problems. Prepare objectives and outlines for courses of study, following curriculum guidelines or requirements of states and schools. Guide and counsel students with adjustment and/or academic problems, or special academic interests. Select, order, store, issue, and inventory classroom equipment, materials, and supplies. **SKILLS**—Instructing; Learning Strategies; Social Perceptiveness; Management of Financial Resources; Persuasion; Service Orientation; Time Management; Management of Personnel Resources.

GOE—Interest Area: 05. Education and Training. **Work Group:** 05.02. Preschool, Elementary, and Secondary Teaching and Instructing. **Other Jobs in This Work Group:** Elementary School Teachers, Except Special Education; Kindergarten Teachers, Except Special Education; Middle School Teachers, Except Special and Vocational Education; Preschool Teachers, Except Special Education; Secondary School Teachers, Except Special and Vocational Education; Special Education Teachers, Middle School; Special Education Teachers, Preschool, Kindergarten, and Elementary School; Special Education Teachers, Secondary School; Teacher Assistants; Vocational Education Teachers, Middle School. **PERSONALITY TYPE:** Social. Social occupations frequently involve working with, communicating with, and teaching people. These occupations often involve helping or providing service to others.

EDUCATION/TRAINING PROGRAM(S)— Technology Teacher Education/Industrial Arts Teacher Education.

WORK ENVIRONMENT—Physical proximity to others; sounds, noise levels are distracting or uncomfortable; contaminants; standing; extremely bright or inadequate lighting.

Water and Liquid Waste Treatment Plant and System Operators

- Education/Training Required: Long-term on-the-job training
- Annual Earnings: $34,850
- Growth: 16.0%
- Annual Job Openings: 9,000
- Self-Employed: 0%
- Part-Time: 1.2%

Age Bracket	Percentage of Workers
45–54 Years Old	31.1%
55–64 Years Old	18.0%
65 or Older	close to 0%

Operate or control an entire process or system of machines, often through the use of control

boards, to transfer or treat water or liquid waste. Add chemicals, such as ammonia, chlorine, and lime, to disinfect and deodorize water and other liquids. Operate and adjust controls on equipment to purify and clarify water, process or dispose of sewage, and generate power. Inspect equipment and monitor operating conditions, meters, and gauges to determine load requirements and detect malfunctions. Collect and test water and sewage samples, using test equipment and color analysis standards. Record operational data, personnel attendance, and meter and gauge readings on specified forms. Maintain, repair, and lubricate equipment, using hand tools and power tools. Clean and maintain tanks and filter beds, using hand tools and power tools. Direct and coordinate plant workers engaged in routine operations and maintenance activities. **SKILLS**—Operation Monitoring; Installation; Operation and Control; Troubleshooting; Management of Material Resources; Operations Analysis; Equipment Maintenance; Management of Personnel Resources.

GOE—Interest Area: 13. Manufacturing. **Work Group:** 13.16. Utility Operation and Energy Distribution. **Other Jobs in This Work Group:** Auxiliary Equipment Operators, Power; Boiler Operators and Tenders, Low Pressure; Chemical Plant and System Operators; Gas Compressor Operators; Gas Distribution Plant Operators; Gas Processing Plant Operators; Gas Pumping Station Operators; Gaugers; Nuclear Power Reactor Operators; Petroleum Pump System Operators; Petroleum Refinery and Control Panel Operators; Power Distributors and Dispatchers; Power Generating Plant Operators, Except Auxiliary Equipment Operators; Ship Engineers; Stationary Engineers. **PERSONALITY TYPE:** Realistic. Realistic occupations frequently involve work activities that include

practical, hands-on problems and solutions. They often deal with plants, animals, and real-world materials like wood, tools, and machinery. Many of the occupations require working outside and do not involve a lot of paperwork or working closely with others.

EDUCATION/TRAINING PROGRAM(S)— Water Quality and Wastewater Treatment Management and Recycling Technology/ Technician.

WORK ENVIRONMENT—Outdoors; contaminants; in an enclosed vehicle or equipment; sounds, noise levels are distracting or uncomfortable; very hot or cold.

Wholesale and Retail Buyers, Except Farm Products

- Education/Training Required: Work experience in a related occupation
- Annual Earnings: $42,190
- Growth: 4.3%
- Annual Job Openings: 24,000
- Self-Employed: 9.9%
- Part-Time: 18.1%

Age Bracket	Percentage of Workers
45–54 Years Old	29.1%
55–64 Years Old	10.8%
65 or Older	4.7%

Buy merchandise or commodities, other than farm products, for resale to consumers at the wholesale or retail level, including both durable and nondurable goods. Analyze past buying trends, sales records, price, and quality of mer-

chandise to determine value and yield. **Select, order, and authorize payment for merchandise according to contractual agreements. May conduct meetings with sales personnel and introduce new products.** Examine, select, order, and purchase at the most favorable price merchandise consistent with quality, quantity, specification requirements and other factors. Negotiate prices, discount terms and transportation arrangements for merchandise. Analyze and monitor sales records, trends and economic conditions to anticipate consumer buying patterns and determine what the company will sell and how much inventory is needed. Interview and work closely with vendors to obtain and develop desired products. Authorize payment of invoices or return of merchandise. Inspect merchandise or products to determine value or yield. Set or recommend mark-up rates, mark-down rates, and selling prices for merchandise. Confer with sales and purchasing personnel to obtain information about customer needs and preferences. Consult with store or merchandise managers about budget and goods to be purchased. Conduct staff meetings with sales personnel to introduce new merchandise. Manage the department for which they buy. Use computers to organize and locate inventory, and operate spreadsheet and word processing software. Train and supervise sales and clerical staff. Provide clerks with information to print on price tags, such as price, mark-ups or mark-downs, manufacturer number, season code, and style number. Determine which products should be featured in advertising, the advertising medium to be used, and when the ads should be run. Monitor competitors' sales activities by following their advertisements in newspapers and other media. **SKILLS**—Management of Financial Resources; Management of Material Resources; Negotiation; Service Orientation; Management of Personnel Resources; Learning Strategies; Instructing; Operations Analysis.

GOE—Interest Area: 14. Retail and Wholesale Sales and Service. **Work Group:** 14.05. Purchasing. **Other Jobs in This Work Group:** Purchasing Agents, Except Wholesale, Retail, and Farm Products. **PERSONALITY TYPE:** Enterprising. Enterprising occupations frequently involve starting up and carrying out projects. These occupations can involve leading people and making many decisions. They sometimes require risk taking and often deal with business.

EDUCATION/TRAINING PROGRAM(S)— Apparel and Accessories Marketing Operations; Apparel and Textile Marketing Management; Fashion Merchandising; Merchandising and Buying Operations; Sales, Distribution, and Marketing Operations, General; Sales, Distribution, and Marketing Operations, General.

WORK ENVIRONMENT—Sitting; physical proximity to others; sounds, noise levels are distracting or uncomfortable; indoors.

Shelton State Libraries
Shelton State Community College

Index

Area, Ethnic, and Cultural Studies Teachers, Postsecondary, 165–167

Art Directors, 29, 35, 54, 57, 61, 64, 68, 71, 75, 77, 105, 112, 125, 133, 140, 142, 167–168

Art, Drama, and Music Teachers, Postsecondary, 168–169

Assessors, 29, 39, 46, 55, 61, 75–76, 78–79, 91, 102, 114, 130, 140, 169–170

Atmospheric, Earth, Marine, and Space Sciences Teachers, Postsecondary, 170–172

Audiologists, 30, 36–37, 52, 58, 68, 70–72, 81, 83–85, 105, 116, 126, 133, 142, 172–173

Aviation Inspectors, 32, 44, 55, 89, 101, 115, 123, 173–174

B

Baby Boomers, defined, 1

benefits, 21

Best Jobs for Baby Boomers Employing the Highest Percentage of Men, 87–91

Best Jobs for Baby Boomers Employing the Highest Percentage of Women, 81–82

Best Jobs for Baby Boomers Interested in Agriculture and Natural Resources, 111

Best Jobs for Baby Boomers Interested in Architecture and Construction, 112

Best Jobs for Baby Boomers Interested in Arts and Communication, 112

Best Jobs for Baby Boomers Interested in Business and Administration, 113

Best Jobs for Baby Boomers Interested in Education and Training, 113–114

Best Jobs for Baby Boomers Interested in Finance and Insurance, 114

Best Jobs for Baby Boomers Interested in Government and Public Administration, 115

Best Jobs for Baby Boomers Interested in Health Science, 115–116

Best Jobs for Baby Boomers Interested in Hospitality, Tourism, and Recreation, 116

Best Jobs for Baby Boomers Interested in Human Service, 117

Best Jobs for Baby Boomers Interested in Law and Public Safety, 117

Best Jobs for Baby Boomers Interested in Manufacturing, 118

Best Jobs for Baby Boomers Interested in Retail and Wholesale Sales and Service, 119

Best Jobs for Baby Boomers Interested in Scientific Research, Engineering, and Mathematics, 119–120

Best Jobs for Baby Boomers Interested in Transportation, Distribution, and Logistics, 120

Best Jobs for Baby Boomers Requiring a Bachelor's Degree, 103–104

Best Jobs for Baby Boomers Requiring a Doctoral Degree, 106

Best Jobs for Baby Boomers Requiring a First Professional Degree, 107

Best Jobs for Baby Boomers Requiring a Master's Degree, 105

Best Jobs for Baby Boomers Requiring an Associate Degree, 102

Best Jobs for Baby Boomers Requiring Long-Term On-the-Job Training, 100

Best Jobs for Baby Boomers Requiring Moderate-Term On-the-Job Training, 99

D

E

F

G

V

W–Z